Studies in Jazz

The Institute of Jazz Studies
Rutgers—The State University of New Jersey
General Editors: Dan Morgenstern and Edward Berger

1. BENNY CARTER: A Life in American Music, *by Morroe Berger, Edward Berger, and James Patrick, 2 vols., 1982*
2. ART TATUM: A Guide to His Recorded Music, *by Arnold Laubich and Ray Spencer, 1982*
3. ERROLL GARNER: The Most Happy Piano, *by James M. Doran, 1985*
4. JAMES P. JOHNSON: A Case of Mistaken Identity, *by Scott E. Brown;* Discography 1917–1950, *by Robert Hilbert, 1986*
5. PEE WEE ERWIN: This Horn for Hire, *as told to Warren W. Vaché Sr., 1987*
6. BENNY GOODMAN: Listen to His Legacy, *by D. Russell Connor, 1988*
7. ELLINGTONIA: The Recorded Music of Duke Ellington and His Sidemen, *by W. E. Timner, 1988; 4th ed., 1996*
8. THE GLENN MILLER ARMY AIR FORCE BAND: Sustineo Alas / I Sustain the Wings, *by Edward F. Polic;* Foreword *by George T. Simon, 1989*
9. SWING LEGACY, *by Chip Deffaa, 1989*
10. REMINISCING IN TEMPO: The Life and Times of a Jazz Hustler, *by Teddy Reig, with Edward Berger, 1990*
11. IN THE MAINSTREAM: 18 Portraits in Jazz, *by Chip Deffaa, 1992*
12. BUDDY DeFRANCO: A Biographical Portrait and Discography, *by John Kuehn and Arne Astrup, 1993*
13. PEE WEE SPEAKS: A Discography of Pee Wee Russell, *by Robert Hilbert, with David Niven, 1992*
14. SYLVESTER AHOLA: The Gloucester Gabriel, *by Dick Hill, 1993*
15. THE POLICE CARD DISCORD, *by Maxwell T. Cohen, 1993*
16. TRADITIONALISTS AND REVIVALISTS IN JAZZ, *by Chip Deffaa, 1993*
17. BASSICALLY SPEAKING: An Oral History of George Duvivier, *by Edward Berger;* Musical Analysis *by David Chevan, 1993*
18. TRAM: The Frank Trumbauer Story, *by Philip R. Evans and Larry F. Kiner, with William Trumbauer, 1994*
19. TOMMY DORSEY: On the Side, *by Robert L. Stockdale, 1995*
20. JOHN COLTRANE: A Discography and Musical Biography, *by Yasuhiro Fujioka, with Lewis Porter and Yoh-ichi Hamada, 1995*
21. RED HEAD: A Chronological Survey of "Red" Nichols and His Five Pennies, *by Stephen M. Stroff, 1996*
22. THE RED NICHOLS STORY: After Intermission 1942–1965, *by Philip R. Evans, Stanley Hester, Stephen Hester, and Linda Evans, 1997*
23. BENNY GOODMAN: Wrappin' It Up, *by D. Russell Connor, 1996*

24. CHARLIE PARKER AND THEMATIC IMPROVISATION, *by Henry Martin, 1996*
25. BACK BEATS AND RIM SHOTS: The Johnny Blowers Story, *by Warren W. Vaché Sr., 1997*
26. DUKE ELLINGTON: A Listener's Guide, *by Eddie Lambert, 1998*
27. SERGE CHALOFF: A Musical Biography and Discography, *by Vladimir Simosko, 1998*
28. HOT JAZZ: From Harlem to Storyville, *by David Griffiths, 1998*
29. ARTIE SHAW: A Musical Biography and Discography, *by Vladimir Simosko, 2000*
30. JIMMY DORSEY: A Study in Contrasts, *by Robert L. Stockdale, 1998*
31. STRIDE!: Fats, Jimmy, Lion, Lamb and All the Other Ticklers, *by John L. Fell and Terkild Vinding, 1999*
32. GIANT STRIDES: The Legacy of Dick Wellstood, *by Edward N. Meyer, 1999*
33. JAZZ GENTRY: Aristocrats of the Music World, *by Warren W. Vaché Sr., 1999*
34. THE UNSUNG SONGWRITERS: America's Masters of Melody, *by Warren W. Vaché Sr., 2000*
35. THE MUSICAL WORLD OF J. J. JOHNSON, *by Joshua Berrett and Louis G. Bourgois III, 1999*
36. THE LADIES WHO SING WITH THE BAND, *by Betty Bennett, 2000*
37. AN UNSUNG CAT: The Life and Music of Warne Marsh, *by Safford Chamberlain, 2000*
38. JAZZ IN NEW ORLEANS: The Postwar Years Through 1970, *by Charles Suhor, 2001*
39. THE YOUNG LOUIS ARMSTRONG ON RECORDS: A Critical Survey of the Early Recordings, 1923–1928, *by Edward Brooks, 2002*
40. BENNY CARTER: A Life in American Music, Second Edition, *by Morroe Berger, Edward Berger, and James Patrick, 2 vols., 2002*
41. CHORD CHANGES ON THE CHALKBOARD: How Public School Teachers Shaped Jazz and the Music of New Orleans, *by Al Kennedy,* Foreword *by Ellis Marsalis Jr., 2002*
42. CONTEMPORARY CAT: Terence Blanchard with Special Guests, *by Anthony Magro, 2002*
43. PAUL WHITEMAN: Pioneer in American Music, Volume I: 1890–1930, *by Don Rayno, 2003*
44. GOOD VIBES: A Life in Jazz, *by Terry Gibbs with Cary Ginell, 2003*
45. TOM TALBERT—HIS LIFE AND TIMES: Voices from a Vanished World of Jazz, *by Bruce Talbot, 2004*
46. SITTIN' IN WITH CHRIS GRIFFIN: A Reminiscence of Radio and Recording's Golden Years, *by Warren W. Vaché, 2005*
47. FIFTIES JAZZ TALK: An Oral Retrospective, *by Gordon Jack, 2004*
48. FLORENCE MILLS: Harlem Jazz Queen, *by Bill Egan, 2004*
49. SWING ERA SCRAPBOOK: The Teenage Diaries and Radio Logs of Bob Inman, 1936–1938, *by Ken Vail, 2005*

50. FATS WALLER ON THE AIR: The Radio Broadcasts and Discography, *by Stephen Taylor, 2006*
51. ALL OF ME: The Complete Discography of Louis Armstrong, *by Jos Willems, 2006*
52. MUSIC AND THE CREATIVE SPIRIT: Innovators in Jazz, Improvisation, and the Avant Garde, *by Lloyd Peterson, 2006*
53. THE STORY OF FAKE BOOKS: Bootlegging Songs to Musicians, *by Barry Kernfeld, 2006*
54. ELLINGTONIA: The Recorded Music of Duke Ellington and His Sidemen, 5th edition, *by W. E. Timner, 2007*
55. JAZZ FICTION: A History and Comprehensive Reader's Guide, *by David Rife, 2007*
56. MISSION IMPOSSIBLE: My Life In Music, *by Lalo Schifrin, edited by Richard H. Palmer, 2008*
57. THE CONTRADICTIONS OF JAZZ, *by Paul Rinzler, 2008*
58. EARLY TWENTIETH-CENTURY BRASS IDIOMS: Art, Jazz, and Other Popular Traditions, *edited by Howard T. Weiner, 2008*
59. THE MUSIC AND LIFE OF THEODORE "FATS" NAVARRO: Infatuation, *by Leif Bo Petersen and Theo Rehak, 2009*
60. WHERE THE DARK AND THE LIGHT FOLKS MEET: Race and the Mythology, Politics, and Business of Jazz, *by Randall Sandke, 2010*
61. JAZZ BOOKS IN THE 1990S: An Annotated Bibliography, *by Janice Leslie Hochstat Greenberg, 2010*
62. BENNY GOODMAN: A Supplemental Discography, *by David Jessup, 2010*
63. THE LIFE AND MUSIC OF KENNY DAVERN: Just Four Bars, *by Edward N. Meyer, 2010*
64. MR. TRUMPET: The Trials, Tribulations, and Triumph of Bunny Berigan, *by Michael P. Zirpolo, 2011*
65. HARLEM JAZZ ADVENTURES: A European Baron's Memoir, 1934–1969, *by Timme Rosenkrantz, adapted and edited by Fradley Hamilton Garner, 2012*
66. WHAT IT IS: Conversations with Jazzman Dave Liebman, *by Dave Liebman with Lewis Porter, 2012*
67. BORN TO PLAY: The Ruby Braff Discography and Directory of Performances, *by Thomas P. Hustad, 2012*

Born to Play

The Ruby Braff Discography and Directory of Performances

Thomas P. Hustad

THE SCARECROW PRESS, INC.
Lanham • Toronto • Plymouth, UK
2012

Published by Scarecrow Press, Inc.
A wholly owned subsidiary of The Rowman & Littlefield Publishing Group, Inc.
4501 Forbes Boulevard, Suite 200, Lanham, Maryland 20706
www.rowman.com

Estover Road, Plymouth PL6 7PY, United Kingdom

British Library Cataloguing in Publication Information Available

Library of Congress Cataloging-in-Publication Data
Hustad, Thomas P.
Born to play : the Ruby Braff discography and directory of performances / Thomas P. Hustad.
p. cm. — (Studies in jazz ; 67)
Includes bibliographical references and index.
ISBN 978-0-8108-8264-5 (cloth : alk. paper) — ISBN 978-0-8108-8265-2 (ebook)
1. Braff, Ruby, 1927–2003. 2. Braff, Ruby, 1927–2003—Discography. I. Title.
ML419.B715H87 2012
788.9'6165092—dc23 [B] 2011051806

∞™ The paper used in this publication meets the minimum requirements of American National Standard for Information Sciences—Permanence of Paper for Printed Library Materials, ANSI/NISO Z39.48-1992.

Printed in the United States of America

To my wife, Sherry, who has shared with me the delights of hearing Ruby's music for over 41 years, to all those who enjoy or come to discover the beauty of Ruby's artistry, and to Ruby Braff and his legacy. I hope that this book helps to remind future generations of his marvelous contributions to good music and nice tunes.

Contents

Series Editor's Foreword

When Tom Hustad first proposed a Ruby Braff discography, it seemed like an excellent idea, but neither he nor we (at that time, Ed Berger and I were the series editors) had an inkling just how monumental a task the author had set himself. On the surface, documenting the great cornetist's recorded output seemed manageable--while sizable, the number of issued recordings was not huge. But Tom had not reckoned with the amount of unissued and privately recorded material, which he was determined to track down. He has done so with the tenacity and patience of a latter-day Sherlock Holmes, and I would be very surprised if anything of significance has failed to be detected by Tom—though a discographer's work is never done.

From the start, Tom had the full cooperation of his subject. Ruby was no shrinking violet and thought well of the enterprise. By then, he had somehow managed to overcome the effects of the emphysema that nearly cut him down in 1992 and explains the gap between June of that year and September 1993. Those of us who knew Ruby marveled at his courage, determination, and sheer physical endurance in the struggle to retain his mastery of the horn. It was accomplished, in part, by employing the diaphragm to the fullest, and I doubt that any other cornetist/trumpeter has matched such a demanding breathing technique.

Ruby soldiered on for nearly a decade, until his slight frame no longer could supply the fuel needed to keep the flame of invention burning. Blessedly, this was also the decade of collaboration with Mat Domber, the owner-producer of Arbors Records. This was an ideal partnership, and it resulted in a veritable outpouring of music that has outlived its brave author, made not only in the studio but also live, as Ruby's final birthdays were celebrated in fine style at the Arbors-sponsored March of Jazz festivals. It was after an Arbors record date in New York in the summer of 2000 that Ruby took on a booking at an intimate New Jersey jazz spot, Shanghai Jazz, with a quartet including the veteran guitarist Bucky Pizzarelli. I was lucky to be there, for Ruby played like an angel. Having first heard him in his native Boston in 1953, and countless times since, I thought I knew what he was capable of creating. But this was special, so much so that I sent Ruby what amounted to a fan letter, to which he responded in a most moving way. (At this writing, recently retired and still in the throes of cleaning out 35 years of accumulated stuff in my office, I can't put my hands on it to quote from.)

As a musician and a man, Ruby Braff was a complete original. In these pages, Tom Hustad has not only unveiled and illuminated Ruby's recorded legacy, but also presented us with a detailed record of his life. To this Ruby fan, it is truly a jewel in the Studies in Jazz series.

—Dan Morgenstern

Introduction

This book attempts to document as much of Ruby Braff's performing career as possible. Ruby helped me tremendously during the final four years of his life, pointing me toward unissued recordings at Vanguard, Chaz Jazz, Concord Jazz, and other labels. I never would have discovered the tunes he performed with the Weavers without his help. His fans around the world continue to contribute information and recordings. Their help has made this book possible. Of course, this book is only a beginning. Ruby did not maintain a diary of his performances, so everything I have reported has been built from searching publications, consulting my own collection of Ruby's recordings, and conversing with people who love Ruby's artistry.

It is inevitable that this book is incomplete. Some of the listings lack full information or may even include errors. Certainly, many performances are not even documented. Probably other recordings exist in private collections and other archives. It is my hope that people who can provide further information will contact me. I welcome correspondence with anyone who can provide copies of additional recordings so that Ruby's musical heritage can be preserved. I feel that Ruby's contributions should ultimately be documented in as much detail as accorded the careers of Armstrong, Basie, Ellington, Goodman, Holiday, Hawkins, Young, and other unique artists. For Ruby was a unique artist. His sound and style are immediately recognizable. Perhaps it will be possible to publish a supplement to this book in the future.

This book is not a biography. Ruby wanted to be known for his artistry. He felt that everything about his life had already been published in a number of articles appearing in the jazz press. But this book is more than a discography. It adds details about a number of Ruby's club and concert performances, as well as unissued recordings. Where private recordings are known to exist, they are noted. This book should serve as a guide to the Ruby Braff archive, and I hope that this collection grows over time. Ruby deserves to have his performances gathered in a central location that can be referenced long into the future.

Why is it worthwhile to document Ruby's career? The best answer is because his artistry warrants it. But an equally valid answer is that it is interesting to document the variety of musicians who performed with Ruby. Ruby was an important transitional figure in jazz. He played with a number of both older and younger musicians. He represented a link between musical generations that worked to maintain melodic traditions in jazz music. Bobby

Short put it simply: "If Fred Astaire played cornet, he would aspire to sound like Ruby Braff."

Whitney Balliett consistently praised Ruby's artistry, writing on one occasion that "the heavyweights among the second-generation swing players are Gerry Mulligan, Ruby Braff, Dave McKenna, and Jimmy Rowles."[1] Of course, Ruby played with each of them, since they were all in demand as artists of the highest order, but, of these fine musicians, his paths crossed with Dave McKenna the most often. They were both proud New Englanders.

Will Friedwald took this even further, writing the following passage in his book *Stardust Melodies* as he discussed one of Ruby's recordings:[2]

> A year after Ellis Larkins and Ruby Braff worked on Lee Wiley's wonderful 1954 Rodgers and Hart collection, the piano player and the cornetist bit off 'Funny Valentine' on their own, without any singer at all. Or I should say without a vocalist per se, since Braff sings through his cornet and by any standard is one of the greatest singers of all time. This is an especially lyrical 'Valentine,' yet a buoyant one that creates a relaxed, romantic atmosphere without resorting to a slow, potentially maudlin tempo. Then as now brilliant storytellers, Braff and Larkins give you the full impact of Hart's meaning without uttering so much as one word of his text.

Ruby's playing was filled with unique ideas. He could tell stories with his horn. His style was distinctive. It is easy to identify his musical voice from his sound and phrasing. He had exemplary technique. Jazz musicians strive for this magical combination of unique ideas and technique. In doing so, Ruby mastered the art of performance.

While this book is not a biography of Ruby's life, it does try to capture some of the vivid stories he recounted about some of his musical experiences. Hopefully both his and my comments will help to establish an overall context for some of the details of his many performances. Ruby created music that transcends the words that only capture some of the details of his performing career. To understand what he accomplished in his performances, you must listen to recordings when they are available. Then perhaps you can hear the beauty that these words represent.

I am indebted to a number of Ruby's fans who have graciously provided copies of their treasured private recordings in myriad recording formats. Thank you. When actual performances are available, I have noted that in the manuscript for both issued and unissued recordings. In many cases, private recordings have been provided in confidence, so I have chosen not to identify the sources. Surely, other recordings will surface in the future.

The inevitable errors are my sole responsibility and a testament to my imperfect skills as a proofreader. All comments are welcome, for a book like this can never be completed. I have included all the information I have been able to obtain prior to March 10, 2012 but acknowledge that there is much more to be discovered. I will reply to all contributors and am eager to add missing details that I have not yet uncovered. I hope that Ruby's fans will share with me the responsibility of extending the documentation of his fabulous career. If you can add further information or recordings, please contact me (Thomas P. Hustad, 3101 South Daniel Street, Bloomington, IN 47401, USA or by e-mail: Hustad@Indiana.edu). I will continue to acknowledge all contributions and attempt to provide updates to those individuals who express interest.

I hope to continue to build a comprehensive collection of recordings and memorabilia associated with Ruby's performances. This book indicates when recordings are available. Readers who have access to additional recordings or other memorabilia are encouraged to contact the author. Eventually I will place this archive collection in a suitable library for reference purposes.

Ruby's artistry should not be forgotten. He created an endless supply of ideas to frame his musical stories. He developed a distinctive voice on his instrument. He was able to build variety into each performance, calling on his fellow musicians in ways that created rich musical textures. His superb technical skills allowed him to play everything he could imagine. This has been documented in recordings that span seven decades. Ruby was born to play. He made beautiful music.

Notes

[1] Whitney Balliett, *The New Yorker*, July 31, 1995, 84.

[2] Will Friedwald, *Stardust Melodies* (New York: Pantheon Books, 2002), 373. The recording of "My Funny Valentine" was made on October 14, 1955, for Vanguard Records.

Acknowledgments

Many individuals have helped to make this book possible. Several producers have recorded Ruby during his career. They have been his champions. Several of Ruby's fans have provided copies of private recordings, along with valuable information. Two provided copies of recordings issued only in Japan that I lacked in my collection. Ruby pointed to several undocumented recordings. He played a central role in helping me develop this manuscript, pointing me to recordings I would never have discovered without his help and sharing stories that brought smiles to both our faces. Thanks to all.

In particular, Dan Morgenstern has been a champion for this project since I first mentioned it to him. Dave Bennett, Manfred Selchow, Tony Shoppee, Michael Steinman, and Don Wolff each provided many hours of private recordings made with Ruby's consent over the years. Much of the information in this book, and the great majority of the unissued recordings reported herein, are only available to me because of their incredible help. Tony also sorted out a number of details for various reissues of many of Ruby's recordings. Mat Domber documented Ruby's final decade with a series of marvelous recordings on Arbors Records. When I described my intent to Mat to begin this project, he immediately encouraged me to contact Ruby. This made Mat this book's initial champion. Subsequently I was honored to be asked to write the album notes for three of Ruby's releases on Arbors Records. Vincent Pelote provided access to a number of recordings from the New Jersey Jazz Society stored at the Institute of Jazz Studies. Don Wolff shared his files about Ruby's appearances at a number of jazz parties. Michael Steinman recorded many of Ruby's club performances in New York in the '70s and provided copies of many other recordings that he had acquired over the years. Will Friedwald kindly shared information about Tony Bennett's career during the time he employed Ruby Braff, thus filling an important gap in this book. Dave Bennett was Ruby's manager for several extensive tours in the United Kingdom. He kindly provided copies of many hours of performance recordings from 1999 and 2003. Ruby really enjoyed performing for his British fans, and Dave made that possible for him to enjoy these special times—and to extend his legacy with many recorded performances. George Wein kindly gave his permission to quote many times from his own book, *Myself Among Others*, and also granted permission for me to obtain copies of many of Ruby's unissued performances from the Newport Jazz Festival held at the Library of Congress.

The following individuals and organizations also provided copies of many unique recordings, important information, handbills, or photographs that are included in this book or were instrumental to its development. They all encouraged me to make this book as complete as possible: Paul Adams, Tony Adkins, Frank Alkyer (*DownBeat*'s publisher, granting permission to reprint Ruby's "Blindfold Test"), Susan Atran (Ruby's sister), Brent Banulis, Charles C. Baron, Ed Berger, Joe Boughton, Jack Bradley (one of Ruby's biggest champions), Michael Brooks, Mark Cantor, Reverend Ellen Chahey, Russ Chase, Derek Coller, Sir Lawrence Collins (my host for a wonderful night in London and the source of photos from Nice), D. Russell Connor, Michael Cuscuna, Stephen Didymus, Edward Feutz, Donna Fields (for Mike Douglas and King World Productions), Michael Frohne, Peter Gaudion, Allan Gilmour, Dave Gould, Mona Granager (Storyville Records), Lew Green, David Griffiths, Ben Hafey, Les Harris, Robert Hilbert, Roland Hippenmeyer, Franz Hoffman, Dick Hyman (who created a number of opportunities for Ruby to perform in public and to record), Shin-ichi Iwamoto, Gunnar Jacobsen, Lars Johansson, Leif Karlsson, Roger Kellaway, John Kennedy, Yoichi Kimura, Mel Levine, Al Lipsky, Tom Lord (for *The Jazz Discography*), Peter Lowe, Jack Lyons, Sonny McGown, Marian McPartland, Alun Morgan, John Nelson, Jim Neumann, John Norris, Ralph O'Callaghan, Ted O'Reilly, Dave Robinson, Nick Puopolo, Robert J. Roberts, Peter Rown, Duncan Schiedt (for permitting publication of a wonderful photograph of Ruby with Louis Armstrong), Bo Scherman, Loren Schoenberg (who said that Ruby was responsible for his career in music), James Shacter, Glen Sharp, Chuck Slate, Roger Stubberfield, Richard M. Sudhalter (for providing unique access to a lost recording session, sharing a wonderful recording from the Grande Parade du Jazz, and meeting with me one evening in Bloomington), Yasuuo Utsumi, Paul Verrette (for providing access to the New Hampshire Library of Traditional Jazz's Prescott Collection), Jim Weaver (for providing valuable information about the Prescott recordings), Bob Weir, Robert S. Wessels, Bert Whyatt, and Arthur Zimmerman. The presence of Ruby's champions from the United Kingdom is very visible in this list, and many aspects of his career would not have been captured without their valuable contributions. Derek Coller, David Griffiths, Alun Morgan, Bob Weir, Bert Whyatt, and Arthur Zimmerman are among the major contributors to jazz archiving and research. I am deeply grateful that they so consistently supported this project.

Others provided access to materials and expressed deep interest in this research. First, Andrew Simmons, then the jazz curator of the National Sound Archive for the British Library, was a superb host during my exploration of that library's jazz holdings. Second, Lawrence A. Appelbaum played a similar role at the Library of Congress. All enjoyed Ruby's artistry. Next, Nick Phillips of Concord Records, Hank O'Neal of Chiaroscuro Records, and Karl Emil Knudsen of Storyville Records all provided valuable information about unissued recordings. They, along with Mat Domber and George Wein, were among Ruby's champions, and certainly they captured much of Ruby's recorded legacy. Hank O'Neal also provided several wonderful photographs. Charles Schwartz served as manager for the Ruby Braff–George Barnes Quartet and provided information about a number of engagements. Finally, Sara Beutter allowed me to borrow noncirculating bound volumes of several jazz magazines from Indiana University's Music Library in order to examine them at home in a more comfortable environment, often with Ruby's music playing in the background. Anne Davison also provided some interesting recollections of Ruby from times that Wild Bill Davison and Ruby performed together.

The following individuals have offered their encouragement, provided additional information, and helped me avoid some errors along the way: Howard Alden, George Avakian, Mike Baillie, Donna Byrne, Ron Della Chiesa, Graham Colombe, Charlie DeVore, Scott Edmiston, Bob Erwig, Maddie Gibson, Ira Gitler, David Goldsworthy, Roland Goodbody, Scott Hamilton, Jake Hanna, Kent Hazen, Nat Hentoff, Franz Hoffmann, Dennis Huggard, Leigh Kamman, Mike Lipskin, Gene Mayl, Sonny McGown, Reid McKenzie, Dave Mills, David Niven, Brian Peerless, Larry Ridley, Dave Samuelson, Han Schulte, Lenny Solomon, John Stock, Sunnie Sutton, Eric Townley, Jack Tracy, Warren Vaché, Steve Voce, Al White, Arild Wilderøe, and Marshall Wood.

While others have also helped, contributions from these many individuals have been particularly valuable. I do apologize to those I might have overlooked in this list, for their support has been invaluable. I have tried to honor every contributor. Given the length of time I spent developing the manuscript for this book, several individuals that I have thanked have passed away. I am sorry that they did not see their valuable contributions recognized in print during their lifetimes.

Concluding, Ruby Braff, Sir Lawrence Collins, Mat Domber, Al Lipsky, Hank O'Neal, and Duncan Schiedt permitted me to publish many of their photographs. Duncan's photograph of Ruby with Louis Armstrong is featured on the book's cover. George Wein gave his permission to cite many passages from his book, *Myself Among Others.* Frank Alkyar, publisher of *DownBeat,* and Mark Gilbert, editor of *Jazz Journal*, have graciously provided permission to include excerpts from published articles that appeared in their pages. Steve Voce supplied information from his personal conversations with Ruby. Next, I wish to thank my editor, Bennett Graff, and his professional team at Scarecrow Press, particularly Jayme Reed and Rayna Andrews, for their help in preparing the final manuscript for publication. Devin Watson designed a striking cover. Those who knew Ruby's love for orange will immediately understand the bold colors. I think that the contrasting colors also capture a bit of Ruby's assertive spirit, while highlighting his lifelong love for Louis Armstrong. I also admire the patience of an unidentified proof reader who consistently found many of my typing and compositional errors, amidst an overwhelming amount of detail in my prepublication manuscript pages. I likely overlooked a few of them in my final text.

Finally, I wish to again thank Dan Morgenstern for being the continuing champion of my efforts to develop this book about a truly remarkable artist, Ruby Braff. His forward sets the tone for the book when he writes, "As a musician and a man, Ruby Braff was a complete original."

Chapter 1

A Beginning

Ruby would want to remind us of the debt all musicians owe to Louis Armstrong. That's Louis, as in "Lewis"—not Louie. Ruby was particular about that. His authority in the matter was Louis Armstrong, himself. Louis was Ruby's leading instructor in the Louis Armstrong University. Ruby said he enrolled in more than 100 classes, but that it was impossible for anyone to graduate. There was too much to learn, and too many levels to explore. Today it is fashionable to talk about lifelong learning, but that is what Ruby practiced throughout his wonderful career.

Next, Ruby might want me to mention the thrill he had seeing Jimmie Lunceford, on film and in a live performance. This was, in fact, the first orchestra Ruby saw perform at the RKO Theater in Boston. Ruby's list isn't finished. Certainly he would want me to mention how a number of musicians helped him become established. Pee Wee Russell and Sid Catlett would receive special praise in introducing the young Ruby Braff to established artists in New York, but there were others as well. Ruby never forgot those who helped him. In turn, he helped many younger musicians in early stages of their careers. That list would certainly include Scott Hamilton, Warren Vaché, Howard Alden, Loren Schoenberg, and Jon Wheatley. Ruby gained from support offered by Louis, Sid, and Pee Wee, and he tried to help several future generations of musicians in return. In fact, he even created several musical settings for Pee Wee Russell that resulted in some of Pee Wee's best recordings.

Ruby would also want me to emphasize that artists should use their technique to create beautiful tunes. He felt that wonderful melodies are remembered far longer than proficient solos. In his own career, Ruby was a master of using the tools of a dramatist to create a memorable performance. His music was not about a series of long solos, but of surprise and interplay. He understood texture. He changed backgrounds to sharpen contrast. Changes in tempo and modulation were tools of his trade. But above all, he honored the nice tunes that he loved to play.

I mention these thoughts because Ruby would probably have something to say to me if I didn't include them. I sent him copies of this manuscript as it developed from 20 pages to 80 and over 100. He paged through it, but mostly his pleasure was in knowing that someone treasured his contributions to music enough to make them accessible to future generations. He talked about some of the details, but quickly became bored and wanted to shift to other topics, often current affairs and some of his future plans and dreams.

Ruby was a wonderful musician. Tony Bennett called him the best cornetist in the world. Jack Teagarden, with the scripting assistance of George Simon, pronounced him the Ivy League's Louis Armstrong. But Ruby really wanted to own a club and present a variety of acts to entertain his customers. He often talked about wanting to include a magician, some jugglers, and a comedian, not only musical performers. He loved talking about the *Ed Sullivan Show* for this reason—variety. Those fortunate enough to attend Ruby's concerts and club performances often laughed at Ruby's humor. Some of his lines were familiar. He repeated them if they worked, but his repertoire was large and the repetition is only evident upon listening to hundreds of private recordings. For instance, he liked to say that for all the times he performed tunes by George Gershwin, that George never called him to say thanks. On paper, that isn't a line that would draw laughter, but when Ruby delivered it he knew how to build it up and time his delivery to create hearty chuckles from his audience. The recordings are the proof. Ruby delivered evenings of entertainment beyond "just music" wherever he played.

In music, Ruby fought labels. Too often he was labeled a Dixieland player, mostly by people who did not take the time to listen to his artistry. In later years, Ruby said he played chamber music. He often preferred small groups so that he could play softly. Ruby's tastes were wide. When I mentioned that I liked Miles Davis better in the '50s than the '80s, Ruby replied that this was "my problem." He praised Phil Woods and Georgie Auld. He loved Benny Goodman. He was respected by many musicians. Ruby respected John Coltrane's abilities but told me that Coltrane declared to him that he had gone too far with his style of playing, but that he could not turn back because it would anger his fans.

Ruby drove my wife and me to dinner several nights to various restaurants in Cape Cod, Ruby's home during the latter years of his life. We listened to some of Benny Goodman's recordings on the way. We talked, but upon hearing a particular phrase on Benny's clarinet, Ruby would inject, "Oooh, isn't that beautiful." Whatever he was doing, music was not far away. Ruby was not concerned about styles in music as much as he was committed to talent in any field of music. He was excited to hear young classical performers on *From the Top*, aired on National Public Radio stations. He was a committed listener. Perhaps it brought back memories of the early days of his own career. Certainly he admired these young performers' talent and dedication.

Ruby's standards were incredibly high. Once, when we were talking about Benny Goodman's reputation for staring at some members in his band—a penetrating glance that came to be called "The Ray"—Ruby said to me, "There is absolutely nothing wrong with that. Anyone who doesn't understand that has no idea of what it takes to be a professional musician." Ruby also described a time he was rehearsing with Benny Goodman at Benny's home. Benny's daughter

Rachel entered the room. Benny said something like, "Hi, Pops," and Rachel asserted, "Dad, my name is Rachel." Ruby used this to describe how Benny's life was totally centered on music, to the point he often thought of nothing else, not even his daughter's name.

Ruby applied equally high standards to his playing. He certainly demanded complete commitment from his fellow musicians. Ruby's talent is evident in his earliest recordings. He became a sensation in the jazz community following the release of a series of recordings made for the Vanguard Records label. Ruby was invited to those sessions by none other than John Hammond, whose eye for talent was legendary. Hammond had been impressed by Ruby's playing at a concert at Brandeis University in Boston. Ruby's style evolved during his career, but he retained his artistic commitment to what he called "the adoration of the melody." His fans never forget the Vanguard recordings, but Ruby maintained that "they really weren't very good." For nearly 50 years he worked to improve. His use of lower register became more dramatic. His juxtaposition of musical voices became more varied. He stopped using mutes, saying, "Any good player should be able to create any sound he wants to achieve without using a mute." But he continued to honor the composers of the Great American Songbook.

Because of his standards, Ruby did not often accept engagements where he did not have full control over the selection of musicians and program. Undoubtedly, this eliminated many possibilities for jobs. Without frequent touring, Ruby lost one important means to stimulate sales of his recordings. But his praise for Mat Domber of Arbors Records was unbounded, for Mat continued to allow Ruby to exercise complete artistic control of his recordings. Arbors has captured some of Ruby's finest recordings. Many have won top awards in the annual critics' poll conducted by *Jazz Journal International* and also been praised in other publications.

Ruby said that he hated it when musicians would claim to know a tune but not be able to play it properly. He said, "If a musician gets into trouble, I can usually get them out of it—but they have to know something about music to follow my lead." He loved juxtaposing songs into unique medleys, to create variety for his listeners and the musicians alike. The transitions were often unplanned, and Ruby expected musicians to quickly respond to his shift in direction, often including both key and tempo. In the recording studio, at least in the later years of his career, he wanted to arrange chairs for each musician so that he could have direct eye contact in order to provide cues for the unique combinations of instrumental voices he wished to create. This led to spontaneity in his performances that can easily be heard. Part of that was a result of physical limits to his lung capacity that were a consequence of advanced asthma and emphysema. But no matter how hard to you listen to his recordings, you will never hear him falter for lack of lung power. He did proudly assert, "A good musician doesn't have to play loudly." Ruby had a wide dynamic range regardless.

As mentioned, Ruby suffered from asthma and emphysema in his later years. He only had clear vision in one eye. If you talked with him, he requested that you move to his good side. During the Arbors recording session in 2000 he suffered from two cracked vertebrae and required a pillow on his chair to ease his pain. But the music was marvelous. Both CDs won international awards. All tunes but one were recorded in a single take. There was no splicing. The tune that required a second take was simply too long to fit on the CD. The musicians were enjoying the original performance so much, that time passed too quickly. When one of the musicians asked that his solo from the first take be spliced into the second, Ruby said, "We don't do that Frankenstein stuff around here." What you hear is exactly what was recorded in the studio. Ruby may have been in pain with limited lung power, but there is no sign of that in any of his playing. There is absolutely no indication of impairment. In live performances, Ruby conversed with the audience between tunes in order to regain his breath and clear his throat so that he could strive to create a masterpiece with his next tune. Sometimes he would use an inhaler during the set. During recording sessions, he lingered in the control room between songs for the same reason, listening to the playback and regaling everyone present with his stories before proceeding to the next performance. In the latter stages of his career he reached the stage or studio in a wheelchair. Fans would wonder what they would hear as he labored to climb to the stage. But when the performance began, there was no doubt that Ruby's delivery was unaffected. He simply saved his energy for what mattered most—his fans.

Ruby's final performances were in the United Kingdom. That was fitting, for his fans there were among his most loyal. Dave Bennett recorded virtually the entire tour. Ruby contracted pneumonia as the tour progressed. Even as his health deteriorated, the quality of the performances remained high. His final concert produced a masterpiece. When Ruby returned to his home, he thought he could recover. Hank O'Neal urged me to phone him, but when I did he had already been rushed to a hospital. From there he entered a convalescent home. He felt he would never be able to play again. Since music had been the central part of his life, that was a huge disappointment. He died February 9, 2003, without being able to return home. Steve Voce later reported that he may have been the last of Ruby's friends to talk with him by phone. Tony Bennett called him regularly.

Growing up, Ruby enjoyed listening to music on the radio. He enjoyed describing how he would hide under the covers of his bed in his youth, listening to live broadcasts from clubs across the country after he parents thought he was already asleep. Every 15 minutes would bring a new delight from a different band playing at a different location. Ruby felt that good music suffered when radio programs became more focused on popular playlists in more recent times. The variety was gone. For jazz, that meant less exposure at a time when the labels applied to various musical styles made it harder for novice listeners to determine what recordings to purchase, especially when they could no longer listen before buying. Ruby continued, "You know, I have never been aware that anyone who came to hear me play was disappointed and did not enjoy some very good music. The problem is getting them to come to the club. We don't seem to be able to make them aware that they would enjoy these tunes."

My own time with Ruby was brief. I met him in Toronto in February 1973, between sets at Bourbon Street. I approached him when he was seated beside Carol Britto. He glanced up from his conversation with her but continued talking. I waited. Finally he looked directly at me, and I said, "Sorry to interrupt. I just wanted to tell you that you taught me taste in music." At that, he smiled, shifted his position and invited me to sit down at his table. We talked about his recordings. "Vanguard, they weren't really very good," he said. I replied that they were indeed wonderful, but that he clearly had extended his style. Ruby smiled, and we continued to talk. Soon, it was time for the next set, and I returned to my own seat beside my wife who had waited patiently while I met my musical hero.

I continued to hope that someone else would take the initiative to write this book. There have been two previous Ruby Braff discographies, both limited to issued recordings.[1] Both were published long ago, one in England and the other in the USA, early in Ruby's career. Copies can sometimes still be acquired from specialist dealers. These books demonstrated the enthusiasm of Ruby's British fans. Much later, Peter Lowe, another British fan, began a later project and announced his intent in the jazz press. I offered to contribute some information to him; however that project did not continue due to Peter's declining health. I don't think that his notes survived. Tired of waiting, I contacted Mat Domber, the owner of Arbors Records. Twenty-seven years had passed since my brief talk with Ruby in Toronto, but I described that encounter to Mat. Mat called Ruby and within the hour encouraged me to do the same. Ruby was delighted to hear from me and claimed to remember me from our conversation in Toronto those many years before. I knew that it was certainly time to present a more complete record of Ruby's performing career to his many fans around the world and I promised to try to do so.

Ruby helped me with this manuscript during the final four years of his life. He invited my wife and me to spend a week with him at his modest rented home on Cape Cod (11 Scott Tyler Road, West Dennis, Massachusetts, if you are ever nearby). Every afternoon and evening we visited him at his home, with his strict instructions never to phone before noon. Ruby's bedtime was often about 6 a.m. His walls were covered with photographs of other musicians. Music played in the background during our talks. We talked on the phone every week or so, and he pointed me to a few recordings that had not been listed in discographies over the years. I made many calls to his home both before and after our visit. I certainly learned how weather affected his breathing. He found watching for whales very relaxing. He had considerable time to himself, for his engagements were infrequent. He told many stories. His telephone number (508-394-8077) will never be the same again.

In one of our conversations, I used the word *friend*. Ruby quickly replied, "*Friend* is a very special word, Tom. A person is fortunate to have one or two in an entire lifetime." But at the conclusion of his final studio recording session, he introduced me as his discographer. He and Bucky Pizzarelli invited me to write the notes that accompany that recording for Victoria Records. Invitations to write the notes for other albums followed from Mat Domber and Joe Boughton. Ruby's music has given me tremendous pleasure throughout much of my life, and I was able to see his satisfaction in knowing that his legacy would be documented and preserved for future generations. When I was in his home, I noticed that an early draft of this manuscript was close to his chair. I spotted another version nearby. I think he admired its growing heft. He talked about some of the details, but each conversation soon shifted to a future dream, politics, or some other musicians—or Judy Garland. But, a number of times when Ruby and I finished our telephone conversation, he asked to speak with my wife. She had become a Ruby Braff fan following our marriage in 1971, since his music was frequently heard in our home. Ruby really enjoyed talking with her. In truth, she was delighted to spend some time talking with Ruby, for his comments were always unique. He really was a romantic at heart, and it showed in their talks.

Ruby created beautiful music. He never married because he felt he could not offer his wife the stability that she would deserve, although he did have romantic relationships that he preferred not to discuss. He had opinions on many things—and his positions were strongly held. Sometimes that led to disagreements. When I mentioned that some people found him difficult, he said, "Tom, don't spread rumors about things like that." He felt that when someone asked his opinion, he was empowered and obligated to provide a direct answer. Since he was asked for his opinion, he failed to see why someone might be offended by his response. Needless to say, Ruby's candor was not always welcome. Some talks ended in heated arguments. He was an honest man, even when discretion might have served him better.

Ruby was unique. His voice in jazz is personal and immediately recognizable. His recordings will continue to touch the emotions of people as long as they are willing to listen. We are fortunate that his recorded legacy is so very rich. He set impossibly high standards for everyone, but also applied the same standards to himself.

I phoned Ruby on the eve of his flight to the UK for his final tour. "Tom," he said, "I'll just try to play as well as I can." He played marvelously, and fortunately nearly every note was captured by Dave Bennett. He leaves a large body of work as his legacy. It is my hope that this book helps to draw attention to his enduring artistry.

Benny Goodman once wrote some simple words to describe how some musicians become deeply committed to the art of performance. His words most certainly apply to Ruby Braff, even though the two of them had not yet met at that time. "[For some musicians,] it's in their blood, just as much as it was in mine."[2]

Introducing Ruby Braff

March 16, 1927–February 9, 2003

Ruby was born March 16, 1927, and died at 7 a.m. on Sunday, February 9, 2003. He never recovered from an illness that began near the end of his final tour in the United Kingdom. His performances throughout the tour were superb. Ruby has left a large recorded legacy, including many award winning albums. Many studio recordings have been released, while a few are documented in this book for the first time. Moreover, Ruby's fans around the world have privately recorded a number of his performances themselves. Many have shared copies of their prized recordings, permitting me to extend the documentation of Ruby's career. In addition, a number of jazz publications and major magazines and newspapers have described Ruby's appearances, and this information is included even when there is no known recording available.

Ruby's older brother was killed in WWII. The younger of his two older sisters lives in Massachusetts. His parents immigrated to the US from Russia when they were young. His father was a carpenter. His father's father was a clarinetist. He spent several years of his youth at 94 Devon Street in Roxbury, Massachusetts.

He began playing trumpet in 1935 at age seven or eight. This was the year Louis Armstrong returned to the US from Europe. Ruby claims that he played familiar melodies when his family was present, and only practiced exercises when alone. He did not read music until later in his career. He had no knowledge of jazz at first and "just played." Gradually, often late into the night, he began to enjoy broadcasts featuring the Dorseys and Artie Shaw. His parents were not aware he was awake and listening intently. Soon he discovered Benny Goodman, then Duke Ellington, Billie Holiday, and Louis Armstrong. Ruby said he first heard Louis on the radio when he was about ten years old. He frequently described the sensation as being like brilliant orange coming from the radio and filling the room. A Boston trumpeter and collector, Mayo Duca, played Louis's records for Ruby. Louis stayed with Duca when in Boston. Ruby's musical education accelerated.

Later in life, Ruby claimed that he developed his lower register technique so that people would not understand that it was him if they heard musical sounds coming through the walls of his New York apartment. Even if they knew he played a trumpet, they might think they were hearing a cello late at night, thereby reducing the chance of any confrontation in the elevators and hallways. Ruby also played softly. Sometimes he explained that he longed to make the trumpet sound like a saxophone. Originally, he had dreamed of playing a tenor saxophone because he thought it looked cool; however, he said that his parents were talked out of purchasing a saxophone by a salesman who sold them a trumpet instead, convincing them that the sax would dwarf Ruby and be hard for him to handle. Ruby felt that the salesman must have shown his parents a baritone saxophone. He resented the substitution.

He started playing professionally at clubs as early as nine years old. He played with other musicians for various parties; however, his first job in a club was accompanying Whistling Sam, the Piano Man. He then became a substitute player at the Silver Dollar Grill (Bar) when he was 11 or 12 whenever the regular musicians found a higher paying job on Friday and Saturday nights. The Silver Dollar was located in Boston's downtown. Ruby was paid $1.50 or $2.00 per night, plus cab fare home. Ruby delighted in the cab ride. At that point he was playing by ear and claimed to know all the standards and popular songs of the day. Ruby frequently enjoyed relating how the club's owner told him to be inconspicuous between sets, since he was clearly under age and not legally allowed to be in the club, much less perform. The owner's instruction was simple: "Go stand between two tall guys at the bar and don't move." But one night, Mary Driscoll, the licensing commissioner, spotted Ruby and asked him what he was doing in the club. Ruby replied that he was a musician hired to perform there. The inspector approached the owner, who promptly denied Ruby's claim. That ended his employment at the Silver Dollar.

Next, he performed at Izzy Ort's Grill, a club nearby in Boston's Combat Zone. Ruby felt that Izzy Ort's was particularly notorious. While Ruby's parents tolerated afternoon engagements, they were not pleased with evening ones. They reluctantly approved these jobs, but required Ruby to return home before midnight. As a condition, his employers provided the fare for a taxi. Ruby also substituted for musicians at other venues from time to time.

Nat Hentoff reported that when Ruby was about 15 he impressed Benny Goodman:[3]

> Goodman, walking past Izzy Ort's, heard the horn and sent in his bandboy, Popsie, to recruit the player for an audition. Ruby was awed but, realizing that his inability to read [music] made him useless in a big band, told Popsie with as much bravado as he could ignite, 'Tell Mr. Goodman I'll go with him only if I can be a soloist and not have to play in the section.' Ruby admitted to a friend years afterward, 'I couldn't have gone anyway. I was too young, but I didn't want to admit either reason. He must have thought I was a very arrogant, crazy kid.'

Ruby recalled that when his brother entered the army, he was about 16. While he was sorry to see his brother leave home, he now had his own bedroom and the use of his brother's car, a 1937 Ford. One evening he learned that Duke Ellington was to perform at Egleston Square in Boston, a traditionally Black neighborhood. He drove to the location, an upstairs ballroom, and it was a wreck. Ruby was the only White person seeking admission, and the doorman was reluctant to let him enter. Ruby declared he wanted to hear Duke Ellington, and this prompted considerable conversation when he declared he was a trumpet player. The manager decided to overlook Ruby's age since he was "an aspiring musician" and sat him at a table next to Duke Ellington. They discussed the program *9:20 Club* that aired in Boston. Duke had Ruby's table moved closer to the piano after learning that Ruby played the trumpet. Many years later in Paris, Ruby reminded Duke of this encounter. Duke claimed to recall the meeting: "Didn't I get you a Coke? Weren't you the kid?" Ellington was known to have an excellent memory. When their paths crossed, Ruby said he made a point to rise early in the morning to share breakfast with Duke. Those who know Ruby's habits for sleeping from 6 a.m. until at least noon will understand the extent of Ruby's interest and devotion.

Steve Voce published an interview with Ruby[4] which reflects on these events, but in a slightly different way for both the original encounter and their conversation during breakfast:

> I was about 15 when I went with some friends to a dance hall in Egleston Square in Boston to hear Duke Ellington for the first time. As far as I know we were the only white people in there that night. It was the band with Sonny Greer, Ben Webster, Barney Bigard and one of my most favorite trumpet players in the world, Ray Nance. Also I don't know of anyone who could play the violin like he could. I found it very moving. Much of my playing is influenced by his violin playing, and he was a great singer. I think that his version of 'I Can't Get Started' is greater than anybody's. Was it Jimmy Blanton or Junior Raglin on bass when I saw the band? Later on I played frequently for a while with Junior Raglin when he stopped in Boston.
>
> I disliked the style of Tricky Sam Nanton. I don't like that muted thing. Everybody was part of Duke's palette and it suited his writing, that's what they were there for. But I would not want to play with someone that growls and makes noises. I hate that sort of thing and I don't like Cootie growling. I like the way he played without the mutes. I used mutes all the time years ago, but Louis Armstrong said, 'What do you use those things for? Play with your own sound.' So I did. Even Louis used a straight mute for effect once in a while—on those wonderful records like 'La Vie En Rose' and things like that. Hearing the band that time in Boston was like being in heaven.
>
> I didn't meet Duke until much later on when I happened to be in the same touring package. We were in the hotel in Paris when he said to me, 'You get up for breakfast? You could have breakfast with me tomorrow, but I eat about seven in the morning.' What he meant was that he didn't go to bed before then. I stayed awake all night and then went and had breakfast with him. He always wanted everybody to feel wonderful. He was the master diplomat and deliverer of compliments. But if he'd been in the diplomatic service as he should have been, we'd have lost all that great music. 'You don't know how much it means to me to have breakfast with you,' I said. 'It means a lot to me, too,' he said, 'because I've been trying to be like you for years.'

Ruby's first major engagement was at the Savoy in Boston, with Edmond Hall, Vic Dickenson, Ken Kersey, John Field, and Jimmy Crawford in the late 1940s. He played a one-nighter in Allentown, Pennsylvania (not a jazz date) in the midst of trying to find engagements in New York without success. Back at the

Savoy, Frankie Newton and Pete Brown were occasional guests. Also in Boston, Ruby played at clubs with the names Vanity Fair and the Glass Hat.[5] Later he played with Sid Catlett at George Wein's Storyville Club. Ruby said that George Wein initially reserved the downstairs room (Mahogany Hall) for Sid. Ruby drove his car to New York, giving Sid a ride. Ruby recalled that this was probably in 1947, but it might have been somewhat later. This led to Ruby's early appearances at Central Plaza, Eddie Condon's, Jimmy Ryan's, and Nick's, in addition to occasional work in Boston. At that time, Ruby and Sid were rooming together. Ruby said that Sid helped him obtain a gig in Toronto with Bud Freeman. Catlett sadly died in Chicago on March 25, 1951, and Ruby returned from Toronto to pick up his own clothes from Catlett's wife.

Ruby liked to tell stories about how he drove Vic Dickenson to the Savoy Café during their early days in Boston. Vic timed his arrival at the club just in time to reach the bandstand and begin playing with the opening downbeat. Ruby dropped Vic off at the door but reached the bandstand a bit late after taking time to park, even on nights that were broadcast on local radio. But there is no question that Vic Dickenson was another of Ruby's earliest champions. Ruby later returned the favors, including Vic in his own session for Vanguard in 1955 and for a Bing Crosby tribute album recorded in 1981. Ruby and Dick Hyman performed together at Vic Dickenson's funeral.

Ruby had a break in 1952 at the Brandeis University Arts Festival. The jazz portions of the program were produced by George Wein. Then, John Hammond heard him for the first time, playing "When It's Sleepy Time Down South." The Hammond-produced Vanguard recordings followed, and Ruby became a sudden sensation. John Hammond played one of the recordings with Ellis Larkins for Richard Rodgers, and this led to Ruby being hired for an onstage role in the Broadway production *Pipe Dream*. The musical ran for eight months. It opened October 1, 1955, in New Haven, continued in Boston for three weeks, and arrived at the Schubert Theater in New York on November 30 for a run of 246 performances until June 30, 1956. Ruby wrote record reviews for the magazine *Saturday Review* during late 1957 and 1958. He moved to New York in 1953, living in Greenwich Village, Washington Heights (340 Cabrini Boulevard), Riverdale (above Manhattan, at 3016 Johnson Avenue, 5444 Arlington Avenue, and 679 West 239th Street) and moved to Cape Cod in 1991.

Martin Williams interviewed Ruby in 1964 for an article in *DownBeat*[6] that is reprinted as a chapter in his book *Jazz Changes*. Ruby spoke about learning to read music:[7]

> When I was a kid, no teacher could explain about syncopation. Even if they could read syncopation, they couldn't explain why you didn't play it exactly the way it was written. It just became confusing to me, and I just never paid any more mind to it, you know. And I met this wonderful guy a few years ago [probably early 1960s or late 1950s], Ward Silloway, the trombone player. He was playing with us at Jack Dempsey's. George Wettling had the job. It could have been the greatest. We worked from about 11 to 2 in the morning. Can you

> believe it? That's the way it was. Ward was playing. Pee Wee Russell. And Wettling.
>
> Ward always was afraid to play jazz. In all the bands he had played in—Bob Crosby, Benny Goodman—there was always some star trombonist there before him who would play all the solos. He became very inward about it. I used to encourage him because he plays good. One night he heard me say that I couldn't read, and he said, 'Are you serious? I can read anything—I'm very good really. Why don't you let me show you something about it?' And he took me on, to meet him every Wednesday in the Fred Waring Building, where he had a few pupils.
>
> I didn't know but most of the time he was going there, he was there just for me, however, and paying for the room. He would never let me know things like that. He'd say, 'What's the matter? You play much more than that when you play jazz—why are you tired here? Could it be that you get so busy reading that you're doing everything wrong? Pressing and pinching that thing against your mouth too hard because you're so busy?'
>
> What a patient, wonderful, wonderful person. So I'd go home and try to write out little things based on what he'd shown me.

Louis Armstrong provided the foundation for jazz music, but there will never be another musician like Ruby Braff. Ruby reported that Louis once said, "Anyone can steal anything but my applause."[8] But Ruby developed a unique style, while retaining a sense of melody. He referred to this on occasion as "adoration of the melody."

One of Ruby's dreams was to own a club that would feature musicians, along with jugglers and magicians, all appearing on movable sets with different guests appearing all night long. He called it "improvised musical theater." He enjoyed the *Ed Sullivan Show* on television, because it presented a tasteful variety of acts. Ruby also said he played 10,000 concerts a day, in his mind. Approaching a recording session he would imagine different combinations of players and tunes. Throughout his career he said he had an ability to understand how an audience would react. "I'm a musicmaker. I *know* who should play a chorus and when. I know how long a number should take. I know when it's dragging. I know when it should start. I know when one chorus is enough for somebody—or half."[9] As music evolved, he adhered to his concept of musical "truth" and dismissed fads. In addition to Louis Armstrong, Ruby praised Phil Woods, George Benson, Al Haig, Miles Davis, Conte Candoli, Georgie Auld, Connie Kay, Frankie Newton, Judy Garland, Duke Ellington, and many other musicians, some of whom played in styles that were not usually associated with him. "I always feel that great artists who are really dedicated to what they believe are truths are the people who will survive—musically and artistically. Those are the only people in the world I take seriously."[10] This led Ruby to reject opportunities to perform in musical settings where he was not in control. His musical standards, to the end, were something he would not compromise. At times Ruby's pointed words became his tool, just as "The Ray" had served Benny

Goodman. Just like Goodman, Ruby would sometimes be seen as argumentative and inflexible.

Some Milestones and Accomplishments

Buck Clayton wrote, "Ruby Braff is a brother. I've known Ruby for such a long time—we have recorded together, played together—and I respect Ruby as being one of the most dedicated trumpet players I ever knew. Ruby constantly improves and today, he is one of the really greats."[11]

Warren Vaché told Whitney Balliett, "As far as I'm concerned, the best trumpeter walking now is Ruby Braff. The taste and intelligence! Ruby is inventing a new language. The hardest thing about any brass instrument is the sheer physical effort it takes to play softly and subtly. You can bull your way through the trumpet, and it will sound that way. But to play it right you have to lean all your muscle and emotion into it. Like Ruby."[12]

Ruby won *DownBeat*'s New Star Award in 1955 and *Melody Maker*'s award in 1957. He received "new star" votes from Louis Armstrong, Bobby Hackett, and Bud Freeman in the 1956 *Encyclopedia of Jazz*. He was truly "born to play." He said, "Anywhere I played they liked it." He was often heard to say, "I understand the songs I play," and he sometimes called them "nice tunes."

Ruby Braff, Duke Ellington, and Billy Strayhorn are probably the only jazz musicians to have a unique typeface named in their honor. The designer, Michael Harvey, describes *Braff* as a modern descendant of Sans Serif Shaded designed for use on book jackets.[13] Ruby consented to the use of his name for a font that fills a unique and important niche in publishing, much as Ruby did with his music.

Lists of achievements can only provide limited insight into a musician's success, but what follows are two simple lists. The first shows the number of times Ruby's records were recognized as "Jazz Record of the Year" and the other shows a list of original compositions listed by ASCAP. The first tune in that list should provide a chuckle.

Ruby Braff's Recordings Receiving "Jazz Records of the Year" Awards from the Critics' Poll Sponsored by *Jazz Journal International* (Published between 1967 and 2004)

Year	Album
1967	*Vic Dickenson Showcase*, Fontana FJL 404
1974	Mel Powell, *Thigamagig*, Vanguard VRS 8502
1976	*The Best I've Heard* (Braff–Barnes Quartet), Vogue VJD 519 (double album)
1979	No awards published that year, since the coverage shifted from the last issue of the year to the second issue of the following year

Year	Album
1981	*Ruby Braff and Ralph Sutton*, Chaz Jazz 101 and Chaz Jazz 102
1983	*Easy Now*, RCA-Victor (F) PL 45140
1991	*The Mighty Braff*, Affinity AFF 757
1993	*New England Songhounds, Volume 1*, Concord Jazz Records CCD 4478
1995	*Vic Dickenson Septet*, Vanguard 662221 Ruby Braff–George Barnes Quartet, *Live at the New School*, Chiaroscuro CRD 126 Mel Powell, *Borderline/Thigamagig*, Vanguard 662223
1996	*Controlled Nonchalance at the Regatta Bar, Volume 1*, Arbors Records ARCD 19134
1998	*Inside & Out*, Concord Jazz CD 4691 *Plays Wimbledon*, Zephyr ZECD 15
1999	*You Can Depend on Me*, Arbors Records ARCD 19165 *Ruby Braff and Dick Hyman Play Nice Tunes*, Arbors Records ARCD 19141
2000	*Born to Play*, Arbors Records, ARCD 19203
2002	*The Ralph Sutton Quartet, Volume 4*, Storyville STCD 8312
2003	*I Hear Music*, Arbors Records ARCD 19244
2004	*Watch What Happens*, Arbors Records ARCD 19259 *Variety Is the Spice of Braff*, Arbors Records ARCD 19194

Ruby Braff's Compositions Listed by ASCAP:

Ad Lib Blues
Auld Lang Syne (of course this is traditional, not a Braff composition—but it is attributed to Ruby on the ASCAP website)
Ellie
Flakey (alternate title *Flaky*)
Flowers for a Lady with Bob Wilber
For Now
Here's Freddie
Here's a Tune
Here's Carl
If All Goes Well
Instantly
Just a Groove
Make Sense
Orange
Perfectly Frank (alternate title *Frankly*) with Jane Jarvis

Right Off
Shō-Time
Smart Alec Blues (alternate title *Smart Alex Blues)*
Someone Reminds Me of You
The Doodle King
Think
Thousand Islands
We're All Through
Where's Freddie? (alternate titles: *Everything's George; Here's Carl)*
With Time to Love

Ruby Braff's Other Original Compositions Not Listed on the ASCAP Website:

Big Blue
Blues for Ellis with Ellis Larkins
Blues for John W. with Dick Hyman
Blues for Ruby with Ellis Larkins
Break My Heart
Clear Water
Only a Blues
Ruby Got Rhythm
There's Something in My Mind (Ruby's original introduction to *Downhearted Blues*)

So why did I take time to write this book? To me, the reason is simple. Ruby's performances have given me great pleasure for many years. I simply wanted to find a way to repay him in some way for my enjoyment. This book is my attempt to do so. Ruby was pleased when he saw the manuscript growing at various stages during his lifetime. I am glad for that.

It is inevitable that I have failed, despite over a decade long effort, to document every appearance Ruby Braff made around the world during his career. As an example, here are just two specific details that remain unclear. I do not see those who provide information on my oversights as critics, but, on the contrary, as collaborators who join me in extending the record of Ruby's artistic career.

Examples of a few unresolved mysteries: Alex Alexander of BBC mentioned during a broadcast that Ruby appeared at Braunston, near Leicester, England, and the following day (Sunday) at Cambridge Jazz Club and "almost three years ago in Denver" meaning about early 1999. Ruby did perform extensively in London, Scotland, and Wales during the summer of 1999, but this booking is but one detail that has eluded me as I attempt to document Ruby's career. There is a jazz club called the Looking Glass, located at Braunston Gate, Leicester. Perhaps details will surface. Ruby also mentioned that he once performed at the White House, but I have been unable to find any further information. Several times, published information includes conflicting dates for recordings and appearances. I welcome further information to help resolve these points.

Undated recordings for Vanguard: Early in our conversations, Ruby reported a session created as a tribute to Johnny Mercer that remained unreleased by Vanguard Records. He stated that it included Eddie Condon and other musicians. I entered this session in 1958 on the basis of a report in *DownBeat* that Ruby recorded with Condon for Vanguard although information is incomplete.[14] Two titles with the Weavers, also recorded for Vanguard, are also entered arbitrarily in 1957 until more information becomes available. Fortunately, recordings of these performances are available.

Notes

[1] Albert J. McCarthy, *Ruby Braff: A Biography, Appreciation, Record Survey & Discography* (London: National Jazz Federation, Jazz Information Series, Token Press, Ltd., 1958) and George J. Hall, *Ruby Braff: A Complete Discography* (Laurel, MD: Jazz Discographies Unlimited, Spotlight Series, Volume 2, 1965).
[2] Benny Goodman and Irving Kolodin, *The Kingdom of Swing* (New York: Stackpole Sons, 1939), 264.
[3] Nat Hentoff, "Ruby Braff Missing Link of Jazz," *Esquire*, May 1958, 62.
[4] Steve Voce, *Jazz Journal International*, April 1995, 14.
[5] George A. Borgman, "The One and Only Ruby Braff," *Mississippi Rag*, December 1995, 2.
[6] *DownBeat*, January 30, 1964, 20–21.
[7] Martin Williams, *Jazz Changes* (New York: Oxford University Press, 1992), 31–32.
[8] James Lincoln Collier, *Louis Armstrong: An American Genius* (New York: Oxford University Press, 1983), 202, quoting from a conversation with Marshall Brown.
[9] Martin Williams, *Jazz Changes* (New York: Oxford University Press, 1992), 37.
[10] Martin Williams, *Jazz Changes* (New York: Oxford University Press, 1992), 35.
[11] Buck Clayton, *Buck Clayton's Jazz World* (New York: Oxford University Press, 1987), 173.
[12] Whitney Balliett, *Goodbyes and Other Messages* (New York: Oxford University Press, 1991), 76.
[13] Paul Shaw, "Filling a Niche: Michael Harvey's New Titling Font," *Print: America's Graphic Design Magazine* 57 (March–April 2003): 30–31.
[14] It was also mentioned in *Jazz Journal International,* February 1982, 8 and *Jazz Information* number 1472.

Chapter 2

The Earliest Days: Boston, Trips to New York, and Building a Relationship with George Wein

Ruby's professional performing career may have started as early as 1943, when Ruby was only 16 years old. He said that he began playing with various bands as early as age nine or ten, in 1936 or 1937. Peter Vacher interviewed Ruby about some events during these early years for his article that appeared in *Jazz Journal International*. Ruby described how he traveled by train to New York with other guys and share a hotel room for the weekend. His share of costs was about $5. In the interview, Ruby spoke about meeting Bobby Hackett:

> [Bobby Hackett] would invariably, on Friday, get on the train, and I got to know who he was and I said to him, 'You gonna be playing in Nick's tonight. Huh?' Even then he was looking for someone to substitute for him so he could drink, all of them, they were all the same, they didn't care, so he says, 'You got your horn?' but I says, 'I'll be coming to Nick's to hear you' and he says, 'Bring the horn, it's a hard night for me there.' And you know the truth of the matter was, in those days they went to work from about quarter to nine to four o'clock in the morning. Even Eddie Condon's, when you went to work there, it was nine to three. And no money! It was crappy money. But the guys liked to play and people spurred them on. There was a place next to Nick's called Julius's and that's where everybody went to drink, except Condon who did his drinking in the joint and met everybody so when he opened his (own) joint he knew everybody in the world. Very smart.[1]

Ruby continued this interview, describing one time that he substituted for Hackett, playing with Pee Wee Russell, Brad Gowans, Joe Sullivan, and Joe Grauso. Later, he described playing informally with Willie "The Lion" Smith and listening to many other musicians in various clubs along 52nd Street. He stated that returning to school at the start of the week was quite a letdown and concluded by saying, "I always hoped the day would come that I could live there."

Ruby continued the interview, reporting his joy at hearing Louis Armstrong perform for his first time. This was at the Aquarium in the spring of 1946. Ruby just stood in front of the revolving entrance doors to hear the bits of music that reached the street. Because of his age and inexperience, he was afraid to enter and later described this to Louis:

> I told Pops (later) I had to catch a note or two every time the door revolved. He said, 'Why didn't you just come in and sit down?' I said, 'Because I didn't know what to do,' and he laughed, he thought that was so funny. Even the notes that came out of that revolving door sounded good.[2]

Susan Atran, Ruby's sister, reported that Ruby was voted the best comedian in his high school, a talent that contributed to his success as a club and concert artist. Following graduation from high school in 1945, he began traveling to New York and staying for a week or two while trying to qualify for a union card. On these early trips to New York, he shared the cost of a room at the Hotel St. James on 45th Street with several classmates, packed three to the room as they sometimes took turns to sleep. He said he lived for a dollar a week during this time. Nat Pierce was living in the same hotel, but he reported making $90 per week playing at the USO club. Downstairs at the back of the hotel, there was a closed cocktail lounge with an out-of-tune piano. It also boasted a record player, often with Lester Young's records playing. Stan Getz, Alan Eager, and other tenor players regularly stopped by. Ruby said he picked the St. James because it was one of the few at this price without cockroaches. He often ordered his meals at the White Rose, located at the corner of 6th and 52nd where there was often a line of musicians for every meal.

Ruby reported that his mother sent him a package of things every week at this time, mostly sardines and peanut butter. But they had no bread. "I hated sardines, but I used to take the cans and dump the cans out the window into the alley unless I absolutely needed to eat them at the time." Around the corner was the Automat, a source of food on other occasions. Coffee was a nickel and $1.50 bought a banquet.

Mel Levine, one of Ruby's friends, reports that he probably heard Ruby perform at the Ken Club as early as 1943. Ruby recalled playing with Nat Pierce in 1943 or 1944, when Nat was 15 years old, in a local club owned by Jack Brown.

Ruby tells a story that probably happened about this time. Fortunately he also reported it to Steve Voce, who included it in one of his many fine interviews with Ruby that he published in *Jazz Journal International*:[3]

> I played with Fats, but I had no idea who he was. At that time I used to play my trumpet along with the music that was on the radio. Sunday was traditionally a day for jam sessions in Boston when I was a little kid. I was walking up Tremont Street with my horn one Sunday. There was a club there called the Tick Tock that had a stairway which went absolutely straight up for about a mile. I saw a truck outside unloading a baby grand white piano and there were a couple of guys trying to get it up the stairs. I was very curious and I said, 'Where's this going?' 'If we can manage it it's going upstairs into the club,' said the guy.

'Who wants this piano up there so bad?' I said. 'Fats Waller wants it,' the guy said. 'Who's he?' I asked. 'Get away from me, son,' he said.

I passed that way again later on and the piano had gone. I decided to go up the stairs and see what was going on. I guess what they were having what we would now call a sound check. There was this big, jolly, fat man loading up the piano bench with what seemed to be bottles of whiskey and laughing and singing and whistling to himself. There was nobody else there but the musicians. I just sat down on a chair and watched, and they started warming up. At one point the big man looked at me and said, 'Hey! What you got there?'

I said 'It's a trumpet.'

'Can you play it?'
'Yeah,' I said.
'How good can you play it?'
'I don't know.'
'Would you like to play with me?'
'Yeah.'
'What would you like to play?'

I said, 'Do you know 'Honeysuckle Rose'?' That was one of the tunes I had been playing with the radio. He kept very straight-faced and he said to the other fellows, 'Do we know 'Honeysuckle Rose'?' So I played that with him and then he said, 'What else would you like to play?' I asked if he knew 'The Sheik of Araby.' He turned to his musicians and said, 'Do we know 'The Sheik of Araby'?' We played that and then we did the same with 'Sweet Sue.'. . . And so it went on. Eventually he said, 'Do you know what time it is?'

'Four thirty,' I answered. 'Where do you live?' he asked. 'I live in Roxbury,' I said. 'How do you get there?' 'On the subway.' 'No,' he said. 'That's not very good. It's getting dark. Come with me.' He jumped off the stand and we ran all the way down the stairs out to the street and he called a cab, gave the driver some money, and said, 'Take this boy home.'

Not so many days after I went to the local movie house and I looked up at the screen and—my god!—there he was with a Derby on. I said to my friends, 'I played with him last Sunday!' and they said 'Yeah, yeah, oh sure, sure.' I said, 'I'm *telling* you, I played with this man!' and nobody would believe me. I always hoped that someday when I grew up I would be able to see him and remind him of that afternoon, but sadly he died.

Taken from a column originally written by Steve Voce that appeared in *Jazz Journal International,* November 1995, 9. Used by permission: www.jazzjournal.co.uk.

In this description of events, Ruby probably recalled seeing Fats Waller perform in the film *Stormy Weather*. Fats Waller died December 14, 1943 after the film's release that year, just as Ruby's reputation began to grow in the Boston area.

It is probably impossible to trace details of many of Ruby's earliest appearances in Boston and New York; however, a few details are available to provide a sketchy framework for these early years.

Boston Jazz Society[4]

May 21, 1944, Boston (perhaps Huntington Chambers, a small auditorium near Copley Square)

Johnny Windhurst and Ruby Braff with unnamed other musicians probably including Howie Gadboys (cl), Ralph Ferrigno (tb), Ev Schwarz (p), Inky Ingersoll (bjo), John Field (b), Pen Brown or Bill Burch (dm)

The article continued: "Our local Boston competition was the Beacon Jazz League, which starred one local boy who's made good—Ruby Braff. Buzzy Drootin usually played for them. Not that either society was able to break even—but the music was great."

The Jazz Society Presents the Vinal Rhythm Kings[5] **(see Figure 2.1)**

December 9, 1945, Savoy Café, 410 Massachusetts Avenue, Boston

Ruby Braff, George Schwartz (tp), Ernie Perry (ts), Ralph Ferrigno, and other unknown musicians

NOTE: I have been able to acquire several acetate recordings of tunes performed by the Vinal Rhythm Kings, but unfortunately none include Ruby Braff. One, recorded at Huntington Chambers, does includes Frankie Newton. Perhaps Ruby will be heard on other recordings that remain to be discovered in the future.

Unknown Billing for a Quintet[6]

Mid-1940s, York Beach, Maine

Ruby Braff (tp), Sam Margolis (ts), Ray Frazee (p), Charlie Terrace (b), Izzy Sklar (dm)

NOTE: A photo from this engagement is available from the 2001 March of Jazz program and included in the photo section in this book.

Unknown Billing, Weymouth, Massachusetts

"In 1945 or 1946, Braff worked a weekly gig with Tony Bell, a drummer, in Weymouth, Massachusets. Tiny Ziegler, the owner of the place, liked to serve Brandy Alexanders to the musicians after 10:00 p.m., locking the doors and not letting the musicians go home until they had some drinks with him. It would be close to 1:00 a.m. when Braff arrived home, and this angered his parents."[7]

George Wein wrote about a period in his life in Boston about 1946 in his memoir, *Myself Among Others*:[8]

> To my relief, I discovered that there were still musicians my age in Boston who hadn't tossed swing for bop. The trumpeter Ruby Braff and tenor saxophonist Sammy Margolis were the spirit and backbone behind a cadre of players inspired by Lester Young, Duke Ellington, Count Basie and, of course, Louis Armstrong.
>
> Working with Ruby, in particular, was an education. He was by far the best trumpet player in the Boston area (and, I would later discover, one of the

finest swing-oriented trumpeters in the world). He knew what it was to play in a combo, and had an amazing ear that enabled him to pick up a tune and chord changes. While my musical training couldn't compare with Ruby's talent and knowledge, we were both anachronisms, and this brought us into musical contact.

Ruby and Sammy [Margolis] represented Boston's swing vanguard. But there was a separate contingent of musicians—epitomized by Harvard University's Crimson Stompers—who were dedicated to the Dixieland style. The first-call pianist in this circle was a guy named Ev Schwarz who ran a gas station at Coolidge Corner in Brookline. As I got to know some of the musicians in this crowd, Ev graciously took me under his wing. He taught me many of the Dixieland and Chicago-style standards of the '20s and '30s. By the time he was through with me, I was capable of working with any of the Dixieland bands in town.

Johnny Blowers reported the following events in 1947:[9] "I met a young trumpet player, Ruby Braff, and talked Condon into letting him sit in [at Condon's]. He was great!" The surrounding context suggests that this comment was made in early to mid-May 1947. The other musicians playing in the group at Condon's are listed as the following: Wild Bill Davison (cnt), Pee Wee Russell (cl), Georg Brunis (tb), Gene Schroeder (p), Eddie Condon (g), Morris Raymond (b), and Johnny Blowers (dm). The text continues, "Wednesday was guest night at Condon's, and the stars came out—Bobby Hackett, Sol Yaged, Bud Freeman, Edmond Hall, Herb Hall, Freddie Olms, Jack Teagarden, Hot Lips Page, and Ruby Braff. Ruby would have been playing professionally for about ten years by this time."

Nat Hentoff reported that Ruby had "worked out his Local 802 union card as early as 1947, waiting out the required nonworking residence in New York by borrowing $25 a week from his mother. 'I knew I had to have that card and I knew the place to grow in jazz was New York.'"[10]

George Wein described the following event that occurred about 1947 in his memoir:[11]

Dick Mascott started working on a series of New England college gigs. Dick did the booking, and I put together a band. In addition to the working quartet, I hired Ruby Braff and Dick LeFave, a trombonist who had worked with Sam Donahue's band. [The working quartet refers to Edmond Hall (cl), George Wein (p), John Field (b), and Joe Cochrane (dm), who performed for a month at the Savoy in Boston and performed at colleges on alternate Saturday nights.]

The resulting program, 'Danceable Jazz: Edmond Hall and His Sextet,' was a big success. We played in Middlebury, Vermont, and appeared at the Winter Carnival in Hanover, New Hampshire, on the Dartmouth College Campus. Each night's fee was $750—much more than we could earn during an entire week at the Savoy. . . .

We had a few other Saturdays open, so I called Charlie Shribman, who, with his brother Sy, had controlled virtually all of the New England ballrooms during their prewar heyday. By 1949, their business had diminished, and Sy

> had passed away. But Charlie still owned and controlled the venues, and he was kind enough to give us a gig at the Raymor Ballroom on Huntington Avenue, just down the street from the Savoy. He paid us something in the neighborhood of $400.
>
> On another open Saturday, Mascott couldn't find a gig. I suggested to Edmond [Hall] that it might be time to put on our own concert at Jordan Hall, the New England Conservator's thousand-seat auditorium. I knew the quartet, or even the sextet, was not enough to fill the hall. We had to do something special. [George Wein continued to describe events surrounding the evening billed as *Edmond Hall and George Wein Present: From Brass Bands to BeBop* on March 1, 1949.]
>
> The popularity of the Edmond Hall Quartet had prompted Steve Connelly to make us Savoy headliners. We were soon going to be working with Jimmy Crawford (former drummer with the Jimmie Lunceford Orchestra), Vic Dickenson (my trombone idol), and Ruby Braff (my man on cornet).

George Wein continued, explaining how he gave his notice and was replaced by Ken Kersey in the quartet.

Jordan Hall Concert[12]
October 24, 1947, Boston
Ruby Braff (tp), Al Drootin (cl), Buzzy Drootin (dm), and others including Edmond Hall (cl), Bud Freeman (ts), Carl Rand (sax), Hot Lips Page (tp), John Nicolazzi (tp), Jimmy Welch (tb), Arthur Medoff (p), John Field (b)

George Wein's first Storyville Club was located at 47 Huntington Avenue in the Copley Square Hotel, later moved to Hotel Buckminster at Kenmore Square in Boston. The Mahogany Hall club was located in the Copley Square Hotel.

Ruby said that he was a guest with Frankie Newton, Pete Brown, and Vic Dickenson on several occasions during this time in Boston. George Wein wrote lovingly about his times with Frankie Newton during this period. Vic Dickenson had returned to Boston from California in about March 1949.[13]

The following recordings of Edmond Hall's All Stars were made by Sam Prescott from WMEX broadcasts. The earliest recordings were made using a wire recorder and later transferred to acetate discs. The wire recordings are lost. Later recordings were made using a home disc recorder. All the discs were transferred to audio cassettes and indexed in a document prepared on July 20, 1982. All discs, reel recordings and cassette tapes are now held at the New Hampshire Library of Traditional Jazz in Auburn, New Hampshire. Manfred Selchow wrote that the later broadcasts from May 22, 23, 24, 29, 31 and June 1, 14, 16, 17, 22, 1949, may contain Ruby Braff while earlier sessions not listed here include Johnny Windhurst. Recordings from May 24, May 31, and June 1, 1949, have never been located in the archived collection and are not included in the listing below. Airchecks from June 7 may be held in the collection but were not available for auditioning. Paul Verrette carefully maintained this unique collection during his lifetime and provided access to these uniquely valuable recordings.

Jim Weaver wrote about the background for these recordings:

> The Boston Jazz Society was a big part of our life, in those years. I began the practice of recording jazz from the radio before Sam, and he caught the fever before he moved to New Hampshire. The recordings were transferred to five-inch reel tapes. Some of the recordings may have been made directly to audio tape, rather than acetates. Sam's wife, Dot, founded the New Hampshire Library of Traditional Jazz and made plans for Paul Verrette to manage the collection. She transferred all the reel tapes to cassettes and copied all available text from the reel boxes. There were a total of 47 cassettes of differing length and quality.[14]

Ed Hall's All Stars[15]
Early 1950s or late 1940s, dates unknown, WMEX broadcasts, Boston
Ruby Braff or Johnny Windhurst (tp), Ed Hall (cl), Vic Dickenson (tb), Ken Kersey (p), John Field (b), Jimmy Crawford (dm)

Johnny Windhurst is listed in the printed log sheets for performances from May 8–13, 1949. Audibly, the playing on some of these particular performances is very similar to Ruby Braff's style, so these recordings are included in this listing. Performances from May 22 and later definitely feature Ruby Braff.

May 8, 1949 (listed as Johnny Windhurst in printed log sheets but could be Ruby Braff instead)
On the Sunny Side of the Street
NOTE: A recording of this tune is available but remains unissued.

May 9, 1949 (listed as Johnny Windhurst in printed log sheets, but could be Ruby Braff instead)
Panama
When the Saints Go Marching In
The World Is Waiting for the Sunrise
Robbins' Nest
West End Blues
NOTE: A recording of these tunes is available but remains unissued.

May 11, 1949 (listed as Johnny Windhurst in printed log sheets but could be Ruby Braff instead)
Basin Street Blues
Muskrat Ramble
There'll Be Some Changes Made
Nobody's Sweetheart
NOTE: A recording of these tunes is available but remains unissued.

May 12, 1949 (listed as Johnny Windhurst in printed log sheets but could be Ruby Braff instead)
Ballin' the Jack
Mood Indigo
NOTE: A recording of these tunes is available but remains unissued.

May 13, 1949 (listed as Johnny Windhurst in printed log sheets but could be Ruby Braff instead)
Carry Me Back to Old Virginny
Singing the Blues (definitely Windhurst rather than Braff)
Yesterdays (no tp, Hall and Dickenson feature)
NOTE: A recording of these tunes is available but remains unissued.

Ruby attended a birthday party for Edmond Hall amidst the appearances captured in the Prescott airchecks; however, no recordings have been located.

Ed Hall's Birthday Party[16]
May 15, 1949, home of Mr. and Mrs. Ernest Di Natale, 185 Franklin Street, Cambridge, Massachusetts
Ruby appeared with Frankie Newton, Ev Schwarz, Jimmy Crawford, John Field, Ken Kersey, Joe Battaglia, John Field, and other musicians, some from Harvard University.

The following airchecks definitely include Ruby Braff with Ed Hall's All Stars:

Ed Hall's All Stars[17]
May 22, 1949, WMEX broadcast, Boston
Ruby Braff (tp), Ed Hall (cl), Vic Dickenson (tb), Ken Kersey (p), John Field (b), Jimmy Crawford (dm)
China Boy
I'm Gonna Sit Right Down and Write Myself a Letter, incorporating Struttin' with Some Barbecue
Blues
Struttin' with Some Barbecue (short extract with Ed Hall's solo)
NOTE: A recording of these tunes is available but remains unissued.

Ed Hall's All Stars[18]
May 23, 1949, WMEX broadcast, Boston
Ruby Braff (tp), Ed Hall (cl), Vic Dickenson (tb), Ken Kersey (p), John Field (b), either Jimmy Crawford or Arthur Herbert (dm)
My Gal Sal
Some of These Days
Lazy River
NOTE: A recording of these tunes is available but remains unissued.

Ed Hall's All Stars[19]
May 29, 1949, WMEX broadcast, Boston
Ruby Braff (tp), Ed Hall (cl), Vic Dickenson (tb), Ken Kersey (p), John Field (b), either Jimmy Crawford or Arthur Herbert (dm)
If I Could Be with You (no tp)
More Than You Know
Someday Sweetheart
Lonely Moments (fragment)
Ja-Da
'S Wonderful—program ends
NOTE: A recording of these tunes is available but remains unissued.

The following three tunes are listed in the printed log for this performance but recordings were not available to the author:
Caravan
If I Could Be with You
Bill Bailey

An aircheck is listed in the log for June 7 but has not been available to the author. The log shows the following tunes played:
Keepin' Out of Mischief Now
St. Louis Blues
Panama
Somebody Stole My Gal
Bill Bailey
Lonely Moments
How Come You Do Me Like You Do
Nobody's Sweetheart
Frolic Sam

Ed Hall's All Stars[20]
June 14, 1949, WMEX broadcast, Boston
Ruby Braff (tp), Ed Hall (cl), Vic Dickenson (tb), Ken Kersey (p), John Field (b), either Jimmy Crawford or Arthur Herbert (dm)
The Man I Love
Cherry
NOTE: A recording of these tunes is available but remains unissued.

Ed Hall's All Stars[21]
June 16, 1949, WMEX broadcast, Boston
Ruby Braff (tp), Ed Hall (cl), Vic Dickenson (tb), Ken Kersey (p), John Field (b), either Jimmy Crawford or Arthur Herbert (dm)
Somebody Stole My Gal
Mean to Me

Exactly Like You or Take the "A" Train (fragment Ed Hall)
NOTE: A recording of these tunes is available but remains unissued.

Ed Hall's All Stars[22]
June 17, 1949, WMEX broadcast, Boston
Ruby Braff (tp), Ed Hall (cl), Vic Dickenson (tb), Ken Kersey (p), John Field (b), either Jimmy Crawford or Arthur Herbert (dm)
Solitude
It's Been So Long (fragment Vic Dickenson solo only)
Moonglow (incomplete)
NOTE: A recording of these tunes is available but remains unissued.

Ed Hall's All Stars[23]
June 22, 1949, WMEX broadcast, Boston
Ruby Braff (tp), Ed Hall (cl), Vic Dickenson (tb), Ken Kersey (p), John Field (b), either Jimmy Crawford or Arthur Herbert (dm)
Careless Love
Medley:
  You Made Me Love You (Dickenson feature)
  My Ideal (piano feature)
Jack the Bear (a few bars featuring John Field (b) to close another tune)
Limehouse Blues
Please Don't Talk About Me When I'm Gone
Bugle Call Rag/Ole Miss
Fragment possibly Buddy Bolden's Blues, which was Ed Hall's sign-off theme (no tp)
NOTE: A recording of these tunes is available but remains unissued.

A printed invitation to former members of the Jazz Society and other interested persons is available to the author. It publicizes a "real jam session" to be held at 8:30 at the Savoy Café featuring the Vinal Rhythm Kings (named for Charlie Vinal). It notes the following: "This is the first informal Monday nite session in a long time!" Ruby's last name is incorrectly spelled *Braaf* in the list of musicians who would appear. This would happen several times during the earlier years of his performing career. The details are shown in the next listing.

Vinal Rhythm Kings[24] **(see Figure 2.2)**
November 21, 1949, Savoy Café, 410 Massachusetts Avenue, Boston
Ruby Braff (tp), Paul Watson (cnt), Bob Gay (tb), Vic Dickenson (tb), Edmond Hall (cl), Howie Gadboys (cl), Ken Kersey (p), Joe Battaglia (p), John Field (b), Arthur Herbert (dm), Bob Saltmarsh (dm)

Manfred Selchow published a photograph from this time that shows only a bit of Ruby's face at the right side of the photograph along with Ed Hall, Nat Hentoff, and Vic Dickenson.[25] I have obtained several home acetate recordings of the Vinal Rhythm Kings, but unfortunately Ruby is not audible.

One of Ruby's appearances with the Edmond Hall All Stars was issued by Savoy Records on an early ten-inch LP. This is the first time that Ruby's playing would have been available on a released recording. It has been frequently reissued over the years.

Edmond Hall All Stars: *Jazz at the Savoy Café*
December 1949, Savoy Café, Boston (LP says spring 1949 on SJL 2251)
Ruby Braff (tp), Vic Dickenson (tb), Edmond Hall (cl), Ken Kersey (p), John Field (b), Jimmy Crawford (dm)
Careless Love
 Savoy MG 15028, 12213, SJL 2251, Regent MG 6076
Please Don't Talk About Me When I'm Gone
 Savoy MG 15028, 12213, SJL 2251, Regent MG 6076, Savoy 0277 (CD)
Bugle Call Rag
 Savoy MG 15028, 12213, SJL 2251, Regent MG 6076
Medley:
 Black and Blue (EH feature)
 Savoy MG 15028, 12213, SJL 2251, Regent MG 6076, Savoy 0277 (CD)
 When a Woman Loves a Man (RB feature)
 Savoy MG 15028, 12213, SJL 2251, Regent MG 6076, Savoy 0277 (CD)
 You Made Me Love You (VD feature)
 Savoy MG 15028, 12213, SJL 2251, Regent MG 6076, Savoy 0277 (CD)
 My Ideal (KK feature)
 Savoy MG 15028, 12213, SJL 2251, Regent MG 6076, Savoy 0277 (CD)
 One Bass Hit (Field feature)
 Savoy MG 15028, 12213, SJL 2251, Regent MG 6076
Limehouse Blues
 Savoy MG 15028, 12213, SJL 2251, Regent MG 6076

NOTE: MG 15028 is a ten- inch LP titled *Jazz at the Savoy Café*. All titles on that LP are included on Avid AMSC 1019 (CD titled *Edmond Hall: Four Classic Albums Plus)*. Both Savoy SJL 2251 and 0277 (CD) are titled *Giants of Traditional Jazz*. The CD fades out after the first few notes of "One Bass Hit" and does not include all titles from the double LP version of this album. All titles also issued on London (E) LZ-C 14005 and Savoy (G) WL 70513, both titled *Giants of Traditional Jazz*. "One Bass Hit" is not listed on the record labels and it provides a brief interlude before the start of "Limehouse Blues," as a part of the medley that features individual members of the group. Some of the issues include announcements by Nat Hentoff as master of ceremonies for the performance.

The Savoy LPs were originally mastered by Rudy Van Gelder in one of his earliest projects.

Ed Hall hired Ruby to replace Johnny Windhurst. Ruby was playing opposite Hall's group with piano and drums. Ruby said that he had to learn 12 Teddy Wilson arrangements prior to a broadcast. This was a challenge since he did not read music at that time. He said that he visualized all the arrangements and was able to play them that same night.

Ed Hall's band continued at the Savoy Café during December, with Jimmy Crawford replaced on drums by Arthur Herbert. The band probably performed until late February or early March 1950. Joe Sullivan opened an engagement on December 19, 1949, with the Vinal Rhythm Kings. Following the opening (on a Monday night) Sullivan continued for a limited engagement with Edmond Hall's All Stars. In addition to Edmond Hall, the All Stars included Ruby Braff (spelled *Ruby Bref* in a publicity handbill), Vic Dickenson, Ken Kersey, John Field, and Arthur Herbert.[26] The author has a copy of the handbill.

Joe Sullivan and Edmond Hall's All Stars[27] (see Figure 2.3)
December 19, 1949 (opening night), Savoy Café, Boston
Ruby Braff (tp), Vic Dickenson (tb), Edmond Hall (cl), Ken Kersey (p), John Field (b), Arthur Herbert (dm)

The next performance of the All Stars was in a concert in late December; however, the location has not been traced.

Edmond Hall's All Stars[28]
Late December 1949, concert, Boston
Ruby Braff (tp), Vic Dickenson (tb), Edmond Hall (cl), Ken Kersey (p), John Field (b), Arthur Herbert (dm)
Sister Kate
The World Is Waiting for the Sunrise
NOTE: Other tunes are not mentioned.

Ed Hall returned to New York in late February or early March 1950.[29] Martin Williams wrote that Steve Kuhn worked as an accompanist at Storyville and Mahogany Hall, performing with local players like Ruby Braff as well as visiting stars including Coleman Hawkins, Vic Dickenson, Chet Baker, and Serge Chaloff. Ruby reported that he played regularly at Mahogany Hall with Bob Wilber and Sid Catlett.[30]

Ed Hall returned to Boston for engagements at the Hi-Hat (without Ruby Braff)[31] and at least the following performance from the Savoy Café that included Ruby.

Savoy Jam Session: WMEX
May 16, 1950, Savoy Café, WMEX aircheck, Boston
(Ruby's opening night with Edmond Hall and His All Stars)
Ruby Braff (tp), Edmond Hall (cl), Vic Dickenson (tb), Ken Kersey (p), John Field (b), Jimmy Crawford (dm), Nat Hentoff (emcee, introduced as Lafayette)

Coquette (incomplete)
Please Don't Talk About Me When I'm Gone (incomplete)
It's Only a Paper Moon (incomplete)
After You've Gone (incomplete)
Coquette (incomplete)
NOTE: A recording of these tunes is available but remains unissued.

An advertisement is available that announced Frankie Newton's All Star Orchestra, vocalist Alice Ross Groves, Nat Pierce's Orchestra, the Charlie Mariano Boptet, and the Ruby Braff Quintet, all appearing at the Savoy Café until Joe Marsala opened on May 26. The Savoy Café was billed as "Boston's Hot Spot of Rhythm."[32] Thus, Ruby Braff was billed as the leader of a quintet; however, further details are not known beyond appearances ending before May 26.

Ruby Braff Quintet[33] (see Figure 2.4)
Before May 26, 1950, Savoy Café, Boston
Ruby Braff (tp) with unknown musicians

George Wein describes the opening of his Boston club, Storyville, in late September 1950 in the Copley Square Hotel. The opening band was the Bob Wilber Sextet with Sidney and Wilbur DeParis, Red Richards, John Field, and Sid Catlett.[34] He reported that business was brisk for six weeks and that Catlett was the real star of the show. An advertisement heralding this opening has a handwritten note by Mel Levine that Ruby Braff replaced Sidney DeParis on October 25, the night of the grand opening.[35] This ad is the foundation for the following appearance by Ruby:

Bob Wilber and His Band (see Figure 2.5)
October 25, 1950, Storyville Club, Copley Square Hotel (grand opening), Boston
Ruby Braff (tp), Wilbur DeParis (tb), Bob Wilber (cl), Red Richards (p), John Field (b), Sid Catlett (dm)

Bob Wilber had performed in France in 1948 and had developed a following by the time of these engagements. He had become well known as a young pupil of Sidney Bechet. A copy of another ad is available. It shows information about an upcoming Sunday afternoon Storyville Jam Session that included Ruby Braff as a member of Bob Wilber's band.[36] The cover charge for entry to the club was listed as $1. It is likely that Wilber's band was appearing nightly at Storyville during this period.

Edmond Hall with Bob Wilber and His Band—Storyville Jam Session: WMEX[37] (see Figure 2.6)
November 12, 1950, Storyville Club, WMEX aircheck, Boston

Sidney DeParis (tp), Wilbur DeParis (tb), Edmond Hall (cl), Bob Wilber (cl, ts), Red Richards (p), John Field (b), Sid Catlett (dm), Nat Hentoff, (emcee)
Bugle Call Rag
Fidgety Feet

Edmond Hall (cl), George Wein (p), John Field (b), Sid Catlett (dm)
Clarinet Marmalade

Add Ruby Braff (tp), Dick LeFave (tb); Ernie Furtado (b) replaces Field
'S Wonderful

Sidney DeParis (tp), Wilbur DeParis (tb), Edmond Hall (cl), Bob Wilber (cl), Red Richards (p), John Field (b), Sid Catlett (dm)
High Society
Bugle Call Rag
NOTE: A recording of these tunes is available but remains unissued.

Louis Armstrong and Jack Teagarden were in Boston on this date for a concert at Symphony Hall on Sunday, November 12, 1950.[38] Ruby recalled that he was still playing at Storyville in Boston that night following the afternoon jam session and he reported that a woman rushed the stage and actually tackled Louis Armstrong during the concert in front of the audience. Louis held his instrument in the air but was pushed to the floor while Jack Teagarden was singing. Louis recovered and spoke to the audience, saying something like the following: "I don't know why she went after me, because Jack was singing." After the concert concluded Ruby recalled that people walked by Storyville, discussing what they had seen and heard. Later, Ruby said that Louis acted out the entire episode for him on several occasions, including dramatically falling to the floor with his arm in the air as if holding his trumpet.[39] Nat Hentoff announced during the above broadcast that Jack Teagarden had played with the group the previous evening and that he intended to return to Storyville after the Symphony Hall concert, but that it was not certain that Louis would accompany him.

An ad for the next Sunday jam session features Henry "Red" Allen with Bob Wilber's band, with "overseer" Nat Hentoff guiding the proceedings.[40] Wilber's band, including Ruby, is billed as "appearing nightly."

Henry "Red" Allen with Bob Wilber and His Band
November 19, 1950, Storyville Club, Copley Square Hotel, Boston (still billed as the grand opening)—the band except Allen were appearing nightly at this time
Henry "Red" Allen, Ruby Braff, Sidney DeParis (tp), Dick LeFave, Wilbur DeParis (tb), Bob Wilber (cl), Red Richards (p), John Field (b), Sid Catlett (dm)

Ruby traveled with Sid Catlett to New York about this time and was hired to play at Central Plaza. Starting much earlier, he had traveled by train to New

York on weekends, when the fare was about $4 round trip. He shared a room on the top of the Automat on those occasions and listened to music. Later, Ruby lived in Greenwich Village. He shared an apartment with Nat Pierce, although some reports have them only living in the same building.

George Wein described the circumstances surrounding the closing of Storyville at the Copley Square Hotel at the very end of November 1950 after only six weeks of business. In early February 1951 he reopened the club at Hotel Buckminster on Kenmore Square. He wrote that he organized Sunday afternoon concerts at Storyville that included guests such as Ruby Braff, Vic Dickenson, Edmond Hall, Wild Bill Davison, and Mezz Mezzrow. The band was led by Bob Wilber and included Johnny Windhurst and Ed Hubble.[41]

Ruby's first performance outside the United States may well have occurred in the following engagement in Toronto. The date and location are uncertain, but the engagement likely ended soon after March 25, 1951. That is the date that Sid Catlett died in Chicago. Ruby reported that he returned to New York following his Toronto engagement with Bud Freeman to pick up his clothes from Sid's wife.

Ruby Braff and Bud Freeman in Toronto[42]
Details unknown but engagement probably ended after March 25. Further details are unknown.

Another advertisement announces a Sunday afternoon jam session at Storyville's new location in Hotel Buckminster at Kenmore Square in Boston with Maestro Nat Hentoff as emcee.[43] This anchors the following performance listing which is also available in an issued recording:

Edmond Hall: *Jazz at Storyville* (see Figure 2.8)
April 29, 1951, Storyville, Hotel Buckminster, Kenmore Square, Boston
Ruby Braff (tp-1), Johnny Windhurst (tp-2), Vic Dickenson (tb), Edmond Hall (cl), George Wein (p), John Field (b), Jo Jones (dm)
Introduction (2)
Paradox 6003, Melodisc (E) MLP 502, Storyville STLP 303, (J) PA 3119
Struttin' with Some Barbecue (2)
Stv EP 402, STLP 303, Paradox 6003, Mel (E) MLP 502, Stv (J) PA 3119
Sweet and Lovely (no tp)
Paradox 6003, Storyville STLP 303, (J) PA 3119, Melodisc (E) MLP 502
Sister Kate (voc VD, 1)
Paradox 6003, Stv STLP 303, Mel (E) MLP 502, Stv STLP 908,
Vogue (E) LAE 12051, Black Lion (G) BLP 60908, BLCD 760908 (CD),
Jazz Colours (G) 874716-2, Past Perfect 220321, Avid AMSC 1019
Ad Lib Blues (1)
Paradox 6003, Stv STLP 303, Mel (E) MLP 502, Stv STLP 908,
Vogue (E) LAE 12051, Black Lion (G) BLP 60908, BLCD 760908 (CD),
Past Perfect 220321, Avid AMSC 1019, Pid 947547

'S Wonderful (1)
Stv EP 402, LP 303, Paradox 6003, Mel (E) MLP 502, Stv STLP 908, Vog (E) LAE 12051, Trio (J) PA 6008, Black Lion (G) BLP 60908, 1201 Music 1003 (CD), BLCD 760908 (CD), Jazz Colours (G) 874716-2, Past Perfect 220321, Avid AMSC 1019

NOTE: The trumpet work on "Sister Kate" and "Ad Lib Blues," in my opinion, is by Ruby Braff, not Johnny Windhurst who is frequently credited in many discographies for these tunes. The date is listed differently in different issues and sources. I have used the date supplied by Manfred Selchow. The "Introduction" is included on Storyville STLP 303, although not listed as such in some discographies. Black Lion BLCD 760908 (CD) is titled *Hustlin' and Bustlin'*. The album released on 1201 Music 1003 is titled *Original Jazz Legends: Salute to George Gershwin*, a five-CD box set. Pid 947547 is titled *Power of Jazz*. Avid AMSC 1019 is titled *Edmond Hall: Four Classic Albums Plus*.

Jim Weaver reported a cassette from the Prescott Collection dated May 6, 1951, featuring Ruby Braff with Ed Hall and one of the DeParis brothers. It was recorded on original reel number 19, transferred to cassette number 19, which was renumbered cassette 30. This tape was not available to audition.

Nat Hentoff's notes to Savoy MG 15016 report that Ruby played with Bud Freeman and Frank Orchard in New York prior to performing with Pee Wee Russell in the session below. He also mentions the Georg Brunis–Pee Wee Russell–Joe Sullivan All Star Band and the George Wettling–Joe Sullivan–Ruby Braff Trio. It has not been possible to trace specific information for any of these appearances. Pee Wee Russell asked Ruby to join his band in Chicago to replace his original trumpeter. Pee Wee had been hospitalized in extremely critical condition in January 1951, in San Francisco. He was released at the end of February. He joined the band at Condon's on July 17, 1951.[44] Following his recovery, his relationship with Ruby Braff developed.

Pee Wee Russell[45]
October 1951, Capitol Lounge, Chicago
Ruby Braff (tp), Ephraim "Ephy" Resnick (tb), Pee Wee Russell (cl), Red Richards (p), Irv Manning (b), Kenny John (dm)

Bob Hilbert quoted Ruby saying, "I knew Pee Wee since I was 16 or 17. I used to go down to New York for the weekend, and the first place I'd go was Nick's." The association with Pee Wee Russell continued, with a month-long engagement at George Wein's Storyville Club. This band was one of the first employed at the club.[46] Recordings from several broadcasts survive. In addition to those listed below, Jim Weaver reported that cassette 10 (new number 35) contains performances from January 6 and 22, 1952, that have not been available for audition. That leads to the following general listing:

Pee Wee Russell Sextet
Month of January 1951, Storyville Club, Buckminster Hotel, Kenmore Square, Boston
Ruby Braff (tp), Pee Wee Russell (cl), and others

Details of Pee Wee's broadcasts are shown below when known. Recordings of broadcasts from January 6 and 22 were not available.

Pee Wee Russell Sextet: WMEX Broadcast
January 14, 1952, Storyville Club, Buckminster Hotel, Kenmore Square, Boston
Ruby Braff (cnt), Ephraim "Ephy" Resnick (tb), Pee Wee Russell (cl), Red Richards (p), John Field (b), Kenny John (dm), Nat Hentoff (announcer)
Struttin' with Some Barbecue
Basin Street Blues
'S Wonderful
Someday Sweetheart
Ballin' the Jack
At the Jazz Band Ball
NOTE: A recording of these tunes is available but remains unissued.

Pee Wee Russell Sextet: WMEX Broadcast
January 16, 1952, Storyville Club, Buckminster Hotel, Kenmore Square, Boston
Ruby Braff (cnt), Ephraim "Ephy" Resnick (tb), Pee Wee Russell (cl), Red Richards (p), John Field (b), Kenny John (dm), Nat Hentoff (announcer)
Way Down Yonder in New Orleans
Sentimental Journey
Sunday
Wrap Your Troubles in Dreams
St. Louis Blues
Muskrat Ramble
NOTE: A recording of these tunes is available but remains unissued.

Pee Wee Russell Sextet: WMEX Broadcast
January 21, 1952, Storyville Club, Buckminster Hotel, Kenmore Square, Boston
Ruby Braff (cnt), Ephraim "Ephy" Resnick (tb), Pee Wee Russell (cl), Red Richards (p), John Field (b), Kenny John (dm), Nat Hentoff (announcer)
Muskrat Ramble
Squeeze Me
The Blue Room
The Lady's in Love with You
I Can't Give You Anything but Love
Original Dixieland One-Step
NOTE: A recording of these tunes is available but remains unissued.

Savoy issued a recording from the night of January 27 on two ten-inch LPs. There have been many subsequent releases of these recordings as shown below.

Pee Wee Russell: ***Jazz at Storyville, Volumes 1 and 2***
January 27, 1952, Storyville Club, Buckminster Hotel, Boston
Ruby Braff (tp), Ephraim "Ephy" Resnick (tb), Pee Wee Russell (cl), Red Richards (p), John Field (b), Kenny John (dm)
Love Is Just around the Corner
Savoy MG 12034, Pickwick SPC 3152, Royale 18158
Squeeze Me
Savoy MG 12034, Pickwick SPC 3152, Royale 18158
Ballin' the Four Bar Break (Ballin' the Jack)
Savoy MG 12034
I Would Do Anything for You
Savoy MG 12034, Pickwick SPC 3152
California, Here I Come
Savoy MG 12034, Royale 18158
Baby, Won't You Please Come Home?
Savoy MG 12034, Pickwick SPC 3152
St. James Infirmary
Savoy MG 12034, Royale 18158
The Lady's in Love with You
Savoy MG 12034
Struttin' with Some Barbecue
Savoy MG 12034, Pickwick SPC 3152
St. Louis Blues
Savoy MG 12041
Sweet Lorraine
Savoy MG 12034, Pickwick SPC 3152
Sentimental Journey
Savoy MG 12034, Pickwick SPC 3152
If I Had You
Savoy MG 12034, Pickwick SPC 3152
Coquette
Savoy MG 12034, Pickwick SPC 3152, Royale 18158
The Lady Is a Tramp
Savoy MG 12034, Royale 18158
NOTE: Savoy MG 12034 is Volume 1 and MG 12041 is Volume 2. All titles on Savoy MG 12034 also are included on London (E) LTZ-C 15061, London Savoy (Can) MG 12034, and CBS Realm (E) RM 151. Pickwick SPC 3152 is titled *Pee Wee Russell & His Dixieland All Stars*. Royale 18158 is titled *Dixieland Chicago Style Featuring Pee Wee Russell and His Orchestra*. This ten-inch LP contains a performance of "China Boy" that is by Jack Teagarden and does not include either Pee Wee Russell or Ruby Braff. All titles on MG 12034 and MG 12041 are also on Savoy SJL 2228 *The Individualism of Pee Wee Russell* and

Savoy WL 70538 as *Jazz at Storyville: Pee Wee Russell and Ruby Braff.* The above titles have been issued many more times. Realm RM 189 is titled *Jazz at Storyville, Volume 3* but the author lacks confirmation of the included titles. Drive Archive DE 41052 (CD) titled *Pee Wee Russell Clarinet Strut* includes "California, Here I Come," "Coquette," "St. James Infirmary," "Love Is Just around the Corner," and "The Lady Is a Tramp." The author also owns a ten-inch LP with a WBAL label featuring Pee Wee Russell playing the following tunes: "St. James Infirmary," "The Lady Is a Tramp," "California, Here I Come," "Coquette," "Love Is Just around the Corner," and "China Boy."

The following table shows additional issues:[47]

Song Title	45 rpm	33 1/3 rpm
Love Is Just around the Corner	Royale EP 387, Savoy XP 8070	Allegro LP 1633, Allegro 1745, Ember (E) CJS 806, Galaxy 4802, Manhattan (Au) LMS 48, Pickwick PTP 2026, Roulette LP A2, Savoy 15014
Squeeze Me	Savoy XP 8070	Allegro 1745, Manhattan (Au) LMS 50, Pickwick PTP 2026, Savoy 15016
Ballin' the Four Bar Break (Ballin' the Jack)	Savoy XP 8070	Manhattan (Au) LMS 50, Pickwick PTP 2026, Savoy 15016
I Would Do Anything for You	Savoy XP 8071	Allegro 1633, Ember (E) CJS 806, Galaxy 4802, Manhattan (Au) LMS 48, Pickwick PTP 2026, Savoy 15014
California, Here I Come	Savoy XP 8071	Allegro 1633, Ember (E) CJS 806, Galaxy 4802, Manhattan (Au) LMS 48, Pickwick PTP 2026, Roulette LP A2, Savoy 15014
Baby, Won't You Please Come Home?	Savoy XP 8072	Allegro 1745, Manhattan (Au) LMS 50, Pickwick PTP 2026, Savoy 15016
St. James Infirmary	Royale EP 387, Savoy XP 8071	Allegro 1633, Ember (E) NR 5002, Ember (E) CJS 806, Galaxy 4802, Halo 50268, Hudson 265, Jonaplay (J) RCA 50268, Manhattan (Au) LMS 48, Roulette LP A2, Savoy 15014, Ultraphonic 50268
The Lady's in Love with You	Savoy XP 8072	Allegro 1745, Manhattan (Au) LMS 52, Roulette LP A2, Savoy 15020
Struttin' with Some Barbecue	Savoy XP 8072	Allegro 1745, Manhattan (Au) LMS 52, Pickwick PTP 2026, Savoy 15020
St. Louis Blues	Savoy XP 8073	Manhattan (Au) LMS 52, Savoy 15014
Sweet Lorraine	Savoy XP 8074	Allegro 1745, Manhattan (Au) LMS 50, Pickwick PTP 2026, Savoy 15016

Song Title	45 rpm	33 1/3 rpm
Sentimental Journey	Savoy XP 8074	Allegro 1745, Manhattan (Au) LMS 52, Pickwick PTP 2026, Savoy 15020
If I Had You	Savoy XP 8075	Allegro 1745, Brookville LCA 0002, Everest 1001/5, Manhattan (Au) LMS 50, Pickwick PTP 2026, Savoy 15016
Coquette	Savoy XP 8075	Allegro 1745, Ember (E) CJS 806, Galaxy 4802, Manhattan (Au) LMS 48, Pickwick PTP 2026, Rondolette LP A2, Savoy 15016
The Lady Is a Tramp	Savoy XP 8073	Allegro 1633, Ember (E) CJS 806, Galaxy 4802, Manhattan (Au) LMS 48, Pickwick PTP 2026, Savoy 15014

NOTE: Galaxy 4802 and Royale LP 18158 titled "Love Is Just around the Corner" incorrectly as "Love Is Here to Stay." Savoy EP XP 8070, Savoy MG 15014, Allegro LP 1633, Rondolette LP A2, Manhattan (Au) LMS 48 all list a title "Euphoria Is Here to Stay," which is actually "Love Is Just around the Corner." Brookville LCA 0002 is part of album LCA 5000 (five-LP set). "The Lady Is a Tramp" is included on MG 12041 (not MG 12034) contrary to some discographies.

Broadcasts continue from Storyville. The following performance was led by Georg Brunis and also includes drummer Roy Haynes early in his career.

Georg Brunis Storyville: WMEX Broadcast
February 22, 1952, Storyville Club, Buckminster Hotel, Boston
Ruby Braff (tp), Georg Brunis (tb), Al Drootin (cl), George Wein (p), John Field (b), Roy Haynes (dm)
Theme and Introduction
Muskrat Ramble
Someday Sweetheart
Royal Garden Blues
Ugly Chile
High Society
Closing
NOTE: A recording of these tunes is available but remains unissued.

Ruby returned to Toronto in late March through early April, this time united with his friend Pee Wee Russell. Likely he remained active at Storyville until his departure, but no details are known. From Toronto, he likely traveled to Chicago, although not necessarily directly.

Ruby Braff and Pee Wee Russell[48]
March 31 through April 7, 1952, Colonial Tavern, Toronto

Ruby Braff (tp), Georg Brunis (tb), Pee Wee Russell (cl), Joe Sullivan (p), George Wettling (dm)

Ruby often told me a story about this engagement. Later I found that Steve Voce reported it in one of his many fine articles about Ruby.[49] Ruby told me that he was the only sober one among the group; however, he told Steve Voce that pianist Buck Washington was in the audience one night. Ruby reported that Buck enjoyed his playing.

It is likely that the same musicians appeared with Ruby and Pee Wee in Chicago.

Ruby Braff and Pee Wee Russell[50]
Mid-April 1952 for two-week engagement, Blue Note, Chicago

It is clear that Ruby's reputation was spreading. People were becoming excited about this emerging young trumpet star.

Lee Wiley[51]
circa 1952, rehearsal, Storyville Club, Boston
The Lee Wiley discography lists Ruby Braff as possibly performing in the following recorded rehearsal session, listing Johnny Windhurst as another option.

Ruby Braff told me emphatically that he is not playing on this session that was first issued on Audiophile ACD 170. His comment to me was simple and direct: "That's too good for it to be me. It must be Bobby [Hackett]."

The following handbills depict eight of the performances in this chapter:

Figure 2.1: Handbill December 9, 1945: handwritten notes made by Mel Levine

To former members of the "Jazz Society"
and other interested persons:
MONDAY NITE - November 21 at 8:30
SAVOY CAFE - 410 Mass. Ave.
Edmond Hall's All Stars and
The Vinal Rhythm Kings
in a real JAZZ SESSION --
not a Jazz Concert$!
Hear Hall, Watson, • Braaf, Dickenson,
Gadboys, Gay, Kersey, Saltmarsh
Field, Battaglia and Herbert
playing unrehearsed improvised jazz.
No admission -- No minimum --
This is the first informal Monday
nite session in a long time!

Figure 2.2: Handbill November 21, 1949: handwritten notes made by Mel Levine—note spelling of "Braaf"

Figure 2.3: Handbill December 19, 1949: handwritten notes made by Mel Levine

Savoy Cafe May 26, 1950
410 MASSACHUSETTS AVENUE
BOSTON
KATHRYN C. DONOGHUE, Manager

Boston's Hot Spot of Rhythm
Salutes the Boston Jubilee Jazz Festival

FRANKIE NEWTON'S ALL STAR ORCHESTRA
ALICE ROSS GROVES, Vocalist
NAT PIERCE'S ORCHESTRA
CHARLIE MARIANO, Boptet
• RUBY BRAFF, Quintet
LINDY MILLER, W.B.Z. Commentator

Next Attraction Starting May 26th 1950
JOE MARSALA
Country's most famous Clarinet Player, Television Star, Composer of "Little Sir Echo," "Don't Cry Joe" and others — also his
ALL STAR DIXIE LAND BAND

Open from 10 A. M. Daily **4 ft. x 3 ft. Television Screen**

Figure 2.4: Handbill May 26, 1950: handwritten notes made by Mel Levine

Figure 2.5: Handbill October 25, 1950: handwritten notes made by Mel Levine showing Ruby substituting for Sidney DeParis

Figure 2.6: Handbill November 12, 1950

Courtesy Dorothy Prescott

Figure 2.7: Handbill November 19, 1950: note listing of Nat Hentoff as "overseer"

Figure 2.8: Handbill April 29, 1951: note Maestro Nat Hentoff of WMEX listed as host

Notes

[1] Peter Vacher, "Rappin' with Ruby," *Jazz Journal International,* January 2003, 6–8. A complete version of this interview will appear in Peter's forthcoming book, *Mixed Messages: American Jazz Stories* (Nottingham, England: Five Leaves Publications, forthcoming May 2012).

[2] Peter Vacher, "Rappin' with Ruby," *Jazz Journal International,* January 2003, 6–8. A complete version of this interview will appear in Peter's forthcoming book, *Mixed Messages: American Jazz Stories* (Nottingham, England: Five Leaves Publications, forthcoming May 2012).

[3] Steve Voce, *Jazz Journal International*, November 1995, 9—correcting Ruby's home to Roxbury.

[4] Jim Weaver, "New York Jazz Stars All Came to Boston 1944 to 1968," *IAJRC Journal*, Fall 1992, 69.

[5] Handbill including handwritten notes made by Mel Levine.

[6] Photo, *The March of Jazz Celebrates Ruby Braff's 74th Birthday Party*, Arbors Records, 2001, 13.

[7] George A. Borgman, "The One and Only Ruby Braff," *Mississippi Rag*, December 1995, 2.

[8] George Wein, *Myself Among Others* (Cambridge, MA: Da Capo Press, 2003), 45.

[9] Warren W. Vaché, *Back Beats and Rim Shots: The Johnny Blowers Story* (Lanham, MD: Scarecrow Press), 87.

[10] Nat Hentoff, "Ruby Braff: Missing Link of Jazz," *Esquire*, May 1958, 62.

[11] George Wein, *Myself Among Others* (Cambridge, MA: Da Capo Press, 2003), 51 and 53.

[12] George A. Borgman, "The One and Only Ruby Braff," *Mississippi Rag*, December 1995, 2.

[13] Manfred Selchow, *Ding Ding: A Bio-Discographical Scrapbook on Vic Dickenson* (Germany: Uhle & Kleinmann, 1998), 230.

[14] Jim Weaver in personal correspondence.

[15] These recordings are held in the Sam Prescott Collection held at the New Hampshire Library of Traditional Jazz.

[16] Manfred Selchow, *Profoundly Blue* (Germany: Uhle & Kleinmann, 1988), 243-4

[17] These recordings are held in the Sam Prescott Collection held at the New Hampshire Library of Traditional Jazz.
[18] These recordings are held in the Sam Prescott Collection held at the New Hampshire Library of Traditional Jazz.
[19] These recordings are held in the Sam Prescott Collection held at the New Hampshire Library of Traditional Jazz.
[20] These recordings are held in the Sam Prescott Collection held at the New Hampshire Library of Traditional Jazz.
[21] These recordings are held in the Sam Prescott Collection held at the New Hampshire Library of Traditional Jazz.
[22] These recordings are held in the Sam Prescott Collection held at the New Hampshire Library of Traditional Jazz.
[23] These recordings are held in the Sam Prescott Collection held at the New Hampshire Library of Traditional Jazz.
[24] Mel Levine provided the flyer and underlined the incorrect spelling of Ruby's last name.
[25] Manfred Selchow, *Profoundly Blue* (Germany: Uhle & Kleinmann, 1988), 249
[26] Manfred Selchow, *Ding Ding: A Bio-Discographical Scrapbook on Vic Dickenson* (Germany: Uhle & Kleinmann, 1998), 236.
[27] Copy of advertisement provided by Manfred Selchow and Mel Levine.
[28] Manfred Selchow, *Profoundly Blue* (Germany: Uhle & Kleinmann, 1988), 248.
[29] Manfred Selchow, *Profoundly Blue* (Germany: Uhle & Kleinmann, 1988), 252.
[30] Martin Williams, *Jazz Changes* (New York: Oxford University Press, 1992), 70.
[31] Manfred Selchow, *Profoundly Blue* (Germany: Uhle & Kleinmann, 1988), 255.
[32] Mel Levine provided the handbill and information about the engagement.
[33] Mel Levine provided the handbill and information about the engagement.
[34] George Wein, *Myself Among Others* (Cambridge, MA: Da Capo Press, 2003), 77.
[35] Advertisement provided by Mel Levine.
[36] Manfred Selchow, *Profoundly Blue* (Germany: Uhle & Kleinmann, 1988), 260.
[37] Postcard announcing this performance reproduced in Manfred Selchow, *Profoundly Blue* (Germany: Uhle & Kleinmann, 1988), 260.
[38] Manfred Selchow, *Profoundly Blue* (Germany: Uhle & Kleinmann, 1988), 261.
[39] Ruby described this evening in a radio interview with Steve Voce, December 15, 1994.
[40] Advertisement provided by Mel Levine.
[41] George Wein, *Myself Among Others* (Cambridge, MA: Da Capo Press, 2003), 81.
[42] Ruby Braff radio interview with Steve Voce, December 15, 1994.
[43] A copy of an advertisement for this performance appears in Manfred Selchow, *Profoundly Blue* (Germany: Uhle & Kleinmann, 1988), 254.
[44] Robert Hilbert, *Pee Wee Russell: The Life of a Jazzman* (New York: Oxford University Press, 1993), 195.
[45] Robert Hilbert, *Pee Wee Russell: The Life of a Jazzman* (New York: Oxford University Press, 1993), 197.
[46] Robert Hilbert, *Pee Wee Russell: The Life of a Jazzman* (New York: Oxford University Press, 1993), 197
[47] Robert Hilbert in collaboration with David Niven, *Pee Wee Speaks: A Discography of Pee Wee Russell* (Metuchen, NJ: Scarecrow Press, 1992), 226–228.

[48] Robert Hilbert, *Pee Wee Russell: The Life of a Jazzman* (New York: Oxford University Press, 1993), 198. Hilbert's book only identified Ruby and Pee Wee. In personal conversation, Ruby identified the other musicians.
[49] *Jazz Journal International*, October 1995, 15.
[50] George A. Borgman, "The One and Only Ruby Braff," *Mississippi Rag*, December 1995, 2.
[51] Len Selk and Gus Kuhlman, *Lee Wiley: A Bio-Discography*, published by the authors, 51.

Chapter 3

Ruby Braff Meets John Hammond: At the Threshold of Jazz Stardom

Ruby was continuing to receive increased attention. Clearly, George Wein had given him opportunities to perform and record. Ruby had already appeared with established jazz musicians who also helped spread the word about his talent. The next chapter in his career was about to begin. John Hammond attended the Festival of the Creative Arts at Brandeis University on June 12, 1952, and enjoyed Ruby's performance; however, the famous Vanguard recordings that Hammond supervised were still a year ahead in Ruby's future.

A copy of the Brandeis program is available. It lists Leonard Bernstein as the festival's director. Then, Bernstein was a professor of music at Brandeis. He also served as moderator for a panel discussion that preceded the performances, described as follows in the program: "The jazz symposium will revolve around an exposition of the present crisis in jazz, brought about by its intellectualization. The discussion will be illustrated by the foremost authorities on and exponents of contemporary jazz." Members of the panel included John Mehegan, Lenny Tristano, George Simon, Barry Ulanov, Leonard Feather, George Wein, and Nat Hentoff. A concert followed the panel discussion, described as follows: "The short historical survey will be followed by a presentation of various trends in present-day Bop by Lenny Tristano, John Mehegan, and other leading jazzmen."

John Hammond told Ruby how he was impressed by Ruby's performance of "When It's Sleepy Time Down South" in this concert. Ruby felt that this led to Hammond's invitation to join Vic Dickenson's session for Vanguard Records on December 29, 1953. The Brandeis festival presented the world premier of the English concert version of Kurt Weil's *Threepenny Opera*, translated and narrated by Marc Blitzstein. His work is the source of the English lyrics for the song "Mack the Knife" as popularized by Louis Armstrong. Lotte Lenya was one of the singers, while Leonard Bernstein conducted the orchestra. This anchors the following entry:

Festival of the Creative Arts 1952: Brandeis University Concert[1]
June 12, 1952 (Thursday), 2:15–5:00 p.m., Adolph Lillman Amphitheatre, Brandeis University, Waltham, Massachusetts
Ruby Braff with unknown musicians but likely including George Wein (p)
When It's Sleepy Time Down South
Further details unknown

But surrounding the Brandeis Festival, Ruby spent much of his time during the summer of 1952 performing on Cape Cod with George Wein at the Hawthorne Inn in Gloucester, Massachusetts. *DownBeat* reported the following: "Ruby Braff has taken the trumpet chair at Storyville in Gloucester for most of the summer. Braff scored a large personal success at the Brandeis Jazz Symposium."[2] This supports the following entry:

Ruby Braff at Storyville
Summer 1952, Hawthorne Inn, Gloucester, Massachusetts
Ruby Braff (tp), Ed Hubble (tb), Jack Fuller (cl), Steve Kuhn (p), George Wein (p), Jimmy Woode (b), Peter Littman (dm)

George Wein wrote the following, listing the musicians who performed during the summer and describing both the origins of the Brandeis concert in June and how a major fire destroyed the musicians' instruments later in the summer:[3]

> I closed Storyville for the summer. I had lined up a deal at the Hawthorne Inn in Gloucester for the second year in a row. This time, I assembled a group consisting of Ruby Braff, Eddie Hubble, Jimmy Woode, clarinetist Jack Fuller, and a young Boston drummer named Peter Littman. I shared the piano chair with Steve Kuhn, who was a Harvard student at the time. Charlie Bourgeois joined us. We rented a picturesque summer house on Pigeon Cove in Rockport. The house's owner, a friendly woman named Mrs. Dole, entrusted us with her keys. 'Don't burn the house down,' she said as she left.
>
> Ruby Braff suggested that we get in touch with Leonard Bernstein, for whom we had performed a few months earlier at Brandeis University. Bernstein had organized a jazz symposium there with Lee Konitz and some other modernists. Knowing about the program in advance, Ruby and I had approached Bernstein at the Somerset Hotel, where he was practicing a Mozart piano concerto for a performance with the Boston Symphony later that week. After introducing ourselves, Ruby and I had suggested our services as a complement to his symposium. We offered to perform a capsule history of jazz (from Armstrong through Ellington and Basie) that would lead into his lecture. Bernstein had been thrilled by the idea, and it had been a success. Symposium panelist John Hammond heard Ruby Braff for the first time. He loved his rendition of 'When It's Sleepy Time Down South.'

Well, despite Mrs. Dole's words of caution, the rented cottage where the musicians stayed in Rockport did burn down. This was during a time Sarah Vaughan was visiting. She and Ruby were sitting on the beach at the time, along with

Bourgeois and Woode. All the musicians' clothing and instruments were lost in the fire. George Wein organized a benefit performance on August 13 in Boston with proceeds from the benefit dedicated to the musicians who lost their instruments.

A copy of an ad for that benefit performance is available. It lists an admission charge of $1.50 for the one-night (Wednesday) program, held at the location of George Wein's original Storyville, located at the Hotel Buckminster in Boston. George and Ruby invited Leonard Bernstein to appear and perform, and he graciously accepted. George Wein wrote that 450 people attended that evening[4] and that "Bernstein's one-nighter netted three thousand dollars. We used those funds to purchase new horns for Ruby, Eddie, and Jack."

During the benefit performance, Leonard Bernstein played 'Honky Tonk Train Blues' and was encouraged by the applause. He sat in with Pee Wee Russell and his group including J. C. Higginbotham (tb). They played a few tunes and then went into a slow blues. Mel Levine recorded the performance, starting at that point in the evening. He dubbed a portion of his recording to present to Leonard Bernstein. Eventually Bernstein's abbreviated copy reached the Library of Congress.

Ruby chuckled when recalling this session. He was quick to express his appreciation for Bernstein's heartfelt support but equally quick to state the following: "Bernstein only thought he could play jazz. But he really did enjoy the applause he received following his solo."

Leonard Bernstein Plays Jazz at Storyville[5] (see Figure 3.1)
August 13, 1952, Storyville Club, Hotel Buckminster, Boston
Leonard Bernstein (p), Pee Wee Russell (cl), Jimmy Woode (b), Marquis Foster (dm)
Blues

George Wein (p) replaces Bernstein; Pee Wee Russell out
What Is This Thing Called Love
You Stepped Out of a Dream

Ruby Braff (tp), Al Drootin (cl), George Wein (p), Jimmy Woode (b), Joe Cochrane (dm)
Manhattan
Birth of the Blues

Marquis Foster (dm) replaces Joe Cochrane
The Lady Is a Tramp
Medley
  I Cover the Waterfront
  Sophisticated Lady (Wein feature, incomplete)

Add Alice Ross Groves (voc)
Pennies from Heaven
It's the Talk of the Town
NOTE: A recording of these tunes is available but remains unissued.

The substitution of Marquis Foster for Joe Cochrane is shown in a catalog listing from the Library of Congress but is not shown in Mel Levine's notes made at the time of the performance. An available advertisement shows Mahogany Hall opened on Thursday, September 18 at the Copley Square Hotel in Boston, the site of the original Storyville. Storyville remained at the Hotel Buckminster.

Pee Wee Russell was the leader of an all-star band that was featured when Mahogany Hall opened its doors. The ad promised both evening and Sunday afternoon sessions dedicated to Dixieland jazz. Storyville continued to operate, with one advertisement showing that Maxine Sullivan and Art Tatum opened on October 20. At that time, the billing at Mahogany Hall had become the Pee Wee Russell–Ruby Braff Band. Ruby had presumably been appearing there regularly since the club opened September 18.

Pee Wee Russell–Ruby Braff Band[6]
October 1952, Mahogany Hall (basement of Copley Square Hotel), Boston
Ruby Braff (tp), Russell "Big Chief" Moore (tb), Pee Wee Russell (cl), Ivan Wainwright (p), John Field (b), Marquis Foster (dm)

Two photographs are available from the March of Jazz program that anchor another group of musicians in this long engagement as shown in the next listing. Both photographs are included in this book's photo section.

Pee Wee Russell[7]
Unknown date, Mahogany Hall, Boston
Ruby Braff (tp), Dick LeFave (tb), Pee Wee Russell (cl), Ivan Wainwright (p), John Field (b), Buzzy Drootin (dm)

Sometime in December Ruby began leading a band at the Seaview in Beverly, Massachusetts, just north of Boston. An advertisement is available to the author that promotes the band for a New Year's party at that location. In the ad, Ruby's name is given as "Ruby Brass," continuing some of the problems with the incorrect spelling of his last name that he experienced in printed announcements earlier in his career.

Ruby Braff and His Dixieland Band (billed as Ruby Brass)[8] **(see Figure 3.2)**
December 29, 1952, Seaview, Beverly, Massachusetts

Ruby Braff and His Dixieland Band (billed as Ruby Brass)[9]
December 31, 1952, Seaview, Beverly, Massachusetts

I have not found any information about performances during January, but Ruby returned to the Storyville Club in Boston for the following performance led by Jo Jones.

Jo Jones[10]
February 1953, Storyville Club, Boston
Ruby Braff (tp), Rollins Griffith (p), Jimmy Woode (b), Jo Jones (dm)

Rollins Griffith appeared with Charlie Parker in performances the following year in Boston. This may have helped to extend Ruby's reputation beyond the Dixieland emphasis of the performances at Mahogany Hall. Perhaps George Wein recorded this group at this time for his Storyville record label, joining the group as its pianist.

Jo Jones
1953, Storyville Club, Boston
Ruby Braff (tp), George Wein (p), Jimmy Woode (b), Jo Jones (dm)
Please Don't Talk about Me When I'm Gone
　Storyville EP 409, STLP 307, Stv (J) PA 3119
Pennies from Heaven
　Storyville EP 409, STLP 307, Stv (J) PA 3119

Nat Hentoff reported the following in *DownBeat*: "Brilliant Boston trumpeter Ruby Braff now heads the Storyville relief band."[11] A month later, he also reported that Ruby Braff was rehearsing a new small band.[12]

The First *DownBeat* Critics' Poll[13]
Ruby Braff placed third in the trumpet new star category, with the number of votes shown:

Trumpet: New Star	
Chet Baker	115
Cat Anderson	10
Ruby Braff	10
Jesse Drakes	10
Carl Halen	10
Shorty Rogers	10
Bob Scobey	10
Clark Terry	10
Nick Travis	10
Herb Pomeroy	5

Ruby Phones John Hammond[14]
Nat Hentoff describes a turning point in Ruby's career, emphasizing Ruby's friendship with Pee Wee Russell:

> Hammond told Braff to phone him when Braff next came to New York. Ruby had been emigrating to New York off and on for years, but had never succeeded in being able to stay. . . .
>
> Braff made the trip to New York again, forcing himself into a desperate conviction that he had to make his stay permanent this time or return to Boston and fulfill completely his parents' prophecy. He ran out of rent money again, and took refuge with Pee Wee and Mary Russell in their Greenwich Village apartment [at 37 King Street in Greenwich Village]. Charles Ellsworth 'Pee Wee' Russell is a gentle, perceptive and creatively individual jazzman whose quizzical shyness has usually been mistaken for inarticulateness and whose lonely, introspective integrity had helped bring him an unwelcome reputation of being a 'character. . . .'
>
> Pee Wee became attracted to the young Boston dissident as a musician and as a transparently honest person after playing with him briefly in Chicago, one of the very few jobs for which Ruby was recommended during a previous struggle in New York. Pee Wee had since played with Ruby in Boston, and had encouraged him in his mountain climbing of New York.
>
> Pee Wee's wife, Mary, his primary source of understanding, is a surfacely gruff woman who fails to conceal warmth of spirit akin to Pee Wee's. 'There are times when I've wanted to kill Ruby,' Mary says, 'but by and large I love him very, very much. He's the most honest man Pee Wee has ever worked with in the music business: and in my way of using the word, he's a very graceful man. When he was living with us and didn't have from what to eat, he'd get out of bed in the morning—that's three in the afternoon for him—and disappear until three or four in the morning. He wanted to keep out of our way and he wanted to make it clear he wasn't sponging on us for food. In fact, he'd always come back with containers of coffee and blueberry muffins, his contribution to the house. . . .'
>
> Pee Wee finally emphasized one day [that Ruby should phone Hammond], 'Look, you'll be on the phone. He's not going to hit you. All he can say is no.'
>
> Braff called, and Hammond soon arranged for Braff to appear at the end of 1953 on the first jazz recordings made by the discriminating classical label, Vanguard, for whom Hammond was the new jazz recording director. The sessions, under the leadership of trombonist Vic Dickenson, were well received in this country and rousingly in England, where they did much to spread the use of the term 'jazz mainstream.' Hammond was also partly responsible for Braff's recording with Benny Goodman on a Capitol big-band date, several weekends of playing with Benny at Basin Street in New York in 1955, and several months as a Mexican trumpet player in Rodgers and Hammerstein's *Pipe Dream.*

However, this is getting ahead of events. In the meantime, Ruby returned to Boston and his continuing association with pianist and entrepreneur George Wein. Storyville returned to its summer home on Cape Cod at the Oceanside Hotel in Magnolia, Massachusetts.

George Wein[15] (see Figure 3.3)
Summer 1953, Storyville Club, Oceanside Hotel, Magnolia, Massachusetts
Ruby Braff (tp), George Wein (p), Jimmy Woode (b), Buzzy Drootin (dm)

"This is the first season for a jazz group at the plush Magnolia site."[16]

Storyville at the Beach
September 6, 1953, Oceanside Hotel, Magnolia, Massachusetts
Ruby Braff (tp), Vic Dickenson (tb, voc), Sam Margolis (cl, ts), George Wein (p, voc), Jimmy Woode (b), Buzzy Drootin (dm), George Wein (announcer)
Fine and Dandy
Manhattan (Wein voc)
Muskrat Ramble (incomplete)
Sister Kate (Dickenson vocal)
Tenderly (Dickenson feature)
Some of These Days
Take the "A" Train
Keepin' Out of Mischief Now
Yesterdays (Dickenson feature, incomplete)
Dancing on the Ceiling
I Got Rhythm
Tea for Two (incomplete)
Spain
Ain't Misbehavin' (Vic Dickenson feature, Wein voc)
Medley: (Wein only, p and voc)
  God Bless the Child (incomplete)
  Summertime (incomplete)
Caravan
When the Saints Go Marching In (Wein voc)
Billie's Blues
NOTE: A recording of these tunes is available but remains unissued.

This summer performance likely closed the summer season. Storyville advertised a Sunday performance by the George Shearing Quintet on September 13 in the *Boston Daily Record*, August 6, 1953. A copy is available to the author. Notably, that advertisement announced an appearance by Charlie Parker on September 21.

Ruby Braff Meets Charlie Parker
George Wein reported that he moved Storyville back to the Copley Square Hotel in September 1953. He operated Mahogany Hall downstairs and Storyville at street level. Charlie Parker opened at Storyville at this location, while traditional musicians were featured downstairs. This may be what Ruby meant when he talked about Charlie Parker coming downstairs to hear him and others perform.[17] Ruby reported that they attended several after-hours performances together when Parker was in Boston. Parker was playing with Roy Haynes and Red Garland on this engagement, according to Ruby.

Nat Hentoff reported Ruby Braff's meeting with Charlie Parker, who played at Storyville in Boston from September 21–28, 1953.[18] Ruby described it as follows in that article:

> Charlie Parker, for example, was very close to the blues and had a beautiful melodic conception. I met him once when we were both playing at Storyville. He said he liked my playing, but I thought he was putting me on until I found out as we talked that he liked the same things in music I did. Charlie had great love and respect for all of music, and his playing showed it.

This was Charlie Parker's second engagement at Storyville, since he had appeared in the club (at the earlier location) from March 7–15, 1953.[19] A recording from this engagement on March 10 has been issued on Blue Note.

The following session, organized by John Hammond and issued by Vanguard Records, launched Ruby Braff's career to a much broader public. He was widely acclaimed for his fine contributions to this session. Obviously, Vic Dickenson was very familiar with Ruby's playing by this time, and Hammond had become a recent champion. While it appears that Hammond invited Ruby to join this session, Vic was not likely to have complained in the least. Ruby reported that this was recorded in a Masonic Temple in Brooklyn.

Steve Voce shared his recollections from his conversations with Ruby about this time, elaborating on Ruby's earlier mention of receiving sardines in chapter 2:[20]

> In 1953 [Ruby] and [Nat] Pierce took an apartment in New York expecting great things. Braff was irritated by his parents' habit of sending him tins of sardines and threw them down the building's airshaft when they arrived. Weeks later, as they starved, he and Pierce were desperately salvaging the tins that hadn't been eaten by their also ravenous neighbors. In December that year he made the classic and still selling recordings of 'Russian Lullaby' and 'Jeepers Creepers' with the Vic Dickenson Septet. But one record date, no matter how successful, didn't constitute a living and he and Pierce were trying to stay alive on a diet of tinned plum tomatoes, the cheapest food to be found. But Braff's talent was as a pillar of fire in the night, and within months he was recording with giants like Buck Clayton, Benny Goodman, and Bud Freeman, and his career took off.

Vic Dickenson: *Vic Dickenson Septet, Volumes 1 and 2*
December 29, 1953, Brooklyn, New York
Ruby Braff (cnt), Vic Dickenson (tb), Edmond Hall (cl), Sir Charles Thompson (p), Steve Jordan (g), Walter Page (b), Les Erskine (dm)
Jeepers Creepers
Vanguard VRS 8001, (E) PPT 12000, (J) VY 506, LAX 3069, GXC 3122, 79610-2 (CD), 99/100-2 (CD), Fnt (E) FJL404
Russian Lullaby
Vanguard VRS 8001, (E) PPT 12000, (J) VY 506, LAX 3069, GXC 3122,

79610-2 (CD), 99/100-2 (CD), Fnt (E) FJL404

Keepin' Out of Mischief Now

Vanguard VRS 8002, (E) PPT 12005, Amadeo (Au) AVRS 7001, Vng (J) VY 506, LAX 3069, GXC 3122, 79608-2 (CD), 99/100-2 (CD), Fnt (E) FJL404

I Cover the Waterfront

Vanguard VRS 8002, (E) PPT 12005, Amadeo (Aus) AVRS 7001, Vng (J) VY 506, LAX 3069, GXC 3122, 79608-2 (CD), 99/100-2 (CD), Fnt (E) FJL 404, Vanguard 79571 (CD)

Sir Charles at Home

Vanguard VRS 8002, (E) PPT 12005, Amadeo (Au) AVRS 7001, Vng (J) VY 506, LAX 3069, GXC 3122, 99/100-2 (CD), Fnt (E) FJL 404, Vanguard 79571 (CD)

NOTE: All titles also on Vanguard VRS 8520/1, VSD 99/100, Vog (E) VJD 551, Vng (J) 200 E 6851, (Fr) 662221 (CD), K26Y 6091/6092 (CD), 200E 6851/2 (CD). Vanguard 79610-2, titled *Nice Work* and Vanguard 79608-2 (CD), titled *Linger Awhile* by Ruby Braff. Vanguard 99/100-2, titled *The Essential Vic Dickenson.* Vanguard 79571 is titled *City Nights: Jazz for the Evening.*

So, in sharp contrast with his growing acclaim, Ruby was fighting to survive as Steve Voce reported above. Following the wonderful session for Vanguard, Ruby may have returned to Boston and been in the audience for part of Vic Dickenson's performance at Mahogany Hall in the Copley Square Hotel as shown in an available advertisement. It was New Year's Eve and certainly Ruby might have had an engagement somewhere himself, but we'll never know. Vic led an all-star band that included Doc Cheatham. Certainly, Ruby was being recognized as an emerging star in the world of jazz at this time, very much justifying his place in *DownBeat*'s new star polling category.

The following recording session has escaped the attention of many of Ruby's fans. Clearly it springs from his relationship with the Vanguard label but places him in a very different role. Reissues on CDs may have helped some of Ruby's fans discover this performance for the first time.

Brother John Sellers: *Sings Blues and Folk Songs*

January 22, 1954, Brooklyn, New York

Brother John Sellers (voc), Ruby Braff (tp), Sir Charles Thompson (p), Freddie Green (g), Walter Page (b), Jo Jones (dm)

Farewell Work Life

Vanguard VRS 8005, VRS 9036, Vng (E) EPP 14002

Dorothea Boogie

Vanguard VRS 8005, VRS 9036, Vng (E) EPP 14002

NOTE: Other performances do not include Ruby Braff. All titles also on Vng (E) PP 12008, Vng 79036-2 (CD), Vanguard/Ace VMD 8006 (CD), Fnt (E) TFL6005, (J) KIJJ 2095, Fontana (E) TFL 6005.

Ruby's increasing acclaim through his recordings with Vanguard brought him to a concert appearance with Mel Powell at Carnegie Hall. Surely this was something that signaled not only early achievement, but at least a bit of his future potential. A copy of the program is available to the author in which Gerry Mulligan (spelled *Jerry* in the program), the Gene Krupa Trio, Steve Allen, the Erroll Garner Trio, and Billie Holiday were also featured. The program states that this was to be both a concert and a recording session.

Mel Powell and His All Stars: *Jam Session at Carnegie Hall*
April 9, 1954 Carnegie Hall, New York—benefit concert for the Lighthouse, New York Association for the Blind
Buck Clayton, Ruby Braff (tp), Urbie Green, Vernon Brown (tb), Mel Powell (p), Tony Scott (cl), Lem Davis (as), Buddy Tate, Eddie Shu (ts only on 1), Gene Krupa (only on 1), Jo Jones (dm), Steve Jordan (g), Milt Hinton (b), Teddy Napoleon (p only on 1), Martha Lou Harp (voc)
I've Found a New Baby
Columbia CL 557, Philips B07057L, CBS (J) SONP 50386
Lighthouse Blues
Columbia CL 557, Philips B07057L, CBS (J) SONP 50386
After You've Gone (1)
Columbia CL 557, Philips B07057L, CBS (J) SONP 50386

Add: Jay Brower (tp) and Romeo Penque (as, bar)
When Day Is Done (voc MLH)
Columbia CL 557, Philips B07057L, CBS (J) SONP 50386
NOTE: "After You've Gone" is also on Columbia (J) EM15 (EP) titled *Mel Powell: After You've Gone, Parts 1 and 2*. There is also a two-EP set, probably on European Columbia issues, titled *Mel Powell: Jam Session at Carnegie Hall*, probably containing "Lighthouse Blues" and "After You've Gone." All of the above performances were scheduled for release on Mosaic Records as a single CD; however, Mosaic was forced to cancel plans for this release due to rights issues.

Next, Ruby was selected to accompany Teddi King on a recording for Storyville Records. Several months before, she had recorded the first two albums issued under her name, the first for Storyville with Beryl Booker and the second, on Coral. Before those recordings she had performed and recorded with Nat Pierce in Boston and with George Shearing for MGM in New York.

Teddi King: *Storyville Presents Miss Teddi King*
Spring 1954, New York
Ruby Braff (tp), Jimmy Jones (p), Milt Hinton (b), Jo Jones (dm)
I Saw Stars
Storyville LP 314, 5009, (J) TD7, P-3909

Love Is a Now and Then Thing (Ruby out)
Storyville LP 314, 5009, P-3909
New Orleans
Storyville LP 314, P-3909, Fremeaux 2929
It's the Talk of the Town
Storyville LP 314, P-3909
I Guess I'll Have to Change My Plans
Storyville LP 314, P-3910
Our Love Is Here to Stay
Storyville LP 314, P-3910
Spring Won't Be Around This Season
Storyville LP 314, P-3910
It's All in the Mind (Ruby out)
Storyville LP 314, P-3910
NOTE: All titles also on Storyville (J) PA 3116, Flare ROYCD 275 (CD), and Storyville/Tokuma (J) TKCB 71632 (CD). All titles appeared on Vogue LDE 142 and four on Vogue EPV 1204 (EP) ("Stars," "New Orleans," "Town," "Love Is Here"). Storyville 5009 is a ten-inch 78 rpm record. Jack Bradley enjoyed noting that this is the only time that Ruby appears on a 78. AFRTS basic musical library, a 16 inch transcription, P series P-3909 contains the first four tunes. P-3910 contains the rest. Fremeaux 2929 is titled *50 Sublimes Chanteuses de Jazz, Vol. 2*. Flare ROYCD 275 is titled *'Round Midnight*.

Ruby greatly respected Frankie Newton's playing and performed with him around Boston, including times in George Wein's clubs. Ruby is unfortunately not audible on the acetate recording I have obtained that captures Newton performing with the Vinal Rhythm Kings. A memorial concert was held following Newton's death on died on March 11, 1954. Newton was a lyrical trumpet artist in his own right, and certainly deserves much wider recognition beyond those who already enjoy his recorded performances.

Frankie Newton Memorial[21]
April 26, 1954, Basin Street, New York
Tony Scott played with Ruby Braff, Urbie Green, Marty Napoleon, Buck Clayton, and others, including the following:[22]
Flip Phillips, Miff Mole, Willie "The Lion" Smith, Pee Wee Russell, Pete Brown, Tony Scott, Sonny Greer, Marian McPartland, Art Mardigan, Buster Bailey, Charlie Shavers, Pee Wee Erwin, Billy Maxted, Bobby Hackett, Pops Foster, Cozy Cole
NOTE: No recording known to exist.

There are two dates given for the following session but May 1954 seems more likely than March 1955 in my opinion:

Ruby Braff: *Hustlin' and Bustlin' / Storyville Presents Ruby Braff: Ruby, Sammy and Friends*
c. May 1954, New York
Ruby Braff (tp), Sam Margolis (ts, cl), Ken Kersey (p), Milt Hinton (b), Bobby Donaldson (dm)
There's a Small Hotel
Storyville STEP 432, Jazz Colours (G) 874716-2, Vogue (E) EPV 1221
Hustlin' and Bustlin' for My Baby
Storyville STEP 432, DA Music CD 3701, Vogue (E) EPV 1221
What's the Reason? (I'm Not Pleasin' You)
Storyville STEP 432
Fine and Mellow
Storyville STEP 433, Jazz Colours (G) 874716-2, Vogue (E) EPV 1221
Flakey
Storyville STEP 433, Jazz Colours (G) 874716-2
Shoe Shine Boy
Storyville STEP 433, Jazz Colours (G) 874716-2, Pid 640362
NOTE: Some sources list this session during March 1955. It also referenced under that date in this listing. All titles also on Storyville STLP 320 (titled *Storyville Presents Ruby Braff: Ruby Sammy and Friends*), Storyville STLP 908, (J) PA 6008, Vogue (E) LAE 12051, Black Lion (E) BLCD 760908 (CD), Black Lion BLP 60908, Jazz Colours (G) 874716-2 (titled *Ruby Got Rhythm*), and Past Perfect 220321 (titled *Ad Lib Blues*). EPV 1221, STLP 908, and BLCD 760908 are each titled *Hustlin' and Bustlin'*. DA Music CD 3701 is a five-CD set titled *Jazz Masters, Volume 1*. Pid 640362 is a compilation titled *Jazz Corner*. "Fine and Mellow" is also included in Jazz Hour JHR 73629 titled *A Jazz Hour with the Mainstream Masters*.

Ruby may have traveled to Toronto with George Wein and Vic Dickenson for an engagement at the Colonial Tavern. If so, he would have encountered some people who may have recalled his earlier appearances there in 1951 with Bud Freeman and 1952 with Pee Wee Russell. I have not located any appearance there in 1953. His next documented appearance was in his home base in Boston, where he led a group featured in a live performance recorded for Storyville Records.

George Wein and His Mahogany Hall Five[23]
May 24–29, 1954, Colonial Tavern, Toronto
George Wein (p), Vic Dickenson (tb), and other unknown musicians
Ruby might have been included in this group, but specific details are unknown.

George Wein Presents: *Jazz at the Boston Arts Festival*
Ruby Braff All Stars
June 9, 1954, Boston (at the Public Gardens)

Ruby Braff (tp), Vic Dickenson (tb, voc), Dick LeFave (tb), Al Drootin (cl, ts), Sam Margolis (ts), George Wein (p), John Field (b), Buzzy Drootin (dm)
High Society
Storyville STEP 414, STLP 311
At the Jazz Band Ball
Storyville STEP 414, STLP 311
Swinging the Blues
Storyville STEP 415, STLP 311
You Took Advantage of Me
Storyville STEP 415, STLP 311
After You've Gone
Storyville STEP 415, STLP 311
When It's Sleepy Time Down South (VD voc)
Storyville STEP 414, STLP 311, STLP 908, (J) PA 6008,
Vogue (E) LAE 12051,Black Lion (E) BLCD 760908 (CD),
Past Perfect 220321, Pid 826324
NOTE: All of the above except "When It's Sleepy Time Down South" also included on Storyville (J) PA 3118 titled *Jazz at Storyville I.* That Japanese album also includes five additional tunes by Bob Brookmeyer and Al Cohn. All titles also appear on another Japanese Storyville/Tokuma TKCB 72383 (CD). Black Lion BLCD 760908 and Storyville SLP 908 are titled *Hustlin' and Bustlin'.* Pid 826324 is titled *Great American Songbook, Vol. 7.*

Ruby said that the highly acclaimed Vanguard sessions were typically recorded using one microphone hanging from a 30-foot-high ceiling in the Brooklyn Masonic Temple. The sound from this approach to recording is distinctive. Certainly the enthusiastic reception of the earlier session with Vic Dickenson must have made it easier for John Hammond to pair Ruby with yet another established artist, Buck Clayton, for his next recording session.

Buck Clayton's Band Featuring Ruby Braff: *Buck Meets Ruby*
July 1, 1954, Brooklyn, New York
Buck Clayton, Ruby Braff (tp), Benny Morton (tb), Buddy Tate (ts), Jimmy Jones (p), Steve Jordan (g), Aaron Bell (b), Bobby Donaldson (dm)
Just a Groove (omit Morton and Tate)
Vanguard VRS 8008, (A, E) VRS 8517, (J) SR 3048
I Can't Get Started
Vanguard VRS 8008, (A, E) VRS 8517, (J) SR 3048,
(A) VCD 79608-2 (CD), 79571 (CD)
Kandee
Vanguard VRS 8008, (A, E) VRS 8517, SR 3103
Love Is Just Around the Corner
Vanguard VRS 8008, (A, E) VRS 8517, SR 3048
NOTE: All of the above also on Vanguard (E) PPT 12006, (J) KICJ 187 (CD), Amadeo (Au) VRS 7002, Vanguard (F) VSD 103/104, 519.057, (J) LAX 3074,

KNJ 2079 (CD), Vanguard (A) VCD 103/104, Family (I) SFR-VN 729, Vanguard (J) KICJ 187(CD also contains Ruby's session recorded October 17, 1955. Avid AMSC 1036 (CD) is titled *Three Classic Albums Plus*. Vanguard 79608-2 (CD) is titled *Linger Awhile* by Ruby Braff. Vanguard 103/4-2 is titled *The Essential Buck Clayton*. Vanguard 79571 is titled *City Nights: Jazz for the Evening*.

The New Yorker published an interview with John Hammond and Nat Hentoff about the Vanguard recording session that combined Buck Clayton and Ruby Braff:[24]

> Hammond: 'As far as I know, ours is the first major attempt to return to natural sound through a single microphone. A lot depends on the hall, and we don't want anyone to know about it except us. . . . We had trouble getting a Steinway. Luckily, Fritz Steinway is a jazz fan, and the moment I mentioned natural sound to him, he said he'd do everything he could to help.'
>
> Hentoff: 'We have Buck Clayton and Ruby Braff for you today. Two of the best guys blowing in the business.'
>
> Hammond, speaking to the musicians: 'Just relax and play. No engineers in sight, no flashing lights—nothing but music. Only please keep cigarettes off the piano.'
>
> Hentoff: 'This is the rarest kind of jazz today. These guys are caught in no man's land, somewhere between the people who think jazz died with Johnny Dodds and the people who think it began with Stan Kenton.'

Ruby is clearly gaining momentum with his recordings for two different record labels and his support by both George Wein and John Hammond. Next comes a session with Lee Wiley. While she has recorded with Bobby Hackett before, this is her first time with Ruby. The results are delightful, as one would expect, given Ruby's abilities as a tasteful supporter of jazz vocalists. When I asked Ruby about Lee Wiley, he reported only that she threw a typewriter at him on one occasion and that was the end of their association. He did not wish to elaborate, but I would be surprised if that occurred during this delightful recording session.

Lee Wiley: *Lee Wiley Sings Rodgers and Hart*
July 7, 1954, New York
Ruby Braff (tp), Jimmy Jones (p), Bill Pemberton (b), Jo Jones (dm)
My Heart Stood Still
    Storyville LP 312, Black Lion BLCD 760911, Storyville EP 416, STLP 916
Glad to Be Unhappy
    Storyville LP 312, Black Lion BLCD 760911, Storyville EP 416
My Funny Valentine
    Storyville LP 312, Black Lion BLCD 760911, Storyville EP 417
Give It Back to the Indians
    Storyville LP 312, Black Lion BLCD 760911, Storyville EP 417

My Romance
Storyville LP 312, Black Lion BLCD 760911, Storyville EP 416
You Took Advantage of Me
Storyville LP 312, Black Lion BLCD 760911, Storyville EP 416
Mountain Greenery
Storyville LP 312, Black Lion BLCD 760911, Storyville EP 417, STLP 916
It Never Entered My Mind
Storyville LP 312, Black Lion BLCD 760911, Storyville EP 417

NOTE: All titles also on Storyville EP 416 and EP 417. Both are 45 rpm EPs. All titles also on Storyville STLP 911, Storyville (J) 6003, Trio (Storyville) (J) PA 6132, Jazz Factory JFCD 22811, Black Lion BLP 60911 (LP), and Jazztone J 1248. Storyville STLP 916 is titled *The Women in Jazz*. Storyville (J) PA 1632 is titled *Duologue*. That album includes additional performances by Ellis Larkins. Jazztone J 1248 is titled *The Songs of Rodgers and Hart—As Sung and Played by Lee Wiley & Friends*. That album includes one selection by Milli Vernon with Ruby Braff along with other selections without Ruby that were previously released on Storyville Records by Teddi King, Jackie Cain, and Roy Kral. "My Heart Stood Still," "My Funny Valentine," "My Romance," and "You Took Advantage of Me" are also included in a two-CD set by Lee Wiley titled *Follow Your Heart* on Jasmine 411.

There is considerable doubt about Ruby's presence in the next session. While announced in early advertisements, he did not appear in this engagement. *DownBeat* reported the following:

> The extensive publicity surrounding Benny's return to the New York night club scene after a long hiatus is expected to benefit the young virtually unknown—except to musicians—Braff [and that] Benny heard Ruby play several weeks ago at a Monday night session at Basin Street. Ruby was substituting for Buck Clayton, who had an injured lip that evening.

The August 25 issue of *DownBeat* (page 1) reported that "Benny Goodman has been doing the best business in the history of Basin Street with turn-away crowds. Despite this announcement in *DownBeat*, the only recording from this engagement includes Charlie Shavers, not Ruby Braff. Further, *The New Yorker* listed Charlie Shavers as the trumpet player during this engagement.[25] Also, if Ruby appeared, he would have had to be absent for his appearance at the first Newport Jazz Festival. Consequently, Loren Schoenberg reported that Ruby's appearance was not likely.[26] But Ruby would play with Goodman at Basin Street West the following March, and that performance was extensively documented in released recordings. The Monday night session at Basin Street mentioned by *DownBeat* could have been the Frankie Newton Memorial concert held there on April 26. Certainly Goodman might have attended, and there was no written report of Ruby appearing at Basin Street around that time.

Benny Goodman (Ruby Braff does not appear at this occasion despite press listing)[27]
July 13, 1954, for three weeks, Basin Street, New York
Charlie Shavers (probably not Ruby Braff) (tp) with Benny Goodman (cl) and others reported to include Mel Powell (p), Israel Crosby (b), and Morey Feld (dm) Probably Charlie Shavers replaced Ruby Braff during this long engagement. The only surviving recording from this engagement features Charlie Shavers.

Next began a tradition that would bring Ruby, repeatedly, in various settings, to the Newport Jazz Festival. Once again, he benefited from the support of George Wein who directed what became a summer tradition in Rhode Island and later in New York as well. The first year's festival was held July 17 and 18 at the Casino in Newport. Ruby appeared with Teddy Wilson, Gerry Mulligan, Bill Harris, Milt Hinton, and Jo Jones reflecting a contrast with the opening set on the first day that was led by Eddie Condon and labeled "Traditional Jazz."

Tickets were priced at three levels, ranging from $3 to $5 per concert. *DownBeat* called this "a remarkable set."[28] Unfortunately no recordings were made during the festival's first year. Photographs of the venue were published as part of the 1978 festival program. The same issue reported that Ruby Braff placed second to Clifford Brown in the Trumpet—New Star category.[29]

Newport Jazz Festival: "First Annual American Jazz Festival"[30]
July 18, 1954, Newport Casino (Bellevue Avenue), Newport, Rhode Island (second day of two-day festival)
Teddy Wilson (p), Ruby Braff (tp), Gerry Mulligan (bars), Bill Harris (tb), Milt Hinton (b), Jo Jones (dm)

George Wein wrote the following about the session above:[31]

> After playing with Ruby for years, I felt that he was almost criminally underrated. And I had an instinct that he and Gerry would hit it off. The combination of traditional and modern jazz musicians in this group was in keeping with my idea of unique programming. This set was, not surprisingly, a success.

Lillian Ross described Ruby's contribution as "neither cool nor non-cool, but himself."[32]

Summers at Cape Cod had become a tradition, and Ruby returned to play in the programs at the summer Storyville Club location. But perhaps this year was a bit different, for *DownBeat* reported that Ruby had now become the "drawing card."[33]

Ruby Braff at Storyville[34]
Summer 1954, Storyville Club, Oceanside Hotel, Magnolia, Massachusetts (Summer Storyville)

Sometime in August (or earlier) Ruby returned to New York. Ruby participated in another recording session organized by John Hammond. This one continued to place Ruby in a more modern setting. Clearly this was not bebop, but the musicians were rooted in the broad mainstream of jazz music. In addition, Ruby led a quartet at the Village Vanguard with Pee Wee Russell. The sequence of these events is unknown and certainly the recording for Vanguard may have been concurrent with the engagement.

Urbie Green Octet: *Urbie Green and His Band / Old Time Modern*
August 17, 1954, Brooklyn, New York
Ruby Braff (tp), Urbie Green (tb), Med Flory (as), Frank Wess (ts, fl), Sir Charles Thompson (p), Freddie Green (g), Aaron Bell (b), Bobby Donaldson (dm)
I Got It Bad and That Ain't Good
    Vanguard VRS 8010, 8530
Lullaby of Birdland
    Vanguard VRS 8010, 8530
Old Time Modern
    Vanguard VRS 8010, 8530
Med's Tune
    Vanguard VRS 8010, 8530
NOTE: All titles also on Jazztone J 1259, Vanguard (E) PPT 12021, Amadeo 7003X. Jazztone J 1259 is titled *Slidin' Swing*. It also includes a performance from another Vanguard session led by Vic Dickenson. All of the above are also included on the CD release *Blues and Other Shades of Green* by Urbie Green, released on Jazzbeat 504.

Steve Jordan reports that Ruby Braff was playing at the Village Vanguard in New York during August 1954, leading a group that included Pee Wee Russell, Nat Pierce, and Walter Page.[35] That engagement may be Ruby's first one as a leader in a major New York club. Ruby Braff is shown using a mute in a photo with Steve Jordan during the following Village Vanguard engagement.[36]

Ruby Braff Quartet (?)
August 1954, Village Vanguard (178 Seventh Avenue South at 11th Street), New York
Ruby Braff (cnt), Pee Wee Russell (cl), Nat Pierce (p),Walter Page (b), and perhaps other musicians

Another recording for Vanguard followed. Undoubtedly this was inspired by the earlier Brandeis concert and recording from Carnegie Hall. Ruby was reunited with Mel Powell. They would have several opportunities to perform together in the future as well. Powell is a wonderful compliment to Ruby, and this launched Ruby's desire to perform as a duo with other pianists in the future.

Mel Powell: *Thigamagig*
August 24, 1954, Brooklyn, New York
Ruby Braff (tp), Mel Powell (p), Bobby Donaldson (dm)
Thigamagig
Vanguard VRS 8502, (Fr) 662223 (CD), 79602-2 (CD),
Vogue (E) VJD 572
You're My Thrill*
Vanguard VRS 8502, (Fr) 662223 (CD), Vogue (E) VJD 572, 79571 (CD),
(J) SR 3045
Button Up Your Overcoat*
Vanguard VRS 8502, (Fr) 662223 (CD), 79602-2 (CD),
Vogue (E) VJD 572, (J) SR 3045
Don-Que-Dee
Vanguard VRS 8502, (Fr) 662223 (CD)
Ain't She Sweet
Vanguard VRS 8502, (Fr) 662223 (CD), 79602-2 (CD), Vogue (E) VJD572
Take Me in Your Arms
Vanguard VRS 8502, (Fr) 662223 (CD), Vogue (E) VJD572
California, Here I Come*
Vanguard VRS 8502, (Fr) 662223 (CD), 79602-2 (CD),
Vogue (E) VJD 572, (J) SR 3045
Bouquet*
Vanguard VRS 8502, (Fr) 662223 (CD), 79602-2 (CD),
Vogue (E) VJD572, (J) SR 3045
NOTE: All titles except * also on Vanguard (J) SR 3045. The titles with * are also on Vanguard (J) SR (M) 3102. Vanguard (Fr) 662223 is titled *Mel Powell Trios: Borderline—Thigamagig*. Vanguard 79602-2 (CD) is titled *The Best Things in Life*. All titles also on Vanguard (J) KIJJ 2083, Vanguard (E) PPL 11000, and KICJ 185 (CD). Vanguard 97571 is titled *City Nights: Jazz for the Evening*.

September brought a return to Boston's Storyville Club at the Copley Square Hotel. Ruby had become a strong drawing card for George Wein in this location. Here he is billed as a member of the Mahogany All Stars. An advertisement is available, stating that Mahogany Hall would open September 17 with Wild Bill Davison, Vic Dickenson, and the Mahogany Hall All Stars. Thus the following billing is partly an attempt to create interest for the opening of that club two weeks later. The All Stars are followed into Storyville by Count Basie and His Orchestra, followed by Gerry Mulligan.

Vic Dickenson returned to New York at the end of 1954,[37] and Ruby's career began to focus more and more on New York sessions as well. Ruby physically moved to New York sometime in 1953 or 1954. His multiple performances 1953 in Boston and on Cape Cod suggest either late 1953 or early 1954 for this move. So, probably Ruby returned to Boston to appear at Storyville for his next performance. See Figure 3.4 for an advertisement announcing this engagement.

Ruby Braff, Vic Dickenson, and the Mahogany Hall All Stars
September 3–8, 1954, Storyville Club, Copley Square Hotel, Boston
Ruby Braff (tp), Vic Dickenson (tb), Sam Margolis (ts), and unknown other musicians

After recording for Vanguard and Storyville and appearing on earlier recordings for Savoy, Ruby attracted the interest of Bethlehem Records. His first recording was issued on a ten-inch LP and it featured one of his original compositions, "Ellie."

Ruby Braff Quartet: *Ruby Braff Swings*
October 1954, New York
Ruby Braff (tp), Johnny Guarnieri (p), Walter Page (b), Bobby Donaldson (dm)
Blue and Sentimental
    Bethlehem BEP 110A, BCP 5, Rep LP 204, London (E) EZ-N 19002, FCP4013
This Can't Be Love
    Bethlehem 11078, BEP 110A, FCP 4015, BCP 6043, London (E) EZ-N 19002
Mean to Me
    Bethlehem BEP 110A, BCP 5, BCP 90, BCP 6043, BCP 6043 (new series), R2 75822 (CD), Bethlehem FCP 4004, Rep LP 204, London (E) EZ-N19011
Ellie
    Bethlehem 11078, Rep LP 204, BEP 110A, BCP 5, BCP 90, BCP 6043, BCP 6043 (new series), R2 75822 (CD), London (E) EZ-N 19011, FCP 4007
The Blue Room
    Bethlehem BEP 110B, London (E) EZ-N 19002, Affinity CD PRO 1
I Can't Get Started
    Bethlehem BEP 110B, London (E) EZ-N 19002
You're a Sweetheart
    Bethlehem BEP 110B, BCP 6043, BCP 6043 (new series), London (E) EZ-N 19011, Bethlehem R2 75822 (CD), FCP 4015
Struttin' with Some Barbecue
    Bethlehem BEP 110B, BCP 5, BCP 6043, BCP 6043 (new series), Rep LP 204, London (E) EZ-N 19011, Bethlehem R2 75822 (CD), FCP 4003

NOTE: All titles also on Bethlehem BCP 1005, Affinity (E) AFF 98, and AFF 757 (CD). All titles on EZ-N 19002 also on London (J) LEB 1001. All titles on EZ-N 19011 also on London (J) LEB1007. BCP 1005 titled *Ruby Braff Swings*. BCP 5 titled *Ruby Braff Omnibus*. AFF 757 is titled *The Mighty Braff*. Bethlehem R2 75822 (CD) is titled *The Best of Braff* and BCP 6034 is titled *Smart. . .Luscious. . .Beautiful: Sounds of the Trumpet*. Bethlehem BCP6043 is titled *The Best of Ruby Braff* and BCP 6043 (New Series) is titled *Adoration of the Melody*. Affinity CD PRO1 is titled *The Message: 14 Jazz Masterpieces from the Affinity Catalog*. All of Ruby's recordings for Bethlehem are also included on Solar 2869490 (CD) titled *The Complete Ruby Braff Bethlehem Recordings*.

The following advertisements depict four of the performances in this chapter:

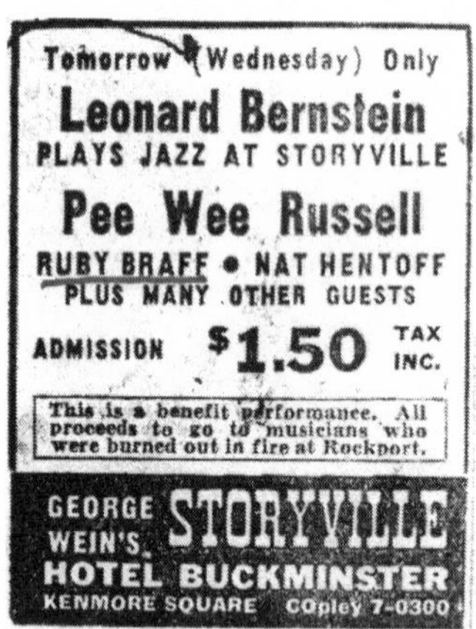

Figure 3.1: Advertisement
August 13, 1952

Figure 3.2: Advertisement
December 29, 1952

Figure 3.3: Advertisement Summer 1953

George Wein's

STORYVILLE

Copley Square Hotel

We are pleased to announce our fifth annual fall opening:

Sept. 3-8 Ruby Braff, Vic Dickenson and the Mahogany Hall All Stars ★
no cover . . . no minimum

Sept. 9-19 COUNT BASIE and his 16 piece orchestra, 1954 Down Beat Critics Poll award winner

Sept. 24 — Oct. 3 GERRY MULLIGAN quartet

Oct. 1 LEE KONITZ quartet (plus Gerry Mulligan through Oct. 3)

Oct. 7-10 TOM LEHRER
Reservations Accepted Now

NOW . . . the best in jazz can be heard on STORYVILLE RECORDS — at your dealers — write for catalog. September releases: "LEE WILEY sings RODGERS and HART", (LP 312) "KONITZ", a new Lee Konitz quartet set, (LP 313). Also on 45's.

★ MAHOGANY HALL opens Sept. 17th WILD BILL DAVISON, Vic Dickenson and The All Stars.

Sunday Matinees 3 P.M. at Storyville and Mahogany Hall

Figure 3.4: Advertisement September 1954

Notes

[1] Program image and information provided by Scott Edmiston, Office of the Arts, Brandeis University.
[2] *DownBeat*, July 30, 1952, 23.
[3] George Wein, *Myself Among Others (*Cambridge, MA: Da Capo Press, 2003), 98, 99, and 100.
[4] George Wein, *Myself Among Others* (Cambridge, MA: Da Capo Press, 2003), 100.
[5] The above recording (but ending with "The Lady Is a Tramp") is held at the Library of Congress, shelf number RGA 3294 track 4-5; record number 127366p+1X; source of

recording beginning with "What Is This Thing Called Love" is from Mel Levine. Mel recorded the concert on a disc recorder and provided the copy to Leonard Bernstein that is now in the Library of Congress. He also provided a copy of a newspaper ad for this performance.

[6] Robert Hilbert, *Pee Wee Russell: The Life of a Jazzman* (New York: Oxford University Press, 1993), 200. A photo of this group, labeled late 1940s, appears in *The March of Jazz Celebrates Ruby Braff's 74th Birthday Party*, Arbors Records, 2001, 13. Ivan Wainwright is listed as Ivan Wright in the photo's caption. The engagement is also mentioned in *DownBeat*, November 19, 1952, 3. This report indicates that Big Chief Russell Moore has just joined the band. The billing in *DownBeat* is reported as the Pee Wee Russell–Ruby Braff Band.

[7] Photo, *The March of Jazz Celebrates Ruby Braff's 74th Birthday Party*, Arbors Records, 2001, 13. Photo caption lists pianist as Ivan Wright.

[8] Source of advertisement: Mel Levine.

[9] Source of advertisement: Mel Levine.

[10] *DownBeat*, March 25, 1953, 3.

[11] *DownBeat*, May 6, 1953, 3.

[12] *DownBeat*, June 3, 1953, 28.

[13] *DownBeat*, August 26, 1953, 7.

[14] Nat Hentoff, "Ruby Braff Missing Link of Jazz," *Esquire*, May 1958, 62.

[15] *DownBeat*, July 15, 1953, 23.

[16] *DownBeat*, August 26, 1953, 20.

[17] George Wein, *Myself Among Others* (Cambridge, MA: Da Capo Press, 2003), 106. The date for Charlie Parker's opening is also from Ken Vail, *Bird's Diary* (England: Castle Communications, 1996), 135.

[18] Nat Hentoff, "Ruby Braff Missing Link of Jazz," *Esquire*, May 1958, 62. Dates for Charlie Parker's engagement are from Ken Vail, *Bird's Diary* (England: Castle Communications, 1996), 135.

[19] Ken Vail, *Bird's Diary* (England: Castle Communications, 1996), 122.

[20] Steve Voce, *The Independent*, February 11, 2003.

[21] *DownBeat*, May 5, 1954, 3. See also Robert Hilbert, *Pee Wee Russell: The Life of a Jazzman* (New York: Oxford University Press, 1993), 205–206 and *Melody Maker*, "Leonard Feather's NY Diary," May 15, 1954 (reproduced in Franz Hoffman's *Henry Red Allen Discography*, self-published by author). This performance is also reported in Manfred Selchow, *Profoundly Blue* (Germany: Uhle & Kleinmann, 1988), 306.

[22] *DownBeat*, June 2, 1964, 4.

[23] Cited in Manfred Selchow, *Ding Ding: A Bio-Discographical Scrapbook on Vic Dickenson* (Germany: Uhle & Kleinmann, 1998), 288.

[24] Brendan Gill and Lillian Ross, *The New Yorker*, July 17, 1954, 17–18.

[25] *The New Yorker*, July 17, 1974, 5.

[26] Personal correspondence with Loren Schoenberg.

[27] *DownBeat*, July 28, 1954, 1.

[28] *DownBeat*, August 25, 1954, 2.

[29] *DownBeat*, August 25, 1954, 7.

[30] Further information not available—Burt Goldblatt, *The Newport Jazz Festival: The Illustrated History* (New York: Dial Press, 1977), 263.

[31] George Wein, *Myself Among Others* (Cambridge, MA: Da Capo Press, 2003), 141.

[32] Lillian Ross, *The New Yorker*, August 14, 1954, 55.
[33] *DownBeat*, August 25, 1954, 21.
[34] *DownBeat*, June 16, 1954, 3
[35] Steve Jordan, *Rhythm Man* (Ann Arbor: University of Michigan Press, 1993), caption on photo by Popsie Randolph printed on unnumbered glossy page.
[36] Steve Jordan, *Rhythm Man* (Ann Arbor: University of Michigan Press, 1993), caption on photo by Popsie Randolph on unnumbered page.
[37] Manfred Selchow, *Ding Ding: A Bio-Discographical Scrapbook on Vic Dickenson (*Germany: Uhle & Kleinmann, 1998), 296.

Chapter 4

Ruby's Growing Reputation: Recording with Teagarden, Goodman, and the Buck Clayton Jam Sessions for Major Record Labels

The Vanguard recordings clearly established Ruby as a new star on the jazz scene. His performance with Mel Powell at Carnegie Hall added to his stature. John Hammond continued to champion Ruby's artistry. Jack Teagarden met Ruby through Louis Armstrong and asked him to join one of his recording sessions. A bit later, Louis joined the two of them on a televised *Timex All Star Jazz Show*. Benny Goodman had become aware of Ruby's potential long ago in Boston, and used Ruby as a soloist on Capitol albums and in several club engagements. John Hammond played a role in recommending Ruby for these recordings, given his long relationship with Benny.

Jack Teagarden and His Orchestra: ***Accent on Trombone***
October 1954, New York
Ruby Braff (tp), Jack Teagarden (tb and vocal on all titles), Sol Yaged (cl), Lucky Thompson (ts), Ken Kersey (p), Sidney Gross (g), Milt Hinton (b), Denzil Best (dm)
The Christmas Song
    Urania 100, Urania UJLP 1002, 1000, Jass Eight, J-CD-3
St. James Infirmary
    Urania 100, Urania UJLP 1001, 1205, 1209, Jazztone J 1254
Blue and Estoric
    Urania UJLP 1002, 1205
After You've Gone
    Urania UJLP 1002, 1205
Stars Fell on Alabama
    Urania UJLP 1002, 1205, 1209, Jazztone J 1254
A Hundred Years from Today
    Urania UJLP 1001, 1205, 1209, Jazztone J 1254

Lover
Urania UJLP 1001, 1205
NOTE: Jazztone J 1254 is titled *Jazz a la Mood* and it also includes selections recorded for Urania by Coleman Hawkins, Ernie Royal, Lucky Thompson, and Willie "The Lion" Smith. Jass Eight and Jass J-CD-3 are both titled *Santa Claus Blues*. Urania UJLP 1205 is titled *Accent on Trombone*. This LP was reissued on Saga (E) XIC 4005, Musidisc (F) 30CV 1073, Society (E) SOC 922, Fresh Sound (Sp) FSR-CD 138 (CD), Fresh Sound FSR 1067 (CD), and Drive Archive DE2 41205 (CD) titled *Personal Choice: Jack Teagarden All Stars*. "Blue and Estoric" and "After You've Gone" are included on *World's Greatest Music*, S3-305 along with selections by other artists recorded for Urania. The album is titled *America's Greatest Jazz*.

Ruby described his recollection of this session to Steve Voce, using words that reflected on his appreciation for being invited to record with these established artists:[1]

> Ruby told me that he was ashamed of it. 'I had no right to be there among such great musicians.' . . . Frank and not given to false modesty, Ruby was wrong of course. He'd made several recordings in the years before, all at the very least serviceable as this one was and of course one of the great performances of his life, the Vic Dickenson Septets. . . . 'I was so unsure of myself and they were all already at the top,' said Ruby.

Clearly many doors were about to open for Ruby, but his sense of modesty would reappear in comments he made to me about his performance in a television special for Timex with Louis Armstrong and Jack Teagarden over three years later in 1958.

Benny Goodman and His Orchestra: *B. G. in HiFi / The Hits of Benny Goodman*
November 9, 1954, New York
Chris Griffin, Ruby Braff, Bernie Privin, Carl Poole (tp), Will Bradley, Cutty Cutshall, Vernon Brown (tb), Benny Goodman (cl), Hymie Schertzer, Paul Ricci (as), Boomie Richman, Al Klink (ts), Sol Schlinger (bars), Mel Powell (p), Steve Jordan (g), George Duvivier (b), Bobby Donaldson (dm), Neal Hefti (arr)—Braff plays solos only and not section parts
20531 Jersey Bounce (no Braff)
Cap W 565, T 1514, Giants of Jazz (It) CD 53054
20532 When I Grow too Old to Dream*
Cap W 565
20533 You Brought a New Kind of Love to Me
Cap W 565, T 1514, Capitol 21145, Giants of Jazz (It) CD 53054, Laserlight 15780 (CD)

20534 Blue Lou (NH arr)
Cap W 565, T 1514, Giants of Jazz (It) CD 53054
20535 Jumpin' at the Woodside
Cap W 565, T 1514, (F) 85202/03, Jazz World JW 77003, Capitol 21145, Giants of Jazz (It) CD 53054, Golden Era 55001
20536 Stompin' at the Savoy
Cap W 565, T 1514, (F) 85202/03, (F) C 054-81713, Laserlight 15780 (CD), Golden Era 55001
20537 Sent for You Yesterday
Cap W 565, T 1514, EMI (F) 1551563, Laserlight 15780 (CD)
NOTE: Entire session on Capitol CDP 7-92864-2, Entertainers CD 0240, and Avid AMBX 151. Entire session except * also on Capitol CDP 7-91212-2. Capitol 21145 (CD) is titled *The Best of Benny Goodman: The Capitol Years.* Laserlight 15780 (CD) is titled *Benny Goodman: Let's Dance.*

Ruby was asked about playing with The Benny Goodman Orchestra. He always replied to me with emphasis, "I never played with Benny's Orchestra. He hired me only as a soloist." Ruby did not read music at this time in his career. At first, Ruby even denied soloing on a few of these tunes until I sent him a tape cassette. Of course, he then agreed and said he enjoyed listening to them again.

A photo from the March of Jazz program[2] is included in the photo section in this book.

Benny Goodman Trio/Quintet: *B. G. in HiFi*
November 16, 1954, New York
Ruby Braff (tp), Benny Goodman (cl), Mel Powell (p), George Duvivier (b), Bobby Donaldson (dm)
20549-14 Rock Rimmon
Cap W 565, T 1514, CDP 7-91212-2, EMI (F) 1551563, Giants of Jazz (It) CD 53054, Entertainers CD 0240, Cap SM 1514, Avid AMBX 151
20550-4 You're a Sweetheart
Cap W 565, Entertainers CD 0240
NOTE: Entire session is on Capitol CDP 7-92864-2, Mosaic MQ6-148, and Mosaic MD4-148 (CD). Ruby Braff does not play on "Rose Room" and "What Can I Say After I Say I'm Sorry." Both titles also on Capitol (F) ED 260426-1 "Sorry" is also on Avid AMBX 151.

Benny Goodman and His Orchestra: *B. G. in HiFi / The Hits of Benny Goodman*
November 17, 1954, New York
Chris Griffin, Ruby Braff, Bernie Privin, Carl Poole (tp), Will Bradley, Cutty Cutshall, Vernon Brown (tb), Benny Goodman (cl), Hymie Schertzer, Paul Ricci (as), Boomie Richman, Al Klink (ts), Sol Schlinger (bars), Mel Powell (p),

Steve Jordan (g), George Duvivier (b), Bobby Donaldson (dm), Neal Hefti (arr)—Braff plays solos only and not section parts

20551 Somebody Stole My Gal
    Cap W 565, T 1514, SM 1514, CDP 7-91212-2, Jazz World JW 77003, EMI (F) 1551563, Laserlight 15780 (CD)

20552 I Would Do Anything for You
    Blu Disc T 1016

20553 Big John's Special
    Cap W 565, T 1514, Giants of Jazz (It) CD 53054, Entertainers CD 0240, EMI (F) 1551563

20554 Let's Dance
    Cap W 565, T 1514, (F) 85202/03, CDP 7-91212-2, EMI (F) 1551563, Laserlight 15780 (CD)

20552 I Would Do Anything for You (breakdown)
    Blu Disc T 1016

NOTE: The three titles on W 565 are also on Capitol CDP 7-92864-2, Capitol (F) ED 260426-1, and Avid AMBX 151.

Vic Dickenson: *Vic Dickenson Showcase*
November 29, 1954, Brooklyn, New York
Ruby Braff, Shad Collins (tp), Vic Dickenson (tb), Edmond Hall (cl), Sir Charles Thompson (p), Steve Jordan (g), Walter Page (b), Jo Jones (dm)

Everybody Loves My Baby
    Vanguard VRS 8012, (E) PPT 12015, Amadeo (Au) AVRS 7012, Vng (J) VY 507, LAX 3070, GXC 3123, Jzt J 1259, Fnt (E) FJL 406, Vng (Fr) 662221 (CD), 99/100-2 (CD), Disco Club DC 3402

Old Fashioned Love
    Vanguard VRS 8013, (E) PPT 12019, Amadeo (Au) AVRS 7006, Vng (J) VY 507, LAX 3070, GXC 3123, 99/100-2 (CD), Fnt (E) FJL 406, Disco Club DC 3402, Vng (Fr) 662221 (CD)

NOTE: Other titles from this album (November session) do not include Ruby Braff. Complete session also on Vanguard (E) VRS 8520/1, VSD 99/100-2, K26Y 6091/6092 (CD), Vog (E) VJD 551, Vng (J) 200E 6851, (J) 66 2221 (CD), 200E 6851/2 (CD), and Vanguard (Fr) 662221 (CD). Vanguard 99/100-2 (CD) is titled *The Essential Vic Dickenson.*

Steve Jordan reports[3] a surprise birthday party for John Hammond was held at the Hammond's summer home in Westport, Connecticut. Ruby Braff, Edmond Hall, Steve Jordan, and Vic Dickenson all performed. George Avakian was among the guests.

Jordan also describes[4] a birthday party in 1954 or 1955 at the home of Bobby Gefaell in Bedford Village, New York, next to Greenwich, Connecticut. Gefaell had been a drummer in college and was an heir to wealth from a family investment in a paper mill. Nat Pierce, Buzzy Drootin, Oscar Pettiford, and Steve Jordan were in the band led by Ruby Braff.

The following appeared in *DownBeat*: "Ruby Braff will be booked by the Gale Agency when he goes on the road with his unit."[5] In addition, Ruby Braff placed 14th in the 18th Annual *DownBeat* Poll on trumpet.[6]

Next, Ruby made another recording for Bethlehem Records.

Ruby Braff Sextet: *Ball at Bethlehem with Ruby Braff*
December 31, 1954/January 1, 1955, New York
Ruby Braff (tp), Eddie Hubble (tb), Sam Margolis (ts), Dick Katz (p), Gene Ramey (b), Izzy Sklar (dm)
Rosetta
    Bethlehem BCP 1034
I'm Gonna Sit Right Down and Write Myself a Letter
    Bethlehem BCP 1034
Sometimes I'm Happy
    Bethlehem BCP 1034, Affinity (E) AFF 757 (CD)
You Can Depend on Me
    Bethlehem BCP 1034
Auld Lang Syne
    Bethlehem BCP 1034, BCP 85, BCP 88, Affinity (E) AFF 757 (CD), FCP 4005
NOTE: All titles, except "You Can Depend on Me," are also on Bethlehem BCP 5 titled *Ruby Braff Omnibus*, Rep LP 204, and London (E) LZ-N 14028. Affinity AFF 757 is titled *The Mighty Braff*. All of Ruby's recordings for Bethlehem are also included on Solar 2869490 (CD) titled *The Complete Ruby Braff Bethlehem Recordings*. This album received three stars in *DownBeat*.

Ruby Braff performed periodically at Eddie Condon's club in New York, beginning in 1955. The club was located on West Third Street, Greenwich Village, in New York. Ralph Sutton was the regular intermission pianist. This was the beginning of a musical friendship that lasted throughout Ruby's lifetime. Condon's club later moved to the Sutton Hotel on East 56th Street.[7] I have not found published reports of Ruby's appearances, so he was likely added as a guest artist on various occasions. But an available advertisement documents Ruby's return to the Blue Note in Chicago in concerts that also included Burl Ives, billed as the "Nation's Leading Folk Singer," and the Al Belletto Quintet. Ruby's group was billed as the Blue Noters Quintet. Admission was $2.

Blue Noters Quintet (see Figure 4.1)
February 6, 1955, 5 p.m. and 9 p.m., The Blue Note, Madison and Clark, Chicago
Lou Levy and Ruby Braff, others unknown, in a program featuring Burl Ives

Ruby tells a story about the following session with Ellis Larkins in an interview with Steve Voce on May 2, 1991. Ruby says that he loved the session Ella Fitzgerald recorded with Ellis Larkins singing Gershwin tunes. When he had a chance to talk to John Hammond, he suggested a pairing with Ellis Larkins for a future Vanguard session.

In later years, Ruby says that Hammond claimed this pairing was his own idea. They were talking in an elevator at the time of a session for Columbia, likely the following year, perhaps the session on March 5, 1956. Given his typical candor, Ruby claimed the idea as his own. Ruby stated that John Hammond became angry. That conversation marked the end of his recording for John Hammond, although they continued to talk from time to time until nearly the time of Hammond's death. Fortunately, there were several excellent recordings on Vanguard, both below and several times in 1956, before that tension arose.

Ruby Braff and Ellis Larkins: ***Two Part Inventions in Jazz, Volumes 1 and 2***
February 17, 1955, Brooklyn, New York
Ruby Braff (tp), Ellis Larkins (p)
Love for Sale
    Vanguard VRS 8019, 79609-2 (CD), Koch 7217 (CD), 7136 (CD)
I've Got a Pocket Full of Dreams
    Vanguard VRS 8019, (J) SR 3106, 79611-2 (CD)
Blues for Ruby
    Vanguard VRS 8019, (J) SR 3106, 79609-2 (CD)
I've Got the World on a String
    Vanguard VRS 8019, 79611-2 (CD), Definitive 11276
Please
    Vanguard VRS 8019, 79609-2 (CD)
Old Folks
    Vanguard VRS 8019, 79611-2 (CD)
Blues for Ellis
    Vanguard VRS8020, (J) SR 3106, 79611-2 (CD)
What Is There to Say?
    Vanguard VRS8020, (J) SR 3106, 79609-2 (CD), 79571 (CD)
When a Woman Loves a Man
    Vanguard VRS8020, 79611-2 (CD), 79571 (CD)
You Are Too Beautiful
    Vanguard VRS8020, (J) SR 3106, 79611-2 (CD)
Skylark
    Vanguard VRS8020, 79609-2 (CD), 79571 (CD)
A Sailboat in the Moonlight
    Vanguard VRS8020, (J) SR 3106, 79609-2 (CD)
A City Called Heaven
    Vanguard VRS8020, 79611-2 (CD), 79571 (CD)

NOTE: All titles also included on *Ruby Braff: The Complete Duets* on Definitive DRCD 11284. This is a two-CD set that also includes performances from October 14 and 17, 1955. All titles on VRS 8019 are also on Vanguard (E) PPT 12010, Amadeo (Eu) AVRS 7009. All titles on VRS 8020 are also on Vanguard (E) PPT 12022, Amadeo (Eu) AVRS 7011. All titles except "A City Called Heaven" are also on VRS 8516 and VRS 8516 (J) (both titled *Pocket Full of Dreams*). Vanguard 79609-2 is titled *Ruby Braff and Ellis Larkins Duets: Volume 1* and 79611-2 is *Volume 2*. Vanguard 97571 is titled *City Nights: Jazz for the Evening*. Koch 7217 is titled *How's Your Romance? Cole Porter in the 1930s Vol. 1* and Koch 7136 is titled *You're the Top: Cole Porter in the 1930s*. The Koch CDs are included in a three-CD box set of the same title with the number A-22701, issued jointly by Koch International Classics and the Indiana Historical Society. Definitive DRCD 11276 is titled *Harold Arlen Songbook: Over the Rainbow*. Each album received five stars in *DownBeat*.

Ruby reported that he severely cut his lip prior to appearing with Goodman at Basin Street. Here is Ruby's story as he related it to me:

> I was rehearsing something with Teddy [Wilson] in Nola Studios above Steinway Hall. I think it was on a Thursday before the weekend engagements started at Basin Street. A door had been removed from its hinges the previous day to allow an organ to be brought in and removed. When the door was replaced, the hinge pins were not inserted, so that when Bobby Donaldson closed the open door, it fell, hitting my trumpet and cutting my lip. Ruby said that Benny made him play throughout the Basin Street engagement and that this probably rescued his career. He described his role in the following way: 'Benny made fine use of what little I could do at the time.' Ruby had limited feeling in his lips for about six months. He repeated part of this story in a radio interview March 2, 1991, with Rob Bamberger and also in a radio interview in London from 1990.

Mosaic Records has published a photo by Popsie showing Ruby Braff, Benny Goodman, Paul Quinichette, and Perry Lopez at Basin Street, February 1955.[8]

Benny Goodman Octet—opening weekend of ten weekend engagement on Friday and Saturday nights[9]
February 25–26, 1955, Basin Street West, New York
Ruby Braff (tp), Urbie Green (tb), Benny Goodman (cl), Paul Quinichette (ts), Teddy Wilson (p), Perry Lopez (g), Milt Hinton (b), Bobby Donaldson (dm)

The Basin Street engagement continued for ten weekends only following this opening weekend; however, only the weekend of March 25–26 was professionally recorded. Thus, no recordings are known for the other weekends.

Benny Goodman Octet—second weekend of ten-weekend engagement
March 4–5, 1955, Basin Street West, New York

Ruby Braff (tp), Urbie Green (tb), Benny Goodman (cl), Paul Quinichette (ts), Teddy Wilson (p), Perry Lopez (g), Milt Hinton (b), Bobby Donaldson (dm)

The Ruby Braff Quintet: *Ruby, Sammy, and Friends / Hustlin' and Bustlin'*
Possibly March 1955, New York but this session is shown in detail on the more likely date of May 1954 given Ruby's busy schedule
Ruby Braff (tp), Sam Margolis (ts, cl), Ken Kersey (p), Milt Hinton (b), Bobby Donaldson (dm)
NOTE: Various sources list both May 1954 and March 1955 as possible recording dates. See May 1954 for details of this session.

Benny Goodman Octet—third weekend of ten-weekend engagement
March 11–12, 1955, Basin Street West, New York
Ruby Braff (tp), Urbie Green (tb), Benny Goodman (cl), Paul Quinichette (ts), Teddy Wilson (p), Perry Lopez (g), Milt Hinton (b), Bobby Donaldson (dm)

Benny Goodman was interviewed for a report in *The New Yorker* about the Basin Street engagement:[10]

> We don't know *what* the hell we're doing. You might say we're having an old-fashioned jam session here, only better. We play sometimes quartet, sometimes octet. Except for Teddy Wilson on piano and Milt Hinton on bass, it's a new group for me. There's Bobby Donaldson on drums, Ruby Braff on trumpet, Urbie Green on trombone, Perry Lopez on guitar, and Paul Quinichette on saxophone. It's kind of what you might call a *big* small group. Very cohesive. We've found we all think the same way, so we just take off and have a lot of fun. Oh, we got ourselves a few basic choruses, but there's an *awful* lot of improvising. We weren't going to have any rehearsals at all before we started, and then I thought, well, maybe one rehearsal, so then we had one and we worked out some arrangements, but we never get around to making much use of them. . . . The most important thing is that I got myself kids with talent. Ruby Braff doesn't read much music, but who cares? He's warm, he feels the way the rest of us feel, and he's having fun. There was a time, a few years back, when all the kids were playing on this bop kick, but they ran up a dead end and now they're coming around to swing. There's a terrific trend to what they call rock and roll, and to race music. As for me, maybe I've been rejuvenated. What I play is still swing, but as a group I guess we have a different sound. When I was playing here last summer, I was just trying to get *back* to something I used to do, but now it's a new thing that grows right out of the past but is new and alive. . . . What I like best about this place is that I like it best when *I'm* playing.

Milt Hinton published a photo showing a young Ruby Braff standing alone in a New York recording studio in 1955.[11] Mosaic Records published two photos of Ruby from the March 15 Buck Clayton Jam Session in its definitive issue of these recordings. The first shows Ruby between Buck Clayton and Bennie

Green.[12] The second shows Ruby seated beside Bennie Green and Dicky Harris.[13] Both show Ruby playing a trumpet.

The Buck Clayton Jam Session recordings were well received by jazz fans and continued to extend Ruby's reputation. It appeared that Ruby had completely recovered from injury to his lip in February.

Buck Clayton: *Jumpin' at the Woodside / All the Cats Join In*
March 15, 1955, New York
Buck Clayton (tp), Ruby Braff (tp), Bennie Green, Dicky Harris (tb), Coleman Hawkins, Buddy Tate (ts), Al Waslohn (p), Steve Jordan (g), Milt Hinton (b), Jo Jones (dm), Jack Ackerman (tap dancing –1)
Rock a Bye Basie –1 (alt tk)
Rock a Bye Basie –1
    Columbia CL 701, JC2L 614, CBS 88031, (J) SONP 50413
Broadway (alt tk)
Out of Nowhere (alt tk)
    Columbia CJ 44291, CBS 463336-1, CK 44291 (CD),
    CBS (E) 46336-2 (CD)
Out of Nowhere
    CL 882, Philips (G) B07905R, Columbia (J) PL 5074, Fresh Sound (Sp) FS 272, FSR 593, 980081-1
Blue Lou (alt tk)
    Columbia CJ 44291, CBS 463336-1, CK 44291 (CD),
    CBS (E) 46336-2 (CD)
Blue Lou
    Columbia CL882, Fresh Sound (Sp) FS 272, FSR 593, 980081-1,
    Philips (E) BBL 7129, (H) B07163L
Broadway
    Columbia CL 701, 413, Philips (E) BBL JC2L614, CBS 88031,
    Columbia (A) B 528 (EP), (I) B 07106L, (I) B 0759S/96L

NOTE: All eight selections are included on Mosaic MD6-144 and MQ8-144. The master take for "Out of Nowhere" is also on CBS (J) SONP 50413, Philips (E) BBL 7129, and (H) B07163L. Philips (E) BBL7087, and (H) B07106L include the master take of "Rock a Bye Basie." Note "Blue Lou" alternate and "Broadway" master takes as originally issued have some splicing from take 1. The four master takes are also included in the following CD: Lone Hill LHJ 10115 titled *Buck Clayton: Complete Legendary Jam Sessions.*

Amidst his continuing weekend appearances with Benny Goodman, Ruby returned to the studio two days later for Bethlehem Records. This reunited him with Bob Wilber. While they had performed together frequently in Boston, this was their first collaboration in a recording studio. Wilber's arrangements provide a rich setting to showcase Braff's lyrical performances.

Ruby Braff and His Orchestra: *Holiday in Braff*
March 17/18, 1955, New York
Ruby Braff (tp), Hymie Schertzer (as), Al Klink, Bob Wilber (cl, ts, arr), Boomie Richman (ts), Sol Schlinger (bars), Ellis Larkins (p), Mundell Lowe, Art Ryerson (g), Walter Page (b), Bobby Donaldson (dm)
Easy Living
Bethlehem BCP 1032, BCP 82, EXLP 6, BCP 6043, R2 75822 (CD)
Flowers for a Lady
Bethlehem 11079, BCP 1032, BCP 5, BCP 86,BCP 6043,FCP 4011, Rep LP 204, R2 75822 (CD)
Foolin' Myself
Bethlehem BCP 1032, BCP 6043, R2 75822 (CD)
I'll Be Around
Bethlehem BCP 1032, BCP 5, BCP 89, BCP 6043, Rep LP 204, R2 75822 (CD)
It's Easy to Blame the Weather
Bethlehem BCP 1032, BCP 6043, R2 75822 (CD)
Pullin' Thru
Bethlehem BCP 1032, BCP 6043, R2 75822 (CD)
When You're Smiling
Bethlehem 11079, BCP 1032, BCP 5, BCP 86, BCP 91, R2 75822 (CD), FCP 4012
You're a Lucky Guy
Bethlehem BCP1032, R2 75822 (CD)
NOTE: All titles also on Bethlehem BCP 6043 (new series), Bethlehem/Toshiba (J) EMI TOJJ 1032 (CD), London (E) LZ-N 14022, Affinity (E) AFF 98 and Affinity (F) AFF 757 (titled *The Mighty Braff*) and R2 75822 (CD) titled *The Best of Braff.* A sampler, *The Stars of Bethlehem Shine Again,* includes "When You're Smiling" on release number 08122 797742. All of Ruby's recordings for Bethlehem are also included on Solar 2869490 (CD) titled *The Complete Ruby Braff Bethlehem Recordings*. This album received four stars in *DownBeat.*

Benny Goodman Octet—fourth weekend of ten weekend engagement
March 18–19, 1955, Basin Street West, New York
Ruby Braff (tp), Urbie Green (tb), Benny Goodman (cl), Paul Quinichette (ts), Teddy Wilson (p), Perry Lopez (g), Milt Hinton (b), Bobby Donaldson (dm)

Benny Goodman did not authorize the release of these recordings from Basin Street West until many years later in a box set distributed by the Book of the Month Club in the US. Additional performances were later released from tapes Goodman donated to Yale University. Groups of reissues of these recordings are noted by the letters A through I below.

Benny Goodman Octet—fifth weekend of ten weekend engagement[14]
March 25–26, 1955, Basin Street West, New York
Ruby Braff (tp), Urbie Green (tb), Benny Goodman (cl), Paul Quinichette (ts), Teddy Wilson (p), Perry Lopez (g), Milt Hinton (b), Bobby Donaldson (dm)

Let's Dance (A)
MusicMasters CIJ 60156Z (CD), 820803-2
Don't Be That Way (B, E)
Philips 870000BFY
Rose Room (RB, UG, PQ, PL out) (B)
Philips 870000BFY
Between the Devil and the Deep Blue Sea (B)
Philips 870000BFY
Body and Soul (RB, UG, PQ, PL out) (A, B, C, I)
Philips 870000BFY, MusicMasters CIJ60156Z (CD), 820803-2, LRC CD9003 (CD)
After You've Gone (RB, UG, PQ, PL out) (B,E,I)
Philips 870000BFY
On the Alamo (B, E, I)
Philips 870000BFY
Just One of Those Things (RB, UG, PQ, PL out) (B, C, E, I)
Philips 870000BFY
Blue and Sentimental (PQ feature) (B, E, H)
Philips 870000BFY
Blue and Sentimental alternate (PQ feature, BG out) (A)
MusicMasters CIJ 60156Z (CD), 820803-2
Air Mail Special (B, I)
Philips 870000BFY
Air Mail Special alternate (A)
MusicMasters CIJ 60156Z (CD), 820803-2
I've Found a New Baby (RB, UG, PQ, PL out) (B, I)
Philips 6379002
I've Found a New Baby alternate (RB, UG, PQ, PL out) (A)
MusicMasters CIJ 60156Z (CD), 820803-2, 65099-2 (a promo CD)
Slipped Disc (B, E, H)
MusicMasters CIJ 60142Z
Slipped Disc alternate (RB, UG, PQ, PL out) (D)
MusicMasters CIJ 60142Z (CD), 820802-2
As Long As I Live (B)
Philips 870001BFY
Flying Home (B, F, I)
Philips 870001BFY
'Deed I Do (B, F, H)
Philips 870001BFY
Avalon (B, F, I)
Philips 870001BFY

Memories of You (B, C, F)
Philips 870001BFY
Memories of You alternate (RB, UG, PQ, PL out) (A)
Philips 870001BFY, MusicMasters CIJ 60156Z (CD)
Stompin' at the Savoy (B, F, H)
Philips 870001BFY
Stompin' at the Savoy alternate (A)
MusicMasters CIJ 60156Z (CD)
If I Had You (B, F)
Philips 870001BFY
Sing, Sing, Sing (B, H)
Philips 870001BFY
Sing, Sing, Sing alternate (A)
MusicMasters CIJ 60156Z (CD)
Lady Be Good (RB, UG, PQ, PL out) (B, C, G, H)
Philips 870002BFY
Stairway to the Stars (UG feature, RB, PQ, BG, PL out) (B, G, I)
Philips 870002BFY, MusicMasters CIJ60156Z (CD)
Honeysuckle Rose (B, G)
Philips 870002BFY
Honeysuckle Rose alternate (A)
MusicMasters CIJ 60156Z (CD)
Nice Work If You Can Get It (RB, UG, PQ, PL out) (B, C, G)
Philips 870002BFY
Nice Work If You Can Get It alternate (RB, UG, PQ, PL out) (A)
MusicMasters CIJ 60156Z (CD)
Rosetta (B, G, H)
Philips 870002BFY
Mean to Me (B)
Philips 870002BFY
Mean to Me alternate (RB feature) (A)
MusicMasters CIJ 60156Z (CD)
Shine (B, G)
Philips 870002BFY
Night and Day (B, G)
Philips 870002BFY
One O'Clock Jump (B, G)
Philips 870002BFY
One O'Clock Jump (A)
MusicMasters CIJ 60156Z (CD)
Goodbye (B, G)
Philips 870002BFY
Goodbye (A)
MusicMasters CIJ 60156Z (CD)

As Long As I Live alternate (C)
Europa Jazz (It) Vol. 75
After You've Gone alternate (RB, UG, PQ, PL out) (C)
Europa Jazz (It) Vol. 75, LRC CD9003 (CD)
If I Had You alternate (C)
Europa Jazz (It) Vol. 75, LRC CD9003 (CD)
On the Sunny Side of the Street alternate (C)
Europa Jazz (It) Vol. 75, LRC CD9003 (CD)
Avalon alternate (C)
Europa Jazz (It)Vol. 75, LRC CD9003 (CD)
Runnin' Wild (RB, UG, PQ, PL out) (A)
MusicMasters CIJ 60156Z (CD)

NOTE: The following key details the content of several of the additional releases of these performances:

(A) These titles also on MusicMasters CIJ 20156F, CIJ 60156Z (CD), and MusicMasters (J) EJD 8001/2. Title of this CD is *Benny Goodman Yale Archives Volume 2: Live at Basin Street—Never Before Released Recordings* and this CD is separately listed below for clarity. Note that this CD includes two titles without Ruby: "Stairway to the Stars" and "Body and Soul." These are the only two titles that were previously issued on LPs according to D. Russell Connor. Loren Schoenberg explained that Benny Goodman selected his favorite versions for earlier LP releases, creating an opportunity to issue more performances from Goodman's archival recordings following his passing.

(B) Also on CLRL SRL 7673 and RL 7673. CRL stands for "Classics Record Library," which is a division of Book of the Month Club. This box set is titled *An Album of Swing Classics*.

(C) Also on HOM HMI 1379. HOM stands for Hall of Music and equals Europa (It) 1045 and Europa Jazz (IT) Vol. 75.

(D) Alternate take from MusicMasters CIJ 60142Z (CD) recorded March 26, 1955, entitled *Benny Goodman Yale Archives Volume 1—Never Before Released Recordings*.

(E) Also on Philips 6379001.

(F) Also on Philips 6379002.

(G) Also on Philips 6379003.

(H) Also on Philips (G) 845324 (part of a two-LP set combined with 845325 below).

(I) Also on Philips (G) 845325 (part of a two-LP set combined with 845324 above).

In addition, Philips 870000/1/2 is equivalent to Classics Record Library (Book of the Month Club) RL 7673 (mono) and SRL 7673 (stereo), Philips (Fr) 6379.0001/2/3, and Phonogram (J) SFL 9087/8/9. Other released compilations are detailed in D. Russell Connor's wonderful book *Benny Goodman—Listen to the Legacy*. His work is a remarkable gift to all discographers as well as a memorial to Benny Goodman's career. MusicMasters releases also appear on related record club labels Jazz Heritage and Musical Heritage Society and are also reissued on Nimbus 2700 titled *Yale Music Library, Volume 1.* All titles on MusicMasters CIJ 60156Z also appear on Limelight 820803-2. The MusicMasters and Limelight CDs are also included in a six-CD (five-volume) box set titled *Swing, Swing, Swing: Rare Recordings from the Yale University Music Library* MusicMasters 65095-2 and also as Limelight 844316-2. LRC CD 9003 (CD) is titled *Teddy Wilson—Sonny Lester Collection.*

Next, I will repeat the listing of alternate takes from the Benny Goodman recordings at Basin Street West. I feel that this adds clarity. Nothing in the listing that follows differs from the comprehensive listing of performances above. Note that the MusicMasters CD lists the date of March 26 from tape boxes, but D. Russell Connor suggests that the actual performances may date from either March 25 or 26 in light of Goodman's "imprecision with dates."

Benny Goodman Octet (alternate takes repeated from above)
March 25–26, 1955, Basin Street West, New York
Ruby Braff (tp), Urbie Green (tb), Benny Goodman (cl), Paul Quinichette (ts), Teddy Wilson (p), Perry Lopez (g), Milt Hinton (b), Bobby Donaldson (dm)
Let's Dance
    MusicMasters CIJ 60156Z (CD), 820803-2
Honeysuckle Rose
    MusicMasters CIJ 60156Z (CD), 820803-2
Runnin' Wild (no Braff)
    MusicMasters CIJ 60156Z (CD), 820803-2
Mean to Me (Braff feature)
    MusicMasters CIJ 60156Z (CD), 820803-2
Memories of You (no Braff)
    MusicMasters CIJ 60156Z (CD), 820803-2
Stompin' at the Savoy
    MusicMasters CIJ 60156Z (CD), 820803-2
Blue and Sentimental (PQ feature, Braff in coda)
    MusicMasters CIJ 60156Z (CD), 820803-2
One O'Clock Jump
    MusicMasters CIJ 60156Z (CD), 820803-2
I've Found a New Baby (no Braff)
    MusicMasters CIJ 60156Z (CD), 820803-2
Stairway to the Stars (LP take, UG feature, no Braff or BG)
    MusicMasters CIJ 60156Z (CD), 820803-2
Body and Soul (LP take, no Braff)
    MusicMasters CIJ 60156Z (CD), 820803-2
Air Mail Special
    MusicMasters CIJ 60156Z (CD), 820803-2

Nice Work If You Can Get It (no Braff)
MusicMasters CIJ 60156Z (CD), 820803-2
Sing, Sing, Sing
MusicMasters CIJ 60156Z (CD), 820803-2
Goodbye
MusicMasters CIJ 60156Z (CD), 820803-2
Slipped Disc
MusicMasters CIJ 60142Z (CD), 820802-2
NOTE: Performances shown as "no Braff" are quartet only consisting of Goodman, Wilson, Hinton, and Donaldson. Two titles listed as LP take are not alternatives from the original LP issues. Other issues are listed on the previous page.

Benny Goodman Octet—sixth weekend of ten weekend engagement
April 2–3, 1955, Basin Street West, New York
Ruby Braff (tp), Urbie Green (tb), Benny Goodman (cl), Paul Quinichette (ts), Teddy Wilson (p), Perry Lopez (g), Milt Hinton (b), Bobby Donaldson (dm)

Ruby again finds time during the week to return to the recording studio, this time accompanying George Wein. This is his fourth recording in just a span of three months amidst his weekend performances with Benny Goodman.

George Wein: *Wein, Women and Song*
George Wein
April 1955, New York
Ruby Braff (tp), Sam Margolis (ts), George Wein (p, voc), Stan Wheeler (b), Marquis Foster (dm)
I'm Gonna Sit Right Down and Write Myself a Letter
Atlantic LP 1221, Atlantic EP 559, Arbors Records ARCD 19268
All Too Soon
Atlantic LP 1221, Atlantic EP 559, Arbors Records ARCD 19268
You're Lucky to Me
Atlantic LP 1221, Atlantic EP 560, Arbors Records ARCD 19268
Back in Your Own Backyard
Atlantic LP 1221, Atlantic EP 560, Arbors Records ARCD 19268
Once in a While
Atlantic LP 1221, Atlantic EP 559, Arbors Records ARCD 19268
You Ought to Be in Pictures
Atlantic LP 1221, Atlantic EP 560, Arbors Records ARCD 19268
Please
Atlantic LP 1221, Atlantic EP 559, Arbors Records ARCD 19268
Did I Remember?
Atlantic LP 1221, Arbors Records ARCD 19268
Who Cares?
Atlantic LP 1221, Atlantic EP 560, Arbors Records ARCD 19268

NOTE: All titles on Atlantic LP 1221 are also issued on Collectables 6525 (CD). Other performances on the original LP do not include Ruby Braff but substitute Bobby Hackett ("Pennies from Heaven," "I'm Through With Love," "Why Try to Change Me Now?," and "I Married an Angel"). These also appear on the Arbors Records release titled *Wein, Women and Song and More: George Wein Plays and Sings*. The CD includes other tracks without Ruby recorded later in a session with Warren Vaché: "Big Butter and Egg Man," "If We Ever Meet Again," "Love You Funny Thing," "When It's Sleepy Time Down South," "I'm Shooting High," "I've Got a Pocket Full of Dreams," "Someday You'll Be Sorry," "Sweethearts on Parade," and "Swing That Music."

Benny Goodman Octet—seventh weekend of 10 weekend engagement
April 9–10, 1955, Basin Street West, New York
Ruby Braff (tp), Urbie Green (tb), Benny Goodman (cl), Paul Quinichette (ts), Teddy Wilson (p), Perry Lopez (g), Milt Hinton (b), Bobby Donaldson (dm)

Benny Goodman Octet—eighth weekend of 10 weekend engagement
April 16–17, 1955, Basin Street West, New York
Ruby Braff (tp), Urbie Green (tb), Benny Goodman (cl), Paul Quinichette (ts), Teddy Wilson (p), Perry Lopez (g), Milt Hinton (b), Bobby Donaldson (dm)

Ruby's appearance at the Stuyvesant Casino overlapped one night with his next weekend with Benny Goodman; however, he likely left Basin Street to join the musicians at the Stuyvasant Casino for some of the late sets. An advertisement listed Chris Connor as the headliner, appearing with Lee Konitz, Buck Clayton, Bobby Hackett, Ruby Braff, Pee Wee Russell, Miff Mole, Joe Sullivan, Pops Foster, Herman Autrey, Manzie Johnson, Milt Jackson, Percy Heath, Urbie Green, Horace Silver, George Wallington, Billy Byers, "and many other jazz stars." This anchors the following listing:

Stuyvesant Casino[15] (see Figure 4.2)
April 22–23, 1955, from 8:30 p.m.–1:00 am, Stuyvesant Casino, 140 2nd Avenue, New York

Benny Goodman Octet—ninth weekend of 10 weekend engagement
April 23–24, 1955, Basin Street West, New York
Ruby Braff (tp), Urbie Green (tb), Benny Goodman (cl), Paul Quinichette (ts), Teddy Wilson (p), Perry Lopez (g), Milt Hinton (b), Bobby Donaldson (dm)

Ruby took time for another recording, this time for Jazztone. Most of the following selections have been reissued; however, "Ruby's Dream" is only issued on a seven-inch diameter LP, probably only in Germany. It is a different melody than the other titles from this session and is one of Ruby's original compositions. It deserves to be included on future reissues.

Ruby Braff All Stars: *Big City Six* / Ruby Braff Sextet: *Little Big Horn / Swinging with Ruby Braff*
April 25, 1955, New York
Ruby Braff (tp), Billy Byers (tb), Sam Margolis (ts), Marty Napoleon (p), Milt Hinton (b), Jo Jones (dm)
Deep River
    Jazztone J 1011, J 1210, J 1265, Hall of Fame JG 601
In the Shade of the Old Apple Tree
    Jazztone J 1011, J 1210, J 1265, Hall of Fame JG 601
'Deed I Do
    Jazztone J 1210, J 1265, (G) J 715
Love Me or Leave Me
    Jazztone J 1210, J 1265, Hall of Fame JG 601
Only a Blues
    Jazztone J 1210, (G) J 715, J 740, Concert Hall SJS 740
Between the Devil and the Deep Blue Sea
    Jazztone J 1210, (G) J 715, J 740
Lonesome Road
    Jazztone J 1210, J 1282, Hall of Fame JG 608, Am. Rec. Society G 452
I'll Never Be the Same
    Jazztone J 1011, J 1210, J 1282,Hall of Fame JG 608,Am. Rec. Society G 452
I'm Shooting High
    Jazztone J 1011, J 1210
Flakey
    Jazztone J 1011, J 1210, Guilde du Jazz (F)J 1011 (?)
Roundelay
    Jazztone J 1011
Ruby's Dream
    Jazztone (G) J 715
NOTE: All titles on J 1210 also on Concert Hall CHJ 1210 and Fresh Sound FSRCD 321 (CD), both titled *Little Big Horn*. Jazztone J 1011 is also titled *Little Big Horn*, while J 1210 is titled *Swinging with Ruby Braff*. Jazztone J 1265 is titled *Swing Lightly*. "Deep River" is also on Jazz Connoisseur JCC 105 (cassette). Jazztone J 740 and Concert Hall SJS 740 are seven-inch diameter LPs that also include tunes by Lionel Hampton, Tony Scott, and Omer Simeon. Both issues are titled *Jazz Parade*. The SJS 740 issues are labeled "syncro stereo" to suggest playing with either a stereo or mono cartridge. This album received five stars in *DownBeat*.

Benny Goodman Octet—final weekend of ten weekend engagement
April 30–May 1, 1955, Basin Street West, New York
Ruby Braff (tp), Urbie Green (tb), Benny Goodman (cl), Paul Quinichette (ts), Teddy Wilson (p), Perry Lopez (g), Milt Hinton (b), Bobby Donaldson (dm)

'Deed I Do
Air Mail Special

The New Yorker carried a report of the final weekend at Basin Street West:[16]

> Some exceptionally gifted jazz musicians are included in the outfit, among them the matchless Teddy Wilson, whose piano solos are still flawless. Benny plays clarinet, of course, and with all his customary finesse and detachment. Among the other standouts are Ruby Braff, a pint-size trumpeter with eyes like large buttons and a soulful address to his horn. . . . I must confess that on the night I dropped in, I arrived toward the end of the ten-o'clock set and heard the octet in only two numbers—'Deed I Do' and 'Air Mail Special Delivery.'

No further information is available for Ruby's appearance at the following benefit performance for children. Likely Ruby's Russian heritage made him very receptive to the invitation to participate in this program.

Summer for Children Dinner Dance[17]
May 26, 1955, Ballroom, Ambassador Hotel, New York
Ruby Braff Quintet, Victor Borge, Rise Stevens, along with a fashion show
The program was for the benefit of the St. Seraphim Foundation (Princess Alexander Obolensky, executive director). The foundation provided benefits for children who come to the U.S. as refugees from communism.

After a very busy time from February through early May, I have found no trace of Ruby's performances until he recorded with Bud Freeman for Bethlehem Records followed by his appearance at the Newport Jazz Festival in the festival's second year.

Bud Freeman Quintet: *Bud Freeman*
July 1955, New York (stated as Hackensack, New Jersey, on Parlophone issue)
Ruby Braff (tp), Bud Freeman (ts), Ken Kersey (p), Al Hall (b), George Wettling (dm)
Newport News
    Bethlehem BCP 29, BCP 6033, Parlophone GEP 8783, Bethlehem 11059
At Sundown
    Bethlehem BCP 29, BCP 6033, Parlophone GEP 8783, Bethlehem 11059
Exactly Like You
    Bethlehem BCP 29, BCP 6033, Parlophone GEP 8783, Bethlehem 11059
Let's Do It
    Bethlehem BCP 29, BCP 6033, Parlophone GEP 8783, Bethlehem 11059
But Not for Me
    Bethlehem BCP 29, BCP 6033, Parlophone GEP 8783
NOTE: Entire session also on London (E) LTZ-N 15030 and Affinity (E) AFF 112 entitled *Stop, Look and Listen.* Bethlehem BCP 6033 also entitled *The Test*

of Time. The session also appeared on a Spanish LP, Maestros del Jazz FM-68 781-1 and a Japanese CD TOCJ 62091. All of Ruby's recordings for Bethlehem are also included on Solar 2869490 (CD) titled *The Complete Ruby Braff Bethlehem Recordings*.

Ruby appeared at the Second Newport Jazz Festival in 1955. This was his second appearance at Newport, and of course George Wein had been familiar with his playing for several years. The program contains a photo of Ruby by Richard Avedon. He is shown standing with his horn draped over his arm while smoking a cigarette. He is listed in the program on Saturday performing in a group led by Al Cohn; however, Chet Baker substituted for him. Ruby was listed in the program for the finale on Saturday but his major appearance was with Count Basie and Lester Young on Sunday. In that session he substituted for Buck Clayton.

Al Cohn and Bob Brookmeyer[18]
July 16, 1955, Second Newport Jazz Festival, Freebody Park, Newport, Rhode Island (second day of three-day festival)
Bob Brookmeyer (vtb), Al Cohn (ts), Chet Baker (tp), Russ Freeman (p), Bob Carter (b), Peter Littman (dm)—Chet Baker replaced Ruby Braff in this session, although some sources continue to list Ruby Braff in error
Co'n Pone
Tiny's Blues
NOTE: A recording of these tunes is available but remains unissued.

The festival program also listed Ruby performing in the finale on July 16. No further details are available and no recording has been located.

Count Basie and Jimmy Rushing[19]
July 17, 1955, Second Newport Jazz Festival, Freebody Park, Newport, Rhode Island (third day of three-day festival)
Count Basie (p), Lester Young (ts), Ruby Braff (tp), Eddie Jones (b), Jo Jones (dm), Jimmy Rushing (voc); Duke Ellington was the master of ceremonies—Ruby Braff substituted for Buck Clayton who was originally scheduled.
Lester Leaps In
I Want a Little Girl (voc JR)
Bye Bye Baby Blues (voc JR)
Bye Bye Baby Blues (encore, voc JR)
NOTE: A recording of these tunes is available but remains unissued.

A photo is available from the March of Jazz program[20] with the date incorrectly given as 1957. This photo is included in the photo section in this book.

DownBeat reviewed this set as follows:[21]

> First up was 'Lester Leaps In,' and he did. Then Jimmy Rushing came up to sing "Little Girl" and two encores, and it was evident to everyone that this group was having fun. Basie was positively beaming, Prez was striding around helping Braff and Rushing with his backgrounds, and it all captured wonderfully the essence of Kansas City jazz. Or any jazz.

Ruby recalls that it took a long time for Jo Jones to change the arrangement of the drums, since the previous drummer was left handed. He told me, "For some reason, Jo Jones played really loud. This was my only time to play with Basie, and I couldn't even hear him over the drums."

The session was originally to have included Buck Clayton instead of Ruby. Burt Goldblatt writes the following:[22]

> A joyous reunion of Count Basie, Lester Young on tenor, Ruby Braff substituting for the ailing Buck Clayton, and Ed Jones on bass with drummer Jo Jones followed. Before the group started, Jo had seated himself at his drums looking disturbed that someone had fouled up his drum setup in some way. The cymbals were not set up correctly or his bass foot pedal was not in place. Whatever it was, it bothered him for a few numbers and Jo vented his annoyance by playing so loudly that he drowned out the soloists. They finally settled into a good groove, and Prez, with his masterly sense of timing, accented by Count Basie, had a natural brilliance and spontaneity. Later, Jimmy Rushing joined them as a surprise guest, adding an emotional depth both moving and beautiful on "I Want a Little Girl," with "Bye, Bye Blues" as an encore.
>
> After the set ended to tumultuous applause, Prez wandered backstage to the large blue-and-white-striped musicians' tent to relax. Jo Jones entered the tent and Prez, looking bemused, gently chided him: 'You're no trouper.'
>
> Jo looked at Prez, his longtime buddy and companion of countless days and years on the road with the Basie band, and replied, 'You couldn't play if your mouthpiece was over there,' glancing to one side of the tent, '. . . 'and your horn was over there,' indicating the opposite side.
>
> 'You're no trouper,' Prez repeated gently.
>
> In desperation Jo knelt and picked up a bass drum, slung it over his back, hunching over like Quasimodo in *The Hunchback of Notre Dame*, and started striding around thumping out intricate rhythms with his hand on the edge of the drum head. 'You know I can play anything I want to on these things,' he pleaded.
>
> Ignoring the display of virtuosity, Prez rose abruptly and started to dance toward the tent door, scat singing, 'Ju jah juboo wah baba jabadoobadoo joobah joobah . . .' past the tent flap and into the sunlight.
>
> Jo turned to musicians Ruby Braff and Sam Margolis, who were sitting nearby, and shouted, 'There goes the greatest drummer in the world!'

Harold C. Schonberg included the following in his review:[23]

> But then along comes a small combination consisting of Count Basie, Lester Young, Jo Jones, and Ruby Braff with an uproarious example of controlled chaos. With Jimmy Rushing doing the vocal solos, the music was earthy and low-down. Anti-intellectual no doubt, but a real emotional experience, backed by a solid rhythm, delivered by superb instrumentalists who were turning their techniques to something else beside abstractions in jazz.

The available recording deserves to be heard, although obtaining rights to release it is likely complicated. The balance on the recording does not allow Jo Jones to overwhelm the other musicians. It is indeed joyous. Ruby speculated that Jo Jones was also disappointed by Ruby's substituting for Buck Clayton.

Newport Jazz Festival Interviews[24]
July 15–17, 1955, Freebody Park, Newport, Rhode Island
Interviews with various artists at the Newport Jazz Festival, including Bud Freeman, Vic Dickenson, Gerry Mulligan, Ruby Braff, Hazel Scott, Billy Taylor, Count Basie, Duke Ellington, Dave Brubeck, Paul Desmond, and George Wein
NOTE: Copies of these recordings have not been available to the author.

Until its recent reissue on CD the following recording was among the rarest of the sessions where Ruby participated.

Nat Pierce: *Jazz Romp*
August 1955, New York
Ruby Braff, Doug Mettome (tp), Billy Byers, Matthew Gee (tb), Phil Woods (as), Sam Margolis (ts), Nat Pierce (p), Freddie Green (g), Jimmy Woode (b), Jo Jones (dm)
Back on the Scene
    Keynote LP 1101, Fresh Sound (CD) 59774
You're Driving Me Crazy
    Keynote LP 1101, Fresh Sound (CD) 59774
Piercin' Thru
    Keynote LP 1101, Fresh Sound (CD) 59774
NOTE: Other performances on this LP do not include Ruby Braff. The album notes show the wrong personnel for some performances. Listening confirms that the above is correct. Fresh Sound 59774 (CD) is titled *Kansas City Memories*.

The following session is Ruby's first recorded encounter with lifelong friend Dave McKenna. Most of the recordings of these tunes are not available to the author except for "Soft Lights and Sweet Music" and "Oh, By Jingo!" For the former, the issued version is spliced from both existing takes. It includes both of Ruby's solos but omits the vocal. A recording of the latter is available.

Steve Jordan praised Ruby's playing on "It's Bad for Me": "I thought it was an exceptional version of a great, tough tune."[25] Hopefully it will be issued some day for these recordings do exist in the Goodman Archive at Yale University.

Ruby recalled that "It's Bad for Me" created problems. He said that Nancy Reed had difficulties and that he urged Benny Goodman to do the vocal himself to reduce the need for more takes.

Benny Goodman Septet[26]
September 8, 1955, New York, for Park Recordings
Benny Goodman (cl), Ruby Braff (tp), Urbie Green (tb), Dave McKenna (p), Steve Jordan (g), Tommy Potter (b), Bobby Donaldson (dm), Nancy Reed, Art Lund (voc)
On the Alamo (warm-up excluding BG)
Soft Lights and Sweet Music (voc NR)
MusicMasters CIJ 60142Z (CD)
Easy to Love (voc AL) (2 takes on tape)
Oh, By Jingo! (voc AL, NR) (3 takes on tape)
It's Bad for Me (voc NR and BG) (4 takes on tape)
'S Wonderful (1 take)
I Cried for You (voc NR) (1 take)
I Want a Little Girl (voc AL) (1 take)
NOTE: "Soft Lights and Sweet Music" is also issued on MusicMasters 20142 (LP), Jazz Heritage, and Musical Heritage 922277 (LP), MusicMasters 40142 (cassette), 5000-4 (cassette), Jazz Heritage and Musical Heritage 322277 (cassette), MusicMasters 5000-2 (CD), Jazz Heritage, Musical Heritage 522277 (CD), and Gambit 69261 (CD) titled *Ruby Braff with Dave McKenna Complete Original Quartet / Quintet Sessions.*

Either about this time or somewhat later, Ruby completed Leonard Feather's questionnaire for the upcoming Encyclopedia of Jazz. The first page of Ruby's response is shown in Figure 4.3. It is discussed in the next chapter.

The following handbills and questionnaire depict two of the performances and one event from this chapter:

OPENING TONIGHT  AL BELLETTO QUINTET BLUE NOTERS QUINTET

2 BIG CONCERTS
5 P.M. & 9 P.M. SUNDAY, FEBRUARY 6
BURL IVES
NATION'S LEADING FOLK SINGER
plus
AL BELLETTO QUINTET
BLUE NOTERS QUINTET
featuring
LOU LEVY RUBY BRAFF
$2.00 ADMISSION
No Cover—No Minimum
For Reservations, Call DEarborn 3-2247
The BLUE NOTE
Madison and Clark SUNDAYS FROM 5 P. M.

Figure 4.1: Advertisement February 1955

Broadway's Best Buy!
This FRI. & SAT., 9 p.m. to 2 a.m.
JAZZ CONCERT & DANCE
at CHILDS PARAMOUNT BALLROOM
1501 Broadway, near 44th St.
The Greatest Names in Jazz!
BUCK CLAYTON COLEMAN HAWKINS
BUD FREEMAN PEEWEE RUSSELL
RUBY BRAFF J. C. HIGGINBOTHAM
JOE MARSALA CLIFF JACKSON
SONNY GREER TOMMY BENFORD
and many other Jazz Stars
Extra! ★ ANNE LEWIS in Sinful Songs
No Minimum or Cover

Figure 4.2: Advertisement April 22, 1955

Jazz Encyclopedia

Horizon Press Inc.

LEONARD FEATHER
340 Riverside Drive
New York 25, N.Y.
MOnument 3-4513

"JAZZ ENCYCLOPEDIA" QUESTIONNAIRE

PLEASE FILL IN VERY CLEARLY IN BLOCK LETTERS:
FULL LEGAL NAME: Reuben BRAFF PROFESSIONAL NAME: Ruby Braff

PERMANENT ADDRESS: 94 DEVON ST. ROXBURY MASS

TELEPHONE: Highlands 2 9443

EXACT DATE OF BIRTH: DAY ___ MONTH March YEAR 1927 WHERE BORN: BOSTON

ANY PARENTS, BROTHERS, SISTERS, OR OTHER RELATIVES MUSICALLY INCLINED? GIVE DETAILS.
GRANDFATHER and many uncles

WHERE AND WHEN DID YOU STUDY MUSIC? WHAT INSTRUMENTS FIRST?
STUDIED in BOSTON By myself
TRUMPET

HOW DID YOU GET INTO THE MUSIC BUSINESS?
HAD TO EARN money and, - wanted to play

GIVE FULL DETAILS AND DATES OF ALL BANDS OR COMBOS YOU HAVE WORKED WITH.
Pee Wee Russell, EDMOND Hall
BUD FREEMAN, Joe Sullivan
Urbie Green, George Wettling
Gene Ramey

Figure 4.3: Leonard Feather's Questionnaire with first page of Ruby's Responses from the Institute of Jazz Studies

Notes

[1] Steve Voce, *Jazz Journal International*, May 2007.
[2] Photo, *The March of Jazz Celebrates Ruby Braff's 74th Birthday Party*, Arbors Records, 2001, 14.
[3] Steve Jordan, *Rhythm Man* (Ann Arbor: University of Michigan Press, 1993), 86.
[4] Steve Jordan, *Rhythm Man* (Ann Arbor: University of Michigan Press, 1993), 111.

[5] *DownBeat*, December 15, 1954, 3.
[6] *DownBeat*, December 29, 1954, 6.
[7] Dan Morgenstern, "Ruby Braff: Long May You Blow," in *The March of Jazz Celebrates Ruby Braff's 74th Birthday Party*, Arbors Records, 2001, 7.
[8] *The Complete Capitol Small Group Recordings of Benny Goodman 1944–1955*, Mosaic Records, 14, photo credit to Popsie Randolph, Frank Driggs Collection.
[9] D. Russell Connor, *Benny Goodman: Listen to His Legacy*, (Metuchen, NJ: Scarecrow Press, 1988), 209. Photo, *The March of Jazz Celebrates Ruby Braff's 74th Birthday Party*, Arbors Records, 2001, 14. It is attributed to circa 1954, further suggesting that Ruby did not appear with Goodman a year earlier.
[10] Lillian Ross and Brendan Gill, *The New Yorker*, March 19, 1955, 32–33
[11] Milt Hinton and David G. Berger, *Bass Line* (Philadelphia: Temple University Press, 1988), 205.
[12] *The Complete CBS Buck Clayton Jam Sessions*, Mosaic Records, 18, photo by Ted Castle, CBS Music.
[13] *The Complete CBS Buck Clayton Jam Sessions*, Mosaic Records, 15, photo by Ted Castle, CBS Music.
[14] This listing is derived from the definitive source, D. Russell Connor, *Benny Goodman—Wrappin' It Up* (Lanham, MD: Scarecrow Press, 1996), 82. Additional issues are also described in D. Russell Connor, *Benny Goodman—Listen to His Legacy* (Metuchen, NJ: Scarecrow Press, 1988), 209–210.
[15] Advertisement in *New York Times*, April 22, 1955.
[16] Douglas Watt, *The New Yorker*, March 26, 1955, 92.
[17] *New York Times*, May 25, 1955.
[18] Voice of America tape at the Library of Congress, Record 101098p+1X, RGA0016 (RWD 5003 B3). Burt Goldblatt, *The Newport Jazz Festival: The Illustrated History* (New York: Dial Press, 1977), 263 lists Ruby Braff in error for this session.
[19] Voice of America tape at the Library of Congress, Record 100893p+1X, RGA0018 (RWD 5005 B2)—"Lester Leaps In" (titled incorrectly as "I Got Rhythm" on the Library of Congress catalog). Michael Frohne lists the first "Bye Bye Baby Blues" as "I May Be Wrong" (probably the same title).
[20] Photos, *The March of Jazz Celebrates Ruby Braff's 74th Birthday Party*, Arbors Records, 2001, 14 and 15.
[21] *DownBeat*, August 24, 1955, 24.
[22] Burt Goldblatt, *The Newport Jazz Festival: The Illustrated History* (New York: Dial Press, 1977), 16–17, carries an interesting account of this session.
[23] Harold C. Schonberg, *New York Times*, July 18, 1955.
[24] Voice of America tapes at the Library of Congress, LC Control Number 89740750, Call Number RWB 1687 A1-B1.
[25] Steve Jordan, *Rhythm Man* (Ann Arbor: University of Michigan Press, 1993), 73.
[26] D. Russell Connor, *Benny Goodman—Wrappin' It Up* (Lanham, MD: Scarecrow Press, 1996), 84–85 for documentation of session.

Chapter 5

Ruby on Broadway and Television: John Hammond Introduces Ruby to Richard Rodgers and Ruby's Vanguard Recordings

For nine months during 1955–1956, Ruby played the trumpet in the non-speaking role of Pancho in the musical *Pipe Dream* by Rodgers and Hammerstein. The production was based on John Steinbeck's novel *Sweet Thursday*. The original Broadway cast recording is available on RCA 09026-61481-2; however, Ruby is not audible on this recording. During the stage performances he played and appeared during an audition scene toward the end of act 1 and also had a solo during the "Bum's Opera" scene during the same act. He also played during a wild party in the second act. He portrayed a comic character. The audition featured a blues that varied nightly, while the other two appearances fit the composed music and accompany dancers. Ruby said that John Hammond shared a copy of the Braff/Larkins Vanguard albums with Richard Rodgers. This led to this non-speaking role. Ruby told me that he regularly brought coffee to John Steinbeck during rehearsals.

Pipe Dream opened October 1 at the Shubert Theatre in New Haven, then continued to Boston on November 7, and opened at the Shubert Theater on Broadway in New York on November 30 for 245 performances during an eight-month run that continued until June 1956. A review appeared in *DownBeat*.[1]

> Braff comes on toward the end of act one to audition for a spot in the band at Helen Traubel's brothel. He also has solo spots during the 'Bum's Opera' scene in that act, and in a wild party during the second act.
>
> Ruby said he was having a ball in the show, but admitted it was harder work than he thought it would be. As for his trumpet playing, Braff's part allows him to improvise, but within bounds. For the audition, he plays a blues which varies nightly. In the other two scenes, his solos must fit the framework of the of the Rodgers music, and back the dancers on stage.

Ruby reported a unique experience one night. Following one of his solos, he said he heard applause. While this would have been commonplace in a jazz club, it was very unusual during these theatrical performances. Ruby looked to the source of the applause that came from the front row of the balcony and saw Benny Goodman loudly clapping for him.

Dom Cerulli interviewed Ruby at this time and published the following remarks:[2]

> These actors have a tremendous responsibility. They've got to be perfect every time. There are very few people who can do this work. No one takes the criticism they do. They are told when to walk, talk ... even breathe. You know, the hardest thing in the world to do is take direction. Someone can show you what to do, but doing it yourself is another thing. I have a tremendous respect for these people, they're wonderful. I thought it was hard to do the bits I have, but you should see the others. If the audience laughs tonight where they didn't laugh last night, these people start checking on the line. They go right down to inflection, to breathing. I've watched Rodgers and Hammerstein giving these people lessons, and you can't buy that.

Copies of the New York *Playbill*, the program sold at those performances, and the earlier program for the world premier in New Haven are available. They list Ruby as a member of the cast. An interesting interview with Jayne Heller, cast as the first actress to appear onstage during the performance, is published in *Steinbeck Studies.*[3] She described John Steinbeck's frequent participation in rehearsals and his delight with the music, along with Richard Rodgers absence during the first few days of rehearsals due to jaw surgery to remove a cancerous growth. She also refers to Ruby's contributions.

> Oh, when the bums came on stage!. . . There was this terrific moment when this trumpet obbligato—this guy was the *Esquire* trumpet player of the year for 1955 [sic]—he was little and he fit into the company: Ruby Braff. Great player. He took us around to see Billie Holiday. Terrific jazz player.

Walter Kerr, the famous drama critic writing for the *Herald Tribune*, described Ruby's key role in his review as reprinted in the same article:

> Sometimes the music is able to take such firm hold of the proceedings that genuine gayety rears its welcome head. As a trumpet blares out the giddy notes of 'A Bum's Opera,' a spindly no-good in red suspenders, bandana, blue flannel shirt, and obtrusive long winter underwear manages to set the stage writing. . . . But the frolicking moments are rare.

The overall tone of reviews was critical and this show is not regarded as one of Rodgers and Hammerstein's successes. But what better time to record more music of Rodgers and Hart, than while appearing in a Rodgers and Hammerstein musical? Ruby found time to return to the recording studio for this and other classic albums, and, at the end, appeared on television in *The Magic Horn*. John Hammond was still providing recording opportunities for Ruby, because tension between them did not arise until March 1956 or later. He organized three very different sessions for Vanguard Records in a single week, reflecting his confidence in Ruby. The first reprised the earlier album recorded with Ellis Larkins, while the second reunited him with Vic Dickenson, Sam Margolis (Ruby's good friend), Nat Pierce, Walter Page, and Jo Jones. The support of this Basie-like rhythm section created a wonderful foundation for that session. The third session returned Ruby to the studio for three tunes during Mel Powell's recording session. This provided Ruby with his first opportunity to record with Oscar Pettiford. Of course, performances of *Pipe Dream* were also occupying time in Ruby's schedule for evening and matinee performances during its run on Broadway.

Ruby Braff and Ellis Larkins: ***Two by Two: Music of Rodgers and Hart***
October 14, 1955, Brooklyn, New York
Ruby Braff (tp), Ellis Larkins (p)
My Funny Valentine
    Vanguard VRS 8507, 79611-2 (CD)
Where or When
    Vanguard VRS 8507, (J) SR 3106, 79609-2 (CD)
I Could Write a Book
    Vanguard VRS 8507, 79611-2 (CD), Definitive DRCD 11281
Thou Swell
    Vanguard VRS 8507, (J) SR 3106, 79609-2 (CD)
My Romance
    Vanguard VRS 8507, 79609-2 (CD), 79571 (CD)
Little Girl Blue
    Vanguard VRS 8507, 79611-2 (CD), 79571 (CD)
The Girl Friend
    Vanguard VRS 8507, 79611-2 (CD)
Mountain Greenery
    Vanguard VRS 8507, (E) EPP 14001, 79609-2 (CD)
Blue Moon
    Vanguard VRS 8507, (E) EPP 14001, 79609-2 (CD)
You Took Advantage of Me
    Vanguard VRS 8507, (E) EPP 14001, (J) SR 3106, 79611-2 (CD),
    (E) EPP14001
I Married an Angel
    Vanguard VRS 8507, (E) EPP14001, 79609-2 (CD)
I Didn't Know What Time It Was
    Vanguard VRS 8507, (J) SR 3106, 79611-2 (CD), 79571 (CD), (J) SR 3106

NOTE: All titles also on Fontana (E) FJL 403 (titled *Two by Two: Ruby Braff and Ellis Larkins Play Rodgers and Hart*), (Eu) 688.902, Vanguard VMD 8507 (CD) (titled *2 x 2—Ruby and Ellis Play Rodgers and Hart*), Vanguard 76909-2 (titled *Ellis Larkins & Ruby Braff Duets Volume 1*), and Vanguard 79611-2 (*Volume 2*). Vanguard 79571 is titled *City Nights: Jazz for the Evening*. All titles also included on *Ruby Braff: The Complete Duets* on Definitive DRCD 11284. This is a two-CD set that also includes performances from February 17 and October 17, 1955. "Mountain Greenery" is also included in a three-CD set *The Complete Rodgers & Hart Songbooks*, Verve 731453326224. Definitive DRCD 11281 is titled *Blue Moon: Rodgers and Hart Songbook.* Vanguard (E) EPP14001 is a seven-inch release. This album received four and one-half stars in *DownBeat.*

Ruby reported that Jo Jones arrived about one hour late to the next session, without his drums. When asked, Jones said that Ruby did not make it clear that this booking was with his drums. "I tell stories, too," he said. Jo was directed to return to his hotel and bring his drums to the session. Perhaps this was the result of some unpleasant memories from the previous Newport Jazz Festival set. Freddie Green was originally scheduled to play on this recording but was unable to appear. Ruby noted his absence by naming one of his compositions, "Where's Freddie?" He gave this melody alternate names in later years, but it is another nice tune.

Despite these events, the recording was another success for Ruby, continuing his tradition with Vanguard Records. Manfred Selchow included a photo of Ruby with Vic Dickenson and Sam Margolis from the Vanguard session in his book, *Ding Ding.*[4]

Ruby Braff Sextet: *The Ruby Braff Special*
October 17, 1955, Brooklyn, New York
Ruby Braff (tp), Vic Dickenson (tb), Sam Margolis (ts, cl-1), Nat Pierce (p), Walter Page (b), Jo Jones (dm)
Romance in the Dark
    Vanguard VRS 8504, (J) SR 3103, 79608-2 (CD)
When You Wish upon a Star (1)
    Vanguard VRS 8504, (J) SR 3103, 79608-2 (CD)
Ghost of a Chance
    Vanguard VRS 8504, (J) SR 3048, 79608-2 (CD)
Where's Freddie?
    Vanguard VRS 8504, (J) SR 3103
Wishing Will Make It So
    Vanguard VRS 8504, (J) SR 3103, 79608-2 (CD)
I'm in the Market for You
    Vanguard VRS 8504, (J) SR 3103, 79608-2 (CD)
Sweet Sue
    Vanguard VRS 8504, (J) SR 3103, 79608-2 (CD)
Linger Awhile
    Vanguard VRS 8504, (J) SR 3048, 79608-2 (CD)
NOTE: All titles also on Vanguard (E) VRS 8504, PPL 11003, (J) LAX 3067, KICJ 187 (CD), ARS G445 (titled *Hey, Ruby*), Amadeo (Au) AVRS 9009, and

(J) K20P 6193. Vanguard 79608-2 (CD) is titled *Linger Awhile.* All titles also included on *Ruby Braff: The Complete Duets* on Definitive DRCD 11284. This is a two-CD set that also includes performances from February 17 and October 14, 1955. Vanguard (J) KICJ 187 also contains the session with Buck Clayton recorded July 1, 1954. Some sources give the recording date for this session as October 19, 1955, linking it to the following session with Mel Powell. All of Ruby's recordings for Bethlehem are included on Solar 2869490 (CD) titled *The Complete Ruby Braff Bethlehem Recordings* and that includes all of the above Vanguard titles as "bonus" recordings. This album received four stars in *Down-Beat.*

Mel Powell: *Out on a Limb*
Mel Powell Quintet
October 19, 1955, Brooklyn, New York
Ruby Braff (tp), Mel Powell (p), Clifton "Skeeter" Best (g), Oscar Pettiford (b), Bobby Donaldson (dm)
Beale Street Blues (SB, OP out)
  Vanguard VRS 8506, VRS 8528 79602-2
The Best Thing for You (Would Be Me)*
  Vanguard VRS 8506, VRS 8528 79602-2
Rosetta
  Vanguard VRS 8506, VRS 8528 79602-2
Three Little Words (RB, BD out)*
  Vanguard VRS 8506, VRS 8528 79602-2
You're Lucky to Me (RB, BD out)*
  Vanguard VRS 8506, VRS 8528 79602-2
Liza
  Vanguard VRS8 506, VRS 8528 79602-2
NOTE: "The Best Thing for You" is incorrectly titled "The Best Things in Life Are Free" on the label and in discographies. Vanguard 79602-2 is titled *The Best Things in Life* (repeating the song title error). The three titles with an asterisk are also issued on Vanguard (J) SR (M) 3102. This release received four stars in *DownBeat.*

A month later, Ruby appeared in another engagement at Storyville in Boston on a Sunday afternoon from 3–7 p.m. that did not interfere with the performance schedule for *Pipe Dream* in New York. That gave him a chance to see old friends and maintain his visibility in jazz circles. Bud Freeman "came upstairs" during a break from performing with Jimmy McPartland at Mahogany Hall. Given the pace of his recent activity, he probably appeared in other venues in New York or even in Boston constrained by his Broadway commitments; however, I have not located any information.

Ruby Braff at Storyville[5]
November 13, 1955, Storyville Club, Boston, Massachusetts

Ruby Braff (tp), Vic Dickenson (tb), Sam Margolis (cl), George Wein (p), John Neves (b), Marquis Foster (dm)
Between the Devil and the Deep Blue Sea*
More Than You Know*
At the Jazz Band Ball (incomplete)
Wrap Your Troubles in Dreams (fragment only)
Sister Kate (VD voc)*

Add Bud Freeman (ts)
'S Wonderful*
NOTE: Recordings of four of these tunes are available and are marked with an asterisk but remain unissued. Two remain unavailable to the author.

It had been less than two months since Ruby's previous recording for Vanguard, and he received a call to rejoin Benny Goodman's Orchestra as a soloist for an album on Capitol timed to take advantage of the release of the motion picture, *The Benny Goodman Story*. He alternated with Harry James as soloist, performing on two tunes during this session. James replaced Braff on "Shine" and "One O'Clock Jump" from this session. Ruby does not appear on the film's soundtrack, for that music was recorded at a different session that was released by Decca Records.

Ruby acknowledged James's abilities but said, "I don't know why he wanted to sound that way," with regard to somewhat sweet sound found in some of his later recordings.

This performance is the earliest recorded meeting between Ruby and Dick Hyman. Of course, this evolved into a very creative partnership that delighted fans in the U.S. and Europe and resulted in a series of memorable recordings.

Benny Goodman and his Orchestra: *Selections Featured in the "Benny Goodman Story"*
December 8, 1955, New York
Chris Griffin, Billy Butterfield, Carl Poole, Ruby Braff, Jimmy Maxwell (tp), Urbie Green, Will Bradley (tb), Benny Goodman (cl), Hymie Schertzer, Phil Bodner (as), Al Klink, Peanuts Hucko (ts), Dick Hyman (p), Tony Mottola (g), Milt Hinton (b), Bobby Donaldson (dm)
20937 Bugle Call Rag
Cap S 706, EMI (J) TOCH 6238, Avid AMBX 151
20946 King Porter Stomp
Blu Disc T 1015
NOTE: Both titles are included on *The Benny Goodman Story*, Capitol CDP 7243 8 33569 2 8. EMI (J) TOCH 6238 (CD) is titled *The Benny Goodman Story Complete*. Avid AMBX 151 titled *The Famous 1938 Carnegie Hall Jazz Concert Plus 1950s Material*.

Ruby participated in a Blindfold Test[6] published in *DownBeat* in 1956. The interview was conducted during the run of *Pipe Dream*. Ruby gave his highest evaluation to Pee Wee Russell in Eddie Condon's recording of "Oh Sister! Ain't That Hot" from 1940, with Fats Waller. Ruby also stated the following: "I also want you to be sure to put in that after Louis Armstrong I consider the greatest jazz musician who ever lived is Bud Freeman. Anybody who hasn't heard Bud, no matter what instrument you play, it is a great loss not to have caught him, and you positively must hear this man. Bud is the greatest." Ruby was one of Bud's biggest fans and enjoyed performing with him.

Perhaps about this time (but possibly earlier), Ruby completed Leonard Feather's questionnaire for the upcoming *Encyclopedia of Jazz*. Collections at the Institute of Jazz Studies collections include original source materials, and Ruby's submission, in his own handwriting, is interesting. As shown in Figure 4.3, one question asked about Ruby's favorite musicians. Ruby listed Louis Armstrong followed by Roy Eldridge, Frankie Newton, Billy Butterfield, Hot Lips Page, Emmett Berry, Bill Coleman, Harold Baker, Bobby Hackett, Ray Nance, Dizzy Gillespie, Joe Newman, Sonny Berman, Buck Clayton, Bix Beiderbecke, Benny Carter, and Henry "Red" Allen. A few of those names may strike some people as unusual choices, but they reflect Ruby's broad appreciation for talent. He also lists his core ambition concisely, namely "to produce great music."

The following is Ruby's first small group encounter on records with lifelong friend Dave McKenna. Their first recorded meeting was in Benny Goodman's session for Capitol. This recording remains a collectors' item, even in reissues. Milli Vernon had previously recorded under the name Pat Cameron.[7]

Milli Vernon: *Introducing Milli Vernon*
February 1956, New York
Ruby Braff (tp), Dave McKenna (p), Jimmy Raney (g), Wyatt Ruther (b), Jo Jones (dm), Milli Vernon (voc)
Weep for the Boys
    Storyville SLP 190
Moments Like This
    Storyville SLP 190
Spring Is Here
    Storyville SLP 190, Jazztone J 1248
Moonray
    Storyville SLP 190, STLP 916
St. James Infirmary
    Storyville SLP 190
This Year's Kisses
    Storyville SLP 190
Everything but You
    Storyville SLP 190

Every Time
    Storyville SLP 190
Blue Rain
    Storyville SLP 190
I Don't Know What Kind of Blues I've Got
    Storyville SLP 190, STLP 916
I Guess I'll Have to Hang My Tears Out to Dry
    Storyville SLP 190
My Ship
    Storyville SLP 190
NOTE: All titles on Trio (J) PA 6130, Tokuma (J) NL 1693261 (CD), and Storyville/Tokuma (J) TKCB 71628 (CD). Storyville STLP 916 is titled *The Women in Jazz*. Jazztone J 1248 is titled *The Songs of Rodgers and Hart – As Sung and Played by Lee Wiley & Friends.*

I presume that the next recording session is the occasion when Ruby argued with John Hammond about the source of the idea that led to pairing Ruby with Ellis Larkins on their two albums for Vanguard. Throughout his life, Ruby stood on principle and would not have been comfortable giving in when he knew himself to be right. Hammond, too, was not one to compromise his beliefs. Likely this came at some cost since Hammond might have continued to create other recording and performance opportunities.

Chip Deffaa reported an amusing conversation with Ruby that included the following words that Ruby described from a telephone conversation with John:[8]

> Hello, Ruby. This is John. How are you?
> Well, I'm in bed with pneumonia and I feel awful.
> Wonderful, Ruby. Now what I called about. . . .

Buck Clayton Jam Session: ***All the Cats Join In***
March 5, 1956, New York
Buck Clayton, Billy Butterfield (tp), Ruby Braff (tp), J. C. Higginbotham (tb), Tyree Glenn (tb, vib), Coleman Hawkins, Julian Dash (ts), Ken Kersey (p), Steve Jordan (g), Walter Page (b), Bobby Donaldson (dm)
All the Cats Join In*
    Columbia CL 882, Columbia (A) CJ 44291, CJ 44380,
    CBS (Eu) 463-336-2, CBS (E) 463-336-1, Mosaic MD6-144, MR8-144
All the Cats Join In (insert)
    Mosaic MD6-144, MR8-144
All the Cats Join In (alt)
    Columbia CJ 44291, CJ 44380, Mosaic MD6-144, MR8-144
After Hours (alt)
    Mosaic MD6-144, MR8-144

After Hours*
Meritt (A) 10, CBS (E) 46336-1, (E) 463.336-2, Columbia (A) CK 44291, CJ 44291, Mosaic MD6-144, MR8-144

Add Jimmy Rushing (voc); omit Tyree Glenn
Don't You Miss Your Baby*
Columbia CL 882, Philips (F) 429411BE, (G) BBL 7129, (H) B07163L, Fresh Sound (Sp) FS 272, FSR 593, 980081-1, CBS (J) SONP 50413, Mosaic MD6-144, MR8-144
Don't You Miss Your Baby (alt)
CBS (E) 46336-1, (E) 46.336-2, Columbia CJ 44291, (A) VL 44291 (CD) Mosaic MD6-144, MR8-144
NOTE: On the following issues, "All the Cats Join In" is spliced from the first version and insert: CL 882, Philips 429.441BE (EP), Columbia (J) PL 5074, Fresh Sound (Sp) FS 272, FSR 593, CBS (EU) 980081-1, CBS (J) SONP 50413, and Philips (E) BBL 7129. The three master takes marked with asterisks are also included in the following CDs: Philips (H) B07163L, Solar 4569904, and Lone Hill LHJ 10115 titled *Buck Clayton: Complete Legendary Jam Sessions*. Columbia (E) 463.336-2 is a CD release, while 464446-1 is an LP.

The following LP was released in conjunction with a television network broadcast on *The Alcoa Hour*. In *The Magic Horn* Ruby played the role of Spencer Lee. Other actors included Ralph Meeker who portrayed the trumpet player and Sal Mineo who supplied him with the trumpet. This was Ruby's first appearance on television. *The Alcoa Hour* was a featured series at the time lasting one hour.

George Wein describes his preparations for *The Magic Horn*:[9]

> The *Alcoa Hour* was a live, hour-long anthology drama series that ran from 1955 to 1957 on NBC. A particular episode, *The Magic Horn*, ran in June 1956. It was the story of an elderly trumpet player who was having a problem until he got a magic horn that changed his whole career. Ralph Meeker played the trumpet player; Sal Mineo was the one who brought the magic horn to him.
>
> I was asked by a record executive at RCA-Victor to put together a band for the show, consisting of musicians who could also act. It was also necessary to have two trumpet players ghosting for Ralph Meeker: before and after the transformation. Now, Jimmy McPartland was very happy to be in this show, but he didn't realize that I cast him as the horn player in decline, and I had Ruby Braff playing the parts with the magic horn. Jimmy was a wonderful musician, and a guy I loved very much. But he didn't have the clarity of sound that Ruby had at that point in his career. I don't think anybody paid attention to this except me; I'm sure Jimmy never thought about it in that light.
>
> Bud Freeman had always wanted to be an actor like his brother, and he would have enjoyed being a part of this show. But of all the musicians I suggested to director Norman Felton—Ruby, Jimmy, Bud, Peanuts Hucko, Vic Dickenson, Buzzy Drootin, Milt Hinton, and Ernie Caceres—Bud was the only guy who didn't make the cut. Norman felt that Bud Freeman, a proper, impeccably dressed man with a little mustache, didn't look enough like a jazz musi-

cian. The show went on without him. It was one of the better jazz stories on television, because we had real musicians playing and portraying themselves. But I missed Bud.

George Wein's Dixie Victors: *The Magic Horn*
May 27, 1956, New York
Ruby Braff (tp), Vic Dickenson (tp), Bill Stegmeyer (cl), Ernie Caceres (bars), George Wein (p), Danny Barker (bjo), Milt Hinton (b), Buzzy Drootin (dm)
G2JB4574 Squeeze Me
RCA-Victor LPM 1332, HMV (E) CLP 1091
G2JB4575 Struttin' with Some Barbecue
RCA-Victor LPM 1332, HMV (E) CLP 1091
G2JB4576 Magic Horn
RCA-Victor LPM 1332, HMV (E) CLP 1091
G2JB4577 A Monday Date
RCA-Victor LPM 1332, HMV (E) CLP 1091

Peanuts Hucko (cl) replaces Stegmeyer; add Jimmy McPartland (1) (tp)
G2JB4578 Sugar
RCA Victor LPM 1332, HMV (E) CLP 1091
G2JB4579 Dippermouth Blues (1)
RCA-Victor LPM 1332, HMV (E) CLP 1091
G2JB4580 Loveless Love (1, but no Braff)
RCA-Victor LPM 1332, HMV (E) CLP 1091
G2JB4581 I Ain't Gonna Give Nobody None of My Jelly Roll (1)
RCA-Victor LPM 1332, HMV (E) CLP 1091
G2JB4582 On the Sunny Side of the Street
RCA-Victor LPM 1332, HMV (E) CLP 1091
NOTE: LPM 1332 titled *The Magic Horn by George Wein's Dixie Victors Featuring Ruby Braff* and HMV (E) CLP 1091 is issued as *Ruby Braff and the Dixie Victors*. All titles included on RCA 74321 13038 2 (CD). I also own a one-sided vinyl 45-rpm test pressing of "Magic Horn" with a handwritten label.

A partial copy of Vic Dickenson's script is available in Manfred Selchow's book *Ding Ding*.[10]

Soundtrack Recording: *The Magic Horn*
June 10, 1956, television broadcast—*The Alcoa Hour—The Magic Horn*— directed by Norman Felton, New York
Ruby Braff (tp-1), Jimmy McPartland (cnt-2), Vic Dickenson (tb), Peanuts Hucko (cl), Ernie Caceres (bars), George Wein (p), Milt Hinton (b), Buzzy Drootin (dm)
The Magic Horn –1
The Magic Horn – piano
The Magic Horn – piano

Squeeze Me –2 (cut off)
Squeeze Me –2 (abrupt end)
Struttin' with Some Barbecue (partly)
Struttin' with Some Barbecue (complete)
Struttin' with Some Barbecue (4 bar coda VD)
When the Saints Go Marching In –2 (cut off)
Everybody Loves My Baby (featuring VD, no trumpets)
Blues (Dickenson and Meeker only)
Blues (Hucko and Meeker only)
Tin Roof Blues (Dickenson, Hucko, Caceres)
The Magic Horn–1 (Meeker, Braff from distance)
The Magic Horn (Meeker)
Two Trumpet Ad Libs –1
My Monday Date –2 (no piano, abrupt end)
My Monday Date –1
Loveless Love –1 (fades)
I Ain't Gonna Give Nobody None of My Jelly Roll (no tp)
The Magic Horn –2 (short part)
The Magic Horn –1
Reprise: Magic Horn
Struttin' with Some Barbecue
NOTE: An audio recording of this program is available but remains unissued. Unfortunately I have not been able to locate a video recording of this program.

The closing of *Pipe Dream* was just ahead in June. Ruby's presence in recording studios had diminished in the first half of 1956, perhaps reflecting the burdens of the performance schedule along with the demands of preparing for *The Alcoa Hour*. The second half of the year would offer him more flexibility, but without a regular paycheck. Indeed recording of what some feel is another of his very finest albums lay just ahead.

Notes

[1] *DownBeat*, December 14, 1955, 11.
[2] *DownBeat*, December 14, 1955, 11.
[3] Anthony Newfield, "*Pipe Dream* Memories," *Steinbeck Studies* 15, No. 2 (Fall 2004): 117–128.
[4] Manfred Selchow, *Ding Ding: A Bio-Discographical Scrapbook on Vic Dickenson* (Germany: Uhle & Kleinmann, 1998), 301.
[5] Manfred Selchow, *Ding Ding: A Bio-Discographical Scrapbook on Vic Dickenson* (Germany, Uhle & Kleinmann, 1998), 302, using listing on that page accompanied by interesting comments.
[6] *DownBeat*, January 25, 1956, 25. From the *DownBeat* Archive. Reprinted by permission of Frank Alkyer.

[7] Geoffrey Wheeler, *Jazz by Mail: Record Clubs and Record Labels 1936–1958* (Manassas, VA, Hillbrook Press, 1999), 135.
[8] Chip Deffaa, *Jazz Veterans* (Fort Bragg, CA: Cypress House, 1996), 101.
[9] George Wein, *Myself Among Others* (Cambridge, MA: Da Capo Press, 2003), 124.
[10] Vic Dickenson's copy of the script is partially reproduced in Manfred Selchow, *Ding Ding: A Bio-Discographical Scrapbook on Vic Dickenson* (Germany: Uhle & Kleinmann, 1998), 310.

Chapter 6

Ruby's Growing Jazz Stardom: Frequent Recordings

Later, there would be periods in Ruby's career when he was not recorded. But he continued to be in the studios frequently in the next few months. Many of Ruby's fans feel that the following session for Epic Records was one of his finest. Mosaic Records issued the recordings, complete with several previously unreleased takes and other alternates that were previously only released on a Philips 45 EP record in England. Note that the next date, June 26, 1956, is also the date of Clifford Brown's tragic death in an automobile accident. By this point, each had won *DownBeat*'s New Star Award, Clifford Brown in 1954 and Ruby in 1955.

Ruby Braff is shown with a big smile in a photo from the book *Jazz Street*. In this book, Dennis Stock wrote the following: "His mother told him never to be a jazzman, that he'd starve. 'She was right,' he says, but he doesn't plan to change."[1]

Pipe Dream closed on Broadway in June 1956 releasing Ruby from the intensive performance schedule from the previous eight months. Nat Hentoff reported events following the closing of *Pipe Dream* on Broadway:[2]

> After *Pipe Dream*, Ruby resumed scuffling, and record sessions have continued to keep him in food. Through the impetus of the Vanguard albums, Braff was enlisted by a number of labels, and in the past year, he has decided to ask for—and has received—$1,000 in lieu of royalties for any album he makes for a major label, but they're not likely to be more than two or three a year.

Ruby Braff's All Stars: *Braff*
June 26, 1956 (date shown on Philips LP; alternate date of October 17, 1956 shown in some discographies), New York
Ruby Braff (tp), Dave McKenna (p), Steve Jordan (g), Buzzy Drootin (dm)
CO56413 As Long As I Live
Philips BBE 12123, (Eu) 429.296BE (both are 45-rpm)
CO56414 Blue Turning Grey Over You
Epic LN 3377, Portrait PJ 44393

CO56415 If I Had You
Philips BBE 12123, (Eu) 429.296BE, 7552.005 (both are 45-rpm)
CO56416 It's Been So Long
Epic LN 3377, Portrait PJ 44393
CO56417 I'm Shooting High
Philips BBE 12123, (Eu) 429.296BE, (Eu) 322.218BF (all are 45-rpm)
C056418 Star Dust
Epic LN 3377, Portrait PJ 44393
CO56419 How Long Has This Been Going On?
Epic LN 3377, Portrait PJ 44393
NOTE: Portrait RJ 44393 (CD) is identical to PJ 44393. Both are titled *Braff.* All titles on Epic also on Philips B07179 titled *Ruby Braff.* All above titles on Mosaic Records MD8-228, titled *Columbia Small Group Swing Sessions 1953–62*, Lone Hill Jazz LHJ 10210 titled *Braff*, and Gambit 69261 (CD) titled *Ruby Braff with Dave McKenna Complete Original Quartet / Quintet Sessions.*

Ruby reported that Coleman Hawkins would not talk to him directly during this session and alcohol played a role in that. Hawkins might have felt that he was an established artist, whereas Ruby was clearly very much his junior. Regardless, this is a fine album.

June 28, 1956, New York
Ruby Braff (tp), Lawrence Brown (tb), Coleman Hawkins (ts), Ernie Caceres (bars), Don Elliott (vib), Nat Pierce (p), Freddie Green (g), Eddie Jones (b), Buzzy Drootin (dm)
C056443-4 Here's Freddie
Epic LN 3377,Philips (E) BBL 7208, (Eu) BO7227L
CO56444-2 You're Lucky to Me (alternate)
Mosaic Records MD8-228
CO56444-3 You're Lucky to Me
Epic LN 3377, Philips (Eu) BO7183L
C056445-3 Just One More Chance
Epic LN3377
C056446-1 'S Wonderful (alternate)
Mosaic Records MD8-228
C056446-2 'S Wonderful
Epic LN 3377, Columbia 65433, Definitive DRCD 11279
NOTE: All titles on Epic LN 3377 are also on Portrait RJ 44393, RK 44393 (CD), and Lone Hill Jazz LHJ 10210 titled *Braff.* Columbia 65433 (CD) is an anthology titled *Gershwin Jazz.* This CD is reissued with the same title on Sony Special Markets 886972499024. All titles including both previously unissued alternate takes are on Mosaic Records MD8-228, titled *Columbia Small Group Swing Sessions 1953–62*. Definitive DRCD 11279 is titled *Summertime: George Gershwin Songbook.* Philips (Eu) BO7183L is titled *This Is Jazz No. 3* while BO7227L is another multi-artist album.

Ruby did not appear at the Newport Jazz Festival in 1956. His session for Epic Records continued.

Ruby Braff's All Stars: *Braff*
July 10, 1956, New York
Ruby Braff (tp), Don Elliott (vib), Nat Pierce (p), Freddie Green (g), Eddie Jones (b), Buzzy Drootin (dm)
CO56311-4 Indian Summer
Epic LN 3377
CO56312-3 Moonglow (alternate)
Philips (E) BBE 12123, (EU) 322.218BF, 429.296BE (all are 45-rpm)
C056312-4 Moonglow
Epic LN 3377
C056313-1 When My Dreamboat Comes Home
Epic LN 3377
CO56314-5 Too Marvelous for Words
Epic LN 3377
NOTE: All titles on LN 3377 are also on Epic (J) NL 525, Philips (E) BBL 7130, (EU) B07179L, CBS RJ 44493, Portrait RK 44493 (CD) (issued as *Braff*), and (J) 25-8P5125 (CD). All titles are on Mosaic Records MD8-228 and Lone Hill Jazz LHJ 10210 titled *Braff*. Philips B07179L and BBE12123 (45-rpm) are both titled *Ruby Braff*. Philips (E) BBE 12123, (EU) 322.218BF, and 429.296BE are all 45-rpm. The first and last are EPs. On BBE 12123, the title "Moonglow" is listed with Don Elliott as the leader. The equivalent issue of 429.296BE does not make this attribution. Session recording logs list master CO56312-1 as "Moonglow and Theme from Picnic."

The following week, Ruby joined his long time friend Dave McKenna in a New York studio to record for ABC-Paramount. While they had both recorded with Benny Goodman and both accompanied Milli Vernon for Storyville Records, this is their first instrumental recording as featured artists. This album received four and one-half stars in *DownBeat*.

Ruby Braff: *Ruby Braff Featuring Dave McKenna*
July 18, 1956, New York
Ruby Braff (tp), Dave McKenna (p), Sam Herman (g), Al Lucas (b), Buzzy Drootin (dm)
5265 Dancing in the Dark
ABC-Para ABC 141, Jasmine (E) JASM 1043, HMV (E) 7EG 8311
5266 It's Wonderful
ABC-Para ABC 141, Jasmine (E) JASM 1043
5267 Louisiana
ABC-Para ABC 141, Jasmine (E) JASM 1043

5268 Blue and Broken Hearted
ABC-Para ABC 141, Jasmine (E) JASM 1043, HMV (E) 7EG8397, Karusell (Swd) KSEP 3054
5269 Almost Like Being in Love
ABC-Para ABC 141, Jasmine (E) JASM 1043, HMV (E) 7EG8311
5270 Blue Prelude
ABC-Para ABC 141, Jasmine (E) JASM 1043
5271 If I Could Be With You
ABC-Para ABC 141, Jasmine (E) JASM 1043, HMV (E) 7EG 8397
5272 Why Was I Born?
ABC-Para ABC 141, Jasmine (E) JASM 1043, HMV (E) 7EG 8397
5273 I Must Have That Man
ABC-Para ABC 141, Jasmine (E) JASM 1043, Karusell (Swd) KDEP 3054
5274 I'm Crazy 'bout My Baby
ABC-Para ABC 141, Jasmine (E) JASM 1043, HMV (E) 7EG 8311, Karusell (Swd) KSEP3054
5275 Lover Come Back to Me
ABC-Para ABC 141, Jasmine (E) JASM 1043, HMV (E) 7EG 8397, Karusell (Swd) KSEP 3054

NOTE: All titles also on ABC-Paramount (J) YW 8536, W&G (Au) BJN 411, Probe (J) IPR-88049, and Gambit 69261 (CD) titled *Ruby Braff with Dave McKenna Complete Original Quartet / Quintet Sessions*. The Gambit CD went out of print soon after its issue in 2006. It now commands a high price. This album received three stars in *DownBeat.*

Ruby returned to network television in a production for the continuing program *Omnibus*. This program has never been issued following its original broadcast; however, the author has viewed a copy held at the Library of Congress.

Omnibus. V, Vol. 9: *Different Drummers* (15-minute segment)[3]
Wesleyan University Collection
1956, TV-Radio Workshop of the Ford Foundation and ABC
Program Producer: Robert Saudek
Musical Consultant: John Hammond
Announcer: Alexander Cook
Telecast: ABC, December 2, 1956
Ruby Braff (cnt), Urbie Green (tb), Tony Scott (cl), Ronnell Bright (p), Walter Page (b), Jo Jones (dm), Chatur Lal (Indian percussion)
Caravan (Urbie Green and Tony Scott solo; ensemble surrounding percussion solo and duet)
Fast Blues (Ruby Braff solo)

Ruby Braff solos on "Fast Blues"—he is quoted by Alexander Cook as joking that the full band would have to play "I Didn't Know What Time It Is."

Ruby Braff: *Bandstand USA* at Storyville
August 4, 1956, Storyville Club, Boston
Ruby Braff (tp), probably Nat Pierce (p), unknown bass, Steve Jordan (g), Buzzy Drootin (dm)
'Deed I Do
Blue and Sentimental
Undecided (incomplete in broadcast)
NOTE: This was part of a six-day booking.[4] A recording of these tunes is available but remains unissued.

DownBeat announced that Ruby Braff placed second to Dizzy Gillespie in the trumpet category in the fourth annual Critics' Poll.[5] Ruby Braff did not appear at the first New York Jazz Festival in August 1956, although his photograph appeared in the printed program. He did return to Boston to appear once again at Storyville for 11 days, opposite Muggsy Spanier. That leads to the following listing.

Ruby Braff[6]
September or October 1956, Storyville Club, Boston
Ruby Braff performed opposite Muggsy Spanier for 11 days.

Ruby's next documented appearance is with an all-star group at Child's Paramount Ballroom in New York. The event was advertised as a concert and dance on Friday and Saturday nights from 9 p.m. to 2 a.m. The advertisement stressed no minimum or cover, noting that it was "Broadway's Best Buy!"[7]

Jazz Concert and Dance (see Figure 6.1)
November 23 and 24, 1956, 9 p.m. to 2 a.m., Child's Paramount Ballroom, 1501 Broadway, near 44th Street, New York
Buck Clayton, Ruby Braff, Coleman Hawkins, Bud Freeman, Pee Wee Russell, J. C. Higginbotham, Cliff Jackson, Joe Marsala, Sonny Greer, Tommy Bedford "and many other jazz stars"

DownBeat reported that Ruby Braff was rehearsing a new band that would be booked by Willard Alexander.[8] His group included the following musicians: Bob Wilber, Buddy Tate, Benny Morton, Walter Page, Nat Pierce, Sam Herman, and Walter Johnson.[9] I have been unable to locate further information, so perhaps no bookings developed as a result; however, in the future, Ruby continued to develop various combinations of musicians that were successful.

The following session is one that Ruby urged me to locate almost from the start of our conversations. He felt that the quality was at least as high at the earlier session for Epic Records, but he had been frustrated by reports that all tapes had been erased.

Reports of a Lost Columbia Recording Session (later issued by Mosaic)
January 1957, New York, George Avakian, producer
Ruby Braff (cnt), Vic Dickenson (tb), Pee Wee Russell (cl), Coleman Hawkins (ts), and others

Ruby reported to me that the tape for this session was rumored to have been destroyed by John Hammond, since he did not supervise the session. Ruby assumed that this happened as a result of their earlier disagreement about the background to the wonderful recordings with Ellis Larkins on Vanguard and John's resentment that this session had taken place under George Avakian's leadership. Of course, that was speculation on Ruby's part; however, I confirmed Ruby's claim that the tapes had been erased in a telephone conversation with George Avakian who earlier had recalled the identities of the musicians for Robert Hilbert.[10]

However, Michael Brooks discovered tapes from April 9 and 11 that have now been issued by Mosaic Records. This is probably the session Ruby praised to me in conversations, and probably the above session recalled by George Avakian. The session released by Mosaic did not include Vic Dickenson and Coleman Hawkins, but Michael Brooks found no trace of other recordings from January. Michael Brooks pointed out that this is proof that it is never a simple matter to erase a master tape once recorded by a major company. But collectors will continue to wonder if there is a further "lost session" from January while they enjoy listening to the newly discovered recordings from April. They are most certainly worth hearing, and details follow below after Ruby's next session for RCA.

Ruby recalled he rehearsed another band including Benny Morton, Sam Margolis, Pee Wee Russell, and Bobby Donaldson about this time. These musicians, in slightly different combinations, appear in the following recordings.

Ruby Braff and His Men: *Hi-Fi Salute to Bunny*
March 26, 1957, RCA Studio 3, New York
Ruby Braff (tp), Benny Morton (tb), Pee Wee Russell (cl), Dick Hafer (ts), Nat Pierce (p), Steve Jordan (g), Walter Page (b), Buzzy Drootin (dm)
H2JB2793 It's Been So Long
RCA-Victor LPM 1510, Bluebird 6456-2 (CD), RCA EPA 1-1510 (45)
H2JB2794 I'm Comin' Virginia
RCA-Victor LPM 1510, Bluebird 6456-2 (CD), RCA EPA 2-1510 (45)
H2JB2795 Keep Smiling at Trouble
RCA-Victor LPM 1510, RCA EPA 3-1510 (45)
NOTE: "It's Been So Long" also appears on RCA 2135736-2, titled *Victor Jazz History, Vol. 17: Mainstream*. Bluebird 6456-2 (CD) is titled *This Is My Lucky Day*. All of the above performances are also included on Mosaic Records CD 1016 with the same title as the LP release and Avid 1011 with the title *Three Classic Albums Plus*. This album received four and one-half stars in *DownBeat*.

Ruby Braff and His Men: *Hi-Fi Salute to Bunny*
April 5, 1957, RCA Studio 3, New York
Same musicians as March 26, 1957
H2JB3273 I Can't Get Started
RCA-Victor LPM 1510, Bluebird 6456-2 (CD), Victor EPA 1-1510 (45)
H2JB3274 Marie
RCA-Victor LPM 1510, Bluebird 6456-2 (CD), Victor EPA 2-1510 (45)
H2JB3275 I Got It Bad and That Ain't Good
RCA-Victor LPM 1510, Bluebird 6456-2 (CD), Victor EPA 3-1510 (45)
NOTE: Bluebird 6456-2 (CD) is titled *This Is My Lucky Day.* All of the above performances are also included on Mosaic Records CD 1016 with the same title as the LP release and Avid 1011 with the title *Three Classic Albums Plus.*

Ruby wrote several arrangements for his tribute to Bunny Berigan. These were his first written arrangements and he featured Pee Wee Russell with a more modern background. It is another delightful album.

As already mentioned, Bob Hilbert's Pee Wee Russell discography cited several sessions produced by George Avakian for Epic Records during January 1957, said to include Coleman Hawkins and Vic Dickenson. He related George Avakian's story that the master tapes had been erased. A letter from Pee Wee Russell is quoted in *Pee Wee Russell: Life of a Jazzman*:[11] "It's the first time in my life that I'm excited about records. We blew our brains out . . . . Ruby is sailing about these records. He got us out of bed a few days ago at two in the morning so he could talk about them. He wanted to try some new stuff, and George Avakian let him do whatever he liked. It was going to be either the world's lousiest or the best. Ruby had been under a strain, so we relaxed with a beer and coffee and talked." As reported, Michael Brooks discovered unissued tapes in Sony's archives in 2003, ending the rumor of their destruction. The session is dated April 9 and 11, 1957. Probably this is the session that was rumored to have taken place in January.

Ruby Braff "Previously Unissued Session" for Columbia Records[12]
April 9, 1957, New York, George Avakian, producer, tapes discovered by Michael Brooks
Ruby Braff (tp), Pee Wee Russell (cl), Jimmy Welch (vtb), Dick Hafer (as, ts, bar), Sam Margolis (ts), Nat Pierce (p), Steve Jordan (g), Walter Page (b), Buzzy Drootin (dm) (Hafer is listed as John Hafer in Sony's files)
Studio chat
unissued, recording available
CO57099-1 No One Else But You (false start)
unissued, recording available
Studio chat
unissued, recording available
CO57099-2 No One Else But You
unissued, recording available

CO57099-3 No One Else But You
unissued, recording available
Studio chat and rehearsal of ending
unissued, recording available
CO57099-4 No One Else But You
Mosaic Records MD8-228
CO57100-1 How Can You Face Me?
Mosaic Records MD8-228
CO57100-2 How Can You Face Me?
Mosaic Records MD8-228
CO57599-1 I Thought I Heard Buddy Bolden Say
unissued, recording available
CO57599-2 I Thought I Heard Buddy Bolden Say
Mosaic Records MD8-228
CO57599-3 I Thought I Heard Buddy Bolden Say
Mosaic Records MD8-228

Ruby Braff Unissued Session for Columbia Records[13]

April 11, 1957, New York, George Avakian, producer
Ruby Braff (tp), Pee Wee Russell (cl), Jimmy Welch (tb), Dick Hafer (as, bar), Sam Margolis (ts), Nat Pierce (p), Steve Jordan (g), Walter Page (b), Buzzy Drootin (dm) (Hafer is listed as John Hafer in Sony's files)
CO57600-1 Keep Young and Beautiful (incomplete)
unissued, recording available
CO57600-2 Keep Young and Beautiful (false start)
unissued, recording available
CO57600-3 Keep Young and Beautiful (breakdown)
unissued, recording available
CO57600-4 Keep Young and Beautiful
Mosaic Records MD8-228
CO57600-5 Keep Young and Beautiful
Mosaic Records MD8-228
CO57601-1 Lady Be Good (end missing)
unissued, recording available
CO57601-2 Lady Be Good
Mosaic Records MD8-228
Brief studio chat
unissued, recording available
CO57645-x Falling in Love With You (false start)
unissued, recording available
CO57645-1 Falling in Love With You
Mosaic Records MD8-228
CO57645-2 Falling in Love With You
Mosaic Records MD8-228

No doubt Ruby was feeling very good about completing this session for Columbia, even though he was subsequently baffled by its lack of release. It is tragic that Ruby died before he could learn that his fans would be able to hear the results of this recording. But it was time for the final session at RCA to complete the Berigan album.

Ruby Braff and His Men: *Hi-Fi Salute to Bunny*
April 12, 1957, New York
Same musicians as March 26, 1957
H2JB3415 Somebody Else Is Taking My Place
RCA-Victor LPM 1510, Victor EPA 3-1510 (45)
H2JB3416 Downhearted Blues
RCA-Victor LPM 1510, Bluebird 6456-2 (CD), Victor EPA 3-1510 (45)
H2JB3417 Did I Remember?
RCA-Victor LPM 1644, Bluebird 6456-2 (CD), (J) RGP 1188,
RCA (G) 74321 18520 2, Victor EPA 945 (45)
NOTE: "Downhearted Blues" is incorrectly titled "There's Something in My Mind" on Bluebird 6456-2 (CD). This likely was done because of Ruby's original introduction to the song. For the three RCA sessions that comprise *Hi-Fi Salute to Bunny*, all titles from LPM 1510 are also on RCA (G) 74321 18520 2, RCA Camden (J) RGP 1188, and (Au) L10822. Bluebird CD 6456-2 is titled *This Is My Lucky Day* and dated December 26, 1957 for the three RCA sessions above. All titles from Bluebird (CD) 6456-2 also appear on Bluebird (CAS) 6456-4. See August 19, 1958 for the balance of this CD. LPM 1644 is titled *Bread Butter & Jam in Hi-Fi* which also appears on RCA (Eu) 74321 36402 2 (CD). All of the above performances are also included on Mosaic Records CD 1016 with the same title as the LP release. The first two titles are also released on Avid 1011 with the title *Three Classic Albums Plus.*

In 1957, Joe Glaser, Louis Armstrong's longtime manager, called Ruby to ask him if he wanted to go to England.[14] Edmond Hall had introduced the two of them at the 1956 Newport Jazz Festival. The call woke Ruby, who later in his life made it known to everyone that there should be "no morning calls because I stay up all night and sleep through the morning." Ruby indicated that he would love to travel with his own octet, but Glaser said Ruby would join with Jack Teagarden and Earl Hines. The exchange quickly heated and insults were exchanged. Ruby suddenly hung up his phone, ending the conversation. Ruby then called back, but ended up exchanging insults again. Nat Hentoff printed Ruby's view of the exchange in *Esquire* magazine, whereupon Joe Glaser phoned and invited Ruby to sign an exclusive representation contract with his booking agency. They met face to face, and Ruby signed. Glaser had a copy of the *Esquire* article on his desk at that moment. Ruby noted it and laughed it off. But Glaser never obtained a booking for Ruby and used his power to reduce Ruby's bookings for the term of the contract. John McDonough called Ruby opinionated and honest and "a PR man's nightmare." Touring the UK with Teagarden and Hines would have brought Ruby some added visibility, although there is no doubt that Ruby's reputation was still growing in jazz circles. In addition to Teagarden and Hines, the tour included Max Kaminsky, Peanuts Hucko, Jack Lesberg, and Cozy Cole. They are all shown in an available copy of the tour's published program. Would this tour have helped Ruby's career? Certainly he later developed a loyal and enthusiastic base of fans throughout England. Did Joe Glaser's actions slow his career? All that is open to speculation.

There is a possible session in June led by George Wein that has remained unissued. No details are known; however, it is certainly possible that George invited Ruby to participate. But clearly the time is rapidly approaching for the summer's Newport Jazz Festival. Ruby was about to appear with Pee Wee Russell, and the performance was to be partially issued on Verve Records.

Unissued George Wein Session, Unknown Personnel (not known if Ruby Braff participated)[15]
June 7, 1957, Boston
2594 Dream a Little Dream of Me
2595 You Are My Lucky Star
2596 Why Try to Change Me Now
2597 Something to Live For

There is a photograph from the 1958 Newport Jazz Festival program that probably dates from the 1957 Festival. It shows Nat Pierce, Pee Wee Russell, Jimmy Welch, Sam Margolis, Ruby Braff, and Steve Jordan performing on stage.[16]

Steve Jordan wrote the following:[17]

> Ruby had rented a nice house in a Bronx suburb and thought it would be a good idea to have us come over and run through some of the tunes we'd play at Newport so we'd sound like a band and not like a half-dozen guys at a jam session. The last guy to arrive was the inimitable Pee Wee Russell. And he had quite an explanation for being late. 'I would have been here sooner but I had trouble on the subway on the way up here. My clarinet case was on the seat beside me and a dirty-looking guy came over and started to pick it up. I said, 'Don't touch that clarinet case' but he started to open one of the latches.' Then Pee Wee drew himself up to his full 5' 9", 120-pound stature and said, 'Now, I'm no Rocky Marciano, you know,' a remark undisputable and one that made us laugh, 'but I hit him good and he ran into the next car. Nobody fools with my clarinet! At the station I had to sit on the bench for awhile to calm down. That's why I'm late.'

The Ruby Braff Octet with Pee Wee Russell and Bobby Henderson at Newport[18]
July 5, 1957, 4th Newport Jazz Festival, Freebody Park, Newport, Rhode Island (second day of four-day festival)

Ruby Braff (tp), Jimmy Welch (vtb), Pee Wee Russell (cl), Sam Margolis (ts), Nat Pierce (p), Steve Jordan (g), Walter Page (b), Buzzy Drootin (dm)
It Don't Mean a Thing
    Verve MGV 8241, Readers' Digest RD4-129
These Foolish Things
    Verve MGV 8241, Verve 845 151-2 (CD)
Lady Be Good
    Verve MGV 8241, Metro (Eu) 2355.015, 2356.017, Readers' Digest RD4-129
No One Else But You
    unissued, recording available

NOTE: All issued titles also on Verve (J) MV 2625 and Verve (LP) MV 2625 with the same title, American Recording Society ARS G439, Columbia (E) 33CX 10104, and Avid 1011 with the title *Three Classic Albums Plus.* Verve 845 151-2 is titled *Jazz Club Mainstream.* The first two titles are also on Verve (G) 845 (CD) and Verve (G) 2150-2 845 150-4 (cassette). The first title is included on *Best of Newport '57: 50th Anniversary Collection,* Verve 000952702.

Ruby introduced the session, stating that there would be "no psychological or psychotic music [and] no fugues." The performance received critical acclaim. Whitney Balliett wrote in *The New Yorker*[19]:

> On Friday, Ruby Braff led an octet that included Pee Wee Russell, the trombonist Jimmy Welch, and the pianist Nat Pierce through four pleasantly and simply arranged selections that offered exceptional solos by Braff and Russell; in 'Nobody Else But You,' Russell took a gentle, barely audible low-register solo that was the equal of any improvisation during the whole weekend.

DownBeat's August 8, 1957, issue also carried a review; however, these pages were removed from the library copy I was able to consult.

Following the Newport Jazz Festival, Ruby Braff performed at Storyville in Boston. At least one broadcast survives from *Bandstand USA* on Mutual Network, while another is referenced in surviving commentary from the program's host, Guy Wallace. The first performance was on July 13, 1957:

Here is the voiceover by Guy Wallace, in conversation with Jean Shepherd, as a *Bandstand USA* segment featuring Miles Davis is closing:

> "The great and unique Miles Davis, and his horn and his quintet, playing for you from Jimmy Garafalo's Café Bohemia at 15 Barrow Street in the Village, and featuring Sonny Rollins on saxophone. How 'bout 'em, Jean, what d'you think?" Shepherd: "Oh, fine." Wallace: "What d'you think of Miles, and the outfit down there?" Shepherd: "Well, they sound very good. As a matter of fact, ah, do you want me to talk about it?" Wallace: "Yeah, I think it'd be wonderful if you did." Shepherd: "Well, you know there's a great deal of misunder-

> standing about jazz among a large number of people who don't know much about it. Y'know it's a strange thing, Guy, I just got back from Europe. I was over about six weeks, I just returned about four or five weeks ago, and one of the things that really impressed me tremendously is something I'd been reading about for years, and that is the appreciation of American jazz all over Europe, not only. . . Hmm?" Wallace: "I wonder why that is." Shepherd: "Well, I think it's because the European approaches it with an open mind, generally. I think most Americans don't. I think most Americans approach the field of jazz—that is, people who do not appreciate it—approach it with a kind of a closed mind; they don't listen to it for what it is." Wallace: "In other words, they're standing around saying 'Condition me to like it'." Shepherd: "Yes, it's more or less like that. And it's the one art form that we've given the world.". . . Wallace: "I guess it is, Jean, and that's true all over the world, too. I just wanna say that we here on the Bandstand are certainly trying to do just that by presenting these live performances of the world's great jazzmen each Saturday night from eight to ten. Coming up on the Bandstand yet tonight, after we break for five minutes of news here, which we're gonna do here in just a few seconds, will be Stan Getz and Jimmy Giuffre from the Village Vanguard, on Seventh Avenue south, near Eleventh Street in New York City. Then we're going up to Storyville in Boston, up to George Wein's pad up there, for, ah, um, Ruby Braff and Pee Wee Russell, and then back here in Manhattan to Birdland for Oscar Pettiford. Jean, stick around here and don't go too far. This is the Bandstand, everybody, Guy Wallace speaking. It's produced by Tommy Reynolds and directed tonight by Tommy [undecipherable], and our guest tonight is the noted author of the book *I, Libertine*, Jean Shepherd. He's a jazz enthusiast, aficionado, buff, critic..." Shepherd: "I'm a pretty good. . . . I'm a pretty good domino man, too." Wallace: "Yeah? And, uh, he's gonna be a snooker." . . . Shepherd: "I'm great at fist-fights." Wallace: "Kelly pool player when we finish with him. Stick with us, everybody, we'll be back after the news with Les Smith. This is Mutual Radio Network, for all America."[20]

The beginning date for Ruby's following engagement at Storyville is unknown, but could have commenced earlier, following his appearance at the Newport Jazz Festival. The following date is taken from the date of the Miles Davis broadcast.

Ruby Braff at Storyville[21]
July 13, 1957, Storyville Club, Boston
Ruby Braff (cnt), Dick LeFave (tb), Pee Wee Russell (cl), Sam Margolis (ts), Ivan Wainwright (p), Johnny Gidano (g), Rowland Smith (b), Marquis Foster (dm)
It Don't Mean a Thing
These Foolish Things
Lady Be Good
NOTE: Ruby's voice is not distinct when he names the guitarist and bass player, so these spellings may be incorrect. A recording of all of the above tunes exists but was not available to the author prior to publication.

Bandstand USA was broadcast on Saturdays. An undated tape recording survives from another *Bandstand USA* broadcast in which Ruby's performance from Storyville is inserted between segments by Chris Connor and Maynard Ferguson that originated from Birdland in New York. *The New Yorker* magazine lists dates for Maynard Ferguson's appearance from July 17–31, 1957.[22] Thus, this broadcast probably dates from July 20. Information from this broadcast provides further details. The musicians who performed on this broadcast probably remained with Ruby throughout this weeklong (or longer) engagement.

Ruby Braff at Storyville[23]
July 20, 1957, Storyville Club, Boston
Ruby Braff (cnt), Dick LeFave (tb), Pee Wee Russell (cl), Sam Margolis (ts), Ivan Wainwright (p), Johnny Gidano (g), Champ Jones (b); Marquis Foster (dm)
Bugle Call Rag
These Foolish Things
Somebody Else Is Taking My Place
Blue and Sentimental (incomplete on broadcast)
NOTE: Ruby's voice is not distinct when he names the guitarist, so this spelling may be incorrect. A recording of all of the above tunes exists but was not available to the author prior to publication.

Ruby could have remained at Storyville following this date prior to his next appearance at the Village Vanguard.

Ruby Braff Sextet[24]
August 10–20, 1957, Village Vanguard (178 Seventh Avenue South at 11th Street), New York (closed Mondays)
Ruby Braff (tp), Pee Wee Russell (cl), Nat Pierce (p), Steve Jordan (g), Walter Page (b), Bobby Donaldson (dm)

Ruby Braff Sextet[25]
August 10, 1957, as part of two week engagement, Village Vanguard (178 Seventh Avenue), New York, broadcast *Bandstand USA* on the Mutual Network
Ruby Braff (tp), Pee Wee Russell (cl), Nat Pierce (p), Steve Jordan (g), Walter Page (b), Bobby Donaldson (dm)
I'm Crazy 'bout My Baby
    Spook Jazz SPJ 6607
Blue Turning Grey Over You (voice over, incomplete on broadcast)
    unissued, recording available
Just You, Just Me
Old Folks
It's Wonderful
NOTE: Recordings of the final three tunes from this performance are not available to the author at the time of publication. A recording of "Blue Turning Grey Over You" is available but remains unissued.

Steve Jordan wrote[26] the following:

> Walter and I were working at the Village Vanguard for two weeks in 1957 with Ruby Braff, and at the bar between sets one night he [Walter Page] kept insisting he was only forty-two years old. We knew damn well that was wrong. Later that evening after a few more tastes, he all but gave his age away when he said, 'You know that lick Ruby was playing on that last tune? Well, that ain't new and Ruby knows it. And it's not as new as Ruby thinks it is, either. Ruby probably heard somebody play it in the thirties. Well, in 1916 I heard it on a gig in New Orleans.' And he kept talking on and on about that gig. 'Wow,' I said, 'you're forty-two years old and you're talking about a gig in 1916!'

Ruby reported that he rehearsed a group consisting of Benny Morton, Sam Margolis, Pee Wee Russell, Steve Jordan, Nat Pierce, and Buzzy Drootin to open a new club, Jazz City. Buddy Rich was the next featured artist. Ruby played opposite Buddy and said that he never left the club, so that he could listen to Buddy between his own sets. This was the first documented meeting between Ruby and Buddy, and Ruby played at a memorial service for Buddy years later. Ruby was one of Buddy's admirers.

DownBeat published a review:

> There's no doubt in my mind that this group, and the octet [meaning the group that performed at Newport] will make it in any location. The music is excellent. The musicians are happy with their lot. And the feeling of professional competence communicates to the audience. The octet is set to open the new club, Jazz City, in Manhattan, and it will stay together at least that long. If more bookings are secured, it quite probably will remain a unit as long as there is a demand. Considering the quality of the music and the genuine happiness created, there is more than a demand for this group. There is a definite need.[27]

The next session is unknown to most of Ruby's fans. Documentation for the recordings with the Weavers is somewhat incomplete. *DownBeat* reported that "Ruby Braff and Walter Page cut an LP with the Weavers for Vanguard."[28] Of course, this report suggests that there may be other unreleased titles. On August 20 Vanguard listed two sessions, with only a change in the string bass player. Ruby recalled Walter Page played on the tunes he recorded. The other session replaced Walter Page with Justin Arndt. But several tunes have been released. Ruby's tone and attack are unmistakable. Nobody can doubt his presence here.

The Weavers

August 20, 1957, Masonic Temple, Brooklyn, New York

Ruby Braff (tp), Pete Seeger (voc, bjo, g), Ronnie Gilbert, Lee Hayes (voc), Fred Hellerman (voc, g), Michael Chimes (electronic harmonica), Michael Rongo (percussion) –Ruby recalled Walter Page (b) played on this recording

Tina
Vanguard VRS 9024, VSD 2030
The Keeper
Vanguard VRS 3014 (45-rpm), VRS 9043, SVD 2022
Joshua Fit the Battle of Jericho
Vanguard VRS 3001, SRV 73001, 79702-2
Hey Lilee Lilee
Vanguard 79707-2

NOTE: Ruby Braff does not appear on other titles from these albums. On LP, VRS 9024 is titled *The Weavers at Home* and VRS 9043 is titled *Traveling On with the Weavers*. Vanguard 79707-2 is a CD release, titled *The Weavers: Rarities from the Vanguard Vault*.

Ruby next appeared at the 2nd Annual New York Jazz Festival, opening the two-day program. The lineup featured many of the finest artists in jazz music, representing a wide range of styles; however, I have not been able to locate details about Ruby's performance on August 23. Given that Ruby had been rehearsing a group to appear in Jazz City, it is quite possible that he was featured with those musicians.

Randall's Island Jazz Festival[29] (2nd Annual New York Jazz Festival)
August 23, 1957, New York
The program also included Count Basie, Joe Williams, Sarah Vaughan, Jimmy Smith, Randy Weston with Cecil Payne, Horace Silver, Carmen McRae, Coleman Hawkins, Miles Davis, Stan Getz, Dave Brubeck, and Maynard Ferguson. Saturday night: Bud Powell, Billie Holiday, the Max Roach Quintet, Anita O'Day, the Gerry Mulligan Quartet, and the Dizzy Gillespie Orchestra

There are two photographs of Ruby visiting Louis Armstrong taken by Lucille Armstrong at their home. The first, dated 1957, shows Louis Armstrong, Charles Graham, and Ruby.[30] The second is taken at the same time but is dated 1960.[31] Two other photos from this occasion were published in the March of Jazz[32] program, and one is included in this book's photo section. All photos show exactly the same setting and must be from the same date. Graham was interviewing Louis Armstrong for an article on his audio taping and his high fidelity sound system. Since that article was published in the magazine *Hi-Fi Music at Home* in March 1958,[33] it appears that the 1957 date is more accurate.

This time, Ruby's rehearsal paid off, and the booking at Jazz City transpired. Ruby followed Buddy Rich into the club. But the outcome was not a happy one. The booking was supposed to have run for one month, but the musicians were not paid for the ten days. Ruby requested that the contract be cancelled. The owners were "gangster-type characters" who were glad to see the band depart.[34]

Ruby Braff and Pee Wee Russell[35]

August 24–September 1, 1957, Jazz City, 157 West 49th Street, near Times Square, New York for two weeks (Mondays off)
Ruby Braff (tp), Benny Morton (tb), Pee Wee Russell (cl), Nat Pierce (p), Steve Jordan (g), Walter Page (b), Bobby Donaldson (dm)

Ruby Braff—Jazz Reviewer:

In 1958, Ruby reviewed jazz recordings for the *Saturday Review*.[36] Ruby was limited to a few lines for each review, filling a single page each time. He said that this was a difficult job, and that he received considerable criticism for his views. That probably explains why he did not continue in this role. His comments on recordings are crisp, and often critical. During this time Ruby's career may have had as much momentum as it ever did. The *DownBeat* New Star Award provided Ruby with some valuable publicity.

A few examples from Ruby's reviews will illustrate his approach:

From January 11:

> Reviewing *Here Come the Swinging Bands* on Verve: And swinging they are. Basie unfailingly has exquisite taste and time, and Williams was wonderful. Some of the arrangements are very tastefully done by Nat Pierce, Quincy Jones, and Ralph Burns. Woody, I admire for his wisdom and strength as an organizer, as well as his talent. Gillespie displays his very schooled ear and complete control of a style only he can play. The star-stealer of the album is Roy Eldridge, whose playing with Krupa on 'Let Me Off Uptown' is the work of a giant. As with every artist of stature, Eldridge never stops growing.

From February 8:

> Reviewing *Chicago/Austin High Jazz in HiFi* by Bud Freeman on RCA: If more people (and critics) could appreciate the classic playing of Freeman, Teagarden, and Pee Wee, the music business probably wouldn't be scuffling as much as it is. The presence of Billy Butterfield, one of the world's finest all around trumpeters, is very gratifying. Wettling keeps everything under control. The rarely heard 'Prince of Wails' is included. Reviewing *CuBop* by Art Blakey on Jubilee: Fine musicians. No message.

From May 17:

> Reviewing *Jazz Giants '58* on Verve: Norman Granz's liner notes give the impression that this is a wonderful album; that Getz, Mulligan, Edison, Bellson, and the Granz house rhythm sectioneers play a gang of music; that everyone's an individual; that the whole thing swings like

> crazy. Well, it's true. Reviewing *Junita Hall Sings the Blues* on Counterpoint: Claude Hopkins, Coleman Hawkins, Buster Bailey, Doc Cheatham, Jimmy Crawford, George Duvivier, were all inspired by Miss Hall. Who wouldn't be! Some of them played better than they ever have. Miss Hall is the living end. Reviewing *The Lion Roars* on Dot: He sure does. [Ruby is of course referring to Willie "The Lion" Smith with his words of praise.]

From June 14:

> Reviewing *The Art of Tatum* on Decca: These are some of the sides that helped win Tatum's reputation for him. They're certainly worth hearing or re-hearing. I've always wanted to have this collection, and thanks to Decca for making it possible. Reviewing *Makin' Whoopee: The Art Tatum, Benny Carter, Louis Bellson Trio* on Verve: Tatum plays a few good measures here and there. It would be unfair to comment on Mr. Carter, since Art gave him no room at all to blow. As a trio, nothing happens. Reviewing *The Soft Touch* by Ellis Larkins on Decca: A breath of cool fresh air.

Writing in *Esquire*, Nat Hentoff, quoted Ruby who described the then current state of his career in music:[37]

> After all these years, I never expect anything to happen good. I'm only concerned with each night. People have been complimenting me since I was ten years old, but I haven't been able to trade the compliments in for cash. I'm still in the same financial panic I've been in all my life. I still don't get a chance to keep a band together of the people I want to play with. But I'm not going to change. I'm hip enough to know you can't be liked by everyone. There's no sense sitting on the fence all your life even if you make a lot of money. You have to be honest, and then at least somebody will know you stand for something.

Hentoff continued, quoting Pee Wee Russell's prescient statement: "Ruby's young. . . . He's still got a way to go, an amount of living as well as playing experience to absorb. When he gets old and grey though, the little giant will be remembered."

At that point, Pee Wee was speaking as a critic might, not only as a friend. This interview provided the first glimpse into some of the principles that guided Ruby during his career. At times, his interpretation of honesty would be seen by some as a lack of necessary flexibility. Here, Ruby was saying that he would not take a job unless he could approve of the people who would accompany him. That is certainly an admirable quality from an artistic point of view, but it may have limited his ability to earn a living in other ways.

There is a photograph from an unknown source that is probably from this period, showing Ruby, Pee Wee, Nat Pierce, and Bud Freeman. Perhaps it relates to the next recording session for Counterpoint led by Pee Wee Russell.

Pee Wee Russell: *Portrait of Pee Wee*
February 18–19, 1958, Belltone Recording Studio, New York
Ruby Braff (tp), Vic Dickenson (tb), Pee Wee Russell (cl), Bud Freeman (ts), Nat Pierce (p, arr), Tommy Potter (b), Karl Kiffe (dm)
That Old Feeling
    Counterpoint CPST 562, CPT 565
I've Got the World on a String
    Counterpoint CPST 562, CPT 565
It All Depends on You
    Counterpoint CPST 562, CPT 565, Sentry (reel tape) 3S-106
Out of Nowhere
    Counterpoint CPST 562, CPT 565
I Used to Love You
    Counterpoint CPST 562, CPT 565, Sentry (reel tape) 3S-106
Oh No!
    Counterpoint CPST 562, CPT 565, Sentry (reel tape) 3S-106
NOTE: Ruby Braff does not play on three more titles: "Exactly Like You," "If I Had You," and "Pee Wee's Blues." All titles on DCC DJZ611 (CD), Fresh Sound (Sp) FSR-CD 126, Rockin' Chair (Sw) no number, Ember CJS 824, Everest FS 233, Globe (J) SMJ 7165, I Grande del Jazz (It) GDJ 07, America (F) 30AM 6097, I Grandi del Jazz (I) GDJ 07, Opus (Arg) OJC 20011, Quadrifoglio (I) VDS 348, Society (E) SOC 1013, Vendette (I) VPA 8099, Prestige 24213-2, Empire Musicwerks 450813, Lone Hill Jazz 10347, and other releases. The Sentry tape is a commercially released pre-recorded tape. "That Old Feeling," "Oh No!," and "It All Depends on You" are also on *Period's Jazz Digest*. Drive Archive DE 41052 is titled *Pee Wee Russell Clarinet Strut* and it includes all titles above except "Out of Nowhere."

Ruby gathered another group of musicians and began rehearsals. I have been unable to find any trace of commercial engagements. Ruby told me that band had hopes for a European tour, but it apparently never performed in public.

Pee Wee Russell and Ruby Braff Rehearsal Band[38]
Ruby Braff (tp), Pee Wee Russell (cl), Bob Wilber (ts), Mickey Crane (p), Bill Takas (b), Buzzy Drootin (dm)

But Ruby was once again on television, performing on the program *Timex All Star Jazz*. This was the second program in that series. Ruby performed with Jack Teagarden. Jack Teagarden describes Ruby Braff as "the Ivy League's Louis Armstrong," likely taking this from George Simeon's script. They were joined by Louis Armstrong. Ruby told me simply, "No one should have been asked to play with Louis Armstrong." Clearly he was honored to appear with his idol.

Television Program: *2nd Timex All Star Jazz Festival*
April 30, 1958, New York
Louis Armstrong (tp, voc), Ruby Braff (tp), Jack Teagarden (tb, voc), Tony Parenti (cl), Marty Napoleon (p), Chubby Jackson (b), Cozy Cole (dm), Bill Hobin (producer), George T. Simon (associate producer)
Basin Street Blues (JT voc)
Kings of Jazz (It) 20.031, MfP MP 211, Windmill WMD 266,
Radiola MR 1095, Giants of Jazz (It) LPJT 69

Add Louis Armstrong (tp, voc), same date
Jeepers Creepers (JT, LA voc)
Kings of Jazz (It) 20.026, MfP MP 211, Windmill (E) WMD 266,
Radiola MR 1095, Giants of Jazz (It) LPJT 69, Phonic (Sp) PHL 5505,
Music for Pleasure (E) MFP2M-146-13270, Windmill (E) WMD 266
NOTE: A video recording also available for all of the above (Kay Jazz Productions KJ 102 is one source). At least one of these titles is also included in Jazz Connoisseur JCC 94 (cassette). The Kings of Jazz LP 20.026 is titled *Here Is Louis Armstrong at His Rare of All Rarest Performances, Volume 2* and Kings of Jazz LP 20.031 is titled *The 50s Rare of All the Rarest, Volume 2*. "Jeepers Creepers" is included on the DVD *Louis Armstrong & His Friends* (Storyville Films Jazz Legends 16014).

Two photos by Jack Bradley exist from the television studio. Both are published in the March of Jazz program,[39] and one is included in this book's photo section.

A month later, and Ruby had returned to Toronto. I have not traced any other visits to Canada since his performances in 1951, 1952, and 1954. Pee Wee filmed a television program with Ruby Braff for the Canadian Broadcasting Corporation. The filming was followed by a wonderful all night jam session according to John Norris.[40]

Pee Wee Russell and His Jazz Band: *Cross-Canada Hit Parade*[41]
May 24, 1958, Toronto, kinescope exists, Canadian Broadcasting Corporation
Ruby Braff (cnt), Steve Richards (tb), Pee Wee Russell (cl), Wally Gurd (p), Jack Richardson (b), Doug McLeod (dm), Phyllis Marshall (voc)
Lady Be Good
Who's Sorry Now? (PM, voc)
NOTE: This program remains unissued; however, a partial video recording is available.

Ruby Braff[42]
June 27–28, 1958 (and perhaps additional dates), Town Tavern, Toronto
No further details available

The next recording is somewhat of a mystery. Ruby mentioned it to me as we discussed unissued studio recordings, although he gave it less emphasis than the April 1957 recording that he feared had been erased by John Hammond at Columbia that later appeared in a deluxe set from Mosaic Records. Ruby described a final recording session for Vanguard Records that was a tribute to Johnny Mercer. Ruby had forgotten many of the details but felt strongly that Eddie Condon had been present. He had less distinct memories about the presence of Nat Pierce, Walter Page, and Jo Jones. I subsequently corresponded with several people at Vanguard Records, now part of the Welk Music Group, and they denied that the following recording was made by Vanguard. But nevertheless I obtained a high quality copy and shared it with Ruby who was delighted to hear it at last. My source for this recording was Richard Sudhalter, long before the prolonged decline in his health. He recalled that he had received a copy made from the master tape to consider for possible preparation of a review or perhaps even album notes. He could not recall if he received his copy in 1958 or at a later time. Even with that information, my discussion with Vanguard did not lead to any claim of ownership of this session.

But the story is not yet over. Alun Morgan wrote me the following note after reviewing a much earlier version of this manuscript:

> Around 1971 RCA in Britain leased the rights to the Vanguard catalogue and the late Albert McCarthy, then editor of the magazine *Jazz Monthly*, was commissioned by RCA to compile a series of 12-inch Vanguard LPs and to write the liner notes. I recall visiting Mac one day when he produced a single-sided 12-inch acetate disc which had, from memory, four tracks on it. He played the disc for me and told me it was Braff with Eddie Condon, the remainder of the group being unknown at the time. In Mac's opinion it was some of the best Braff he'd heard and he wanted to include it somewhere in his RCA/Vanguard compilations but had been told that these were the only tracks made. With the absence of any further tracks, and the problem with the "unknown" personnel details Mac reluctantly dropped the idea from his schedule. . . . Mac had been given the acetate disc by RCA as part of the Vanguard leasing package so it may well have been done for Vanguard.

Listening to the recording there is one possible explanation for its remaining unissued. There is certainly no problem with the performance; however, there is somewhat less immediacy to the miking of the musicians. The recording has the "Vanguard sound" associated with Ruby's other releases, but the music levels are lower and somewhat less defined. This seems to improve as the session continues. Perhaps Ruby was being moved closer to the microphone as the session progressed in order to obtain better sound balance? Of course, it is also possible that Ruby was correct in thinking that John Hammond remained angry. But why would there have been in investment in creating the session in the first place? Anyhow, I have a high quality digital audio tape of this recording that was professionally transferred from Richard's copy at my expense. Perhaps someday others will hear this fine recording.

Tribute to Johnny Mercer[43]
Date and location unknown—perhaps 1958—probably Brooklyn, New York
Ruby Braff (tp), unknown p, b, dm, Eddie Condon (g). Ruby thought that the others were Jo Jones (dm), Nat Pierce (p), Walter Page (b)
You Must Have Been a Beautiful Baby
And the Angels Sing
Jeepers Creepers
When a Woman Loves a Man
Goody Goody
When I Take My Sugar to Tea
Mandy Is Two
Mister Meadowlark
If You Were Mine
NOTE: A recording of these tunes is available but remains unissued. "When I Take My Sugar to Tea" is not a Mercer composition but this performance sounds like that the chords of that song.

Ruby is captured in broadcasts in July, and airchecks were captured for subsequent issue on an LP record that is more accessible than the original 16-inch transcription. Max Kaminsky is listed as playing in the Gothic Room on May 10 in *The New Yorker*. Braff is not listed at this location for the July 11 date either. While this July 11 date is suspect, it is taken from Bob Hilbert's research and therefore it remains the best available information at this time.

Ruby Braff—Pee Wee Russell Sextet: *American Bandstand*[44]
July 11, 1958 (possible date), Gothic Room, Hotel Duane, 237 Madison Avenue, New York
Ruby Braff (tp), Wayne Andre (tb), Pee Wee Russell (cl), Jimmy Jones (p), Bill Takas (b), Nat Ray (dm)
Theme (Blues)
Shoestring SS 109, AFRS *Bandstand USA* 37 16-inch transcription
Medley:
When You're Smiling
Shoestring SS 109, AFRS *Bandstand USA* 37 16-inch transcription
What Is There to Say?
Shoestring SS 109, AFRS *Bandstand USA* 37 16-inch transcription
I Would Do Anything for You (incomplete)
Shoestring SS 109, AFRS *Bandstand USA* 37 16-inch transcription
NOTE: "What Is There to Say?" is briefly interrupted by a news report and is incomplete on the LP release. "I Would Do Anything for You" is faded out just before the end of the performance. A recording of the transcription is available.

The following record is another favorite among some of Ruby's fans. It was issued in both monaural and stereophonic versions. Strangely, a CD version is labeled stereo but plays mono. While the music is identical on both versions, there is a special excitement in the stereophonic version when Roy Eldridge and Ruby Braff are clearly heard in different speakers. There was never an occasion when Roy did not rise to the challenge of competing with another trumpeter. Ruby was up to every challenge, responding in his own unique way.

This album was nominated for a Grammy Award in 1960. The winner was Ella Fitzgerald's album, *Ella Swings Lightly*. See the listing for the balance of this album in August 19 and for a listing of other issued recordings.

Ruby Braff and His Men: *Easy Now*
August 11, 1958, Webster Hall, New York
Ruby Braff, Emmett Berry (tp), Vic Dickenson (tb), Bob Wilber (cl, ts), Marty Napoleon (p), Mundell Lowe (g), Leonard Gaskin (b), Don Lamond (dm)
J2JB6217 For Now
RCA Victor LPM 1966, LSP 1966
J2JB6218 When My Sugar Walks Down the Street
RCA Victor LPM 1966, LSP 1966
J2JB6219 I Just Couldn't Take It, Baby
RCA Victor LPM 1966, LSP 1966
J2JB6220 My Walking Stick
RCA Victor LPM 1966, LSP 1966
J2JB6221 Little Man You've Had a Busy Day
RCA Victor LPM 1966, LSP 1966
J2JB6222 Give My Regards to Broadway
rejected
NOTE: See the comments following the August 19 session for additional issues of these tunes. This album received four and one-half stars in *DownBeat*. The LPM issue is monaural, while the LSP issue is stereophonic.

Residents of New York and the surrounding area were fortunate to be able to view a live jazz program, aired weekly on Thursday nights from 9 to 10:30 on WNTA from New Jersey and also made available for broadcasting on U.S Armed Forces TV in 31 other countries. Art Ford, a well known disc jockey, hosted this series of programs, and Ruby Braff was included among the guests on August 14. I would love to see a video version of this program, but I have located an audio recording. Each program in this series was spontaneous, and there were inevitable moments where musicians took a bit of time to determine who would play what. In my opinion, that just adds to the excitement. Kinescopes of a number of the programs, or at least portions of programs, have appeared in limited circulation. Perhaps there will be a comprehensive video issue someday. The Jazz Connoisseur label from England did issue a comprehensive set of audio recordings on cassettes years ago. That is the source of my recording of the following program.

Television Broadcast: ***Art Ford's Jazz Party***[45]
August 14, 1958, WNTA TV-Radio Broadcast, Newark, New Jersey
Ruby Braff (cnt), Tyree Glenn (tb), Hank D'Amico (cl), Georgie Auld (ts), Stuff Smith (v), Harry Shepherd (vib), Marty Napoleon (p), Mary Osborne (g), Vinnie Burke (b), Roy Burns (dm), Maxine Sullivan (voc and vtb-1), Art Ford (emcee)
Bugle Call Rag (theme)
  Jazz Connoisseur Cassette AF16-DP
Tea for Two
  Jazz Connoisseur Cassette AF16-DP
Sophisticated Lady (Osborne feature, with p, b, dm)
  Jazz Connoisseur Cassette AF16-DP
Keepin' Out of Mischief Now (v MS)
  Jazz Connoisseur Cassette AF16-DP
Sidewalks of New York (Glenn feature with rhythm section)
  Jazz Connoisseur Cassette AF16-DP
Out of Nowhere (Auld and Napoleon feature)
  Jazz Connoisseur Cassette AF16-DP
It's Only a Paper Moon (D'Amico feature, with rhythm section)
  Jazz Connoisseur Cassette AF16-DP
It's Wonderful (MS voc, with v, vib, and rhythm section)
  Jazz Connoisseur Cassette AF16-DP
Happy Birthday (for Stuff Smith)
  Jazz Connoisseur Cassette AF16-DP
Humoresque (Smith feature with rhythm section)
  Jazz Connoisseur Cassette AF16-DP
Sweetheart of Sigma Chi (Shepherd and Burns feature, with rhythm section)
  Jazz Connoisseur Cassette AF16-DP
You're Driving Me Crazy (Braff feature)
  Jazz Connoisseur Cassette AF16-DP
I Cover the Waterfront (Auld feature, with rhythm section)
  Jazz Connoisseur Cassette AF16-DP
S'posin'-1 (MS voc and vtb)
  Jazz Connoisseur Cassette AF16-DP
Jumpin' at the Woodside
  Jazz Connoisseur Cassette AF16-DP
NOTE: On "Sidewalks" and "Humoresque" the other horn players play only on the final chord. On "Crazy" the other horn players play only supporting ensemble parts. The full group plays on "Bugle," "Tea," "Mischief," "Nowhere," "Birthday," "S'Posin'," and "Woodside." One audio channel from the program was broadcast on AM and FM radio to permit television viewers to hear the performance in stereophonic sound if they simultaneously listened to their radio while watching.

The next session completes Ruby's album titled *Easy Now*. It is the first time he recorded with Hank Jones.

Ruby Braff and His Men: *Easy Now*
August 19, 1958, Webster Hall, New York
Ruby Braff (tp), Roy Eldridge (tp, flgh), Hank Jones (p), Mundell Lowe (g), Leonard Gaskin (b), Don Lamond (dm)
J2JB6222 Give My Regards to Broadway
RCA Victor LPM 1966, LSP 1966, Franklin Mint GMY 065
J2JB6393 Willow Weep for Me
RCA Victor LPM 1966, LSP 1966, (F) 75.578
J2JB6394 This Is My Lucky Day
RCA Victor LPM 1966, LSP 1966
J2JB6395 Someday You'll Be Sorry
RCA Victor LPM 1966, LSP 1966
J2JB6396 Yesterdays
RCA Victor LPM 1966, LSP 1966
J2JB6397 The Song Is Ended
RCA Victor LPM 1966, LSP 1966, (F) 75.578, 430.633
NOTE: All titles also on Bluebird 6456-2 (CD) titled *This Is My Lucky Day* and Avid 1011 with the title *Three Classic Albums.* Franklin Mint is a four-LP set titled *The Official Grammy Awards Archive Collection: Jazz Instrumentals* and other selections are by other artists. All titles on LPM/LSP 1966 also on RCA (F) PL 45140, RCA (G) 74321 18522 2 (while stereo master is indicated, it plays as monaural) and RCA (J) 5016. All titles except "The Song Is Ended" also are included on *Ruby Braff Complete Recordings with Hank Jones Featuring Jim Hall* on Gambit 69260. "The Song Is Ended" is included on Gambit (CD) 69261 titled *Ruby Braff with Dave McKenna Complete Original Quartet / Quintet Sessions.* RCA (F) 75.578 is titled *Jazz de Poche No. 22.* All titles are also included on Avid 1011 with the title *Three Classic Albums Plus*. Both monaural and stereophonic versions of the RCA LP were issued as shown.

Ruby next recorded an album for Warner Brothers, continuing the relationship he began with Hank Jones at RCA and beginning one with Al Cohn. But first there are hints of at least two other performances that are not specifically traced.

Ruby Braff and Pee Wee Russell[46]
Probably October 1958, unknown date and location
"A nice band at a New Jersey spot some weeks ago for 7 days."
Ruby Braff (tp), Vic Dickenson (tb), Pee Wee Russell (cl), Buzzy Drootin (dm)

A published photograph shows an early version of the Newport All Stars in 1958 showing Bud Freeman (ts), Ruby Braff (cnt), Pee Wee Russell (cl), George Wein (p), and Jack Lesberg (b).[47]

Ruby Braff and the Shubert Alley Cats: *Ruby Braff Goes Girl Crazy*
December 4, 1958, New York
Ruby Braff (tp), Al Cohn (cl, ts), Hank Jones (p), Jim Hall (g), George Duvivier (b), Buzzy Drootin (dm)
A50063 I Got Rhythm
    Warner Bros. W 1273, WS 1273
A50064 Bidin' My Time
    Warner Bros. W 1273, WS 1273, Valiant VS 104
A50065 But Not for Me
    Warner Bros. W 1273, WS 1273, Valiant VS 104

December 5, 1958, New York
Bob Haggart (b) replaces Duvivier
A50066 Could You Use Me
    Warner Bros. W 1273, WS 1273
A50067 Treat Me Rough
    Warner Bros. W 1273, WS 1273
A50068 Boy What Love Has Done to Me
    Warner Bros. W 1273, WS 1273
A50069 Embraceable You
    Warner Bros. W 1273, WS 1273, Valiant VS 104
A50070 Barbary Coast
    Warner Bros. W 1273, WS 1273
NOTE: All of the above also issued on AFRS Basic Musical Library 16-inch P series (popular) transcription 6669/70, Gambit 69260 (CD) which is titled *Ruby Braff Complete Recordings with Hank Jones Featuring Jim Hall* and Wounded Bird WOU 1273 bearing the original album title *Ruby Braff Goes Girl Crazy.* Master number A50071 was allocated to a medley spliced from master A50064/65/69 and issued as "Medley" on Warner Bros. W/WS 1281 titled *Jazz Festival in Hi-Fi.* It is also issued on AFRS P6535 16-inch P series, (E) WM 4015, WS8015, and Valiant (E) VS104. "Could You Use Me" is the correct title and it is listed on album jacket, but "Could You See Me" is listed incorrectly in some discographies.[48] Contrary to other published suggestions clarinet and/or tenor saxophone appear with trumpet/cornet on each track. This album received four stars in *DownBeat.*

Ruby next recorded for the Stere-o-craft label. I talked with jazz clarinetist Bobby Gordon during the 2001 March of Jazz program, and he said that his father was responsible for this label and these recordings. This is a very nice session that brings together musicians who have not performed with Ruby.

Ruby Braff Sextet: *You're Getting to Be a Habit with Me*
1958/59, New York
Ruby Braff (tp), Don Elliott (vib), Hank Jones (p), Mundell Lowe (g), Milt Hinton (b), Don Lamond (dm)

Let's Do It
Stere-o-craft RMC/RSC 507, Bell BLP 43, SLP 43, 206, Gambit 69260 (CD)
When Your Lover Has Gone
Stere-o-craft RMC/RSC 507, Bell BLP 43, SLP 43, 206, Gambit 69260 (CD)
Taking a Chance on Love
Stere-o-craft RMC/RSC 507, Bell BLP 43, SLP 43, 208, Gambit 69260 (CD)
You're Getting to Be a Habit With Me
Stere-o-craft RMC/RSC 507, Bell BLP 43, SLP 43, RSC 500, 205, Gambit 69260 (CD)

Nat Pierce (p) replaces Jones
1958/59, New York but a different date
Someday Sweetheart
Stere-o-craft RMC/RSC 507, Bell BLP 43, SLP 43, SS106 (45-rpm), 205
Swing That Music
Stere-o-craft RMC/RSC 507, Bell BLP 43, SLP 43, 207
You'd Be So Nice to Come Home To
Stere-o-craft RMC/RSC 507, Bell BLP 43, SLP 43, SS106 (45-rpm), 207
Cabin in the Pines
Stere-o-craft RMC/RSC 507, Bell BLP 43, SLP 43, 208
Lazy
Stere-o-craft RMC/RSC 507, Bell BLP 43, SLP 43, RSC500, 209
If Dreams Come True
Stere-o-craft RMC/RSC507, Bell BLP 43, SLP43, 209
NOTE: All titles on RMC/RSC 507 also on Hi-Life HL 43, Fresh Sound FSRCD 1614-2 with the same title as the original LP, and World Record Club (E) T312 (correcting the number in some discographies). The session also appears on a five-inch diameter prerecorded tape from World Record Club with the same issue number. Stere-o-craft 206–209 are all seven-inch diameter 33 1/3-rpm records for jukeboxes. The issue came complete with a miniature cover and title strips. Gambit 69260 is titled *Ruby Braff Complete Recordings with Hank Jones Featuring Jim Hall.* All titles are also on Avid 1011 with the title *Three Classic Albums Plus.*

Ruby next appeared one or more Monday nights at the Embers in New York, reuniting him with Ellis Larkins. The coverage in *DownBeat* mentioned musicians and tunes listed below but also continued, "Judging by the performance, the phone answerers should soon stop calling him *Rudy Brass* and get the name right. Good crowd reception." During the time, other nights featured Bobby Hackett's quartet and Teddy Wilson's trio.[49]

Ruby Braff at the Embers
January 1959 (first Monday night in 1959 and perhaps additional Monday performances thereafter, Embers, New York
Ruby Braff (cnt), Ellis Larkins (p), John Simmons (b), Bobby Donaldson (dm)
Sentimental Journey
St. James Infirmary
Gone with the Wind
Mean to Me
I Can't Give You Anything but Love
Just You, Just Me
NOTE: Other titles are not mentioned.

Ruby next traveled to Washington, D.C., to perform at the Bayou Club. Partial audience recordings survive to allow us to enjoy portions of these otherwise undocumented performances. It is unclear how long the engagements ran or whether they were only performing a single night on each occasion.

Ruby Braff at the Bayou Club
February 22, 1959, Bayou Club, Washington, D.C.
House band led by Wild Bill Whelan (tp, voc), Bobby Hackett, Ruby Braff (cnt), Bill Decker (tb), Val Scannell (cl), John Sweet (p), Bob Decker (b), Walt Gifford (dm)
St. James Infirmary
When the Saints Go Marching In (voc RB)
Other titles at this session feature Bobby Hackett, and Ruby Braff is not audible.
NOTE: A recording of these tunes is available but remains unissued.

Ruby finally appeared at the Metropole. This was a well known club for traditional jazz performances in New York. This is his earliest documented performance there, but it is certain that other appearances have gone undocumented.

Ruby Braff at the Metropole: Ruby Braff and Bobby Hackett Quartets Alternated[50]
Easter 1959: opening Good Friday (March 27, 1959) upstairs and performing on Friday and Saturday nights, Metropole, New York
Ruby Braff (tp), Al Williams (p), Whitey Mitchell (b), Marquis Foster (dm)

Ruby Braff at the Bayou Club
April 1959, Bayou Club, Washington D.C.
House band led by Wild Bill Whelan (tp, voc), Bobby Hackett, Ruby Braff (cnt), Bill Decker (tb), Val Scannell (cl), John Sweet (p), Bob Decker (b), Walt Gifford (dm)
Muskrat Ramble
NOTE: A recording of this tune is available but remains unissued.

No other details are known for the next listing, reportedly for a Bayou Club in New York. It appeared in a book about Bobby Hackett's career. Probably this location is actually the Bayou Club in Washington, D.C. If so, it extends the previous listing.

Bobby Hackett and Ruby Braff at the Bayou Club[51]
After April 25, 1959, for "part of the time" with Ruby Braff, Bayou Club, New York

Ruby's next recordings with Larry Adler are curiosities. Many people are not aware of Ruby's appearance since he is not credited on either of the LPs released from these recording sessions. Larry Adler told Gary Giddins that Bill Pemberton (b) and Bobby Donaldson (dm), who are generally listed in the personnel for this session, couldn't make the date and that they were replaced by Benjamin and Motian as listed below. Ruby just said to me, "Adler thought he knew how to play jazz." These were not among Ruby's favorite recordings, but they provide interesting listening and they do reunite Ruby with Ellis Larkins. Like Ruby's upcoming 1960 recording with Jackie Gleason, there are some interesting moments.

Larry Adler: *Larry Adler*
Larry Adler Quartet / Sextet
May 11–14, 1959, New York
Larry Adler (hca) acc. by Ruby Braff (tp-1), Ellis Larkins (p), Clifton "Skeeter" Best (el-g), Joe Benjamin (b), Paul Motian (dm)
How High the Moon-1
    Audio Fidelity AFSD 5916, Music & Memories MMD 1101
Blues in the Night-1
    Audio Fidelity AFSD 5916, Music & Memories MMD 1101
The Girl Friend-1
    Audio Fidelity AFSD 5916
Love for Sale-1
    Audio Fidelity AFSD 5916, Music & Memories MMD 1101
My Funny Valentine-1
    Audio Fidelity AFSD 5916, Music & Memories MMD 1101
Grisbi-1
    Audio Fidelity AFSD 5916, Music & Memories MMD 1101
This Can't Be Love-1
    Audio Fidelity AFSD 5916, Music & Memories MMD 1101
Summertime-1
    Audio Fidelity AFSD 5916, Music & Memories MMD 1101
There's a Boat That's Leavin' Soon for New York
    Audio Fidelity AFSD 5916, Music & Memories MMD 1101
Sophisticated Lady
    Audio Fidelity AFSD 5916, Music & Memories MMD 1101

Little Girl Blue
Audio Fidelity AFSD 5916
Genevieve
Audio Fidelity AFSD 5916, Music & Memories MMD 1101
Begin the Beguine-1
Audio Fidelity AFSD 5916, Music & Memories MMD 1101
NOTE: Other titles on MMD 1101 do not include Ruby Braff. The Music & Memories CD is titled *The Magic of Larry Adler*. All of the above are also included on *The Golden Era of Larry Adler, Volume 2* (E) Prestige B000024FQQV (CD). All of the above except "There's a Boat That's Leavin' Soon for New York," "Little Girl Blue" and "Genevieve" are also on Larry Adler, *The Best of Summertime,* Castle Pulse (E) PLS CD 131 (CD). The following record is even less well known than the first. Locating copies may pose a challenge for some of Ruby's fans.

Larry Adler Quartet/Sextet: *Larry Adler Again!*
Probably same dates and personnel
May 11–14, 1959, New York
Larry Adler (hca) acc. by Ruby Braff (tp-1), Ellis Larkins (p), Clifton "Skeeter" Best (el-g), Joe Benjamin (b) and Paul Motian (dm)
Night and Day
Audio Fidelity AFSD 6193, Castle Pulse (E) PLS CD 131 (CD)
September Song-1
Audio Fidelity AFSD 6193
Malaguena
Audio Fidelity AFSD 6193
Speak Low
Audio Fidelity AFSD 6193
But Not for Me-1
Audio Fidelity AFSD 6193
I've Got You Under My Skin
Audio Fidelity AFSD 6193
Someone to Watch Over Me
Audio Fidelity AFSD 6193
Falling in Love with Love
Audio Fidelity AFSD 6193
Love Walked In-1
Audio Fidelity AFSD 6193
Do It Again
Audio Fidelity AFSD 6193

Soon thereafter, Ruby returned to Toronto for a weeklong engagement at Basin Street. Further details remain unknown beyond brief coverage in the *Globe and Mail* newspaper.[52]

Basin Street Imperials
May 1959 (one week engagement), Basin Street, Toronto
Ruby Braff (tp), others unknown
My Monday Date

The following advertisement depicts one of the performances in this chapter:

Broadway's Best Buy!
This FRI. & SAT., 9 p.m. to 2 a.m.
JAZZ CONCERT & DANCE
at CHILDS PARAMOUNT BALLROOM
1501 Broadway, near 44th St.
The Greatest Names in Jazz!
BUCK CLAYTON COLEMAN HAWKINS
BUD FREEMAN PEEWEE RUSSELL
RUBY BRAFF J. C. HIGGINBOTHAM
JOE MARSALA CLIFF JACKSON
SONNY GREER TOMMY BENFORD
and many other Jazz Stars
Extra! ★ ANNE LEWIS in Sinful Songs
No Minimum or Cover

Figure 6.1: Advertisement from November 1956

Notes

[1] Dennis Stock, *Jazz Street* (New York: Doubleday, 1960), 86.
[2] Nat Hentoff, "Ruby Braff Missing Link of Jazz," *Esquire*, May 1958, 62.
[3] 90 minutes, black & white, 3/4" two videocassettes (this segment is the start of the second tape) Unissued but held at the Library of Congress with the listing VBE 2395-96.
[4] *DownBeat*, September 5, 1956, 36.
[5] *DownBeat*, August 8, 1956, 11.
[6] *DownBeat*, October 31, 1956, 45.
[7] Advertisement, *New York Times*, November 22, 1956.
[8] *DownBeat*, January 23, 1957, 8.
[9] *DownBeat*, February 6, 1957, 8.
[10] Robert Hilbert, *Pee Wee Russell: The Life of a Jazzman* (New York: Oxford University Press, 1993), 215. Robert Hilbert in collaboration with David Niven, *Pee Wee Speaks: A Discography of Pee Wee Russell* (Metuchen, NJ: Scarecrow Press, 1992), 249.
[11] Robert Hilbert, *Pee Wee Russell: The Life of a Jazzman* (New York: Oxford University Press, 1993), 215.
[12] Michael Brooks, CBS/Sony, and Michael Cuscuna, Mosaic Records, brought this discovery to my attention prior to its long overdue release.

[13] Michael Brooks, CBS/Sony. Michael Cuscuna of Mosaic Records brought this discovery to my attention prior to its long overdue release.
[14] John McDonough, "Salty Dog with a Hot Lip," *DownBeat*, January 27, 1977, 27–28 and my personal conversations with Ruby Braff.
[15] Michael Ruppli, *Atlantic Records*: *Volume 1 1947–1966* (Westport, CT: Greenwood Press, 1979), 95.
[16] Photo published in opening article for official 1958 festival program by Dom Cerulli, "Newport Past and Present," *5th Annual Newport Jazz Festival*, 7. Ruby did not perform in 1958, the year this program was published.
[17] Steve Jordan, *Rhythm Man* (Ann Arbor: University of Michigan Press, 1993), 116.
[18] Unissued titles recorded by Voice of America and held at the Library of Congress, Record 104612p+1X, shelf number RGA0032 (RWD 5023 A-B1). The Library of Congress catalog incorrectly shows "No One Else But You" as "Nobody Else But You."
[19] Whitney Balliett, *The New Yorker*, July 20, 1957, 83.
[20] The transcribed comments are taken from Miles Ahead: A Miles Davis Website: http://www.plosin.com/milesAhead/Sessions.aspx?s=570713. This is the source that lists the date of July 13, 1957.
[21] Information from Art Zimmerman.
[22] *The New Yorker* listed performances at Birdland in the issues of July 13, 20 and 27, 1957.
[23] Information from Art Zimmerman.
[24] *The New Yorker*, August 10, 1957, 7 and August 17, 1957, 8 (reporting that Ruby is "trumpeting at last in a band of his own"). Robert Hilbert, *Pee Wee Russell: The Life of a Jazzman* (New York: Oxford University Press, 1993), 217.
[25] Engagement reported in *DownBeat*, September 5, 1957, 8; reviewed in *DownBeat*, September 19, 1957, 39, where the tune titles are mentioned. According to the description in the review, the broadcast was probably the opening night for the engagement.
[26] Steve Jordan, *Rhythm Man* (Ann Arbor: University of Michigan Press, 1993), 114.
[27] *DownBeat*, September 19, 1957, 39.
[28] *DownBeat*, October 3, 1957, 58.
[29] *DownBeat*, October 3, 1957, 49 and *New York Times* August 24, 1957.
[30] Michael Cogswell, *Louis Armstrong: The Offstage Story of Satchmo* (Portland, OR: Collectors Press), 35.
[31] Charles Graham and Dan Morgenstern, *The Great Jazz Day* (Emeryville, CA: Woodford Press, 2000), 142.
[32] Photo, *The March of Jazz Celebrates Ruby Braff's 74th Birthday Party*, Arbors Records, 2001, 15–16.
[33] Michael Cogswell, *Louis Armstrong: The Offstage Story of Satchmo* (Portland, OR: Collectors Press), 42.
[34] George A. Borgman, "The One and Only Ruby Braff," in *Mississippi Rag*, December 1995, 5.
[35] Robert Hilbert, *Pee Wee Russell: The Life of a Jazzman* (New York: Oxford University Press, 1993), 217, *The New Yorker*, August 24, 1957, 8, and *The New Yorker*, August 31, 1957, 8.
[36] Reviews were published in the following issues of *Saturday Review* during 1958: January 11, February 8, April 12, May 17, June 14, and September 13.
[37] Nat Hentoff, "Ruby Braff Missing Link of Jazz," *Esquire*, May 1958, 62.
[38] Robert Hilbert, *Pee Wee Russell: The Life of a Jazzman* (New York: Oxford University Press, 1993), 221.

[39] Photo, *The March of Jazz Celebrates Ruby Braff's 74th Birthday Party*, Arbors Records, 2001, 15–16.
[40] *Coda Magazine*, June 1958, 10. Also cited in Robert Hilbert, *Pee Wee Russell: The Life of a Jazzman* (New York: Oxford University Press, 1993), 221, and *Coda Magazine*, August/September 1986, 33.
[41] Robert Hilbert in collaboration with David Niven, *Pee Wee Speaks: A Discography of Pee Wee Russell* (Metuchen, NJ: Scarecrow Press, 1992), 267–268.
[42] *The Globe and Mail*, June 28, 1958.
[43] *DownBeat*, August 21, 1958, 38, mentioned that "Ruby Braff and Eddie Condon cut a Vanguard LP."
[44] Robert Hilbert, *Pee Wee Russell: The Life of a Jazzman* (New York: Oxford University Press, 1993), 221, and Robert Hilbert in collaboration with David Niven, *Pee Wee Speaks: A Discography of Pee Wee Russell* (Metuchen, NJ: Scarecrow Press, 1992), 270.
[45] *Art Ford's Jazz Party 1958 TV and Radio Broadcasts,* by Bob Weir, self-published.
[46] Dan Morgenstern, *Coda Magazine*, December 1958, 6.
[47] George Wein, *Myself Among Others* (Cambridge, MA: Da Capo Press, 2003), unnumbered page in glossy photo section.
[48] Pointed out by Russ Chase.
[49] *DownBeat*, February 19, 1959, 44.
[50] John Norris, *Coda Magazine*, May 1959, 9–10.
[51] Harold Jones, *Bobby Hackett: A Bio-Discography* (Westport, CT: Greenwood Press, 1999), 13.
[52] *The Globe and Mail*, May 1959 (no date known).

Chapter 7

The Growing Role of Festivals and the Newport Jazz Festival All Stars: George Wein's Festivals and International Tours: July 1959–October 1964

Ruby had developed a relationship with George Wein in Boston from the early days of his performing career. Already he had performed at three Newport Jazz Festivals; however, George Wein had been working hard to extend the concept of jazz festivals to other cities and countries. George was truly a uniquely skilled entrepreneur in addition to his musical talents. Their early association led to a relationship that was mutually beneficial. The following performance of the Newport Jazz Festival All Stars united Ruby with a number of his musical friends. This was the first time Ruby performed at Newport with a group officially named the Newport All Stars. Ruby performed and recorded in Europe, Japan, and Mexico as part of various Newport All Star groups, building on the reputation that had continued to grow since the release of his Vanguard recordings.

The Newport Festival All Stars performed on the first day of the four-day festival and the set was broadcast on CBS and the Voice of America. This was the first time I can document that Ruby had performed with Ray Bryant.

Newport Jazz Festival All Stars[1]
July 2, 1959, 6th Newport Jazz Festival, Freebody Park, Newport, Rhode Island
Buck Clayton (tp), Vic Dickenson (tb), Pee Wee Russell (cl), Bud Freeman (ts), Ray Bryant (p), George Wein (p), Freddie Green (g), Champ Jones (b), Buzzy Drootin (dm)

Blues 1
    unissued, recording available
Blues 2
    unissued, recording available
Avalon
    Musica Jazz (It) MJP 1071

Wrap Your Troubles in Dreams
Musica Jazz (It) MJP 1071
Sweet Sue
Europa Jazz (It) EJ 1023, Curcio/I Giganti del Jazz (It) GJ 29,
Los Grandes del Jazz (Sp) GJ 29, complete session recording available

Add Ruby Braff (tp) and Jimmy Rushing (voc)
I'm Gonna Sit Right Down and Write Myself a Letter (voc JR)
Avid 1011
Goin' to Chicago (voc JR)
Avid 1011
St. Louis Blues (voc JR)
Avid 1011
NOTE: Musica Jazz (It) MJP 1071 is titled *Pee Wee Russell.* Film clips may exist from WJAR-TV held at Rhode Island Historical Society Library.[2] Avid 1011 is titled *Three Classic Albums Plus.* A complete recording of the performance is available.

There are several media references to George Wettling leading a group including Ruby when he performed at Jack Dempsey's Restaurant in New York. The date is unknown but stated to be a few years before 1964, in the late 1950s or early 1960s.[3] That anchors the next entry.

George Wettling
Unknown date, late '50s or early '60s but a few years before 1964, Jack Dempsey's Restaurant, Broadway, New York
Ruby Braff (tp), Ward Silloway (tb), Pee Wee Russell (cl), George Wettling (dm)

Braff was living in the same building at this time as Johnny Windhurst. He encouraged Pee Wee Russell to play the alto saxophone he had acquired from Peanuts Hucko.[4] Ruby and Pee Wee had an engagement "somewhere in New Jersey" during July.

Ruby Braff with Pee Wee Russell[5]
July 1959, "somewhere in New Jersey"
Ruby Braff (tp), Pee Wee Russell (as) and unknown others

During 1959, George Wein produced a festival held at the CNE Grandstand (Canadian National Exposition). About 5,000 people attended. The festival did not continue following 1959. Ruby Braff's appearance is described below. The festival's program showed that he performed the first evening, Friday, July 23.

Toronto Jazz Festival, Ruby Braff Quartet[6]
July 23, 1959, Toronto

Ruby Braff (tp), George Wein (p), Carne Bray (b), Buzzy Drootin (dm)
I Got Rhythm
Blue and Sentimental
Mean to Me
Fine and Mellow
Just You, Just Me

George Wein had created a festival tour, and Ruby was scheduled to perform as a member of the Newport All Stars on Friday afternoon, July 30 in French Lick Indiana. The event was named the Midwest Jazz Festival. Other musicians included Miles Davis, Sarah Vaughan, Jimmy Smith Trio, Sonny Stitt, The Kingston Trio, Horace Silver, Harry "Sweets" Edison, Toshiko, Roy Eldridge, and Pee Wee Russell. However, *DownBeat* reported that he did not appear in this festival despite the scheduled listing.[7]

Newport All Stars: Midwest Jazz Festival—Sheraton Jazz Festival[8]
July 30, 1959, French Lick, Indiana
Thursday evening, July 30 to Sunday evening, August 2, 1959, French Lick, Indiana, organized by George Wein
Ruby Braff did not perform

The festival in Indiana was followed three weeks later with the 1st Boston Jazz Festival where Ruby did appear.

1st Boston Jazz Festival[9]
August 23, 1959 (Sunday, final evening), Boston
Ruby Braff (tp), other details unknown but may have included Pee Wee Russell, Vic Dickenson, Buck Clayton, Bud Freeman, Eddie Condon, or Jimmy Rushing, all of whom appeared in other parts of the program

Bud Freeman reported the following story:[10]

> Vic Dickenson, Ruby Braff, and I were driving from New York City to Baltimore to play on a television show. As we reached the outskirts of Wilmington, we spotted a diner just off the highway. Ruby suggested that we stop at the diner for some coffee and a snack. Vic said that he didn't think that he'd be served there (this was about fifteen years ago) and we argued that they'd have to serve him so we went into the diner and sat down at a booth. Surely enough, the waitress called Ruby and me into the kitchen and asked, "Is that fellow colored?" "We all are," snapped Ruby. Before the waitress had a chance to say anything, we were all out the door.

Ruby returned to Toronto a month after the Toronto Jazz Festival, presumably capitalizing on the visibility from his performance as well as previous appearances. There are no details available beyond a date and location.

Ruby Braff[11]
August 31, 1959, Westover Hotel, Toronto

Ruby's next partner was Bob Brookmeyer. I have not found information about when they may have begun rehearsing, and there are no traces of performances other than the following recording for United Artists. Roy Decarava published a picture of Ruby with Bob Brookmeyer from an unknown date and location. Ruby looks downcast for some reason.[12]

Ruby Braff Quintet: *Blowing Around the World*
1959, New York
Ruby Braff (tp), Bob Brookmeyer (p), Barry Galbraith (g), Joe Benjamin (b), Buzzy Drootin (dm)
In a Little Spanish Town
    United Artists UAL 3045, UAS 6045
April in Paris
    United Artists UAL 3045, UAS 6045
Russian Lullaby
    United Artists UAL 3045, UAS 6045
Too-Ra-Loo-Ra-Loo-Ra
    United Artists UAL 3045, UAS 6045
Nagasaki
    United Artists UAL 3045, UAS 6045
Song of India
    United Artists UAL 3045, UAS 6045
Come Back to Sorrento
    United Artists UAL 3045, UAS 6045
South of the Border
    United Artists UAL 3045, UAS 6045
Loch Lomond
    United Artists UAL 3045, UAS 6045
Chinatown, My Chinatown
    United Artists UAL 3045, UAS 6045
NOTE: All titles also on United Artists (J) UAT 5014. This album received three stars in *DownBeat*.

Ruby Braff's Blindfold Test
Ruby Braff completed his second Blindfold Test for Leonard Feather, published in *DownBeat*. Feather cited Ruby's fifth place in the *DownBeat* Readers' Poll:[13]

> **Blindfold Test: Ruby Braff**
>
> An Exclusive Online Extra
>
> By Leonard Feather—01/21/1960

It came as something of a shock to Ruby Braff to learn recently that he had come fifth on trumpet in the 1959 *DownBeat* readers' poll—ahead of Harry James, Roy Eldridge, Louis Armstrong, Shorty Rogers, and many other big names. There is irony in the situation, for Ruby, as reported here some months ago, has been chronically unemployed—apparently a victim of the fact that he is a young exponent of an early style.

Most of the country's jazz clubs at present cater either to strictly modern audiences or to a no less rigid Dixieland crowd. Since Ruby falls into neither category (his playing smacks more of Buck Clayton than either Louis Armstrong or Miles Davis) things have been rugged for him in New York.

As his LPs indicate, Ruby has too individual a style and is too good a musician to change or subvert his personality. He is also a man of firm opinions, as the comments below indicate. Ruby was given no information about the records before or during the test.

The Records

1. Dukes of Dixieland. *Sweet Georgia Brown* (Audio Fidelity). Frank Assunto, trumpet.

I don't like scrambled eggs kind of music. Also, it sounds like a real commercial attempt, like one of those crowd pleasers where everybody's screaming and yelling and trying to keep up to the noise of the whole general confusion.

I think the outstanding guy on the record is the trumpet player. He sounds very good to me, and I'd like to see that guy put to better use than playing that kind of music.

It reminded me of sort of a Phil Napoleon kind of a thing—or the Dukes of Dixieland, although I've never heard them sound that fierce, that definite. And I don't think the trumpet player's up to being able to play like this fellow, though he's good. I'd give it two.

2. Charles Mingus. *Boogie Stop Shuffle* (Columbia). Horace Parlan, piano; Charles Mingus, bass, composer.

That's an interesting thing. I'd say that whoever did the writing for that, or put it together, was very influenced by Duke—and to me that automatically makes it a serious enough thing to discuss, you know?

Of course Duke would never have ended anything that way—he never would have let it get out of hand—but I'm nuts about the arrangement. I think it's very, very nice and I really enjoyed it, but I wish the solos were up to the magnificence of the arrangement. Like the piano player, when he started playing it got very unsettled and very weak—very confused—but the bass player sounded wonderful.

I don't know who it is but he sure sounds good. So just for the arrangement and for the spirit of it, I'll give it three.

3. Louis Armstrong/Oscar Peterson. *Moon Song* (Verve). Armstrong, trumpet, vocal; Peterson, piano; Herb Ellis, guitar; Ray Brown, bass; Louis Bellson, drums.

That was the boss, huh? The boss took over and it was just beautiful—wonderful to hear him do something different—you know, a different kind of song for a change. Gee, he just can't do anything but the greatest.

The accompaniment sounded just a little too busy behind him—a little bit on the noisy kick, you know? Outside of that it was wonderful, although this was not a good key for him to sing in; he was straining. He'd sound better with a more modern, Basie-type rhythm section. This is too busy.

But even if I hadn't heard the record and his name was on it I'd give it five stars anyway. Is that the most stars you can give? Yes? Okay—give it five and a half.

4. **Quincy Jones**. *Tickle-Toe* (Mercury). Clark Terry, Harry Edison, trumpet solos.

What a wonderful record—all stars for those guys. That's *Tickle-Toe,* isn't it? Beautiful band! I thought I heard Clark Terry—did I hear him? It sounded awfully good, and the other trumpet player sounded good, too. I don't know who it was, but they all sounded good to me.

Just let me ask you one thing: that isn't a band that's together all the time, is it? The reason I say it is because it's amazing, very often today they record bands right on the spot and they sound so wonderful, and people take them for granted because they hear a lot of it; but in the old days, if they heard a band that sounded *one-half* as good, they'd say "Wow—the greatest band in the world!" It's just that their musicianship is so far above what it used to be.

Wonderful music! Five stars.

5. **Ornette Coleman**. *Mind And Time* (Contemporary). Coleman, alto; Don Cherry, trumpet; Percy Heath, bass; Shelly Manne, drums.

Wow—saved by the bass player! Once I heard Charlie Parker sound a little bit like that when he was completely sick—as sick as he could possibly be. Well, I'm sure this could never be anybody like that and I hope this guy doesn't play like this all the time—it sounded like utter confusion and madness—terrible! What is that?

I think the trumpet player unfortunately got hung up, or influenced, by the first chorus of the alto player—he sounded pretty panicky too. I have never heard anything as disjointed and mixed-up and crazy as that in my life. Good heavens!

As for the composition, I think it was a very poor exercise, that's all. No stars except for the bass player—he was good, so a half a star because of him.

6. **Count Basie**. *I Ain't Got Nobody* (from *Spirituals To Swing*; Vanguard). Piano solo rec. 1939, with Walter Page, bass; Jo Jones, drums.

That has to be the greatest. That sounds like Count, Jo Jones—huh? Wonderful, anything he does. Five and a half stars for him too! He sounds a little reluctant to do a whole piano bit there by himself. He sounds a little as though he's saying, "Oh, do I have to?" But it's Count, it's got to be him. I liked him on the slow chorus; I like him on everything because every time he touches a chord he seems to be an expert on how to voice it on the piano. You know that's a very hard thing to do: when he touches a chord, even if it's three lousy notes, he makes them sound beautiful.

7. **Horace Silver**. *Swingin' The Samba* (Blue Note). Blue Mitchell, trumpet; Louis Hayes, drums.

Well, if it was a showcase for the drummer, it was all right, because the drums sounded very, very good. But jazz being an American music, I don't think they have to borrow from any of the Latin-American countries for their themes. Aside from the trumpet player, I didn't like anything on there. The head itself didn't make it—I can't think of anything good about it except the drums and trumpet—that's about all. I'd give it about one and a half stars for the drums and the trumpet.

8. **Buck Clayton/Harry Edison.** *Come With Me* (Verve). Jimmy Forrest, tenor.

Gee, that was nice, very enjoyable. I thought I heard some Buck Clayton on there somewhere—sounded very nice—and I heard someone that sounded a little like Diz, but not quite. I got the feeling it could have been Shad Collins—I've heard him play that way. He's a very talented cat too—very, very good. The tenor man is familiar to me but I can't place him—I've played with him, I think, but I just don't know who it is. It's a very swinging record—very nice. I'd give that four stars.

9. **Cootie Williams.** *On The Sunny Side of the Street* (Jaro). Williams, trumpet and vocal.

That's a rather strange record—never heard anything like that. I don't like that lick they were playing together—that unison thing. It sounded kind of muddy. All in all, it's a good performance, but I don't know, the singer doesn't seem too comfortable about that song, or else he's trying too hard. It's kind of forced. He should have sung it slower. He loses the picture of the song in that tempo.

I enjoyed the trumpet solo—it sounded very, very good—I don't know who that could be, but you know who I've heard play like that, at different times in his life? I've heard Red Allen sound like that. On that kick, you know. It's a good record—I'd give it three.

DownBeat published a two-page article January 21, 1960 titled "Stereo Shopping with Ruby Braff" in which Ruby expressed his opinions about his stereo equipment. An accompanying photo showed Ruby seated in a chair with his horn beside his turntable, with records in the background.

Ruby Braff appeared at the Tally-Ho Club in Pennsylvania and Storyville Club in Boston during early 1960. John Hammond reportedly planned to record Ruby at the Embers during the engagement the week of March 13 for Columbia Records. The article also reported that Ruby would tour the Midwest with Kenny Davern (cl and as) and Buzzy Drootin (dm).[14] Ruby and Kenny both lived in the same building at the time in Riverdale. They appeared at the Roundtable in Toledo, Ohio, in April with a group that also included Bobby Pratt (tb and p) and Russell George (b).[15] This was Ruby's first documented engagement with Kenny Davern; however, the group failed to find other jobs. Ruby also performed at the Embers before recording with Jackie Gleason in a session in the long-running series for Capitol Records.

Ruby Braff[16]
Early 1960 for "a week or two," Storyville Club, Boston
Details unknown

Ruby Braff and Pee Wee Russell[17]
Early 1960 for "an occasional weekend job," Tally-Ho Club, Philadelphia, PA
Ruby Braff (cnt), Pee Wee Russell (cl), and other musicians

Ruby Braff Quartet[18]
March 7–12, 1960, (except Sundays), Embers, New York
Ruby Braff (cnt), Ellis Larkins (p), Aaron Bell (b), Buzzy Drootin (dm)

The New Yorker announced Ruby's appearance at the Embers with the following words: "The unmitigated trumpet of Ruby Braff, a fine broth of a boy, will be added to the menu, along with his foursome." This group once again unites Ruby with Ellis Larkins. John Hammond obtained this booking for Ruby. He alternated with the Dorothy Donegan Trio as reported in the available advertisement.

Ruby Braff Quartet[19] **(see Figure 7.1)**
March 14–19, 1960, Embers, New York
Ruby Braff (cnt), Ellis Larkins (p), Aaron Bell (b), Buzzy Drootin (dm)

Ruby's principles surfaced again in an article from *Melody Maker*.[20] They are largely unchanged from Nat Hentoff's earlier interview published in 1958 in *Esquire* magazine already quoted. Ruby was often unyielding on points that reflected on the quality of his performances. Simply put, he set high standards and applied them both to himself and to others.

> The only thing that bothers me a bit is working in front of people, after a period of inactivity. However, I suppose I'll get over this touch of nervousness after the first couple of nights. Convictions can get you in hot water. Before long, it's on the grapevine that you're 'difficult.' But despite the cost, I will not cheat people by playing in a way that is not natural for me or by playing with musicians whom I don't care for. All I want to do is play good music. And I don't believe it's necessary to change my personality or playing in order to do so.

The article continued, indicating that Ruby planned to tour under the auspices of a booking agent from Columbus, Ohio, with Buzzy Drootin (dm) and Kenny Davern (cl, as), perhaps with Ronnie Ball (p). Ruby continued, "Frankly, I'd like to have Basie for the piano chair, but I guess he's pretty busy these days. I have been trying to get a group over to England ever since Louis Armstrong told me that the jazz fans over there were interested in me. A few times in recent years it looked as if I would be able to make it. But now, I don't know just when I'll be able to do the trip. George Wein has spoken to me about a tour in the future but nothing is definite. It would make me very happy if it worked out."

Ruby Braff—As Part of Midwest Tour[21]
April 4, 1960, for an unknown number of days, Roundtable, Toledo, Ohio
Ruby Braff (cnt), Kenny Davern (cl, as), Bobby Pratt (tb, p), and Russell George (b), Buzzy Drootin (dm)

Kenny Davern returned to New York after this engagement. Further bookings on Ruby's hopes for a Midwest Tour have not been traced.

Jackie Gleason: *Lazy Lively Love*
Jackie Gleason (conducting)
Large string orchestra or small jazz group featuring Ruby Braff, Buck Clayton, Yank Lawson (tp), Lawrence Brown, Tyree Glenn (tb), Buster Bailey, Andy Fitzgerald (cl), Claude Hopkins (p), Al Caiola (g), Milt Hinton (b), unknown (dm)—perhaps Specs Powell (dm), George Williams (arr)
April 25, 1960 (released 1961)
Speak Low
    Capitol W 1439, Capitol CDP 7243 8 52541 2 3
Limehouse Blues
    Capitol W 1439
Lover Man
    Capitol W 1439, Capitol CDP 7243 8 52541 2 3
Too Close for Comfort
    Capitol W 1439
It Had to Be You
    Capitol W 1439
I'm Gonna Sit Right Down and Write Myself a Letter
    Capitol W 1439
Brokenhearted
    Capitol W 1439
Breezin' Along With the Breeze
    Capitol W 1439
Smile
    Capitol W 1439, Capitol CDP 7243 8 52541 2 3
On the Street Where You Live
    Capitol W 1439
Because of You
    Capitol W 1439
Exactly Like You
    Capitol W 1439
NOTE: Ruby is not featured on all titles but is audible throughout. Capitol CDP 7243 8 52541 2 3 is a two- CD compilation titled *The Romantic Moods of Jackie Gleason.* The recording date is listed in that release.

The Gleason album's arrangements provide interludes for short solos against an admittedly rigid but steady rhythmic foundation. Having said that, this is worth a listen for some nice moments throughout the session. Woody Allen incorporated this version of "Limehouse Blues" in the soundtrack of his 1990 feature film *Alice*. To me, Ruby is the most comfortable on "Exactly Like You."

Ruby described the Jackie Gleason session in an interview in *Cadence*:[22]

> That was a very rare situation where he specifically wanted me to play. As a matter of fact, I told him I wouldn't even finish the date and I only did a few of them. He said, 'Aren't you going to do the rest of them?' I said, 'No, because you're the worst.' It was such a strange thing, he had two of everything. Two trumpets, two clarinets, a bunch of violins, if I'm not mistaken, and about 2000 trombones. It was just silly, really silly. So I just stood there that day because of my friend Yank Lawson. He said, 'Don't go away. Jesus don't leave me here.' So I says, 'Okay, but I'm not comin' back. Jesus Christ this guy's weird.'

But of course this was an example of Ruby's artistic principles overriding his choices of relationships that might have led to earning income from future recording sessions involving Gleason. Ruby was guided by artistic rather than practical or commercial considerations. Uncompromising behavior can be seen by some as strength of commitment while others may view it as a sign of inflexibility. There can be no doubt how Ruby saw it. He was unyielding and felt that his reputation gave him the right to his commitment to his standards, although he did express some envy of Bobby Hackett's ability to gain financially from participating in Gleason's recordings.

George Wein reported that Ruby Braff would once again open the season at the summer location for Storyville on Cape Cod on June 24, 1960.[23] The group likely continued there following the Newport Jazz Festival.

Ruby Braff at Storyville
June 24 through at least July 1, 1960, Storyville Club, Cape Cod, Massachusetts
Ruby Braff (cnt), Don Kenney (b), perhaps including Pee Wee Russell, George Wein, and Buzzy Drootin during at least part of the engagement

Burt Goldblatt published a photo of Ruby with Pee Wee Russell and George Wein. Ruby and Pee Wee are shown after exchanging instruments before they performed as a joke for this photo.[24] It is nice to see Ruby's sense of humor captured in this picture.

Newport All Stars[25]
July 2, 1960, 7th Newport Jazz Festival, Freebody Park, Newport, Rhode Island (first day of three-day festival)
Jazz USA telecast WJAR-TV released in 26 film series made for US Information Services and World Jazz Series, CBS broadcast July 3, 1960, Ruby Braff included in program numbers 2, 8, 21
Ruby Braff (cnt), Pee Wee Russell (cl), George Wein (p), Don Kenney (b), Buzzy Drootin (dm)
Just You, Just Me
Fine and Mellow
Rosetta
Mean to Me
Three Little Words

NOTE: Both audio and video recordings of four of these tunes are available but remain unissued. "Mean to Me" has only been available to the author as an audio recording. "Just You, Just Me" and an incomplete version of "Rosetta" are part of the second part of the filmed series *Jazz USA*. This film also included the Newport Youth Band, Cannonball Adderley, and Herbie Mann.[26] The eighth film included the Newport Youth Band, Ruby Braff, and Andy Marsala. The 21st film included the Newport Youth Band, Ruby Braff, and Cannonball Adderley.[27] Ruby's comments on the Library of Congress audio recording refer to Don Kenney currently appearing with him at Storyville. At the time of publication, an audio version of this performance is available for downloading from WolfgangsVault.com.

The Saturday night festival performance was shortened by rioting. As a result, George Wein was not involved in planning a Newport Festival for 1961. Perhaps this provided him some extra time to tour with the Newport All Stars.

Ruby Braff at Storyville
Following Newport Jazz Festival through perhaps mid or late July 1960, Storyville Club, Cape Cod, Massachusetts
Ruby Braff (cnt), Don Kenney (b), perhaps including Pee Wee Russell, George Wein, and Buzzy Drootin during at least part of the engagement

Following his engagement at Storyville on Cape Cod, Ruby returned to Toronto to perform for his growing base of fans.

Ruby Braff[28]
August 1, 1960, for one week, Town Tavern, Toronto
Ruby Braff (cnt), Nat Pierce (p), Don Kenney (b), Buzzy Drootin (dm)

As the year progressed, *DownBeat* magazine carried an ad announcing that Ruby Braff and Bobby Hackett were accepting a limited number of jazz trumpet students in the New York area (see Figure 7.2).[29] Ruby demonstrated some qualities associated with entrepreneurs when he worked to organize various musical groups and this may be another aspect of this side of his behavior. One of his inspirations may have even been George Wein's successes with promoting jazz festivals and bringing good music to the attention of celebrities and business leaders. While later tension developed between them, there is no doubt that they had a very symbiotic relationship for many years.

George Wein wrote about a New Year's Eve party at his New York apartment:[30]

> That night [December 31, 1960] we threw a grand New Year's Eve party; there were maybe thirty or forty people in attendance, half of them friends of Judy Brown. I think I had Ruby Braff and Pee Wee Russell playing. Joyce cooked dinner at 10 o'clock. At midnight everybody kissed each other, and most of Ju-

> dy's friends said goodnight; the party half dispersed. I didn't tell anyone about our special guests. They simply arrived: Richard Burton, Sir Laurence Olivier, Peter Brook, Clive Revill, Elizabeth Seal, a whole coterie of stars from the English theater. People were coming up to me and whispering, 'I thought I just saw you walk in with someone. Was it?' I replied, 'If it looks like who you think it is, it probably is.' The electricity was palpable.

The following performance probably falls within Ralph Sutton's appearance at Condon's for three weeks in January 1961; however, it could come during Ruby's later stand at that club that began in early July.[31] This is Ruby's earliest recorded performance with Ralph Sutton. Part of this lively performance has been commercially issued.

Ruby Braff and Ralph Sutton at Condon's: *Recovered Treasures*
Unknown date, perhaps 1961 during the above engagement, Condon's, New York
Ruby Braff (cnt), Ralph Sutton (p), Bill Takas (b), and unknown (dm)—perhaps Buzzy Drootin (dm)
You Meet the Nicest People in Your Dreams
    Jump JCD 12-29
Sugar
Undecided
Medley:
  I've Got a Right to Sing the Blues
  Beale Street Blues
  St. James Infirmary
Two Sleepy People
    Jump JCD 12-29
I Would Do Anything for You
You're Lucky to Me
Save It Pretty Mama
    Jump JCD 12-29
Jeepers Creepers
Lazy River
    Jump JCD 12-29
NOTE: Four tunes have been issued on Jump JCD 12-29. Audio recordings of the other eight tunes are available but remain unissued. Jump JCD 12-29 bears the title I created for it, *Ruby Braff and His Musical Friends: Recovered Treasures.* See the album notes I wrote for this release in the appendix for background information on this session.

Ruby began rehearsing with Marshall Brown to form yet another new group, beginning in late December or early January.[32] Perhaps his recent work with Bob Brookmeyer stimulated his search for an ongoing partner who played the trombone.

Ruby Braff–Marshall Brown Sextet[33]
Week of February 20, 1961, Town Tavern, Toronto
Ruby Braff (cnt), Marshall Brown (vtb), Tommy Newsom (ts), Howard Collins (g), Don Kenney (b), Buzzy Drootin (dm)
The following tunes were among those played on February 24:
Satin Doll
Easy Living
Mood Indigo
Royal Garden Blues
Caravan

The following reference probably refers to an engagement at Condon's beginning in July; however, it is included here as well, based on Bob Hilbert's research.

Pee Wee Russell and Ruby Braff at Condon's[34]
Spring 1961, Condon's, New York
Ruby Braff (tp), Marshall Brown (vtb), Pee Wee Russell (cl), plus unknown others

Ruby is not listed in *The New Yorker* from January to June 1961 for Condon's so Hilbert's reference probably pertains to the engagement beginning July 6. Of course it is quite possible that Ruby would have been a guest at Condon's during these months.

Ruby did join Bobby Hackett who was listed in *The New Yorker* during this time for at least the following night. A portion of this performance has been released on compact disc and, at the time of publication, it is the only commercially issued recording that pairs these two fine cornetists.

Ruby Braff and Bobby Hackett at Condon's: *Recovered Treasures*
March 2, 1961, Condon's, New York
Ruby Braff, Bobby Hackett (cnt), Peanuts Hucko (cl), Dave McKenna (p), unknown (b), Jake Hanna (dm)—perhaps Bill Takas (b)
Struttin' with Some Barbecue
Jump JCD 12-29
Medley:
Sugar
Jump JCD 12-29
I Can't Give You Anything but Love
Jump JCD 12-29
Lover Come Back to Me
Jump JCD 12-29

Medley:
Sweet Lorraine (Braff feature)
Jump JCD 12-29
Makin' Whoopee (Hucko feature)
unissued but a recording is available
Keepin' Out of Mischief Now (Hackett feature)
Jump JCD 12-29
Sweet Georgia Brown
Jump JCD 12-29
NOTE: Jump JCD 12-29 is titled *Ruby Braff and His Musical Friends: Recovered Treasures.* See the album notes I wrote for this release in the appendix for background information on this session.

Bobby Hackett closed at Condon's on March 11 after opening for the final week in January. During this time Eddie Condon did not play, but circulated among the patrons many evenings. Condon returned to the bandstand March 13 (club was closed Sundays) with Max Kaminsky, Bob Wilber, and others following Hackett's departure. It is likely that Ruby and Peanuts were guest artists the night the above performance was recorded and not appearing on a nightly basis.[35]

Ruby was a member of the Newport All Stars for a European tour that ran from April 8 until April 22. George Wein planned to discontinue the Newport Jazz Festival in 1961, following the rioting that shortened the Saturday night performance and ended the festival prematurely. Subsequently, different organizers did present a festival at Newport that year.

A photo exists of the Newport All Stars performing in Berlin, April 8, 1961, and includes George Wein, Pee Wee Russell, Ruby Braff, Jimmy Woode, Vic Dickenson, and Buzzy Drootin.[36] With the photo is a reproduction of a poster announcing the concert program.[37]

Newport All Stars[38]
April 8, 1961, Sportpalast, Berlin, Germany
Ruby Braff (cnt), Vic Dickenson (tb), Pee Wee Russell (cl), George Wein (p), Jimmy Woode (b), Buzzy Drootin (dm)
Royal Garden Blues
Exactly Like You
Basin Street Blues (featuring VD)
Other tunes not mentioned

Newport All Stars[39]
April 9, 1961, Audi-Max, Hamburg, Germany
Ruby Braff (cnt), Vic Dickenson (tb), Pee Wee Russell (cl), George Wein (p), Jimmy Woode (b), Buzzy Drootin (dm)

A copy of another poster provides another date on this tour in Cologne, Germany.

Newport All Stars[40]
April 12, 1961, Gürzenich, Cologne, Germany

Newport All Stars[41]
April 1961, Copenhagen
Ruby Braff (cnt), Vic Dickenson (tb), Pee Wee Russell (cl), George Wein (p), Jimmy Woode (b), Buzzy Drootin (dm)

Newport All Stars
April 14, 1961, Essen Jazz Festival, WDR (Westdeutscher Rundfunk) broadcast in two parts, Essen, Germany
Ruby Braff (cnt), Vic Dickenson (tb), Pee Wee Russell (cl), George Wein (p), Jimmy Woode (b), Buzzy Drootin (dm)
Royal Garden Blues (incomplete)
Blue and Sentimental
Just You, Just Me
Exactly Like You
Sugar
I've Found a New Baby
Basin Street Blues (VD feature)
NOTE: A recording of these tunes is available but remains unissued.

A photograph exists of the Newport All Stars performing in Tilburg on April 15, 1961. It shows Pee Wee Russell, Jimmy Woode, Ruby Braff, and Vic Dickenson.[42] This supports the following entry, but no recordings are available to the author.

Newport All Stars[43]
April 15, 1961, Tilburg, The Netherlands

Newport All Stars
April 17–19, 1961 Baden-Baden, Germany, SWF-TV (Suedwestfunk)—telecast October 9, 1961
Ruby Braff (cnt), Vic Dickenson (tb), Pee Wee Russell (cl), George Wein (p), Jimmy Woode (b), Buzzy Drootin (dm)
Way Down Yonder in New Orleans*
C Jam Blues
Jazz Train Blues*
Sugar (Russell feature)
Lover Come Back to Me (Dickenson feature)
When Your Lover Has Gone (Braff feature)

NOTE: From the 23rd edition of a telecast produced by Joachim E. Berendt, *Jazz Heard and Seen.* The balance of the program featured Roland Kirk. A video recording of this program is available and a separate audio recording is available for the two tunes marked with an asterisk. The basis for the title of the tune "Jazz Train Blues" becomes obvious when you see the unusual stage setting for the broadcast. The bandstand is designed to resemble an old steam locomotive.

Newport All Stars: *Midnight Concert in Paris*[44]
April 22, 1961, Olympia Theater, Paris
Ruby Braff (tp), Vic Dickenson (tb), Pee Wee Russell (cl), George Wein (p), Jimmy Woode (b), Buzzy Drootin (dm)
(PB 8943) I've Found a New Baby
    Smash (F) 27023, SRS 67023
(PB 8944) When Your Lover Has Gone
    unissued
(PB 8945) Ain't Misbehavin'
    unissued
(PB 8946) When My Sugar Walks Down the Street
    Smash (F) 27023, SRS 67023
(PB 8947) If I Had You
    unissued
(PB 8948) Sweet Georgia Brown
    Smash (F) 27023, SRS 67023
(PB 8949) Lover Come Back to Me
    Smash (F) 27023
(PB 8950) Blue and Sentimental
    Smash (F) 27023, SRS 67023, Philips
(PB 8951) I May Be Wrong
    unissued
(PB 8952) Basin Street Blues
    unissued
(PB 8953) Jeepers Creepers
    unissued
(PB 8954) These Foolish Things
    unissued
(PB 8955) Sugar
    Smash (F) 27023, SRS 67023
(PB 8956) Everyone's Blues
    unissued
(PB 8957) Blues Pour Commencer
    Smash (F) 27023, SRS 67023, Philips 7552005 (cassette)
(PB 8958) Everyone's Blues
    unissued
(PB 8959) Blues Pour Commencer
    unissued

NOTE: All performances also on Mercury (F) 134614, Mercury International (E) 21047, Philips (E) BL7665, and (J) SM 7104. Smash (F) SRS 67023 is a stereo version of the above. All of the above issued performances are included in the 109th release in the Jazz in Paris CD series from Universal Music, titled *Midnight Concert at the Olympia*, Gitanes 984 596-9. One of the above selections was included on a Japanese release prepared by Dan Morgenstern for a 50th Anniversary of Mercury Records compilation. "Blues Pour Commencer" can be translated as "Blues to Begin." This album received three stars in *Down-Beat.*

Two concerts were performed. The Newport All Stars played the first part of each concert, and the Buck Clayton All Stars followed. Specifically, the Newport All Stars performed at 5–6:30 p.m. on April 22 and from midnight to 1:30 a.m., so the midnight concert was actually on April 23.[45] Bob Hilbert's Pee Wee Russell discography incorrectly lists the date as April 15, 1961.[46] That incorrect date was from album notes signed by George Wein where he reported the following:

> April 15, 1961 was a momentous day in French history . . . the day the generals of the French Army in Algiers chose to revolt against the government of Charles de Gaulle. That spring day also saw the Newport Jazz Festival All Stars making their first concert appearance in Paris at the Olympia Theater. We gave two concerts that fateful day and, fortunately, the advance ticket sale for both had been good. It would have been a dismal evening for both the musicians and the promoters if this had not been the case. After 12 noon on that day of revolution, not a single ticket was sold at the box office. . . . We did completely different programs for each of the two concerts as we knew we were to be recorded. The selections in this album represent the best of both performances.

George Wein is undoubtedly correct on all other details; however, the failed uprising of some retired French generals against Charles De Gaulle began on April 21, 1961, during the Algerian War.

Beyond the caption for a published photograph, there is no further information about Ruby appearing with Bud Freeman sometime in 1961 in Steubenville, Ohio. That engagement is listed here arbitrarily.

Ruby Braff and Bud Freeman[47]
1961, Steubenville, Ohio
Ruby Braff (tp), Bud Freeman (ts), Chuck Folds (p), Bill Crow (b), Buzzy Drootin (dm)

George Wein did not produce the 1961 jazz festival held in Newport, Rhode Island, as a consequence of the rioting in 1960. He returned as producer in 1962. So, Ruby did not appear at Newport in 1961. The following may also be the engagement listed for spring 1961 by Bob Hilbert and Dan Morgenstern[48] since there was no engagement listed in *The New Yorker* from January–June 1961 for

Ruby Braff appearing at Condon's. This is the first time I have documented Ruby playing with John Bunch.

Eddie Condon's All Stars[49]
July 6–September 13, 1961, Condon's, 330 East 56th Street, New York (closed Sundays)—except July 15
Ruby Braff (cnt), Marshall Brown (tb), Pee Wee Russell (cl), Jack Keller or John Bunch (p), Eddie Condon (g), Ronnie Bedford (dm), and possibly others at various times
Mean to Me
As Long As I Live
I'm Yours
Birth of the Blues
Moonglow

John S. Wilson wrote the following:[50]

> For the first time in more than a year, the band at Condon's is under Mr. Condon's leadership and he is celebrating the occasion by mounting the stand for every set, giving the downbeat for fast numbers with several reckless raps on the shell of his guitar and starting the slower ones with commanding thumps of his heal.

While Marshall Brown and Ruby were waiting for a September engagement in Toronto they agreed to appear in Eddie Condon's band. The Ruby Braff–Marshall Brown Sextet did appear in at least one jazz festival during this time, so it is likely that Ruby did not appear every night at Condon's during this period.

Ruby Braff–Marshall Brown Sextet[51]
July 15, 1961, Virginia Beach Jazz Festival, Alan B. Shepard Convention Dome, Virginia Beach, Virginia
Ruby Braff (tp, voc), Marshall Brown (vtb), Tommy Newsom (ts), Howard Collins (g), Don Kenney (b), Buzzy Drootin (dm)—the program credits arrangements to Marshall Brown, Don Sebesky, and Cy Johnson
Crazy Rhythm

Condon's[52]
Continuing August–September 13, 1961, Condon's, New York "until further notice"
Ruby Braff (cnt), Marshall Brown (vtb), Pee Wee Russell (cl), John Bunch (p), Eddie Condon (g), Ronnie Bedford (dm)

Ruby recorded his second LP for United Artists, this time with Marshall Brown instead of Bob Brookmeyer. Since they had been playing together some time, this appears to be a successful partnership. Probably the recording preceded a three-week engagement in Toronto, marking Ruby's latest return to that city.

Ruby Braff–Marshall Brown Sextet: *Ruby Braff–Marshall Brown Sextet*[53]
Ruby Braff (tp, voc), Marshall Brown (vtb), Tommy Newsom (ts), Howard Collins (g), Don Kenney (b), Buzzy Drootin (dm)
1961, (probably July or August during engagement at Condon's), New York
Just in Time
 United Artists UAL 4093, UAS 5093, Fresh Sound (Sp) 2609.411
Cinnamon Kisses
 United Artists UAL 4093, UAS 5093, Fresh Sound (Sp) 2609.411
In a Sentimental Mood
 United Artists UAL 4093, UAS 5093, Fresh Sound (Sp) 2609.411
Like Someone in Love (voc)
 United Artists UAL 4093, UAS 5093, Fresh Sound (Sp) 2609.411
Crazy Rhythm
 United Artists UAL 4093, UAS 5093, Fresh Sound (Sp) 2609.411
I Got It Bad and That Ain't Good
 United Artists UAL 4093, UAS 5093, Fresh Sound (Sp) 2609.411
Love Is Just around the Corner
 United Artists UAL 4093, UAS 5093, Fresh Sound (Sp) 2609.411
You're Lucky to Me (voc)
 United Artists UAL 4093, UAS 5093, Fresh Sound (Sp) 2609.411
Easy Living (voc)
 United Artists UAL 4093, UAS 5093, Fresh Sound (Sp) 2609.411
I'm Beginning to See the Light
 United Artists UAL 4093, UAS 5093, Fresh Sound (Sp) 2609.411
I Let a Song Go Out of My Heart
 United Artists UAL 4093, UAS 5093, Fresh Sound (Sp) 2609.411
Sweet Georgia Brown
 United Artists UAL 4093, UAS 5093, Fresh Sound (Sp) 2609.411

Ruby Braff–Marshall Brown Sextet[54]
Three-week engagement including weeks of September 11, 18, 25, 1961, Town Tavern, Toronto
Ruby Braff (cnt), Marshall Brown (vtb), Tommy Newsom (ts), Howard Collins (g), Bill Crow (b), Buzzy Drootin (dm)
Nobody Else But You
Hear Me Talkin' to You
Rockin' in Rhythm

Ruby and Marshall Brown had very different ideas about the performance of jazz music. Ruby said that at one engagement, probably this one in Toronto, that Marshall dropped to a knee during one of his solos for theatrical effect. Ruby claimed that he exclaimed, "For God's sake, Marshall, just stand up and play."

The growing tension between them spelled the end of this musical association, although they continued to appear together as members of the Newport All Stars for nearly another year because of Marshall's relationship with the Newport Jazz Festival.

Condon's[55]
October 12–November 4, 1961, New York
Ruby Braff (cnt), Marshall Brown (vtb), Pee Wee Russell (cl), Eddie Condon (g), Buzzy Drootin (dm), and perhaps others
(Condon and Drootin also appeared in December at the Colonial in Toronto with Buck Clayton.)[56]

George Wein wrote the following[57]:

> The story of the Ohio Valley Jazz Festival begins in the bitter-cold winter of 1961, more than six months before the Newport Jazz Festival's resurrection. Times were hard—I had no club or festival—and I found myself falling back on the piano as a means of income. With Ruby Braff, Pee Wee Russell, Marshall Brown, and Jack Six on bass, I managed to book a series of gigs for the Newport All-Stars in the Corn Belt. There wasn't much money in touring, but it kept us alive. One of our extended engagements had been in a Xenia, Ohio, club called Kenkels. As leader the gig paid me about $400 a week—just enough money for the rent of my office-apartment at Fifty Central Park West.

Newport All Stars
Winter 1961, Midwest tour, unknown locations and dates
Ruby Braff (cnt), Pee Wee Russell (cl), Marshall Brown (vtb), George Wein (p), Jack Six (b), and probably a drummer

Newport All Stars
Winter 1961, Kenkels, Xenia, Ohio
Ruby Braff (cnt), Pee Wee Russell (cl), Marshall Brown (vtb), George Wein (p), Jack Six (b), and probably a drummer

Ruby Braff and Marshall Brown[58]
George Wein announced plans to open Storyville in Greenwich Village, New York, before the end of March. He stated that Ruby Braff and Marshall Brown would be the first musicians to play there.

George Wein wrote the following:[59]

> My Newport All-Star band, which had toured the Midwest during much of the long, cold winter of 1961–62, now began to serve a handy promotional purpose. When Rhode Island's U.S. Senator Claiborne Pell, a former Newport Festival board member, invited us to play a concert in the rotunda of the old Senate Office Building in Washington, it made news. The group—which consisted of

> Ruby Braff, Pee Wee Russell, Marshall Brown, Eddie Phyfe, Billie Taylor (the bassist, not the pianist), and myself—played a lunch-hour show on Monday June 18, to some 500 senatorial staff members. It was the first such concert in the rotunda; the occasion was noteworthy enough to prompt an AP Wire Service photo that was distributed to newspapers across the country. We appeared the following morning on NBC's *Today Show*. We also made a series of appearances leading up to the Newport Festival—the first at the Boston Arts Festival on July 2. For the following week, we played nightly at Nick Cannarozzi's Cliff Walk Manor in Newport, the former rebel-festival site. We shared this engagement with 'Charles Mingus and the Newport Rebels,' which featured Toshiko Akiyoshi (then Mariano) on piano.

The above quotation anchors the following bookings, leading up to the 1962 edition of the Newport Jazz Festival, again led by George Wein. Ruby also mentioned that he once performed at the White House, but I have been unable to find any further information. It is possible that Ruby was referring to the next performance.

Newport All Stars
June 18, 1962, Old Senate Office Building—some reports state U.S. Capitol Rotunda, Washington, D.C.
Ruby Braff (cnt), Marshall Brown (vtb), Pee Wee Russell (cl), George Wein (p), Billy Taylor, Sr. (b), Eddie Phyfe (dm)

Newport All Stars
June 19, 1962, *Today Show*, NBC Television, New York
Ruby Braff (cnt), Marshall Brown (vtb), Pee Wee Russell (cl), George Wein (p), Billie Taylor, Sr. (b), Eddie Phyfe (dm)

Newport All Stars (see Figure 7.3)
June 29–July 1, 1962 (before the Newport Jazz Festival), Cliff Walk Manor, Newport, Rhode Island
Ruby Braff (cnt), Marshall Brown (vtb), Pee Wee Russell (cl), George Wein (p), John Neves (b), Jo Jones (dm)

Newport All Stars
July 2, 1962, Boston Arts Festival, Boston

Ruby also recalled that he appeared on the *Tonight Show* (NBC) in New York, probably about this time.

Newport All Stars[60]
July 8, 1962, 9th Newport Jazz Festival, Freebody Park, Newport, Rhode Island (second day of three-day festival)
Ruby Braff (cnt), Marshall Brown (vtb), Pee Wee Russell (cl), George Wein (p), John Neves (b), Buzzy Drootin (dm), Louise Tobin (voc)—some listings incor-

rectly show Jo Jones on drums since he was listed in the preliminary program but did not appear with the group

Sweet Georgia Brown
    unissued, recording available
I'm Crazy 'bout My Baby
    unissued, recording available
Unknown title
    unissued
You Can Depend on Me
    Toshiba EMI TOLW 3162*, unissued, recording available
Blue and Sentimental
    unissued, recording available

Add Bud Freeman (ts)
Crazy Rhythm
    unissued, recording available
St. Louis Blues
    unissued, recording available
Pee Wee's Blues
    unissued, recording available
Should I (LT voc)
    unissued, recording available
I Got It Bad and That Ain't Good (LT voc)
    unissued, recording available
'Deed I Do (LT voc)
    unissued, recording available
Take the "A" Train (joined by Duke Ellington Orchestra)
    unissued, recording available

NOTE: Toshiba EMI TOLW 3162 is a laserdisc and VHS videotape release titled *Newport '62* showing most of Ruby's solo and part of Pee Wee's solo. This same program was also released on DVD as Quantum Leap DJ 863 (which prints Ruby's name as *Ruby Bratt*). While Duke Ellington and His Orchestra joined the Newport All Stars on the final title, Ruby and Bud soloed first. Willis Conover mentioned Ruby Braff's reviewing of jazz records for the *Saturday Review*. He wrote reviews during late 1957 and 1958. The tape recording from the Library of Congress does not include the unknown title and "You Can Depend On Me." Film clips may exist from WJAR-TV and WPRI-TV held at Rhode Island Historical Society Library.[61]

A photo exists from the March of Jazz program[62] showing Ruby with Bud Freeman. A few performances in New York may have followed the Newport festival, but one with Pee Wee and Dickie Wells is placed below arbitrarily. These are followed by appearances by the Newport All Stars at the Ohio Valley Jazz Festival and, afterwards, at the Surf Club in Cincinnati. In conjunction with that appearance, the Surf Club provided an opportunity for Ruby's reunion with

Jack Teagarden. The Newport All Stars then recorded for Impulse Records in New York.

Gene Sedric Benefit Concert[63]
July 25, 1962, Central Plaza, New York
Ruby Braff (cnt), Dickie Wells (tb), Pee Wee Russell (cl), and other musicians including Estell Williams (voc) (she was daughter of Fess Williams)

Ruby Braff and Pee Wee Russell[64]
1960s, unknown date and location, New York
Ruby Braff (cnt), Dickie Wells (tb), Pee Wee Russell (cl), Mickey Sheen (dm)

Newport All Stars[65]
August 25, 1962, Ohio Valley Jazz Festival, Carthage Fairgrounds, Cincinnati, Ohio (the festival ran from August 24–26)
Ruby Braff (cnt), Marshall Brown (vtb), Pee Wee Russell (cl), George Wein (p), and other musicians
Keepin' Out of Mischief Now
Performance ended due to heavy rain

Newport All Stars[66]
August 26, 1962, Ohio Valley Jazz Festival, Carthage Fairgrounds, Cincinnati, Ohio (the festival ran from August 24–26)
Ruby Braff (cnt), Marshall Brown (vtb), Pee Wee Russell (cl), George Wein (p), and other musicians
Slow Blues
Indiana

Duncan Schiedt photographed Ruby talking with Louis Armstrong at the Ohio Valley Jazz Festival. This photo is included in this book's photo section and a cropped version is shown on the cover.

Jack Teagarden Sextet with Guests Ruby Braff and Pee Wee Russell[67]
August 26, 1962, Ohio Valley Jazz Festival, Carthage Fairgrounds, Cincinnati, Ohio (the festival ran from August 24–26)

Jack Teagarden Sextet with Guests Ruby Braff and Pee Wee Russell[68]
August 26, 1962, Surf Club, Cincinnati, Ohio, following performance at the Ohio Valley Jazz Festival

Whitney Balliett asked Ruby Braff about Jack Teagarden. Ruby reported the following conversation with Jack, starting with his opening question[69]:

> I said to him, 'You're always consistent, no matter where you play. If I play in a room with a lot of rugs and drapes—as opposed to a nice, empty wooden

> room—it ruins me, and I might as well go home.' He said, 'That's because you bring a certain sound to work with you. Forget that sound and just bring your horn and trust the fact that your sound will just naturally drop in on you, no matter how closed up the room is. Just play nice notes and don't worry and it will happen to you.' He was always cool.

The Newport All Stars appeared at the Surf Club in addition to Ruby's appearance with Jack Teagarden.

Newport All Stars[70]
August 1962 Surf Club, Cincinnati, Ohio, for one or more days following the Ohio Valley Jazz Festival
Probably Ruby Braff (cnt), Marshall Brown (vtb), Pee Wee Russell (cl), George Wein (p), and other musicians

Newport All Stars[71]
October 8 (Columbus Day), 1962, Englewood Cliffs, New Jersey
Note: This led to the Impulse recording below.

Newport All Stars: *George Wein and the Newport All Stars*
October 12, 1962, New York
Ruby Braff (cnt), Marshall Brown (vtb, bass tp), Bud Freeman (ts), Pee Wee Russell (cl), George Wein (p), Bill Takas (b), Marquis Foster (dm)
At the Jazz Band Ball
    Impulse A (S) 31, (E) IMPL 8046
Crazy Rhythm
    Impulse A (S) 31, (E) IMPL 8046
Blue Turning Grey Over You
    Impulse A (S) 31, (E) IMPL 8046
Lulu's Back in Town
    Impulse A (S) 31, (E) IMPL 8046
The Bends Blues (no Braff)
    Impulse A (S) 31, (E) IMPL 8046
Keepin' Out of Mischief Now
    Impulse A (S) 31, (E) IMPL 8046
Ja-Da
    Impulse A (S) 31, (E) IMPL 8046
Slowly (no Braff)
    Impulse A (S) 31, (E) IMPL 8046
NOTE: All of the above also on Impulse 1A-9359/2, Impulse/Sparton (Can) A (S) 31, HMV (E) CLP 1651. This album received three stars in *DownBeat.*

Condon's[72]
February 4–16, 1963 (closed Sundays), 330 East 56th Street, New York
Ruby Braff (cnt), Ralph Sutton (p), Buzzy Drootin (dm)

A photo taken by Jack Bradley exists as Jack Crystal presents Ruby Braff with an award at Central Plaza.[73] This anchors the following entry. This photo is included in this book's photo section.

Ruby Braff at Central Plaza[74]
Details unknown, photo dated 1963

Ruby Braff[75]
Two weeks until June 23, 1963, Lennie's, West Peabody, Massachusetts
No details available

The 1963 Newport Jazz Festival program includes a photograph by Jack Bradley that shows Pee Wee Russell, Buzzy Drootin, and Ruby Braff.

Newport All Stars: *That Newport Jazz*[76]
Newport Jazz Festival All Stars
July 6, 1963, 10th Newport Jazz Festival, Freebody Park, Newport, Rhode Island (third day of four-day festival)
Ruby Braff (cnt), Al Grey (tb), Bud Freeman (ts), George Wein (p), Wendell Marshall (b), Roy Haynes (dm)
Exactly Like You
    unissued, recording available
You Can Depend on Me (inc. Grey)
    Columbia C2-38262
Rosetta
    Columbia CL 22179, CS 8979, CBS (Eu) 21139
Just You, Just Me
    Columbia CL 22179, CS 8979, CBS (Eu) 21139, Col/Legacy C3K 89076
When Your Lover Has Gone
    Columbia CL 22179, CS 8979, CBS (Eu) 21139
Lester Leaps In (inc. Grey)
    Columbia CL 22179, CS 8979, CBS (Eu) 21139
NOTE: This recording was also issued on a seven-inch reel-to-reel tape with the same number as the original stereo LP, Columbia Stereo Tape CS 8979. Columbia/Legacy C3K 89076 is titled *Happy Birthday Newport: 50 Swinging Years.* Other performances on this three-CD set are by other artists. This CD lists the date incorrectly as July 4, not July 6.

Ruby Braff and His Associates[77]
July 13, 1963, 7–12 p.m., broadcast on WRVR-FM, New York from an unknown location

George Wein organized a festival in Detroit, Michigan, from August 3–4, 1963, but there is no specific indication that Ruby appeared.[78]

Nick's, located on 7th Avenue and 10th Street closed in August 1963, changing an important part of the jazz music scene in New York City. Dick Wellstood had been performing there with Sol Yaged, and that led to the following week long engagement in Foxborough, Massachusetts, at the Bay State Race Track. The band played a long set each night before the first race and short sets between races thereafter. This was the first time I have identified Ruby performing with Dick Wellstood and Zoot Sims. A photo from the March of Jazz program is included in this book's photo section. Then the Newport All Stars traveled for the second year to Ohio. I have not located information that points to any other appearances on this trip apart from the Ohio Valley Jazz Festival. Afterwards, the Newport All Stars continued to perform in New York, New Hampshire, and perhaps other locations throughout New England.

Newport All Stars[79]
One week in August 1963, Bay State Race Track, Foxborough, Massachusetts
Ruby Braff (cnt), Shorty Baker (tp), Benny Morton (tb), Zoot Sims, Bud Freeman (ts), Pee Wee Russell (cl), Dick Wellstood, George Wein (p), Alex Cirin (b), Buzzy Drootin (dm) (George Wein departed during the engagement to prepare for the Ohio Valley Jazz Festival.)

Newport All Stars[80]
August 24, 1963, Ohio Valley Jazz Festival, Cincinnati, Ohio
Ruby Braff (cnt), Bud Freeman (ts), George Wein (p), Lee Tucker (b), Philip Paul (dm)
At Sundown
Keepin' Out of Mischief Now
St. Louis Blues
Blue and Sentimental (Braff feature)
Three Little Words (Freeman feature)

Jam Session[81]
August 24, 1963, Ohio Valley Jazz Festival, Cincinnati Ohio
Ruby Braff (cnt), Maynard Ferguson, Howard McGhee (tp), Bud Freeman (ts), Paul Desmond (as), Dave Brubeck (p), and other musicians

George Wein organized a festival in Monterey, California from September 20 – 22, 1963, but there is no indication that Ruby appeared.[82]

Newport All Stars[83]
February 1964, Wagonwheels, New York
Ruby Braff (cnt), Bud Freeman (ts), George Wein (p), and other unnamed musicians

Newport All Stars[84]
February 1964, Newport Comes to the University of New Hampshire, Durham, New Hampshire
Ruby Braff (cnt), Bud Freeman (ts), George Wein (p), Alex Cirin (b), Marquis Foster (dm), Bunny Briggs (dancer, on the final three numbers performed by this group)

This festival performed at five different college locations in New England, but details of the other four locations were not reported.

Perhaps due to Ruby's self-promotion, *DownBeat* reported plans to produce a film, *The Ruby Braff Story*.[85] The coverage cited plans by Hillman Productions of New York. The company's president, Norma Valleau, was to be the film's producer. Sam Margolis was named as an advisor, and script writing was under way. Barry Harvey was listed as the film's director and assistant producer. Ruby would record the soundtrack, and the soundtrack would also incorporate existing recordings. Shooting was scheduled to begin at the end of May. Ruby would portray himself onscreen. His comment was, "It's all right as long as they don't cast me as the heavy."[86] Apart from these mentions in the jazz press, there are no further reports of any activity on this project.

Ruby probably continued to perform in New York clubs, but only two reports have been located. One is an imprecise date for an appearance with Paul Gonsalves. But festival season was again approaching, leading with the Pittsburgh Jazz Festival where the All Stars appear with the title of the Newport Jazz Festival Orchestra.

Teddy Napoleon Benefit[87]
May 24, 1964, Central Plaza, New York, Willis Conover, master of ceremonies
Ruby Braff (cnt), Phil Olivella (cl), John Murtaugh (ts), Dick Katz or Dave McKenna (p), Dante Martucci (b), Harry DiVito (tb), Buzzy Drootin (dm)
Struttin' with Some Barbecue
Three Little Words

Metropole[88]
About 1964, Metropole, New York
Ruby Braff (cnt), Paul Gonsalves (ts), possibly Nat Pierce (p), Buzzy Drootin (dm)

Newport Jazz Festival Orchestra[89]
June 20, 1964, Pittsburgh Jazz Festival, Pittsburgh, PA
Ruby Braff (cnt), Bud Freeman (ts), Pee Wee Russell (cl), Wendell Marshall (b), Charlie Persip (dm)
Crazy Rhythm
Ain't Misbehavin'

Add Bennie Benack (tp)
Two unnamed Dixieland numbers
C Jam Blues

Ruby's nearly annual string of appearances continued for the 1964 Newport Jazz Festival. This provided Ruby with his first opportunity to appear with Ben Webster and renewed his association with Buck Clayton. It is possible that Ruby accompanied the All Stars to Japan immediately after this appearance. Sadly, I did not have an opportunity to discuss this with Ruby during his lifetime. Ruby said that he toured Japan twice, and this is the most likely candidate for his first trip.

It is clear that Ruby did appear in a tribute to Eddie Condon held at Carnegie Hall on July 20. This marked Ruby's return to Carnegie Hall after a wonderful appearance with Mel Powell in 1954. He would return frequently later in his career when the Newport Jazz Festival moved to New York City. The Newport All Stars returned to Ohio in August where Ruby performed with Woody Herman for the first time.

Newport All Stars[90]
July 5, 1964 (Sunday evening), 11th Newport Jazz Festival, Freebody Park, Newport, Rhode Island (final day of four-day festival)
Buck Clayton (tp), Ben Webster (ts), Al Grey (tb), Sir Charles Thompson (p), Slam Stewart (b), Ben Riley (dm)
Perdido
Star Dust
Take the "A" Train
Ruby Braff (cnt) replaces Buck Clayton and Ben Webster out
Sunday
Mean to Me

Add Ben Webster (ts)
Lover Come Back to Me
NOTE: A recording of these tunes is available but remains unissued. At the time of publication, "Sunday," "Mean to Me," "Lover Come Back to Me" and "Take the 'A' Train" are all available for download from WolfgangsVault.com.

George Wein's and Jimmy Lyons's Tokyo Jazz Festival[91]
Six days starting July 10, 1964, Tokyo, then Osaka, Kyoto, Nagoya, and Sapporo
Ruby Braff may have toured with the Newport All Stars but this is not confirmed.

Tribute to Eddie Condon[92]
July 20, 1964, Carnegie Hall, New York

Musicians appearing included Henry "Red" Allen, Wild Bill Davison, Buck Clayton, Dizzy Gillespie, Max Kaminsky, Ruby Braff, Johnny Windhurst (tp),Georg Brunis, Lou McGarity, Cutty Cutshall (tb), Pee Wee Russell, Peanuts Hucko (cl), Bud Freeman (ts), Joe Bushkin, Joe Sullivan, Jess Stacy (p), George Wettling, Zutty Singleton (dm), Helen Ward (voc), scheduled master of ceremonies is Sammy Davis, Jr.

Newport All Stars[93]
August 16, 1964, Ohio Valley Jazz Festival, Crosley Field, Cincinnati, Ohio
Ruby Braff (cnt), Bud Freeman (ts), George Wein (p), Alex Cirin (b), Philip Paul (dm)
Several unknown tunes

Add Woody Herman (cl)
Two additional selections performed

Newport All Stars[94]
August 31, 1964, possibly New York
Ruby Braff (cnt), Pee Wee Russell (cl), Bud Freeman (ts), George Wein (p), unknown bass and drums
Three Little Words
St. Louis Blues
NOTE: A recording of these tunes is available but remains unissued.

Ruby Braff attended performances by Louis Armstrong at Freedomland during Labor Day weekend 1964. Also present were Johnny Windhurst, Dan Morgenstern, Max Kaminsky, Danny and Blue Lu Barker, Dick Wellstood, and Kenny Davern.[95] Then, George Wein brought the Newport All Stars to Europe for another extensive tour, the first since 1961.

Newport All Stars[96]
European Tour, September 24–October 11, 1964
Tour included Berlin, Zurich, Paris, Milan, Stockholm, Copenhagen, Helsinki, and other unnamed cities. Specific information is shown below for five of these cities, but not for Zurich and Helsinki.

One of these concerts was presented as the 1964 USA Jazz Festival in Stockholm, Sweden, organized by George Wein in cooperation with Swedish jazz magazine *Estrad*. The festival featured the Miles Davis Quintet (Miles, Wayne Shorter, Herbie Hancock, Ron Carter, Tony Williams), the Dave Brubeck Quartet (Brubeck, Desmond, Eugene Wright, and Joe Morello), and the Roland Kirk Quartet (Kirk, Tete Montoliu, Tommy Potter, and Kenny Clarke) performing. At the end of the show there was a special tribute to Charlie Parker called "In Memoriam Charlie Parker" featuring J. J. Johnson, Sonny Stitt, Howard McGhee, and Walter Bishop, Jr. Other participants that night included Sister Rosetta

Tharpe, George Russell, Thad Jones, Garnett Brown, Joe Farrell, Barre Phillips, Al Heath, Harry Edison, Coleman Hawkins, Sir Charles Thompson, Jo Jones, Ruby Braff, Pee Wee Russell, Bud Freeman, George Wein, Jimmy Woode, and Joe Nay.

Pee Wee Russell's Chicagoans (aka Newport All Stars)[97]
September 26, 1964, Berlin
Ruby Braff (cnt), Pee Wee Russell (cl), Bud Freeman (ts), George Wein (p), Jimmy Woode (b), Joe Nay (dm)
Royal Garden Blues
Ain't Misbehavin'
Just You, Just Me
Pee Wee's Blues (omit Braff, Freeman)
Indiana
NOTE: A recording of these tunes is available but remains unissued.

Newport All Stars[98]
September 28, 1964, broadcast, Basel, Switzerland
Same personnel
Indiana
Birth of the Blues
I've Found a New Baby
St. Louis Blues
Omit Ruby Braff and Freeman
Pee Wee's Blues
NOTE: There are additional titles without Pee Wee Russell, some of which probably include Ruby Braff.

Newport All Stars[99]
Perhaps September 29 or 30, 1964, but during this tour, Milan, Italy
Ruby Braff (tp), Pee Wee Russell (cl), Bud Freeman (ts), George Wein (p), Jimmy Woode (b), Joe Nay (dm)
I've Found a New Baby
Ain't Misbehavin'
Three Little Words (Freeman with rhythm)
Pee Wee's Blues (Russell with rhythm)
Just You, Just Me (Braff with rhythm)
Undecided
St. Louis Blues
NOTE: A video recording of these tunes is available but remains unissued.

All above titles are included in a film titled *The Newport All-Stars in Milan*, Italy, 1964. George Wein mentions that they had been traveling through the South of France prior to this performance; however, no details have surfaced.

Chicago All Stars
October 1, 1964, Salle Pleyel, Paris
Ruby Braff (tp), Pee Wee Russell (cl), Bud Freeman (ts), George Wein (p), Jimmy Woode (b), Joe Nay (dm)
Pee Wee's Blues
    Blu Jazz (G) BJ 036CD
Three Little Words
    Blu Jazz (G) BJ 036CD
St. Louis Blues
    Blu Jazz (G) BJ 036CD
NOTE: Remaining titles on this CD are by George Russell Sextet and Uptown All Stars (Coleman Hawkins). The CD indicates that it is manufactured in Germany; however, the production is Italian.

Newport All Stars[100]
October 3, 1964, Stockholm
Ruby Braff (tp), Pee Wee Russell (cl), Bud Freeman (ts), George Wein (p), Jimmy Woode (b), Joe Nay (dm)
Ain't Misbehavin'
Pee Wee's Blues (Russell feature)
I Can't Give You Anything but Love (Freeman feature)
I've Found a New Baby
Royal Garden Blues
NOTE: A recording of these tunes is available but remains unissued.

A photography of Ruby Braff and Bud Freeman was published in the Copenhagen Jazz Festival program. The Newport All Stars, billed as the Chicago All Stars, opened the program. On the first day they were followed by Henrik Johansen, Sister Rosetta Tharpe, the Original Tuxedo Jazz Band with Alvin Alcorn, Arnvid Meyers Orkester, and an all-star group including Harry Edison, Coleman Hawkins, Jo Jones, and Sir Charles Thompson. The Miles Davis Quintet opened the second day. They were followed by the George Russell Sextet, Niels Henning Ørsted with Kenny Drew, the Roland Kirk Quartet, and the Dave Brubeck Quartet. A tribute to Charlie Parker concluded the festival, featuring Howard McGhee, Sonny Stitt, J. J. Johnson, Walter Bishop, Jr., Tommy Potter, and Kenny Clarke. Quite a program.

Chicago All Stars, a.k.a. Newport All Stars[101]
October 4, 1964, Copenhagen
Ruby Braff (cnt), Bud Freeman (ts), Pee Wee Russell (cl), George Wein (p), Tommy Potter (b), Joe Nay or Tony Williams (dm)
I've Found a New Baby
Ain't Misbehavin'
Just You, Just Me (Braff feature)

Omit Braff and Freeman
Pee Wee's Blues
NOTE: A recording of these tunes is available but remains unissued.

A photograph likely taken during the next performance was published in *Crescendo*. It shows Brian Brocklehurst, Lennie Hastings, Pee Wee Russell, Ruby Braff, and Bud Freeman performing at the Marquee Club in London from February 1968. This was Ruby's first appearance in Britain.

Newport All Stars
October 11, 1964, 60-minute BBC television program *Jazz 625*, recorded at Marquee Club, London—the first of two programs, Terry Henebery, producer, introduced by Steve Race. The air date was probably December 12, 1964.
Ruby Braff (cnt), Bud Freeman (ts), Pee Wee Russell (cl), George Wein (p), Brian Brocklehurst (b), Lennie Hastings (dm)
Royal Garden Blues
Ain't Misbehavin'
Three Little Words (Freeman with rhythm)
Pee Wee's Blues (Russell with rhythm)
Just You, Just Me (Braff with rhythm)
St. Louis Blues
NOTE: An audio recording of these tunes is available but remains unissued.

"Royal Garden Blues" also appeared in a compilation broadcast, *Jazz 625: Christmas Special*, Terry Henebery, director. The broadcast date for this program was probably December 26, 1964, aired as a Christmas special. The following program was likely broadcast on March 13, 1965. Both programs, and the compilation, apparently exist in BBC's archives on 35-mm film.

Newport All Stars
October 11, 1964, BBC television program *Jazz 625*, recorded at Marquee Club, London—second of two programs
Ruby Braff (cnt), Bud Freeman (ts), Pee Wee Russell (cl), George Wein (p), Brian Brocklehurst (b), Lennie Hastings (dm)
Blues
I've Found a New Baby
Undecided
Sugar
You Took Advantage of Me
I'm Crazy 'bout My Baby
Blues
NOTE: An audio recording of these tunes is available but remains unissued.

Ruby Braff, Bud Freeman, and George Wein returned to the U.S. following the taping of the *Jazz 625* programs, but Pee Wee Russell remained to perform at the Manchester Sports Guild. But Ruby returned to England in May 1965. I have been unable to locate details of any performances until that time, a gap in his recordings and performances of seven months—it appears to be a prolonged period of inactivity which of course was both economically and emotionally challenging for him.

The following handbill and advertisements depict three of the performances in this chapter:

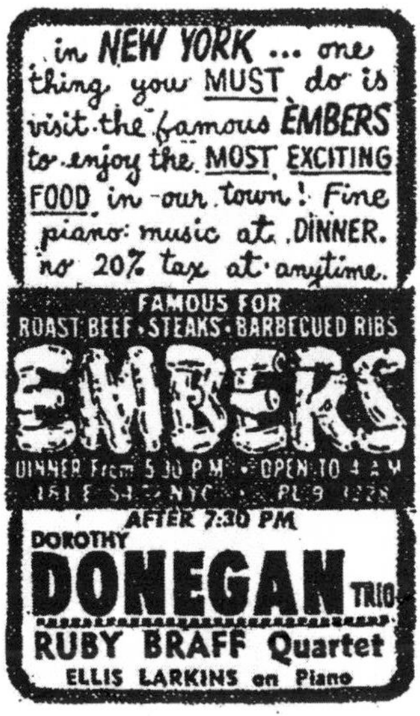

Figure 7.1: Advertisement
March 1960

ANNOUNCING

THAT

RUBY BRAFF

and

BOBBY HACKETT

will accept limited number of jazz trumpet students in the New York area.

Call KIngsbridge 8-2572

Figure 7.2: Advertisement
December 1960

Figure 7.3: Handbill
June & July 1962

Notes

[1] All titles are available complete from the Library of Congress as shown below. Source of session: Voice of America tape at the Library of Congress, Record 134158p+1X, RGA 0047 (RWD 5707-5708 A1), and RGA 0067 (RWD 5742 A2-B1).

[2] Anthony J. Agostinelli, *The Newport Jazz Festival: Rhode Island 1954–1971—A Bibliography, Discography and Filmography* (Providence, Rhode Island: privately printed, October 1977), 62. John S Wilson reviewed in *New York Times*, July 3, 1959.

[3] Martin Williams writing in January 1964 and Martin Williams, *Jazz Changes* (New York: Oxford University Press, 1992), 31-32. The band played from 11 p.m. to 2 a.m. to entertain the after-fight crowds. Also mentioned in *DownBeat*, January 30, 1964, 20.

[4] Robert Hilbert, *Pee Wee Russell: The Life of a Jazzman* (New York: Oxford University Press, 1993), 224.

[5] Robert Hilbert, *Pee Wee Russell: The Life of a Jazzman* (New York: Oxford University Press, 1993), 225.

[6] *Coda Magazine*, August 1959, 12–13.

[7] *DownBeat*, September 3, 1959, 15.

[8] Midwest Jazz Festival program.

[9] Boston Jazz Festival program.

[10] Bud Freeman, *You Don't Look Like a Musician (*Detroit: Balamp Publishing, 1974), 85.

[11] *DownBeat*, October 1, 1959, 53.

[12] Roy Decarava, *The Sound I Saw* (London: Phaidron Press Limited, 2003), pages are unnumbered.

[13] Leonard Feather, "Blindfold Test," *DownBeat*, January 21, 1960. Reproduced courtesy of the *DownBeat* Archive.

[14] *Melody Maker*, March 19, 1960, 14.

[15] Edward N. Meyer, *The Life and Music of Kenny Davern* (Lanham, MD: Scarecrow Press, 2010), 44.

[16] *Melody Maker*, March 19, 1960, 14.

[17] *Melody Maker*, March 19, 1960, 14.
[18] Copy of article from unknown newspaper, March 13, 1960, *Melody Maker*, March 19, 1960, 14, and *The New Yorker*, March 5, 1960, 8, and March 12, 1960, 8. Advertised in the *New York Times*, March 8, 1960.
[19] Don Nelson, unknown newspaper (*NY Daily News* perhaps), March 13, 1960.
[20] *Melody Maker*, March 19, 1960, 14.
[21] Advertisement in *Toledo Blade*, April 4, 1960: "Ruby Braff, jazz trumpeter and his combo, will be featured at the Roundtable starting tonight."
[22] *Cadence*, June 1983, 13.
[23] *Coda Magazine*, July 1960, 12.
[24] Burt Goldblatt, *The Newport Jazz Festival: The Illustrated History* (New York: Dial Press, 1977), 72.
[25] Anthony J. Agostinelli, *The Newport Jazz Festival: Rhode Island 1954–1971—A Bibliography, Discography and Filmography* (Providence, Rhode Island: privately printed, October 1977), 60, 61, lists the content of the other film programs: program 8 includes the Newport Youth Band, Ruby Braff, Pee Wee Russell, and Andy Marsala while program 21 includes the Newport Youth Band, Ruby Braff, and Cannonball Adderley. Source of audio session tape: Voice of America tape at the Library of Congress, Record 159395p+1X, RGA 0067 (RWD 5742 A2—B1).
[26] David Meeker, *Jazz in the Movies: New Enlarged Edition* (New York: Da Capo, c. 1981), entry number 1677, unnumbered pages.
[27] Anthony J. Agostinelli, *The Newport Jazz Festival: Rhode Island 1954–1971—A Bibliography, Discography and Filmography* (Providence, Rhode Island: privately printed, October 1977), 60, 61.
[28] *The Globe and Mail*, August 6, 1960, *Coda Magazine* August 1960, 2, and *Coda Magazine*, September 1960, 4.
[29] *DownBeat*, December 22, 1960, 55.
[30] George Wein, *Myself Among Others* (Cambridge, MA: Da Capo Press, 2003), 208–9.
[31] *The New Yorker*, January 7, 1961, 8.
[32] *Toronto Daily Star*, February 25, 1961.
[33] *Toronto Telegram*, February 24, 1961 (this was reported as the professional engagement for this group) and *Globe and Mail*, February 25, 1961. A review appears in *Coda Magazine*, March 1961, 5–6. The engagement is also reported in *DownBeat*, April 13, 1961, 46.
[34] Robert Hilbert, *Pee Wee Russell: The Life of a Jazzman*, New York (New York: Oxford University Press, 1993), 240 and quote from Dan Morgenstern's review in *Metronome* that praised "Moonglow."
[35] *The New Yorker*, March 11, 1961, 8.
[36] Manfred Selchow, *Ding Ding: A Bio-Discographical Scrapbook on Vic Dickenson* (Germany: Uhle & Kleinmann, 1998), 293.
[37] Manfred Selchow, *Ding Ding: A Bio-Discographical Scrapbook on Vic Dickenson* (Germany: Uhle & Kleinmann, 1998), 392.
[38] Manfred Selchow, *Ding Ding: A Bio-Discographical Scrapbook on Vic Dickenson* (Germany: Uhle & Kleinmann, 1998), 391, 393.
[39] Manfred Selchow, *Ding Ding: A Bio-Discographical Scrapbook on Vic Dickenson* (Germany: Uhle & Kleinmann, 1998), 391.
[40] Poster image.
[41] Robert Hilbert, *Pee Wee Russell: The Life of a Jazzman* (New York: Oxford University Press, 1993), 240.

[42] Photograph from Han Schulte and Manfred Selchow, *Ding Ding: A Bio-Discographical Scrapbook on Vic Dickenson (*Germany: Uhle & Kleinmann, 1998), 397.
[43] Han Schulte and Manfred Selchow, *Ding Ding: A Bio-Discographical Scrapbook on Vic Dickenson (*Germany: Uhle & Kleinmann, 1998), 397–398.
[44] Source of information for matrix numbers and unissued titles: Michel Ruppli and Ed Novitsky, *Mercury Records: A Discography: Volume II, the 1956-1964 Era (*Westport, Connecticut: Greenwood Press, 1993), 438.
[45] Bob Weir provided this information. The date is also from Manfred Selchow, *Ding Ding: A Bio-Discographical Scrapbook on Vic Dickenson (*Germany: Uhle & Kleinmann, 1998), 399, which notes that these titles are drawn from two different concerts on that day. The corrected date is also published in the recent CD reissue in Gigantes (Universal Music) in the Jazz in Paris series of recordings.
[46] Robert Hilbert in collaboration with David Niven, *Pee Wee Speaks: A Discography of Pee Wee Russell* (Metuchen, NJ: Scarecrow Press, 1992), 298.
[47] Photo by Jack Bradley in *The March of Jazz Celebrates Ruby Braff's 74th Birthday Party*, Arbors Records, 2001, 16.
[48] Robert Hilbert, *Pee Wee Russell: The Life of a Jazzman* (New York: Oxford University Press, 1993), 240, and quote from Dan Morgenstern's review in *Metronome* that praised "Moonglow."
[49] *DownBeat*, August 17, 1961, 13 and 52. *The New Yorker*, July 8, 1961, 6, July 15, 1961, 7, July 22, 1961, 7, noting "a splendid all-out and clattering evening," July 29, 1961, 6, August 5, 1961, 7, August 12, 1961, 6, August 19, 1961, August 26, 1961, 6, September 2, 1961, 7, September 9, 1961, 6, September 16, 1961, 6, and John S. Wilson, *New York Times*, July 13, 1961.
[50] John S. Wilson, *New York Times*, July 13, 1961.
[51] *DownBeat*, June 22, 1961, 51, and a review in *DownBeat*, August 31, 1961, 12–13. Tom Gwaltney was the festival's promoter and the sextet opened the second night of the festival. Tommy Newsom received an award for being the "Most Outstanding Virginia-Born Musician" at the festival. A copy of printed festival program is available and includes photos of Braff and Brown.
[52] *DownBeat*, August 17, 1961, 13 and 52, August 31, 1961, 45, and September 14, 1961, 45.
[53] This album was mentioned as "just recorded" in *DownBeat*, August 31, 1961, 13.
[54] *Toronto Telegram*, September 15, 1961 (article reports that the recording for United Artists is soon to be released) and *Globe and Mail*, September 16, 1961. *Coda Magazine* announced the engagement in the September 1961 issue, on page 2 and reviewed the performance in the October 1961 issue, on page 5. Also see a mention in *DownBeat*, November 9, 1961, 42.
[55] *DownBeat*, December 7, 1961, 54, *The New Yorker*, October 14, 1961, 8, October 21, 1961, 8, October 28, 1961, 8, November 4, 1961, 8, November 11.1961, 8.
[56] *DownBeat*, December 21, 1961, 60.
[57] George Wein, *Myself Among Others* (Cambridge, MA: Da Capo Press, 2003), 429.
[58] *DownBeat*, March 1, 1962, 44.
[59] George Wein, *Myself Among Others* (Cambridge, MA: Da Capo Press, 2003), 233.
[60] Source of session: Voice of America tape at the Library of Congress, Record 181437p+1X, RGA 0084 (RWD 5760 B2—6085 A1). Additional film may exist from July 8 at the Rhode Island Historical Society Library, with the catalog codes of RI-2, RI-5, and RI-7.

[61] Anthony J. Agostinelli, *The Newport Jazz Festival: Rhode Island 1954–1971—A Bibliography, Discography and Filmography* (Providence, Rhode Island: privately printed, October 1977), 62 and 63.
[62] Photo by Jack Bradley, *The March of Jazz Celebrates Ruby Braff's 74th Birthday Party*, Arbors Records, 2001, 17.
[63] Robert Hilbert, *Pee Wee Russell: The Life of a Jazzman* (New York: Oxford University Press, 1993), 247.
[64] Photo by Jack Bradley, *The March of Jazz Celebrates Ruby Braff's 74th Birthday Party*, Arbors Records, 2001, 17.
[65] *DownBeat*, October 11, 1962, 12; Robert Hilbert, *Pee Wee Russell: The Life of a Jazzman* (New York: Oxford University Press, 1993), 247.
[66] *DownBeat*, October 11, 1962, 12; Robert Hilbert, *Pee Wee Russell: The Life of a Jazzman* (New York: Oxford University Press, 1993), 247.
[67] *DownBeat*, October 11, 1962, 12; Robert Hilbert, *Pee Wee Russell: The Life of a Jazzman* (New York: Oxford University Press, 1993), 247.
[68] Robert Hilbert, *Pee Wee Russell: The Life of a Jazzman* (New York: Oxford University Press, 1993), 247.
[69] Whitney Balliett, *The New Yorker*, April 2, 1984, 54.
[70] *DownBeat*, September 27, 1962, 55.
[71] George A. Borgman, "The One and Only Ruby Braff," in *Mississippi Rag*, December 1995, 5.
[72] *The New Yorker*, February 2, 1963, 8, February 9, 1963, 11, February 16, 1963, 8.
[73] Photo by Jack Bradley, *The March of Jazz Celebrates Ruby Braff's 74th Birthday Party*, Arbors Records, 2001, 17.
[74] Photo by Jack Bradley, *The March of Jazz Celebrates Ruby Braff's 74th Birthday Party*, Arbors Records, 2001, 17.
[75] *DownBeat*, July 4, 1963, 44 and 46.
[76] Voice of America tape at the Library of Congress, Record number 187695p+1X, shelf number RGA 0094 (RWD 6094 B2) (tape excludes "Rosetta," "Just You, Just Me" and "When Your Lover Has Gone") perhaps due to the Columbia's recording contract.
[77] Radio schedule, *New York Times*, July 13, 1963.
[78] John S. Wilson, *New York Times*, June 23, 1963.
[79] Edward N. Meyer, *Giant Strides* (New York: Scarecrow Press, 1999), 72, *DownBeat*, September 26, 1963, 47, and article by Martin Williams in *Jazz Journal*, January 1964, 25–26. Also photo *The March of Jazz Celebrates Ruby Braff's 74th Birthday Party*, Arbors Records, 2001, 16 (photo is dated from late 1950s but probably corresponds to this point in time).
[80] Manfred Selchow, *Ding Ding: A Bio-Discographical Scrapbook on Vic Dickenson* (Germany: Uhle & Kleinmann, 1998), 423, and *DownBeat*, October 10, 1963, 13.
[81] *DownBeat*, October 10, 1963, 42.
[82] John S. Wilson, *New York Times*, June 23, 1963.
[83] *DownBeat*, April 11, 1962, 10.
[84] *DownBeat*, April 11, 1962, 34 (review of concert), and *DownBeat*, March 28, 1963, 54 (mentioning Pee Wee Russell was booked for this appearance but he was not mentioned in the review and probably did not appear).
[85] *DownBeat*, March 26, 1964, 11.
[86] *Coda Magazine*, June 1964, 19.
[87] *DownBeat*, July 30, 1964, 17 and 39. *Coda Magazine* July 1964, 23, gives exact date but says that Dave McKenna was the pianist.

[88] George A. Borgman, "The One and Only Ruby Braff," in *Mississippi Rag*, December 1995, 5.
[89] *DownBeat*, July 30, 1964, 13, and advertisement from June 18, 1964, 27.
[90] Burt Goldblatt, *The Newport Jazz Festival: The Illustrated History* (New York: Dial Press, 1977), 270. Note: Bob Weir reports that the session was broadcast by Voice of America on the program *Jazz Hour*. Film clips may exist from WPRI-TV held at Rhode Island Historical Society Library. Anthony J. Agostinelli, *The Newport Jazz Festival: Rhode Island 1954–1971—A Bibliography, Discography and Filmography, Filmography* (Providence, Rhode Island: privately printed, October 1977), 63.
[91] *DownBeat*, June 4, 1964, 8, and March 26, 1964, 11.
[92] *DownBeat*, July 30, 1964, 9–10.
[93] George Wein, *Myself Among Others* (Cambridge, MA: Da Capo Press, 2003), 433, details mentioned in *DownBeat*, October 8, 1964, 21–22, and ad in *DownBeat*, June 18, 1964, 27.
[94] Robert Hilbert in collaboration with David Niven, *Pee Wee Speaks: A Discography of Pee Wee Russell* (Metuchen, NJ: Scarecrow Press, 1992), 326.
[95] *Coda Magazine*, October/November 1964, 16.
[96] *DownBeat*, July 30, 1964, 11.
[97] Robert Hilbert in collaboration with David Niven, *Pee Wee Speaks: A Discography of Pee Wee Russell* (Metuchen, NJ: Scarecrow Press, 1992), 327. Joe Nay is listed in Robert Hilbert, *Pee Wee Russell: The Life of a Jazzman* (New York: Oxford University Press, 1993), 263.
[98] Robert Hilbert in collaboration with David Niven, *Pee Wee Speaks: A Discography of Pee Wee Russell* (Metuchen, NJ: Scarecrow Press, 1992), 327.
[99] David Meeker, *Jazz in the Movies*, the Library of Congress website, 2005.
[100] Correspondence with Manfred Selchow; Robert Hilbert, *Pee Wee Russell: The Life of a Jazzman* (New York: Oxford University Press, 1993), 64, says that Tony Williams sat in on drums.
[101] Listed in Robert Hilbert in collaboration with David Niven, *Pee Wee Speaks: A Discography of Pee Wee Russell* (Metuchen, NJ: Scarecrow Press, 1992), 328, but only as "early October."

Chapter 8

The Growing Role of Festivals and the Newport Jazz Festival All Stars: George Wein's Festivals and International Tours: May 1965–December 1967

Ruby's next documented performances were in the program *Jazz from Kansas City* held at Royal Festival Hall in London. This program was produced by Harold Davison and created by Humphrey Lyttelton. I cannot locate any performances during the seven months following his return from England following his appearance on British television in October 1964.

Jazz from Kansas City[1]
May 8, 1965, Royal Festival Hall, London

Ben Webster (ts), Stan Tracey (p), Rick Laird (b), Ronnie Stephenson (dm)
Our Love Is Here to Stay
Over the Rainbow
Gone with the Wind

Ruby Braff (cnt), Stan Tracey (p), Rick Laird (b), Ronnie Stephenson (dm)
Mean to Me
These Foolish Things
Just You, Just Me

Ruby Braff (cnt), Vic Dickenson (tb), Bruce Turner (as), Stan Tracey (p), Rick Laird (b), Ronnie Stephenson (dm)
Keepin' Out of Mischief Now
Jeepers Creepers

Buck Clayton (tp), Bruce Turner (as), Ben Webster (ts), Stan Tracey (p), Rick Laird (b), Ronnie Stephenson (dm)
I Can't Get Started

Perdido

Joe Turner (voc), Ruby Braff (cnt), Buck Clayton (tp), Vic Dickenson (tb), Bruce Turner (as), Ben Webster (ts) and the Humphrey Lyttelton Band for the finale
Roll 'Em Pete (voc JT)
NOTE: A recording of these tunes is available but remains unissued.

There were two concerts, both with the same program. One was at 6:15 p.m. and the other, at 9:00. The available recording is from the second concert. Buck Clayton wrote, "Later in the month the show had split into smaller groups for other engagements."[2]

The concert program for *Jazz from Kansas City*[3] states that Ruby performed in a jam session with Ben Webster, Buck Clayton, Vic Dickenson, and Bruce Turner with the Stan Tracey Trio. The program also listed Ruby as a member of a big band with Buck Clayton, Humphrey Lyttelton (tp), Vic Dickenson, Ed Harvey (tb), Ben Webster, Bruce Turner, Tony Coe, Joe Temperley (saxes), Stan Tracey (p), Dave Green (b), Johnny Butts (dm), and Joe Turner (voc). The available recording indicates that the actual performance varied slightly from the published program.

Ruby promptly returned to the US and several performances in New York and Pittsburgh have been traced before he returned to England in June.

Morey Feld's All Stars[4]
May 23, 1965, Mondi's Crystal Ship, Glen Cove, New York
Ruby Braff (cnt), Cutty Cutshall (tb), Hank D'Amico (cl), Dave McKenna (p), Jack Lesberg (b), Morey Feld (dm)

Ruby Braff[5]
June 7, 1965, Ruby ended "a long engagement" when Joe Newman opened on June 21, 1965, Embers West located at 224 West 49th Street, New York
Ruby Braff (cnt), Ross Tompkins (p), Russell George (b), Jake Hanna (dm)

Among Ruby's stories was one about Judy Garland. He spoke of her frequently and with great fondness, although they never performed together. Ruby reported that Judy Garland phoned him one day to report that she had been locked inside her dressing room at a New York theater, between her matinee and evening performances. This was at a time in her life where the theater's manager may have felt the need to assure that she would return for the evening concert. She asked Ruby to come to unlock the door. Ruby replied that he was unable to do so, but that he would "call Frank." He reached Frank Sinatra on the West Coast. Ruby reported that two large men subsequently appeared at the New York theater to lead Judy Garland to her freedom. Ruby featured his "Judy Garland

Medley" several times in performances, but did not always include the same tunes.

Ruby said that Judy had discussed recording with him at some point. Of course, that never happened. They both understood how to create drama and contrast within a musical performance, so this could have been a remarkable recording. Both conveyed a sense of innocence in their performances, while experiencing disappointment in parts of their lives. Certainly, Ruby would have treasured the experience for the rest of his life.

Newport All Stars[6]
June 18, 1965, 2nd Annual Pittsburgh Jazz Festival (festival ran from June 18–20), Pittsburgh, Pennsylvania
Ruby Braff (cnt), Bud Freeman (ts), George Wein (p), Larry Gales (b), Ben Riley (dm)
'Deed I Do
You Took Advantage of Me
When It's Sleepy Time Down South
Take the "A" Train

Ruby returned to England for his next appearance at the Manchester Sports Guild. Copies of tickets are available for both June 25 and 27, 1965, as well as July 10 and 11.

Ruby Braff with Alex Welsh Band[7]
June 25, 1965, Manchester Sports Guild (Cellar), Manchester, England
Ruby Braff (cnt), Alex Welsh (tp), John Barnes (bars), Roy Williams (tb), Fred Hunt (p), Jim Douglas (g), Ron Mathewson (b), Lennie Hastings (dm)
Royal Garden Blues
You Took Advantage of Me
The World Is Waiting for the Sunrise
Medley:
 I Can't Give You Anything but Love
 Sugar
Where's Freddie?
Wolverine Blues
Keepin' Out of Mischief Now
Struttin' with Some Barbecue
Blue and Sentimental
After You've Gone
NOTE: A recording of these tunes is available but remains unissued.

It is probable that the musicians who perform in Manchester continued on the tour for the dates that followed. Certainly, *Jazz Journal International* reports that Lennie Hastings was present on the tour.[8] Jack Swinnerton organized the tour.[9] Swinnerton wrote the following and his words are a clear tribute to Ruby's professionalism:[10]

> Braff instantly set about organizing his numbers with the Welsh band, so that every member of the group was heard to best advantage. An adept presenter, and one who instantly gelled with the audience, Braff was as passionately against what he saw as false show business gimmicks as anyone I have ever encountered. (How many ever succeeded in persuading him to autograph? I did, but only after encouraging him to place his signature alongside those of Vic Dickenson, Bud Freeman, and Pee Wee Russell on a record that they were all on.) That Ruby was interested in producing good band sessions with fine solos and no salesmanship was quickly apparent. What we got, in total, and personal preferences aside, was really just about the best integrated tour of the lot, and the professional standards outshone most other visitors. Braff's imagination and dynamic approach set a standard very hard to follow—this I have long considered to be the finest hour of the full Welsh band and guest musician on tour.

Ruby Braff with Alex Welsh Band[11]
June 26, 1965, Bath Jazz Festival, Regency Ballroom, Sawclose, Bath, England

Ruby Braff with Bruce Turner's Jump Band[12]
June 27, 1965, Manchester Sports Guild, Manchester, England
Bruce Turner, Ray Crane (tp), Ronnie Gleave (vib) plus unnamed rhythm section

The *Just Jazz* article also reports that backing was provided by the Gary Cox Quartet in some performances.

Ruby Braff with Alex Welsh Band[13]
June 30, 1965, 100 Club, 100 Oxford Street, London

Ruby Braff with Alex Welsh Band[14]
July 2, 1965, Osterley Jazz Club, Osterley Rugby Football Club, Club Pavilion, Tentelow Lane, Southall, Middlesex, England

Ruby Braff with Alex Welsh Band[15]
July 3, 1965, Dancing Slipper, Nottingham, England

Ruby Braff with Alex Welsh Band[16]
July 4, 1965, Coatham Hotel, Redcar, England
The Redcar Jazz Club operated in the hotel during the 1950s and '60s.

Ruby Braff with Alex Welsh Band[17]
July 5, 1965, Woodside Hall, Glasgow, Scotland

Ruby Braff with Alex Welsh Band[18]
July 7, 1965, Dolphin Hotel, Botley, Southampton, Hampshire, England

Ruby Braff with Alex Welsh Band[19]
July 9, 1965, Leofric Hotel, Coventry, England

Ruby Braff with Alex Welsh Band[20]
July 10, 1965, Conway Hall, Red Lion Square, London

Ruby Braff with Alex Welsh Band[21]
July 11, 1965, Manchester Sports Guild, Manchester, England

Sinclair Traill wrote the following editorial comment on Ruby's next engagement. Ruby's photograph was featured on the cover of *Jazz Journal* that month. Traill described Ruby's performance as being "compact and competent" with a deep feeling for jazz and "marvelous control and most enviable technique." He continued, emphasizing Ruby's range of dynamics (drawing a comparison to Miles Davis in that regard) and a tone that is both "large and warm" while placing "great store on melody" like Louis Armstrong. He concludes, writing, "I know of no cornetist playing today, who by his control and powerful pulse, makes better use of a good melody. In addition, Ruby Braff has a most pleasant stage presence, his friendly announcements, spoken with a pixielike grin, doing much to communicate a warm, friendly personality to his audience."[22]

The following performance is the first time that Ruby performed with Allan Ganley, a drummer who continued to provide Ruby with excellent support on Ruby's subsequent tours of the UK.

Ruby Braff Quartet
July 1965 (during this interval and suggested to be on a Sunday in Traill's editorial), Bull's Head, Barnes, London
Ruby Braff (cnt), Art Ellefson (ts), Alan Branscombe (p), Allan Ganley (dm)
No further details available

Upon his return to the U.S., Ruby began a three-week engagement at the Embers West in New York City.

Ruby Braff[23]
July or August 1965, Embers West, West 49th Street, New York
Ruby Braff (cnt), Ross Tompkins (p), Russell George (b), Jake Hanna (dm)
No further details available

His next appearance was at the *DownBeat* Jazz Festival in Chicago. Again, Ruby was in excellent company. The program opened Friday night with Gary McFarland leading a large orchestra that featured Stan Getz as a soloist, followed by the Miles Davis Quintet and the Stan Getz Quartet. Ruby was next, performing once again with the Newport Jazz Festival All Stars. The evening continued with the Earl Hines Trio and the Dave Brubeck Quartet. This is Ruby's first appearance with Stan Getz; however, it is not clear that they performed together during this set.

***DownBeat* Chicago Jazz Festival: Newport All Stars**[24]
August 13, 1965, Soldiers' Field, Chicago
Ruby Braff (cnt), Bud Freeman (ts), Pee Wee Russell (cl), George Wein (p), Steve Swallow (b), Joe Morello (dm)
Just You, Just Me
St. Louis Blues
I Want a Little Girl

Add Stan Getz
Blues (featuring Getz and Russell)

While in Chicago, Ruby told Art Hodes that he was flying to Texas for another performance after his appearance at the *DownBeat* Festival. He then headed to New Orleans and onward to San Antonio; however, I have been unable to trace further details.

Newport All Stars[25]
August 1965, an unknown club in San Antonio, Texas
Ruby Braff (cnt), Bud Freeman (ts), George Wein (p), with other unnamed musicians

Ruby returned to Toronto in early November. John Norris[26] wrote the following in his review for the following Club 76 engagement: "The variety of moods that Braff can project within a single solo of several choruses is refreshing." Bill Smith published a photograph of Ruby in an issue of *Coda*.[27] The rest of November was a busy time for Ruby with a series of different performances in New York, Chicago, and Boston.

Ruby Braff with the Jimmy Coxson Trio[28]
November 8–13, 1965, Club 76, Toronto
Ruby Braff (cnt), Jimmy Coxson (p), Harold Holmes (b), Ricky Marcus (dm)
You've Changed
Easy Living
Wolverine Blues
Royal Garden Blues
Struttin' with Some Barbecue
I Can't Give You Anything but Love

Jack Bradley published a photograph that was taken at the next performance. It shows Jack Lesberg, Tony Aless, Morey Feld, Hank D'Amico, and Cutty Cutshall performing in Glen Cove, New York.[29] This was probably the last engagement Hank D'Amico played prior to his death. This photograph is included in this book's photo section as is Jack Bradley's studio portrait of Ruby that also appeared in the program that may be from about this time.

Morey Feld's All Stars[30]
November 1965, Mondi's Crystal Ship, Glen Cove, New York
Ruby Braff (cnt), Cutty Cutshall (tb), Hank D'Amico (cl), Tony Aless (p), Jack Lesberg (b), Morey Feld (dm)

Ruby Braff and George Wein[31]
November 1965, private party in Chicago
Ruby Braff (cnt), Bud Freeman (ts), George Wein (p), and unknown others

Shorty Baker died November 8, 1966 and 114 musicians participated in a tribute concert from 3 p.m. until 4 a.m. including Duke Ellington, Roland Kirk, Henry "Red" Allen, Ruby Braff, Max Kaminsky, Eddie Heywood, and Ray Bryant.

Tribute to Harold (Shorty) Bake—Benefit Concert[32]
December 5, 1965, Luigi's, Greenwich Village, New York

Morey Feld Quintet: Dixieland Versus Rock and Roll[33]
December 12, 1965, Sunrise Village, Belmore, Long Island, New York
Ruby Braff (cnt), Cutty Cutshall (tb), Hank D'Amico (cl), Tony Aless (p), Morey Feld (dm)
Details unknown but Feld's group battled an unnamed rock band

Pete Johnson died March 23, 1967, and this led to Ruby's appearance at another memorial concert.

Pete Johnson Memorial Concert[34]
December 22, 1965, Palm Gardens, Ballroom, on West 52nd Street at 8th Avenue, New York
Published reports state that Ruby Braff headed a delightful band including Bob Wilber (ss), Eddie Barefield (as), Chuck Folds (p), Bill Crow (b), and Eddie Dougherty (dm)
Sometimes I'm Happy
Medium Blues
Take the "A" Train
Undecided
Between the Devil and the Deep Blue Sea
Other titles were not reported

Ruby Braff Sextet[35]
Late December 1965, Jazz Workshop, Boston
Ruby Braff (cnt), Gene DiStasio (tb), Jimmy Mosher (ts), Ray Santisi (p), Tony Eira (b), Dick Berk (dm)

Ruby next appeared at the Boston Globe Jazz Festival. The program opened at 8:30 p.m. on January 14 with the Zoot Sims–Sonny Stitt Quartet, followed by the Newport Jazz Festival All Stars. The Dave Brubeck Quartet was next, followed by the Dizzy Gillespie Quintet and the Stan Getz Quartet. The evening closed with a grand finale that included Getz, Gillespie, Sims, Stitt, Bud Freeman, James Moody, Ruby Braff, and Toshiko Mariano. Ruby's appearance is reflected in the next two listings, including his first performance with Dizzy Gillespie, Sonny Stitt, and James Moody.

Newport All Stars at the Boston Globe Jazz Festival[36]
January 14, 1966, War Memorial Auditorium (now named Hynes Auditorium), Boston
Ruby Braff (cnt), Pee Wee Russell (cl), Bud Freeman (ts), George Wein (p), Jack Lesberg (b), Morey Feld (dm)

Finale at the Boston Globe Jazz Festival[37]
January 14, 1966, War Memorial Auditorium (now named Hynes Auditorium), Boston
Ruby Braff (cnt), Dizzy Gillespie (tp), Sonny Stitt (as), Stan Getz, Bud Freeman, Zoot Sims, James Moody (ts), Toshiko Mariano (p), and unknown rhythm section

Performances on January 15 at the festival were by the Duke Ellington Orchestra, Joe Williams with Duke Ellington, the Benny Goodman Quintet, and the Herbie Mann Octet.

Dick Creeden[38]
January 1966, Village Green, Danvers, Massachusetts
Ruby Braff (cnt) sitting in one night with Dick Creeden, Stan Montero (cl, ts), Cas Brodsky (tb), Bob Pillsbury (p), unknown (b), Dave Markell (dm)

Ruby Braff[39]
January 28–29, 1966, Village Green, Danvers, Massachusetts

Where Is Jazz Going: WBAI Interview[40]
February 5, 1966, WBAI Studio, New York
Bob Messenger interviewed Ruby Braff, Jake Hanna, and other musicians

Ruby's next documented appearance was at Town Hall in New York. The occasion was a memorial concert for Hank D'Amico. Ruby had performed in a group with D'Amico in November that may have been his final performance. Musicians performing in the memorial concert included Ruby Braff, George Barnes, Bob Brookmeyer, Clark Terry, Billy Butterfield, Al Cohn, Roy Eldridge, Stan Getz, Peanuts Hucko, Thad Jones, Mel Lewis, Max Kaminsky, Elliot Lawrence, Gerry Mulligan, Marian McPartland, Joe Newman, Kai Winding, Glen Osser, Vincent Abato, Tony Aless, Mousey Alexander, Vernon Brown, Bill Crow, Cutty Cutshall, Kenny Davern, Tony Faso, Morey Feld, Mickey Gravine, Jim Hall, Jake Hanna, Milt Hinton, Bernie Leighton, Jack Lesberg, Jimmy Maxwell, Don Lamond, Dave McKenna, Lou McGarity, Marty Napoleon, Tommy Newsom, Gene Quill, Boomie Richman, Ernie Royal, Sal Salvador, Tony Scott, Bill Stegmeyer, Lou Stein, Buddy Weed, Joe Wilder, Phil Woods, and others, with Willis Conover serving as the master of ceremonies. A copy of the concert program is available.

Hank D'Amico Memorial Concert[41]
March 20, 1966, Town Hall, New York
Marian McPartland and Ruby Braff performed together as they did in 1954 for Frankie Newton's memorial concert.

Ruby next returned to Texas for the second year in a row with the Newport All Stars. This was his first documented performance with Gerry Mulligan. Then he returned to New York before continuing to appear with the Newport All Stars in Kansas City and Atlanta before returning to the Newport Jazz Festival.

Newport All Stars[42]
April 2–3, 1966, Longhorn Jazz Festival, Disch Field, Houston
Ruby Braff (cnt), Bud Freeman (ts), Gerry Mulligan (bar), George Wein (p), Jack Lesberg (b), Morey Feld (dm)

Benefit Show at the Village Gate[43]
April 26, 1966, Village Gate, 160 Bleeker Street, New York
Ruby Braff appeared in a benefit show that also included the Max Roach Quintet, the Thad Jones–Mel Lewis Orchestra, the Art Farmer Quintet, the Jimmy Giuffre Quartet, Roy Eldridge, Roland Kirk, and Carol Sloane.

The Jazz Interactions sessions were held each Sunday from 5–9 p.m. at the Village Gate. This may have included Ruby Braff on some occasions but no specific information is available at this time.

Newport All Stars[44]
May 1, 1966, Kansas City Jazz Festival, Kansas City, Missouri
Ruby probably performed with this group

Newport All Stars[45]
May 27, 1966, Atlanta Jazz Festival, Atlanta Stadium
Ruby Braff (cnt), Lou McGarity (tb), Pee Wee Russell (cl), George Wein (p), Eddie Condon (g), Jack Lesberg (b), Dick Berk (dm)
Indiana
At the Jazz Band Ball
Blues from the Delta
Oh, Baby

Peanuts Hucko Sextet[46]
June 9–August 3, 1966, Eddie Condon's, 330 East 56th Street, New York (closed Sundays)
Ruby Braff (cnt), Cutty Cutshall (tb), Peanuts Hucko (cl), Dave McKenna or Ray Bryant (p), Gene Ramey (b), Cliff Leeman (dm)

Dave McKenna played the first week of this engagement, replaced by Ray Bryant for the balance. Ruby had replaced Herman Autrey in this group and Autrey, in turn, replaced Ruby in August. Ruby would have been absent for other appearances in June and July.

Ruby Braff Septet at the Museum of Modern Art: *Jazz in the Garden*[47]
June 23, 1966, Museum of Modern Art Courtyard, 11 West 53rd Street, New York (co–sponsored by *DownBeat* magazine, opening concert in the series, produced by Dan Morgenstern, Herbert Bronstein, and Charles Graham)
Ruby Braff (cnt), Buddy Tate (ts), Bob Wilber (ss), Phil Woods (as), George Wein (p), Jack Lesberg (b), Marquis Foster (dm)
Undecided
Keepin' Out of Mischief Now
C Jam Blues
These Foolish Things
Museum Blues
Lullaby of the Leaves
I Would Do Anything for You
Mean to Me
Take the "A" Train
NOTE: A photograph from this concert appeared in the *New York Times*.

Ruby reported that he played at a country club with Eddie Condon the day before the Newport Jazz Festival. When lying on the grass lawn, he relaxed but later developed allergy symptoms for the first time in his life. Upon reaching Newport Buddy Rich helped him recover. Allergies would become part of the Ruby's life in later years, making it difficult for him to travel. He became very sensitive to both temperature and humidity. In later years, he asked that electric fans be placed in front of the stage in some clubs to blow smoke away from the bandstand.

Ruby Braff and Eddie Condon[48]
June 30, 1966, unknown country club location
Details unknown

A photograph exists of Ruby Braff, Gerry Mulligan, Bud Freeman, Buddy Rich, and George Wein, performing on the first day of the four-day Newport Jazz Festival in 1966.[49]

Newport All Stars
July 1, 1966, 13th Newport Jazz Festival, Festival Field, Newport, Rhode Island
Ruby Braff (cnt), Bud Freeman (ts), Gerry Mulligan (as, bar), George Wein (p), Jack Lesberg (b), Buddy Rich (dm)
Rose Room
  Jazz Band EBCD 2120-2 (CD), LRC CDC 8520, Denon (J) C38-7682,
  DC 8520, LRC (J) YX 7563, LRC CDC7682, CDC 8520,
  Europa Jazz EJ 1034, EJ 42, I Giganti Del Jazz 42, Hallmark CD 310872
  Weton-Wesgram MCPS CD PACK 017
Bernie's Tune
  Jazz Band EBCD 2120-2 (CD), Bluenite CD BN 078,
  Hallmark CD 310872, Weton-Wesgram MCPS CD PACK 017
I Can't Give You Anything but Love (BF feature)
  Jazz Band EBCD 2120-2 (CD)
Yesterdays (RB feature)
  Jazz Band EBCD 2120-2 (CD)
Out of Nowhere (GM feature)
  Jazz Band EBCD 2120-2 (CD), Bluenite CD BN 078, Hallmark CD 310872
I Never Knew
  Jazz Band EBCD 2120-2 (CD), I Giganti Del Jazz (It) 30,
  Europa Jazz EJ 1024, Bluenite CD BN 078, Hallmark CD 310872,
  Weton-Wesgram MCPS CD PACK 017
NOTE: Jazz Band EBCD 2120-2 (CD) is titled *Newport Jazz All Stars July 1966*. I Giganti Del Jazz (It) 30 lists the incorrect date of 1961 for the above tune. Tom Lord's *Jazz Discography* gives different rhythm section (Billy Taylor, Benny Moten, Osie Johnson for Wein, Lesberg, and Rich on "Rose Room" and "Bernie's Tune" only; however, the drummer sounds like Buddy Rich and George Wein handles all announcements. There are a number of other releases of several of these tunes. Sometimes they are released as part of recordings by Gerry Mulligan. For example, Weton-Wesgram MCPS CD PACK 017 is titled *Gerry Mulligan: The Saxophone Player* and Hallmark (E) CD 310872 is titled *West Coast Sax*.

There is a photo available from the March of Jazz program.[50] These recordings are the earliest I have found where Ruby performs with Jack Lesberg although they had performed together since at least 1958.

George Wein wrote about the above session, further confirming Buddy Rich's presence on "Rose Room":[51]

> After the struggle of the past months, I was hungry for the joyous feeling that the 1966 Newport Jazz Festival was all about. So I did an opening-night set with the Newport All Stars—which, this year, featured not only the usual cast of Bud Freeman, Jack Lesberg, and Ruby Braff, but also Gerry Mulligan and Buddy Rich. I had never played with either Buddy or Gerry and I was looking forward to it. We started with "Rose Room," my piano leading into the tune.
>
> From the first few measures, it was clear that Buddy was steering the ship. His drumming was so exacting and propulsive that it took us all to another level. It brought things out of the group that surprised everybody. It seemed to inspire Ruby in particular. . . .
>
> Gerry was another revelation. His baritone saxophone swung through "Out of Nowhere" with lightness, like a soft-shoe tap dancer with an intricate, delicate routine. And Gerry surprised everyone when, counting off "Bernie's Tune," he switched to alto, an instrument he had not played publicly in nearly twenty years.
>
> Gerry and Buddy were on the gig because they had asked to play with us. . . . John Wilson of the *New York Times* noted with some surprise that our little band had been the 'stars' of the program.

Whitney Balliett reported the following in *The New Yorker*:[52] "Braff played as if he might never play again; each solo had a thousand good notes, a dozen leaping intervals, run upon graceful run, and a beseeching passion."

Next, Ruby performed in a group that gathered many notable trumpeters. A photograph shows Billy Taylor, Jimmy Owens, Clark Terry, Bobby Hackett, Gene Taylor, Kenny Dorham, Dizzy Gillespie (partially obscured), Howard McGhee, Ruby Braff, Sid Shaeffer, and Kenny Burrell performing on the Newport stage in the next session.

Trumpet Workshop[53]
July 4, 1966, 13th Newport Jazz Festival, Festival Field, Newport, Rhode Island (fourth day of four-day festival)
Dizzy Gillespie, Bobby Hackett, Clark Terry, Kenny Dorham, Henry "Red" Allen, Howard McGhee (tp), Thad Jones (cnt), Ruby Braff (cnt), Billy Taylor, George Wein (p), Kenny Burrell (g), Sid Shaeffer (dm)

Featuring Kenny Dorham, Thad Jones, and Howard McGhee
Bag's Groove
    Solar (Sp) 4569903
My One and Only Love (Kenny Dorham)
    Solar (Sp) 4569903

I Can't Get Started (Thad Jones)
    Europa Jazz (I) EJ 1039
I'll Remember April (Howard McGhee)
    unissued, recording available
Wee Dot
    unissued, recording available
Kenny Dorham, Thad Jones, Howard McGhee out

Featuring Henry "Red" Allen (tp, voc), Ruby Braff (cnt), and Clark Terry (flgh and pocket trumpet)
Lover Come Back to Me*
    unissued, recording available
Summertime* (Allen feature)
    unissued, recording available
All of Me* (Allen feature)
    unissued, recording available

Featuring Ruby Braff (cnt), Ross Tompkins (p), Gene Taylor (b), Mike Deluse (dm), and Teddi King (voc)
Our Love Is Here to Stay
    unissued, recording available
Keepin' Out of Mischief Now
    unissued, recording available

Clark Terry (flgh, pocket trumpet) and Billy Taylor (p) replace Braff and Tompkins
Days of Wine and Roses (Terry feature)
    unissued, recording available
Rhythm-a-ning (Terry feature)
    unissued, recording available

Dizzy Gillespie (tp) and Bobby Hackett (cnt) replace Clark Terry
'S Wonderful
    Giganti Del Jazz (I) GJ 30, Europa Jazz (I) EJ 1024
On Green Dolphin Street (Hackett feature)
    unissued, recording available
I Got It Bad and That Ain't Good (Hackett feature)
    unissued, recording available
Struttin' with Some Barbecue (Hackett, Gillespie)
    unissued, recording available

Add: Kenny Burrell (g)
Siboney (Gillespie, Burrell)
    unissued, recording available

What's New? (Gillespie, Burrell, Sid Shaeffer (dm))
unissued, recording available

Dorham, Jones, McGhee, Hackett, Braff, Terry, return
Add Gene Taylor (b), Billy Taylor (p), Jimmy Owens (flgh)
Disorder at the Border
Unissued, recording available
NOTE: Solar (Sp) 4569903 is titled *Sharp Edge* by Howard McGhee. The CD lists the following personnel: Howard McGhee, Kenny Dorham (tp), Billy Taylor (p), Gene Taylor (b), Connie Kay (dm), and lists the performance as "live in New York, ca. 1960." David Meeker[54] also lists "St. Louis Blues" (Henry "Red" Allen) but this is apparently an error. Film may exist from this performance. *Jazz from Newport, 1966* from National Educational Television contains "Struttin' with Some Barbecue," "Siboney," "Lover Come Back to Me," and "Days of Wine and Roses."[55] At the time of publication, audio recordings of selections marked with an asterisk are available for viewing from YouTube.com. Each is shown with non-synchronized video clips of the performers.

A photo is available from the March of Jazz program.[56]

Ruby appeared with the Newport All Stars on Sunday evening, July 17 at a concert at Lewisohn Stadium, 138th Street and Amsterdam Avenue in New York. Others performing that night were the Dave Brubeck Quartet, the Thelonious Monk Quartet, and the Jimmy Smith Trio. This was part of a five-day program. Next, he appeared with Teddy Wilson at an unknown location in New Jersey before returning to Condon's in New York.

Newport All Stars at the Metropolitan Opera Summer Concert[57]
July 17, 1966, Lewisohn Stadium, New York
Bobby Hackett, Ruby Braff (cnt), Edmond Hall, Pee Wee Russell (cl), Zoot Sims (ts), George Wein (p), Jack Lesberg (b), Jake Hanna (dm)
The Man I Love
When You're Smiling

Teddy Wilson with Ruby Braff[58]
Mid–July 1966, unknown location in New Jersey
Ruby Braff (cnt), Clifton "Skeeter" Best (g), Teddy Wilson (p), Knobby Totah (b)

Ruby Braff and Peanuts Hucko[59]
Late August–Mid September 1966, Condon's, New York
Ruby Braff (cnt), Peanuts Hucko (cl), and unnamed other musicians

This reference could pertain to the June 9–August 3 engagement above since this club closed for vacation from August 20–September 6; however, the musicians could have returned in early September.

The next two reports involve an overlapping date, September 17. It is possible that Ruby did not appear in Toronto on the 17th (Saturday); however, it is not currently possible to resolve this apparent conflict. Perhaps Ruby obtained a substitute that allowed him to leave Toronto for the single date in Pittsburgh but the 17th was a Saturday making that unlikely for the final weekend of his appearance. Perhaps the Pittsburgh appearance was in the morning or afternoon, permitting him to return to Toronto for his evening appearance.

Ruby Braff[60]
Two-week stay including September 14–20, 1966, Plaza Room, Park Plaza Hotel, Toronto
Ruby Braff (cnt), Jimmy Coxson (p), Harold Holmes (b), John Connell (dm)
I've Got the World on a String
Pennies from Heaven
Just You, Just Me
Yesterdays

Ruby Braff Quartet[61]
September 17, 1966, Pittsburgh, Pennsylvania
Ruby Braff (cnt), Buddy Tate (ts), Don Coates (p), Jake Hanna (dm)

Ruby Braff[62]
Fall 1966, Playboy Club, New York
Ruby Braff played a "recent Friday" at the Playboy Club

Ruby Braff Quintet[63]
October 17, 1966, Condon's, New York—This may have continued on other Monday nights.
Ruby Braff (cnt), Dick Rath (tb), Joe Muranyi (cl), Don Coates (p), Johnny Blowers (dm)

These Monday sessions are not listed in *The New Yorker.*

Ruby began rehearsing with Bob Wilber in the hope of developing another group that could tour both in the US and abroad. A recording is available of one of their rehearsals, part of which has been issued commercially.

Rehearsal: Ruby Braff and Bob Wilber[64]**: *Private Treasures from the Allegheny Jazz Concerts***
November 9, 1966, Bob Wilber's home, New York City
Ruby Braff (cnt), Bob Wilber (cl, ss), Wayne Wright (g), unknown bass, with conversation between tunes

Everybody Loves My Baby (slow version)
unissued, recording available
Everybody Loves My Baby (false start)
unissued, recording available
Everybody Loves My Baby (fast version)
unissued, recording available
Mandy, Make Up Your Mind
unissued, recording available
I'm a Little Blackbird
unissued, recording available
Coal Cart Blues (incomplete performance)
unissued, recording available
Down in Honky Tonk Town
Jump JCD 12-35
China Boy
unissued, recording available
Cake-Walking Babies from Home (version 1)
unissued, recording available
Cake-Walking Babies from Home (version 2)
unissued, recording available
Cake-Walking Babies from Home (version 3)
unissued, recording available
Cake-Walking Babies from Home (version 4)
unissued, recording available
Cake-Walking Babies from Home (version 4)
unissued, recording available
Cake-Walking Babies from Home (version 5)
unissued, recording available
Blues (incomplete on recording)
unissued, recording available
NOTE: Jump JCD 12-35 is titled *Private Treasures from Allegheny Jazz Concerts 1950's–2000*. Other titles from this two-CD release are by other artists.

Bob Wilber was performing at Eddie Condon's throughout this period. It is certainly possible that Ruby sat in with the group at times, even though this was not listed in *The New Yorker*. *DownBeat* did mention Ruby's appearance, though.

Ruby Braff Quintet[65]
Late November or early December 1966, Condon's, New York

No other references to Ruby appear in *The New Yorker* at this time

Buddy Tate Band: Whitney Balliett's Party Celebrating Publication of *Such Sweet Thunder*[66]
December 1966, Five Spot Café, New York
Ruby Braff (cnt), Henry "Red" Allen (tp on several numbers), Buddy Tate (ts), George Wein (p), Tommy Potter (b), Jo Jones (dm), Buddy Rich (dm) substituting for Jones on several numbers

George Wein and the Newport All Stars Presented by Jazz Interactions[67]
"This Sunday" during December 1966 (December 3 or 10 are possible), Five Spot Café, 2 St. Mark's Place and 3rd, New York (see Figure 8.1)
Ruby Braff (cnt), Buddy Tate (ts), George Wein (p), Jack Lesberg (b), Don Lamond (dm)

Bob Wilber: Pharmaceutical Advertising Club's Annual Dinner Dance[68]
December 16, 1966, Waldorf-Astoria, New York
Ruby Braff (cnt), Buck Clayton, Johnny Glasel (tp), Vic Dickenson, Cutty Cutshall (tb), Rudy Powell (as), Bud Freeman (ts), Bob Wilber (cl, ss), Dave McKenna (p), Wayne Wright (g), Milt Hinton (b), Morey Feld (dm)
One O'Clock Jump
Goodnight Sweetheart
Basin Street Blues
Other tunes not mentioned

Ruby Braff Interview with Elwood Glover
January 1967? Date and location unknown, CBC–TV
NOTE: A recording of this interview is available but remains unissued.

Newport All Stars at the 2nd Annual Boston Globe Jazz Festival[69]
January 20, 1967, City of Boston War Memorial Auditorium (now named Hynes Auditorium), evening concert, Boston
Ruby Braff (cnt), Lou McGarity (tb), Edmond Hall, Pee Wee Russell (cl), Bud Freeman (ts), George Wein (p), Jack Lesberg (b), Don Lamond (dm)
Blues
Little Rock Getaway (Braff feature)
Stars Fell on Alabama (McGarity feature)
Sugar (Russell feature)
As Long As I Live (Hall feature)

Add Marian McPartland, with Lesberg and Lamond only
Autumn Leaves

Add Jimmy McPartland to above
Unnamed tune

All musicians return
Undecided

Further details are unknown; however, a photograph showing Lou McGarity, Ruby Braff, Bud Freeman, Ed Hall, and Pee Wee Russell exists.[70] Yet another exists by Jack Bradley, although incorrectly dated from the late 1960s[71] in the March of Jazz program. A copy is included in this book's photo section.

Newport All Stars at the 2nd Annual Boston Globe Jazz Festival[72]
January 21, 1967, City of Boston War Memorial Auditorium (now named Hynes Auditorium), afternoon concert, Boston
Ruby Braff (cnt), Lou McGarity (tb), Edmond Hall, Pee Wee Russell (cl), Bud Freeman (ts), George Wein (p), Jack Lesberg (b), Don Lamond (dm)
I've Found a New Baby
Other tunes not mentioned

Ruby Braff[73]
March 3, 1967, Mystic Motor Inn, Mystic, Connecticut
Ruby Braff(cnt) as guest artist featured with other musicians

Newport All Stars[74]
April 30, 1967, Longhorn Jazz Festival, Longhorn, Texas (festival ran from April 28–30)
Ruby Braff (cnt), Lou McGarity (tb), Pee Wee Russell (cl), Buddy Tate (ts), Ernie Caceres (bars), George Wein (p), Jack Lesberg (b), Don Lamond (dm)
If I Had You
Lester Leaps In (Tate feature)
Stars Fell on Alabama (McGarity feature)
Honeysuckle Rose
I Can't Give You Anything but Love (Braff feature)
Just You, Just Me
NOTE: Other titles not listed in review.

Newport All Stars[75]
May 1967, Five Spot Café, 2 St. Marks Place, just east of 3rd Avenue, New York
(as a part of the Sunday-only Jazz Interactions program that ran from 5–10 p.m.)
NOTE: Musicians not listed in article.

The Jazz Interactions series ended Sunday, August 13, 1967.[76] Ahead was a tour that included several performances in Mexico. George Wein wrote the following:[77]

> This included a massive Newport Jazz Festival tour of Europe with an aggregate of artists as diverse as Sarah Vaughan, Thelonious Monk, Miles Davis, and Archie Shepp. I accompanied the tour on every date, heard most of the music and spent time with the musicians. [Perhaps the tour Wein describes is the Jazz Expo '67 tour that began in October 1967, not in the spring, which would closely follow the concerts he described in Mexico.]
>
> In addition to a Newport tour of Europe, the spring 1967 brought the first "Newport Jazz Festival in Mexico"—an event produced in conjunction with that nation's leading concert agency, Conciertos Daniel. American Airlines had chosen to sponsor the festival as a celebration of its 25th anniversary of service to Mexico. . . .
>
> We presented two concerts in the city of Puebla, two concerts at Belles Artes (a lovely 2,000-seat opera house in Mexico City), and one at the National Auditorium in Mexico City (which had a capacity of 14,000). The festival was a huge success; our concerts in Puebla [two concerts, April 13] and at Belle Artes [two concerts, April 12 in Mexico City] sold out, and we drew 10,000 people to the National Auditorium [April 14, Mexico City].

Some of the performances were recorded and are shown for the May dates that correct the April dates listed above. The dates for the performances in Mexico are inconsistently reported in various sources. *DownBeat* reviewed the Puebla Jazz Festival, reporting the date as being on May 12 and thus is the most reliable source for dates.[78]

Newport All Stars[79]

May 12, 1967, Puebla Jazz Festival, Auditorio De La Reforma, Puebla, Mexico
Ruby Braff (tp), Pee Wee Russell (cl), Bud Freeman (ts), George Wein (p), Jack Lesberg (b), Don Lamond (dm)

'Deed I Do
    unissued and unavailable
Blue and Sentimental
    Columbia CS 9631, Mosaic MCD-1018
Rosetta
    Mosaic MCD-1018
Blues for Puebla
    Mosaic MCD-1018

At some point during a tour by the Newport All Stars, Ruby was to meet Bud Freeman in Bud's hotel room. He arrived, pretty much on time, and knocked on the door. Bud said, "Come in." Ruby was surprised to see Bud standing in front of a floor standing mirror, completely naked. Bud slowly turned from side to side, never taking his eyes from his reflection. He said to Ruby, "Pretty good for a sixty-year-old, don't you agree." For perhaps the only time in his life, Ruby did not say a word in reply.

Newport All Stars[80]
May 13, 1967, Palace of Fine Arts, Mexico City (two concerts, but Newport All Stars only played the first concert)
Ruby Braff (tp), Pee Wee Russell (cl), Bud Freeman (ts), George Wein (p), Jack Lesberg (b), Don Lamond (dm)
I Never Knew
    Columbia CS 9631, Mosaic MCD-1018
All of Me
    Columbia CS 9631, Mosaic MCD-1018
Have You Met Miss Jones?
    Columbia CS 9631, Mosaic MCD-1018
Take the "A" Train
    Columbia CS 9631, Mosaic MCD-1018
I Can't Give You Anything but Love
    Columbia CS 9631, Mosaic MCD-1018
Honeysuckle Rose
    Mosaic MCD-1018
The World Is Waiting for the Sunrise
    Columbia CS 9631, Mosaic MCD-1018

Newport All Stars[81]
May 14, 1967, National Auditorium, Mexico City
Ruby Braff (tp), Pee Wee Russell (cl), Bud Freeman (ts), George Wein (p), Jack Lesberg (b), Don Lamond (dm)
If I Had You
    Columbia CS 9631, Mosaic MCD-1018
'S Wonderful
    Mosaic MCD-1018
NOTE: The LP and CD include performances drawn from the three concerts. Both are titled *George Wein Is Alive and Well in Mexico.* Note that the dates listed by Columbia and Mosaic are all in April rather than May. I have used the date published in the contemporary review in *DownBeat* instead. All titles on Columbia CS 9631 also are included on Mosaic MCD-1018. The Mosaic release included previously unissued performances, probably selected from the list below.

Newport All Stars[82]
Several additional titles were recorded but remain unissued on Columbia LP, *George Wein Is Alive and Well in Mexico,* or the subsequent Mosaic CD issue with three possible exceptions as shown below:
These Foolish Things
'Deed I Do
Blue and Broken Hearted
Rose Room

Blues for Puebla
    probably same performance as issued on Mosaic MCD-1018 from May 12
Rosetta
    probably same performance as issued on Mosaic MCD-1018 from May 12
Undecided
'S Wonderful
    probably same performance as issued on Mosaic MCD-1018 from May 14
Sugar
Lullaby of the Leaves
Just One of Those Things

George Wein wrote: "Dizzy Gillespie, one of the festival's better-known attractions, later confessed to me that he had wanted to walk out onstage to join us in Mexico City. I told him that he should have."[83]

Newport All Stars[84]
May 25, 1967, US National Day, Place de Nations, Expo '67 *Jazz Festival USA*, Montreal
Ruby Braff (cnt), Pee Wee Russell (cl), Bud Freeman (ts), George Wein (p), Jack Lesberg (b), Don Lamond (dm)
Royal Garden Blues
Les Blues Fait Froid Aujourd'hui*
Just You, Just Me
The World Is Waiting for the Sunrise
NOTE: A recording of "Les Blues Fait Froid Aujourd'hui" is available but remains unissued and is marked with an asterisk. That title can be translated as "The Blues Is Cold Today."

Newport All Stars[85]
June 16 or 17, 1967, Atlanta Jazz Festival, Atlanta, Georgia
Musicians not listed in article

Newport All Stars[86]
June 29, 1967, NBC *Today Show*, New York
Ruby Braff (cnt), Pee Wee Russell (cl), Bud Freeman (ts), George Wein (p), Jack Lesberg (b), Don Lamond (dm)
St. Louis Blues
Honeysuckle Rose
Just One of Those Things
Sugar (omit Braff and Freeman)
I Can't Give You Anything but Love
NOTE: A recording of "Sugar" is available but remains unissued. A recording is reported to exist for "Just One of Those Things" and "I Can't Give You Anything but Love."

Ruby returned to the Newport Jazz Festival, performing twice on opening night, Friday, June 30. The evening began with Olatunji and Company and continued to Earl Hines with Ruby Braff who substituted for Roy Eldridge in that performance. This was their first performance together. Ruby then continued with the All Stars. After an intermission, the evening continued with Count Basie, Thelonious Monk, Dizzy Gillespie, Max Roach, the Modern Jazz Quartet, and the Albert Ayler Quintet. This clearly represented a wide range of styles.

Ruby also appeared during the closing evening of the festival with Red Norvo, following Illinois Jacquet with Milt Buckner. The program then continued, featuring the Dave Brubeck Quartet, Sarah Vaughan, and the Wes Montgomery Trio, closing with Lionel Hampton and His Alumni Orchestra.

Ruby Braff and Earl Hines[87]
June 30, 1967, Schlitz Salute to Jazz: The 14th Newport Jazz Festival, Festival Field, Newport RI
Ruby Braff (cnt), Earl Hines (p)
You Can Depend on Me (Hines solo)
These Foolish Things
Rosetta

Whitney Balliett wrote the following in *The New Yorker*:[88]

> The two men, both fearless, self-preoccupied ornamentalists, had never played together before, but they got off a graceful 'These Foolish Things' and a fast, intent 'Rosetta' Hines' solos were full of his arrhythmic whirlpools and upper-register, single-note jubilations, and Braff managed to move in opposite parallels.

Newport All Stars[89]
June 30, 1967, Schlitz Salute to Jazz: The 14th Newport Jazz Festival, Festival Field, Newport, Rhode Island
Ruby Braff (cnt), Bud Freeman (ts), Budd Johnson (ss, ts), Pee Wee Russell (cl), George Wein (p), Jack Lesberg (b), Don Lamond (dm)
Royal Garden Blues
Sugar (Pee Wee Russell feature)
Singing the Blues
These Foolish Things

Add Budd Johnson (ss)
Summertime

Ruby flew to Wisconsin for the following performance and then returned to Newport in time for his appearance with Red Norvo on the closing day of the Newport Jazz Festival.

Newport All Stars[90]
July 2, 1967, Washington Park, Milwaukee, Wisconsin
Ruby Braff (cnt), Bud Freeman (ts), Pee Wee Russell (cl), George Wein (p), Jack Lesberg (b), Don Lamond (dm)

Red Norvo All Stars[91]
July 3, 1967, 14th Newport Jazz Festival, Festival Field, Newport, Rhode Island, starting at 7:30
Ruby Braff (cnt-1), Red Norvo (vib), George Wein (p), Jack Lesberg (b), Don Lamond (dm)
I Love You
I Surrender Dear (Norvo switches to xylophone after his first chorus and returns to vibraphone)
Ida, Sweet as Apple Cider
Rosetta (1)
When It's Sleepy Time Down South (1)
NOTE: This may have been recorded by Voice of America on program number MUSA 4740B.[92] It is not clear if Ruby's other performances from the 14th festival were recorded. They are not presently listed in the Library of Congress collection.

Newport All Stars
Autumn 1967, location unknown but probably New York
Ruby Braff (cnt), Buddy Tate (ts), George Wein (p), Jack Lesberg (b), Don Lamond (dm)
Pan Am Blues
    Soundsheet Promotional Record
Strolling at Newport
    Soundsheet Promotional Record
NOTE: This is a promotional record for Pan American Airlines. It was issued on flexible Soundsheet (seven-inch LP) and made to promote the Newport Jazz Festival in Europe. This disc was also included with each boxed set of David Redfern photographs published by Doug Dobell from his shop at 77 Charing Cross Road in London.[93] One copy is available in the author's collection.

Newport All Stars[94]
Summer 1967, reported engagements for Newport Festival packages in Detroit, St. Louis, Memphis, Cleveland, Cincinnati, and Buffalo. Some may involve the Newport All Stars, perhaps with Ruby Braff.

Ruby next flew to England to tour with Alex Welsh. A number of engagements were listed in *Jazz Journal International*. In a few cases, additional information is available.

Ruby Braff with Alex Welsh[95]: Tour Begins
September 22 Osterley Rugby Football Club, Osterley, Middlesex, England
September 23 Nottingham, England following an afternoon rehearsal in Manchester (postponing Manchester to October 6–7 from the original schedule)[96]—details follow:

Ruby Braff with Alex Welsh Band[97]
September 23, 1967, Dancing Slipper, Central Avenue, West Bridgeford, Nottingham, England—the performance followed an afternoon rehearsal in Manchester
Ruby Braff (cnt), Alex Welsh (tp), Roy Williams (tb), John Barnes (bars), Fred Hunt (p), Jim Douglas (g), Ronnie Rae (b), Lennie Hastings (dm)
Shiny Stockings (Braff out)
    unissued, recording available
Please (Braff out)
    Lake LACD 223
When My Sugar Walks Down the Street
    Lake LACD 223
I Can't Give You Anything but Love
    Lake LACD 223
Between the Devil and the Deep Blue Sea
    Lake LACD 223
You've Changed
    Lake LACD 223
No One Else But You
    Lake LACD 223
Stan's Dance (Braff out, start missing)
    unissued, recording available
Just One More Chance (Braff out)
    Lake LACD 223
Where's Freddie?
    Lake LACD 223
Medley:
  Nobody Knows You When You're Down and Out
    Lake LACD 223
  Buddy Bolden's Blues
    Lake LACD 223
Ruby Got Rhythm (Ruby's Tune)
    unissued, recording available
Foolin' Myself
    Lake LACD 223
Hear Me Talkin' to You
    Lake LACD 223

After You've Gone
unissued, recording available
NOTE: Alex Welsh announced "Ruby's Tune" but they later recorded this with the title "Ruby Got Rhythm." It is a variation on "I Got Rhythm." Lake LACD223 is titled *Ruby Braff with Alex Welsh & His Band.*

At the beginning of the second set of this performance Alex Welsh announced, "Ruby Braff is certainly the finest musician we have ever worked with." Placing this in context, Ruby's tour with this band came after prior tours that featured Henry "Red" Allen, Pee Wee Russell, Bud Freeman, and Earl Hines. Whether you agree with Welsh or not does not really matter. The clear message is that Ruby, in 1965, was recognized as a member of an elite group of jazz musicians with an international reputation among musicians and the jazz audience.

Ruby Braff with Alex Welsh Band: Tour Continues[98]
September 24 Rotterdam, The Netherlands
September 25 and 26 100 Club, London
September 27 Amersham, Buckinghamshire, England
September 28 Haywards Heath, West Sussex, England
September 30 Birmingham, West Midlands, England
October 1 Boston, Lincolnshire, England
October 3 Purcell Room, London (7:30)

The Times of London included a short review of Ruby's performance at Purcell Room with Alex Welsh:[99]

> Art Farmer, the fine modern jazz trumpeter, once wrote that he could see no reason why Ruby Braff, a musician the same age as himself, should have turned his back on modern jazz and based his cornet style on an earlier era. But as Braff has proved over the past decade and a half, most recently at the Purcell Room last night, he has managed to develop his style in ways which would have been impossible in a modern jazz context.
>
> This can be heard most obviously in his tone, which is much fuller and richer than that of any modern trumpeter and a good deal more flexible. Only occasionally on slower number does it slip from a beautiful roundness into a slightly plump sound.
>
> But the most valuable development lies in his rhythmic approach. Although modern jazz is rhythmically more sophisticated than earlier styles, its sophistication is tied to an increasingly minute and strict subdivision of the basic beat and has thus lost sight of the earlier tendency to phrase freely across the beat. It is this aspect which Braff has taken almost to an ultimate conclusion with a constant departure and return to the pulse which is judged to a hair's breadth and probably has no parallel in modern jazz.
>
> The accompanying Alex Welsh Band played as well as ever, in spite of Lennie Hastings' ugly drumming. It was especially interesting to hear Roy Williams's trombone beside Braff's cornet because it is something of the same

> rhythmic independence in his playing that makes him the most original soloist in the Welsh Band.

It is worthwhile to note that Lennie Hastings received favorable reviews in other performances when he appeared with Ruby.

Ruby Braff with Alex Welsh Band: Tour Continues[100]
October 4 Dolphin, Botley, Oxfordshire, England
October 5 Town Hall, Wandsworth, England

Ruby Braff and Alex Welsh[101]
October 6, 1967, Manchester Sports Guild (Ballroom), Manchester, England
Ruby Braff (cnt), Alex Welsh (tp), John Barnes (bars), Roy Williams (tb), Al Gay (cl, ts), Fred Hunt (p), Jim Douglas (g), Ronnie Rae (b), Lennie Hastings (dm)
When My Sugar Walks Down the Street
I Can't Give You Anything but Love
Between the Devil and the Deep Blue Sea
Exactly Like You
No One Else But You
Buddy Bolden's Blues
Look Out Here Comes Jenks
You've Changed
Hear Me Talkin' to You
You Took Advantage of Me
NOTE: A recording of these tunes is available but remains unissued.

Ruby Braff and Alex Welsh[102]
October 7, 1967, Manchester Sports Guild (Cellar), Manchester, England (replacing Nottingham which shifted to September 23)
Ruby Braff (cnt), Alex Welsh (tp), Roy Williams (tb), John Barnes (bars), Al Gay (cl, ts), Fred Hunt (p), Jim Douglas (g), Ronnie Rae (b), Lennie Hastings (dm); Guests: Nat Pierce (p), Eddie Jones (b), Jake Hanna (dm)
When My Sugar Walks Down the Street
I Can't Give You Anything but Love
Between the Devil and the Deep Blue Sea
Exactly Like You
You've Changed
No One Else But You
Where's Freddie? (with Jake Hanna)
Just You, Just Me (with Hanna, Jones, and Pierce)
Foolin' Myself (With Hanna, Jones, and Pierce)
Hear Me Talkin' to You (with Hanna, Jones, and Pierce)
Keepin' Out of Mischief Now (with Hanna, Jones, and Pierce)
Nobody Wants You When You're Down and Out

Ruby Got Rhythm
You've Changed
NOTE: A recording of these tunes is available but remains unissued. The final three tunes are from a different source but are labeled as coming from this same concert.

Roy Williams commented about the Manchester Sports Guild engagement:[103]

> The first time we met Ruby was in 1967 and again the first gig was the Manchester Sports Guild. We all had to get up there early because he wanted to meet us and he wanted to talk about a program and to rehearse. I can always remember that when we got there he was sitting on a high stool with the manager of the place, Jenks, in his carpet slippers and pullover. We were all introduced to Ruby and he seemed quite affable. He said 'Ok, let's get down to business,' so we went down into the cellar. We were all a little bit nervous. We'd heard the records, his famous Vanguard sides, but I don't think we did any of those tunes. He would say, 'Right, d'you guys know this?' It would be something vaguely familiar, but he wasn't having that. You either knew it or you didn't. We started to play something and one or two of us weren't very sure. Fred Hunt on piano was very nervous. Ruby said, 'Stop! Now listen. I'm only going to tell you guys this once. Don't *ever* say you know a tune when you don't. Remember, there have been thousands and thousands of tunes and you're not expected to know them all. So if I call a tune and you're not a hundred per cent sure, you tell me and we won't do it. Because if *you* suggest something and I don't know it, then I'll tell you the same. Anyway, it worked well and we came to an amicable conclusion. He wrote out keys and things, fine, and he did a couple of features and it was wonderful, it really was. He introduced all that interplay between himself and bass or guitar, and all those lovely colors going on, which made it so interesting.

Those remarks echoed yet another of Ruby's principles, namely that you should always admit if you don't know a tune in advance. Once again, this was an aspect of his professionalism and his requirement that everyone conform to his musical standards. The next performance appears to have been added to this tour and may be the final concert; however, there is a gap in the record of Ruby's performances and it is likely he remained in England. Given his love of performing, he probably appeared somewhere before the Jazz Expo '67 tour began on October 19. That tour was extensive, covering twenty cities in twelve countries and lasting nearly a month. Ruby recorded with Alex Welsh after the Jazz Expo '67 tour, on November 8 before returning to the United States.

Ruby Braff with Alex Welsh: Tour Continues[104]
October 8, 1967, Carlisle, Cumbria, England

The Jazz Expo program took advantage of the presence of several American musicians in Europe to form the center of a festival. *The Times* described some of the background leading to this program, noting that Jack Higgins was the central figures from the Harold Davidson organization that planned this event. The article quoted him as follows:[105]

> 'This really came about through a series of well-placed coincidences. At the same time as George Wein was bringing over some Americans for the Berlin Jazz Festival, Charles Lloyd was to be on his way back from Prague, a German promoter had planned a tour of his American Folk Blues Festival, and I myself was bringing in Dave Brubeck, Budd Johnson, Earle Warren and others.' Once the idea of combining them all in one festival had been born, it was then a matter of hard work and organization to fit them together and to add what further attractions were needed to make a full week of jazz concerts.

Various musicians performed in this tour arranged by George Wein and co-sponsored by Pan American Airways and the United States Travel Service of the US Department of Commerce. Ruby's biography and a photograph by David Redfern appeared in the program used at least for the October 24 concert in London. Part of the text reflects Ruby's humor:

> Braff was unfortunate enough never to have worked for Al Capone, never to have experienced the bootleg era, never to have taken part in primitive pre-electric recordings, never to have become part of a folk lore which was already on the decline when he was still at school. Historically he has always been out of his time, and in the jazz world, where dates and eras are often more important to the followers than the actual merit of the music, this was a fatal handicap. But for those listeners enlightened enough not to care about such matters, and who listen only for the professional performance, Braff is one of the outstanding trumpeters.[106]

Jazz Expo '67 Tour[107]

October 19–November 12, 1967, in over 20 cities in 12 countries including London, England; Ireland; Helsinki, Finland; Copenhagen, Denmark; Stockholm, Sweden; Berlin, Germany; Rotterdam, The Netherlands; Belgium; Italy; Paris, France; and Barcelona, Spain

Ruby Braff (cnt), Buddy Tate (ts), George Wein (p), Jack Lesberg (g), Don Lamond (dm)

Trumpeter Bill Coleman wrote the following:

> [After playing in a festival in Birmingham, England, on May 29] I came back also to London to play a festival at the Hammersmith theater. . . . Ben Webster was there also, and it was my first time to become acquainted with a fine trumpet player whom I had heard on records but never met him. His name was Ruby Braff and when we met, the feeling between us was like we had known each other for years. Ruby was with George Wein's Newport All Stars. He played more horn in person than I had heard him do on records and he had a beautiful style.[108]

Jazz Expo '67 Festival: Newport All Stars[109]
October 24, 1967, Odeon, Hammersmith, London
Ruby Braff (cnt), Buddy Tate (ts), George Wein (p), Jack Lesberg (b), Don Lamond (dm)
'Deed I Do
I Want a Little Girl
I Can't Give You Anything but Love
Undecided
Pan Am Blues

Hear Me Talkin'
October 28, 1967, London
Ruby Braff (cnt), George Wein (p), Jack Lesberg (b), Don Lamond (dm)
Don't Blame Me
    Black Lion BLCD760138 (CD), Polydor 2460 127,
    Black Lion (US) BL 127, Jazz Colours 874773-2

Add Buddy Tate (ts) same date
Mean to Me (take 1)
    Black Lion BLCD 760138 (CD), Polydor 2460 127,
    Black Lion (US) BL 127, Jazz Colours 874773-2, Jazz Colors 874713-2
Body and Soul (no Tate)
    Black Lion BLCD 760138 (CD), 1201 Music 1001
I Surrender Dear (no Braff)
    Black Lion BLCD 760138 (CD), Jazz Colors 874713-2
My Monday Date
    Black Lion BLCD 760138 (CD), Jazz Colors 874713-2
Take the "A" Train (take 2)
    Black Lion BLCD 760138 (CD), Jazz Colors 874713-2
Pan Am Blues
    Black Lion BLCD 760138 (CD), Jazz Colors 874713-2,
    St. Clair/Excelsior EXL 10252
These Foolish Things (no Braff)
    Black Lion BLCD 760138 (CD)
The Sheik of Araby (take 2)
    Black Lion BLCD 760138 (CD)
Lullaby of the Leaves (no Braff)
    Black Lion BLCD 760138 (CD)
Mean to Me (take 2)
    Black Lion BLCD 760138 (CD)
Take the "A" Train (take 1)
    Black Lion BLCD 760138 (CD)
Please Don't Talk About Me When I'm Gone (no Braff)
    Black Lion BLCD 760138 (CD)

The Sheik of Araby (take 1)
Black Lion BLCD 760138 (CD)
NOTE: Black Lion BLCD 760138 (CD) issued as *Ruby Braff—Buddy Tate with the Newport All Stars*. Polydor 2460 127 and BL 127 are both titled *Hear Me Talkin'*. "The Sheik of Araby" (probably take 1) is also on Black Lion BLP 30188 titled *Ruby Got Rhythm*, and Jazz Colours (G) 874720-2 *Introducing Jazz Colours*. "Mean to Me" and "Take the 'A' Train" (probably take 1 for each) are also on DA Music CD 3702 titled *Jazz Masters, Volume 2*. The album released on 1201 Music 1001 is titled *Original Jazz Legends Featuring Torrid Trumpeters*. Polydor 2460 138 is titled *Hear Me Talkin'*, and it includes "'A' Train," Foolish," "Monday," "Body," "Mean," "Surrender," "Please Don't," and "Pan Am Blues." Jazz Colors 874713-2 (Ger) is titled *Buddy Tate with Humphrey Lyttelton and Ruby Braff*, and it includes "Mean to Me" (take 1), "I Surrender Dear," "My Monday Date," "Take the 'A' Train" (take 2), and "Pan Am Blues." Jazz Colours 874773-2 is titled *Where's Freddie?* St. Claire/Excelsior EXL 10252 is titled *Jazzin' the Blues*. The National Sound Archive (British Library) catalog indicates the date for this performance is October 20, 1967, eight days before the date listed on the album.

Given the large number of reissues of these recordings, it is helpful to include the following helpful summary prepared by Tony Shoppee:

Timing	Song	A	B	C	D	E	F	G
4:32	Don't Blame Me		X		X		X	
6:31	Mean to Me (take1)		X		X		X	X
4:43	Body and Soul	X			X			
5:10	I Surrender Dear (Ruby out)	X			X			X
6:07	My Monday Date	X			X			X
3:57	Take the "A" Train (take 2)	X			X			X
3:18	Pan Am Blues	X			X			X
5:12	These Foolish Things	X			X			
5:24	The Sheik of Araby (take 2)				X			
2:43	Lullaby of the Leaves (no Braff)				X			
7:42	Mean to Me (take 2)	X			X			
4:20	Take the "A" Train (take 1)				X			
4:20	Please Don't Talk About Me When I'm Gone (no Braff)	X			X			
4:37	The Sheik of Araby (take 1)			X	X			

Key to various issues on Polydor, Black Lion, and DA Music (Jazz Colours):

A. Polydor 2460 138; Black Lion BLP 30115 etc (LP)
B. Polydor 2460 127; Black Lion BLP 30110 etc (LP)
C. Black Lion BLP 30188 (LP)
D. Black Lion BLCD 760138
E. Black Lion BLCD 760161

F. DA Music (Jazz Colours) 874773-2
G. DA music 874713-2

Newport All Stars
October 29, 1967, De Doelen Concert Hall, Rotterdam, The Netherlands

Newport All Stars[110]
November 5, 1967, Berlin Jazz Festival, Philharmonie, Berlin
Ruby Braff (cnt), Buddy Tate (ts), George Wein (p), Barney Kessel (g), Jack Lesberg (b), Don Lamond (dm)
Rose Room

Newport All Stars
November 7, 1967, Paris Jazz Festival, Paris
Ruby Braff (cnt), Buddy Tate (ts), George Wein (p), Barney Kessel (g), Jack Lesberg (b), Don Lamond (dm)
Take the "A" Train
    Blu Jazz (It) BJ 009CD
Pan Am Blues
    Blu Jazz (It) BJ 009CD
These Foolish Things
    Blu Jazz (It) BJ 009CD
I Can't Give You Anything but Love
    Blu Jazz (It) BJ 009CD
Indiana
    Blu Jazz (It) BJ 009CD

Hear Me Talkin'! and **Ruby Got Rhythm**
Ruby Braff with Alex Welsh and His Band
November 8, 1967, London
Ruby Braff (tp), Alex Welsh (tp), Roy Williams (tb), Al Gay (ts), John Barnes (bars), Fred Hunt (p), Jim Douglas (g), Ronnie Rae (b), Lennie Hastings (dm)
You've Changed (omit Welsh, Williams)
    Polydor (E) 2460.127, Jazz Colours (G) 874708-2, 874773-2
No One Else But You
    Polydor (E) 2460.127, 874773-2
Medley:
  Nobody Knows You When You're Down and Out
    Polydor (E) 2460.127, Intercord/Black Lion (G) 155.00, 874773-2
  Buddy Bolden's Blues
    Polydor (E) 2460.127, Intercord/Black Lion (G) 155.00, 874773-2
Where's Freddie?
    Polydor (E) 2460.127, 874773-2
Hear Me Talkin' to You (take 1)
    Polydor (E) 2460.127, Jazz Colours (G) 874708-2, 874773-2

Hear Me Talkin' to You (take 2)
  Black Lion (E) BLP 30188
Ruby Got Rhythm
  Polydor (E) 2460.127, Jazz Colours (G) 874708-2
When My Sugar Walks Down the Street
  Polydor (E) 2460.127, Jazz Colours (G) 874708-2,
  Bell Records BLR 89.059
Between the Devil and the Deep Blue Sea
  Polydor (E) 2460.127, Jazz Colours (G) 874708-2, Jazz Colours 874773-2
Smart Alex Blues
  Polydor (E) 2460.127, Jazz Colours (G) 874708-2, Jazz Colours 874773-2
Foolin' Myself (omit Welsh, Williams, Barnes, Gay)
  Black Lion (E) 2661.006, BLP 30188, (G) 157.001,
  (Am) BLP20101/102, (Sp)4263/64, Polydor Select 2661.006,
  Jazz Colours (G) 874716-2

NOTE: BLP 30188 is titled *Ruby Got Rhythm.* All titles on Polydor (E) 2460.127 are also on Black Lion (E) BLP 30110, BLCD 760161 (titled *Hear Me Talkin'*), (Sp) 4284, (G) 28405, 127.004, (US) BL 127 (also titled *Hear Me Talkin'*). "Hear Me Talkin'" (probably main take) is also on DA Music CDE 3702 titled *Jazz Masters, Volume 2.* Jazz Colours 874708-2 is titled *Ballads for Trumpet.* Intercord (G) 155.002 is titled *Dixieland Jubilee, Volume 1.* Jazz Colours 874773-2 is titled *Where's Freddie?* Two additional titles ("Mean to Me" and "Don't Blame Me") are also on Polydor (E)2460.127 attributed to the George Wein Newport All Stars actually recorded on October 28, 1967. Tony Shoppee prepared the following helpful guide to these issued recordings.

Timing	Song	A	B	C	D	E	F	G	H
4:42	You've Changed		X			X	X		
5:44	No One Else But You		X			X	X		
6:07	Medley		X			X	X		
6:24	Where's Freddie?		X			X	X		
5:53	Hear Me Talkin' to You (take 1)		X			X			X
5:48	Hear Me Talkin' to You (take 2)			X		X	X		
4:02	Ruby Got Rhythm			X		X			X
4:57	When My Sugar Walks Down the Street			X		X			X
10.25	Between the Devil and the Deep Blue Sea			X		X	X		X
5:39	Smart Alex Blues			X		X	X		X
4:04	Foolin' Myself			X		X			X

Key to various issues on Polydor, Black Lion, and DA Music (Jazz Colours):

A. Polydor 2460 138; Black Lion BLP 30115 etc (LP)
B. Polydor 2460 127; Black Lion BLP 30110 etc (LP)

C. Black Lion BLP 30188 (LP)
D. Black Lion BLCD 760138
E. Black Lion BLCD 760161
F. DA Music (Jazz Colours) 874773-2
G. DA Music 874713-2
H. DA Music 874716-2

Ruby had clearly extended his reputation in Europe, even beyond his previous impact. His next documented performance pairs him with Teddy Wilson at Carnegie Recital Hall in a very diverse performance series collectively called *Jazz the Personal Dimension.* Subsequent concerts in this series featured the Gary Burton Quartet, the Archie Shepp Quintet, and the Freddie Hubbard Quartet.

Teddy Wilson's Trio with Ruby Braff: *Jazz the Personal Dimension*[111]
December 15, 1967, 8:30, Carnegie Recital Hall, New York (co sponsored by The Institute of Jazz Studies and Carnegie Hall Corporation) (see Figure 8.2)
Ruby Braff (cnt), Teddy Wilson (p), Jack Lesberg, Don Lamond (dm)
Trio without Braff:
Stompin' at the Savoy
Satin Doll
Body and Soul
Moonglow
Undecided

Add Ruby Braff
I Can't Give You Anything but Love
Ain't Misbehavin'
Just You, Just Me
You Took Advantage of Me
This Year's Kisses
Sweet Georgia Brown (encore)

The following advertisements depict two of the performances in this chapter:

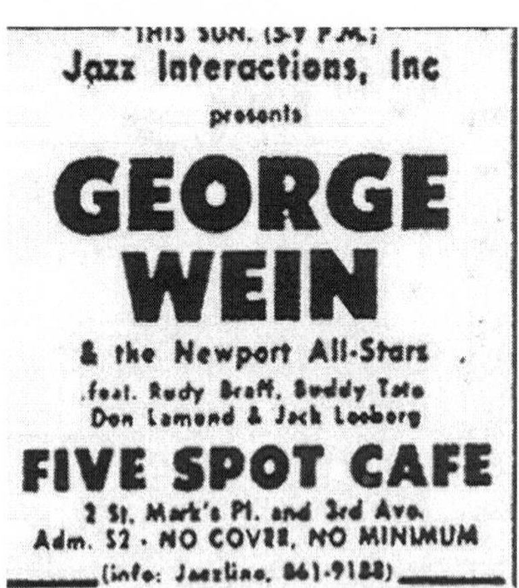

Figure 8.1: Advertisement December 1966

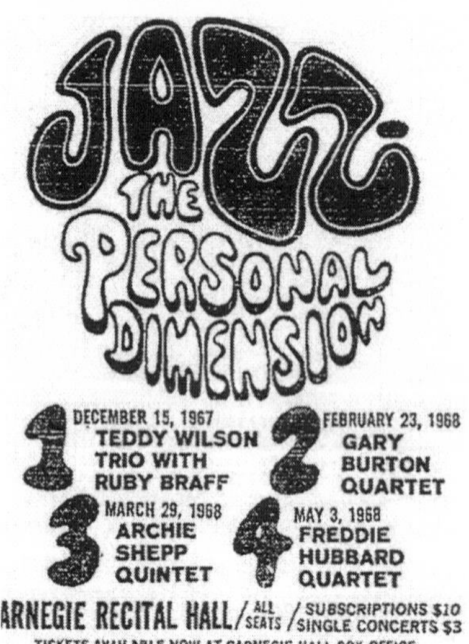

Figure 8.2: Advertisement November 26, 1967

Notes

1 Manfred Selchow, *Ding Ding: A Bio-Discographical Scrapbook on Vic Dickenson* (Germany Uhle & Kleinmann, 1998), 452–453. Further Information from Alun Morgan, citing forthcoming discography of Stan Tracey by Stephen Didymus. Also concert review article published as "Mainstream at the Festival Hall," *Jazz Journal International*, June 1965, 10–13 (including photographs).

2 Buck Clayton, *Buck Clayton's Jazz World* (New York: Oxford University Press, 1987), 175.

3 Published concert program Jazz from Kansas City.

[4] *Coda Magazine*, June/July 1965, 24.
[5] *DownBeat*, September 23, 1965, 18, *DownBeat* July 29, 1965, 10, and *New York Times*, June 7, 1965.
[6] *DownBeat*, July 29, 1965, 11.
[7] Ticket provided by Tony Adkins—additional information provided by David Griffiths from ad in *Jazz Times,* June 1965.
[8] *Jazz Journal International*, October 1965, 22–23.
[9] Jack Swinnerton's name was supplied by David Griffiths and Swinnerton is the author of the following report.
[10] "The Manchester Sports Guild Part 7: Wild Bill Davison and Others," *Just Jazz*, by Jack B. Swinnerton, April 2003, 30–31.
[11] Information on date and location prior to CD release provided by David Griffiths from ad in *Jazz Times,* June 1965. Paul Adams provided details on musicians.
[12] Some details unknown—ticket provided by Tony Adkins; information provided by David Griffiths from ad in *Jazz Times*, June 1965; personnel listed in "The Manchester Sports Guild Part 7: Wild Bill Davison and Others," *Just Jazz*, by Jack B. Swinnerton, April 2003, 30–31.
[13] Details unknown—information provided by David Griffiths from ad in *Jazz Times*, June 1965.
[14] Details unknown—information provided by David Griffiths from ad in *Jazz Times*, June 1965.
[15] Details unknown—information provided by David Griffiths from ad in *Jazz Times*, June 1965.
[16] Details unknown—information provided by David Griffiths from ad in *Jazz Times*, June 1965.
[17] Details unknown—information provided by David Griffiths from ad in *Jazz Times*, June 1965.
[18] Details unknown—information provided by David Griffiths from ad in *Jazz Times*, June 1965.
[19] Details unknown—information provided by David Griffiths from ad in *Jazz Times*, June 1965.
[20] Details unknown—information provided by David Griffiths from ad in *Jazz Times*, June 1965.
[21] Information provided by Bob Weir.
[22] Sinclair Traill, "Editorial," *Jazz Journal*, August 1965, 3.
[23] *DownBeat*, July 29, 1965, 10
[24] Robert Hilbert, *Pee Wee Russell: The Life of a Jazzman (*New York: Oxford University Press, 1993), 266. Art Hodes, writing about the festival and reporting a conversation with Ruby Braff in his column in *DownBeat*, December 16, 1965, 22. He said that Ruby reported he just returned from England and was about to fly to San Antonio. The festival is reviewed in an article in *DownBeat*, September 23, 1965, 19–23 with comments about the Newport All Stars reported on 20. A preannouncement is contained in "Top Jazz Names on *DownBeat* Festival," *Chicago Tribune*, August 8, 1965, E8.
[25] Art Hodes stated that he had played opposite Ruby and Bud at a club in San Antonio "this summer" and before the date of the *DownBeat* Jazz Festival reported in his column—see *DownBeat*, December 16, 1965, 22. Further details were published in *DownBeat*, August 26, 1965, 43. The date followed Hodes June 1965 recording session with Mama Yancey for Verve/Folkways.

[26] *Globe and Mail,* November 11, 1965.
[27] Bill Smith, *Coda Magazine*, December/January 1965/66, 28.
[28] *Globe and Mail,* November 11, 1965, *DownBeat*, January 13, 1966, 43, and *Coda Magazine*, December 1965/January 1966, 28 (includes photo).
[29] Jack Bradley from *Coda Magazine*, February/March 1966, 28 and also published in *The March of Jazz Celebrates Ruby Braff's 74th Birthday Party*, Arbors Records, 2001, 20.
[30] Jack Bradley reporting in *Coda Magazine*, February/March 1966, 23 includes photo of the group at this location (this was probably the last engagement played by Hank D'Amico prior to his death). The photo also appears in *The March of Jazz Celebrates Ruby Braff's 74th Birthday Party*, Arbors Records, 2001, 20.
[31] *DownBeat*, November 4, 1965, 42—article states that the private party will be "later this month."
[32] Abbreviated article by Dan Morgenstern, "The New York Jazz Benefit Scene," *DownBeat*, March 10, 1966, 21, reprinted in Franz Hoffmann, *The Henry Red Allen & J.C. Higgenbotham Collection, Part 3*, self-published, 144.
[33] *DownBeat*, December 16, 1965, 14.
[34] Abbreviated article by Dan Morgenstern, "The New York Jazz Benefit Scene," *DownBeat*, March 10, 1966, 21, reprinted in Franz Hoffmann, *The Henry Red Allen & J.C. Higgenbotham Collection, Part 3*, self-published, 144. Ken Vail, *Duke's Diary Part Two (*Lanham, MD: Scarecrow Press, 2002), 276.
[35] *DownBeat*, January 13, 1966, 42.
[36] Concert program, George Wein, *Myself Among Others* (Cambridge, MA: Da Capo Press, 2003), 262 and Jack Bradley reporting in *Coda Magazine*, February/March 1966, 22.
[37] Boston Globe Jazz Festival program.
[38] Jack Bradley reporting in *Coda Magazine*, February/March 1966, 22.
[39] Jack Bradley reporting in *Coda Magazine*, February/March 1966, 22, reporting that after sitting in previously Ruby was hired on the spot for these two nights. Other musicians were not listed in Bradley's report.
[40] *New York Times*, February 5, 1966.
[41] Jack Bradley, *Coda Magazine*, February/March 1966, 22.
[42] Jack Bradley, *Coda Magazine*, February/March 1966, 20. Ruby is not specifically mentioned in the brief report. Also mentioned in general is the Kansas City Jazz Festival May 1, 1966. See also *DownBeat* June 2, 1966, 37.
[43] *The New Yorker*, April 23, 1966, 11.
[44] Jack Bradley, *Coda Magazine*, Feb/Mar 1966, 20. Ruby is not specifically mentioned in this brief report.
[45] Listed in Robert Hilbert in collaboration with David Niven, *Pee Wee Speaks: A Discography of Pee Wee Russell* (Metuchen, NJ: Scarecrow Press, 1992), 338 and also reported in *DownBeat*, July 14, 1966, 55 (reporting, "Braff has never been in better form").
[46] *DownBeat*, July 28, 1966, 12, *The New Yorker*, June 11, 1966, 8, June 18, 1966, 8, June 25, 1966, 8, July 2, 1966, 8, July 9, 1966, 6, July 16, 1966, 8, July 23, 1966, 7, July 30, 1966, 7, and August 6, 1966, 7.
[47] *DownBeat*, August 11, 1966, 34 (review by Stanley Dance) and John S. Wilson, *New York Times*, June 24, 1966 and photo in *New York Times*, July 3, 1966 and *The New Yorker*, June 18, 1966, 13.

[48] Interview with Ruby Braff

[49] George Wein, *Myself Among Others* (Cambridge, MA: Da Capo Press, 2003)—photo appears on an unnumbered page in the glossy photo section.

[50] Photo by Jack Bradley, *The March of Jazz Celebrates Ruby Braff's 74th Birthday Party*, Arbors Records, 2001, 18.

[51] George Wein, *Myself Among Others* (Cambridge, MA: Da Capo Press, 2003), 264.

[52] Whitney Balliett, *The New Yorker*, July 16, 1966, 95.

[53] Film exists of the trumpet and guitar workshops. Billy Taylor MC, broadcast on NET as "*Jazz from Newport*" included "Struttin' with Some Barbecue" (Bobby Hackett with rhythm section), "Lover Come Back to Me" (Clark Terry, Ruby Braff, Henry Red Allen), "Summertime" (Feature: Henry Red Allen), "Siboney" (Duet: Dizzy Gillespie, Kenney Burrell) and "Disorder at the Border" (all trumpeters with rhythm section, Billy Taylor replaced George Wein). Details reported in *Henry Red Allen Discography* by Franz Hoffmann. Audio: Voice of America tape at the Library of Congress, Record number 196632p+1X, shelf number RGA 0105—0106 (RWD 6105 A1. 6106 A1—B1); "Lover Come Back to Me" and "Summertime" are incomplete on the Library's tape due to tape change at time of recording. Complete versions of "Disorder at the Border," "Summertime" and "Lover Come Back to Me" obtained from private source.

[54] David Meeker, *Jazz in the Movies: New Enlarged Edition* (New York: Da Capo, 1982), entry 1658, unnumbered pages.

[55] Anthony J. Agostinelli, *The Newport Jazz Festival: Rhode Island 1954–1971—A Bibliography, Discography and Filmography* (Providence, RI: privately printed, October 1977), 63–64.

[56] Photo by Jack Bradley, *The March of Jazz Celebrates Ruby Braff's 74th Birthday Party*, Arbors Records, 2001, 18.

[57] Harold Jones, *Bobby Hackett: A Bio-Discography* (Westport, CT: Greenwood Press, 1999) probably based on *DownBeat* from September 22, 1966, 33, and this article is also cited by Manfred Selchow, *Profoundly Blue* (Germany: Uhle & Kleinmann, 1988), 535—lists only these tunes from others played. The performance is also mentioned by Jack Bradley reporting in *Coda Magazine*, August/September 1966, 27 giving the following specific dates: July 15: Duke Ellington Orchestra, Miles Davis Quintet; July 16: Lionel Hampton All Star Reunion (with Teddy Wilson, Gene Krupa, Coleman Hawkins, Roy Eldridge, Clark Terry, Illinois Jacquet, Frank Foster, Wes Montgomery, and Milt Buckner); July 17: Special Jazz Concert (with Dave Brubeck Quartet, Thelonious Monk Quartet, Jimmy Smith Trio, and the Newport All Stars with Bud Freeman, Ruby Braff, Bobby Hackett, George Wein, Pee Wee Russell, and Edmond Hall). Ken Vail reports (in *Duke's Diary: Part Two* (Lanham, MD: Scarecrow Press), 293, that the Ellington concert was recorded, but the recording may extend to other artists. (No tape is known to exist except for Vail's claim above and a claim in Harold Jones, *Bobby Hackett: A Bio-Discography*, Greenwood Press, 1999 that the two listed tunes are available.) Ad published in *New York Times*, July 5, 1966, and also listed in *The New Yorker*, July 16, 1966, 10.

[58] Jack Bradley reporting in *Coda Magazine*, August/September 1966, 27–28.

[59] *DownBeat*, September 8, 1966, 44—vacation dates for Condon's published in *The New Yorker*, September 3, 1966, 8.

[60] *The Telegram*, September 14, 1966, and September 20, 1966; also mentioned by John Norris in *Coda Magazine*, October/November 1966, 15 and *DownBeat*, November 3, 1966, 50. Ruby is interviewed in *The Telegram*, September 24, 1966.

[61] Jack Bradley reporting in *Coda Magazine*, October/November 1966, 24.
[62] Jack Bradley reporting in *Coda Magazine*, October/November 1966, 23.
[63] Jack Bradley reporting in *Coda Magazine*, December/January 1966/67, 23.
[64] *DownBeat*, December 15, 1966, 15, reports Bob Wilber and Ruby Braff have been working on an LP project with the working title "Ruby Braff and Bob Wilber Play the Music of Louis Armstrong and Sidney Bechet." The article continues, "The titles would be culled from the 1924 Blue Fives and Red Onion Jazz Babies records which had Armstrong and Bechet, plus the 1940 session they did for Decca."
[65] *DownBeat*, December 29, 1966, 15.
[66] *DownBeat*, January 12, 1967 extracted in Franz Hoffmann, *The Henry Red Allen & J.C. Higgenbotham Collection, Part 3*, self-published, 159.
[67] Advertisement reproduced in Franz Hoffmann, *The Henry Red Allen & J.C. Higgenbotham Collection, Part 3*, self-published, 159.
[68] Jack Bradley reporting in *Coda Magazine*, March 1967, 22 and also cited in Manfred Selchow, *Ding Ding: A Bio-Discographical Scrapbook on Vic Dickenson (*Germany: Uhle & Kleinmann, 1998), 465, and *DownBeat*, February 9, 1967, 13.
[69] Jack Bradley reporting in *Coda Magazine*, March 1967, 31, and *DownBeat*, March 23, 1967, 26–27; photo appears in *The March of Jazz Celebrates Ruby Braff's 74th Birthday Party*, Arbors Records, 2001, 20.
[70] Manfred Selchow, *Profoundly Blue (*Germany: Uhle & Kleinmann, 1988), 553
[71] Photo, *The March of Jazz Celebrates Ruby Braff's 74th Birthday Party*, Arbors Records, 2001, 20.
[72] *DownBeat*, March 23, 1967, 26–27, and Manfred Selchow, *Profoundly Blue (*Germany: Uhle & Kleinmann, 1988), 552.
[73] *Coda Magazine*, May 1967, 26, Jack Bradley reporting that Ruby was the guest star.
[74] Robert Hilbert, *Pee Wee Russell: The Life of a Jazzman* (New York: Oxford University Press, 1993), 277, and review in *DownBeat* June 15, 1967, 28–29. Note that *DownBeat*'s review lists Ernie Caceres while Robert Hilbert, *Pee Wee Russell: The Life of a Jazzman* (New York: Oxford University Press, 1993) lists Bud Freeman instead. *DownBeat*'s review lists the tune titles.
[75] *DownBeat*, June 15, 1967, 14.
[76] *The New Yorker*, August 12, 1967, 7.
[77] George Wein, *Myself Among Others* (Cambridge, MA: Da Capo Press, 2003), 274.
[78] *DownBeat*, July 13, 1967, 26, contains review of the Puebla Jazz Festival at Auditorio De La Reforma. See next footnote for associated dates reported by *DownBeat.*
[79] *Down Beat*, April 20, 1967, page 14, reported different dates: May 12 at Puebla, May 13 Belles Artes Theater in Mexico City and May 14 at Auditorio Nacionale in Mexico City.
[80] *Down Beat*, April 20, 1967, page 14, reported different dates: May 12 at Puebla, May 13 Belles Artes Theater in Mexico City and May 14 at Auditorio Nacionale in Mexico City.
[81] *Down Beat*, April 20, 1967, page 14, reported different dates: May 12 at Puebla, May 13 Belles Artes Theater in Mexico City and May 14 at Auditorio Nacionale in Mexico City.
[82] Robert Hilbert in collaboration with David Niven, *Pee Wee Speaks: A Discography of Pee Wee Russell* (Metuchen, NJ: Scarecrow Press, 1992), 345, with dates adjusted to match the *DownBeat* review cited in previous footnote.
[83] George Wein, *Myself Among Others* (Cambridge: MA: Da Capo Press, 2003), 275.

[84] All unissued—listed in Robert Hilbert in collaboration with David Niven, *Pee Wee Speaks: A Discography of Pee Wee Russell* (Metuchen, NJ: Scarecrow Press, 1992), 346 (except "Ain't Misbehavin'" and "Sugar"). This concert was organized by the Institute for Jazz Studies.
[85] *DownBeat*, April 20, 1967, 14.
[86] All unissued—listed in Robert Hilbert in collaboration with David Niven, *Pee Wee Speaks: A Discography of Pee Wee Russell* (Metuchen, NJ: Scarecrow Press, 1992), 346–347.
[87] Burt Goldblatt, *The Newport Jazz Festival: The Illustrated History* (New York: Dial Press, 1977), 271, identifies the session and Whitney Balliett, *Ecstasy at the Onion (*Indianapolis: Bobbs-Merrill Company, Inc., 1971), 22, mentioning tunes.
[88] Whitney Balliett, *The New Yorker*, July 22, 1967, 74.
[89] Burt Goldblatt, *The Newport Jazz Festival: The Illustrated History* (New York: Dial Press, 1977), 271, Whitney Balliett, *Ecstasy at the Onion (*Indianapolis: Bobbs-Merrill Company, Inc., 1971), 23, mentioning tunes, Robert Hilbert, *Pee Wee Russell: The Life of a Jazzman*, New York (New York: Oxford University Press, 1993), 281 and Jack Bradley, *Coda Magazine*, August/September 1967, 4. John S. Wilson, *New York Times*, July 6, 1957, mentioning "These Foolish Things."
[90] Robert Hilbert, *Pee Wee Russell: The Life of a Jazzman* (New York: Oxford University Press, 1993), 281, date stated in *DownBeat*, June 29, 1967, 15, and *The Milwaukee Journal*, June 29, 1967, 37.
[91] Burt Goldblatt, *The Newport Jazz Festival: The Illustrated History* (New York: Dial Press, 1977), 272, for session and Michael Frohne for titles of tunes played. Jack Bradley, *Coda Magazine*, August/September 1967, 5, mentions "When It's Sleepy Time Down South" as especially well performed.
[92] Anthony J. Agostinelli, *The Newport Jazz Festival: Rhode Island 1954–1971—A Bibliography, Discography and Filmography* (Providence, Rhode Island: privately printed, October 1977), 3 in appendix 1.
[93] Information from correspondence with Alun Morgan.
[94] *DownBeat*, July 27, 1967, 11.
[95] *Jazz Journal International*, September 1967, 23. The October 3 engagement is also listed in *The Times*, October 2, 1967.
[96] "Blowing in . . . Horn men Ruby and Bill," *Nottingham Evening Post*, September 15, 1967, 14. Tony Shoppee provided a copy of this article and associated listing, *Nottingham Evening Post*, September 23, 1967, 2.
[97] Details provided by Paul Adams. Earlier information provided by David Griffiths from ad in *Jazz Times*, June 1965. The Lake CD shows a possible date of Summer 1967 but the tape box did not include any date. Ruby's fans will enjoy this unique recording.
[98] *Jazz Journal International*, September 1967, 23. The October 3 engagement is also listed in *The Times, October 2, 1967.*
[99] *The Times*, October 4, 1967, 8.
[100] *Jazz Journal International*, September 1967, 23. The October 3 engagement is also listed in *The Times, October 2, 1967.*
[101] Information from Tony Adkins.
[102] Earliest information from Tony Adkins. Paul Adams kindly provided additional information details.
[103] Steve Voce, "Roy Williams, Acclaimed International Trombonist," *Jazz Journal International*, February 2001, 21.

[104] *Jazz Journal International*, September 1967, 23.
[105] *The Times*, October 12, 1967, 7.
[106] Jazz Expo ‘ 67 program.
[107] *DownBeat*, July 27, 1967, 11, and December 26, 1967, 13.
[108] Bill Coleman, *Trumpet Story* (Boston: Northeastern University Press, 1981), 214.
[109] *Jazz Journal International*, October 1967, 15, and *DownBeat*, December 28, 1967, 18 (*DownBeat* gives the date as October 25).
[110] Michael Frohne and listing in *Jazz Journal International,* October 1967. An extensive review of the festival was written by Leonard Feather, *Los Angeles Times*, November 10, 1967, noting Sarah Vaughan, Miles Davis, Don Ellis, Tony Scott, Thelonious Monk, and many others. He called Ruby a “splendid soloist,” singling him out for praise. Feather also contributed a review published in *DownBeat*, January 11, 1968, 23-24 and 42.
[111] Jack Bradley reporting in *Coda Magazine*, March 1968, 37, and *DownBeat*, May 2, 1968, 16. The concert opened the second season of programs in this series. Also listed in *The New Yorker*, December 9, 1967, 18. *DownBeat*, January 11, 1968, 13, gives the year as 1968 apparently in error. Advertised in *New York Times*, November 26, 1967.

Chapter 9

The Growing Role of Festivals and the Newport Jazz Festival All Stars: George Wein's Festivals and International Tours: January 1968–May 1970

January brought an exciting opportunity. The following recording comes from a party held in the Penthouse of Benny Goodman's apartment in New York to commemorate the 30th Anniversary of the famous Goodman Carnegie Hall Concert. Ruby reports that January 16 was "freezing cold." Benny Goodman phoned him and asked if he wanted to stop by and play. Ruby asked who would be there, and was told that it would be Jess Stacy, Gene Krupa, Lionel Hampton, and a few other guys. Ruby's impression was that it was just an informal gathering for fun; however, when he arrived the doorman directed him to the Penthouse. When he left the elevator, Ruby saw many people present and then decided that Goodman had invited him informally in order to avoid paying for his appearance. Ruby repeated much of this story in a radio interview March 2, 1991, with Rob Bamberger.

A copy of the engraved invitation to the party is available, directing people to the Roof Garden at 200 East 66th Street for cocktails and a buffet dinner from 6 p.m. This location is one floor above Goodman's apartment. There is a photo by John McDonough showing Benny Goodman with Ruby Braff from this occasion. Also visible are George Avakian and John S. Wilson.

30th Anniversary Party of Benny Goodman's Carnegie Hall Concert[1]
January 16, 1968, New York taped by D. Russell Connor and broadcast on WNEW, January 27, 8:05–10 p.m. (see Figure 9.1)
Benny Goodman (cl), Ruby Braff (tp), Lionel Hampton (vib), Jess Stacy (p), George Simon (cymbal while Krupa's drums were being set up)
Unknown blues (warm-up)
Sweet Lorraine

Add: Gene Krupa midway through "I Want to Be Happy" after the pedal was attached to his bass drum
I Want to Be Happy
If I Had You
Avalon
Someday Sweetheart
Rosetta
Body and Soul (trio only: Goodman, Stacy, Krupa)
I Would Do Anything for You
Don't Be That Way
Stompin' at the Savoy
NOTE: An audio recording of these tunes is available but remains unissued. A video recording of "Avalon" also exists as filmed by CBS on this occasion.

Published photos exist in the March of Jazz program.[2] One is included in this book's photo section.

Newport All Stars[3]
February 14, 1968, Scranton, Pennsylvania
Ruby Braff (cnt), Pee Wee Russell (cl), George Duvivier (b), Jake Hanna (dm)

Ruby returned to the Boston Globe Jazz Festival on February 17, where he performed two Ellington compositions with George Wein. Later, Ruby and Gerry Mulligan were featured as soloists with Duke Ellington and His Orchestra. Ruby then prepared to travel to Aspen, Colorado, for an extended engagement with Ralph Sutton. In many ways, this recalled their earlier collaborations at Eddie Condon's club in New York.

3rd Annual Boston Globe Jazz Festival[4]
February 17, 1968, War Memorial Auditorium (now named Hynes Auditorium), Boston (second night of the festival)
Duke Ellington and His Orchestra with Ruby Braff and Gerry Mulligan guest soloists
Duke Ellington (p), Gerry Mulligan (bar), bass, and drums
Star Dust

Add Harry Carney for following title only
Unnamed tune

Ruby Braff (cnt) and George Wein (p), with bass and drums
Don't Get Around Much Anymore
In a Sentimental Mood

Add full orchestra with Mulligan and perhaps Braff
I Got It Bad and That Ain't Good
Things Ain't What They Used to Be

Sunnie Sutton said that Ruby's engagement at her club lasted a total of six weeks. Recording only took place during the nights listed below.[5] There were times when alcohol flowed freely; however, we are fortunate that Karl Emil Knudsen released many of the performances on Storyville Records.

The Ralph Sutton Quartet[6]
February 26, 1968, Sunnie's Rendezvous, Aspen, Colorado
Ruby Braff (cnt), Ralph Sutton (p), Milt Hinton (b), Mousey Alexander (dm)
'Deed I Do
A Good Man Is Hard to Find
Swing That Music
Medley:
  Body and Soul
  Everything Happens to Me
  These Foolish Things
The Lady Is a Tramp
Just Friends
The World Is Waiting for the Sunrise
Honky Tonk Train Blues (Sutton solo)
The Sheik of Araby
Someday You'll Be Sorry
I've Found a New Baby
I Can't Give You Anything but Love
Beale Street Blues
Someday Sweetheart
Blue and Broken Hearted
St. Louis Blues
I'm Crazy 'bout My Baby
Blue Lou
Ain't Misbehavin'
Old Folks
My Monday Date
Lady Be Good
NOTE: An audio recording of these tunes is available but remains unissued.

The Ralph Sutton Quartet[7]
February 27, 1968, Sunnie's Rendezvous, Aspen, Colorado
Ruby Braff (cnt), Ralph Sutton (p), Milt Hinton (b), Mousey Alexander (dm)
When the Saints Go Marching In
You're Driving Me Crazy
Sugar

Jumpin' at the Woodside
If I Had You
I Never Knew
Blue Lou
St. Louis Blues
Shoe Shine Boy
Blue Turning Grey Over You
I've Got My Love to Keep Me Warm
Honeysuckle Rose
I've Found a New Baby
NOTE: An audio recording of these tunes is available but remains unissued.

Ruby told a funny story about one of his meetings with Karl Emil Kundsen, owner of Storyville Records. They met in Ruby's New York hotel room at a time when Knudsen was making further plans to release more of Ruby's recordings, probably the final volumes of the sessions from Aspen listed below. This meeting probably occurred in the late 1990s. Karl asked Ruby for permission. Ruby said that he replied, "But you haven't paid me yet for the previous release." At this point, Karl opened his briefcase and showed a large amount of money. He said to Ruby, "Just take what you want." At this point, Ruby smiled and said that he reached into the briefcase and withdrew a large handful of bills. "Not that much!" Karl retorted. Ruby returned most of the money and retained what they agreed would be appropriate compensation.

The Ralph Sutton Quartet, Volume 1
February 28, 1968, Sunnie's Rendezvous, Aspen, Colorado
Ruby Braff (cnt), Ralph Sutton (p), Milt Hinton (b), Mousey Alexander (dm)
Gone with the Wind
    Storyville STCD 8243
Exactly Like You
    Storyville STCD 8243
Keepin' Out of Mischief Now
    Storyville STCD 8243
Rosetta
    Storyville STCD 8243
You Can Depend on Me
    Storyville STCD 8243
Limehouse Blues
    Storyville STCD 8243
Memories of You
    Storyville STCD 8243
Liza
    Storyville STCD 8243

Louisiana
    Storyville STCD 8243
Wang Wang Blues
    Storyville STCD 8243
On the Sunny Side of the Street
    Blue Angel Jazz Club BAJC 501, Storyville STCD 8243
Shine
    Storyville STCD 8243

The Ralph Sutton Quartet, Volume 2
February 28, 1968, Sunnie's Rendezvous, Aspen, Colorado
Ruby Braff (cnt), Ralph Sutton (p), Milt Hinton (b), Mousey Alexander (dm)
I'm Gonna Sit Right Down and Write Myself a Letter
    Storyville STCD 8246
Oh, Baby
    Storyville STCD 8246
Ain't Misbehavin'
    Storyville STCD 8246
Don't Blame Me
    Storyville STCD 8246
What a Little Moonlight Can Do
    Storyville STCD 8246
Can't We Be Friends?
    Blue Angel Jazz Club BAJC 501, Storyville STCD 8246
Medley:
  I Wished on the Moon
    Storyville STCD 8246
  If You Were Mine*
    Storyville STCD 8246
I've Got a Pocket Full of Dreams**
    Storyville STCD 8246
Medley:
  Diane
    Storyville STCD 8246
  All by Myself
    Storyville STCD 8246
  You Are My Lucky Star***
    Storyville STCD 8246
The Sheik of Araby
    Storyville STCD 8246
* Session log shows this title as "Ace in the Hole" but CD plays as listed above.
** Title listed incorrectly as "I've Got a Pocket Full of Money" on the CD. Title is correct in session log.
*** Title not listed in session log.

NOTE: Storyville STCD 8243 and STCD 8246 include all titles recorded on February 28 in the order recorded.

The Ralph Sutton Quartet Featuring Ruby Braff, Milt Hinton, and Mousey Alexander, Volume 3
February 29, 1968, Sunnie's Rendezvous, Aspen, Colorado
Ruby Braff (cnt), Ralph Sutton (p), Milt Hinton (b), Mousey Alexander (dm)
Undecided
unissued (intended for issue on the CD below but not released)
I Believe in Miracles
Storyville STCD 8301
It's Wonderful
Storyville STCD 8301
I Never Knew
Storyville STCD 8301
Sweethearts on Parade
Storyville STCD 8301
Shine
Storyville STCD 8301
A Hundred Years from Today
Blue Angel Jazz Club BAJC 501, Storyville STCD 8301
Take the "A" Train
Storyville STCD 8301
I Would Do Anything for You
Storyville STCD 8301
Love Is Just Around the Corner
Storyville STCD 8301
Someday Sweetheart
Blue Angel Jazz Club BAJC 501, Storyville STCD 8301
I've Found a New Baby
Blue Angel Jazz Club BAJC 501, Storyville STCD 8301

The Ralph Sutton Quartet Featuring Ruby Braff, Volume 4
February 29, 1968, Sunnie's Rendezvous, Aspen, Colorado
Ruby Braff (cnt), Ralph Sutton (p), Milt Hinton (b), Mousey Alexander (dm)
I Surrender Dear
Storyville STCD 8312
Jeepers Creepers
Storyville STCD 8312
Just One of Those Things
Storyville STCD 8312
I'm Crazy 'bout My Baby
Blue Angel Jazz Club BAJC 501, Storyville STCD 8312

Coquette
  Storyville STCD 8312
Lady Be Good
  Storyville STCD 8312
Speak Well of Me (Sutton solo)
  unissued
A Cottage for Sale (omit Braff, Alexander)
  Storyville STCD 8312
Ol' Pigeon-Toed Joad (Sutton solo)
  unissued
I Got Rhythm
  Storyville STCD 8312
Dinah
  Storyville STCD 8312
St. Louis Blues
  Blue Angel Jazz Club BAJC 501, Storyville STCD 8312
NOTE: Storyville STCD 8301 and STCD 8312 include all titles recorded February 29 in order of recording, with the exception of "Undecided" and the two solos by Ralph Sutton shown above. Unissued titles are included in master tapes owned by Storyville Records.

Ralph Sutton with Ruby Braff: *On Sunnie's Side of the Street*
The following listing summarizes the original Blue Angel Jazz Club LP created from the above session tapes. The album was issued with two different cover designs. The original LP had the release number CD 501S printed vertically, only on the rear cover. The label had no release number, but CD 501S was pressed in the vinyl.
February 27–29, 1968, Sunnie's Rendezvous, Aspen, Colorado
Ruby Braff (cnt) Ralph Sutton (p) Milt Hinton (b) Mousey Alexander (dm)
Someday Sweetheart
  Blue Angel Jazz Club BAJC 501, Storyville STCD 8301
A Hundred Years from Today
  Blue Angel Jazz Club BAJC 501, Storyville STCD 8301
I've Found a New Baby
  Blue Angel Jazz Club BAJC 501, Storyville STCD 8301
Can't We Be Friends?
  Blue Angel Jazz Club BAJC 501, Storyville STCD 8246
I'm Crazy 'bout My Baby
  Blue Angel Jazz Club BAJC 501, Storyville STCD 8312
On the Sunny Side of the Street
  Blue Angel Jazz Club BAJC 501, Storyville STCD 8243
St. Louis Blues
  Blue Angel Jazz Club BAJC 501, Storyville STCD 8312

Jack Bradley photographed Ruby with Zoot Sims at the next engagement at Kenny's Pub in New York. His photo appears in the March of Jazz program and is included in this book's photo section.[8]

New York Hot Jazz Society Concert[9]
April 21, 1968, Kenny's Pub, New York
Ruby Braff (cnt), Pee Wee Russell (cl), Zoot Sims (ts), Nat Pierce (p), Milt Hinton (b), Mousey Alexander (dm)
Don't Blame Me
Ain't Misbehavin'
I Want to Be Happy

Omit Russell from the following selections:
Just You, Just Me
Sunday
I Want a Little Girl
NOTE: A recording of these tunes is available but remains unissued.

Whitney Balliett wrote in *The New Yorker*:[10]

> The affair at Kenny's resembled a night on Fifty-second street.... Braff played with his customary red-hot lyricism, and Sims was extraordinary.... All Russell's solos were notable.

Charlotte Jazz Festival[11]
May 10-11, 1968, Charlotte, North Carolina
Ruby Braff may have appeared with the Newport All Stars in this festival produced by George Wein

I have one tangible reminder of Ruby's next appearance at the Half Note in the form of a table card where he wrote his address and phone number as 5444 Arlington Avenue, Riverdale, NY 10471, phone, 575-8436. The card announced a $3.50 minimum charge per person for drinks only.

Ruby Braff[12]
Ending May 19, 1968, Half Note, New York
Further details unknown

Newport All Stars[13]
June 23, 1968, Pennsylvania Dutch Jazz Festival, Lancaster Riding Club, Lancaster, Pennsylvania
Ruby Braff (cnt), Buddy Tate (ts), Nat Pierce (p), George Duvivier (b), Jake Hanna (dm)
Just You, Just Me
Sometimes I'm Happy

Blue and Sentimental
Take the "A" Train

It remains unclear if Ruby participated in all the performances that comprised the Schlitz Salute to Jazz tour. One of the bookings where some further information is available was named the Hampton Jazz Festival. The performance in Lancaster above may have also been part of this tour. A photo of Ruby with Buddy Tate appears in the program. The festival program listed the following other appearances: Winston Salem (June 21), Pittsburgh (June 23), Dallas (July 12), Austin (July 13), Houston (July 14), Omaha (July 18), Denver (July 20), Oklahoma City (July 21), Phoenix (July 26), Oakland (July 27), San Diego (July 28), Rochester (August 2), Madison (August 3), Detroit (August 3, 4), Kansas City (August 9), St. Louis (August 10), Cleveland (August 11), Chicago (August 16), Cincinnati (August 17), and Memphis (August 18).[14]

Newport All Stars at the Hampton Jazz Festival[15]
June 28–29, 1968, Hampton Institute, Hampton, Virginia
Ruby Braff (cnt), Illinois Jacquet (ts), George Wein (p), and other musicians
Flying Home
Note: This was the final selection played. No other information is available.

Atlanta Jazz Festival[16]
June 29-30, 1968, Atlanta, Georgia
Ruby Braff may have appeared with the Newport All Stars in this festival produced by George Wein

However, it was again time for the Newport Jazz Festival. The program repeated the cover design and incorporated the name of the Schlitz Salute to Jazz. Ruby performed on the third day of the festival as one of the guests who performed with Alex Welsh's band. Two other notable guests were Bud Freeman and Joe Venuti.

Alex Welsh Band with Guests[17]
July 6, 1968, 15th Newport Jazz Festival, Festival Field, Newport, Rhode Island (third day of four-day festival)
Alex Welsh (tp), Ruby Braff (cnt), Roy Williams (tb), Bud Freeman (ts), Pee Wee Russell (cl), John Barnes (cl, bar), Joe Venuti (v), George Wein, Fred Hunt (p), Jim Douglas (g), Tony Bayless (b), Lennie Hastings (dm)
Welsh Band opens the set:
Oh, Baby
Between the Devil and the Deep Blue Sea
Open Country

Add Bud Freeman
Exactly Like You (Freeman featured with rhythm section)

I Got Rhythm (with full band)

Add Pee Wee Russell; Freeman out
Pee Wee's Blues
Love Is Just around the Corner

Add Ruby Braff; Russell out
No One Else But You

Add Joe Venuti and George Wein (p); Braff out
Body and Soul
Sweet Georgia Brown

All guests return, with full band:
Royal Garden Blues

A photo is available in the March of Jazz program.[18]

Ruby Braff and Zoot Sims Quintet[19]
August 6–September 1, 1968, Half Note, New York (closed Mondays)
Ruby Braff (cnt), Zoot Sims (ts), Nat Pierce (p), Mousey Alexander (dm)—bass players rotated through the engagement and included the following: Herb Mickman, Herbie Lewis, Ron Markowitz, and Jack Lesberg

Ruby Braff and Brew Moore[20]
September 3–15, 1968, Half Note, Hudson Street at Spring Street, New York
Ruby Braff (cnt), Brew Moore (ts), Nat Pierce (p), Reggie Johnson (b), Gus Johnson (dm)

Ruby Braff told a story about driving Brew Moore home after closing, when Moore lived in a very bad neighborhood. When they pulled up in Ruby's car, Ruby noticed a tough looking man lingering at the entrance. He said, "Brew, wait in the car." However, Moore insisted on getting out. While reaching for his key, the man attempted to rob him. At that point, Moore said, "But man that isn't fair. You robbed me last night." At that point, the man apologized and left.

George Wein Quintet[21]
October 14–19, 1968, opening performance for engagement, Ronnie Scott's, London
Ruby Braff (cnt), Red Norvo (vib), George Wein (p), Kenny Napper (b), Ronnie Stephenson (dm)

Ronnie Scott's club opened October 3 and George Wein's Quintet opened its engagement a few nights later.

Hank Mobley sat in with Ruby, likely during this engagement. Hank arrived in England April 22, 1968. He was sponsored by Ronnie Scott during much of his time in England. Mobley appeared at Ronnie Scott's club several times.[22] Ruby also participated in the Jazz Expo '68 program that was positioned as the Newport Jazz Festival in London in the concert's program.

The Times reviewed a performance:[23]

> This week Ronnie Scott's Club makes one of its rare forays into pre-modern jazz with the arrival of Ruby Braff, Red Norvo and the George Wein Trio. Norvo, who has never played in Britain before, was the only vibraphonist in the thirties and forties who could be mentioned in the same breath as Lionel Hampton, thanks to an extremely nimble and light style. The nimbleness is still there, but rather inflexible now, as if beautifully polished patterns are being automatically slotted together.
>
> Ruby Braff is a different matter. Not only is he one of those rare musicians who sound as if they never stop looking for new phrases, new ways of surprising themselves, he has in addition a mastery of the cornet which allows him to translate his ideas into immediate achievement. Occasionally, at the extremes of his range, he becomes raucous or plummily soft, but even within these limits he has more light and shade than most.
>
> George Wein plays very good piano for one who is actually an impresario, and his two English accompanists, Ronnie Stephenson and Kenny Napper, complete a deft quintet. The main complaint is that in Scott's newly established club it needs a good audience to provide the atmosphere without which even the best jazz falls into a pit; it may be that Braff's brand of perfection is too unfashionable to attract the numbers it deserves.

Several photographs exist from the next concert. A photograph by Valerie Wilmer shows Benny Carter with Ruby Braff,[24] and another by David Redfern is printed in the Jazz Expo '68 program. It shows Ruby performing with Alex Welsh's Band, probably from the previous July's performance at the Newport Jazz Festival.[25] The Jazz Expo '68 program also includes an uncredited photo of Ruby by Jack Bradley. This photo was also published in the March of Jazz program, attributed to 1965. A copy of that photo is included in this book's photo section.

Ruby's biography in the program includes the following:

> Perhaps the most remarkable example in jazz today of a musician who has completely mastered a style whose heyday was over before he was even beginning to play, Braff stands as a contradiction of the theory that younger men should concern themselves with younger styles. . . . If one analyses his trumpet style, one finds all the classic attributes, a thick, resonant tone, facility over the range of the instrument, complete confidence in striding from one harmony to the next, and, most important of all, an imp of originality which makes him in-

stantly recognizable and is probably due most to the texture of the sound he produces.

Newport All Stars: Jazz Expo '68[26]

October 25, 1968, The Odeon, Hammersmith, London
Ruby Braff (cnt), Benny Carter (as), George Wein (p), Red Norvo (vib), Barney Kessel (g), Kenny Baldock (b), Tony Crombie (dm)
Undecided
Don't Blame Me
You Stepped Out of a Dream (Kessel solo)
I Can't Give You Anything but Love (Braff feature)
Body and Soul (Carter feature)
Ida (Norvo feature)
Take the "A" Train

This was a weeklong staging of the Newport Jazz Festival in London. Other performers included Dave Brubeck, Gerry Mulligan, Count Basie, Don Rendell, Ian Carr, Dizzy Gillespie, James Moody, Mike Westbrook, Art Blakey, Max Roach, Ginger Johnson, Muddy Waters, Otis Spann, Ronnie Scott, Gary Burton, Michael Garrick, Jimmy Reed, John Lee Hooker, T-Bone Walker, Curtis Jones, Big Joe Williams, Earl Hines, Budd Johnson, Alex Welsh, Salena Jones, Ed Harvey, Roy Budd, Horace Silver, and Stan Tracey. Total attendance was reported to exceed 32,000, and the cost of the festival was reported as $48,000.

The Jazz Expo '68 tour was organized by George Wein under auspices of the *Visit USA* program of the US Travel Service of the Department of Commerce and Pan American World Airways, duplicating the sponsorships from 1967. Various combinations of musicians performed in 36 cities. Performances for this tour in England include London, Wakefield, and Bristol. The tour also reached cities in Germany, Switzerland, France, and Italy, including concerts scheduled in Berlin (Philharmonie), Munich, Düsseldorf, Frankfurt, Cologne, Stuttgart, and Hildesheim, Basel, Lausanne, Geneva, Montreux, Zurich, Yverdon, Freiberg, Neufchatel, Milan, Prato, Reggio Emilia, Paris, Lyons, and Strasbourg. Other cities included Copenhagen (at Tivoli), Aarhus, Madrid, Barcelona, Brussels, Oslo, Rotterdam at De Doelen, Stockholm, and Helsinki. The tour also reached Ireland and Finland. Ruby's participation is only verified for some of those locations.[27] Obviously, this was a very extensive tour.

Newport All Stars[28]

October 26, 1968, The Maltings, Aldeburgh Festival Concert Hall, Snape, Suffolk, England[29]
BBC-2 TV Broadcast April 3, 1969 for Program 1 and December 12, 1968 for program 2– the televised titles are from the BBC series *Jazz at the Maltings*, Terry Henebery, producer, Benny Green, master of ceremonies
Ruby Braff (cnt), Benny Carter (as), George Wein (p), Red Norvo (vib), Barney Kessel (g), Kenny Baldock (b), Tony Crombie (dm)

Program 1
All of Me
All the Things You Are
What Kind of Fool Am I?
Undecided
Blues
NOTE: A recording of these tunes is available but remains unissued.

Program 2
I Want to Be Happy
I Can't Give You Anything but Love
Sunday
Rose Room (fades after BC solo)
NOTE: An audio recording of these tunes is available but remains unissued.

"Undecided" was also included in a rebroadcast, *Jazz at the Maltings Spectacular*, producer, Terry Henebery. This program presented a compilation drawn from the series and included performances by Buddy Rich, Dave Brubeck with Gerry Mulligan, Oscar Peterson, Dizzy Gillespie, Gary Burton, Earl Hines, and Count Basie. Video recordings for these programs apparently no longer exist at the BBC.

Only two additional performances are documented at this time from the tour; however, there are likely others since I am unable to trace Ruby's presence for the balance of November and much of December.

Newport All Stars[30]
October 27–29, 1968, Copenhagen, as part of George Wein's "Newport Tour"
Details unknown

Ruby next is known to have performed in a two-week engagement at Plaza 9 in New York, again as a member of the Newport All Stars. Two photos exist from this engagement. One is a posed photograph showing Larry Ridley, Barney Kessel, Ruby Braff, George Wein, Red Norvo, and Don Lamond while the other captures a moment during one of the performances. This second photo was published in the 1978 Newport Jazz Festival program, ten years later. A number of publications mentioned this appearance, and it is the first known engagement that brings Ruby together with Tony Bennett. Soon thereafter, Tony retained Ruby for various tours and recordings. Of course, Tony had already performed regularly with Bobby Hackett.

Newport All Stars[31] **(see Figure 9.2)**
December 26, 1968–January 12, 1969, Plaza 9—And All That Jazz, New York
Ruby Braff, Bobby Hackett (cnt), Red Norvo (vib), Barney Kessel (g), Larry Ridley (b), George Wein (p), Don Lamond (dm)—Guests Bobby Hackett (cnt) and Tony Bennett (voc)

Royal Garden Blues
All of Me
C Jam Blues
Am I Blue?
Undecided
Jumpin' at the Woodside
Somebody Else Is Taking My Place
These Foolish Things
Swing That Music

Add Bobby Hackett
Struttin' with Some Barbecue
Pennies from Heaven
I'm Comin' Virginia
Undecided
In a Mellotone

Add Tony Bennett
Fools Rush In
I Left My Heart in San Francisco

Newport All Stars[32]
January 13, 1969, *Tonight Show*, NBC Television Network, New York
Ruby Braff (cnt), Red Norvo (vib), George Wein (p), Barney Kessel (g), Don Lamond (dm), Larry Ridley (b)

Ruby had become a regular at the Boston Globe Jazz Festival. Once again, he performed with the Newport All Stars, opening the first night of the festival at 8 p.m. The All Stars were followed by Roland Kirk, the Dave Brubeck Quartet, and the Mothers of Invention, providing exposure to a wide range of styles within a single evening. The All Stars returned on February 1 for an afternoon performance, adding Gerry Mulligan to the group.

The Newport All Stars: 4th Annual Boston Globe Jazz Festival[33]
January 31, 1969, evening, Boston
Ruby Braff (cnt), Red Norvo (vib), Barney Kessel (g), George Wein (p), Larry Ridley (b), Don Lamond (dm)
Just You, Just Me
Sunday
Days of Wine and Roses

The Newport All Stars: 4th Annual Boston Globe Jazz Festival[34]
February 1, 1969, afternoon, 4th Annual Boston Globe Jazz Festival, Boston

Ruby Braff (cnt), Gerry Mulligan (bar), Red Norvo (vib), Barney Kessel (g), George Wein (p), Larry Ridley (b), Don Lamond (dm)

Pee Wee Russell died on February 15. Of course, Ruby's relationship with Pee Wee was a special one. Ruby wanted me to list this in recognition of their relationship.

Pee Wee Russell's Funeral[35]
February 1969, Maplewood, New Jersey
Ruby Braff was a pallbearer

The Newport All Stars appeared at Plaza 9, from February 18–March 2, 1969. This was the second two-week engagement in two months. Details are known for February 26.[36] Whitney Balliett wrote, "Braff's monolithic eloquence is lightened by Norvo's pinpoint embroidery."

Newport All Stars[37]
February 18–March 2, 1969, Plaza 9—And All That Jazz, New York
Ruby Braff (tp), Red Norvo (vib), George Wein (p, el-p, voc), Barney Kessel (g), Tal Farlow (b, el-b), Larry Ridley (b), Don Lamond (dm)

Newport All Stars[38]
February 26, 1969, New York
Ruby Braff (tp), Red Norvo (vib), George Wein (p, el-p, voc), Barney Kessel (g), Tal Farlow (b, el-b), Larry Ridley (b), Don Lamond (dm)
Blue Boy
    Atlantic SD 1533, Collectables 6194 (CD)
Ja-Da
    Atlantic SD 1533, Collectables 6194 (CD)
Sunny
    Atlantic SD 1533, Collectables 6194 (CD)

February 27, 1969, same personnel.
Am I Blue?
    Atlantic SD 1533, Collectables 6194 (CD)
Melancholy Baby
    Atlantic SD 1533, Collectables 6194 (CD)
Exactly Like You
    Atlantic SD 1533, Collectables 6194 (CD)
These Foolish Things
    Atlantic SD 1533, Collectables 6194 (CD)
Nobody Knows You When You're Down and Out
    Atlantic SD 1533, Collectables 6194 (CD)
In a Little Spanish Town
    Atlantic SD 1533, Collectables 6194 (CD)

Topsy
Atlantic SD 1533, Collectables 6194 (CD)
Body and Soul
unissued

The next venue for the Newport All Stars was unusual, the Fillmore East in New York. This was a four-hour program that also included the Herbie Hancock Sextet, Thelonious Monk's Quartet, Clark Terry's Rehearsal Band, and the Billy Taylor Trio. Probably the Newport All Stars performed early and then returned to Plaza 9 in time to close their two-week engagement at that club.

Newport All Stars: George Wein Concert (the first of eight Sunday evening concerts)[39] (see Figure 9.3)
March 2, 1969, Fillmore East, New York, starting at 7 p.m.
Ruby Braff (tp), Red Norvo (vib), George Wein (p, el-p, voc), Barney Kessel (g), Tal Farlow (b, el-b), Larry Ridley (b), Don Lamond (dm)
Topsy (Farlow and Kessel feature)
These Foolish Things (Norvo, Farlow)
Exactly Like You (Norvo)
Melancholy Baby (Braff)
Medium Blues (Braff feature)

Newport All Stars: Morgan State Jazz Festival[40]
June 21–22, 1969, Morgan State College, Baltimore, Maryland
Ruby Braff (cnt), Red Norvo (vib), Tal Farlow (g), George Wein (p), Larry Ridley (b), Don Lamond (dm)
Take the "A" Train
Other titles not mentioned in review

Ruby again performed as a member of the Newport All Stars at the 16th Newport Jazz Festival. This time, they opened the afternoon program on the third day of the festival. The group was followed by Miles Davis, John Mayall, Gary Burton, and the Mothers of Invention, again reflecting the considerable range of styles that had become evident at these annual festivals. The program contains a photo of Ruby with George Wein and the following descriptive quote from Mr. Wein: "We play the kind of jazz that most musicians want to play, but don't."[41]

The program also listed other festivals produced by Festival Productions: Morgan State Jazz Festival (June 21–22 in Baltimore), Hampton Jazz Festival (June 26–28, Hampton, VA), Miami Jazz Festival (June 27–29), Blind Faith Festival (July 11 in Newport, RI), Laurel Pop Festival (July 11–12, Laurel, MD), Philadelphia Pop Festival (July 11–12), Longhorn Jazz Festival (July 18–20, Dallas), Newport Folk Festival (July 16–20), Rutgers Jazz Festival (July 26–27, New Brunswick, NJ), and Laurel Jazz Festival (August 1–3, Laurel, MD). It is unknown if Ruby participated in any of these festivals beyond his appearances at the Newport Jazz Festival at Rutgers Jazz Festival below.

Newport All Stars: 16th Newport Jazz Festival[42]
July 5, 1969, Festival Field, Rhode Island (third day of four-day festival)
Ruby Braff (cnt), Red Norvo (vib), Tal Farlow (g), Larry Ridley (b), Jack DeJohnette (dm), Mavis Rivers (voc)
Avalon
I Wished on the Moon
Slow Blues
What a Little Moonlight Can Do

Add Mavis Rivers
Dearly Beloved
But Beautiful
George Wein wrote that Don Lamond had been unable to appear for this performance. They called on Jack DeJohnette, who was appearing with Miles Davis at the time.[43]

Teddy Wilson Trio with Guest Ruby Braff[44]
June or July 1969, Downbeat Club, New York
Ruby Braff (cnt), Teddy Wilson (p), Jack Lesberg (b), Cliff Leeman (dm)
Wild Bill Davison alternated with Teddy Wilson during this engagement. Woody Allen was a surprise guest with Wilson on some occasions.

The 1st Annual Rutgers Jazz Festival followed and the Newport All Stars performed during the second night of this two-night festival. George Wein was the festival's producer. Also appearing that night were the following: Buddy Rich Orchestra, Nina Simone, Miles Davis Quintet, Donald Byrd, and Blood Sweat and Tears. Ralph Burton reviewed the Rutgers Jazz Festival for DownBeat and had considerable praise for Ruby's performance:[45]

> Ruby Braff, just about my favorite of all living pre-bop horns, led off, with that incredibly rich tone of his, on a swinging "'A' Train" that was like a drink of cool sparking spring-water, ravishingly backed by Red Norvo, Tal Farlow, Larry Ridley, Cliff Leeman, and George Wein at the piano. Oh, man, how those guys swing! You tend to forget, when you haven't looked through *Macbeth* or *David Copperfield* for awhile, just how great they really are. That's somewhat the way I felt listening to this incomparable brand of jazz. . . . Every song was a story, a little work of art, complete and final, and all too short.

Newport All Stars: Rutgers Jazz Festival[46]
July 27, 1969, Rutgers Stadium, New Brunswick, New Jersey
Ruby Braff (cnt), Red Norvo (vib), George Wein (p), Tal Farlow (g), Larry Ridley (b), Cliff Leeman (dm)

Take the "A" Train
Mean to Me
Undecided
Exactly Like You

There is a possible appearance of Ruby Braff with Bobby Hackett at Grande Parade du Jazz: Nice Jazz Festival in 1969; however, I have not been able to verify that with information about performances at the festival that year. It is likely that a published photo actually dates from 1975 when Ruby and Bobby were featured together in many sets at the Grande Parade du Jazz. Therefore, the following performance is unlikely.

Grande Parade du Jazz: Nice Jazz Festival[47]
Ruby Braff, Bobby Hackett (cnt)

Newport All Stars[48]
August 15, 1969, The Spectrum, Philadelphia
Ruby Braff (cnt), Red Norvo (vib), Tal Farlow (g), George Wein (p), Larry Ridley (b), Don Lamond (dm)

I have been unable to trace the actual date of the following performance, so I have arbitrarily placed the engagement here, in 1969, until a more specific date can be determined. Ruby would have cringed on being photographed under a banner that read "The Dukes of Dixieland"; however, he certainly enjoyed performing with the group of musicians shown in the photograph and listed in the next set. This photo is included in this book's photo section.

Metropole[49]
Late 1960s, Metropole, New York
Ruby Braff (ct), Cutty Cutshall (tb), Bob Wilber (cl), John Giuffrida (dm)

Newport All Stars[50]
Fall 1969 for one week, Plaza Hotel, New York
Ruby Braff (cnt), Red Norvo (vib), Barney Kessel (g), George Wein (p), Larry Ridley (b), Lenny McBrowne (dm)
Other artists are listed in various issues of *The New Yorker* for this club at this time. Therefore, this date may or may not be correct.

Newport All Stars[51]
Fall 1969 for four weeks, Economy Hall, located in the basement of the Royal Sonesta Hotel, New Orleans
Ruby Braff (cnt), Red Norvo (vib), Barney Kessel (g), George Wein (p), Larry Ridley (b), Lenny McBrowne (dm)

This was the engagement when plans began for the New Orleans Jazz & Heritage Festival.[52]

Ruby returned to England for what has become at least an annual visit.

Jam Session at Ronnie Scott's[53]
October 10, 1969, London, BBC Television broadcast
Ruby Braff (cnt), Bill Coleman (tp, flgh), Charlie Shavers (tp, voc), Buddy Tate (ts), Albert Nicholas (cl), Jay McShann (p), Barney Kessel (g), Spike Heatley (b, announcer), Oliver Jackson (dm)
Perdido (solo BC and AN)
In a Mellotone (solo BC)
Please Don't Talk About Me When I'm Gone (solo RB)*
Sooner or Later (solo RB and BK)*
Indiana (voc CS)*
Bye Bye Blackbird (voc CS)
Nature Boy (voc CS)
Body and Soul (solo BT)
Jumpin' at the Woodside (sole BT and OJ)
NOTE: Audio recordings of three tunes marked with an asterisk are available but remain unissued. This is probably the source of tunes rebroadcast in August 13, 1970 for "Please Don't Talk about Me When I'm Gone" and "Sooner or Later."

Jazz Expo at Wakefield: Newport All Stars[54]
October 1969, Wakefield Theater Club, Wakefield, England
Ruby Braff (cnt), Benny Carter (as), Barney Kessel (g), George Wein (p), Kenny Baldock (b), Tony Crombie (dm)
Details are unknown.

Ruby Braff Plays Louis Armstrong
October 20, 1969, Paris
Ruby Braff (tp), George Wein (p), Barney Kessel (g), Larry Ridley (b), Don Lamond (dm)
Cornet Chop Suey
BYG (F) 529.123
(Was I to Blame for) Falling in Love With You
BYG (F) 529.123
I've Got a Feelin' I'm Fallin'
BYG (F) 529.123
It's Wonderful
BYG (F) 529.123
When It's Sleepy Time Down South
BYG (F) 529.123

I'm Thankful
BYG (F) 529.123
Swing That Music
BYG (F) 529.123
Someday You'll Be Sorry
BYG (F) 529.123
NOTE: All titles also on Affinity (E) AFF 45 and AFF 776, titled *Swing That Music* (double LP and CD). Red Norvo replaces Ruby Braff on other performances on those releases. BYG LP correctly lists "It's Wonderful," while some discographies list "'S Wonderful" in error. "It's Wonderful" also is included on two anthology releases, *Either Side of Midnight*, Charley Lakeside 082333238428, and *Late Night Jazz, Volume 1*, Pazzazz 883717012326.

Some of Ruby's fans are aware of a curious recording by Steve Lacy in a solo album called *The Cryptosphere*, recorded in Paris in September 1971. It was first issued on an LP titled *Lapis* on Saravah (Fr) 10031. The album has been reissued on Saravah (Fr) SHL 1069 (titled *Saravah Jazz!*) and Denon-Saravah (J) YQ7914SH. On this title, Lacy plays his accompaniment to Ruby's recording from the above session of "(Was I to Blame for) Falling in Love With You." Lacy's recording has been reissued on *Scratching the Seventies*, a three-CD set on Saravah (F) SHL 2082.

Larry Ridley reported that George Wein actively sought out local recording opportunities while touring with the Newport All Stars to augment the musicians' incomes as much as possible.[55]

Jack Bradley's photo from the March of Jazz program dates from about this time and shows the next group.[56] This photo is included in this book's photo section.

Newport All Stars[57]
October 24, 1969, Ronnie Scott's, London
Ruby Braff (cnt), Red Norvo (vib), Joe Venuti (v), Barney Kessel (g), George Wein (p), Larry Ridley (b), Don Lamond (dm)
Sweet Georgia Brown (features Venuti)*
Undecided*
Please Don't Talk About Me When I'm Gone
Soon
NOTE: Recordings of two tunes marked with an asterisk are available but remain unissued. Video recordings may exist of first two tunes as *Jazz Scene at the Ronnie Scott Club: Clarke-Boland, Teddy Wilson, Newport All-Stars and Oscar Peterson,* UK 1970, director and producer Terry Henebery and for the next two tunes as *Jazz Scene at the Ronnie Scott Club: Gary Burton, Newport All-Stars and Oscar Peterson,* UK 1970, Terry Henebery.

Jazz Expo '69 was billed as the Newport Jazz festival in London, running from October 25–1 November 1. Performing artists included Sarah Vaughan, Maynard Ferguson, Gary Burton, Charlie Shavers Quartet, Salena Jones, the Newport All-Stars, Dakota Staton, Bill Coleman, Lionel Hampton, Dave Shepherd, Lionel Hampton and his band, Thelonious Monk Quartet, Cecil Taylor, Alan Skidmore, Miles Davis, and Mary Lou Williams. Thursday October 30 was the *American Folk, Blues and Gospel Festival '69* with Albert King, Otis Spann, John Lee Hooker, Champion Jack Dupree, and the Robert Patterson Singers. Ruby was again present as a member of the Newport All Stars.

The program once again includes Ruby's biography and also a photograph by David Redfern.[58]. These biographical sketches have increased in length each year of the Jazz Expo series. The text again reveals a bit about Ruby as follows:

> The old psychiatric cliché about small men who compensate for their size by being aggressive undergoes an interesting mutation in the case of Ruby Braff. When it comes to music, he has one of the most honest tongues I have ever come across, although on second thought it may not be lack of inches that is wholly responsible for this. . . . Benny Carter told me how astonished he had been when he played with Braff for the first time, how this trumpeter, relatively unknown to most people, including Carter himself, had played music so mature that Carter scratched his head and wondered how such things could be.

Newport All Stars: Jazz Expo 1969[59]
October 27, 1969, Royal Festival Hall, Odeon, Hammersmith, London
Ruby Braff (cnt), Red Norvo (vib), Joe Venuti (v), Barney Kessel (g), George Wein (p), Larry Ridley (b), Don Lamond (dm)
Spider's Web
I Got It Bad and That Ain't Good
You're Driving Me Crazy
Other titles not mentioned

The Times reported on the concerts, praising the Newport All Stars, especially Ruby:[60]

> Certainly the most satisfying set was that by the Newport All Stars on Monday, when Ruby Braff, Red Norvo and Barney Kessel demonstrated the advantages of knowing each other's playing, Braff in particular displaying a superb poise of a kind that only Roy Williams, Alex Welsh's trombonist, came near to emulating.

Tribute to Duke
Newport All Stars
October 29, 1969, Stadt-Casino, Basel, Switzerland
Ruby Braff (cnt), Joe Venuti (v), Red Norvo (vib), George Wein (p), Barney Kessel, Kenny Burrell (g), Larry Ridley (b), Don Lamond (dm)

Sweet Georgia Brown (no Braff)
    MPS (G) 15255
Undecided (no Braff)
    MPS (G) 15255
Sophisticated Lady (no Braff)
    MPS (G) 15255
Daybreak (Kessel solo)
    MPS (G) 15255
I Got It Bad and That Ain't Good
    MPS (G) 15255
Just a Sittin' and a Rockin'
    MPS (G) 15255
'Deed I Do
    MPS (G) 15255
If I Could Be with You
    MPS (G) 15255
Things Ain't What They Used to Be
    MPS (G) 15255
Rose Room
    MPS (G) 15255

Newport All Stars
November 1, 1969, Paris Jazz Festival, Paris
Ruby Braff (cnt), Red Norvo (vib), George Wein (p), Barney Kessel (g), Larry Ridley (b), Don Lamond (dm)
Blue Boy
    Blu Jazz (It) BJ009CD
The Girl from Ipanema
    Blu Jazz (It) BJ009CD
I Got It Bad and That Ain't Good
    Blu Jazz (It) BJ009CD
And Now My Love
    Blu Jazz (It) BJ009CD

Newport All Stars: Copenhagen Jazz Festival[61]
Probably November 2, 1969, Copenhagen, Denmark
Ruby Braff (cnt), Red Norvo (vib), George Wein (p), Barney Kessel (g), Larry Ridley (b), Don Lamond (dm)
Love Me or Leave Me
Lady Be Good*

Ruby Braff and George Wein out
The Girl from Ipanema

Ruby Braff and George Wein return; Red Norvo, out
I Got It Bad and That Ain't Good*

Ruby Braff and George Wein out
Samba de Orpheu

Add Joe Venuti (v), George Wein returns
Sweet Georgia Brown*
I Want to Be Happy*

Ruby Braff and Red Norvo return
Timmie's Blues*
NOTE: "Timmie's Blues" is the same melody as "Fine and Mellow." Film was released with the title *Copenhagen Jazz Festival 1969.*[62] A video recording of all listed titles is available. At the time of publication selections marked with an asterisk can be seen on www.YouTube.com.

The following date cannot be correct since it corresponds to the date of the performance in the Netherlands on that day; however, it likely did occur during early November. Likely candidates would be November 3, 4, 6, or 7. The only other remote possibility is that one performance was scheduled as a matinee and the other, at night, allowing time for travel between cities.

Newport All Stars: European Concert
Perhaps November 5, 1969, Stockholm, Sweden[63]
Ruby Braff (cnt), Red Norvo (vib), Joe Venuti (v), Barney Kessel (g), Kenny Burrell (g), Larry Ridley (b), Don Lamond (dm)
C Jam Blues
    Unique Jazz (It) UJ 28
Satin Doll
    Unique Jazz (It) UJ 28
Don't Get Around Much Anymore
    Unique Jazz (It) UJ 28
Rockin' in Rhythm
    Unique Jazz (It) UJ 28
Perdido
    Unique Jazz (It) UJ 28
Medley:
  In a Sentimental Mood
    Unique Jazz (It) UJ 28
  Take the "A" Train
    Unique Jazz (It) UJ 28
Medley:
  Sophisticated Lady
    Unique Jazz (It) UJ 28

I Want to Be Happy
Unique Jazz (It) UJ 28

An available copy of a poster announces the Newport Jazz Festival in Rotterdam and the presence of Duke Ellington, Sarah Vaughan, Miles Davis, Lionel Hampton, Cecil Taylor, and the Newport All Stars.

Newport All Stars: Newport Jazz Festival in Rotterdam[64]
November 5, 1969, De Doelen, Rotterdam, The Netherlands

I have located three photographs from the next performance in Berlin in 1969. One is a close up shot of Barney Kessel, Ruby Braff, and George Wein while the others show everyone performing except for Don Lamond.[65] Another photograph, although attributed to the 1970s, shows this group including Don Lamond but without Joe Venuti.

Newport Jazz Festival All Stars: Berlin Jazz Festival[66]
November 8, 1969, Berlin
Ruby Braff (cnt), Joe Venuti (v), Red Norvo (vib), George Wein (p), Barney Kessel (g), Larry Ridley (b), Don Lamond (dm)
C Jam Blues
In a Mellotone
Unknown
Daydream
Unknown
Sweet Georgia Brown
Sophisticated Lady
Unknown

Larry Ridley recalled that he sat with Ruby at a bar in the Berlin airport. Larry ordered schnapps, which the burley bartender served in a shot glass. The glass was chipped on one side, so Larry asked for a replacement. The bartender retorted with words to the effect that "you will drink it or go somewhere else" whereupon Ruby became incensed and swore at him, taking this as an extreme insult to his companion.[67] Yet again, we see Ruby's principles in action.

The following engagement is probably the occasion George Wein recalled when he reported that Frank Sinatra was in the audience for a performance in fall 1969.[68]

Newport All Stars[69]
December 30, 1969–January 25, 1970, Plaza 9—All That Jazz, Fifth Avenue at 59th Street, New York (closed Mondays)
Ruby Braff (cnt), Red Norvo (vib), Chuck Wayne (g), George Wein (p), Barney Kessel (g), Larry Ridley (b), Lenny McBrowne (dm)

Newport Jazz Festival All-Stars[70]
Late January 1970, Downbeat, New York
Ruby Braff and others, with Cliff Leeman replacing Don Lamond (dm)

Ruby Braff Interview with Henry Whisten
1970? Date and location unknown, CBC Radio
NOTE: A recording of this interview is available but remains unissued.

Cliff Leeman, Ruby Braff, Larry Ridley, George Wein, and Barney Kessel are shown performing in concert in Japan from this tour in a photo from Larry Ridley's website.[71] The photo is dated "Tokyo 1969." Tom Lord dates this as October 8, 1969; however, this was a time that the group was in Europe with Don Lamond as the drummer, so I have entered it following the European tour. Of course, it is also possible that this recording and the associated tour occurred prior to the European tour. However, Cliff Leeman replaced Don Lamond prior to late January, so that suggests a later date in early 1970 for the following recording and the undocumented performances on tour in Japan. Of course, very few people have been fortunate to hear the following recording.

Newport All Stars in Japan
Exact date not known, Tokyo
Ruby Braff (cnt), Joe Venuti (v), Red Norvo (vib), George Wein (p), Barney Kessel (g), Larry Ridley (b), Cliff Leeman (dm)
Honeysuckle Rose
    Union (Teichiku) (J) UPS-49
Russian Lullaby
    Union (Teichiku) (J) UPS-49
Autumn Leaves
    Union (Teichiku) (J) UPS-49
I Surrender Dear
    Union (Teichiku) (J) UPS-49
Fly Me to the Moon
    Union (Teichiku) (J) UPS-49
Perdido
    Union (Teichiku) (J) UPS-49
Star Dust
    Union (Teichiku) (J) UPS-49
Summertime
    Union (Teichiku) (J) UPS-49
Body and Soul
    Union (Teichiku) (J) UPS-49

Larry Ridley reported that on this tour Ruby became upset at one point because the beds in the hotel were too short. Of course, Ruby sometimes joked about his small stature, so Larry recalled this irony with a smile in his voice as he elaborated upon how much he enjoyed playing with Ruby during various engagements. He expressed highest praise for Ruby's melodic style and said that it was always a joy to play with him. "Ruby," he said, "never took half-steps with his music and expected the same commitment from other musicians." When that did not happen, Ruby could become "crusty."[72]

Louis Armstrong and His Friends
May 29, 1970, New York
Louis Armstrong (voc) with large ensemble
We Shall Overcome
    Flying Dutchman AMS-12009, Bluebird 8310-2-RB,
    Bluebird 09026-63961-2, Jazz Heritage 512984H (CD),
    Bluebird (Eu) 2663961-2 (CD), Philips (Eu) 6073.700, RCA 090266388929
NOTE: RCA 090266388929 is titled *God Bless America: Only Patriotic Album.*

Ruby was reported to have been included in a large vocal chorus but is not audible on this recording. Stanley Dance[73] writes that Ruby Braff dropped into Louis Armstrong's recording session for Flying Dutchman on the second day (May 27, 1970, with the titles "His Father Wore Long Hair," "Everybody's Talking," and "The Creator Has a Master Plan"). Dance was present all three days, and the third day has the group vocal chorus that includes Ruby on "We Shall Overcome" on May 29. Interestingly, Ruby stated that he did not recall participating in the recording of the chorus on this session when I asked him about it. For that reason the musicians and other members of the vocal chorus are not listed even though the musicians are documented in other discographies. Mike Lipskin also does not recall Ruby being present in the studio for this recording.[74]

The following invitation and advertisements depict three of the performances in this chapter:

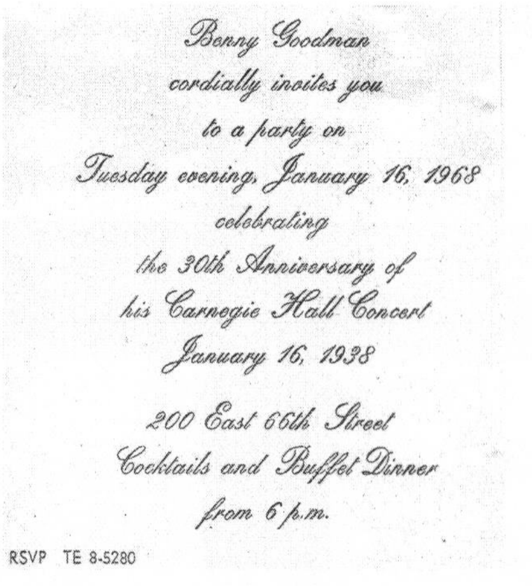

Benny Goodman
cordially invites you
to a party on
Tuesday evening, January 16, 1968
celebrating
the 30th Anniversary of
his Carnegie Hall Concert
January 16, 1938

200 East 66th Street
Cocktails and Buffet Dinner
from 6 p.m.

RSVP TE 8-5280

Figure 9.1: Invitation
January 16, 1969

By Popular Demand
Newport Jazz All-Stars
Red Norvo • Ruby Braff
BarneyKessel • GeorgeWein
"Mousey" Alexander's Trio
Dinner at 8
Plaza 9
& all that JAZZ
at The Plaza
Plaza 9-3933

Figure 9.2: Advertisement
January 1, 1969

Figure 9.3: Advertisement
February 21, 1969

Notes

[1] Source for session documentation D. Russell Connor, *Benny Goodman: Listen to His Legacy* (Metuchen, NJ: Scarecrow Press, 1988), 254. An extensive review is published in *DownBeat*, March 7, 1968, 20–22 that includes a photo of Ruby with Benny Goodman. John S. Wilson, *New York Times*, January 17, 1968, describes the evening and lists the broadcast.

[2] Photo, *The March of Jazz Celebrates Ruby Braff's 74th Birthday Party*, Arbors Records, 2001, 19.

[3] Jack Bradley reporting in *Coda Magazine*, March 1968, 37.

[4] *DownBeat*, April 18, 1968, 47, and Jack Bradley's report in *Coda Magazine*, March/April 1968, 37, along with published festival programs.

[5] Sunnie Sutton, personal conversation, July 1, 2004.

[6] Karl Emil Knudsen has provided extensive information on the following Aspen sessions. Performance dates are taken from copies of the session logs he provided. Master tape owned by Storyville Records.

[7] Master tape owned by Storyville Records.

[8] Photos by Jack Bradley published in *The March of Jazz Celebrates Ruby Braff's 74th Birthday Party*, Arbors Records, 2001, 18.

[9] Coverage by Whitney Balliett, *The New Yorker*, May 4, 1968, 173. Balliett mentions the first three song titles in his review.

[10] Whitney Balliett, *The New Yorker*, May 4, 1968, 173.

[11] Festival and dates listed in *Salute to Jazz 1968* program published by Festival Productions.
[12] *DownBeat*, May 30, 1968, 46.
[13] *DownBeat*, August 8, 1968, 29.
[14] Copy of festival program available includes photo of Ruby in a collage.
[15] George Wein, *Myself Among Others* (Cambridge, MA: Da Capo Press, 2003), 278.
[16] Festival and dates listed in *Salute to Jazz 1968* program published by Festival Productions.
[17] Burt Goldblatt, *The Newport Jazz Festival: The Illustrated History (*New York: Dial Press, 1977), 273 (for session) and Whitney Balliett's *Ecstasy at the Onion (*Indianapolis: Bobbs-Merrill Company, Inc., 1971), 29 (for tunes performed), and Jack Bradley reporting in *Coda Magazine,* December 1968, 38, (for mention of "Royal Garden Blues" as the finale). Dan Morgenstern's enthusiastic review is in *DownBeat*, September 5, 1968, 34, and John S. Wilson echoed his feelings, *New York Times*, July 8, 1968. *Coda Magazine*, August 1969, 3, for photo of Ruby with Joe Venuti at a Schlitz Salute to Jazz from about this time.
[18] Photo by Jack Bradley, *The March of Jazz Celebrates Ruby Braff's 74th Birthday Party*, Arbors Records, 2001, 18.
[19] *DownBeat* August 8, 1968, 44 and October 3, 1968, 39. *The New Yorker*, August 3, 1968, 4, August 10, 1968, 4, August 17, 1968, 4, reporting that on August 18 Buck Clayton and the All-Stars would perform for the New York Hot Jazz Society before the 10 p.m. set with Braff and Sims, August 34, 1968, 4, August 31, 1968, 4, and John S. Wilson, *New York Times*, September 11, 1968.
[20] *DownBeat* August 8, 1968, 44 and October 3, 1968, 39. *The New Yorker*, September 3, 1968 (reporting that Moore would replace Braff rather than join him in error), September 7, 1968, 4, and September 11, 1968, 4.
[21] *Jazz Journal International*, November 1968, 1. Dates published in *DownBeat*, November 28, 1968, 41.
[22] Simon Spillett, "Hank Mobley in Europe 1968–1970," *Jazz Journal International*, January 2004, 7. Thanks to Glen Sharp for pointing out this article.
[23] *The Times*, October 17, 1968, 19.
[24] Charles Fox, *The Jazz Scene* (London: Hamlyn, 1972), 12, photo by Valerie Wilmer.
[25] Jazz Expo '68 program.
[26] Advertisement for Jazz Expo '68 published in *Jazz Journal International*, September 1968, 9. *Jazz Journal International,* December 1968, 1, reports on the concert and mentions George Wein, Ruby Braff, Benny Carter, and Barney Kessel. Source of information: Derek Coller. A review appears in *DownBeat*, December 26, 1968, 42.
[27] *New York Times*, October 20, 1968, and *DownBeat*, December 12, 1968.
[28] Ed Berger in correspondence for the date listed for the performance. Note: The British Library listing incorrectly lists "The Party's Over" rather than "What Kind of Fool Am I?" as a title. In addition, that listing states that the location is The Maltings, Aldeburgh, Suffolk. It also says that the broadcast date for "All of Me" through "Blues" is April 3, 1969, and for the other titles is December 12, 1969. My own reel tapes have a date of December 12, 1968 for the broadcast of "I Want to Be Happy" through "Rose Room" and April 3, 1969, for the broadcast that includes "All of Me" through "Blues."
[29] The Aldeburgh Festival Concert Hall and date of October 26 are listed by David Meeker, *Jazz in the Movies*, 2005, an online resource from the Library of Congress and *Jazz Journal International*, October 1968, 18.

[30] *DownBeat*, February 6, 1969, 45.
[31] Harold Jones, *Bobby Hackett: A Bio-Discography* (Westport, CT: Greenwood Press, 1999) and *DownBeat*, February 8, 1969, 42, and the tune titles for a particular evening's performance are listed in *DownBeat*, March 6, 1969, 18–19 with photo and also John Norris reporting in *Coda Magazine*, March 1969, 35. *The New Yorker*, December 21, 1968, 8, December 28, 1968, 8, January 4, 1969, 8, January 11, 1969, 8, and *DownBeat*, January 9, 1969, 46. John S. Wilson, *New York Times*, December 30, 1968 and *New York Magazine*, December 23, 1968, 14.
[32] *Washington Post*, January 13, 1969.
[33] *DownBeat*, May 1, 1969, 36–37 and published festival program.
[34] *DownBeat*, March 20, 1969, 44, and *DownBeat*, May 1, 1969, 36–37 and published Boston Globe Jazz Festival program.
[35] Robert Hilbert, *Pee Wee Russell: The Life of a Jazzman* (New York: Oxford University Press, 1993), 292.
[36] Whitney Balliett, *The New Yorker*, March 15, 1969, 171, February 15, 1969, 7, February 22, 1969, 6, and March 1, 1969, 8, *DownBeat*, April 3, 1969, 15, ads in *New York Times*, February 19, 26, and 28, 1969.
[37] Source of location: Whitney Balliett, *Ecstasy at the Onion* (Indianapolis: Bobbs-Merrill Company, Inc., 1971), 34, reprinted from *The New Yorker*, March 15, 1969, 173.
[38] Source of location: Whitney Balliett, *Ecstasy at the Onion (*Indianapolis: Bobbs-Merrill Company, Inc., 1971), 34, reprinted from *The New Yorker*, March 15, 1969, 173.
[39] Whitney Balliett, *Ecstasy at the Onion (*Indianapolis: Bobbs-Merrill Company, Inc., 1971), 35. Also reported in *DownBeat*, March 20, 1969, 14, and *New York Times*, February 13, 1969, and John S. Wilson, *New York Times*, March 3, 1969, and ad in *New York Times*, February 21, 1969.
[40] *DownBeat*, June 12, 1969, 46, and *DownBeat*, September 18, 1969, 30.
[41] 1969 Newport Jazz Festival Program.
[42] Burt Goldblatt, *The Newport Jazz Festival: The Illustrated History* (New York: Dial Press, 1977), 274, and Whitney Balliett, *Ecstasy at the Onion (*Indianapolis: Bobbs-Merrill Company, Inc., 1971), 48, and *DownBeat*, August 21, 1969, 25, which mentioned the tunes performed. Advertisement in *New York Times*, June 1, 1969.
[43] George Wein, *Myself Among Others* (Cambridge, MA: Da Capo Press, 2003), 283.
[44] Leonard Feather, *Los Angeles Times*, July 12, 1969.
[45] *DownBeat*, October 2, 1969, 24–25, including photo, 25, and mentioning Cliff Leeman in the review.
[46] Ad in *New York Times*, June 29, 1969, July 20, 1969, and July 24, 1969; *DownBeat*, October 2, 1969, 24–25, including photo, 25, and mentioning Cliff Leeman in the review.
[47] Photo by Jack Bradley, *The March of Jazz Celebrates Ruby Braff's 74th Birthday Party*, Arbors Records, 2001, 21, and also contained in press release for April 9, 2002, Bobby Hackett tribute performance in Boston. As noted in the text, the correct date is likely 1975.
[48] *DownBeat*, October 16, 1969, 42, and *DownBeat*, August 21, 1969, 47.
[49] Photo, *The March of Jazz Celebrates Ruby Braff's 74th Birthday Party*, Arbors Records, 2001, 21.
[50] George Wein, *Myself Among Others* (Cambridge, MA: Da Capo Press, 2003), 351. George Wein wrote that Frank Sinatra attended one night.
[51] George Wein, *Myself Among Others* (Cambridge, MA: Da Capo Press, 2003), 351. On 358 the date is referenced as late in the year.

[52] *Jazz Journal International*, December 1993, 7.
[53] Information from David Griffiths.
[54] *Jazz Journal International*, December 1969, 23.
[55] Larry Ridley in personal conversation February 7, 2006.
[56] Photo, *The March of Jazz Celebrates Ruby Braff's 74th Birthday Party*, Arbors Records, 2001, 21.
[57] David Meeker, *Jazz in the Movies*, the Library of Congress website, 2005.
[58] Jazz Expo '69 program showing page with Braff's bio and photo by David Redfern.
[59] *DownBeat*, January 8, 1970, 26.
[60] *The Times*, October 30, 1969, 13.
[61] Date from David Meeker, *Jazz in the Movies*, the Library of Congress website http://lcweb2.loc.gov/cocoon/ihas/loc.natlib.ihas.200023340/default.html.
[62] David Meeker, *Jazz in the Movies*, the Library of Congress website, 2005.
[63] Correspondence with Leif Karlsson. He identifies Stockholm as the location for this performance.
[64] Information provided by Han Schulte.
[65] At the time of publication other photos can be seen at http://www.jazzpages.com/KarlheinzKlueter/ but the ones cited are not currently shown.
[66] Information provided by Michael Frohne, and this is probably the session mentioned on the MPS album jacket.
[67] Larry Ridley in personal conversation, February 7, 2006.
[68] George Wein, *Myself Among Others* (Cambridge, MA: Da Capo Press, 2003), 351.
[69] *DownBeat*, February 19, 1970, 40 and *The New Yorker*, December 27, 8, January 3, 1970, 7, January 10, 1970, 6, January 17, 1970, 8.
[70] Jack Bradley writing in *Coda Magazine*, December 1969, 61 (following a six-week booking by Bobby Hackett that began November 28).
[71] This photo can be seen at http://www.larryridley.com/photos.htm at the time of publication.
[72] Larry Ridley in personal conversation February 7, 2006.
[73] *Jazz Journal International*, July 1970, 11.
[74] Mike Lipskin in personal conversation. Mike was present for that session in his role with RCA Records.

Chapter 10

Tony Bennett and New York Clubs: Ruby Reaches New Audiences

Ruby was a featured soloist with Tony Bennett during the period 1970–1974, although the only released recordings from this long association date from 1973. Will Friedwald has very kindly contributed extensive information drawn from contemporary press coverage that has extended documentation of this period beyond what I was able to capture from other sources. He gathered these reports while researching Tony Bennett's career for their book *The Good Life*. When reports specifically mention Ruby Braff, they are included in the regular style. Reports that do not explicitly mention Ruby Braff are also included, but are indented to reflect the uncertainty about Ruby's presence. While Ruby's presence cannot be verified in these performances at this time, it is nonetheless likely that he appeared on some of those occasions.

Tony Bennett with Ruby Braff[1]
June 20, 1970, Place des Nations, Montreal
Tony Bennett performed with an orchestra directed by John Bunch including Ruby Braff (cnt) and John Christie (ts)
Something
What the World Needs Now Is Love
I Left My Heart in San Francisco
Everybody's Talking
The Shadow of Your Smile
Little Green Apples

Jazz at Ronnie Scott's: Likely Rebroadcast of October 10, 1969
Newport All Stars
August 13, 1970, BBC, London
Ruby Braff (cnt), Red Norvo (vib), George Wein (p), Barney Kessel (g), Larry Ridley (b), Don Lamond (dm)
Please Don't Talk About Me When I'm Gone
Sooner or Later

NOTE: An audio recording of these tunes is available but remains unissued. This is probably a rebroadcast of the program dated October 10, 1969, during the Newport All Star's previous European tour.

Roy Eldridge opened at Ryan's in New York in September 1970 on a Tuesday. Ruby Braff was the only New York musician on hand for the occasion; however, there is no indication that he was invited to play since the evening would have focused on Roy.[2]

Tony Bennett[3]
September 26, 1970, 8 and 11 p.m., Philharmonic Hall, Lincoln Center, New York
Ruby Braff (cnt), John Bunch (p and musical director), Louis Bellson (dm), Bunny Briggs (tap dancing to open the show), and a large orchestra
I Left My Heart in San Francisco
Something
The Shadow of Your Smile
San Francisco
It Had to Be You
Get Happy (included Braff solo)
People

Braff filled with obbligatos with his only solo coming on "Get Happy." In his review, John S. Wilson wrote the following:[4]

> And yet when it was over, there were really just a few songs to remember and one question to carry away: Why was Ruby Braff there? He got one short chorus in a slam-bang version of "Get Happy" and the rest of the night he sat there noodling. Even when Bix Beiderbecke was buried in Paul Whiteman's band, he got more than one chorus a night.

The Boy from New Orleans: A Tribute to Louis Armstrong[5]
Late October 1970, CBS, London
Louis Armstrong (tp), Ruby Braff (cnt), John Bunch (p) with large orchestra during rehearsal, Finley Hund, and Phil Schultz, directors
Aired on Columbia Broadcasting System
Pretty Little Missy
God Save the Queen

Tony Bennett (voc), Ruby Braff (cnt), John Bunch (p), and large orchestra
They All Laughed
I'll Begin Again
NOTE: A video recording of this program is available but remains unissued. Ruby did not solo on any of the above titles but was introduced by Tony Bennett and bows to the audience on camera. *Jazz Journal International*[6] reported a Lou-

is Armstrong concert in October that probably served as the basis for part of this film and said that other musicians include Danny Moss (cl), Arthur Watts (b), Eric Delaney (dm), and Tyree Glenn (tb).

Tony Bennett[7]
November 23, 1970, Shoreham Blue Room, Washington, D.C.
Ruby Braff (cnt), John Bunch (p), and the Bob Cross Orchestra (32 musicians)
If I Ruled the World
Get Happy
Autumn Leaves
Little Green Apples
Medley:
One for My Baby
It Had to Be You

Contemporary reports do not mention Ruby Braff explicitly in the following performance:

> **Tony Bennett** (reported in *Variety*, February 17, 1971)
> February 2, 1971, Royal Albert Hall, London
> Dennis Farnon conducted the London Philharmonic Orchestra for the first half of the program. Tony Bennett performed for the second half (60 minutes):
> I Left My Heart in San Francisco
> What the World Needs Now
> I'll Begin Again
> This performance was a one-night stand benefiting the London Philharmonic Orchestra's National Appeal Fund.

Upstairs at the Downstairs
Ruby says he sat in, probably sometime during 1971, when George Barnes and Bucky Pizzarelli performed together at the club Upstairs at the Downstairs in New York.[8] This eventually led, starting in perhaps 1973, to Ruby rehearsing at George Barnes's home, later adding Wayne Wright and John Giuffrida. For several years Ruby had worked to identify other artists who could be combined in order to explore new performance possibilities. The work with Tony Bennett created flexibility to create a new working group that became the Ruby Braff–George Barnes Quartet. Many critics have felt that this became one of the finest small groups in the history of jazz. Barnes and Pizzarelli also performed together at the Guitar (754 Tenth Avenue at 51st Street) in New York for four weeks during the months of October 1970 and March 1971 on Wednesdays through Sundays, so Ruby would have had other opportunities to hear them as well.[9]

Your Father's Mustache[10]
February 21, 1971, 7th Avenue South and 10th Street, New York
Ruby Braff (cnt) featured with Balaban & Cats: Red Balaban (b) and unidentified musicians—about this time this band included the following musicians: Ed Polcer (tp), Dick Rath (tb), Herb Hall or Kenny Davern (cl), Red Richards (p), Red Balaban (b), Connie Kay or Buzzy Drootin (dm)[11]

Your Father's Mustache[12]
March 1971, 7th Avenue South and 10th Street, New York
Probably Ruby performs with same musicians as on February 21.

Your Father's Mustache[13]
April 4, 1971, 7th Avenue South and 10th Street, New York
Probably Ruby performs with same musicians as on February 21.

Tony Bennett with Ruby Braff[14]
April 13–23, 1971, Empire Room, Palmer House Hotel, Chicago

Will Leonard reviewed one of Mr. Bennett's performances:[15]

> Tony Bennett sings nearly two dozen songs each show, these evenings in the Empire room of the Palmer house, and about two-thirds of them are numbers he has sung repeatedly on the same floor. But there is new power in this one, new delicacy in that one, new nuances here, new phrasing there, as he overwhelms the big room with a vocal torrent alternately torrid and tender.
>
> The instrumental music, with John Bunch conducting and Ruby Braff blowing a wide open cornet, is as exciting as Bennett's swinging voyage thru all the old ones, and a lot of new ones.

Jazz Interactions[16]
April 25, 1971, at 5 p.m., Jazz Center, New York
Ruby Braff (cnt) performed with unknown musicians
The concert program also included the Chico Hamilton Quartet, Roland Hanna, Roy Haynes, Jimmy Heath, Milt Jackson, Howard McGhee, Marian McPartland, and others.

Contemporary reports do not mention Ruby Braff explicitly in the following performance:

> **Tony Bennett** (reported in *Variety*, May 5, 1971, and *The New Yorker*, page 8)
> Opening April 28, 1971, Empire Room, Waldorf-Astoria, New York (except Sundays and Monday)
> Musicians include John Bunch (p), the George Cort Orchestra, and the Felipe Yanez Orchestra. The following tune was mentioned:

Love Story

Klaus Stratemann[17] reported that Duke Ellington performed in Newark on April 12 and at Lincoln Center (Philharmonic Hall) on April 16, so the Waldorf appearance probably includes this interval. Tony Bennett's engagement opened April 28 and ran through May 22 except Sundays and Mondays.[18] Duke Ellington at the piano offered a "few words and cheek kissing, four to a customer."

Tony Bennett at Philharmonic Hall[19]
1971 (two concerts), Lincoln Center, New York
Louis Bellson Orchestra, Ruby Braff featured
I Left My Heart in San Francisco
I Wanna Be Around
Come Saturday Morning
They All Laughed
Medley:
 One for My Baby
 It Had to Be You

Connoisseur Concerts: Tribute to Louis Armstrong[20]
July 10, 1971, Town Hall, New York
Ruby Braff (cnt), Dizzy Gillespie, Clark Terry, Jimmy McPartland (tpt), Dickie Wells (tb), Pepper Adams, Bobby Brown (s), Joe Muranyi (cl), Bob Haggart (b), Marian McPartland, Jaki Byard (p), Al Cohn–Willis Conover New York Band including Eddie Bert and Bill Watrous (tb), Ben Aronov (p), Carmen Leggio, George Dorsey (as), Charlie Fowlkes (bar)
Blues for Pops (Gillespie)
Solitude (Fowlkes)
Other selections not named
Blues (all)

Contemporary reports do not mention Ruby Braff explicitly in the following performance:

> **Tony Bennett** (reported in *Variety*, July 23, 1971)
> Probably July 1971, Caesar's Palace, Las Vegas
> Musicians include John Bunch (p)

Tony Bennett with Count Basie and His Orchestra[21]
July 26–August 1, 1971, Westbury Music Fair, Westbury, Long Island, New York
Ruby Braff (cnt), John Bunch (p and musical director), along with Count Basie and His Orchestra

Tony Bennett[22]

August 4–8, 1971, Shady Grove Music Fair, Rockville, Maryland
Ruby Braff (cnt), John Bunch (p), and Buddy Rich and His Orchestra

Contemporary reports do not mention Ruby Braff explicitly in the following performances:

> **Tony Bennett** (reported in *Billboard* and *Variety*, October 20, 1971 and *The New Yorker*, October 2, 1971, page 13)
> October 9, 1971, two concerts (8:00 and midnight), Carnegie Hall, New York
> Robert Farnon conducting
> I Want to Be Happy
> Love Story
> Because of You
> Something
> Autumn Leaves
> Medley:
> Just in Time
> One for My Baby
> I Left My Heart in San Francisco
>
> **Tony Bennett** (reported in *Variety*, November 3, 1971)
> Probably mid-October 1971, Riviera, Las Vegas
> John Bunch, Pat Henry (comic), Jack Cathcart Orchestra (29 musicians)
> Love Story
> Something
> Let There Be Love
> The Lady's in Love with You
> Just in Time
> I Left My Heart in San Francisco
> It Had to Be You
> One for My Baby
> For Once in My Life

Tony Bennett in London[23]

Perhaps October 27, 1971, Palladium, London
The first half of the concert featured a variety of acts including Lonnie Donegan, Arthur Worsley (a ventriloquist), Ugo Garrido (a juggler), Doriss Dancers (16), Robert Lowe conducting the Palladium Orchestra
The second half of the concert featured Tony Bennett with Ruby Braff, John Bunch, and Joe Cocuzzo
I'll Begin Again

If I Ruled the World
Old Devil Moon
For Once in My Life
I Left My Heart in San Francisco
NOTE: This was the Palladium debut for Tony Bennett who was featured during the second half of the bill.

Ruby Braff Quartet at the Half Note[24]
October 24, 1971, 289 Hudson Street, at Spring Street, New York (one night only)
Ruby Braff (cnt) and unknown other musicians but probably similar to October 30 engagement that follows.

The one night engagement at the Half Note was extended to run from October 27–November 7, 1971 (except Monday nights when Clark Terry's 17-piece band was featured). The regular bassist was reported to be Victor Sproles. Jimmy Rushing returned to perform on November 5–7, 1971.[25] The Half Note was located at 289 Hudson Street in New York.

Ruby Braff Quartet at the Half Note with James Rushing[26]
October 27–November 7, 1971, 289 Hudson Street, at Spring Street, New York
Ruby Braff (cnt), Ken Ascher (p), Victor Sproles (b), Dottie Dodgion (dm), add Jimmy Rushing (voc) on November 5–7

Ruby Braff Quartet at the Half Note
October 30, 1971, New York
Ruby Braff (cnt), Ken Ascher (p), Frank Clayton (b), Dottie Dodgion (dm)
Just You, Just Me
When Your Lover Has Gone
Take the "A" Train
Ain't Misbehavin'
Yesterdays
When You're Smiling
Don't Get Around Much Anymore
Between the Devil and the Deep Blue Sea
When I Fall in Love
Tea for Two
Softly, As in a Morning Sunrise (Braff out)
In a Mellotone
Don't Be That Way
I Can't Get Started
The Man I Love
Somebody Loves Me
Blue and Sentimental

Add Sam Margolis (ts)
I Never Knew
These Foolish Things
Them There Eyes
Cocktails for Two
Rosetta
NOTE: A recording of these tunes is available but remains unissued.

Ruby Braff Quartet at the Half Note[27]
Unknown date, probably from the same engagement, New York
Ruby Braff (cnt), Ken Ascher (p), Michael Moore (b), Dottie Dodgion (dm)
Hustlin' and Bustlin' for My Baby
You Are Too Beautiful

Despite meeting George Barnes, Ruby continued to experiment with other combinations of musicians. His creative appetite was unbounded. His relationships with Tony Bennett and Jimmy Rushing provided regular employment as he continued his search, with the International Jazz Quartet becoming his next group.

Jack Bradley mentioned one such rehearsal: "Ruby Braff's new group is shaping up nicely. With him are Sam Margolis (cl, ts), Earle Warren (as, bar), Benny Morton (tb), and rhythm. The arrangements are by Ruby and it's great to hear Louis's 'You Are My Lucky Star' and 'You're Lucky to Me,' Fat's 'Sweet and Slow,' Duke's 'Mood Indigo' and 'Solitude,' and Braff's 'Where's Freddie?'"[28]

Ruby Braff Quartet at the Half Note with James Rushing[29]
February 22–March 11, 1972, New York
Ruby Braff (cnt), Ken Ascher (p), Bill Pemberton (b), Oliver Jackson (dm), Jimmy Rushing (voc, on weekend nights only)

Ruby did not appear on Mondays, when Clark Terry's big band appeared. Probably Ruby closed on March 11 but could have also performed on Tuesday, March 14 before James Moody opened on March 15.

Ruby Braff at Your Father's Mustache[30]
March 12, 1972, New York
Ruby Braff (cnt), Dick Rath (tb), Sal Pace (cl), Chuck Folds (p), Red Balaban (b), Marquis Foster (dm)
Sunday
Ain't Misbehavin'
You Can Depend on Me
Sugar
Sweet Georgia Brown
Indiana

Pennies from Heaven
Louisiana
New Orleans
Way Down Yonder in New Orleans
I've Found a New Baby
If I Could Be with You
Rosetta
Basin Street Blues
Tea for Two
Please Don't Talk About Me When I'm Gone
Someday Sweetheart
Big Butter and Egg Man
Blues
Lady Be Good
Rose Room
When It's Sleepy Time Down South
Swing That Music
The Song Is Ended
NOTE: A recording of these tunes is available but remains unissued.

Ruby Braff Quartet at the Half Note with James Rushing
April 4, 1972, New York
Ruby Braff (cnt), Jimmy Rushing (voc), Don Friedman (p), Roland Wilson (b), Dottie Dodgion (dm)
Don't Get Around Much Anymore
Tea for Two
When Your Lover Has Gone
Wrap Your Troubles in Dreams
Foolin' Myself
When You're Smiling (JR voc)
Exactly Like You (JR voc)
See See Rider (JR voc)
All of Me (JR voc)
This Can't Be Love
Over the Rainbow
Mean to Me
Blue Skies (JR voc)
Trouble in Mind (JR voc)
On the Sunny Side of the Street (JR voc)
Goin' to Chicago (JR voc)
St. James Infirmary (JR voc)

Substitute Jake Hanna (dm) for Dottie Dodgion
Sent for You Yesterday (JR voc)

Dottie Dodgion (dm) returns for Jake Hanna
They Can't Take That Away from Me
The Man I Love
Here, There and Everywhere
You're Driving Me Crazy
Am I Blue? (JR voc)
I Can't Believe That You're in Love with Me (JR voc)

Substitute Bill Pemberton (b) for Roland Wilson
Melancholy Baby (JR voc)
Don't You Miss Your Baby (JR voc)

Add Judy Canterino (voc)
Who's Sorry Now? (JR, JC voc)

Out Judy Canterino (voc)
Happy Birthday to Bill Pemberton
You Took Advantage of Me
NOTE: A recording of these tunes is available but remains unissued.

Contemporary reports do not mention Ruby Braff explicitly in the following performances; however, given Ruby's schedule in New York it is unlikely he was with Mr. Bennett in London in March for the first two events described below:

Tony Bennett (reported in *Variety*, March 29, 1972)
(this is a long *Variety* story on Tony Bennett owning masters, controlling TV shows)
United Kingdom for 13-week television series, including guests Billy Eckstine and Sarah Vaughan

Tony Bennett (reported in *Variety*, March 29, 1972)
March 26 and 31, 1972, April 2, 1972, Palladium, London

Tony Bennett (reported in *Variety*, May 3, 1972)
April 28, 1972, Las Vegas Hilton, Las Vegas
John Bunch (p), Lennon Sisters (voc), Joe Guercio Orchestra (31 musicians)
Smile

Tony Bennett (reported in *The New Yorker,* May 6, 1972, May 13, page 8, May 27, page 8)
Opening May 12 until May 27, 1972, Empire Room, Waldorf-Astoria, New York—performing for dinner and supper, except Sundays and

Mondays—Ruby was performing in a different room in the same hotel and therefore may have joined these performances.

Ruby Braff International Quartet at the Half Note with James Rushing[31]
May 18–21, 1972, Half Note, New York
Ruby Braff (cnt) with other musicians. Jimmy Rushing is added on Friday and Saturday nights. Clark Terry's big band takes over on Monday nights.

Ruby Braff International Quartet at the Half Note[32]
May 1972, New York
Ruby Braff (cnt), Hank Jones (p), Milt Hinton (b), Dottie Dodgion (dm)
No further information is available.

Ruby Braff Quartet at the Half Note
May 21, 1972, New York
Ruby Braff (cnt), Ben Aronov (p), George Mraz (b), Dottie Dodgion (dm)
Sunday
Struttin' with Some Barbecue
That Old Feeling
No Moon at All
Love Walked In
Body and Soul
Thou Swell
Out of Nowhere
Somebody Loves Me
When I Fall in Love
Mean to Me
Over the Rainbow
Lover Come Back to Me

John Bunch (p) replaces Ben Aronov
Nice Work If You Can Get It
Here, There and Everywhere
Take the "A" Train
Just You, Just Me
Easy Living
Tea for Two

Add Jerry Dodgion (as); Ben Aronov (p) returns for John Bunch
It's Only a Paper Moon
Jeepers Creepers
Jive at Five
Confessin'
Them There Eyes
NOTE: A recording of these tunes is available but remains unissued.

Ruby Braff International Quartet[33]
May 23, 1972, Peacock Alley, Waldorf-Astoria, New York
Ruby Braff (cnt), Hank Jones (p), George Duvivier (b), Dottie Dodgion (dm)

No further information is available about the above appearance at Peacock Alley, but this booking probably extended into June in light of the next published reports. An ad in the *New York Times* billed the group as "Tony Bennett's favorite jazz artists under the direction of Ruby Braff."[34] John Wilson wrote the following in his review: "At Mr. Braff's request, a dance floor has been spread in front of the bandstand and the almost forgotten pleasures of dancing to excellent jazz is available to New Yorkers once again." He also reported that this was the first time jazz was performed in Peacock Alley. Also, Ruby asked that a dance floor be installed especially for his performance.[35]

Jimmy Rushing passed away on June 8 during Ruby's appearance at the Waldorf-Astoria. His appearances on weekends at the Half Note must have been among his very last performances since they extended on weekends through mid-May. His final appearance there with Ruby was advertised for May 19 and 20. The next chapter will provide details of a concert held to honor his legacy.

Ruby Braff International Quartet[36] **(see Figure 10.1)**
Early June 5–10, 1972 (the week that includes the 9th), Peacock Alley, Waldorf-Astoria, New York
Ruby Braff (cnt), Hank Jones (p), George Duvivier (b), Dottie Dodgion (dm)
Watch What Happens
When a Woman Loves a Man
Other titles not listed
NOTE: Tony Bennett obtained this booking for Ruby while he was performing at the Empire Room in the same hotel. Further details are unknown.

Ruby Braff Quartet at the Half Note[37]
June 16–18, 1972, New York (the engagement ran from at least June 16 "through Sunday"—it was reported to come one week after closing at Peacock Alley)
Ruby Braff (cnt), Dill Jones (p), Victor Gaskin (b), Dottie Dodgion (dm)
Sunday
New Orleans
Someday You'll Be Sorry
A Hundred Years from Today
Keepin' Out of Mischief Now
You're Lucky to Me
Sugar
I've Got a Feelin' I'm Fallin'
Save It Pretty Mama
My Monday Date

Louisiana
NOTE: A recording of these tunes is available but remains unissued.

Ruby Braff Quartet at the Half Note
June 25, 1972, New York
Ruby Braff (cnt), Don Friedman (p), Victor Sproles (b), Dottie Dodgion (dm)
Lover Come Back to Me
Mean to Me
Them There Eyes
Confessin'
Lester Leaps In
Jive at Five
Indiana
Mood Indigo
This Can't Be Love
In a Mellotone
But Not for Me
Blues
NOTE: A recording of these tunes is available but remains unissued.

Contemporary reports do not mention Ruby Braff explicitly in the following performance:

> **Tony Bennett** (reported in *Variety* July 19, 1972)
> July 13, 1972, Harrah's, Lake Tahoe
> John Bunch (p), Liz Torres (comic), Chris Kirby (ventriloquist), Brian Farnon Orchestra (32 musicians) performing 17 songs
>> The Summer Knows
>> O Sole Mio
>> I Left My Heart in San Francisco
>> Just in Time
>> Once Upon a Time
>> Smile

Ruby Braff Quartet at the Half Note[38]
June 25, 1972, Half Note, New York
Ruby Braff (cnt), others unknown

Mike Longo with Ruby Braff at the Half Note[39]
July 6, 1972, Half Note, New York
Ruby Braff (cnt), Mike Longo (p), plus two unknown members of Longo's Trio
Clark Terry was featured with Longo's Trio on July 5, with Ruby following on July 6. Around this time Mike Longo recorded with Ron Carter (b) and Mickey Roker (dm) so they may be two possibilities for this engagement.

Ruby Braff Quartet at the Half Note[40]
July 18–30, 1972, New York (closed Mondays)
Ruby Braff (cnt), others unknown

Ruby Braff Quartet at the Half Note
July 19, 1972, New York
Ruby Braff (cnt), Dill Jones (p), George Mraz (b), Dottie Dodgion (dm)
You Are My Lucky Star
Foolin' Myself
I Believe in Miracles
I Can't Get Started
Big Butter and Egg Man
Linger Awhile
You're a Lucky Guy
Quiet Nights
What Is There to Say?
I Want to Be Happy
Easy Living
Lover Come Back to Me

Add Pepper Adams (bars)
A-Flat Blues
Pepper Adams out
Just You, Just Me
Keepin' Out of Mischief Now
Melancholy Baby
Save It Pretty Mama
Take the "A" Train
NOTE: A recording of these tunes is available but remains unissued.

Ruby Braff Quartet at the Half Note
July 21, 1972, New York
Ruby Braff (cnt), Dill Jones (p), George Mraz (b), Dottie Dodgion (dm)
You're a Lucky Guy
Blue and Sentimental
Jeepers Creepers
Pennies from Heaven
Them There Eyes
'Deed I Do
I Cover the Waterfront

Add Jerry Dodgion (as)
I Would Do Anything for You
Sometimes I'm Happy
Just You, Just Me

Autumn Leaves
My Blue Heaven
Take the "A" Train
NOTE: A recording of these tunes is available but remains unissued.

The Half Note moved to 149 West 54th Street and Ruby probably did not appear in the new location, ending a dependable series of engagements and setting the stage for the development of some new relationships. George Wein led the Newport Ensemble at the Half Note in April 1973, but Ruby is not listed in *The New Yorker* in conjunction with those appearances. The Newport Ensemble included Wein (p), Al Harewood (dm), and Larry Ridley (b).[41]

Contemporary reports do not mention Ruby Braff explicitly in the following performance:

> **Tony Bennett** starring at benefit (reported in *Billboard*)
> August 4, 1972, Princess Grace of Monaco's gala for benefit of the Red Cross

The following advertisement depicts one of the performances in this chapter:

Figure 10.1: Advertisement
May 25, 1972

Notes

[1] David Smith, "While Bennett Swings Nice and Low," *The Gazette* (Montreal), June 22, 1970.
[2] Source Roy Bolden Memoir (1998) cited in John Chilton, *Roy Eldridge, Little Jazz Giant* (New York: Continuum), 258.
[3] John S. Wilson, *New York Times*, September 28, 1970, and *The New Yorker*, September 19, 1970, 14.
[4] John S. Wilson, *New York Times*, September 28, 1970.

[5] Details in Klaus Stratemann, *Louis Armstrong on the Screen* (Copenhagen: Jazz Media, 1996), 585–587.
[6] *Jazz Journal International*, December 1970, 3.
[7] Hollie I. West, *Washington Post*, November 25, 1970.
[8] George Barnes cited by Bert Whyatt and Derek Coller, "The Ruby Braff–George Barnes Quartet," *Jazz Journal International*, August 2001, 12–14.
[9] *The New Yorker*, October 3, 1970, 4 and March 13, 1971, 7.
[10] *The New Yorker*, February 20, 1971, 6.
[11] *DownBeat*, June 10, 1971, 33.
[12] *DownBeat*, April 1, 1971, 38.
[13] *The New Yorker*, April 3, 1971, 6.
[14] Wayne Jones writing in *Coda Magazine*, June 1971, 41.
[15] Will Leonard, *Chicago Tribune*, April 11 and 16, 1971.
[16] *The New Yorker*, April 24, 1971, 14.
[17] Klaus Stratemann, Duke *Ellington: Day By Day and Film By Film* (Copenhagen: JazzMedia, c. 1992), 615.
[18] *The New Yorker*, April 24, 1971, 8, May 1, 1971, 8, May 8, 1971, 8, and May 15, 1971, 8. Ruby gained a nice mention from a review of this engagement in *Billboard*, May 15, 1971: "one of the most tasteful jazz artists" who "injects all too few crackling solos through the evening."
[19] Correspondence with Will Friedwald mentioning coverage in *Billboard* from an unspecified issue.
[20] John S. Wilson, *New York Times*, July 13, 1971.
[21] Advertisement in *New York Times*, June 20, 1971.
[22] Advertisement, *Washington Post*, June 20, 1971.
[23] Correspondence with Will Friedwald referencing his concert flyer from 1971. This is probably the concert reported in *Variety* on October 27 (year of issue not certain).
[24] *The New Yorker*, October 23, 1971, 6.
[25] *The New Yorker*, October 30, 1971, 7, and November 6, 1971, 6.
[26] *The New Yorker*, October 30, 1971, 7.
[27] Dan Morgenstern writing in *DownBeat*, January 20, 1972, 15. He probably refers to the October/November engagement, since *The New Yorker* does not mention Ruby playing at the Half Note in December or January.
[28] Jack Bradley reporting in *Coda Magazine*, January/February 1972, 40, and Dan Morgenstern's article in *DownBeat*, January 20, 1972, 15.
[29] *The New Yorker*, February 19, 1972, 6, February 26, 1972, 7 (which also mentions that George Barnes ended his longtime relationship with Bucky Pizzarelli), March 4, 1972, 6, March 11, 1972, 6 (mentioning that Ruby will not appear on March 12), and March 18, 1972, 6. *DownBeat*, May 25, 1972, 36. Jimmy Rushing entered the Flower Fifth Avenue Hospital on May 12 and died on June 8. He had worked weekends at the Half Note following an earlier heart attack. These dates are included in his obituary published in *DownBeat*, August 17, 1972, 10, and a listing in the *New York Times*, March 4, 1972.
[30] Ruby's recent guest appearances are mentioned in *DownBeat*, April 27, 1972, 36, so there are probably other bookings around this time.
[31] *The New Yorker*, April 22, 1972, 6, and May 20, 1972, 6.
[32] Letter from Shin-ichi Iwamoto.

[33] Letter from Shin-ichi Iwamoto and coverage in *DownBeat*, June 22, 1972, 11 and 36. Zoot Sims and the JPJ Quartet appeared at the Half Note between Ruby's May and June bookings.
[34] Advertisement in the *New York Times,* May 25, 1972.
[35] *New York Times*, May 26, 1972.
[36] *New York Times*, June 16, 1972.
[37] *New York Times*, June 16, 1972.
[38] *The New Yorker*, July 1, 1972, 5.
[39] *The New Yorker*, July 8, 1972, 4, and *New York Magazine*, July 10, 1972, 17.
[40] *The New Yorker*, July 15, 1972, 4, July 22, 1972, 3, and July 29,1972, 4.
[41] *The New Yorker*, March 31, 1973, 6, April 7, 1973, 6, and April 14, 1973, 6.

Chapter 11

Ruby Braff and Two of His Next Champions: Carl Jefferson and Hank O'Neal—Beginning the Relationships with Concord Jazz and Chiaroscuro Records

Ruby had already benefited from long-standing relationships with George Wein (Storyville Records) and John Hammond (Vanguard Records). He was fortunate to have had every one of those relationships as well as those that followed. A special friendship with Jack Bradley was also important in extending his visibility. Of course, his relationship with George Wein continued and led to additional tours throughout Europe and Japan. In addition, Dick Hyman would create a number of opportunities for them to perform together, earning necessary income while delighting the public.

Ruby's recording relationship with Hank O'Neal and Chiaroscuro Records began in 1972 and extended for over eight years. Another recording relationship began with Carl Jefferson in 1974 and ran for over 20 years; however, Ruby performed at the Concord Jazz Festival in 1972 before Jefferson issued his first record. By 1985, the recordings on Concord Records provided most of Ruby's ongoing visibility in the US. Without the support of these men, starting in 1972, Ruby would not have been as successful in keeping his name in front of the jazz community. Hank O'Neal was based on the East Coast, while Carl Jefferson was based in California.

However, this is getting ahead of Ruby's story, for he was now working with his International Quartet, a group that had been performing regularly at the Blue Note and Waldorf-Astoria Hotel in New York City where Tony Bennett had helped arrange bookings.

Dottie Dodgion said the following about Ruby Braff, probably in conjunction with the following appearance:[1]

> Ruby Braff is not an easy person. He would *never* hire you just because you were a girl. God! Somebody said that one time. I played the Concord Jazz Festival with Ruby, Milt Hinton, and Hank Jones. We'd been playin' all over for about two years. Philip Elwood of the *San Francisco Chronicle* said, 'Well, it's obvious to see why Dottie's there, it's for visual effects.' Well, Ruby was *furious*! He called him up and he says, 'How dare you say that I would hire somebody for any other reason than music!' Ruby gave it to him good.

That provided another glimpse into Ruby's principles.

Ruby Braff Quartet[2]
August 12, 1972, Concord Jazz Festival, Concord, California
Ruby Braff (cnt), Hank Jones (p), probably Milt Hinton (b), and Dottie Dodgion (dm)
No further information available but this is the first documented association with Carl Jefferson.

Ruby Braff International Quartet[3]
Wednesday–Sunday including August 23-27, 1972, Tony's Place, 241 East 86th Street, New York
Ruby Braff (cnt), Hank Jones (p), George Mraz (b), Dottie Dodgion (dm)
Blues
Sugar

John S. Wilson wrote the following in his review:

> As for Mr. Braff, he is to the cornet what Erroll Garner is to the piano—a romantic, a swinger, a melodist and a musician with a very positive sense of personal style. His solos are anecdotal songs, filled with asides, comments, and sudden gay, little dances. He is basically a product of the influence of Louis Armstrong, but when the quartet went into a gorgeous, slow, shuffling blues the other night, he suddenly became the image of Frankie Newton playing behind Billie Holiday.

Contemporary reports do not mention Ruby Braff explicitly in the following performance:

> **Tony Bennett** (reported in *Variety*, August 22, 1973, article reported he was at Harrah's in Reno "last year")
> Perhaps August 1972, Harrah's, Reno, Nevada

10th Annual Gibson Jazz Party[4]
September 2–4, 1972, Broadmoor Hotel, Colorado Springs, Colorado
Participating artists included Ruby Braff, Pee Wee Erwin, Bobby Hackett, Joe Newman, Clark Terry, Joe Wilder (tp or cnt), Urbie Green, Benny Morton, Frank Rosolino, Trummy Young (tb), Barney Bigard, Peanuts Hucko, Johnny

Mince (cl), Kenny Davern (cl, ss), Benny Carter (as), Budd Johnson (ts, ss), James Moody (ts, flute), Al Cohn, Flip Phillips, Zoot Sims (ts), Howard Johnson (bar, tuba), Dick Hyman, Hank Jones, Roger Kellaway, Teddy Wilson (p), Les Paul, Bucky Pizzarelli (g), Lyn Christie, George Duvivier, Milt Hinton, Larry Ridley, Slam Stewart (b), Alan Dawson, Bert Dahlander, Oliver Jackson, Cliff Leeman, Bobby Rosengarden, and Grady Tate (dm).

A photograph of the grand finale shows Ruby Braff, Ross Tompkins, Johnny Mince, Milt Hinton, Clark Terry, Buster Cooper, Frank Rosolino, Carl Fontana, James Moody, Zoot Sims, and Al Cohn. This was probably Ruby Braff's first appearance at a Gibson party. This year's party became known as the birthplace of Soprano Summit after Bob Wilber and Kenny Davern performed a set together.

Ruby Braff International Quartet[5]
September 13–16 and 20–23, 1972, Tony's Place, New York
Ruby Braff (cnt), Hank Jones (p), George Mraz (b), Dottie Dodgion (dm)
No further information available but this appears to be a continuing engagement Wednesday through Saturday each week.

Charles Schwartz, who managed the Braff–Barnes Quartet, wrote the following:[6]

> Ruby and I became friends at Tony's which led Ruby later on to insist that I was the only manager to handle the group [Ruby Braff–George Barnes Quartet]. Lee Konitz walked in one night with his horn to sit in. Ruby was playing as only Ruby could play. Konitz tried warming up and after listening to Ruby packed up his horn and left without playing a note. Ruby and I had a great laugh.

Contemporary reports do not mention Ruby Braff explicitly in the following performance:

> **Tony Bennett** (reported in *Variety*, September 22, unknown year)
> Probably September 22, 1972, Hilton International, Las Vegas
> Count Basie (13 musicians), John Bunch, Joe Guercio Orchestra (28 musicians), Frank Sinatra introduced Tony Bennett
> Smile
> Don't Get Around Much Anymore
> Get Happy

Ruby had not spent time in recording studios since his departure from the Newport All Stars. His most recent records with that group were recorded in Europe. While Ruby was already thinking about possibly forming a group with George Barnes, he was still enjoying his work with his International Jazz Quartet. After their performances at the Half Note and Waldorf-Astoria Hotel, it was time to record the group, augmented for the occasion.

Ruby Braff: *Ruby Braff and His International Quartet Plus Three*
Ruby Braff (cnt), Dick Hyman (p), Milt Hinton (b), Dottie Dodgion (dm) with Sam Margolis (cl, ts), Jerry Dodgion (cl, as), Howard Collins (g)
September 27, 1972, New York
This Year's Kisses
    Chiaroscuro CR 115, Vogue VJD 524
Medley:
  Chicago
    Chiaroscuro CR 115, Vogue VJD 524
  I Can't Give You Anything but Love
    Chiaroscuro CR 115, Vogue VJD 524
Swan Song
    Chiaroscuro CR 115, Vogue VJD 524
Bugle Call Rag
    Chiaroscuro CR 115, Vogue VJD 524
All Alone
    Chiaroscuro CR 115, Vogue VJD 524
I Know That You Know
    Chiaroscuro CR 115, Vogue VJD 524, Chiaroscuro CR (D) 219
NOTE: Chiaroscuro CR (D) 219 is *The Judge at His Best.* Hank O'Neal reports that additional performances exist on tape from this session. This was the 15th release on the Chiaroscuro label. The label began with recordings by jazz pianists and then featured music by Eddie Condon, reflecting O'Neal's long-standing friendship. It developed into one of the finest jazz specialist labels.

Ruby Braff International Quartet[7]
Wednesday–Sunday including September 27–30, 1972, Tony's Place, 241 East 86th Street, New York
Ruby Braff (cnt), Hank Jones (p), George Mraz (b), Dottie Dodgion (dm)

Your Father's Mustache[8]
October 1, 1972, New York
Ruby Braff (cnt), Kenny Davern (ss), Dick Rath, Bobby Pratt (tb), Johnny Varro (p), Red Balaban (g), Marquis Foster (dm)
Love Me or Leave Me
Basin Street Blues
Oh, Baby
High Society

Substitute Bobby Pratt (tb) for Dick Rath
When It's Sleepy Time Down South
I Would Do Anything for You

When the Saints Go Marching In
NOTE: A recording of these tunes is available but remains unissued.

Ruby Braff: *Ruby Braff and His International Quartet Plus Three*
Ruby Braff (cnt), Dick Hyman (p), Milt Hinton (b), Dottie Dodgion (dm), Jerry Dodgion (as, cl), Sam Margolis (ts, cl), Howard Collins (g)
October 9, 1972, New York
Right Off
    Chiaroscuro CR 115,Vogue VJD 524
With Time to Love
    Chiaroscuro CR 115,Vogue VJD 524
I Ain't Got Nobody
    Chiaroscuro CR 115,Vogue VJD 524
Lonely Moments
    Chiaroscuro CR 115,Vogue VJD 524
NOTE: Vogue VJD 524 is titled *Bugle Call Rag.* The above titles do not appear on Vogue VJD 519, contrary to some listings. Hank O'Neal indicates that out-takes exist from this session and supplied the recording dates that are used in this listing.

The John S. Wilson wrote a story in the *New York Times* about Dottie and Jerry Dodgion's move to a new home in Park Ridge, New Jersey, and their acquisition of "a nine-foot Steinway grand piano from Phil Woods, who moved to Paris and asked the Dodgions to take his piano." To celebrate, they invited a number of musicians to their home. The article continues as follows:[9]

> To celebrate the acquisition, the Dodgions invited some of their friends to a party. It resulted in an unusual mass assemblage of jazz pianists, each of whom took turns trying out the instrument. The performers included Marian McPartland, Dill Jones, Max Morath (a nearby neighbor), Patti Bown, Tommy Flanagan, Dick Katz, John Bunch, Pat Rebillot, Walter Norris, and Ruby Braff, normally a cornetist but who, according to Mrs. Dodgion, 'can hold his own among any group of pianists.'

Ruby did not display his piano skills often; however, he had an upright piano in his home on Cape Cod later in his life. He used it to create compositions and explore some of the harmonies that he incorporated into some of the arrangements he made for his later recordings. He did play piano on a later *Piano Jazz* program hosted by Marian McPartland and some other occasions. However, this is getting ahead of the events of 1972.

Benefit Concert for Widow of Jimmy Rushing[10]
October 29, 1972, Your Father's Mustache, New York
The following musicians were scheduled to appear: Ruby Braff, Al Casey, Buck Clayton, Doc Cheatham, Al Cohn, Eddie Condon, Kenny Davern, Wild Bill

Davison, Vic Dickenson, Roy Eldridge, Milt Hinton, Gene Krupa, Jo Jones, Jimmy McPartland, Zoot Sims, Buddy Tate, Dick Wellstood, Bob Wilber, Sol Yaged's Quartet, the Saints and Sinners, and Balaban & Cats, with music starting at 4 p.m. Further details are not available.

Ruby's second release on Chiaroscuro reflected both Hank O'Neal's focus on recordings by pianists and Ruby's long-standing association with Ellis Larkins. They had not recorded tougher since the two memorable releases on Vanguard.

Ruby Braff and Ellis Larkins: *The Grand Reunion*[11]
November 4 and 11, 1972, WARP Studios, New York
Ruby Braff (cnt), Ellis Larkins (p)
Fine and Dandy
    Chiaroscuro CR 117, CR (D) 117
I Want a Little Girl
    Chiaroscuro CR 117, CR (D) 117
Skylark
    Chiaroscuro CR 117, CR (D) 117
The Very Thought of You
    Chiaroscuro CR 117, CR (D) 117
If Dreams Come True
    Chiaroscuro CR 117, CR (D) 117, CR 204
Liza
    Chiaroscuro CR 117, CR (D) 117
Easy Living
    Chiaroscuro CR 117, CR (D) 117
Love Walked In
    Chiaroscuro CR 117, CR (D) 117
Things Ain't What They Used to Be
    Chiaroscuro CR 117, CR (D) 117
Ain't Misbehavin'
    Chiaroscuro CR 117, CR (D) 117
Exactly Like You
    CR (D) 117
Don't Get Around Much Anymore
    CR (D) 117
I'm Confessin'
    CR (D) 117
Don't Be That Way
    CR (D) 117
NOTE: CR204 also exists as a pressing issued by Radio Shack as an LP and eight-track tape. All titles from CR 117 also on Chiaroscuro (J) ULS 1858 and Vogue (E) VJD 524. A different date is listed on the CD (October 14, 1972) but the November 4 date above was supplied by Hank O'Neal. David Griffiths add-

ed the date of November 11 to the date from Hank O'Neal. The LP record jacket states that the recording session took place in October 1972.

Off to England? Or Was It California?[12]
Ruby reported in a radio interview with Rob Bamberger on March 2, 1991, that he jumped in a cab to the airport to fly to England seconds after the above session with Ellis Larkins was completed. There does not appear to be media reports of a Braff UK tour at this time or a report of a concert by Tony Bennett, so Ruby was probably recalling the long flight to California for his next club engagement. If he did fly to the UK, it was probably between the two sessions with Larkins. But it is possible that the flight to California to appear at Donte's and for the Blue Angel Jazz Club is what he was recalling.

Ruby Braff and Nat Pierce[13]
November 13, 1972, Donte's, Hollywood, California
Ruby Braff (cnt), Nat Pierce (p), Barney Kessel (g), Herb Mickman (b), Jake Hanna (dm)
Leonard Feather's review mentioned the following tunes:[14]
Jeepers Creepers
Mood Indigo
Lester Leaps In
Blue and Sentimental
I Want to Be Happy
Lady Be Good

For the next performance, Ruby recalled that Jake Hanna arrived late. Terry Gibbs played drums for this session, explaining Ruby's comment on the recording that Gibbs played only half of the session on his vibes. There are no vibes audible on this recording.

Ruby Braff and Nat Pierce[15]
November 14, 1972, Donte's, Hollywood, California
Ruby Braff (cnt), Nat Pierce (p), Barney Kessel (g), Herb Mickman (b), Terry Gibbs (dm)
Rosetta

Add Terry Gibbs (dm)
Ghost of a Chance
The World Is Waiting for the Sunrise
There's a Small Hotel
Somebody Loves Me

Jake Hanna (dm) replaces Gibbs
Jeepers Creepers

Medley:
  Mood Indigo
  C Jam Blues
  I Got Rhythm
Medley:
  Blue and Sentimental
  I Want to Be Happy
Over the Rainbow
Lady Be Good
Just You, Just Me
Mood Indigo
Unknown Title
For All We Know
Undecided
Love Me or Leave Me
These Foolish Things
Blues
I Can't Give You Anything but Love
I've Got the World on a String
This Can't Be Love
Just You, Just Me
Am I Blue?
NOTE: A recording of these tunes is available but remains unissued.

Blue Angel Jazz Club—5th Annual Meeting[16]
November 18, 1972, 3 p.m.–2 a.m., The University Club, Pasadena, California (organized by Dr. and Mrs. William MacPherson)

"Joe Venuti is a last-minute addition to the list of 23 stars set to take part." Other musicians included Ruby, Joe Pass, Supersax (Med Flory, Bill Perkins, Jay Migliori, Warne Marsh, and Jack Nimitz), John Best, Abe Most, Ray Sherman, Red Norvo, Flip Phillips, Herb Ellis, Sonny Criss, Ronnell Bright, Nat Pierce, Jimmy Rowles, and Mavis Rivers.

Contemporary reports do not mention Ruby Braff explicitly in the following performance:

Tony Bennett with Count Basie and 14 Strings (reported in *Billboard*, unknown date)
Probably late 1972, Miami Beach Auditorium, Miami Beach, Florida
Count Basie (p), Sonny Payne (dm), Al Grey (tb), Jimmy Forrest (ts)
    Just in Time
    If I Ruled the World
    I Left My Heart in San Francisco
    Something
    My Love

Chris Sheridan[17] reports that Jimmy Forrest temporarily joined Basie in June 1972, departed, and then returned full time for a Basie tour with Tony Bennett following October 1972. Harold Jones left the band following a concert on October 23, being replaced by Sonny Payne.

Ruby Braff and Roy Eldridge: Jazz Ramble[18]
December 12, 1972, New School, New York
Other concerts in this series were by Eddie Condon and the Gene Krupa All Stars (November 21), the Jack Reilly Trio (November 28), and the Earl Hines Group (December 5).

Ruby Braff–Dottie Dodgion Quartet[19]
January 1973, Gulliver's, West Patterson, New Jersey
Ruby Braff (cnt), Tommy Flanagan (p), George Mraz (b), Dottie Dodgion (dm)

Tony Bennett on *Mike Douglas Show*
February 2, 1973, Philadelphia
Ruby Braff appeared with Tony Bennett on the television show.
Bernie Leighton (p and musical director), Ruby Braff (cnt), Tony Bennett (voc), with studio orchestra
Watch What Happens
On the Sunny Side of the Street
NOTE: A video recording of this program is available but remains unissued.

Ruby is interviewed by Mike Douglas in the above program: Mike Douglas: "Is there any word you would use to describe your style?" Ruby Braff: "Mine." Ruby did not elaborate, leaving Mike Douglas without an opening to a follow-up question. Ruby probably felt that this was a silly question undeserving an answer. In retrospect, it was a lost opportunity to build a relationship.

Tony Bennett on *Merv Griffin Show*[20]
February 9, 1973 (this was the air date in Chicago—taping was likely before Ruby's Toronto appearance that follows)
Tony Bennett with Ruby Braff—other guests are Eli Wallach, Anne Jackson, Tommy Leonetti, and Hal David

Ruby Braff Quartet[21]
Week of February 5–10, 1973, Bourbon Street, Toronto
Ruby Braff (cnt), Carol Britto (p), David Young (b), unknown drummer
Sweethearts on Parade
Jeepers Creepers
In a Mellotone

This engagement in Toronto is when I met Ruby for the first time. It established a connection that has made this book possible. Jack Batten wrote the following in his review:

> 'What that performance, and all the others in the set, too, got across was a sense of how much Braff loves to play. You can't miss the joy in his jazz.' He continued, 'Sadly he hasn't appeared much in Toronto, except for a couple of local Newport All-Star dates and as a guest with the old Mike White band in its days at the Westover.'[22]

I can find no documentation of that earlier visit to the Westover Hotel. Earlier visits to Toronto are reported in earlier chapters.

Contemporary reports do not mention Ruby Braff explicitly in the following performance:

Tony Bennett (reported in *Variety*, April 4, 1973)
Probably March 1973, Palladium, London
Stan Reynolds Orchestra (32 musicians)

"Jazz Ramble" at the New School[23]
April 3, 1973, 8 p.m., New School, 66 West 12th Street, New York
Ruby Braff (cnt), Sam Margolis (cl, ts), Ben Aronov (p), Milt Hinton (b), Dottie Dodgion (dm)
Romance in the Dark
Mean to Me
Rose Room
When I Fall in Love (SM out)
Do Nothin' Till You Hear From Me (rhythm section)
Them There Eyes
I Can't Give You Anything but Love
Just You, Just Me
Ghost of a Chance (RB out)
Lover Come Back to Me (SM out)
Over the Rainbow (MH feature)
Rosetta
Take the "A" Train
NOTE: A recording of these tunes is available but remains unissued.

Ruby Braff and George Barnes began rehearsals for the Braff–Barnes Quartet. Hank O'Neal wrote that they used his studio in Greenwich, New York, once, then twice, and finally three times each week starting in May 1973 and continuing until the quartet's debut at the Newport Jazz Festival on June 29.[24] Ruby said he sat in several years before when George Barnes and Bucky Pizzarelli performed together at the club Upstairs at the Downstairs.[25]

This quartet can legitimately be called one of the finest small bands in the entire history of jazz.

Jazz Interactions 8th Birthday Celebration[26]
Probably May 1973, Village Gate, New York
Ruby Braff Quintet performed along with many other artists in both the upstairs and downstairs clubs

"Interlude" Concert at Town Hall[27]
May 23, 1973, New York
Ruby Braff (cnt-1), Dick Hyman (p), George Barnes (g), George Duvivier (b), Jo Jones (dm), Peter Snakehips Dean (voc)
My Honey's Lovin' Arms
Funky Blues
Thou Swell
Harlem Strut (Hyman)
Ooh, That Kiss (1)
I'm Nuts about Screwy Music (voc PD)
Baby, Won't You Please Come Home? (voc PD)
I'm Gonna Sit Right Down and Write Myself a Letter (voc PD)
Ding Dong Daddy (voc PD) (incomplete)
B Flat Blues (1)
Just You, Just Me (1)
Where's Freddie? (1)
NOTE: A recording of these tunes is available but remains unissued.

Tony Bennett on *Mike Douglas Show*
May 25, 1973, Philadelphia (television air date in New York, June 1, 1973)[28]
Tony Bennett (voc), Ruby Braff (cnt), unknown p, b, g, dm
You Took Advantage of Me
NOTE: Audio and video recordings of this program are available but remain unissued.

Contemporary reports do not mention Ruby Braff explicitly in the following performances:

> **Tony Bennett** (reported in *Variety*, May 30, 1973)
> May 26, 1973, Las Vegas Hilton, Las Vegas
> Nevada Philharmonic (100 musicians), conducted by Joe Guercio
> Smile
> I Left My Heart in San Francisco

Tony Bennett appeared with Joey Heatherton and the Mike Curb Congregation in a 60-minute television program from an unknown date. The first half is filmed on the beach, while the second half is indoors with a big band. At about 26 minutes into the program, Tony introduces Ruby for the following number, saying: "Ruby Braff is my very favorite musician on this entire planet." The remaining selections begin about 39 minutes into the program.

Aloha! Tony Bennett in Hawaii
Tony Bennett with Ruby Braff and His International Jazz Quartet
Ruby Braff (cnt), plus piano, saxophone, bass, drums (probably Jerry Dodgion (s), and Dottie Dodgion (dm))
I Left My Heart in San Francisco (TB voc)

Tony Bennett with Ruby Braff (cnt) soloist with orchestra directed by Bernie Leighton with arrangements by Don Costa
The Shadow of Your Smile (TB voc)
There Will Never Be Another You (TB voc)
NOTE: Audio and video recordings of this program are available but remain unissued.

Tony Bennett wrote that Ruby Braff sat in with George Barnes and Bucky Pizzarelli when they performed at the St. Regis Hotel in New York.[29] Tony Bennett continued, describing their working relationship in two separate comments:

> [Ruby Braff has] a sound that's as precious as a string of pearls or a rare diamond. And fortunately [he's] made records that audiences will enjoy forever.[30]
>
> My main focus in late 1973 became the brilliant trumpet playing of Ruby Braff. I'd known Ruby since 1951 when I first played Chicago. . . . [Ruby] loved the way that combination sounded, and he suggested to George that they start a group. They gradually worked out a lineup of two guitars, a trumpet, and a bass. When I heard about this group, I had to check them out. I thought they were great, and Ruby said to me, 'Why don't you come and sing a couple of tunes with us, and relax for awhile, you know?' I was singing almost exclusively with big bands then, and even with a good sound system, I always had to belt it out to be heard above the music. I liked the groove I got into with this intimate group so much that I did two special concerts with them at Alice Tully Hall in New York.[31]

So, it is time for the debut of one of the finest small groups in the entire history of jazz music.

Notes

[1] Dottie Dodgion interviewed in Wayne Enstice and Janis Stockhouse, *Jazzwomen* (Bloomington, IN: Indiana University Press, 2004), 116.
[2] Letter from Shin-ichi Iwamoto and above statement from Dottie Dodgion, op. cit.

[3] *New York Times*, August 26, 1972 (article refers to "Sugar"). *Jazz Journal International*, October 1972, 23, refers to a continuing engagement and it continues into September.
[4] *DownBeat*'s *Music '73* (Chicago: Maher Publications, 1973), 26–30 and *DownBeat*, November 9, 1972, 10; Leonard Feather, *Los Angeles Times*, September 6, 1972.
[5] Letter from Shin-ichi Iwamoto and *The New Yorker*, September 9, 1972, 6, September 16, 4.
[6] Charles Swartz in private correspondence dated August 1, 2004.
[7] *New York Magazine*, September 25, 1972, 22.
[8] *The New Yorker*, September 30, 1972, 6.
[9] John S. Wilson, *New York Times*, November 5, 1972.
[10] *DownBeat*, November 9, 1972, 11, and *The New Yorker*, October 28, 1972, 6.
[11] A different date is listed on the CD but the date above was supplied by Hank O'Neal. David Griffiths added the date of November 11 to the date from Hank O'Neal.
[12] Interview in Washington, D.C., on March 2, 1991.
[13] Correspondence with Manfred Selchow. This engagement is mentioned in *DownBeat*, December 21, 1972, 44. This is Ruby's first engagement in California reported in this book. The appearance at Donte's is listed in an advertisement in the *Los Angeles Times*, November 12, 1972.
[14] Leonard Feather, *Los Angeles Times*, November 18, 1972.
[15] Engagement mentioned in *DownBeat*, December 21, 1972, 44.
[16] Leonard Feather, *Los Angeles Times*, November 18, 1972, and November 24, 1972; *DownBeat*, January 18, 1973, 43.
[17] Chris Sheridan, *Count Basie: A Bio-Discography* (New York: Greenwood Press, c. 1986), 794.
[18] *DownBeat*, November 9, 1972, 41, advertised in *New York Times*, September 4, 1972.
[19] *DownBeat*, February 15, 1973, 11.
[20] *Chicago Tribune*, February 9, 1973.
[21] Jack Batten, *Globe and Mail*, February 7, 1973.
[22] Jack Batten, *Globe and Mail*, February 7, 1973.
[23] Hank O'Neal recorded this session in two- and four-track format. It is mentioned in *DownBeat*, May 24, 1973, 13, and *New York Times*, April 1, 1973.
[24] Album notes for Chiaroscuro records CR 121, *The Ruby Braff–George Barnes Quartet*.
[25] George Barnes cited by Bert Whyatt and Derek Coller, "The Ruby Braff–George Barnes Quartet," *Jazz Journal International*, August 2001, 12–14.
[26] *DownBeat*, June 21, 1973, 11.
[27] John S. Wilson, *New York Times* May 25, 1973.
[28] Television list, *New York Times*, June 1, 1973.
[29] Tony Bennett with Will Friedwald, *The Good Life* (New York: Pocket Books, 1998), 216.
[30] Tony Bennett with Will Friedwald, *The Good Life* (New York: Pocket Books, 1998), 145.
[31] Tony Bennett with Will Friedwald, *The Good Life* (New York: Pocket Books, 1998), 216.

Chapter 12

The Ruby Braff–George Barnes Quartet: One of the Finest Small Groups in the History of Jazz

Ruby's growing relationship with Hank O'Neal was particularly timely because Ruby had been working informally with George Barnes since 1971 to create a new group, and Hank O'Neal became an early champion of this emerging quartet. Ruby's fans owe Hank O'Neal a debt of gratitude for preserving these creative performances. He had become familiar with Ruby's playing with George Barnes since some of the quartet's rehearsals were in his studio, beginning in May 1973, while also releasing three of Ruby's recordings. During this time, Ruby continued his association with Tony Bennett, and Tony became one of the earliest champions of the Ruby Braff–George Barnes Quartet.

The group's debut was at Carnegie Hall. Ruby claimed that the audience was indeed wonderful. He told me simply, "They loved everything we did that night." Fortunately, the performance was recorded. George Wein scheduled the quartet not only to open for Benny Goodman, but also to open the first night of the entire festival. Hank O'Neal has a photograph taken at his studio, Downtown Sound, in New York in June 1973 showing Tony Bennett singing with the quartet during one of those rehearsals. This photograph is included in this book's photo section.

Ruby Braff–George Barnes Quartet[1]
June 29, 1973, 7:30 p.m., 20th Newport Jazz Festival, Carnegie Hall, New York
Ruby Braff (cnt), George Barnes, Wayne Wright (g), John Giuffrida (b)
Ooh, That Kiss
With Time to Love
Looking at You
Old Folks
Liza
Here, There and Everywhere
Our Love Is Here to Stay
Nobody Else But You

It's Like the Fourth of July
Everything's George (Where's Freddie?)
NOTE: The Ruby Braff–George Barnes Quartet opened the concert. A recording of these tunes is available but remains unissued. There is prolonged applause following the conclusion of the performance. The concert then continued, featuring the original Benny Goodman Quartet. At the time of publication, the complete concert is available for downloading from WolfgangsVault.com.

As mentioned, this performance opened the evening's concert, followed by Benny Goodman. Benny was experiencing considerable back pain at the time. John S. Wilson later wrote that the Braff–Barnes Quartet upstaged the reunion of Benny Goodman's original quartet, although his comments did not appear until after he reviewed the group's first recording for Chiaroscuro Records.[2] Ruby recalled that while he climbed the stairs as he left the stage, he passed Benny Goodman walking down to begin his performance. Benny said, "Ruby, you're going the wrong way." Ruby tried to explain that he just opened the concert, and that Benny would love the audience. Goodman did not understand and continued to presume that Ruby was scheduled to perform with him. He repeated, "Ruby, you're going the wrong way." When Ruby did not reply, Goodman said, "Well, then, you're fired."

In just over a week, the Quartet performed at the Jazz Museum.

Braff-Barnes Quartet at Jazz Museum
July 8, 1973, New York
Ruby Braff (cnt), George Barnes, Wayne Wright (g), John Giuffrida (b)
Ooh, That Kiss
The 4th of July
Struttin' with Some Barbecue
It's Wonderful
Someday You'll Be Sorry
Keepin' Out of Mischief Now
No One Else But You
You're a Lucky Guy
Basin Street Blues
Liza
Old Folks
Them There Eyes
Where's Freddie?
Our Love Is Here to Stay
Lady Be Good
Sweethearts on Parade
Exactly Like You

Add Rudy Rutherford (cl)
Swing That Music

Rutherford out
When It's Sleepy Time Down South (fragment)
NOTE: A recording of these tunes is available but remains unissued.

The Braff–Barnes Quartet performed at the Rainbow Room for three weeks in New York about this time[3] Jack Bradley's photo from the March of Jazz program may have been taken between sets.[4] Hank O'Neal was able to arrange a recording session in late July, less than a month after the group's debut.

The Ruby Braff–George Barnes Quartet
Late July 1973, New York
Ruby Braff (cnt), George Barnes, Wayne Wright (g), John Giuffrida (b)
Ooh, That Kiss
Chiaroscuro CR 121
With Time to Love
Chiaroscuro CR 121
Looking at You
Chiaroscuro CR 121
Old Folks
Chiaroscuro CR 121
Liza
Chiaroscuro CR 121
Here, There and Everywhere
Chiaroscuro CR 121
Our Love Is Here to Stay
Chiaroscuro CR 121
Nobody Else But You
Chiaroscuro CR 121
It's Like the Fourth of July
Chiaroscuro CR 121
Everything's George (Where's Freddie?)
Chiaroscuro CR 121
NOTE: All titles from CR 121 are also on Chiaroscuro (J) ULS 1683, ULS 1842, Jazz Lips JL 765, Vogue (E and F) VJD 519. The Vogue double album is titled *The Best I've Heard.* This Vogue album received a jazz record of the year award from *Jazz Journal International.* The Jazz Lips release is titled *To Fred Astaire With Love* and includes all selections from February 3, 4, and 5, 1975. "Looking at You" also appears in the three-CD box set *You're Sensational: Cole Porter in the 30s, 40s, and 50s* from the Indiana Historical Society and Koch International Classics, with the issue number A-33714.

Hank O'Neal confirmed the July date above to be correct. The album's notes said the recording preceded another recording date with Tony Bennett by a day or two, incorrectly suggesting that the Chiaroscuro recording date should be in mid-September rather than in July. David Griffiths added "late July" to Hank O'Neal's "July" dating. O'Neal also indicated that unissued performances exist from this session in private correspondence.

Album notes to CR 121 also report that a film featuring Tony Bennett with this group "should be in full production" by the release of this album, produced by Elliott Kastner. Portions of the production were filmed at Madison Square Garden (the Honeydreamers Ball in New York), Buffalo, New York (both at a concert and during a two-week engagement at Buffalo Hilton Hotel), and Alice Tully Hall at Lincoln Center in NYC (September 14 and 15, 1973). Tony Bennett presumably still owns the film, which has never been released. It was originally developed as a potential 90-minute television special.[5] This supports the following listing.

Film: *This Funny World*[6]
1971–1973 (date unknown)
Tony Bennett, Ruby Braff and others

The *DownBeat* International Critics Poll results showed that the Ruby Braff–George Barnes Quartet placed first in the category of combo talent deserving wider recognition.[7] Ruby felt the group should have won the best combo award instead.[8]

Contemporary reports do not mention Ruby Braff explicitly in the following performance:

> **Tony Bennett** (reported in *Variety*, August 22, 1973)
> August 17, 1973, Harrah's, Reno, Nevada
> Norm Crosby, John Carlton Orchestra (28 musicians)
> The program featured 20 songs, including the following:
>
> > Just in Time
> > The Shadow of Your Smile
> > What the World Needs Now
> > On the Sunny Side of the Street
> > Don't Get Around Much Anymore
> > Sophisticated Lady

At 3 p.m., the day prior to the upcoming September programs at Alice Tully Hall, Tony Bennett held a rehearsal with the Ruby Braff–George Barnes Quartet in a studio on Christopher Street.

The quartet opened a concert at Alice Tully Hall in Lincoln Center to a packed house with one hour of Rodgers and Hart tunes. Tony Bennett joined the quartet to sing 21 Rodgers and Hart tunes. There are rumors of an existing recording, but I have not been able to locate a copy. There is an advertisement available.[9] The ad indicates "Be in the Movies with Tony Bennett as both performances will be filmed."

Tony Bennett Sings an Evening of Rodgers and Hart[10] **(see Figure 12.1)**
September 14 and 15, 1973 (two concerts at 8:00 p.m.), Alice Tully Hall, Lincoln Center, New York
Tony Bennett with the Ruby Braff–George Barnes Quartet
Ruby Braff (cnt), George Barnes (g), Wayne Wright (g), John Giuffrida (b), Tony Bennett (voc)
Blue Moon
There's a Small Hotel
The Most Beautiful Girl in the World
I Wish I Were in Love Again
Lover
Spring Is Here
Have You Met Miss Jones?
Encore: I Left My Heart in San Francisco

Whitney Balliett reviewed the concert:

> The concert at Alice Tully the next evening . . . is a smooth and engaging success. The hall is sold out, and the audience is hip. Bennett sings the verses of most of the songs, and by the time he gets a note or two into the chorus there is the applause of recognition. . . . He sings twenty-one Rodgers and Hart tunes, and many are memorable. He sings a soft, husky 'Blue Moon,' and then comes a marvelous, muted Ruby Braff solo. 'There's a Small Hotel' is even softer, and Braff and George Barnes react with pianissimo statements. The group, indeed, is impeccable. The solos are beautiful, and the dynamics all anticipate Bennett. During Braff's solo in 'The Most Beautiful Girl in the World,' Bennett sits on a stool to the musicians' right, and near the end of 'I Wish I Were in Love Again' he forgets his lyrics and soars over the wreckage with some good mumbo-jumbo and a fine crescendo. 'Lover' is ingenious. Bennett sings it softly, at a medium tempo (it is usually done at top speed), then briefly takes the tempo up, and goes out sotto voce. He does 'I Left My Heart in San Francisco' as an encore. The ovation is long and standing.[11]

Ed Sullivan Show[12]
Unknown date, Tony Bennett, with Ruby Braff and an orchestra that included Milt Hinton (b) and Joe? (dm)
NOTE: A video recording of this performance is available but remains unissued.

Tony made a recording for his own label, Improv, featuring a selection of the Rodgers and Hart songs, issued on two separate records and later reissued with alternate takes by Concord Jazz. These performances are impeccable. I have dated Ruby's next live performance with Tony Bennett to the year 1977.

Tony Bennett: *Tony Bennett Sings 10 Rodgers and Hart Songs*
September 28–30, 1973, CBS Studios, New York (CD set says July 12 and 16, 1973)
Ruby Braff (cnt), George Barnes (g), Wayne Wright (g), John Giuffrida (b), Tony Bennett (voc)
This Can't Be Love
    Improv 7113, DRG CDXP 2102, Crimson Productions 160, Concord CCD 6023-2, Concord Jazz CCD4 2255-2
This Can't Be Love (alt tk #1)
    Concord Jazz CCD4 2255-2
Blue Moon
    Improv 7113, DRG CDXP 2102, Concord Jazz CCD4 2255-2
The Lady Is a Tramp
    Improv 7113, DRG CDXP 2102, Crimson Productions 160, DBM (E) DBM 1001C, Concord Jazz CCD4 2255-2
Lover
    Improv 7113, DRG CDXP 2102, Concord CCD 6023-2, Concord Jazz CCD4 2255-2
Manhattan
    Improv 7113, DRG CDXP 2102, Crimson Productions 160, DBM (E) DBM 1001C, Concord Jazz CCD4 2255-2
Spring Is Here
    Improv 7113, DRG CDXP 2102, Concord Jazz CCD4 2255-2
Have You Met Miss Jones?
    Improv 7113, DRG CDXP 2102, Concord Jazz CCD4 2255-2
Isn't It Romantic
    Improv 7113, DRG CDXP 2102, Concord CCD 6023-2, Concord Jazz CCD4 2255-2
Wait 'Til You See Her
    Improv 7113, DRG CDXP 2102, Crimson Productions 160, Concord Jazz CCD4 2255-2
I Could Write a Book
    Improv 7113, DRG CDXP2102, Concord CCD 6023-2, Concord Jazz CCD4 2255-2
I Could Write a Book (alt tk #2)
    Concord Jazz CCD4 2255-2

NOTE: All original takes plus listed alternate takes are included in *The Complete Improv Recordings* Concord Jazz CCD4 2255-2. All but the two alternative takes are also issued on DRG DARC-2-2102 (double LP) as *The Rodgers and Hart Songbook*, Horatio Nelson (E) CYU 108 (LP), CDSN 1129 (CD), Improv (E) IMP 7113, and Rhino 75838 (CD). Crimson Productions CRIMCD 160 is titled *Hollywood and Broadway* by Tony Bennett. Music Club (E) 238 (CD) includes the first five originally issued titles above. "Spring Is Here" and "I Could Write a Book" are also included in *Classic Tony Bennett, Vol. 1* (EMI-

Capitol Special Markets 72438184352). Concord CCD 6023-2 is titled *Tony Bennett Sings for Lovers*. All the above performances (including alternate takes) are also available on *Tony Bennett Sings the Rodgers and Hart Songbook*, Concord CCD 2243-2.

Tony Bennett: *Tony Bennett Sings . . . More Great Rodgers and Hart*
September 28–30, 1973, CBS Studios, New York
Ruby Braff (cnt), George Barnes (g), Wayne Wright (g), John Giuffrida (b), Tony Bennett (voc)
Thou Swell
    Improv 7120, DRG CDXP 2102, Crimson Productions 160,
    Concord CCD 6023-2
Thou Swell (alt tk # 1)
    Concord Jazz CCD4 2255-2
The Most Beautiful Girl in the World
    Improv 7120, DRG CDXP 2102, Crimson Productions 160,
    DBM (E) DBM 1001C
The Most Beautiful Girl in the World (alt tk #4)
    Concord Jazz CCD4 2255-2
There's a Small Hotel
    Improv 7120, DRG CDXP 2102, Crimson Productions 160,
    DBM (E) DBM 1001C
I've Got Five Dollars
    Improv 7120, DRG CDXP 2102, Crimson Productions 160,
    DBM (E) DBM 1001C
You Took Advantage of Me
    Improv 7120, DRG CDXP 2102
I Wish I Were in Love Again
    Improv 7120, DRG CDXP 2102, Crimson Productions 160,
    DBM (E) DBM 1001C
I Wish I Were in Love Again (alt tk #1)
    Concord Jazz CCD4 2255-2
This Funny World
    Improv 7120, DRG CDXP 2102
This Funny World (alt tk #3)
    Concord Jazz CCD4 2255-2
My Heart Stood Still
    Improv 7120, DRG CDXP 2102, Concord CCD 6023-2
My Romance
    DRG CDXP 2102, DBM (E) DBM 1001C
Mountain Greenery
    Improv 7120, DRG CDXP 2102, Crimson Productions 160,
    DBM (E) DBM 1001C

NOTE: All original takes plus listed alternate takes are included in *The Complete Improv Recordings* Concord Jazz CCD4 2255-2. "I Wish I Were in Love Again" is also issued on Improv (45 rpm) TB 713106 and Verve 526448-2 titled *My Funny Valentine*, accompanied *by* "Mountain Greenery." All originally issued takes are also issued on DRG DARC-2-2102 (double LP) as *The Rodgers and Hart Songbook* and Rhino 75838 (CD). Music Club (E) 238 (CD) includes five titles from above: "World," "Hotel," "Again," "Still," and "Greenery." Crimson Productions 160 is titled *Hollywood and Broadway* by Tony Bennett. "I Wish I Were in Love Again" and "Mountain Greenery" also appear on a compilation with other artists on Verve 52644802 (titled *My Funny Valentine*) and Concord 01343152272 (titled *Jazz Moods: Sounds of Spring*) and in a three-CD set *The Complete Rodgers & Hart Songbooks*, Verve 731453326224. "The Most Beautiful Girl in the World," "You Took Advantage of Me," and "Thou Swell" are also included on *Classic Tony Bennett, Vol. 1* (EMI-Capitol Special Markets 72438184352). "My Romance" is also included in Concord Jazz 27518, titled *Playboy Jazz After Dark, Volume 2.* Concord CCD 6023-2 is titled *Tony Bennett Sings for Lovers*. All the above performances (including alternate takes) are also available on *Tony Bennett Sings the Rodgers and Hart Songbook*, Concord CCD 2243-2.

The following recording is a separate release, available only on two 45-rpm issues.

Tony Bennett with the Ruby Braff–George Barnes Quartet
Date and location unknown (probably New York)—from the motion picture *A Touch of Class*
Ruby Braff (cnt), George Barnes, Wayne Wright (g) with string section arranged by Torrie Zito
All That Love Went to Waste
    Philips 45: 6006 372, Brut 45: BR 813
Some of These Days
    Philips 45: 6006 372, Brut 45: BR 813
NOTE: The Brut 45 has been issued with two label designs, green and black.

Charles Schwartz reported the growing tension between Ruby and George Barnes:[13]

> There are a lot of ugly stories about Ruby and George such as at a concert with Tony when George was drunk and ripped up Tony's music and said, 'This is what I think of boy singers.' Ruby picked up the pieces of music and was trying to stuff them down George's throat while Wayne and John played valiantly on. Ruby also destroyed a 50 concert tour with Tony by calling Tony's manager names. Ruby also destroyed a tour that George Wein and I were planning. George felt that with the disbanding of the Modern Jazz Quartet we were the logical successors, and was willing to back it up with cash.

Eventually, Ruby came to hate George, but they continued to perform together, making wonderful music. But it was likely the above events that ended the relationship Ruby had enjoyed with Tony Bennett. Their work together had extended Ruby's visibility to other audiences and provided additional income. But they did remain in contact until Ruby's death and performed together at least once in Chicago in 1977. Michael Moore replaced John Giuffrida in the Braff–Barnes Quartet when Giuffrida remained with Tony Bennett in Las Vegas.[14]

Ruby next performed with Buzzy Drootin and then at a benefit concert to raise funds for Gene Krupa's Retarded Children's Foundation.

Ruby Braff with Buzzy Drootin[15]
Late 1973 or early 1974, Scotch 'n Sirloin Restaurant, 77 North Washington Street, Boston
Ruby Braff was a guest artist in a six-piece band built around Al Drootin (cl, ss), Sonny Drootin (p), and Buzzy Drootin (dm)

World of Music Tribute to Gene Krupa[16] **(see Figure 12.2)**
January 17, 1974, 8 p.m., The Felt Forum, Madison Square Garden, New York
Musicians appearing include the following: George Barnes, Ruby Braff, Lionel Hampton, Louis Bellson, Buddy Rich, Sonny Igoe, Elvin Jones, Roy Burns, Cozy Cole, Tyree Glenn, Pee Wee Erwin, Max Kaminsky, Buddy Miles, Anita O'Day, Bobby Scott, Grady Tate, Charlie Ventura, Helen Ward, Teddy Wilson, Roy Eldridge, Urbie Green, Bobby Hackett, Dizzy Gillespie, Milt Hinton, and Roy Haynes, host: William B. Williams

Ruby performed the afternoon of February 17 at the Longshore Country Club. This was followed by a two week engagement with George Barnes at the Half Note that moved to the Rainbow Room.

All Star Jazz Concert[17] **(see Figure 12.3)**
February 17, 1974, Longshore Country Club, Westport, Connecticut
Ruby Braff (cnt), Vic Dickenson (tb), Johnny Mince (cl), Lou Stein (p), George Barnes (g), Milt Hinton (b), Cliff Leeman (dm)

Ruby Braff–George Barnes Quartet[18]
February 25–March 9, 1974, Half Note, 149 W 54th Street, New York
Ruby Braff (cnt), George Barnes (g), Wayne Wright (g), Michael Moore (b)

Damita Jo with the Ruby Braff–George Barnes Quartet at the Rainbow Grill[19]
March 11–30, 1974, 30 Rockefeller Plaza, New York (closed Sundays)

Ruby Braff (cnt), George Barnes (g), Wayne Wright (g), Michael Moore (b)—Damita Jo also appeared on the billing for these dates
With Time to Love (Braff composition)
Nobody Else But You
NOTE: No other titles are mentioned. This was reported as the quartet's first engagement in a New York nightclub but it followed the previous weeks at the Half Note.

Ruby Braff–George Barnes Quartet[20]
Probably Spring 1974, Jazz Emporium, Mendota, Minnesota

New York Jazz Repertory Company 1st Season[21]
Ruby Braff was one of the members of the company of over 100 musicians—George Wein, executive director

Concerts in this series were publicized for at least the following dates: February 3, February 17, April 16, April 22, May 12, June 8, and June 15, 1974. The first season ran from January 26 to June 28, with 15 concerts in total. Ruby participated in the April 26 concert as shown below, and perhaps on other occasions. Ruby also appeared in a November concert during the second season.

Ruby Braff–George Barnes Quartet at Monmouth County Library[22]
April 12, 1974, Monmouth County Library, Route 35, Shrewsbury, New Jersey
Ruby Braff (cnt), George Barnes (g), Wayne Wright (g), Michael Moore (b)

Hank O'Neal recorded the Quartet at a concert in the Jazz Ramble series at the New School for Social Research for his second release.

Ruby Braff–George Barnes Quartet: *Live at the New School*
April 22, 1974, Jazz Ramble–New School for Social Research, New York
Ruby Braff (cnt), George Barnes (g), Wayne Wright (g), Michael Moore (b)
This Can't Be Love
    Chiaroscuro CR (D) 126
With Time to Love
    Chiaroscuro CR (D) 126
There Will Never Be Another You
    Chiaroscuro CR (D) 126
Solitude
    Chiaroscuro CR 126, CR 204, Chiaroscuro CR (D) 126
Struttin' with Some Barbecue
    Chiaroscuro CR 126, CR 204, Chiaroscuro CR (D) 126
On the Sunny Side of the Street
    Chiaroscuro CR 126, CR 204, Chiaroscuro CR (D) 126
Thou Swell
    Chiaroscuro CR (D) 126

Body and Soul
Chiaroscuro CR 126, CR 204, Chiaroscuro CR (D) 126
Just Squeeze Me
Chiaroscuro CR (D) 126
It Don't Mean a Thing
Chiaroscuro CR 126, CR 204, Chiaroscuro CR (D) 126
Rockin' in Rhythm
Chiaroscuro CR 126, CR 204, Chiaroscuro CR (D) 126
Sugar
Chiaroscuro CR 126, CR 204, Chiaroscuro CR (D) 126
Liza
Chiaroscuro CR (D) 126
You're a Lucky Guy
Chiaroscuro CR 126, CR 204, Chiaroscuro CR (D) 126
Don't Blame Me
Chiaroscuro CR (D) 126
Cheek to Cheek
Chiaroscuro CR (D) 126
Mean to Me
Chiaroscuro CR 126, CR 204, Chiaroscuro CR (D) 126
Here, There and Everywhere
Chiaroscuro CR (D) 126
Goose Pimples
Chiaroscuro CR 126, CR 204, Chiaroscuro CR (D) 126
Nobody Else But You
Chiaroscuro CR (D) 126

NOTE: Chiaroscuro CR (D) 126 is titled *Live at the New School: The Complete Concert*. All titles on CR 126, Chiaroscuro (J) ULS 1847, and Vogue (E and F) VJD 519. The Vogue double album is titled *The Best I've Heard*, which is a quote from Eubie Blake. His complete reaction to this quartet was "The best I've heard in seventy-two years."[23] CR 204 also exists as a pressing issued by Radio Shack as an LP and eight-track tape. "Just Squeeze Me" is incorrectly titled "Squeeze Me" on the CD. In addition, the CD lists "With Time for Love" whereas Ruby's composition is titled "With Time to Love." The LP jacket incorrectly lists "A Ghost of a Chance" "for Body and Soul," whereas the label is correct. "Body and Soul" is correctly titled on Vogue (E and F) VJD 519 and Franklin Mint 90, album No. 23.

New York Jazz Repertory Company: Duke Ellington Tribute[24]
April 26, 1974, 8 p.m., Carnegie Hall, New York
The concert featured a large group directed by Sy Oliver and a small one led by Bob Wilber. Guests included the Ruby Braff–George Barnes Quartet, Stan Getz, Jimmy Rowles, Vic Dickenson, the Billy Taylor Trio, and Brooks Kerr leading a

group including Russell Procope, Sonny Greer, and Joya Sherrill. Duke Ellington was hospitalized at the time.

Tribute to Vic Dickenson at the Jazz Week in Boston: Ruby Braff with Buzzy Drootin[25]
April 29th to May 5th, 1974, Scotch 'n Sirloin Restaurant, Boston—on Friday Ruby Braff performed
Ruby Braff (cnt), Babe Donahue (tp), Vic Dickenson, Dick LeFave (tb), Al Drootin (cl, ss), Sonny Drootin (p), Tony Jordan (b), Buzzy Drootin (dm)
Mean to Me
Ain't Misbehavin'
I Can't Get Started (Braff feature)
Medley:
  Exactly Like You
  Four or Five Times

Brew's: Mike Burgevin with Guests[26]
"A Friday Evening in May, 1974," probably May 10 or 17, Brew's, 156 East 34th Street, New York
Ruby Braff (cnt), Vic Dickenson, Rudy Powell, Sam Margolis (ts), Jimmy Andrews (p), Mike Burgevin (dm)
Sophisticated Lady
Other tunes were not reported.

Jack Bradley photographed the Quartet at the Bryant Park performance below.[27]

Braff–Barnes Quartet at Bryant Park (6th Avenue at 42nd Street)[28]
June 3, 1974, New York
Ruby Braff (cnt), George Barnes, Wayne Wright (g), Michael Moore (b)
Rockin' in Rhythm
On the Sunny Side of the Street
Here, There and Everywhere
The 4th of July
Looking at You
Sugar
Just Squeeze Me
Goose Pimples
It Don't Mean a Thing
I'm Putting All My Eggs in One Basket
Solitude
Mean to Me
Old Folks
Cheek to Cheek*
Body and Soul*
Ooh, That Kiss*

NOTE: A recording of all but the three final tunes is available but remain unissued. The ones marked with an asterisk were not available to the author.

Ruby Braff–George Barnes Quartet[29]
June 15 and 16, 1974, 4 p.m. both days, North End Major Stage, Lakefront Festival of the Arts, Milwaukee, Wisconsin
Ruby Braff (cnt), George Barnes (g), Wayne Wright (g), Michael Moore (b)

Ruby Braff–George Barnes Quartet: *Today Show* (NBC Television)
June 21, 1974, NBC, New York, (appeared on both hours of the program)
Ruby Braff (cnt), George Barnes (g), Wayne Wright (g), Michael Moore (b)
Ooh, That Kiss
Here, There and Everywhere
NOTE: A recording of these tunes is available but remains unissued. I was only able to tape one of the two segments.

Film Soundtrack: *The Switch or How to Alter Your Ego*[30] (released as *Oversexed* in the UK)
Ruby Braff–George Barnes Quartet
Summer 1974–specific date unknown
Director: Joe Sarno—Producers: Sidney Ginsberg and Peter Kares—Distributor: Scotia International-American

The Ruby Braff–George Barnes Quartet received a screen credit in the opening sequence; however, Ruby is only heard in an improvised slow blues performance that lasts just under two minutes. Joe Sarno, in a telephone conversation, said he enjoyed working with Ruby. He reported that the quartet recorded original compositions in a studio for the soundtrack after Ruby viewed the film. He does not recall further details, and both the film and the soundtrack appeared to be lost until a recent DVD issue. The film ran 100 minutes in the US release but only 75 minutes in the UK. The version on the DVD runs 92 minutes and it is said to be "the only known element for the film." It is not known if the musical portion of the soundtrack was longer in the original US theatrical or more recent shortened DVD release, given Mr. Sarno's reference to multiple compositions. This is probably the most unusual recording in Ruby's career. This soft core pornographic film borrows from Robert Louis Stevenson's classic story *The Strange Case of Dr. Jekyll and Mr. Hyde*.

When I mentioned this film to Ruby, he blushed. He quickly said that this had been one of his mistakes and that he wished I had not learned of it. Ruby's fans would agree with him. Yet, given Ruby's musical standards, his short performance is easily recognized, but it is not performed in the style of the Braff–Barnes Quartet. We'll probably never know if there was more music recorded for the soundtrack.

Next, The Ruby Braff–George Barnes Quartet closed both the early and late performances at Avery Fisher Hall on July 2 in a featured concert during the Newport Jazz Festival. The program featured a number of notable artists, and Ruby was delighted by the emphasis on melody in the design of the program. The quartet was featured in performances of tunes by George Gershwin and Irving Berlin. Other musicians performing in this concert program include Johnny Mathis, Gerry Mulligan, Bobby Short, Bobby Hackett, Vic Dickenson, Jackie Cain, and Roy Kral, with Dave Garroway as master of ceremonies. Stan Getz was scheduled to appear but withdrew due to food poisoning.

The program opened with Bobby Short performing a selection Duke Ellington and Billy Strayhorn songs ("Daydream," "Love Like This Can't Last," "I'm Satisfied," "Drop Me Off in Harlem," "Something to Live For," and "Jump for Joy"), then continued as Gerry Mulligan performed Kurt Weill tunes ("My Ship," "Lost in the Stars," and "September Song"). Jimmy Rowles played a medley of two Jerome Kern melodies ("Remind Me" and "All the Things You Are") and Jackie Cain and Roy Kral followed with two tunes by Alec Wilder ("It's So Peaceful in the Country" and "While We're Young"). Then it was time for the Ruby Braff–George Barnes Quartet.

The Quartet was included in two performances at the Newport Jazz Festival in Avery Fisher Hall.

Ruby Braff–George Barnes Quartet: Newport Jazz Festival *Jazz Salute to the American Song*[31]
July 3, 1974, 7:30 and 11:30 p.m., Avery Fisher Hall, New York
Ruby Braff (cnt), George Barnes, Wayne Wright (g), Michael Moore (b)
First Concert: 7:30 p.m.
I'm Putting All My Eggs in One Basket
They Can't Take That Away from Me
Isn't It a Lovely Day to Be Caught in the Rain?
Cheek to Cheek

Second Concert: 11:30 p.m. *Jazz Salute to the American Song*
I'm Putting All My Eggs in One Basket
They Can't Take That Away from Me
Isn't It a Lovely Day to Be Caught in the Rain?
Cheek to Cheek
NOTE: A recording of these tunes is available but remains unissued. The program closed with a performance by Bobby Hackett and Vic Dickenson ("Alexander's Ragtime Band," "What'll I Do," "Together," "Blue Skies," "Goodbye Darling," and "Mimosa and Me").

Brew's
July 4, 1974, New York
Ruby Braff (cnt), Marshall Brown (vtb), Sam Margolis (cl), Jimmy Andrews (p), Wayne Wright (g), Mike Burgevin (dm)

Struttin' with Some Barbecue
Someday You'll Be Sorry

Add tenor, probably Sam Margolis
I Want to Be Happy
NOTE: A recording of these tunes is available but remains unissued.

The Grande Parade du Jazz began in 1974, and this provided an opportunity for Ruby to return to Europe a number of times. Given the extent of his reputation, he was certainly a logical choice to perform, both with the Braff–Barnes Quartet and in other combinations. A published photograph shows Ruby watching as Vic Dickenson solos during a performance captioned "Nice, France 1969." It is more likely that it comes from the following performance since I have been unable to verify that Ruby appeared in Nice in 1969.[32] However, Max Jones published a photograph taken by Beryl Bryden which is undoubtedly from the next performance. It shows onstage, Ruby performing with Earl Hines, Bobby Hackett and Pee Wee Erwin.[33] A bust of Louis Armstrong was unveiled during this event, and this was the first concert in the festival.

Tribute to Louis Armstrong : Grande Parade du Jazz (Nice Jazz Festival)[34]
July 15, 1974, Nice, France (This was the first day of the first Grande Parade du Jazz.)
Wallace Davenport (tp), Bill Coleman (tp, flgh), Jimmy McPartland, Wild Bill Davison (cnt), Vic Dickenson (tb), Barney Bigard (cl), Budd Johnson (ts, ss), George Wein (p), Arvell Shaw (b, voc), Cozy Cole (dm)
When It's Sleepy Time Down South
    unissued, recording available
Struttin' with Some Barbecue (featuring BC on flgh)
    unissued, partial recording available
Them There Eyes (featuring WBD)
    Unissued, no recording available
Confessin' (featuring WD)
    RCA FXL1 7159
Creole Love Call (featuring BB)
    unissued, recording available

Add Ruby Braff (cnt)
All of Me (voc JM)
    RCA FXL1 7159
Memories of You (featuring BC)
    Unissued, no recording available
Sugar (featuring VD)
    RCA FXL1 7159

I Can't Give You Anything but Love (featuring RB)
RCA FXL1 7159
Sweet Georgia Brown
Unissued, no recording available

Ruby Braff was not listed in personnel on the front and rear album cover; however his solo is described in the liner notes by J. P. Guiter, who wrote the following: ". . . for our taste we would admit to a slight preference for Ruby Braff's contribution."

Ruby Braff–George Barnes Quartet at the Grande Parade du Jazz[35]
July 16, 1974, Nice, France
Ruby Braff (cnt), George Barnes, Wayne Wright (g), Michael Moore (b)
Ooh, That Kiss*
Old Folks
Goose Pimples
Looking at You
Solitude
Liza
Struttin' with Some Barbecue
Cheek to Cheek
Just Squeeze Me
Rockin' in Rhythm*
No One Else But You
You're Lucky to Me
NOTE: Brief fragments of two of the tunes marked with an asterisk are available but remain unissued. I have not located a complete recording of this performance or any of the next three sets.

Ruby Braff–George Barnes Quartet at the Grande Parade du Jazz[36]
Ruby Braff (cnt), George Barnes, Wayne Wright (g), Michael Moore (b)
July 17, 1974, Nice, France
Them There Eyes
It's Like the Fourth of July
Struttin' with Some Barbecue
Ain't Misbehavin'
Cheek to Cheek
Liza
Old Folks
Ooh, That Kiss
Our Love Is Here to Stay
Everything's George (Where's Freddie?)

Ruby Braff at the Grande Parade du Jazz: Nice Jazz Festival[37]
July 1974, Nice, France

Ruby Braff (cnt), Wallace Davenport (tp), Benny Morton (tb), Bud Freeman (ts), Maxim Saury (cl), Eddie Vinson (as), Earl Hines (p), Jimmy Leary (b), Panama Francis (dm)
Unknown tunes performed

Tribute to Sidney Bechet: Ruby Braff–George Barnes Quartet at the Grande Parade du Jazz[38]
July 18, 1974, Nice, France
Ruby Braff (cnt), George Barnes, Wayne Wright (g), Michael Moore (b)
No One Else But You
With Time to Love
Mean to Me
Don't Blame Me
How Long Has This Been Going On?
It Don't Mean a Thing
It's Wonderful
I'm Putting All My Eggs in One Basket
They Can't Take That Away from Me
Rockin' in Rhythm
Blues in A Flat

Tribute to Count Basie: Grande Parade du Jazz[39]
July 18, 1974, Nice, France
Ruby Braff (cnt), Wallace Davenport, Bill Coleman (tp), Vic Dickenson (tb), Buddy Tate, Eddie "Lockjaw" Davis, Gérard Badini (ts), George Wein (p), Jimmy Leary (b), Panama Francis (dm), Willie Mabon (voc)
Swinging the Blues
  RCA (Fr) FXL1 7158
Broadway
  RCA (Fr) FXL1 7158
Blue and Sentimental
  RCA (Fr) FXL1 7158
Goin' to Chicago (WM voc)
  RCA (Fr) FXL1 7158
Lester Leaps In
  RCA (Fr) FXL1 7158
One O'Clock Jump
  RCA (Fr) FXL1 7158

Jack Bradley's photo taken during the above performance appears in the March of Jazz program.[40]

Ruby Braff with Lennie Felix, Maxine Sullivan, and Wayne Wright: Grande Parade du Jazz

July 18, 1974, Nice, France (informal performance, club setting, not onstage)
Ruby Braff (cnt), Lennie Felix (p)
At Sundown
Blue and Sentimental

Add Maxine Sullivan (voc)
I've Got the World on a String
That Old Feeling
I Could Write a Book*

Add Wayne Wright
On the Sunny Side of the Street*
I Want to Be Happy

Omit Maxine Sullivan
Ain't Misbehavin'
NOTE: A complete recording of five of these tunes is available but remains unissued. Only partial recordings are available for the two tunes marked with an asterisk.

Ruby Braff–George Barnes Quartet at the Grande Parade du Jazz[41]

July 19, 1974, Nice, France
Ruby Braff (cnt), George Barnes, Wayne Wright (g), Michael Moore (b)
Unknown title
Summertime
Bidin' My Time
On the Sunny Side of the Street
I Can't Give You Anything but Love
Unknown title
Somebody Loves Me
Them There Eyes
Goose Pimples

Ruby Braff at the Grande Parade du Jazz[42]

July 19, 1974, Nice, France
Ruby Braff, Wild Bill Davison (cnt), Kenny Davern (ss), Joe Venuti (v), Marian McPartland (p), Tiny Grimes (g), Bob Haggart (b), Gus Johnson (dm), Maxine Sullivan (voc)
Exactly Like You
You Took Advantage of Me
Rockin' Chair (voc MS)
That Old Feeling (voc MS)
C Jam Blues

'S Wonderful

Ruby Braff–George Barnes Quartet at the Grande Parade du Jazz
July 1974, Nice, France (The Grande Parade du Jazz: Nice Jazz Festival ended on July 21, so this appearance was no later than that date.)
Ruby Braff (cnt), George Barnes, Wayne Wright (g), Michael Moore (b)
No One Else But You
On the Sunny Side of the Street
The Man I Love
Don't Blame Me
NOTE: A recording of these tunes is available but remains unissued.

Shortly after his return from France, Ruby flew to California. The 1974 Concord Jazz Festival ran for two weekends, July 26–28 and August 2–4.[43] The Ruby Braff–George Barnes Quartet performed on the first night. This was the West Coast debut for the quartet, and the performance was released on Concord Jazz records. Ruby had a very successful 20-year relationship with Carl Jefferson that resulted in a succession of excellent released on the Concord Jazz label through 1995. Their relationship had begun in 1972 in preparation for the Concord Summer Festival that August. It continued until Ruby performed a single tune in a 1995 tribute concert that celebrated Jefferson's career, followed by his final recording session for the label, both with Roger Kellaway. This relationship produced many memorable recordings. Ruby had gained from Hank O'Neal's support on the East Coast and now he had gained an active champion on the West Coast.

Ruby Braff–George Barnes Quartet: *Plays Gershwin*
July 26, 1974, Concord Boulevard Park, Concord Summer Festival, Concord, California
Ruby Braff (cnt), George Barnes, Wayne Wright (g), Michael Moore (b)
'S Wonderful
    Concord CJ 5, GRT 5378H (tape)
I Got Rhythm
    Concord CJ 5, Concord 013431-21822-7
They Can't Take That Away from Me
    Concord CJ 5
Nice Work If You Can Get It
    Concord CJ 5
Somebody Loves Me
    Concord CJ 5
But Not for Me
    Concord CJ 5

Medley:
  Summertime
    Concord CJ 5
  Bidin' My Time
    Concord CJ 5, Concord CCD 6013
Love Walked In
    Concord CJ 5, Concord CCD 6013, Snapper Music SMDCD 271 (CD)
Embraceable You
    Concord CJ 5, Concord CCD 6013
Liza
    Concord CJ 5, Snapper Music SMDCD 271 (CD)
NOTE: All titles also on Concord (J) ICJ 80053, K25Y 19551 (CD), and CCD 6005. Concord 013431-21822-7 is titled *Concord Records 30th Anniversary* and Snapper Music SMDCD 271 is titled *I'm Shooting High.* The Snapper release is a reissue of tunes from various Concord Jazz releases. Concord CCD 6013 is titled *Concord Jazz: Collector's Series Sampler.*

Ruby Braff–George Barnes Quartet at El Matador[44]
July/August 1974, two-week engagement following Concord Jazz Festival, El Matador, San Francisco

Charles Schwartz wrote the following:[45]

> [Audiences were small at the El Matador and Ruby criticized the club's management.] Ruby as usual was running his mouth about creeps from San Quentin. They were going to hurt him. I had to plead with them on bended knee to prevent this.
>
> When we were in California our agency called. In an unusual move I had placed them [Braff–Barnes Quartet] with a classical agency who had never handled a jazz group before. I had a definite direction in mind. These people had strong connections for the college circuit which was the way I wanted to go. When we signed with these people, I told them we needed a national TV show. They said this was very difficult. I said, 'Keep trying.' When they called us in California I knew it had to be something good as I had kept the group working. Anyway they had gotten the Griffin show, which for a jazz group was nearly unheard of. Now I revealed to all what my plan was. It was to send press kits to every college in the country and to use the Griffin show as an audition for all. The agency was ecstatic and thought we would get about 200 gigs at $3000 a shot. This was more money than Ruby had ever made before and reaching more people than Ruby had ever played for in his entire career. There was a minor problem that Griffin only would pay one leader and two sidemen, a difference of only $100. Over this $100 Ruby flipped out. He screamed that he would not play Griffin's show on that basis. That was the last straw. Ruby eventually fired me.

Ruby Braff–George Barnes Quartet at the St. Lawrence Center[46]
August 7, 1974, St. Lawrence Center, Toronto
Ruby Braff (cnt), George Barnes, Wayne Wright (g), Michael Moore (b)

I was present at this concert. Although the audience was small (probably about 800) in a much larger hall, the music was grand. No recording has surfaced.

Ruby Braff–George Barnes Quartet[47]
August 13, 1974, on the steps at Federal Hall National Memorial, 26 Wall Street, New York

Jack Bradley's photo from this performance appears in the March of Jazz program[48] and is included in this book's photo section.

Ruby Braff–George Barnes Quartet[49]
Performances for two weeks in Boston and one week in Washington, D.C.

Ruby Braff–George Barnes Quartet: *Salutes Rodgers & Hart*
October 1974, A&R Recording Studios, New York
Ruby Braff (cnt), George Barnes (g), Wayne Wright (g), Michael Moore (b)
Mountain Greenery
    Concord CJ 7, Connoisseur Collection VSOPCD 240
Isn't It Romantic
    Concord CJ 7, CJ 93
The Blue Room
    Concord CJ 7
There's a Small Hotel
    Concord CJ 7, CCD 4833-2
Thou Swell
    Concord CJ 7
I Wish I Were in Love Again
    Concord CJ 7, CCD 6013
Lover
    Concord CJ 7
You Took Advantage of Me
    Concord CJ 7, Snapper Music SMDCD 271
Spring Is Here
    Concord CJ 7, Concord CCD 6013
The Lady Is a Tramp
    Concord CJ 7, Snapper Music SMDCD 271
NOTE: All titles also on Concord (J) ICJ 80060, K25Y 19553 (CD) and CCD 6007. Concord Jazz CCD 4833-2 is titled *Ruby Braff: The Concord Jazz Heritage Series*. CJ 93 is titled *A Taste of Jazz* and Snapper Music SMDCD 271 is

titled *I'm Shooting High.* The Snapper release is a reissue of tunes from various Concord Jazz releases. Concord CCD 6013 is titled *Concord Jazz: Collector's Series Sampler.*

Album notes state that "one concert [with Tony Bennett] was filmed at Alice Tully Hall." Likely this comment refers to the September 1973 concerts included in Tony Bennett's unreleased film *This Funny World.*

Ruby Braff–George Barnes Quartet[50]
October 14–19, 1974, Blues Alley, 1073 Wisconsin Avenue NW (rear), Georgetown (Washington, D.C., area)
Ruby Braff (cnt), George Barnes (g), Wayne Wright (g), Michael Moore (b).

Ruby Braff–George Barnes Quartet[51]
November 1, 1974, Jazz Gehört und Gesehen, Berlin Jazztagen (The broadcast on Germany's Radio Three is titled *Jazz Heard and Seen* and the performance is part of *Berlin Jazz Days.*)
Ruby Braff (cnt), George Barnes (g), Michael Moore (b), Wayne Wright (g)
Ooh, That Kiss
In My Solitude*
But Not for Me*
Gershwin Medley:
  Summertime*
  Bidin' My Time*
They Can't Take That Away from Me*
I Got Rhythm
Sugar*
Liza*
There's a Small Hotel (available recording ends during this tune)
Everything's George (Where's Freddie?)
NOTE: Both audio and video recordings exist from this broadcast but remain unissued. Selections available in the video recording are marked with an asterisk. The audio recording is complete except for the final portion of "There's a Small Hotel" and all of "Everything's George." An interview with Ruby Braff is included in broadcast. At the time of publication, all selections marked with an asterisk are available for downloading from www.YouTube.com.

New York Jazz Repertory Company: *Satchmo Remembered—The Music of Louis Armstrong at Carnegie Hall*[52]
November 8, 1974, 8 p.m., Carnegie Hall, New York
Dick Hyman and the New York Jazz Repertory Company
Ray Nance (cnt, voc), Ruby Braff (cnt), Vic Dickenson, (tb), Kenny Davern (ss), Dick Hyman (p), Milt Hinton (b), Carmen Mastren (g), Bobby Rosengarden (dm)

Struttin' with Some Barbecue (voc RN)
unissued, recording available

Omit Ray Nance
Big Butter and Egg Man (CS voc)
Atlantic SD 1671

Ruby Braff (cnt), Dick Hyman (p), Milt Hinton (b), Carmen Mastren (g), Bobby Rosengarden (dm)
Someday
Atlantic SD 1671

Ruby Braff (cnt), Dick Hyman (p)
Rosetta
Atlantic SD 1671

Full personnel (no soloists audible)
When It's Sleepy Time Down South
unissued, recording available
NOTE: Other performances in this concert (and on this LP) do not include Ruby Braff

Ruby Braff attended the special Preview Party for a new exhibit featuring *Count Basie and His Bands* at the New York Jazz Museum on November 11, 1974. The exhibit commemorated the 40th anniversary of the founding of Basie's band in Kansas City. Earle Warren led a performance by the Count Basie Alumni Band, with Count Basie in attendance with his wife, Catherine.[53]

A second Armstrong tribute concert in this series was performed at Carnegie Hall on November 15 but probably did not include Ruby Braff. Listed performers included Bernie Privin, Joe Newman, Doc Cheatham, Ernie Royal, Jimmy Owens, Yank Lawson, Ray Nance, Bobby Hackett, and others.[54]

Ruby recalled being involved in a horrible evening on Long Island with Carmen Mastren and maintained that they were the only two musicians who could play at a professional level. They paired on a number of the tunes from that evening.[55]

A recent recording has surfaced that comes from the performance of the Ruby–Braff George Barnes Quartet for a convention of the National Academy of Recording Artists, held an RCA studio in New York. The group was booked by Mike Lipskin. Mike is an accomplished stride pianist in his own right. He was a student of Willie "The Lion" Smith. Then, he was a staff producer for RCA Records working on the acclaimed Vintage Series among other projects. Ruby would encounter Mike again in February, when he produced the Braff–Barnes Fred Astaire tribute album for RCA and then again in 2004, when Mike was musical director for a series of Stride Summit concerts in San Francisco. The musicians were introduced by Leonard Feather.

Ruby Braff–George Barnes Quartet at the NARAS Convention with Mike Lipskin

November 19, 1974, RCA Studios, New York
Ruby Braff (cnt), George Barnes (g), Mike Lipskin (p), Wayne Wright (g)
Wrap Your Troubles in Dreams
    Buskirk Records 007
One Hour
    Buskirk Records 007
'S Wonderful
    Buskirk Records 007
Unknown title
    Unissued

Mike Lipskin shared his thoughts on Ruby in personal correspondence:

> Ruby Braff was a unique jazz artist giving much pleasure to his listeners and imbued with what Whitney Balliett used to call 'the sound of surprise.' Several facets of his artistry made the word "unique" most applicable to this great jazzman.
>
> In a broad sense, his overall style contained a sophistication of phrasing that transcended any particular jazz period. Anyone well versed in the evolution of pre bop jazz trumpet would have trouble chronologically placing him or the musical tools he seemed to gravitate toward. There's often a smattering of off-hand, sparse, almost post bop phrasing, followed by a warm and legato passage harking back to the 1930s. (Hence the Balliett *sound of surprise*.)
>
> Probably without knowing it he set himself up for difficult challenges, one was to honor his idol, Louis Armstrong and create originality within that tradition. Unlike some who idolized Pops, Ruby did not try to sound like Louis, did not repeat many of the pioneer's phrases, and had his own tone and dynamics.
>
> Another challenge was to created variations on a song while respecting its melodic line and the intent of the composer, harder to do than trying to dazzle with 16th note arpeggios along a harmonic framework.
>
> Along with fine tone and dynamics, he had a special way of taking liberties with any song but always showing respect for its melody and the composer's intent. Ruby did this consistently for the longest time, without ever sounding stale or devoid of freshness.
>
> As staff producer for RCA Records, I was lucky enough to record him when he was part of the Braff–Barnes Quartet. During these sessions his consistently relaxed stance while playing was almost ironic considering the subtle profundity of his musical ideas. Some artists become tense when a 'take' is being made in the studio. Ruby was as much at ease there as when performing in a jazz joint.
>
> I also had the honor of accompanying him twice. First was in 1974 at an impromptu jam session with the Braff–Barnes Quartet, and then in 1988 as mu-

sical director and performer for the first San Francisco Jazz Stride Summit. Both experiences were great musical highlights for me.

Ruby Braff Quintet[56]
December 7, 1974, Brew's, 156 East 34th Street, New York
Ruby Braff (cnt), Tom Artin (tb), Dill Jones (p), Al Hall (b), Mike Burgevin (dm)
Them There Eyes
I Ain't Got Nobody
When You're Smiling
Ghost of a Chance
Rosetta
Baby, Won't You Please Come Home?
The World Is Waiting for the Sunrise (incomplete)
Love Me or Leave Me
NOTE: A recording of these tunes is available but remains unissued.

The Ruby Braff–George Barnes Quartet opened at Buddy's Place on December 9, 1974, through December 21.[57] The club was closed on Sundays. Buddy Rich performed there with his band when in New York, but other musicians were booked when he was touring. Performances were scheduled at 10 p.m. and midnight Mondays through Thursdays, and 8:45, 10:45 and 12:45 p.m. Fridays and Saturdays. The location was at 1220 Second Avenue at 64th Street, New York.

Ruby Braff–George Barnes Quartet at Buddy's Place
December 9–21, 1974, New York
Ruby Braff (cnt), George Barnes, Wayne Wright (g), Michael Moore (b)

Ruby Braff–George Barnes Quartet at Buddy's Place
December 10, 1974, Buddy's Place, New York
Ruby Braff (cnt), George Barnes (g), Wayne Wright (g), Michael Moore (b)
It Don't Mean a Thing
Spring Is Here
You Took Advantage of Me
Take the "A" Train
Looking at You
Sunny Side of the Street
Love Walked In
Mountain Greenery
Medley:
  Summertime
  Bidin' My Time
Them There Eyes

Lover
Nice Work If You Can Get It
Where's Freddie?

Set Two:
But Not for Me
Old Folks
Just Squeeze Me
The Lady Is a Tramp
In My Solitude
You're a Lucky Guy
Medley:
  What's New
  The Man I Love
There's a Small Hotel
Thou Swell
Sugar
The Lady's in Love with You
They Can't Take That Away from Me
Rockin' in Rhythm
NOTE: A recording of these tunes is available but remains unissued.

Ruby Braff–George Barnes Quartet at Buddy's Place
December 20, 1974, Buddy's Place, New York
Ruby Braff (cnt), George Barnes (g), Wayne Wright (g), Michael Moore (b)
Jeepers Creepers
Medley:
  Summertime
  Bidin' My Time
Love Me or Leave Me
Mountain Greenery
Sugar
But Not for Me
Ooh, That Kiss
Body and Soul
Lady Be Good
Keepin' Out of Mischief Now
Goose Pimples
I Got Rhythm
Love Walked In
Rockin' in Rhythm
The Man I Love
Take the "A" Train
NOTE: A recording of these tunes is available but remains unissued.

Ruby Braff–George Barnes Quartet at Buddy's Place
December 21, 1974, Buddy's Place, New York City (this was final night of a two–week booking)
Ruby Braff (cnt), George Barnes, Wayne Wright (g), Michael Moore (b)
It Don't Mean a Thing
They Can't Take That Away from Me
It's Wonderful
Jeepers Creepers
Summertime
Bidin' My Time
Love Me or Leave Me
Mountain Greenery
Lover
Nice Work If You Can Get It
But Not for Me
Ooh, That Kiss
Over the Rainbow
Lady Be Good
Spring Is Here
Thou Swell
Keepin' Out of Mischief Now
Solitude
Goose Pimples
I Got Rhythm
Love Is Just around the Corner
Love Walked In
Rockin' in Rhythm
NOTE: A recording of these tunes is available but remains unissued.

Ruby Braff–George Barnes Quartet
January 17, 1975, Downtown Room, Statler-Hilton Hotel, Buffalo, New York
Ruby Braff (cnt), George Barnes, Wayne Wright (g), Michael Moore (b)
Ooh, That Kiss
I Want a Little Girl
They Can't Take That Away from Me
The Lady Is a Tramp
Sweethearts on Parade
Keepin' Out of Mischief Now
Love Walked In
Goose Pimples
Nice Work If You Can Get It
Lover Come Back to Me
Nobody Else But You

When Your Lover Has Gone
Love Is Just around the Corner
Mood Indigo
Somebody Loves Me
I'm Getting Sentimental Over You
The World Is Waiting for the Sunrise
Spring Is Here
Between the Devil and the Deep Blue Sea
Medley:
  Liza
  Melancholy Baby
  Over the Rainbow
NOTE: A recording of these tunes is available but remains unissued.

The quartet's next recording was for RCA Records before flying to England to appear in Ronnie Scott's Club.

Ruby Braff–George Barnes Quartet: *To Fred Astaire with Love*
February 3/4/5, 1975, New York
Ruby Braff (cnt), George Barnes, Wayne Wright (g), Michael Moore (b)
EPA1-1101 Cheek to Cheek
    RCA APL 1-1008, (F) FXL 3.7343, Reader's Digest RD 4A-017, RCA (F) PM 43267
EPAl-1102 They Can't Take That Away from Me
    RCA APL 1-1008, (F) FXL 3.7343
EPA1-1103 Easter Parade
    RCA APL 1-1008, (F) FXL 3.7343
EPA1-1104 A Shine On Your Shoes
    RCA APL 1-1008, (F) FXL 3.7343
EPA1-1105 I'm Putting All My Eggs in One Basket
    RCA APL 1-1008, (F) FXL 3.7343
EPA1-1106 They All Laughed
    RCA APL 1-1008, (F) FXL 3.7343, Reader's Digest RD 4A-017
EPAl-1107 Be Careful, It's My Heart
    RCA APL 1-1008, (F) FXL 3.7343
EPA1-1108 I'm Old Fashioned
    RCA APL 1-1008, (F) FXL 3.7343
EPA1-1109 Isn't It a Lovely Day to Be Caught in the Rain?
    RCA APL 1-1008, (F) FXL 3.7343
EPA1-1110 Top Hat, White Tie and Tails
    RCA APL 1-1008, (F) FXL 3.7343
NOTE: All titles also on RCA (E) SF 8442 and Jazz Lips JL 765 with the same album title. That album also includes all tunes from the late July 1973 Chiaroscuro session. Reader's Digest RD 4A-017 is titled *All-Star Jazz Festival* and

consists of eight LPs. RCA (F) PM 43267 is titled *From Chicago to New York (1923-1975)* and consists of three LPs.

Ruby Braff–George Barnes Quartet[58]
February 24, 1975, opening of engagement that lasts three weeks, Ronnie Scott's Club, London
Ruby Braff (cnt), George Barnes, Wayne Wright (g), Michael Moore (b)
Undecided
Pennies from Heaven
I'm Old Fashioned
Rockin' in Rhythm
Them There Eyes
Jeepers Creepers
Over the Rainbow
It Don't Mean a Thing
I Want a Little Girl
Top Hat, White Tie and Tails
The World Is Waiting for the Sunrise
The Blue Room
Take the "A" Train
There's a Small Hotel
But Not for Me
I'm Putting All My Eggs in One Basket
NOTE: No recordings are known to exist.

Bud Freeman was in the audience at least one night. Ken Gallacher wrote the following:[59]

> I remember once going into Ronnie's along with Bud Freeman to listen to the Braff–Barnes Quartet, one of the most lyrical groups ever to grace jazz music. Braff, always a booster for the legendary Chicago tenor sax stylist, made Bud take a bow as he told the audience just how wonderful a musician he was. It was almost a repeat of what he had once told Leonard Feather in a *DownBeat* Blindfold Test. In that interview he declared that Bud Freeman had been the most important musical influence on him after Louis Armstrong and Fats Waller.
>
> Later in the downstairs bar there were signs that the co-leaders were building towards the personality clash which ended the group's short but glorious life. As the sparks threatened to fly Barnes eventually turned away from the cornetist and told me a wonderful story about the lead trumpeter Jimmy Maxwell.
>
> Barnes had recognized the accent and told me that Maxwell, who led the Benny Goodman trumpet section as well as others and was one of the most sought-after studio musicians in New York, was distinctly proud of his Scottish ancestry. So much so that on occasions when he had imbibed a little too much

> he would get out his bagpipes—which he could play—and walk around his Manhattan block entertaining the neighbors.
>
> A few years later at the Nice Festival Maxwell, then playing in a small group with Teddy Wilson and Barney Bigard, confirmed the story to me and grinned: 'You've been speaking to George Barnes, haven't you?'

One media report noted the following:[60]

> When the group visited London, to play at Ronnie Scott's club, the RCA executive who invited them to dinner to meet useful media contacts was obliged to give two dinner parties, since Braff and Barnes were no longer on speaking—let alone dining—terms.

In conversations with many people, Ruby said the following: "I hated George and he hated me. When we were playing, that was fine. But when we stopped, we would see the hate in each other's eyes. It became intolerable."

But, whatever the tension that was indisputably about to lead to a crisis for the group, the performance was praised by Miles Kington writing for *The Times*:[61]

> Jazz people generally think it is unmanly to do without a drummer, so Ruby Braff's current group, with George Barnes on guitar, Wayne Wright on rhythm guitar and Michael Moore on bass, runs the risk of being called effeminate behind its back. Judging from Monday, the first night of a three-week run, I like it just the way it is, and those who don't can make up for it mentally—all round me in the club I could sense the mental sizzle of cymbals and hiss of wire brushes. It's one of those rare groups in jazz, in the Goodman, John Kirby and Gerry Mulligan tradition, that have the right sort of chamber approach—lots of tight arrangements, short ripe solos, constant interplay and a dynamic level that makes a fortissimo come as a shock—and they do it superbly well.
>
> Braff's cornet is the glory of the group, of course. It can be no coincidence that it has just made an LP of Fred Astaire themes, because Braff has the same effortless floating quality, the same ability to make the impossible look too easy to bother about. (His lower register work must be the best in jazz.) Having once made the decision over twenty years ago not to follow modernist trends and remain a Peter Pan Clifford Brown-who-never-grew-up, Braff has shown against the odds and the critics that it is possible to advance without being progressive.
>
> One of the great lightweight champions of jazz, Barnes's playing is more foursquare, but he makes his lines sing as few guitarists have since Django (not so much of a compliment when you think how few have tried) and provides a witty foil to Braff besides, I suspect, being responsible for the unusual items such as Bix's 'Goose Pimples' and Duke's 'Rockin' in Rhythm.'

Later that year, Mr. Kington listed the album *Live at the New School* as one of his three choices for record of the year. His words are worth recalling:[62]

> Braff is a pugnacious little American reputed not to suffer fools gladly and thus not to stay in one group for long; he is also the most gifted cornetist I have ever heard, with a magical tone and madcap imagination, so I'm glad that this group has stuck together long enough to make six LPs. (Rumor has it that it is now breaking up.)

Ruby Braff–George Barnes Quartet[63]
Following the return from London, Buddy's Place, 133 West 33rd Street, New York
Ruby Braff (cnt), George Barnes, Wayne Wright (g), Michael Moore (b)

Vinnie Corrao watched this performance prior to joining the group and beginning rehearsals. *The New Yorker* did not report any other engagements at Buddy's Place until a month later. The club had closed to move to this new location.

Dick Hyman: *Charleston: The Song That Made the Twenties Roar*
April 29, 1975, probably New York
Ruby Braff (cnt), Dick Hyman (organ)
If I Could Be with You
    Columbia M 33706

Ruby Braff (cnt), Dick Hyman (p)
Snowy Morning Blues
    Columbia M 33706
Just Before Daybreak
    Columbia M 33706

May 21, 1975
Ruby Braff (cnt), Dick Hyman (p), Vic Dickenson (tb), Bob Wilber (ss), Everett Barksdale (bjo), Bob Haggart (b), Bobby Rosengarden (dm)
Carolina Balmoral
    Columbia M 33706
Carolina Shout
    Columbia M 33706
Steeplechase Rag
    Columbia M 33706
NOTE: Other titles do not include Ruby Braff. All titles also on *Jelly & James*, Sony Masterworks, MDK 52552 (CD).

Eddie Condon's[64]
May 26, 1975, Eddie Condon's, New York
Ruby Braff (cnt), Vic Dickenson (tb), Herb Hall (cl), Jimmy Andrews (p), Red Balaban (b), Ronnie Cole (dm)

You Made Me Love You
Way Down Yonder in New Orleans
Do You Know What It Means to Miss New Orleans
Fidgety Feet
I Want a Little Girl
Midnight in Moscow
Rose Room (Herb Hall feature)
California, Here I Come
Squeeze Me
Who's Sorry Now?

An article written by John S. Wilson from the *New York Times* is reprinted in *Eddie Condon's Scrapbook of Jazz,* titled "Eddie Condon Is Back at the Old Stand":[65]

> Mr. Braff is an unusually rewarding cornetist. He is now almost without a peer as an exponent of richly melodic jazz. His soft, low-register solos, his manner of slithering slyly form note to note and the brilliance of his biting attack when he moves into the upper register give his playing a constant sense of excitement. [The group then appearing at Condon's at 320 East 56th Street included Pee Wee Russell (cl), Marshall Brown (vtb), Ruby Braff (cnt), Jack Keller (p) and Ronnie Bedford (dm).]

That delightful book, coauthored with Hank O'Neal, also includes a photo from about this time of Ruby Braff (cnt), Cutty Cutshall (tb), Herb Hall (cl), and Leonard Gaskin (b).[66]

Eddie Condon's[67]
May 27, 1975, New York
Ruby Braff (cnt-1), Ed Polcer (cnt-2), Vic Dickenson (tb), Herb Hall (cl), Jimmy Andrews (p), Red Balaban (b), Ronnie Cole (dm)
Rosetta (1)
I Can't Give You Anything But Love (1)
Wrap Your Troubles in Dreams (1)
Struttin' with Some Barbecue (1, 2)

Ruby Braff (cnt), Jimmy Andrews (p), Red Balaban (b), Ronnie Cole (dm)
Just You, Just Me
Ain't Misbehavin'
Lover Come Back to Me
Someday You'll Be Sorry
Medley:
  Dinah
  I Got Rhythm

Add Ed Polcer (cnt-2), Vic Dickenson (tb), Herb Hall (cl)
Exactly Like You (1, 2)

Ruby Braff (cnt –1, voc), Ed Polcer (cnt-2), Vic Dickenson (tb), Herb Hall (cl), Jimmy Andrews (p), Red Balaban (b), Ronnie Cole (dm)
Japanese Sandman (2)
Keepin' Out of Mischief Now (2) (Braff voc but not cnt)
Love Me or Leave Me (2)
Mood Indigo (2)
Lady Be Good (1, 2)

Ruby Braff (cnt), Jimmy Andrews (p), Tommy Bryant (b), Ronnie Cole (dm)
Them There Eyes
Medley:
  I've Got a Right to Sing the Blues
  You've Changed
  The World Is Waiting for the Sunrise
Medley:
  Ghost of a Chance
  You Are Too Beautiful

Add Ed Polcer (cnt-2), Vic Dickenson (tb), Herb Hall (cl)
When You're Smiling (1, 2)

Ruby Braff (cnt-1), Ed Polcer (cnt-2), Vic Dickenson (tb), Herb Hall (cl), Brooks Kerr (p), Red Balaban (g), Tommy Bryant (b), Dottie Dodgion (dm)
My Honey's Lovin' Arms (2)
Baby, Won't You Please Come Home? (2)
Slow Boat to China (2)
I Would Do Anything for You (1, 2)

Ruby Braff (cnt), John Bunch (p), Red Balaban (g), Tommy Bryant (b), Dottie Dodgion (dm)
Sometimes I'm Happy
This Can't Be Love
Mean to Me (fragment)*
Blue and Sentimental *
I Want to Be Happy*
Cocktails for Two*
I Want a Little Girl*
Take the "A" Train*
NOTE: Recordings of all but the final six tunes, marked with an asterisk, are available but remain unissued.

Ruby Braff with Buzzy Drootin[68]
Two appearances during June 1975, Scotch 'n Sirloin Restaurant, Boston
Ruby Braff was a guest artist in a six piece band built around Al Drootin (cl, ss), Sonny Drootin (p), and Buzzy Drootin (dm)

The New Yorker[69] reported that Michael Moore was occasionally appearing with John Bunch during his engagement at Bradley's. The report mentioned that Moore was available because the "Ruby Braff–George Barnes Quartet [is], mystery of mysteries, unable to find work in New York." But fortunately, the group did perform at Carnegie Hall as part of the 1975 Newport Jazz Festival. Other performers in this program included Harry James and His Orchestra, and Buddy Rich and His Band. A stock photo of Ruby and George appears in the festival's program. The text includes a short description as follows:[70]

> Cornetist Ruby Braff and guitarist George Barnes have appeared on the past two Newport Festivals and have on both occasions won acclaim from audience and critics with a warm well-balanced program of material and a blending of instruments that is rarely heard in this day of watts and volts. The very lyrical style of Ruby has become legend in the past years. This combination is creating its own legend at every appearance.

John S. Wilson wrote the following in his review:[71]

> The Newport Jazz Festival which has eight big bands on tap this year, presented the first two, Buddy Rich's and Harry James's, on Sunday evening at Carnegie Hall. But although Mr. Rich's band is representative of the aggressively virtuosic present-day big jazz ensembles, and Mr. James's group typifies the steam-roller power of the swing-era bands, they were both upstaged by a foursome, the Ruby Braff–George Barnes Quartet, which slipped into the program between the two bands. Mr. Braff and Mr. Barnes are old hands at stealing other people's thunder. The quartet made its debut two years ago on the opening night of the 1973 Newport Festival as the appetizer preceding a reunion of the original Benny Goodman Quartet. And although the packed house had obviously come to hear Mr. Goodman, Teddy Wilson, Lionel Hampton, and Gene Krupa, the Braff–Barnes Quartet was the hit of the evening.

Ruby Braff–George Barnes Quartet: Newport Jazz Festival *The Trumpet and the Drum*[72]
June 29, 1975, Carnegie Hall, New York
Ruby Braff (cnt), George Barnes, Vinnie Corrao (g), Michael Moore (b)
Them There Eyes
They Can't Take That Away from Me
I'm Old Fashioned
Isn't It a Lovely Day to Be Caught in the Rain?
Why Was I Born

Nice Work If You Can Get It
Love Walked In
Ooh, That Kiss
NOTE: A recording of these tunes is available but remains unissued. At the time of publication, the complete concert, including the portions featuring Harry James and Buddy Rich is available for downloading from WolfgangsVault.com.

Summertime meant that the group could travel to Europe where audiences eagerly awaited them at the Grande Parade du Jazz in Nice.

Ruby Braff–George Barnes Quartet at the Grande Parade du Jazz[73]
July 20, 1975, 8–9 p.m., Dance Stage, Nice, France
Ruby Braff (cnt), George Barnes, Vinnie Corrao (g), Michael Moore (b)
Them There Eyes
Nice Work If You Can Get It
Spring Is Here
Unknown title
Take the "A" Train
They Can't Take That Away from Me
It Don't Mean a Thing
With Time to Love
You're Lucky to Me
Basin Street Blues
No One Else But You
I'm Old Fashioned
Ooh, That Kiss

Next, Ruby performed his first of two sets with Bobby Hackett. This one featured the two friends with only a rhythm section anchored by George Wein. A published photograph showing Ruby playing while Bobby listened is dated from 1969 but more likely it was taken during the following performance.[74] A copy is included in this book's photo section.

Grande Parade du Jazz: Nice Jazz Festival[75]
July 21, 1975, 8–9 p.m., Garden Stage, Nice, France
Ruby Braff, Bobby Hackett (cnt), George Wein, (p) Larry Ridley (b), Ray Mosca (dm)
There'll Be Some Changes Made
Someday You'll Be Sorry*
Am I Blue?
Big Butter and Egg Man*
Blues
You Stepped Out of a Dream (Hackett solo)

I Want to Be Happy
NOTE: Recordings of two tunes shown with an asterisk are available but remain unissued.

A photo from the March of Jazz program was taken in a restaurant in Nice in 1975.[76]

Grande Parade du Jazz: Nice Jazz Festival[77]
July 21, 1975, 11–12 midnight, Arena Stage, Nice, France
Ruby Braff (cnt), George Barnes, Vinnie Corrao (g), Michael Moore (b)
Love Walked In*
Goose Pimples
Here, There and Everywhere
Rockin' in Rhythm*
Love Me or Leave Me*
I Want a Little Girl
Unknown title
Solitude*
But Not for Me*
NOTE: Recordings of five tunes shown with an asterisk are available but remain unissued.

Trumpet Talk: Grande Parade du Jazz[78]
July 22, 1975, 10–11 p.m., Garden Stage, Nice France
Ruby Braff (cnt), Pee Wee Erwin (tp), Red Norvo (vib), Dorothy Donegan (p), Panama Francis (dm)
NOTE: Michael Moore was scheduled to be the bassist, but he appeared on a Benny Carter/Joe Venuti set, so bassist, if any, is not known. No documentation of titles performed has been located.

Ruby Braff Rehearsal for Evening Session at the Grande Parade du Jazz[79]
Ruby Braff, Bobby Hackett (cnt), George Barnes, Vinnie Corrao (g), Michael Moore (b)
Conversation
Undecided

Ruby Braff–George Barnes Quartet with Bobby Hackett at the Grande Parade du Jazz[80]
July 22–23, 1975, 12–1:00 a.m., Dance Stage, Nice, France
Ruby Braff, Bobby Hackett (cnt), George Barnes, Vinnie Corrao (g), Michael Moore (b)
NOTE: No documentation of titles performed has been located.

Ruby Braff–George Barnes Quartet: Music of Fred Astaire at the Grande Parade du Jazz[81]
July 23, 1975, 8–9 p.m., Dance Stage, Nice, France
Ruby Braff (cnt), George Barnes, Vinnie Corrao (g), Michael Moore (b)
NOTE: No documentation of titles performed has been located.

Remember Louis Armstrong: Grande Parade du Jazz[82]
July 23, 1975, Arena Stage, 10–11 p.m., Nice France
Bobby Hackett, Ruby Braff (cnt), Pee Wee Erwin, Joe Newman (tp), Earl Hines (p), Harley White (b), Eddie Graham (b)
NOTE: No documentation of titles performed has been located.

Grande Parade du Jazz: Nice Jazz Festival[83]
July 25, 1975, 12–1 a.m., Arena Stage, Nice, France, (started just after midnight, a moment after the end of July 24)
Ruby Braff (cnt), Red Norvo (vib), George Barnes, Vinnie Corrao (g), Michael Moore (b), Bobby Rosengarden (dm)
Lady Be Good
Sometimes I'm Happy
Exactly Like You
These Foolish Things
Tea for Two
NOTE: A recording of these tunes is available but remains unissued. Corrao takes first guitar solo on "Exactly Like You."

Ruby Braff–George Barnes Quartet with Pee Wee Erwin: Grande Parade du Jazz[84]
July 25, 1975, 7–8 p.m., Garden Stage, Nice, France
Ruby Braff (cnt), Pee Wee Erwin (tp), George Barnes, Vinnie Corrao (g), Michael Moore (b)
Unknown title
Misty (Braff out)
Jeepers Creepers
NOTE: The three tunes listed above closed the set; however, no documentation of earlier titles has been located.

Grande Parade du Jazz: Nice Jazz Festival[85]
July 25, 1975, 10–11 p.m., Arena Stage, Nice, France
Ruby Braff (cnt), Benny Carter (as), George Barnes, Vinnie Corrao (g), Michael Moore (b), Ray Mosca (dm)
Wrap Your Troubles in Dreams
Just You, Just Me

Mean to Me
Take the "A" Train
I Can't Get Started (Carter feature)
Sugar (Carter out)
Love Me or Leave Me
Lover Come Back to Me
NOTE: An audio recording of these tunes is available but remains unissued. A television broadcast was probably limited to "Just You, Just Me," "Mean to Me," and "Take the 'A' Train." Ruby said that he encouraged Benny Carter to play trumpet during part of this session; however, Carter declined, saying that he would not be as good as Ruby on this occasion. Of course, Benny Carter was a marvelous trumpeter player, so his remarks likely reflected his desire to avoid any sort of competition during this performance. Carter was being polite. It would have been fascinating to hear them perform together on brass instruments.

A photograph is available showing George Barnes, Ruby Braff, Vinnie Corrao, Bobby Hackett, Michael Moore, and Richard Sudhalter performing onstage during the next set.

Grande Parade du Jazz: Nice Jazz Festival[86]
July 26, 1975, Nice, France
Ruby Braff, Bobby Hackett (cnt), George Barnes, Vinnie Corrao (g), Michael Moore (b)
Rose Room, interpolating In a Mellotone

Add Dick Sudhalter
Sweet Lorraine
Sweet Georgia Brown
Once in a While* (Sudhalter with rhythm)
Sometimes I'm Happy (Braff with rhythm)
I Can't Get Started (Hackett with rhythm)

Add Ed Hubble (tb)
Them There Eyes
NOTE: A recording of these tunes, except one title marked with an asterisk, is available but remains unissued. My source for this recording was Dick Sudhalter. He omitted "Once in a While" due to his own modesty, knowing that my focus was on obtaining recordings by Ruby. I have very fond memories of my meeting and correspondence with Dick. He was truly, as is sometimes said, a gentleman and a scholar, as well as a sensitive musician.

Much later, Richard Sudhalter published an excellent book, *Lost Chords*. Steve Voce, in one of his columns, described Ruby's reactions to that book:[87]

> When Ruby decided to read Dick Sudhalter's magnificent 900-page book *Lost Chords* he found the huge tome unwieldy for one of his small stature. His solution was to rip each page out after he had read it and thus the book became lighter as he progressed through it. 'I thought it was excellent,' he told Dave Bennett, 'but don't tell Sudhalter.'

Grande Parade du Jazz: Nice Jazz Festival
July 26, 1975, Nice, France
Ruby Braff (cnt), Johnny Guarnieri (p), Michael Moore (b), Ray Mosca (dm)
Blue and Sentimental
NOTE: A recording of this tune is available but remain unissued. This is the first time Ruby performed with Johnny Guarnieri since their LP on the Bethlehem label that was recorded in 1954.

Ruby Braff: Grande Parade du Jazz[88]
July 27, 1975, 8–9 p.m., Dance Stage, Nice, France
Ruby Braff (cnt), Buddy Tate (ts), Kenny Drew (p), Major Holley (b), Eddie Graham (dm)
NOTE: No documentation of titles performed has been located.

Dixieland Jam Session: Grande Parade du Jazz[89]
July 28, 1975, 12–1 a.m., Dance Stage, Nice France, (started just after midnight, a moment after the end of July 27)
Maxim Saury (cl) with Ruby Braff (cnt), Wingy Manone (tp), Kenny Davern (ss), Herb Hall (cl), Joe Venuti (v), and others
NOTE: No documentation of titles performed has been located. The list of performing musicians is incomplete. July 27 was the closing day of the festival; however this set starts moments after midnight, making the date technically July 28.

Vinnie Corrao also recalled performances by the Braff–Barnes Quartet in Barcelona and in a castle along the France–Spain border.[90] Details are not traced at the time of publication.

The Ruby Braff–George Barnes Quartet performed for the final time at the Concord Jazz Festival. Ruby performed only one more time with George Barnes, at Dick Gibson's jazz party that began on August 30, just one month after their successes at the Grande Parade du Jazz. Truly this was one of the finest groups in the entire history of improvised music. Other performers in the Sunday program in Concord included Helen Humes, Teddy Wilson, and Bobby Hackett. The group had lasted since early rehearsals in 1973 and their debut at Carnegie Hall in July that year. It is perhaps fitting that the group's final performance was recorded at the Concord Summer Festival. While Ruby and George hated each other personally, they continued to produce beautiful music together. They both enjoyed the stimulating act of creating each performance.

Ruby Braff–George Barnes Quartet[91]
August 3, 1975, Concord Summer Festival, Concord, CA
Ruby Braff (cnt), George Barnes, Vinnie Corrao (g), Michael Moore (b)
NOTE: It is likely that the performances at the Concord Festival were recorded, but I have not been able to trace any details or to confirm that possibility.

The following three advertisements depict performances in this chapter:

Figure 12.1: Advertisement September 1973

THE WORLD OF MUSIC TRIBUTE

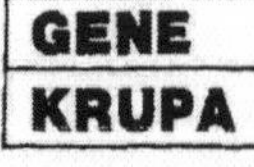

For the benefit of
THE GENE KRUPA RETARDED CHILDREN'S FOUNDATION
Starring
LIONEL HAMPTON • BUDDY RICH • LOUIS BELLSON
featuring
GEORGE BARNES • RUBY BRAFF • LEE CASTLE • JOHNNY DESMOND • DOC GOLDBERG • SONNY IGOE • ELVIN JONES • ROY BURNS • COZY COLE • TYREE GLENN • PEE WEE IRWIN • MAX DAMINSKY • BUDDY MILES • ANITA O'DAY • BOBBY SCOTT • GRADY TATE • CHARLIE VENTURA • HELEN WARD • TEDDY WILSON • and other friends, and the GENE KRUPA ALUMNI BAND directed by EDDIE SHU and WNEW STAR PERSONALITY—WILLIAM B. WILLIAMS. Produced by Peter C. Mallon and Bill Titone
THURSDAY, JANUARY 17, 1974—8 P.M.
at the

For Ticket Information call (212) 594-4400
TICKETS: $7.00-$10.00-$15.00
Tickets also at over 150 Ticketron outlets.
Call (212) 644-4400 for location near you.

Figure 12.2: Advertisement January 6, 1974

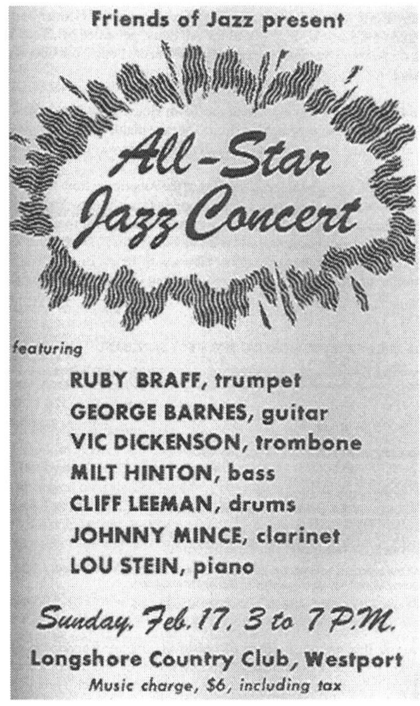

Figure 12.3: Advertisement February 17, 1974

Notes

[1] Voice of America tapes at Library of Congress, Record 238560p+1X, shelf number RGA 0189 (RWD 6580).
[2] John S. Wilson, *The New York Times*, January 23, 1974.
[3] Bert Whyatt and Derek Coller, "The Ruby Braff–George Barnes Quartet," *Jazz Journal International*, August 2001, 12–14.
[4] Photo by Jack Bradley, *The March of Jazz Celebrates Ruby Braff's 74th Birthday Party*, Arbors Records, 2001, 24.
[5] Bert Whyatt and Derek Coller, "The Ruby Braff–George Barnes Quartet," *Jazz Journal International*, August 2001, 12–14.
[6] Leonard Feather and Ira Gitler, *The Biographical Encyclopedia of Jazz* (New York: Oxford University Press, 1999), 76.
[7] *DownBeat*, August 15, 1974, 15.
[8] Charles Schwartz in private correspondence dated August 1, 2004.
[9] Advertisement, *The March of Jazz Celebrates Ruby Braff's 74th Birthday Party*, Arbors Records, 2001, 22.
[10] Will Friedwald citing *Variety*, September 19, 1973, and concert advertisement reproduced in *The March of Jazz Celebrates Ruby Braff's 74th Birthday Party*, Arbors Records, 2001, 22. Also Whitney Balliett published a review of the concert in *The New Yorker*, January 7, 1974, 42, mentioning many of the songs and a standing ovation at the end.

Advertised in *New York Times*, August 12, 1973 and August 26, 1973. Will Friedwald reported in private correspondence that half of the Lincoln Center concert was Rodgers and Hart material with the Braff-Barnes Quartet and half was Tony Bennett's regular concert set at the time.

[11] Whitney Balliett, *The New Yorker*, January 7, 1974, 42.

[12] Interview with Ruby Braff.

[13] Charles Schwartz in private correspondence dated August 1, 2004.

[14] Album notes for Concord Jazz CJ 7 *Braff/Barnes Quartet Salutes Rogers and Hart.*

[15] *Coda Magazine*, February 1974, 28 (the article reports Ruby's appearance in the past tense so it was prior to the publishing deadline for the issue).

[16] Advertisement, *New York Times*, January 6, 1974, and additional listing of musicians appearing in Bruce H. Klauber, *The World of Gene Krupa* (Ventura, CA: Pathfinder Publishing of California, 1990), 191.

[17] Manfred Selchow, *Ding Ding: A Bio-Discographical Scrapbook on Vic Dickenson* (Germany: Uhle & Kleinmann, 1998), 606. An advertisement for this concert is reproduced on 605.

[18] *New York Magazine*, February 11, 1974, 17, and February 4, 1974, 17.

[19] *New York Times*, March 16, 1974 with ending date of engagement published in *DownBeat* erroneously as March 23, March 28, 1974, 43. The opening date published in *The New Yorker*, March 11, 1974, 8. The closing date was published in *The New Yorker*, April 1, 1974, 7. Likely the engagement was extended, accounting for the differences in reports of the closing date. John S. Wilson, *New York Times*, March 16, 1974. Advertised in *New York Times*, March 6, 13, 16, 20, 23, 27, and 30, 1974, closing date listed in *New York Times*, March 10, 1977, March 17, 1977, and *New York Magazine*, March 18, 1974, and March 25, 1974, 20, and April 1, 1974, 19.

[20] *DownBeat*, February 14, 1974, 35—the quartet was announced to appear at some future time during 1974.

[21] Manfred Selchow, *Ding Ding: A Bio-Discographical Scrapbook on Vic Dickenson* (Germany: Uhle & Kleinmann, 1998), 608. An advertisement is reproduced on that page.

[22] *Jersey Jazz*, May 1974, 21, and Joseph Sullivan, *New York Times*, December 9, 1979. That article states that the concert was recorded by John Livingston, director of the library system.

[23] Eubie Blake is quoted on the jacket for the Concord Records album CR 126, *Live at the New School.*

[24] John S. Wilson, *New York Times*, April 28, 1974.

[25] Manfred Selchow, *Ding Ding: A Bio-Discographical Scrapbook on Vic Dickenson* (Germany: Uhle & Kleinmann, 1998), 611.

[26] Manfred Selchow, *Ding Ding: A Bio-Discographical Scrapbook on Vic Dickenson* (Germany: Uhle & Kleinmann, 1998), 612.

[27] George A. Borgman, "The One and Only Ruby Braff," *Mississippi Rag*, December 1995.

[28] Photo reproduced in *The March of Jazz Celebrates Ruby Braff's 74th Birthday Party*, Arbors Records, 2001, 22, and listed in *New York Times*, June 3, 1974, for "today at 12:15."

[29] *Milwaukee Journal*, Friday, June 14, 1974.

[30] David Meeker, *Jazz in the Movies, New Enlarged Edition* (New York: Da Capo, 1981), entry number 2422 on unnumbered page and personal conversation with Joe Sarno.

[31] Library of Congress, shelf number RGA 0251 (RWD 7073 A2-B4) and RGA 0257-02258 (RWD 7074-7057A1). The first tape excludes the titles with Bobby Hackett and Vic Dickenson.
[32] *The Jazz Family Album* 5 (East Stroudsburg, PA: Al Cohn Memorial Jazz Collection, 1997), 13.
[33] Max Jones, *Talking Jazz*, (New York: W. W. Norton and Company, 1988), photo number 16, published in unnumbered pages in second photo section in the book.
[34] Manfred Selchow, *Ding Ding: A Bio-Discographical Scrapbook on Vic Dickenson* (Germany, Uhle & Kleinmann, 1998), 620–621.
[35] Notes prepared by Eric Townley and supplied by Derek Coller.
[36] Notes prepared by Eric Townley and supplied by Derek Coller.
[37] Notes prepared by Eric Townley and supplied by Derek Coller.
[38] Notes prepared by Eric Townley and supplied by Derek Coller.
[39] Photo of this session reproduced in *The March of Jazz Celebrates Ruby Braff's 74th Birthday Party*, Arbors Records, 2001, 23.
[40] Photo, *The March of Jazz Celebrates Ruby Braff's 74th Birthday Party*, Arbors Records, 2001, 23.
[41] Notes prepared by Eric Townley and supplied by Derek Coller.
[42] Notes prepared by Eric Townley and supplied by Derek Coller.
[43] *DownBeat*, July 18, 1974, 10.
[44] Charles Swartz in private correspondence dated August 1, 2004.
[45] Charles Swartz in private correspondence dated August 1, 2004.
[46] *Coda Magazine*, July 1974, 28 and September 1974, 25.
[47] Bert Whyatt and Derek Coller, "The Ruby Braff–George Barnes Quartet," *Jazz Journal International*, August 2001, 12–14, and schedule in *New York Times*, August 11, 1974.
[48] Photo by Jack Bradley, *The March of Jazz Celebrates Ruby Braff's 74th Birthday Party*, Arbors Records, 2001, 22.
[49] Bert Whyatt and Derek Coller, "The Ruby Braff–George Barnes Quartet," *Jazz Journal International*, August 2001, 12–14, drawn from report in album notes.
[50] *DownBeat*, October 24, 1974, 50, listing in *Washington Post*, October 18, 1974.
[51] The German host announces the date as November 1; however, some sources list this performance on November 11, 1974. The video program was broadcast on WDR as *Jazz for Fun*, showing a copyright of 1990.
[52] John S. Wilson, *New York Times*, November 10, 1974.
[53] Howard E. Rischer, *Jazz Exposé: The NY Jazz Museum and the Power Struggle That Destroyed It* (Nashville, TN: Sundog Ltd., 2004), 62.
[54] *The New Yorker*, November 11, 1974, 17.
[55] Ruby mentioned this performance in a radio interview with Steve Voce from December 15, 1994.
[56] Joe Boughton (Joe reported that Jack Fine (cnt) played the first set as leader prior to Ruby's arrival).
[57] Ads in *New York Times*, December 2, 1974, and December 20, 1974, and listing in *New York Magazine*, December 23, 1974, 23, and *New York Magazine*, December 16, 1976, 29.
[58] Bert Whyatt and Derek Coller, "The Ruby Braff–George Barnes Quartet," *Jazz Journal International*, August 2001, 12–14. Sinclair Traill reviewed one performance in *Jazz Journal International*, April 1975, 22, but did not mention tunes played. *DownBeat*,

March 13, 1975 for closing date and June 19, 1975, 33–34 for review that included additional tune titles for one night of the performance (three sets).
[59] Ken Gallacher, *The Herald* (England), January 4, 1997.
[60] Ruby Braff's obituary, published in *The Daily Telegraph*, February 11, 2003.
[61] Miles Kington, *The Times*, February 26, 1975, 11.
[62] Miles Kington, *The Times*, December 13, 1975.
[63] Bert Whyatt and Derek Coller, "The Ruby Braff–George Barnes Quartet," *Jazz Journal International*, August 2001, 12–14.
[64] Information from Roland Hippenmeyer.
[65] Eddie Condon and Hank O'Neal, *Eddie Condon's Scrapbook of Jazz* (New York: Galahad Books, 1973) in the section "Third Street and Points North," pages are unnumbered.
[66] Eddie Condon and Hank O'Neal, *Eddie Condon's Scrapbook of Jazz*, New York, Galahad Books, 1973, in the section "Third Street and Points North," pages are unnumbered.
[67] Partially listed in Manfred Selchow, *Ding Ding: A Bio-Discographical Scrapbook on Vic Dickenson* (Germany: Uhle & Kleinmann, 1998), 653. *The New Yorker*, May 26, 1975, 6, lists this engagement.
[68] George A. Borgman, "The One and Only Ruby Braff," in *Mississippi Rag*, December 1995, 6.
[69] *The New Yorker*, June 23, 1975, 4.
[70] 1975 Newport Jazz Festival program, 1975, 31.
[71] *New York Times*, June 29, 1975.
[72] Library of Congress, MUSA7536B (1975 Newport Jazz Festival/NYC #4, Various Composers, Buddy Rich and His Orchestra, Ruby Braff–George Barnes Quartet, broadcast date August 18, 1975—presumably MUSA is Music USA?—also Library of Congress RGA 0282 (RWD7500 A2-7501). This is the debut of Vinnie Corrao with the quartet. Source of Corrao's comment: Bert Whyatt and Derek Coller, "The Ruby Braff–George Barnes Quartet," *Jazz Journal International*, August 2001, 12–14.
[73] Notes prepared by Derek Coller.
[74] Photo, *The March of Jazz Celebrates Ruby Braff's 74th Birthday Party*, Arbors Records, 2001, 21.
[75] Notes prepared by Derek Coller.
[76] Photo, *The March of Jazz Celebrates Ruby Braff's 74th Birthday Party*, Arbors Records, 2001, 23.
[77] Notes prepared by Derek Coller.
[78] Notes prepared by Derek Coller.
[79] Information from Roland Hippenmeyer.
[80] Notes prepared by Derek Coller.
[81] Notes prepared by Derek Coller.
[82] Notes prepared by Derek Coller.
[83] Notes prepared by Derek Coller.
[84] Notes prepared by Derek Coller.
[85] Information from Ed Burger and notes prepared by Derek Coller.
[86] While I have chosen not to mention the names of individuals who provided copies of each available recording, I will make an exception this time. Dick Sudhalter provided a copy of his recording during his lifetime, but he said that he had deleted his own performance. He told me of his delight in being included in this set with Ruby and Bobby but said he did not want to be compared to either of them. Dick helped me in other ways as well.

[87] Steve Voce, *Jazz Journal International*, May 2007.
[88] Notes supplied by Derek Coller.
[89] Notes prepared by Derek Coller.
[90] Source of Corrao's comment: Bert Whyatt and Derek Coller, "The Ruby Braff–George Barnes Quartet," *Jazz Journal International*, August 2001, 12–14.
[91] Leonard Feather, "Take Two Bands, Mix, Boil and Savor," *Los Angeles Times*, August 5, 1975.

Chapter 13

New York Clubs and International Tributes to Louis Armstrong

Ruby returned to Condon's following the final performance of the Braff-Barnes Quartet in California. A recording is available for the second night of his engagement that began on August 25. George Wein and Helen Humes joined the group for part of the performance. Then Ruby flew to Colorado for Dick Gibson's jazz party where he performed once again with George Barnes, in a group reminiscent of their famous quartet.

Eddie Condon's[1]
August 25–August 29, 1975, 144 West 54th Street, New York
Ruby Braff (cnt), Ed Polcer (tp), Vic Dickenson (tb), Herb Hall (cl), Jimmy Andrews (p), Red Balaban (b), Ronnie Cole (dm)
Performing Friday noon and evenings from Monday, August 25 through Saturday, August 29. This is the first time I have documented Ruby playing with Frank Tate.

Eddie Condon's[2]
August 26, 1975, New York
Ruby Braff (cnt), Dick Rath (tb), Herb Hall (cl), Red Richards (p), Red Balaban (b), Ronnie Cole (dm)
I've Found a New Baby
Am I Blue?
You're Driving Me Crazy
Ain't Misbehavin'
Sweethearts on Parade
Indiana
Muskrat Ramble
Sweet Georgia Brown
I Can't Give You Anything but Love
Struttin' with Some Barbecue
I Got Rhythm

Rosetta
Medley:
  Over the Rainbow
  When You're Smiling

Substitute George Wein (p) for Red Richards
Rose Room
When My Sugar Walks Down the Street
Medley:
  Basin Street Blues
  Lester Leaps In
All of Me

Ruby Braff (cnt), Dick Rath (tb), Herb Hall (cl), Red Richards (p), Frank Tate (b), Red Balaban (g), Ronnie Cole (dm), Helen Humes (voc)
Someday You'll Be Sorry
If I Could Be with You (voc HH)
On the Sunny Side of the Street (voc HH)
I Want to Be Happy
Sweet Lorraine

Substitute Jackie Williams (dm) for Ronnie Cole
Between the Devil and the Deep Blue Sea
Them There Eyes
The Song Is Ended
NOTE: A recording of these tunes is available but remains unissued.

Dick Gibson's 13th Annual Jazz Party: Ruby Braff with George Barnes[3]
August 30–September 1, 1975 Dick Gibson's Labor Day Party, Broadmoor Hotel, Colorado Springs, Colorado
Ruby Braff (cnt), George Barnes, Herb Ellis (g), Ray Brown (b)
Exactly Like You
These Foolish Things
Undecided
NOTE: A recording of these tunes is available but remains unissued.

A photo is available in the March of Jazz program that shows the following group of musicians that likely performed in another set at this party; however, it could come from another year at this event.[4]

Ruby Braff (cnt), Kenny Davern (ss), Flip Phillips (ts), George Barnes (g), Milt Hinton (b, possible), Gus Johnson (dm)
No further details are known.

The Gibson Jazz Party is the last documented time that Ruby Braff and George Barnes appeared on the same program. Ruby reflected on their relationship at length. He felt that they produced superb music, but hated each other. Ruby felt much of their conflict was rooted in George's drinking. He also resented that he did a disproportionate amount of the work to obtain engagements. Ruby told me that the group failed because it never had "good management." In the end, this developed into a mutual lack of personal respect. This ended their wonderful artistic partnership. Many feel that this collaboration was one of the finest small groups in the entire history of jazz music.

John McDonough wrote in *Coda Magazine* and *DownBeat* that he asked Ruby Braff to perform in the special *Soundstage* program taped by Public Television as a tribute to John Hammond. This program featured Benny Goodman, George Benson, Benny Carter, Teddy Wilson, Red Norvo, Milt Hinton, Jo Jones, and other artists. Ruby was upset that his fee would have been nominal ($250 plus travel expenses) while Hammond was a wealthy man. McDonough apologized for the low fee he could offer.[5] Ruby continued, speaking very directly, "Look. When I play anywhere, I pick the musicians. I pick the songs. Nobody else. I don't accompany anybody. I'm not interested in your goddam show. Anything else you want to say?"

Ruby played in a number of benefit performances for musicians, but avoided tributes of the sort represented by this program. The national exposure in such a friendly setting would have probably brought Ruby favorable press, and perhaps more engagements and record sales, but that was not how he saw his choice. He felt underappreciated.

I remember watching the original broadcast of this spirited program on television. Perhaps Ruby's refusal to participate was still a carryover from his much earlier argument with John Hammond while they were together at Columbia records.

John McDonough continued, mentioning an engagement he attended featuring Ruby with Teddy Wilson a few months later. I have not been able to trace that engagement.

Soundstage: Tribute to John Hammond[6]
Fall, 1975, WTTW Television Studios, Chicago
Ruby did not appear.

Ruby Braff Quartet[7]
September 21, 1975, Eddie Condon's, 144 West 54th Street, New York

Jimmy Ryan's
October 1, 1975, 154 West 54th Street, New York
Ruby Braff (cnt), Bobby Pratt (tb), Joe Muranyi (ss, cl), Mickey Crane (p), Ted Sturgis (g), Eddie Locke (dm)
Lover Come Back to Me (incomplete)
When It's Sleepy Time Down South

Rosetta

Norman Simmons (p) replaces Mickey Crane
When You're Smiling
I Want a Little Girl
Just You, Just Me
Dick Katz (p) was the pianist on some nights[8]
NOTE: A recording of these tunes is available but remains unissued.

Ruby Braff Sextet[9]
October 6–22, 1975, Jimmy Ryan's, 154 West 54th Street, New York
Ruby appeared nightly except Sundays when Max Kaminsky led the band. He replaced Roy Eldridge who was away from his long-term engagement.

Ruby Braff and Teddy Wilson[10]
Unknown performance mentioned by John McDonough

Ruby few to Europe in mid-October for the Satchmo Remembered Tour. The tour covered 12 countries in 30 days. That alone brought to mind Louis Armstrong's pace as he traveled the world.

Louis Armstrong's Music: George Wein's Satchmo Remembered Tour[11]
Beginning late October 1975
Performances also included Umea, Sweden, Warsaw, Poland, Gothenburg, Sweden, Aarhus, Denmark (Jazzhus), Stockholm (Ballet Theater on the Square, performance televised), and Brussels (October 31, 1974).

Louis Armstrong's Music[12]
November 1, 1975, De Doelen, Rotterdam, The Netherlands
Charles Mingus Quintet also performed at this concert.

Louis Armstrong's Music: George Wein's Satchmo Remembered Tour[13]
November 2, 1975, Ostend, Belgium

Performances continued in Paris (Theatre Nationale de Chaillot, televised), Kamen, Germany, and Baden, Switzerland.

New York Jazz Repertory Company[14]
November 9, 1975, Philharmonic Hall, Berlin
Joe Newman, Pee Wee Erwin, Jimmy Maxwell (tp), Ed Hubble (tb), Kenny Davern (cl, sax), Dick Hyman (p, org), Marty Grosz (g), George Duvivier (b), Bobby Rosengarden (dm), Blanche Thomas (voc)
West End Blues
New Orleans Function
Chimes Blues

St. Louis Blues
Medley:
  Ain't Misbehavin'
  Laughin' Louis

Ruby Braff (cnt) with Hyman, Grosz, Duvivier, Rosengarden
Medley:
  I'm Shooting High
  Save It Pretty Mama

Ruby Braff (cnt) with full New York Jazz Repertory Company
Song of the Islands
Hello Dolly
Mack the Knife
When It's Sleepy Time Down South

Marty Grosz recounted the following story from about this time:[15]

> [Rosengarden] used to do a thing during a performance of this Louis Armstrong thing on 'Mack the Knife' that morphed into a bongo solo. What that had to do with anything was anybody's guess. But it was an accommodation to feature Rosengarden's bongos. About a week into the trip the bongos disappeared. It wasn't me. I don't think it was Kenny [Davern]. I can't speak for Ruby.

There are suggestions of two additional performances in Berlin that would have been on either November 9 or 10. Information about locations is lacking at the time of publication. November 9 falls on a Sunday, so there is a possibility of both matinee and evening performances on that date. It is also possible, but unlikely, that the group returned to Berlin later in the tour, perhaps accounting for the following reports.

New York Jazz Repertory Company[16]
November 1975, Berlin
Joe Newman, Pee Wee Erwin, Jimmy Maxwell (tp), Ed Hubble (tb), Kenny Davern (cl, sax), Dick Hyman (p, org), Marty Grosz (g), George Duvivier (b), Bobby Rosengarden (dm), Blanche Thomas (voc)
West End Blues
Free as a Bird
Oh, Didn't He Ramble
Chimes Blues
Cake Walking Babies from Home
Potato Head Blues
St. Louis Blues
You've Been a Good Old Wagon
Willie the Weeper

Wild Man Blues
Weather Bird Rag
SOL Blues
Ding Dong Daddy

New York Repertory Company[17]
November 1975, Berlin
Joe Newman, Pee Wee Erwin, Jimmy Maxwell (tp), Ed Hubble (tb), Kenny Davern (cl, sax), Dick Hyman (p, org), Marty Grosz (g), George Duvivier (b), Bobby Rosengarden (dm), Blanche Thomas (voc)
Ding Dong Daddy
Pennies from Heaven
Medley
  Laughin' Louis
  Two unknown titles
Jeepers Creepers
Unknown title
Song of the Islands

Louis Armstrong's Music: George Wein's Satchmo Remembered Tour[18]
November 1975
Performances continued at Lausanne, Switzerland (November 11, 1974); Belgrade, Yugoslavia; Zagreb, Yugoslavia; Bologna, Italy; Genoa, Italy; Teatro Comunale Dell'Opera); Barcelona, Spain (10th Festival Internacional de Jazz); Marseilles, France (Theatre des varietes); Cascais, Portugal (5th Festival Internacional de Jazz de Cascais). There is a conflicting report of dates, listing November 11 for the performance in Marseilles.[19]

Pee Wee Erwin wrote the following: "The performances turned in by Ruby Braff, who did a 20-minute solo spot on every program, were likewise superb. Ruby is a very creative musician, and his performances kept me pretty happy musically."[20]

The tour ended with the concert in Portugal. Kenny Davern and Marty Grosz left the tour immediately rather than travel to Portugal due to rumors of political unrest.[21] Ruby returned home and appeared as a guest artist for one night at Eddie Condon's club. There were other guests that evening, so the combinations of musicians changed frequently. The collective personnel were Ruby Braff (cnt), Vic Dickenson (tb), Herb Hall (cl), John Bunch (p), Red Balaban (b), Connie Kay (dm), Wayne Wright (g), Jo Jones (dm), Joe Bushkin (p), Milt Hinton (b), and Jane Harvey (voc).

Eddie Condon's[22]
January 6, 1976, New York
Ruby Braff (cnt), Vic Dickenson (tb), Herb Hall (cl), John Bunch (p), Red Balaban (b), Connie Kay (dm)

Exactly Like You
These Foolish Things
Sometimes I'm Happy
Indiana

Ruby Braff (cnt), John Bunch (p), Red Balaban (b), Connie Kay (dm)
You're Driving Me Crazy
It's Only a Paper Moon
The World Is Waiting for the Sunrise
What Is There to Say?

Add Herb Hall (cl)
Keepin' Out of Mischief Now

Add Vic Dickenson (tb)
Please Don't Talk About Me When I'm Gone

Ruby Braff (cnt), John Bunch (p), Wayne Wright (g), Milt Hinton (b), Connie Kay (dm)
Tea for Two
All of Me
My Funny Valentine

Ruby Braff (cnt), Joe Bushkin (p), Wayne Wright (g), Milt Hinton (b), Jo Jones (dm)
You're Driving Me Crazy interpolating Moten Swing

Add Jane Harvey (voc)
She's Funny That Way

Ruby Braff (cnt), John Bunch (p), Wayne Wright (g), Red Balaban (b), Connie Kay (dm)
Linger Awhile
Medley:
  Basin Street Blues
  I Got Rhythm

Add Herb Hall (cl), Vic Dickenson (tb)
Sugar
Them There Eyes
NOTE: A recording of these tunes is available but remains unissued.

Eddie Condon's[23]
Ruby Braff sat in with house band—no further details

Scott Hamilton reported that he appeared as a guest sitting in a few times at Condon's during 1976 and 1977;[24] however, I have not located information about specific dates.

Bob Wilber and His Champs[25]

January 18, 1976, 6–10 p.m., New Jersey Jazz Society, Watchung View Inn, Routes 202–206, Pluckemin, New Jersey
Ruby Braff (cnt), Bob Wilber (cl, ss), Wayne Wright (g), George Duvivier (b), Fred Stoll (dm)

Sunday
    unissued, recording available
Somebody Stole My Gal
    unissued, recording available
Sugar
    Arbors Records ARCD 19328
Lady Be Good
    unissued, recording available
When You're Smiling
    Arbors Records ARCD 19328
Somebody Loves Me
    unissued, recording available
Here's That Rainy Day (Wilber feature)
    unissued, recording available
These Foolish Things
    Arbors Records ARCD 19328
All of Me
    Arbors Records ARCD 19328
Jeepers Creepers
    unissued, recording available
I Would Do Anything for You
    unissued, recording available
As Long As I Live
    unissued, recording available
Warm Valley (Wilber and Duvivier)
    unissued, recording available
Skylark (Wright solo)
    unissued, recording available
Bass Improvisation (Duvivier)
    unissued, recording available
Fine and Mellow
    Arbors Records ARCD 19328
Swing That Music
    unissued, recording available

NOTE: Arbors Records ARCD 19328 is titled *Soprano Summit—1995. . . . And More*. It contains other performances recorded by the New Jersey Jazz Society in 1975. A complete recording of the above performance is available. I was delighted to point out the quality of this performance to Mat Domber following my auditioning it for this book while visiting the Institute of Jazz Studies.

George Wein opened his Storyville Club in New York in early 1976, located at 41 East 58th Street.[26] As a policy, he stated that he did not plan to advertise performers and that the performers would change every night. The club operated with various musicians' styles on various nights during this time. Musicians were encouraged to sit in. People were encouraged to phone for information about the musicians who would appear on a given evening. Given the lack of advertising, I have not determined if Ruby Braff performed in this club. If he did, probably it would have been in an appearance with other musicians he selected. This policy changed a few months later. Then, engagements were extended and publicized: however, Ruby was not listed among those musicians.

Ruby Braff[27]
February 18–28, 1976 (Wednesdays through Saturdays, alternating with Max Kaminsky), Jimmy Ryan's, 154 West 54th Street, New York

Ruby Braff Quartet[28]
February 22, 1976, 8 p.m., Eddie Condon's, 144 West 54th Street, New York
Red Balaban (b) was the owner of the club and often led the house band. The band often included Vic Dickenson (tb), Herb Hall (cl), Ed Polcer (tp), Jimmy Andrews (p), and Connie Kay (dm)

Notes

[1] *New York Times*, August 24, 1975.
[2] Date listed in *The New Yorker*, August 25, 1975, 4, and *New York Magazine*, September 1, 1975, 17.
[3] Stanley Dance mentioned Ruby's appearance in *Jazz Journal International*, October 1975, 10. A photo of Ruby with Ray Brown and George Barnes is reproduced in *The March of Jazz Celebrates Ruby Braff's 74th Birthday Party*, Arbors Records, 2001, 23.
[4] Photo is reproduced in *The March of Jazz Celebrates Ruby Braff's 74th Birthday Party*, Arbors Records, 2001, 24.
[5] John McDonough, *DownBeat*, January 27, 1977, 17–18.
[6] *Coda Magazine*, November 1975, 33 (John McDonough wrote "Ruby Braff was curt and totally uninterested unless he could pick his sidemen [to appear on the *Soundstage* tribute to John Hammond program]." Also, *DownBeat*, January 27, 1977, 17–18 and 38–39.
[7] *New York Times*, September 21, 1975, but not mentioned in *The New Yorker*, September 22, 1975, 4.
[8] *New York Magazine*, October 13, 1975, 23.
[9] *New York Times*, October 5, 1975 and *The New Yorker*, October 6, 1975, 6, October 13, 1975, 6, and October 20, 1975, 6, and *New York Magazine*, October 27, 1975, 20.

[10] John McDonough, *DownBeat*, January 27, 1977, 17–18.
[11] See Warren W. Vaché, Sr., *Pee Wee Erwin: This Horn for Hire* (Metuchen, NJ: Scarecrow Press, 1987), 329–333, for further information about this tour.
[12] Information from Han Schulte.
[13] See Warren W. Vaché, Sr., *Pee Wee Erwin: This Horn for Hire* (Metuchen, NJ, Scarecrow Press, 1987), 331–332, for further information about this tour.
[14] Information from Michael Frohne.
[15] Marty Grosz, quoted in Edward H. Meyer, *The Life and Music of Kenny Davern: Just Four Bars* (Lanham, MD: Scarecrow Press, 2010), 122.
[16] Information from Michael Frohne.
[17]Information from Michael Frohne.
[18] See Warren W. Vaché, Sr., *Pee Wee Erwin: This Horn for Hire* (Metuchen, NJ, Scarecrow Press, 1987), 329–333, for further information about this tour.
[19] Edward H. Meyer, *The Life and Music of Kenny Davern: Just Four Bars* (Lanham, MD: Scarecrow Press, 2010), 122.
[20] Warren W. Vaché, Sr., *Pee Wee Erwin: This Horn for Hire* (Metuchen, NJ: Scarecrow Press, 1987), 329-333
[21] Edward H. Meyer, *The Life and Music of Kenny Davern: Just Four Bars* (Lanham, MD: Scarecrow Press, 2010), 122
[22] Listed in *The New Yorker*, January 5, 1976, 6.
[23] *New York Magazine*, January 12, 1976, 24.
[24] Scott Hamilton in private correspondence.
[25] New Jersey Jazz Society Archive, restricted tapes held at the Institute for Jazz Studies.
[26] Reported in consecutive issues of *The New Yorker* starting in March 1976.
[27] *The New Yorker*, February 16, 1976, 6, February 23, 1976, 6, March 1, 1987, 6 and *New York Magazine*, February 26, 1976, 24.
[28] *New York Times*, February 22, 1976, and *The New Yorker*, February 23, 1976, 6.

Ruby Braff in late teens in mid-1940s in York Beach, Maine. Charlie Terrace, Ray Frazee, Ruby, Izzy Sklar, Sammy Margolis (from the March of Jazz program).

Mahogany Hall, probably from 1952. Dick LeFave, Buzzy Drootin, Ruby, John Field, Ivan Wainwright, Pee Wee Russell (from the March of Jazz program).

Another view at Mahogany Hall, Boston probably from 1952, John Field, Ruby, Ivan Wainwright, Pee Wee Russell (from the March of Jazz program).

Ruby (standing at far right) as jazz soloist with the Benny Goodman Orchestra, November 9, 1954. Trumpets: Carl Poole, Chris Griffin, Bernie Privin; Trombones: Will Bradley, Cutty Cutshall, Vernon Brown; Drums: Bobby Donaldson; Bass: George Duvivier; Piano: Mel Powell; Guitar: Steve Jordan; Saxes: Hymie Schertzer, Paul Ricci, Boomie Richman, Al Klink, Sol Schlinger (not necessarily in that order); Benny and Ruby (from the March of Jazz program).

Ruby and Lester Young at Newport, July 17, 1955. Photo by Bill Spilka (from the March of Jazz program).

Ruby with Louis Armstrong, 1957 (from the March of Jazz program).

Timex Television Show, April 30, 1958. Ruby, Louis Armstrong, Jack Teagarden. Photo by Jack Bradley (from the March of Jazz program).

Ruby with Louis Armstrong at Ohio Valley Jazz Festival, Cincinnati, Ohio, August 1962. Photo by Duncan Schiedt.

Jack Crystal presents an award to Ruby at Central Plaza, New York City, in 1963. Crystal produced weekly sessions at Central Plaza and was Milt Gabler's brother-in-law. Milt was the owner of the Commodore Music Shop. Photo by Jack Bradley (from the March of Jazz program).

Ruby at the Bay State Race Track in Foxborough, Massachusetts, August 1963 with Benny Morton, Zoot Sims, possibly Buzzy Drootin, Ruby, possibly Alex Cirin, Bud Freeman, Pee Wee Russell, Dick Wellstood (from the March of Jazz program).

Ruby, circa 1965, Photo by Jack Bradley (from the March of Jazz program). This photo appeared in the Jazz Expo '68 program and may have been taken in 1966 or 1967.

Mondi's Crystal Ship, Greenvale, New York, November 1965. Jack Lesberg, Tony Aless, Morey Feld, Hank D'Amico, Ruby, Cutty Cutshall. Photo by Jack Bradley (from the March of Jazz program).

Boston Globe Jazz Festival, January 20, 1967. Pee Wee Russell, George Wein, Lou McGarity, Ruby, Don Lamond, Bud Freeman, Edmond Hall. Photo by Jack Bradley (from the March of Jazz program).

Benny Goodman party celebrating 30th anniversary of Carnegie Hall concert, January 16, 1968. Benny, Ruby, Jess Stacy, Lionel Hampton. John S. Wilson (with glasses behind Ruby) and George Avakian (smiling above Benny). Photo by Popsie (from the March of Jazz program).

Zoot Sims and Ruby at Kenny's Pub, April 21, 1968. Photo by Jack Bradley (from the March of Jazz program).

Newport All Stars Tour, 1969. Red Norvo, Don Lamond, Ruby, George Wein, Larry Ridley, Barney Kessel. Photo by Jack Bradley (from the March of Jazz program).

Metropole, New York City, late '60's, Johnny Giuffrida, Cutty Cutshall, Ruby, Bob Wilber. Photo by Jack Bradley (from the March of Jazz program).

Tony Bennett, Wayne Wright, John Giuffrida, Ruby, and George Barnes at Downtown Sound, New York, June 1973. Photo by Hank O'Neal.

Ruby Braff–George Barnes Quartet, August 13, 1974. Michael Moore, Wayne Wright, Ruby, and George. Photo by Jack Bradley (from the March of Jazz program).

Ruby and Bobby Hackett at Nice, July 21, 1975 (from the March of Jazz program).

Ruby and Tony Bennett at Pizza Express, London, July 1976. Photo by Tim Motion (from the March of Jazz program).

Dick Hyman and Ruby at Downtown Sound, New York, April 1977. Photo by Hank O'Neal (from the March of Jazz program).

Woody Herman and Ruby at Downtown Sound, March 13, 1980. Photo by Hank O'Neal.

Ruby and Bud Freeman on a Swedish ferry boat in 1980. Photo by Gunnar Holmberg (from the March of Jazz program).

Ruby and Slam Stewart, Nice, France, July 21, 1980. Photo by Sir Lawrence Collins.

Ruby, Nice, France, July 21, 1980. Photo by Sir Lawrence Collins.

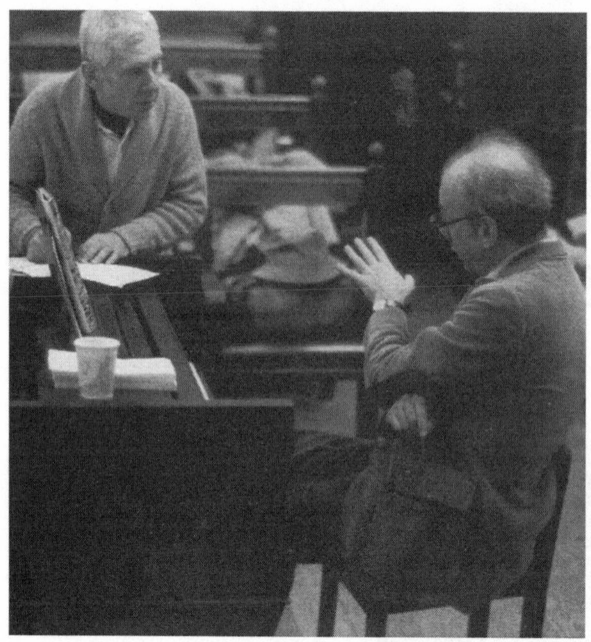

Rehearsing with Dick Hyman at the Church of the Heavenly Rest, New York City, April 1982 (from the March of Jazz program). Photo by Nancy Miller Elliott.

Ruby, John Bunch, Phil Flanigan, Chris Flory at Vanguard Recording Studio, New York, December 15, 1983. Photo by Hank O'Neal.

October 21, 1984 (from left: Benny Carter, Scott Hamilton, Bob Haggart, and Ruby. Ruby penciled in Hag's jacket in his copy of the photo because everyone was supposed to wear a black tux and Hag didn't. Photo by Hank O'Neal (from the March of Jazz program).

Clark Terry and Ruby, October 11, 1985, on the S/S *Norway* during the Floating Jazz Festival. Photo by Hank O'Neal (from the March of Jazz program).

Ruby's smile shows his satisfaction following four days of recording session for Arbors Records. From left: Sherry Hustad, Mat Domber, Ruby, Tom Hustad, and Rachel Domber outside Nola Studios in New York on July 28, 2000. Photo by Al Lipsky.

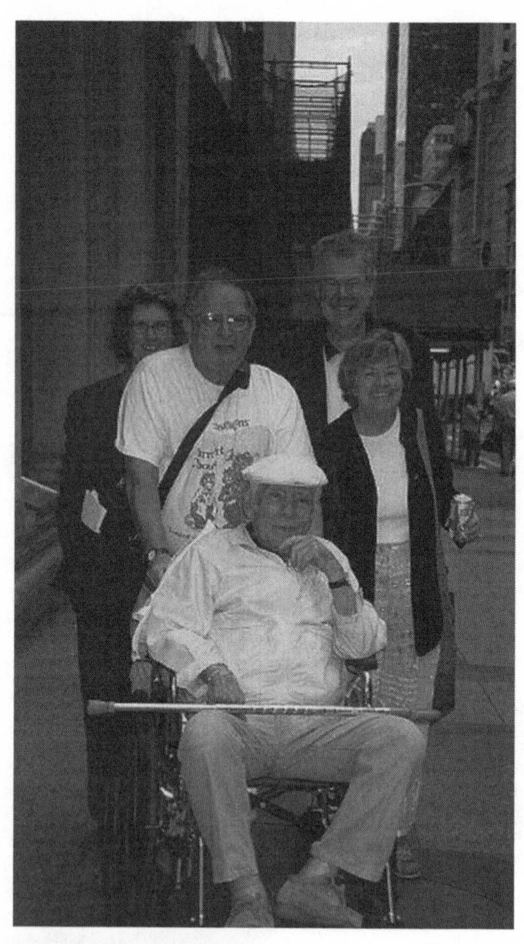

Ruby with boyhood friend, Nat Hentoff, at the March of Jazz, March 2001. Photo by Al Lipsky.

Ruby at the piano during sound check prior to the start of the March of Jazz, March 17, 2001. Photo by Al Lipsky.

At Nola Studios following completion of Ruby's last day in a recording studio, June 14, 2002. The Victoria Records session followed two days of recording for Arbors Records. Tom Hustad, Ruby, Bucky Pizzarelli. Photo by Al Lipsky.

THE MARCH OF JAZZ CELEBRATES

RUBY BRAFF'S

74TH BIRTHDAY PARTY

Featuring the All-Stars

Howard Alden
Harry Allen
John Allred
Ben Aronov
Joe Ascione
Dan Barrett
Ruby Braff
John Bunch
Joe Bushkin
Bill Charlap
Anat Cohen
Greg Cohen
Joe Cohn
Jackie Coon
Kenny Davern
Tony DeNicola
Lorraine Desmarais
Peter Ecklund
Eddie Erickson
Phil Flanigan
Dave Frishberg
Allan Ganley
Bobby Gordon
Wycliffe Gordon
Dave Green
Marty Grosz
Jake Hanna
Dick Hyman
Nobuo Ishida
Jane Jarvis
Jerry Jerome
Jon-Erik Kellso
Rebecca Kilgore
Yoichi Kimura
Jack Lesberg
Sherrie Maricle
George Masso
Dave McKenna
Ed Metz Jr.
Tommy Newsom
Michiko Ogawa
Nicki Parrott
Ken Peplowski
Flip Phillips
Bucky Pizzarelli
Randy Reinhart
Randy Sandke
Bryan Shaw
Daryl Sherman
Karolina Strassmayer
Ralph Sutton
Frank Tate
Johnny Varro
Jon Wheatley
Joe Wilder
Jackie Williams
Chuck Wilson

Friday, March 16 to Sunday, March 18, 2001

at the Sheraton Sand Key Resort, Clearwater Beach, Florida

With special performances by **The Johnny Varro Swing 7 • Joe Bushkin**
Marty Grosz and The Orphan Newsboys • Sherrie Maricle's Five Play • The Yo Kimura Trio
Sonny LaRosa & America's Youngest Jazz Band • The Howard Alden-Dan Barrett Quintet

And a Special Recital by Honoree Jane Jarvis celebrating her 85th year.

PRESENTED BY

ARBORS  RECORDS

Cover of the March of Jazz program from 2001 honoring Ruby on his 74th birthday. Presented by Arbors Records. Ruby autographed my copy writing, "To my wonderful friends Tom and Sherry from your buddy, Ruby Braff." The photo shows Ruby's head matched with Marlon Brando's body from *The Godfather*. Ruby was very pleased with this design, created for his Arbors release *The Cape Godfather*. That title was derived from Ruby's residence on Cape Cod.

Chapter 14

Ruby Braff: European Tours

Ruby had toured internationally for a decade; however, his reputation had grown to the point that he had become a major attraction, especially in Europe. His success at George Wein's annual festivals in Nice, France, provided an opportunity for his British fans to record many of his performances. In turn, this led to UK tours with increasing frequency. Ruby delighted in the support of his fans in the United Kingdom, where he performed to enthusiastic audiences in all his engagements. His recordings for Sonet, while made in New York, had broader distribution in Europe than in the US. The following session is the first time that Ruby recorded with Bucky Pizzarelli, an association they both maintained for many years. They had been together in clubs on previous occasions. This is also his first recording with Jimmy Rowles, although their paths had also crossed in the past. In April, Ruby traveled to Chicago for a booking at Rick's Café Americain followed by his departure for England in June.

Ruby Braff: Them There Eyes
March 23, 1976, Downtown Sound, New York
Ruby Braff (cnt), Dick Katz (p), Bucky Pizzarelli (g), Bill Crow (b), Connie Kay (dm)
Swinging on a Star
    Sonet (E) SNTF 713, (E) SNTCD 713, (G) 0602498148891 (CD)
It's the Same Old South
    Sonet (E) SNTF 713, (E) SNTCD 713, (G) 0602498148891 (CD)
I've Grown Accustomed to Her Face
    Sonet (E) SNTF 713, (E) SNTCD 713, (G) 0602498148891 (CD)
I've Grown Accustomed to Her Face (alternate take)
    Sonet (E) 0602498148891 (CD)
Love Lies
    Sonet (E) SNTF 713, (E) SNTCD 713, (G) 0602498148891 (CD)
Love Lies (alternate take)

Sonet (E) 0602498148891 (CD)
I Must Have That Man
Sonet (E) 0602498148891 (CD)

March 24, 1976
Jimmy Rowles (p) replaces Dick Katz

Add: Vic Dickenson (tb)
Yesterdays
Sonet (E) SNTF 713, (E) SNTCD 713, (G) 0602498148891 (CD)
Medley
I'm Pulling Through
Sonet (E) SNTF 713, (E) SNTCD 713, (G) 0602498148891 (CD)
It's the Little Things That Mean So Much
Sonet (E) SNTF 713, (E) SNTCD 713, (G) 0602498148891 (CD)
Them There Eyes
Sonet (E) SNTF 713, (E) SNTCD 713, (G) 0602498148891 (CD)
Why Was I Born?
Sonet (E) SNTF 713, (E) SNTCD 713, (G) 0602498148891 (CD)
Dream Dancing
Sonet (E) SNTF 713, (E) SNTCD 713, (G) 0602498148891 (CD)
Tea for Two
Sonet (E) SNTF 713, (E) SNTCD 713, (G) 0602498148891 (CD)
Dinah
Sonet (E) 0602498148891 (CD)
Big Blue
Sonet (E) 0602498148891 (CD)
NOTE: All titles also on Sonet (Sp) 4358, (F) VG 408-SNTF 713, (J) KUX-17N. "It's the Same Old South" also released on a sampler LP Sonet JUB-5 titled *Sonet's Jublieum Serie 5. Jazz 1956-1976.*

Ruby Braff[1]
April 13, 1976, Eddie Condon's, 144 West 54th Street, New York
Ruby performed with the regular sextet, perhaps unchanged from his February appearance.

Ruby Braff Quartet
April 23, 1976 as part of a longer booking, Rick's Café Americain, Holiday Inn, Lake Shore Drive, Chicago
Ruby Braff (cnt), Joe Johnson (p), Joe Levenson (b), Marshall Thompson (dm)

Will Leonard attended one performance and wrote the following review:[2]

> Ruby Braff is one of those artists who is a giant in his own realm, although he is an unknown to devotees of the Johnny Carson and Merv Griffin shows. He's

> a big fish in a little pond—a jazz man whose name is known nationwide, but only within the intimate circles of the 'righteous' music.
>
> His appearance at Rick's Café Americain, in the Holiday Inn on Lake Shore Drive, is a momentous occasion for jazz fans who know of him only by reputation or by phonograph records. It seems as if he hasn't played this town since an occasion in his youth when he opened at the late, lamented Blue Note, and either quit or was fired within hours of his inaugural set.
>
> Reuben plays one of the gentlest trumpets, cajoling and consoling, sweet talking you at the same time that it sounds cynical. It's in low key, it's thoughtful, it noodles along as if it doesn't give a rip what you think—it's just telling you how Ruby Braff feels at the moment. And that's mighty impressive, for Ruby has been around. [It is] a mighty fine quartet. And that's the way it sounds.

Ruby had appeared with Tony Bennett in Chicago at the Palmer House in April 1971 for a ten-day engagement. He did appear a few times in the 1950s (including three times at the Blue Note) and 1960s in Chicago, but not on a regular basis.

Ruby Braff toured the UK from June 14 through July 8.[3] Twenty-one engagements were scheduled. The following locations are noted: 100 Club in London; the Louis Armstrong Memorial Concert at Fairfield Hall, Croydon; the Crown, Codsall; Jazz Cellar, Stockport; and other venues. The Lennie Felix Trio provided accompanyment on at least nine dates, but other accompanists included the Alex Welsh band, the Eddie Thompson Trio, and Benny Simkins's Sextet. *Melody Maker*[4] also reported that Ruby played with Brian Lemon, Keith Ingham, and Lennie Hastings during this tour at various times. The following specifics were published prior to the performances, although Brian Lemon is not listed on any of these published dates.

Ruby Braff Tour:

June 14, 1976: Ruby Braff with the Lennie Felix Trio, County Arms, Blaby, England (near Leicester)
June 15, 1976: Ruby Braff with the Kenny Stewart Trio, McLellan Galleries, Glasgow, Scotland

Ruby Braff in Edinburgh
June 16, 1976, 127 Club, Edinburgh, Scotland
Ruby Braff (cnt) plus the Kenny Stewart Trio, other musicians unknown
Lady Be Good
Sweet Lorraine
Hey Lawdy Mama
I Can't Get Started
Take the "A" Train
I Can't Give You Anything but Love (incomplete)
You Took Advantage of Me (incomplete)

Medley:
  Mood Indigo
  I Got Rhythm
Jeepers Creepers
NOTE: A recording of these tunes is available but remains unissued.

Ruby Braff at Seven Dials Pub[5]
June 17, 1976, Seven Dials Pub, Covent Garden, London
Ruby Braff (cnt), Lennie Felix (p), Harvey Weston (b), Johnny Richardson (dm)
Lady Be Good
These Foolish Things
Exactly Like You
Sugar
Moonglow
Take the "A" Train
Pennies from Heaven
In a Mellotone
I Cover the Waterfront
Them There Eyes
Medley:
  My Funny Valentine
  I Would Do Anything for You
Medley:
  Cocktails for Two
  But Not for Me
  When It's Sleepy Time Down South
NOTE: A recording of these tunes is available but remains unissued.

Ruby Braff Tour Continues
June 18, 1976: Ruby Braff with the Lennie Felix Trio, Grasshoppers F.C., Preston, England
June 19, 1976: Ruby Braff with the Lennie Felix Trio, the Crown, Codsall, England
June 20, 1976: Ruby Braff with Malcolm Gooding's Band, Belfast. Malcolm Gooding recalled that Ruby mentioned that he was very pleased with Tony Drennan's piano playing the night before in Dublin, but that remark must have been made on June 22.[6]

A copy of a poster publicizing Ruby's next performance is available and a recording of the concert has appeared on CD from Nagel Heyer. The performance ran from 8:30–11:30 p.m., with admission charged at the door of £1.50. A photograph of Ruby with Jack Daly in the background is also available.

Ruby Braff and the Fair City Jazzmen in Dublin (see Figure 14.1)
June 21, 1976, Slattery's Lounge Terenure, Dublin, Ireland

Ruby Braff (cnt), Tony Drennan (p), Jimmy McKay (b), Jack Daly (dm)
Just You, Just Me
Nagel Heyer CD 104
Sweet Lorraine
Nagel Heyer CD 104
Medley:
Solitude
Nagel Heyer CD 104
I Got Rhythm
Nagel Heyer CD 104
These Foolish Things
Nagel Heyer CD 104
I Want to Be Happy
Nagel Heyer CD 104
Sugar
Nagel Heyer CD 104
The Man I Love
Nagel Heyer CD 104
I Can't Get Started
Nagel Heyer CD 104
Mean to Me
Nagel Heyer CD 104
Hey Lawdy Mama
Nagel Heyer CD 104
NOTE: Ruby called Tony Drennan "Tommy" on the recording, in error. At this point, Ruby was joined by the Fair City Jazzmen, led by Colie Walsh. They played a few numbers together to close the concert. No information has been located about that portion of this engagement. On the CD release "Hey Lawdy Mama" is titled "Ruby's Blues," and "These Foolish Things" is erroneously titled "Little Things Mean a Lot." Nagel Heyer CD 104 is titled *Little Things: Live in Dublin 1976.*

Ruby Braff with the Blue Note Jazz Band[7]
June 22, 1976, Failand Hall, Bristol, England
Ruby Braff (cnt), John Skuse (tb), Wayne Chandler (g), Geoff Hancock (b)—other musicians not named
Just You, Just Me
Mood Indigo
I Got Rhythm
Indiana
My Sweet Tooth (Braff out)
Ain't Misbehavin'
When You're Smiling
I Can't Give You Anything but Love
Muskrat Ramble

Honeysuckle Rose

Ruby Braff Tour Continues:

June 24, 1976: Ruby Braff with the Lennie Felix Trio, Great Harwood F.C., Lancashire, England
June 25, 1976: Ruby Braff with the Lennie Felix Trio, 100 Club, London[8]
June 26, 1976: Ruby Braff with the Lennie Felix Trio, 100 Club, London
June 27, 1976 (Lunchtime): Ruby Braff with Tony Mann's Trio, Blindley Heath, Surrey, England

Benny Simkins Band
June 27, 1976 (evening), St. Francis Hospital, Haywards Heath, Sussex, England
Ruby Braff (cnt), Roy Bower, (tp), rest of personnel unknown
Lady Be Good
You've Changed
Someday You'll Be Sorry
Pennies from Heaven
If I Could Be with You
Undecided
'S Wonderful
Medley:
  I Cover the Waterfront
  Ain't Misbehavin'
Hey Lawdy Mama
Medley (short versions of each title):
  Danny Boy
  Struttin' with Some Barbecue
  I've Grown Accustomed to Her Face
  I Can't Give You Anything but Love
Sweethearts on Parade
Muskrat Ramble
Medley:
  Basin Street Blues
  When It's Sleepy Time Down South
NOTE: A recording of these tunes is available but remains unissued.

Ruby Braff Tour Continues
June 29, 1976: Ruby Braff with Alex Welsh's Band, Newcastle Festival, Newcastle upon Tyne, England
July 1, 1976: Ruby Braff with the Lennie Felix Trio, Isle of Man

Ruby Braff at the Jazz Cellar[9]
July 2, 1976, Jim Jacob's Jazz Cellar, Warren Bulkeley Hotel, Stockport, England

Ruby Braff (cnt), Eddie Thompson (p), Pete Taylor (b), Pete Staples (dm)
'Deed I Do
Yesterdays
Lover Come Back to Me
Ja-Da (rhythm only)
Pennies from Heaven (incomplete)
You Make Me Feel So Young*
These Foolish Things*
Solitude*
NOTE: Recordings of the first four of these tunes along with an incomplete recording of the fifth are available but remain unissued. The final three tunes are marked with an asterisk. They were performed but have not been available for audition.

Ruby Braff Tour Continues
July 4, 1976, Ruby Braff with the Lennie Felix Trio, Wellesley Hotel, Leeds, England

Ruby Braff at the Red Lion[10]
July 5, 1976, Red Lion (Pub), Hatfield, Hertfordshire, England
Lennie Felix (solo piano)
Medley:
  Rosetta
  Chelsea Bridge
  The Sheik of Araby

Add Harvey Weston (b), Johnny Richardson (dm)
Just One of Those Things
Medley:
  Prelude to a Kiss
  If Dreams Come True

Add Ruby Braff (cnt)
Sugar
In a Mellotone
I've Got a Right to Sing the Blues
Them There Eyes

Braff out
Little Rock Getaway
Do You Know What It Means to Miss New Orleans
Wolverine Blues

Add Ruby Braff (cnt)
Medley:
  Ain't Misbehavin'
  Melancholy Baby
Medley:
  But Not for Me
  Cheek to Cheek
Jeepers Creepers
Medley:
  I'm Getting Sentimental Over You
  I've Got a Feelin' I'm Fallin'
One Hour
Medley of "several tunes simultaneously":
  Please
  Stairway to the Stars
  You've Changed
Medley:
  Danny Boy
  What's New?
The Man I Love
Medley:
  Memories of You
  Keepin' Out of Mischief Now
  Pennies from Heaven
  When It's Sleepy Time Down South
  Georgia on My Mind
Medley:
  Hey Lawdy Mama
  When the Saints Go Marching In
  Goodnight Sweetheart
Medley:
  If You Were Mine*
  I Wished on the Moon*
NOTE: Recordings of all but the final two tunes marked with an asterisk are available but remain unissued.

The above recording ends with the following words: "We would like to see Ruby back sometime in the very near future. Ruby will appear Thursday night at the Pizza Express on Dean Street and has been working very hard for the past three weeks or so."

The Louis Armstrong Anniversary Concert[11] (see Figure 14.2)
July 6, 1976, 8 p.m., Fairfield Hall, Park Lane, Croydon, England

Ruby Braff appearing with the Keith Ingham Trio and also on the program were Alex Welsh and His Band, Humphrey Lyttelton, and the Lennie Hastings Trio (with Peter Ind)

Ruby Braff Tour Continues
July 7, 1976: Ruby Braff with the Lennie Felix Trio, Concorde, Southampton, England

Pizza Express[12]
July 8, 1976, London
Ruby Braff (cnt), Lennie Felix (p), Harvey Weston (b), Johnny Richardson (dm)
Sometimes I'm Happy
These Foolish Things
The Man I Love
Medley:
  Please
  Three Little Words

Jake Hanna (dm) replaces Richardson
Mean to Me
Medley:
  Tea for Two
  I Can't Give You Anything but Love
In a Mellotone
Over the Rainbow

Same location and date
Keith Ingham (p) replaces Felix
Romance in the Dark
Medley:
  You've Changed
  I Got Rhythm
You Can Depend on Me
Medley:
  Foolin' Myself
  Easy Living
You're a Sweetheart
Medley:
  The Very Thought of You
  Cocktails for Two
You're Driving Me Crazy
Medley:
  If You Were Mine (incomplete)
  I Wished on the Moon*

NOTE: Recordings of these tunes are available but remain unissued; however, the recording ends during the performance of "If You Were Mine" and does not include the final tune as marked with an asterisk.

Pizza Express, when it appears in this manuscript, refers to the location at 10 Dean Street, Soho, London. Musicians in the audience that night included Jake Hanna, who agreed to perform, Johnny Smith, Joe Bushkin, Keith Ingham, Larry Adler, and Susannah McCorkle. Ruby Braff, quoted in interview with Max Jones, described that evening:

> I played deliberately for an hour and a half last night because I didn't want to stop. It was so good and I was afraid if I did, something would happen that would interrupt that situation; if I stopped something would go wrong or somebody would be missing. . . . I told myself I owed it to me to have a good time on my final night. So I says to Jake after a long while: 'Do you want to run off or do you want to stay on?' He says: 'Let's stay on.' So I said: 'Great.' So we played on until one in the morning.[13]

A photo from the March of Jazz program shows Ruby with Tony Bennett from Pizza Express.[14] A copy appears in this book's photo section.

There is a gap of just over two weeks until the next documented performance. Whether Ruby had other engagements or perhaps enjoyed some personal time while in England is unknown. After the next performance at the 100 Club, he returned to Condon's, followed by a month-long return to Rick's Café Americain in Chicago.

Ruby Braff at the 100 Club
July 25–26, 1976, 100 Club, London
Ruby Braff (cnt), Lennie Felix (p), Harvey Weston (b), Johnny Richardson (dm)
Sweet Lorraine
When You're Smiling
Keepin' Out of Mischief Now
Rose Room
Medley:
  Mood Indigo
  I Got Rhythm
Ain't Misbehavin'
St. Louis Blues
Sugar
Love Me or Leave Me
Medley:
  Tea for Two
  Over the Rainbow
Sweet Georgia Brown
If I Could Be with You

C Jam Blues
NOTE: A recording of these tunes is available but remains unissued.

Ruby Braff Quartet[15]
August 1, 1976 (Sunday), Condon's, West 54th Street, New York

Ruby had a four-week engagement from August 3–28, 1976 at Rick's Café Americain in Chicago.[16] Performances were taped by members of the audience on two nights. Will Leonard reviewed one of the earliest nights in the engagement:[17]

> This is the second engagement within four months at Rick's for Braff, who hadn't been seen here for many seasons until the Holiday Inn Lake Shore invited him to town last spring.
>
> If memory serves (and we're pretty sure it does), the current quartet is far more fascinating than that selected for Ruby's recent stint in the room. . . . They're a fine trio on their own, as they demonstrate smoothly in a brief set before Ruby surfaces.
>
> Ruby, of course, is a gentle trumpeter, who can blow sweet and cynical at the same time, telling you the way it is without pestering your eardrums. He dominated the scene last spring. Now he's definitely the leader of the quartet as well as an earnest teammate.

Ruby Braff Quartet
August 12, 1976 (as part of a four week engagement from August 3–28), Rick's Café Americain, Holiday Inn Lakeshore Drive, Chicago
Ruby Braff (cnt), Bobby Wright (p), Jim Atlas (b), Jerry Coleman (dm)
Fly Me to the Moon
This Year's Kisses
Don't Be That Way
I Ain't Got Nobody
I'm Crazy 'Bout My Baby
Romance in the Dark
Medley:
  Please
  I Want a Little Girl
Old Folks
Nice Work If You Can Get It
Our Love Is Here to Stay
Medley:
  Easy Living
  Coquette
Sweethearts on Parade
NOTE: A recording of these tunes is available but remains unissued.

Ruby Braff Quartet
August 18, 1976 (as part of a four week engagement from August 3–28), Rick's Café Americain, Holiday Inn Lakeshore Drive, Chicago
Ruby Braff (cnt), Bobby Wright (p), Jim Atlas (b), Jerry Coleman (dm)
Love Me or Leave Me
Medley:
  You're My Thrill
  What's New?
Medley:
  Easy Living
  Foolin' Myself
Louisiana
Take the "A" Train
This Can't Be Love
Sweethearts on Parade
Medley:
  You've Changed
  C Jam Blues
Why Was I Born?
High Society
Sweet Georgia Brown
Medley:
  Georgia on My Mind
  Ole Miss
Someday You'll Be Sorry
Royal Garden Blues
NOTE: A recording of these tunes is available but remains unissued.

This was a four-week engagement, his second in Chicago in a year. Ruby had initiated the name artist policy in this club. which began with his first appearance.[18] John McDonough reviewed a performance from another evening during this engagement in a *DownBeat* article, listing the following tunes from that program:

Foolin' Myself
Just You, Just Me
Cocktails for Two
I Got Rhythm
Them There Eyes
NOTE: No recording is known to exist for these performances.

In addition, John McDonough speculated that Ruby would return again very soon after this engagement after already appearing for four weeks the previous August.

Ruby had become a regular at Dick and Maddie Gibson's Labor Day jazz parties. Over 60 hours of performances were filmed during the 1996 event; however, only an edited version of this film ever appeared. In a personal conversation, Maddie Gibson said that she had no access to those filmed performances. The final version of the film was released 1977, directed by Vilis Lapenieks. It was shown at Cannes Film Festival. The listing below summarizes the parts of the film that include Ruby Braff. The film opens with a staged sequence of some musicians arriving before the party begins. Performance footage is drawn from actual sessions during the party which ran from September 4–6 at the Broadmoor Hotel in Colorado Springs, Colorado.

Gibson Jazz Party: The Great Rocky Mountain Jazz Party
September 3, 1976, Gibson's home in Denver
Ruby Braff audible with other musicians during opening credits
I Can't Believe That You're in Love with Me (fragment on soundtrack)

September 3, 1976, Gibson's home in Denver
Ruby and Clark Terry briefly duet on the street after Ruby is filmed arriving in an antique automobile.
Struttin' with Some Barbecue (fragment on soundtrack)

Ruby Braff (cnt), Al Grey (tb), Benny Carter (as), Flip Phillips (ts), Roger Kellaway (p), Bucky Pizzarelli (g), Milt Hinton (b), Gus Johnson (dm)
Rosetta
NOTE: A video recording of the entire film is available but remains unissued.

Some information is available about Ruby's performances during the Gibson Jazz Party. A photograph was published showing Ruby with Jerry Fuller and Buddy Tate in 1976.[19] This anchors the following performance:

Gibson Jazz Party: The Great Rocky Mountain Jazz Party
Ruby Braff (cnt), Buddy Tate (ts) and Jerry Fuller (cl) with other unknown musicians

Ruby probably performed with many other groups during the party. In addition to Ruby and the musicians already listed appearing with him, the following musicians are also visible during the film: Frank Rosolino, Zoot Sims, Major Holley, Phil Woods, Eubie Blake, Jon Faddis, Bob Wilber, Kenny Davern, Pee Wee Erwin, Peanuts Hucko, Joe Venuti, Buddy Tate, Billy Butterfield, Trummy Young, Budd Johnson, Al Cohn, Tommy Flanagan, Roy Haynes, Dick Hyman, Joe Wilder, Ray Brown, Roland Hanna, Buddy DeFranco, Joe Newman, Ralph Sutton, Carl Fontana, Bill Watrous, and George Duvivier.

Ruby Braff at Condon's[20]
October 12, 1976, Eddie Condon's, New York

Ruby Braff (cnt) as a guest with Balaban & Cats, the house band: Jimmy Andrews (p), Vic Dickenson (tb), Red Balaban (b), Connie Kay (dm), Herb Hall (cl), Ed Polcer (tp)

The published listing of the above performance included the following statement: "With the death of Bobby Hackett, Braff stands almost alone as a richly romantic jazz cornetist."

Ruby Braff Quartet[21]
November 14, 1976, Stryker's, 103 West 86th Street, New York
Ruby Braff (cnt) and unknown others

Ruby Braff Quartet[22]
November 19–20, 1976, Stryker's, 103 West 86th Street, New York
Ruby Braff (cnt), Joe Puma (g), and unknown others

Ruby Braff at Condon's[23]
November 30, 1976, Eddie Condon's, 144 West 54th Street, New York
Ruby Braff (cnt) as a guest with Balaban & Cats, the house band: Jimmy Andrews (p), Vic Dickenson (tb), Red Balaban (b), Connie Kay (dm), Herb Hall (cl), Ed Polcer (tp)

Ruby Braff at Condon's
December 5, 1976, Eddie Condon's, 144 West 54th Street, New York
Ruby Braff (cnt), John Bunch (p), Wayne Wright (g), Michael Moore (b), Connie Kay (dm)
Sunday
Days of Wine and Roses
Always
I Can't Explain
It's All Right with Me
Medley:
  Ghost of a Chance
  Quiet Nights of Quiet Stars (Corcovado)

Set 2:
I Know That You Know
What Is There to Say?
Autumn Leaves
In a Mellotone
I've Grown Accustomed to Her Face
Tea for Two
You Can Depend on Me
Dinah
You're Driving Me Crazy

Medley:
  Georgia
  I Want a Little Girl
  Them There Eyes
NOTE: A recording of these tunes is available but remains unissued.

Kind words from Ed Polcer reported in an interview conducted by John S. Wilson:[24] "Many listeners hear in his [Ed Polcer's] playing reflections of Louis Armstrong and of Bobby Hackett. But his favorite of all trumpet players is Ruby Braff who, Mr. Polcer says, 'has a tremendously tasteful mix of good, hard swing and nice modern ideas.'"

Ruby Braff Quartet[25]
January 9, 1977, Free Public Library, Springfield, New Jersey
Ruby Braff (cnt), Johnny Morris (p), Milt Hinton (b), Bobby Rosengarden (dm)
Medley:
  I've Grown Accustomed to Her Face
  I Would Do Anything for You
Love Me or Leave Me
I Got Rhythm
Them There Eyes
Yesterdays
St. Louis Blues
Medley:
  Over the Rainbow
  Chicago (incomplete)
Sunday
NOTE: A recording of these tunes is available but remains unissued.

Ruby Braff Quartet[26]
January 16, 1977, 3 p.m., Monmouth County Library, Shrewsbury (Route 35), New Jersey
Ruby Braff (cnt), Johnny Morris (p), Milt Hinton (b), Bobby Rosengarden (dm)
Them There Eyes
Yesterdays
St. Louis Blues
Medley:
  Over the Rainbow
  Chicago
Sunday
Medley:
  I've Grown Accustomed to Her Face
  I Would Do Anything for You
Love Me or Leave Me
NOTE: A recording of these tunes is available but remains unissued.

Ruby Braff Interview with Ted O'Reilly
January 20, 1977, CJRT-FM, Toronto
NOTE: A recording of this interview is available but remains unissued.

Ruby Braff[27]
Early 1977 and prior to February 28 (probably January), Bourbon Street
Further details are unknown.

American Popular Song Miniseries: Michael's Pub[28]
February 1 through end of March 1977, Michael's Pub, New York
Ruby Braff (cnt), Dick Hyman (p), Howard Alden (g), Michael Moore (b), Bob Jones (announcer) – Contrary to reports, Howard Alden said he was not present.
As Time Goes By
All That Love Went to Waste
NOTE: This eight-week series began February 1, 1977, but it unclear when Ruby might have participated. So this listing is somewhat speculative. Howard states that he did not perform with Ruby until 1984, so he is not present.

Ruby Braff at Condon's[29]
February 15, 1977, Eddie Condon's, 144 West 54th Street, New York
Ruby Braff (cnt) as a guest with Balaban & Cats, the house band: Jimmy Andrews (p), Vic Dickenson (tb), Red Balaban (b), Connie Kay (dm), Herb Hall (cl), Ed Polcer (tp)

The New Jersey Jazz Society organized what became three annual multi-day events called the Strides of March. Ruby was featured each year, playing with other well-known jazz musicians. The programs were recorded, and these recordings are held in the collections of the Institute for Jazz Studies at Rutgers University. That makes it possible to document every set when Ruby performed. Listening to these recordings makes it clear that the audience was very enthusiastic and that the musicians enjoyed themselves.

Ruby Braff Quintet[30]
March 25, 1977, Strides of March #1, New Jersey Jazz Society, Playboy Resort, McAfee, New Jersey
Ruby Braff (cnt), John Bunch (p), Wayne Wright (g), George Duvivier (b), Bobby Rosengarden (dm)
I Want to Be Happy
Tea for Two (interpolating Two Sleepy People)
Medley:
  I Want a Little Girl
  Mean to Me
I Ain't Got Nobody
NOTE: A recording of these tunes is available but remains unissued.

Ruby Braff Quintet[31]
March 26, 1977, Strides of March #1, New Jersey Jazz Society, Playboy Resort, McAfee, New Jersey
Ruby Braff (cnt), Zoot Sims (ss, ts), John Bunch? (p), unknown (b), (dm)
Rosetta
The Very Thought of You
Lady Be Good
Ain't Misbehavin'
NOTE: A recording of these tunes is available but remains unissued.

Ruby Braff Quintet[32]
March 27, 1977 Strides of March #1, New Jersey Jazz Society, Playboy Resort, McAfee, New Jersey
Ruby Braff (cnt), Ed Hubble (tb), John Bunch (p), Wayne Wright (g), George Duvivier (b), unknown (dm)
I Would Do Anything for You
Sugar
I'm Getting Sentimental Over You (Hubble feature)

Add Chris Lowell (voc), Braff and Hubble out
Cherokee
Ain't Misbehavin'

Add Braff, Hubble; Lowell out
Love Me or Leave Me
NOTE: A recording of these tunes is available but remains unissued.

Ruby Braff Quintet[33]
April 1–2 and 8–9, 1977, Stryker's, 103 West 86th Street, New York
Ruby Braff (cnt), Sam Margolis (cl, ts), Bucky Pizzarelli (g), Bill Crow (b), Ronnie Bedford (dm) for the first weekend and Connie Kay (dm) the second

A photograph of Ruby exists from his performance at Stryker's. John S. Wilson quoted Ruby in his review:[34]

> I was never a fan of mine. You won't get better if you don't recognize the truth about your playing. Now I think I'm playing good. But it takes a long time to learn to play great. My yardstick is Lester Young and Louis Armstrong. By this yardstick, I'm growing. I'm getting to be very good. But I've still got another 50 years to go to be great.
>
> Playing beautiful tunes by Cole Porter or Duke Ellington makes you play better. No one could play a song like Charlie Parker. He'd play a melody that would make you cry. And then he'd improvise on it. He'd heard Lester, Louis, Benny Goodman—everything wonderful. But if a guy growing up in this era turns on the radio to learn something, God help him.

The article notes that Braff was planning to record a collection of Stevie Wonder songs with strings accompaniment. While I am extremely comfortable interpreting this remark as a joke, you can never be completely sure with Ruby. For instance, I have seen a video recording of Dave McKenna performing a medley of early Stevie Wonder songs for a group of junior high school students.

Ruby Braff: Jazz Uptown[35]
April 15–17, 1977, Café Burgundy, 50431 Connecticut Avenue NW, Washington, D.C.
Ruby Braff (cnt) with unknown musicians

1st Annual Pacific Kool Jazz Fair[36]
May 2, 1977, Honolulu
Musicians appearing included Woody Herman Orchestra, Chuck Mangione's Quartet, Wallace Davenport's New Orleans Band, Pee Wee Erwin, Ruby Braff, John Bunch, Al Cohn, Kenny Davern, Vic Dickenson, George Duvivier, Mickey Gravine, Marty Grosz, Major Holley, Dick Hyman, Ed Hubble, Cliff Leeman, Bobby Rosengarden, Zoot Sims, Jack Six, Fred Stoll, Warren Vaché, Jr., Dick Wellstood, Bob Wilber, Wayne Wright, and Carrie Smith.

Ruby Braff[37]
Sometime in 1977, likely during first half of the year, the Barber Shop, Broadway, Off Route 35, Point Pleasant Beach, New Jersey

Ruby Braff: *Fats Waller's Heavenly Jive*
Spring (likely May) 1977, two days, New York
Ruby Braff (cnt), Dick Hyman (org)
Soothin' Syrup Stomp
    Chiaroscuro CR 162
I Can't Give You Anything but Love
    Chiaroscuro CR 162
Got a Brand New Suit
    Chiaroscuro CR 162
Chloe
    Chiaroscuro CR 162
I'm Gonna See My Ma
    Chiaroscuro CR 162
I Ain't Got Nobody
    Chiaroscuro CR 162
Sweet and Slow
    Chiaroscuro CR 162
I Believe in Miracles
    Chiaroscuro CR 162

Willow Tree
 Chiaroscuro CR 162
Sugar
 Chiaroscuro CR 162
Persian Rug
 Chiaroscuro CR 162
Boo Hoo
 Chiaroscuro CR 162

Hank O'Neal indicates that outtakes exist from the *Heavenly Jive* session and supplied the approximate date. He photographed Ruby with Dick Hyman playing the organ at Downtown Sound in April 1977. If that date is correct, it moves the date of the *Heavenly Jive* recording to April from the listed date in May. This photograph is included in this book's photo section.

Ruby Braff at the Cincinnati Jazz Club
May 1977, Maggie's Opera House, 4901 Vine Street, St. Bernard, Cincinnati, Ohio
Ruby Braff (cnt), John Ulrich (p), Sid Townsend (b), Glen Kimmel (dm)
Sunday*
Medley:
 These Foolish Things
 I Would Do Anything for You
Sweethearts on Parade
I Ain't Got Nobody
Big Butter and Egg Man
Sometimes I'm Happy
When You're Smiling
You Can Depend on Me
When It's Sleepy Time Down South
I Know That You Know
Tea for Two
Someday You'll Be Sorry
Lover Come Back to Me
Blue Lou
Pennies from Heaven
Cocktails for Two
Over the Rainbow (incomplete)
Them There Eyes (missing start)
The Very Thought of You
Mean to Me
Sugar
Medley:
 I've Grown Accustomed to Her Face
 Chicago

Dinah*
NOTE: A recording of these tunes is available but remains unissued. The opening and closing tunes are incomplete in the recording and are marked with an asterisk.

Jimmy Ryan's[38]
May 17-21 and 24-29, 1977, Jimmy Ryan's, 154 West 54th Street, New York
Ruby Braff (cnt), Bobby Pratt (tb), Clarence Hutchenrider (cl), Johnny Morris (p), Ted Sturgis (b), Ernie Hackett (dm)
Max Kaminsky replaced Ruby on Monday and Sunday nights during this period.

Jimmy Ryan's[39]
June 7–11, 14–18 and 21–23, 1977, Jimmy Ryan's, 154 W. 54th Street, New York
Ruby Braff (cnt), Bobby Pratt (tb), Clarence Hutchenrider (cl), Johnny Morris (p), Ted Sturgis (b), Ernie Hackett (dm)

Max Kaminsky replaced Ruby on Monday and Sunday nights during this period. as Ruby substituted for Roy Eldridge in this engagement.

Today Show[40]
June 23, 1977, NBC Studios, New York
Ruby Braff was a guest but further details are unavailable at time of publication.

Ruby Braff on the *Today Show*
July 1977, NBC Studios, New York (the date was announced as the day before the start of the 1981 Newport Jazz Festival)
Ruby Braff (cnt), Johnny Morris (p), Bill Mollenhoff (vib), Jay Leonhardt (b), Ronnie Bedford (dm)
Medley:
  When It's Sleepy Time Down South
  Someday You'll Be Sorry*
NOTE: A recording of these tunes is available but remains unissued, although the final tune is incomplete and marked with an asterisk.

For the 1977 Newport Jazz Festival, Ruby performed at a Jazz Picnic in Waterloo Village in Stanhope, New Jersey. This program was hosted by the New Jersey Jazz Society as an integral part of the festival, and this was the second year for this event. Obviously the members of the society had enjoyed Ruby's performances in the past. The program showed that tickets were $6 in advance, with a 50 percent discount for children. The program began at noon and was scheduled to continue until 10:00 p.m. Other musicians appearing included John Bunch, Kenny Davern, Harry "Sweets" Edison, Marty Grosz, Bob Haggart, Scott Hamilton, Milt Hinton, Connie Kay, Michael Moore, Bucky Pizzarelli, Ed Polcer, Warren Vaché, Jr., Zoot Sims, Dick Wellstood, and many others. Clearly this represented a wide range of styles within the jazz mainstream and a wonderful value for fans of good music.

Ruby Braff Quintet[41]
July 3, 1977, Newport Jazz Festival at Waterloo Village (sponsored by Newport Jazz Festival and New Jersey Jazz Society), Stanhope, New Jersey
Ruby Braff (cnt), Bob Wilber (as), Johnny Morris (p), George Duvivier (b), Bobby Rosengarden (dm)
Sunday
Ain't Misbehavin'
Rocks in My Bed (Wilber feature)
Lover Come Back to Me
When I Fall in Love
Lady Be Good
NOTE: A recording of these tunes is available but remains unissued.

Commemorating Louis Armstrong: Ruby Braff at Michael's Pub[42]
July 4–16, 1977 for two weeks, Michael's Pub, 211 East 55th Street, New York (closed Sundays, Woody Allen appeared Mondays)
Ruby Braff (cnt), Bill Mollenhoff (vib), Johnny Morris (p), Jay Leonhardt (b), Ronnie Bedford (dm)
Jeepers Creepers
Swing That Music
I Can't Give You Anything but Love
Exactly Like You

"On a recent evening, [Eubie] Blake and his wife Marian took another couple to see *Unsung Cole* off-Broadway in New York and then on to supper at Michael's Pub where trumpeter Ruby Braff was playing. Braff, seeing them come in, immediately swung into Blake's 'You're Luck to Me.'"[43]

A short review in *The New Yorker* included the following words:[44]

> During the past twenty-five years, Braff has both refined and embellished his style, which derives from Louis Armstrong with assists from Buck Clayton and Wild Bill Davison. The refinements: a wiser choice of notes, a general rhythmic and tonal toughening, and the relaxation brought on by middle age and late-blooming confidence. The embellishments: an increasingly daring and dramatic sense of dynamics, a lower register large enough to house a blimp, and an unerring and graceful prolixity. Braff's melodic lines are Gothic tracery, and his tone is velvet and damask and silk. . . . Braff continually tilts and tips the group, and there are a lot of welcome a-cappella passages, four-and eight-bar exchanges, and stop-time sections. According to the club's management, Braff is supposed to be celebrating Louis Armstrong while he is here, and it's an unfortunate gimmick. Braff is a wizard with Porter and Rodgers and Hart and Gershwin, few of whom Armstrong ever touched.

Ruby Braff[45]
July 19–August 6, 1977, Jimmy Ryan's, 154 West 54th Street, New York
Ruby Braff (cnt), Bobby Pratt (tb), Sam Margolis (cl), Johnny Morris (p), Ted Sturgis (b), Eddie Locke (dm)
Max Kaminsky replaced Ruby on Monday and Sunday nights during this period

Ruby Braff at Michael's Pub[46]
On a Tuesday–Saturday during August 1977, Michael's Pub, 211 East 55th Street, New York
Further details are unknown.

Soprano Summit with Ruby Braff[47]
August 21, 1977, 3 p.m., Liberty State Park, New Jersey
Soprano Summit: Bob Wilber, Kenny Davern (ss), Marty Grosz (g), George Duvivier (b), Bobby Rosengarden (dm)
Rockin' in Rhythm
Ruby Braff (cnt), Kenny Davern (ss, cl), Marty Grosz (g, voc), George Duvivier (b), Bobby Rosengarden (dm)
Exactly Like You
Ain't Misbehavin' (Grosz vocal)
Caravan
Sunday*
Lady Be Good
Keepin' Out of Mischief Now (Grosz vocal)
I Wish That I Were Twins (Grosz vocal, Braff out)
Sometimes I'm Happy (Davern out)
NOTE: A recording of these tunes is available but remains unissued. The recording of "Sunday" is incomplete and marked with an asterisk.

Jazz Galaxy's Festival[48]
September 3, 1977, Mitchell Park, Milwaukee, Wisconsin
Ruby Braff appeared as a teacher at a workshop

I asked Ruby about his interest in leading workshops in university settings and he simply replied, "I'm not very good at that." He did not elaborate.

Ruby Braff Quartet[49]
October 28, 1977, The Continental Restaurant, Kings Highway, Turnpike Exit 24, Fairfield, Connecticut
Ruby Braff (cnt), Johnny Morris (p), with bass and drums

Midland Jazz Party,[50]
November 1977, Hilton Hotel, Midland, Texas (organized by Max Christensen)
Musicians included Bucky Pizzarelli, Dave McKenna, Derek Smith, Dick Hyman, Red Norvo, Jack Lesberg, Milt Hinton, Mousey Alexander, Jake Hanna,

Cliff Leeman, Kenny Davern, Johnny Mince, Flip Phillips, Eddie Miller, Scott Hamilton, Carl Fontana, Ed Hubble, Bill Watrous, Ed Polcer, Warren Vaché, Jr., Ruby Braff, and Pee Wee Erwin.

George Barnes had been scheduled to appear in this program; however, he died September 4. We'll never know if he and Ruby would agree to be reunited onstage. Scott Hamilton recalled that this is when Ruby learned of George's passing.

This is the first documented time that Ruby appeared on the same program as Scott Hamilton, although Scott reported to me that he sat in with Ruby a few times at Condon's in 1976 and earlier in 1977. At this time, Scott was exciting the jazz community and had performed and recorded with Warren Vaché, John Bunch, Red Norvo, Dave McKenna, Joe Venuti, and Benny Goodman. Scott also reported that this was just his second appearance at a jazz party. The other was the Concord Jazz Festival, where he appeared August 4, 1977. Ruby and Scott would not record together until 1983; however, they performed together on many other occasions before that time, some of which have been privately recorded. Ruby encouraged talented young musicians just has he had found his own champions in the decades of the '40s and '50s, earlier in his own career. Of course, Ruby and Scott were also recorded together in Ruby's final performance.

Jimmy Ryan's[51]

Occasional dates during October and November 1977, 154 West 54th Street, New York

Ruby Braff was a regular substitute for Roy Eldridge at Jimmy Ryan's during this time. Roy was usually scheduled to appear on Tuesday–Saturday nights.

The following posters depict two of the performances in this chapter:

Figure 14.1: Poster, June 1976

TW Enterprises present

The Louis Armstrong Anniversary Concert

TUESDAY, 6th JULY 1976 at 8.00 p.m.

at

THE FAIRFIELD HALL, PARK LANE, CROYDON

(General Manager: Michael Tearle)

with

ALEX WELSH AND HIS BAND
HUMPHREY LYTTELTON
THE LENNIE HASTINGS TRIO

and

RUBY BRAFF

Tickets: £2.00, £1.75, £1.50, £1.25, £1 & 75p

Figure 14.2: Poster June/July 1976

Notes

[1] *The New Yorker*, April 12, 1976, 6.
[2] Will Leonard, *Chicago Tribune*, April 23, 1976.
[3] Information supplied by Derek Coller. Copy of listing with dates supplied by David Griffiths.
[4] *Melody Maker*, August 19, 1978.
[5] Reviewed by Max Jones in *Melody Maker*, June 26, 1976.
[6] Ralph O'Callaghan reporting conversation with Malcolm Gooding—photo and handbill from Ralph O'Callaghan.
[7] Copy of ticket and published concert review supplied by Bert Whyatt—the article states that Ruby traveled from Dublin to Bristol by air through London and mentioned the musicians and titles listed.
[8] A copy of the club's calendar of performances for May and June is available.
[9] Concert review by Eddie Lambert published in *Jazz Journal International,* August 1976, 21, which mentions the titles not available on the recording.
[10] Information from Tony Adkins; program notes on "Rosetta" through "Saints" prepared by Derek Coller and used with minor changes.
[11] Display ad published in *Jazz Journal International*, June 1976, 17.
[12] Joe Buskin performed solo piano with Larry Adler added on one tune in remainder of this session but this was not available for audition at the time of publication.
[13] Max Jones, *Talking Jazz*, (New York: W. W. Norton and Company, 1988), 93.
[14] Photo, *The March of Jazz Celebrates Ruby Braff's 74th Birthday Party*, Arbors Records, 2001, 22.
[15] *New York Times*, August 1, 1976, and *The New Yorker*, August 2, 1976, 5, and *New York Magazine*, August 2, 1976, 20.
[16] Will Leonard, *Chicago Tribune*, June 20, 1976.
[17] Will Leonard, *Chicago Tribune*, August 6, 1976.
[18] John McDonough, "Ruby Braff: Salty Dog with a Lip," *DownBeat*, January 27, 1977, 18. The article mentions other tunes listed, probably from another evening.
[19] *Jazz Journal International*, December 1976, 9 includes a photo caption from Great Rocky Mountain Jazz Party 1976.
[20] *New York Times*, October 10, 1976, and *The New Yorker*, October 11, 1976, 6.
[21] *New York Times*, November 14, 1976.
[22] *The New Yorker*, November 15, 1976, 8, and November 22, 1976, 8.
[23] *The New Yorker*, November 29, 1976, 8.
[24] John S. Wilson, *New York Times*, January 7, 1973.
[25] Chuck Slate provided the information.
[26] Chuck Slate provided information about location and a *New York Times* classified ad, January 16, 1977, mentioning that the concert was "today."
[27] John Norris reporting in *Coda Magazine*, April 1977, 27.
[28] Dick Hyman mentioned this series but only the singers are listed in contemporary press reports, starting with the *New York Times*, February 1, 1977, and mentioned periodically thereafter including a mention of the program being "last winter" in a further article by John S. Wilson dated August 28, 1977.
[29] *The New Yorker*, February 14, 1977, 8.
[30] New Jersey Jazz Society Collection, Institute of Jazz Studies.

[31] New Jersey Jazz Society Collection, Institute of Jazz Studies.
[32] New Jersey Jazz Society Collection, Institute of Jazz Studies.
[33] Press release from Ivan Black and John S. Wilson, *New York Times*, April 1, 1977, and listed in *New York Times*, April 3, 1977, and *The New Yorker*, March 28, 1977, 8, April 4, 1977, 8, and April 11, 1977, 8.
[34] John S. Wilson, *New York Times*, April 1, 1977, and listed in *New York Times*, April 3, 1977.
[35] *Washington Post*, April 15, 1977.
[36] Warren W. Vaché, Sr., *Pee Wee Erwin: This Horn for Hire* (Metuchen, NJ: Scarecrow Press, 1987), 341.
[37] John S. Wilson, *New York Times*, August 21, 1977.
[38] *The New Yorker*, May 23, 1977, 8, May 30, 1977, 8, and *New York Magazine*, June 20, 1977, 20 and June 27, 1977, 25.
[39] *The New Yorker*, June 6, 1977, 8, June 13, 1977, 6, and June 20, 1977, 6.
[40] *New York Times*, June 23, 1977, and *Chicago Tribune*, June 23, 1977.
[41] New Jersey Jazz Society tape in restricted archive at the Institute for Jazz Studies. Photo reproduced in *The March of Jazz Celebrates Ruby Braff's 74th Birthday Party,* Arbors Records, 2001, 25, caption says circa 1979. Listed in *New York Times*, June 24, 1977, and listed in *The New Yorker*, July 4, 1977, 8.
[42] John S. Wilson, *New York Times*, July 3, 1977, July 7, 1977, July 10, 1977, and July 15, 1977. *The New Yorker*, July 4, 1977, 6, July 11, 1977, and July 18, 6, and *New York Magazine*, July 18, 1977, 22.
[43] "Listeners Are Wild about Eubie Blake," *The News and Courier* (Charleston, SC) July 30, 1977, 17c.
[44] *The New Yorker*, July 18, 1977, 4.
[45] *The New Yorker*, July 18, 6, July 25, 1977, 6, August 1, 1977, 4, and August 8, 1977, 6.
[46] *Jersey Jazz*, August 1977 but this does not appear in *The New Yorker* and may have been a reference to the July engagement.
[47] *New York Times*, August 21, 1977.
[48] *Milwaukee Sentinel*, August 19, 1977, 21, and August 4, 1977, 4
[49] Information is taken from an available copy of a printed handbill.
[50] Warren W. Vaché, Sr., *Pee Wee Erwin: This Horn for Hire* (Metuchen, NY, Scarecrow Press, 1987), 345–346.
[51] *The New Yorker*, November 7, 1977, 8, and November 14, 1977, 8.

Chapter 15

The Pianists and the Growth of Jazz Parties: November 1977–June 1979

Ruby had performed with Dick Hyman, Ellis Larkins, Dave McKenna, Nat Pierce, Mel Powell, and Ralph Sutton in the 1950s. His first documented performance with John Bunch dates from 1961. Beginning perhaps in 1974, Dick Hyman created a number of opportunities for recordings and performances that involved Ruby. Ralph Sutton and John Bunch also became more frequent collaborators. Roger Kellaway stimulated Ruby in different ways. In this era of jazz parties, Ruby found himself performing in many combinations, but much of the foundation was built from a growing partnership with a few pianists who he felt provided appropriate and sympathetic support. As jazz disappeared from many radio stations and the number of jazz clubs declined, jazz parties began to occupy a growing importance in bringing live performances to people who loved this music. They were an alternative to clubs that booked featured artists to perform with a local rhythm section of, sometimes, uneven ability, or different approaches to music. Ruby's attention to chamber music fit into this growing trend. Ruby continued to exercise control over the musicians on the bandstand, and economics dictated that he could not travel with a large group. Therefore, a core of pianists was perhaps a natural way for Ruby to balance artistic goals, control, and new economic realities. Whatever the reason they produced many musical treasures together.

Jack Kleinsinger produced a number of jazz concerts in a series called Highlights in Jazz. A few recordings have been released from various performances, so perhaps others will be in the future. No known recording of the opening portion of the first half of the next concert is available. Those performance featured Braff–Hyman duets, including "Got a Bran' New Suit" and "Soothing Syrup Stomp." The first half of the concert concluded with solos by Marty Grosz, which are included in a recording available to the author, but these tunes do not include Ruby Braff. Thus, those solos are omitted from the listing below.

Ruby Braff and Dick Hyman: Highlights in Jazz / Jazz at the New School[1]
November 10, 1977, Eisner and Lubin Auditorium, New York University, New York, Jack Kleinsinger, producer (see Figure 15.1)
Ruby Braff (cnt), Dick Hyman (org)
Sugar
Dinah
I Believe in Miracles
One Hour

Add Marty Grosz (g)
Jeepers Creepers (voc MG)
Keepin' Out of Mischief Now (voc MG)
NOTE: A recording of these tunes is available but remains unissued.

Ruby Braff and Dick Hyman[2]
November 12, 1977, 8 p.m., Monmouth County Library, Route 35, Shrewsbury, New Jersey
Ruby Braff (cnt), Dick Hyman (org)

Ruby next appeared in a concert at the Chicago Opera House presented as a fund raiser to retire a mortgage for the Mother Cabrini Old Age Home. Frank Sinatra flew to Chicago for this short performance before returning to an unnamed engagement. Mother Cabrini was the first American citizen to be canonized by the Roman Catholic Church. Tony Bennett performed in the second part of the program. The surviving seven-inch reel recording in the author's collection includes Sinatra's entire performance; however, the tape ends during Tony Bennett's performance. Both singers performed with a large band. Ruby Braff soloed during one tune on the available recording.

Tony Bennett with Will Friedwald wrote the following about this evening:[3]

> Frank and I met up another time in Chicago. There was a home for Italian-American senior citizens there called the Mother Cabrini Old Age Home. They were putting on a big benefit so they could raise enough money to pay off their mortgage. Originally Frank was going to do the show, but when he canceled because of an arm injury, they called me, and I agreed to do it. But Frank decided he could do the show with his arm in a sling. Since I was already booked, we decided to do it together.
>
> When we were planning the show, Frank decided that he'd go on first. I don't know why; maybe there was someplace he wanted to be. When he finished he turned to the crowd and said, 'Ladies and gentlemen, the greatest singer in the business, Tony Bennett.' It was just about the greatest honor I've ever received.

This performance is the last one I have been able to document in which Ruby accompanies Tony Bennett. Further, I believe this is their first documented appearance together since 1973. Certainly this was a wonderful artistic collaboration. They will next appear on the same program in 1979, but there is no indication that they performed together. That program honored the vocalist Teddi King and raised money for lupus research.

Frank Sinatra and Tony Bennett at the Opera House
Unknown date, perhaps 1977, Chicago Opera House, Chicago
Ruby Braff (cnt), Tony Bennett (voc), other musicians unknown
Get Happy
NOTE: Ruby Braff is not audible on other selections on this available recording. The available recording mostly contains Sinatra's half of the concert.

Ruby Braff Quintet[4]
November 25–26, 1977, Stryker's, 103 West 86th Street at Columbus Avenue, New York
No further details are available.

Ruby Braff[5]
January 2–21, 1978, Bourbon Street, 180 Queen Street West, Toronto
No further details are available.

Ruby apparently had problems at Canadian Immigration on a visit prior to July 1978. He was refused entry to Canada for a TV appearance and was told he could be banned for a year.[6] This event may have been the basis for comments he made much later to Lenny Solomon at a recording session in 1991.

Ruby Braff[7]
January 25–28, 1978, Jimmy Ryan's, 154 West 54th Street, New York
Ruby Braff (cnt), Bobby Pratt (tb), Joe Muranyi (cl), Johnny Morris (p), Ted Sturgis (b), Eddie Locke (dm)

The New Jersey Jazz Society produced the second annual Strides of March jazz weekend, held at the Playboy Club in McAffee, New Jersey, the weekend of March 31, 1978. Ruby was again invited and recordings are again available in the collections of the Institute of Jazz Studies. A copy of the flyer announcing the program is available along with photos of Zoot Sims playing with Ruby Braff and Warren Vaché listening intently to Ruby Braff. This is Ruby's first documented appearance with Eddie Miller, although they both performed at the Midland Jazz Party in Texas five months previously.

Ruby Braff Sextet[8]
March 31, 1978, Strides of March #2, New Jersey Jazz Society, Playboy Club, Great Gorge Hotel, McAfee, New Jersey
Ruby Braff (cnt), Vic Dickenson (tb), Eddie Miller (ts), John Bunch (p), Bucky Pizzarelli (g), George Duvivier (b), Bobby Rosengarden (dm)
I Want to Be Happy

Sophisticated Lady (Eddie Miller feature)
Pennies from Heaven
NOTE: A recording of these tunes is available but remains unissued.

Ruby Braff and Zoot Sims[9]
March 31, 1978, Strides of March #2, New Jersey Jazz Society, Playboy Club, Great Gorge Hotel, McAfee, New Jersey
Ruby Braff (cnt), Zoot Sims (ts), Bucky Pizzarelli (g), Dave McKenna (p), Jack Lesberg (b), Bobby Rosengarden? (dm)
Love Me or Leave Me
Medley:
  Body and Soul (Sims feature)
  The Very Thought of You (Braff feature)
Lady Be Good
NOTE: A recording of these tunes is available but remains unissued.

Ruby Braff and Dick Hyman[10]
April 1, 1978, Strides of March #2, New Jersey Jazz Society, Playboy Club, Great Gorge Hotel, McAfee, New Jersey
Ruby Braff (cnt) and Dick Hyman (org)
Got a Brand New Suit
Sugar
Black Beauty
Medley:
  If I Could Be with You
  I Know That You Know
Dinah
NOTE: A recording of these tunes is available but remains unissued.

Ruby Braff Quartet[11]
April 1, 1978, Strides of March #2, New Jersey Jazz Society, Playboy Club, Great Gorge Hotel, McAfee, New Jersey
Ruby Braff (cnt), Ed Hubble (tb), Eddie Miller (ts), Bucky Pizzarelli (g), Dick Hyman? (p), Slam Stewart (b), Cliff Leeman (dm)
Struttin' with Some Barbecue
I Got It Bad and That Ain't Good (Eddie Miller feature)
Just You, Just Me
Just a Closer Walk with Thee (Braff out)
Indiana
NOTE: A recording of these tunes is available but remains unissued.

With the weekend behind him, Ruby returned to the recording studio for a second LP for Sonet. This one has never been reissued on CD.

Ruby Braff: *Pretties*
April 4–5, 1978, New York
Ruby Braff (cnt, voc), Harry Shepherd (vib), John Bunch (p), Remo Palmier (g), Earl May (b), Mousey Alexander (dm)
If I Ruled the World
    Sonet (E) SNTF 777
Please
    Sonet (E) SNTF 777
I'm Shooting High
    Sonet (E) SNTF 777
Nancy (With the Laughing Face)
    Sonet (E) SNTF 777
This Could Be the Start of Something Big
    Sonet (E) SNTF 777
Love Me or Leave Me
    Sonet (E) SNTF 777
Dreams
    Sonet (E) SNTF 777
Tangerine (voc Braff)
    Sonet (E) SNTF 777
This Is All I Ask
    Sonet (E) SNTF 777
S'posin'
    Sonet (E) SNTF 777
NOTE: All titles also on Vogue (F) VG408-SNTF777.

Ruby Braff[12]
April 26–29, 1978, Jimmy Ryan's, 154 West 54th Street, New York
Ruby Braff (cnt), Bobby Pratt (tb), Joe Muranyi (cl), Johnny Morris (p), Ted Sturgis (b), Ernie Hackett (dm)

Ruby was interviewed by George Hall for his radio program in conjunction with his next reported engagement in Annapolis.

Ruby Braff Quartet[13]
May 2–14, 1978, King of France Tavern, Maryland Inn, 22 Church Circle, Annapolis, Maryland
Ruby Braff (cnt), Johnny Morris (p), Bill Nelson (b), Bill Rickenbach (dm)

Joe Boughton made a cassette recording at Condon's during a performance on May 17, 1978, by Randy Reinhart, Vic Dickenson, Bobby Gordon, Jimmy Andrews, Phil Flanigan, and Connie Kay. His notes report that Ruby, Warren Vaché, and Roy Eldridge were in the audience that night, although Ruby is not audible on the available recording but he may have joined the group on subsequent sets. Certainly, Ruby was back home in New York after his appearance in Annapolis.

Ruby returned to Carnegie Hall for the Newport Jazz Festival in 1978 in a program celebrating titled *Jazz Salute to the American Song*. Other performers in the program included Mel Tormé (performing Harold Arlen tunes), Stan Getz (Alec Wilder), Jimmy Rowles (Harry Warren), Gerry Mulligan (Arthur Schwartz), Irene Kral (Cole Porter), Marian McPartland, Urbie Green, Warren Vaché, Jr., Ken Peplowski, Dave Frishberg, Bobby Short, and Alberta Hunter. Ruby and Dick Hyman joined in a short program of tunes by Fats Waller. Following Newport, he had an engagement at Jimmy Ryan's before flying to England.

Newport Jazz Festival:[14] ***Jazz Salute to the American Song***
June 27, 1978, Carnegie Hall, New York
Ruby Braff (cnt), Dick Hyman (org)
How Can You Face Me?
Ain't Misbehavin'
Honeysuckle Rose

Ruby Braff[15]
June 27?–July 1, 1978, Jimmy Ryan's, 154 West 54th Street, New York
Ruby Braff (cnt), Bobby Pratt (tb), Joe Muranyi (cl), Johnny Morris (p), Ted Sturgis (b), Eddie Locke (dm)

Ruby was off to London again for an extended engagement at Pizza Express. The following performance is Ruby's earliest encounter with Brian Lemon that I have discovered with the possible exception of Ruby's UK tour in 1976. Brian provided Ruby with excellent support on many of his future tours and several of his recordings. Several nights, Ruby performed with Eddie Thompson and his trio. The two of them performed unaccompanied on the closing night of the engagement. Only two recordings appear to exist.

Pizza Express[16]
July 27, 1978, London
Ruby Braff (cnt), Brian Lemon (p), Kenny Baldock (b), Derek Hogg (dm)
Thou Swell
Sweethearts on Parade
Somebody Loves Me
Body and Soul
You Took Advantage of Me
Exactly Like You
Muskrat Ramble
I'm Putting All My Eggs in One Basket
Don't Get Around Much Anymore
Old Folks

As Long As I Live
Easy Living
You're Driving Me Crazy
White Waves (?)
Struttin' with Some Barbecue
Love Is Just around the Corner
Ain't Misbehavin'
What's New?
Three Little Words
I've Got a Right to Sing the Blues
I Know That You Know
Unknown blues
Love Walked In

A photo from the March of Jazz program by Jack Bradley exists from the time of this engagement.[17]

Melody Maker, in the issue dated August 19, 1978, refers to an engagement at Pizza Express (and unspecified other dates in Britain) with Eddie Thompson, Len Skeat, and Russ Bryant. It specifically mentioned one night at Pizza on the Park with Eddie Thompson. I have not been able to locate further details for these appearances; however, the next recording probably corresponds to the July 30 performance. Perhaps further information about this tour will surface later. There were likely other nights at Pizza Express as well that I have been unable to document.

Ruby Braff with Eddie Thompson
Probably July 30, 1978, Pizza Express, London
Ruby Braff (cnt), Eddie Thompson (p)
It's the Same Old South
Medley:
  Old Folks
  On the Sunny Side of the Street
Medley:
  Pennies from Heaven
  I Cover the Waterfront
Medley:
  Loveless Love
  If I Could Be with You One Hour Tonight
I've Got a Feelin' I'm Fallin'
Medley:
  I Can't Give You Anything but Love
  Thinking of You
  Coquette

NOTE: A recording of these tunes is available but remains unissued. "Loveless Love" is announced as "Old Fashioned Love" on this recording. This recording closed the engagement.

Ruby referred to this as his happiest tour to the UK to this point in conversation with Max Jones.[18] ". . . this is the best place I've ever worked in. It's been the most enjoyable gig I've had in my life—ever, anywhere. The best gig I've worked in 40 years, I'm telling you. There were no hassles at all." Ruby singled out Eddie Thompson for praise. Referring to other evenings, he also said, "And there were two very nice people playing with us: Len Skeat and Russ Bryant, they're both wonderful too, you know. And, of course, last night at the Pizza on the Park I worked with just Eddie. I really enjoyed that." Max Jones continued, "So Ruby is a most happy fella right now. Which is good, because his exceptional musicianship should bring him satisfaction as well as recognition from musicians and critics. Recognition he has had from the start, as I recall, but it has been reported frequently that he has felt disillusioned with the music business from time to time. Ruby said yes, with the business, never with the music." Ruby next performed in London in November 1978, resuming his relationship with Eddie Thompson, but for now it was back to the United States.

Ruby Braff with Buddy Tate: King of France Tavern[19]
Week of August 8, 1978, Maryland Inn, Annapolis, Maryland

Al White published two photos of Ruby Braff performing at Dick Gibson's Jazz Party. The first shows him with Benny Carter[20] and the second with Trummy Young, Al Grey, and Marshall Royal[21]. Apart from a review by Leonard Feather, there is no further information available about specific performances.

Dick Gibson's Colorado Jazz Party[22]
September 1-4, 1978, Broadmoor Hotel, Colorado Springs, Colorado
Ruby Braff with others including Benny Carter, Trummy Young, Marshall Royal, and Al Grey
I've Grown Accustomed to Her Face

Ruby Braff[23]
September 12?–September 20, 1978, Jimmy Ryan's, 154 West 54th Street, New York
Ruby Braff (cnt), Bobby Pratt (tb), Joe Muranyi (cl), Johnny Morris (p), Ted Sturgis (b), Eddie Locke (dm)

Ruby Braff with Warren Vaché: King of France Tavern[24]
Week of October 17, 1978, Maryland Inn, Annapolis, Maryland

Once again, Ruby flew to London. He recorded two albums for Pizza, a label associated with Pizza Express, but only the first was issued due to technical problems with the second session. The label shows, appropriately, a photograph of a pizza. Only one live appearance has been documented beyond this recording. Likely he made additional appearances on this trip to offset the time and cost of travel.

Ruby Braff with the Neil Richardson Strings: *Swinging on a Star: Ruby Braff Plays Bing, Volume One*
November 1978, Maida Vale, London
Ruby Braff (cnt), Brian Lemon (p), Len Walker (g), Lennie Bush (b), Terry Jenkins (dm), the Neil Richardson strings led by Sydney Sax. Music arranged and conducted by Neil Richardson.
Swinging on a Star
    Pizza (E) 5501
Old Folks
    Pizza (E) 5501, Pizza 1 (45-rpm)
Did You Ever See a Dream Walking (A)
    Pizza (E) 5501
I've Got a Pocket Full of Dreams (A)
    Pizza (E) 5501
Moonlight Becomes You
    Pizza (E) 5501
Pennies from Heaven
    Pizza (E) 5501
Go Fly a Kite
    Pizza (E) 5501
Please
    Pizza (E) 5501
All Alone
    Pizza (E) 5501
You're Sensational
    Pizza (E) 5501
Too-Ra-Loo-Ra-Loo-Ra
    Pizza (E) 5501
White Christmas
    Pizza (E) 5501, Pizza 1 (45-rpm)
NOTE: All of the above except (A) also on Arbors ARCD 19219 titled *Ruby Braff and Strings: In the Wee, Small Hours in London and New York*. See March 1999 for the balance of the performances on this CD. "You're Sensational" also appears in the box set *You're Sensational: Cole Porter in the 30s, 40s and 50s*.

Pizza Express[25]
November 28, 1978, Pizza Express, London
Ruby Braff (cnt), Eddie Thompson (p), Len Skeat (b), Ted Pope (dm)

Love Walked In
I've Got the World on a String
Nancy (With the Laughing Face)
Mean to Me
What a Little Moonlight Can Do
But Not for Me (omit Braff)
Lady Be Good
This Could Be the Start of Something Big
Ghost of a Chance
Three Little Words
Russian Lullaby
Jeepers Creepers
Medley:
  Old Folks
  How Long Has This Been Going On?
Struttin' with Some Barbecue
They Can't Take That Away from Me
Medley:
  Star Dust
  Solitude
Unknown title
Isn't She Lovely (omit Braff)
The Very Thought of You (omit Skeat and Pope)
Medley:
  Blue Lou
  Chicago
  The Man That Got Away
  Over the Rainbow

Pizza: Unissued session
November 1978, live, Pizza Express, London
Ruby Braff (cnt), Brian Lemon (p), Louis Stewart (g), Len Skeat (b), Bobby Rosengarden (dm)
Yesterdays
Watch What Happens
Sometimes I'm Happy
The Man I Love
'S Wonderful
Ain't Misbehavin'
I Guess I'll Have to Change My Plans
Poor Butterfly
I've Got a Right to Sing the Blues
Dinah

NOTE: The above tunes were scheduled for release on Pizza (E) PE 5503; however, according to Dave Bennett, the master tape was judged not satisfactory due to poor recording balance. The record was never produced.

Ruby discussed the following recording session. He found the approach very unusual, saying that in many cases only fragments of tunes were recorded at times as directed by William Savory, Helen Ward's husband. According to Ruby, Savory was very enthusiastic, frequently interrupting performers to say words like, "That's just what we wanted" and slowing the progress of making the overall album. Despite Ruby's recollections, the record is very enjoyable. While it is labeled "Volume 1," inquires by the author have led to no signs of further material or master tapes held in Savory's personal archive. Savory was known, among many other things, for being part of a team at Columbia Records that developed the first 33 1/3-rpm long-playing records and pioneering in the transfers of 78 rpm masters to LPs for reissue. He was Helen Ward's husband.[26]

Helen Ward: *Helen Ward Songbook, Volume 1*[27]
January 9, 1979, Chiaroscuro Studios, Christopher Street, New York
Bucky Pizzarelli (g and leader), Steve Jordan (g), Ruby Braff (cnt), Vic Dickenson (tb), Al Cohn (ts), Mickey Crane (p), Milt Hinton (b), Butch Miles (dm), Helen Ward (voc)
Someone to Watch Over Me
    Lyricon 1001
The Glory of Love
    Lyricon 1001
NOTE: See also March 26 and 27, 1970, for additional titles from this album that include Ruby Braff. Ruby Braff does not perform on all selections on this album. Dates and personnel as reported in Tom Lord, *The Jazz Discography*. The album only provided collective information. Ruby said that this, together with the subsequent dates, was one of the strangest recording sessions he ever experienced. The musicians were asked to perform the music in segments. Savory exclaimed words like, "This is just want we wanted to hear." Then, they would resume. Ruby did not claim that the entire session was done in this manner, but this was his dominant recollection of the proceedings.

Heavenly Jazz Concert Series: *Zoot Sims and Friends*[28]
March 18, 1979, 5 p.m., Church of the Heavenly Rest, 5th Avenue and 90th Street, New York
Ruby Braff (cnt), Zoot Sims (ts), Jimmy Rowles (p), Bucky Pizzarelli (g), Major Holley (b), Bobby Rosengarden (dm)

Further details are not known for the above performance. Proceeds went to support the day school at the church. This series of concerts was organized by Paul Weinstein, whose father was a close friend of Eddie Condon and Ernie Anderson during the era of Condon's Town Hall Concerts. His son attended the day school. Ruby was quite open to donating his time to supporting charitable groups of this sort.

Ruby continued to be called whenever Roy Eldridge was unavailable to perform at Jimmy Ryan's.

A year had passed for Ruby, and the third Strides of March program was scheduled for the weekend of March 23. Ruby again appeared in several sets. The actual personnel appeared to depart from the available copy of the published program.

Ruby Braff Quintet[29]
March 23, 1979, Strides of March #3, New Jersey Jazz Society, Somerset Marriott Hotel, Somerset, New Jersey
Ruby Braff (cnt), Herb Ellis (g), Derek Smith (p), Michael Moore (b), Bobby Rosengarden (dm)
Thou Swell
Medley:
  The Very Thought of You
  Tea for Two
I Love You (Ellis feature)
Lover Come Back to Me
NOTE: A recording of these tunes is available but remains unissued.

The above medley and "I Love You" were broadcast on the National Public Radio Program *Jazz Alive* on September 12, 1980. Air dates may differ in different cities.

Ruby Braff Octet[30]
March 23, 1979, Strides of March #3, New Jersey Jazz Society, Somerset Marriott Hotel, Somerset, New Jersey
Ruby Braff (cnt), Vic Dickenson (tb), Bob Wilber (ss), Bobby Gordon (cl), Remo Palmier (g), Derek Smith (p), Jack Lesberg (b), Jake Hanna (dm)
Mood Indigo*
Struttin' with Some Barbecue
Someone to Watch Over Me (Dickenson feature)
Apex Blues
Blues My Naughty Sweetie Gave to Me
Jeepers Creepers
NOTE: With the exception of "Mood Indigo," which is marked with an asterisk and may not be part of this set, a recording of these tunes is available but remains unissued.

Ruby Braff Octet[31]
March 23, 1979, Strides of March #3, New Jersey Jazz Society, Somerset Marriott Hotel, Somerset, New Jersey (start of afternoon of second day at 1 p.m.)

Ruby Braff (cnt), Vic Dickenson (tb), Bob Wilber (cl), Zoot Sims (ts), Remo Palmier (g), Dick Hyman (p), Michael Moore (b), Jake Hanna (dm)
Lady Be Good
Jealous
Come Sunday (Michael Moore feature)
I Can't Believe That You're in Love with Me
Wequasset Wail (Limehouse Blues) (Wilber feature)
Love Me or Leave Me
NOTE: A recording of these tunes is available but remains unissued.

Ruby Braff Septet[32]
March 24, 1979, Strides of March #3, New Jersey Jazz Society, Somerset Marriott Hotel, Somerset, New Jersey (afternoon session)
Ruby Braff (cnt), Bob Wilber (cl), Zoot Sims (ts), Herb Ellis (g), Derek Smith (p), Michael Moore (b), Jake Hanna (dm)
I'm Getting Sentimental Over You
The More I See You (Ellis feature)
Between the Devil and the Deep Blue Sea
Gravy Waltz (Smith feature)
A Child Is Born (Smith feature–incomplete on recording)
The Sheik of Araby (Smith feature–incomplete on recording)
Lady Be Good
NOTE: A recording of these tunes is available but remains unissued. "The More I See You" may have been incorrectly reported as "For All We Know" in a review of this session.

Ruby Braff Septet[33]
March 24, 1979, Strides of March #3, New Jersey Jazz Society, Somerset Marriott Hotel, Somerset, New Jersey (final evening after midnight, so actually March 25)
Ruby Braff (cnt), Vic Dickenson (tb, voc), Zoot Sims (ss, ts), Herb Ellis (g), Dick Wellstood (p), Michael Moore (b), Bobby Rosengarden (dm)
Linger Awhile
Mean to Me
I Never Knew (Sims feature)
Medley:
  For All We Know (Braff feature)
  Chicago
Cherry (Dickenson feature tb and voc)
Keepin' Out of Mischief Now (Zoot plays ss)
NOTE: A recording of these tunes is available but remains unissued.

Helen Ward: *Helen Ward Songbook Volume 1*
March 26, 1979, New York

Bucky Pizzarelli (g and leader), Steve Jordan (g), Ruby Braff (cnt), Vic Dickenson, George Masso (tb), Phil Bodner (cl), Al Cohn (ts), Tony Monte (p), Milt Hinton (b), Bobby Rosengarden (dm), Helen Ward (voc)
There'll Be Some Changes Made
    Lyricon 1001
I Thought About You
    Lyricon 1001
In a Little Spanish Town
    Lyricon 1001

March 27, 1979, New York
Bucky Pizzarelli (g and leader), Steve Jordan (g), Ruby Braff (cnt), George Masso (tb), Phil Bodner (cl), Al Cohn (ts), Tony Monte (p), Milt Hinton (b), Bobby Rosengarden (dm), Helen Ward (voc)
Keepin' Out of Mischief Now
    Lyricon 1001
The Second Time Around
    Lyricon 1001
NOTE: See also January 9, 1970, for additional titles from this album that include Ruby Braff. Ruby Braff does not perform on all selections on this album. Dates and personnel as reported in Tom Lord, *Jazz Discography*. The album only provided collective information. While the record is labeled Volume 1, there is no trace of additional recordings from these sessions.

Ruby Braff[34]
March 28–31, 1979, Jimmy Ryan's, 154 West 54th Street, New York
Ruby Braff (cnt), probably with the following musicians: Bobby Pratt (tb), Joe Muranyi (cl), Johnny Morris (p), Ted Sturgis (b), Eddie Locke (dm)

Unknown Jazz Party
Possibly 1979 but it has not been possible to trace the date and location of this recording more precisely
Ruby Braff (cnt), John Bunch (p), Milt Hinton (b), Bobby Rosengarden (dm)
Yesterdays
Sunday
Medley:
  I've Grown Accustomed to Her Face
  I Would Do Anything for You
St. Louis Blues
NOTE: A recording of these tunes is available but remains unissued.

Jazz Interactions Annual Fund Raising Concert and Tribute to Ed Beach[35]
April 29, 1973, Village Gate, New York

Performing musicians include Ruby Braff, Randy Brecker, the Countsmen with Jo Jones and Earle Warren, the Jimmy Giuffre Trio, Chico Hamilton Quintet, Jimmy Heath, Lee Konitz, Harold Mabern, Attila Zoller, and others.

Ruby Braff Quartet[36]
May 6, 1979, 8 p.m., Bargemusic, Fulton Ferry Landing, Brooklyn, New York

Ira Gitler produced a jazz party in Kansas City for June 1–3 and invited Ruby to participate. On June 1, in his opening announcement, Ira Gitler announced, "The last time we had Ruby here we had him, with Al Cohn, in a snowstorm." So this points to an unknown previous winter engagement in Kansas City in an earlier year that I have been unable to trace. Scott Hamilton reported to me that Al Cohn told him about the snowstorm many times. They were stranded for several days at that time. The reference may have been to the severe winter storms and blizzards that affected many parts of the US in February 1978.

Jazz Olympics: Kansas City Jazz Festival[37]
June 1–3, 1979, Muehlebach Hotel, Kansas City, Missouri. This was the first "Jazz Olympics" Festival
Festival producer: Ira Gitler

Jazz Olympics: Kansas City Jazz Festival: June 1, 1979

Ruby Braff Sextet:
Ruby Braff (cnt), Bob Kindred, Scott Hamilton (ts), Dave Frishberg (p, voc), Michael Moore (b), Jake Hanna (dm)
Just You, Just Me
Sweet and Lovely (Hamilton feature)
Love Me or Leave Me
Drop Me Off in Harlem (Frishberg feature)
Mean to Me
I'm Getting Sentimental Over You (Kindred feature)
Blues*
NOTE: A recording of these tunes is available but remains unissued. One tune is incomplete in the recording and is marked with an asterisk.

This is the earliest recording that I have located which unites Ruby and Scott Hamilton in performance although this was not their first time performing together.

Ruby Braff Sextet
Ruby Braff (cnt), Bob Kindred, Scott Hamilton (ts), Dave Frishberg (p), Michael Moore (b), Jake Hanna (dm)
You're Driving Me Crazy
You've Changed (Moore feature)

Jive at Five
I've Grown Accustomed to Her Face (Braff feature)
All the Things You Are (Hamilton feature)
The Crave (Frishberg solo)
Keepin' Out of Mischief Now*
NOTE: A recording of these tunes is available but remains unissued. One tune is incomplete in the recording and is marked with an asterisk.

Ruby Braff Sextet
Ruby Braff (cnt), Bob Kindred, Scott Hamilton (ts), Dave Frishberg (p), Michael Moore (b), Jake Hanna (dm)
You Turned the Tables on Me
Time After Time (Hamilton feature)
Wrap Your Troubles in Dreams

Add Jack Ackerman (tap dancing)
My Funny Valentine

Ackerman out
I Got It Bad and That Ain't Good (Moore feature)
Them There Eyes
NOTE: A recording of these tunes is available but remains unissued.

Jazz Olympics: Kansas City Jazz Festival: June 2, 1979

Ruby Braff Sextet
3 p.m.
Ruby Braff (cnt), Bob Kindred, Scott Hamilton (ts), Dave Frishberg (p), Michael Moore (b), Jake Hanna (dm)
Exactly Like You
Dear Bix (Frishberg solo and vocal)

Add Jack Ackerman (tap dancing)
Jeepers Creepers

Ackerman out
Don't Blame Me (Hamilton feature)
Sometimes I'm Happy*
NOTE: A recording of these tunes is available but remains unissued. One tune is incomplete in the recording and is marked with an asterisk.

Ruby Braff Sextet
5 p.m.
Ruby Braff (cnt), Bob Kindred, Scott Hamilton (ts), Dave Frishberg (p), Michael Moore (b), Jake Hanna (dm)

The Man I Love
Body and Soul (Kindred feature)
Medley
  Cocktails for Two
  On the Sunny Side of the Street
My Romance (Moore feature)
Medley:
  I Can't Give You Anything but Love
  The Very Thought of You
I Thought About You (Hamilton feature)
Blues
NOTE: A recording of these tunes is available but remains unissued.

Ruby Braff Sextet
Evening
Ruby Braff (cnt), Bob Kindred, Scott Hamilton (ts), Dave Frishberg (p), Michael Moore (b), Jake Hanna (dm)
Medley:
  Rose Room
  In a Mellotone
Ain't Misbehavin'
Let's Do It (Frishberg feature)
Yesterdays (Hamilton feature)
Lover Come Back to Me
Keepin' Out of Mischief Now
Way Down Yonder in New Orleans
NOTE: A recording of these tunes is available but remains unissued.

Ruby Braff Sextet
Ruby Braff (cnt), Bob Kindred, Scott Hamilton (ts), Dave Frishberg (p), Michael Moore (b), Jake Hanna (dm)
Thou Swell
Blues
I Got It Bad and That Ain't Good (Moore feature)

Add Jack Ackerman (tap dancing)
Between the Devil and the Deep Blue Sea

Ackerman out
For All We Know
NOTE: A recording of these tunes is available but remains unissued.

Jazz Olympics: Kansas City Jazz Festival: June 3, 1979

Ruby Braff Sextet
Ruby Braff (cnt), Scott Hamilton, Bob Kindred (ts), Nat Pierce (p), Michael Moore (b), Jake Hanna (dm)
Sunday
Struttin' with Some Barbecue
In a Sentimental Mood (Kindred feature)
Jeepers Creepers
My Romance (Moore feature)
Stuffy (Hamilton feature)
When You're Smiling
NOTE: A recording of these tunes is available but remains unissued.

Ruby Braff Quartet
Ruby Braff (cnt), Nat Pierce (p), Michael Moore (b), Gus Johnson (dm)
Sometimes I'm Happy

Replace Gus Johnson with Jake Hanna (Jake Hanna arrived late for the opening number)
These Foolish Things
I Never Knew
Blue and Sentimental
NOTE: A recording of these tunes is available but remains unissued.

Ruby flew to Toronto directly from Kansas City for another appearance at Bourbon Street for a two-week engagement.

Ruby Braff at Bourbon Street[38]
June 4–17, 1979, Bourbon Street, 180 Queen Street West, Toronto
Ruby Braff (cnt), Ed Bickert (g), David Young (b), Jerry Fuller (dm)
NOTE: John Norris reviewed the performance on June 7 during this engagement and mentioned the following tunes:[39]
You've Changed
Lester Leaps In
Pennies from Heaven
Take the "A" Train
Easy Living

Jerry Fuller reported the following in an interview during this engagement: "I can't take it anymore, he's so funny." Mark Miller continued, writing, "When a request for "Tea for Two" must be filled, it becomes a nice joke, complete with the appropriate soft-shoe routine from brushman Fuller; when the revue upstairs at Basin Street begins to shake the walls below, Braff counters with the softest ballad of the evening. Complex fellow. Marvelous musician."[40]

Ruby Braff Interview with Ted O'Reilly
June 11, 1979, CJRT-FM, Toronto, Ontario
NOTE: A recording of this interview is available but remains unissued.

Ruby Braff with the Ed Bickert Trio
June 14, 1979, Toronto
Ruby Braff (cnt), Ed Bickert (g), Don Thompson (b), Terry Clarke (dm)
True Love
    Sackville (Ca) 3022, Sackville SK2CD 5005 (CD)
I've Got a Feelin' I'm Fallin'
    Sackville (Ca) 3022, Sackville SK2CD 5005 (CD)
This Year's Kisses
    Sackville (Ca) 3022, Sackville SK2CD 5005 (CD)
The World Is Waiting for the Sunrise
    Sackville (Ca) 3022, Sackville SK2CD 5005 (CD)
The Very Thought of You
    Sackville (Ca) 3022, Sackville SK2CD 5005 (CD)
After Awhile
    Sackville (Ca) 3022, Sackville SK2CD 5005 (CD)
What Is There to Say?
    Sackville (Ca) 3022, Sackville SK2CD 5005 (CD)
My Funny Valentine
    Sackville (Ca) 3022, Sackville SK2CD 5005 (CD)
Medley:
  The Song Is Ended
    Sackville (Ca) 3022, Sackville SK2CD 5005 (CD)
  When I Fall in Love
    Sackville (Ca) 3022, Sackville SK2CD 5005 (CD)
I Must Have That Man
    Sackville SK2CD 5005 (CD)
If Dreams Come True
    Sackville SK2CD 5005 (CD)
NOTE: See January 17, 1984 and January 23, 1984 for other sessions included on the above Sackville CD, titled *The Canadian Sessions*.

Ruby Braff Interview with Ted O'Reilly
June 16, 1979, CJRT-FM, Toronto
NOTE: A recording of this interview is available but remains unissued.

Ruby performed at both Waterloo Village and in Carnegie Hall for the 1979 Newport Jazz Festival. He was captured in several sets at Waterloo and was also featured in a tribute to Billie Holiday in an evening concert.

Newport Jazz Festival
June 23, 1979, 5–10 p.m. Newport Jazz Festival, Waterloo Village, Stanhope, New Jersey
Ruby appeared at Waterloo Village as part of the Newport Jazz Festival, in a program called *Swing'n Pianos*. This program was co-sponsored by the New Jersey Jazz Society.

Ruby Braff Quartet[41]
June 23, 1979, 5-10 p.m. Newport Jazz Festival, Waterloo Village, Stanhope, New Jersey
New Jersey Jazz Society
Ruby Braff (cnt), Dick Wellstood (p), Michael Moore (b), Bobby Rosengarden (dm)
Keepin' Out of Mischief Now
Sugar
Carolina Shout (Wellstood solo)
You Can Depend on Me
NOTE: A recording of these tunes is available but remains unissued.

Ruby Braff–Dick Hyman[42]
June 23, 1979, Newport Jazz Festival, Waterloo Village, Stanhope, New Jersey
New Jersey Jazz Society
Ruby Braff (cnt), Dick Hyman (org)
Persian Rug
If I Could Be with You
Rosetta
I've Got a Feelin' I'm Fallin'
Love Me or Leave Me
NOTE: A recording of these tunes is available but remains unissued.

Ruby Braff–Dick Hyman–Dick Wellstood[43]
June 23, 1979, Newport Jazz Festival, Waterloo Village, Stanhope, New Jersey
New Jersey Jazz Society
Ruby Braff (cnt), Dick Wellstood, Dick Hyman (p)
Medley:
  The Very Thought of You
  Liza
  I've Found a New Baby
NOTE: A recording of these tunes is available but remains unissued.

Bob Wilber and Four Pianos[44]
June 23, 1979, Newport Jazz Festival, Waterloo Village, Stanhope, New Jersey
Bob Wilber (ss), Sammy Price, Derek Smith, Dick Wellstood, Dick Hyman (p)
Sweet Georgia Brown

Add Ruby Braff (cnt), Jack Lesberg (b), Mousey Alexander (dm)
That's a Plenty
No Gas Boogie
NOTE: A recording of these tunes is available but remains unissued.

No Gas Boogie is a name supplied by Sammy Price. There was a gasoline shortage at the time of this concert and the audience responded to his humor.[45] A photograph is available from the March of Jazz program.[46]

Newport Jazz Festival: *We Remember Billie*[47]
June 28, 1979, Carnegie Hall, New York
Ruby Braff (cnt), Buddy Tate (ts), Lionel Hampton (vib), Ray Bryant (p), George Duvivier (b), Wayne Wright (g), Bobby Rosengarden (dm)
Why Was I Born
Romance in the Dark
I Must Have That Man
I'm Pulling Through
Unidentified blues

Roy Eldridge declined an invitation to appear and was reported to be "particularly upset to learn that Ruby Braff had played on numbers that Roy had originally recorded with Lady Day."[48] This may be the reason that Ruby was not listed in *The New Yorker* ever again as appearing as Roy's regular replacement at Jimmy Ryan's. Eventually Max Kaminsky expanded his role in that club.

The following handbill depicts one of the performances in this chapter:

Figure 15.1: Handbill November 10, 1977

Notes

[1] John S. Wilson, *New York Times*, August 28, 1977, and *New York Magazine*, November 14, 1977, 35.
[2] *New York Times*, November 6, 1977.
[3] Tony Bennett with Will Friedwald, *The Good Life* (New York: Pocket Books, 1998) 228–229.
[4] *The New Yorker*, November 28, 1977, 8.
[5] *Globe and Mail*, January 4, 1978, and January 11, 1978, reporting engagement ends Saturday.
[6] David Lancashire, *Globe and Mail*, July 10, 1978.
[7] *The New Yorker*, January 23, 1978, 8, and January 30, 1978, 6.
[8] New Jersey Jazz Society Collection, Institute of Jazz Studies.
[9] New Jersey Jazz Society Collection, Institute of Jazz Studies.
[10] New Jersey Jazz Society Collection, Institute of Jazz Studies.
[11] New Jersey Jazz Society Collection, Institute of Jazz Studies.
[12] *The New Yorker*, April 24, 1978, 8, and May 1, 1978, 8.
[13] *Washington Post*, April 28, 1978, May 5, 1978, and May 12, 1978. Ruby featured in radio interview with George Hall.
[14] Whitney Balliett, *Night Creature* (New York: Oxford University Press, 1981), 177 reprinted from *The New Yorker*, July 17, 1978, 97. Library of Congress, RGA 0361 (RWD 8397-8398). *The New Yorker*, June 26, 1978, 7, and *New York Magazine*, July 3, 1989, 3.
[15] *The New Yorker*, July 3, 1978, 5–only the closing date was published for the ongoing engagement.
[16] Information provided by Derek Coller.
[17] Photo by Jack Bradley, *The March of Jazz Celebrates Ruby Braff's 74th Birthday Party*, Arbors Records, 2001, 24.
[18] Max Jones, *Talking Jazz*, (New York: W. W. Norton and Company, 1988), 94–95.
[19] Scott Hamilton talking with Mel Levine on July 13, 1978.
[20] Al White, *Jazz Party* (Little Rock, AR: August House Publishers, 2000), 22.
[21] Al White, *Jazz Party* (Little Rock, AR: August House Publishers, 2000), 76.
[22] Al White, *Jazz Party* (Little Rock, AR: August House Publishers, 2000), 76; Leonard Feather, *Los Angeles Times*, September 6, 1978.
[23] *The New Yorker*, September 18, 1978, 7. Only the closing date was published for the ongoing engagement.
[24] Scott Hamilton talking with Mel Levine on July 13, 1978.
[25] Notes from Derek Coller.
[26] Of course Bill Savory was also in the news when his collection of original private recordings of jazz performances from the 1930s was acquired by the National Jazz Museum in Harlem. At the time of publication, the following link provides a fascinating glimpse into these historical recordings: http://www.nytimes.com/2010/08/17/arts/music/17jazz.html?pagewanted=all. Savory was instrumental in preparing the LP releases of Benny Goodman's 1938 Carnegie Hall concert.
[27] This session is described by John S. Wilson, *New York Times*, September 7, 1979.
[28] Advertisement in *Jersey Jazz* March 1979, *The New Yorker*, March 19, 1979, 10, and listing in *New York Times*, March 16, 1979, and *New York Magazine*, March 19, 1979, 32.

[29] New Jersey Jazz Society Collection, Institute of Jazz Studies Strides of March Program from New Jersey Jazz Society contained on tapes 147–155 in a restricted archive at the Institute for Jazz Studies.
[30] New Jersey Jazz Society Collection, Institute of Jazz Studies. "Mood Indigo" is listed in the National Public Radio archive but is not on the reel tapes at the Institute of Jazz Studies. Thus, it may come from a different part of the program.
[31] New Jersey Jazz Society Collection, Institute of Jazz Studies.
[32] New Jersey Jazz Society Collection, Institute of Jazz Studies.
[33] New Jersey Jazz Society Collection, Institute of Jazz Studies.
[34] *The New Yorker*, March 26, 1979, 8, and April 2, 1979, 8, and *New York Magazine*, April 2, 1979, 24.
[35] *Village Voice*, April 26, 1973, 18.
[36] *New York Times*, May 6, 1979.
[37] Concert organized by Ira Gitler who holds master tapes and reviewed by Jerry Adkins in *Coda Magazine*, August 1979, 36.
[38] Mark Miller writing in the *Globe and Mail*, June 8, 1979, and August 16, 1980, when he stated that this engagement ran two weeks.
[39] John Norris, writing in *Coda Magazine*, August 1979, 37.
[40] Mark Miller writing in the *Globe and Mail*, June 8, 1979.
[41] New Jersey Jazz Society archive held at the Institute of Jazz Studies and ad in *New York Times*, May 29, 1979.
[42] Original tape held in New Jersey Jazz Society archive held at the Institute of Jazz Studies. Advertised in *New York Times*, June 22, 1979.
[43] Original tape held in New Jersey Jazz Society archive held at the Institute of Jazz Studies.
[44] Original tape held in New Jersey Jazz Society archive held at the Institute of Jazz Studies.
[45] John S. Wilson, *New York Times*, June 25, 1979.
[46] Photo, *The March of Jazz Celebrates Ruby Braff's 74th Birthday Party*, Arbors Records, 2001, 25.
[47] Manfred Selchow, *Ding Ding: A Bio-Discographical Scrapbook on Vic Dickenson* (Germany: Uhle & Kleinmann, 1998), 740–741. Library of Congress RGA 0389 (RWD 8511).
[48] John Chilton, *Roy Eldridge, Little Jazz Giant* (New York: Continuum, 2002), 294.

Chapter 16

The Pianists and the Growth of Jazz Parties: July 1979–February 1982

John S. Wilson reported that Scott Hamilton and Ruby toured with George Wein's Newport All Stars following the Newport Jazz Festival's *Tribute to Billie Holiday* concert.[1] No information is available, but this probably refers to the festival performances at Nice and in London that follow. Ruby had not performed with George Wein since 1975; however, Scott did tour with the Newport All Stars.

Ruby's documented appearances at New York clubs never again reached the frequency of the years during the 1970s. By the early 1980s, Warren Vaché was appearing regularly at Broadway Joe's and even before this Scott Hamilton was featured regularly at Eddie Condon's. The 1980s did feature expanded opportunities for Dick Wellstood, Ralph Sutton, and Dave McKenna, and Ruby did join them on at least a few documented occasions. Bucky Pizzarelli, Bob Wilber, and Dick Hyman also continued to remain active in Manhattan clubs.

So, once again it was time for Ruby to fly to France for the 1979 Grande Parade du Jazz. The festival offered him a chance to play with many top-level musicians that had never joined him in recording sessions. Among the many matchups, Ruby was scheduled to perform with Stan Getz at the end of the festival. They discussed the tunes they would play in the performance; however, Stan then only called on Ruby to join in the first two tunes in the set, upsetting Ruby since he, rightly, felt slighted. A partial recording of that set is available; however, another featuring Ruby with Dave Brubeck has not been located at the time of publication. The contrast of styles would certainly be interesting to hear. But Ruby begins with several of his longtime musical friends in his first set at the festival.

Ruby Braff Quintet: Grande Parade du Jazz
July 5, 1979, Grande Parade du Jazz, Nice, France
Ruby Braff (cnt), Vic Dickenson (tb), Jimmy Rowles (p), Slam Stewart (b), Alan Dawson (dm)
The Very Thought of You
Keepin' Out of Mischief Now

Someone to Watch Over Me (featuring VD)
Lady Be Good (featuring SS)
Linger Awhile
NOTE: A recording of these tunes is available but remains unissued.

Newport All Stars: Grande Parade du Jazz
July 6, 1979, Jardin des Arénes de Cimiez, Grande Parade du Jazz, Nice, France
Ruby Braff (cnt), Vic Dickenson (tb), George Wein (p), Jack Sewing (b), Bobby Durham (dm)
You're Lucky to Me
Blue and Sentimental
When You're Smiling
You Can Depend on Me

Add Sonny Stitt (as, ts)
Just You, Just Me
NOTE: A recording of these tunes is available but remains unissued. Michael Frohne lists "Just You, Just Me" on July 5 and adds Bucky Pizzarelli to the above personnel. Perhaps that is a different performance but not likely.

Ruby Braff–Jimmy Rowles: Grande Parade du Jazz
July 6, 1979, Grande Parade du Jazz, Nice, France
Ruby Braff (cnt), Jimmy Rowles (p), Slam Stewart (b), Shelly Manne (dm)
Between the Devil and the Deep Blue Sea
These Foolish Things
Love Me or Leave Me
I've Grown Accustomed to Her Face
Joshua Fit the Battle of Jericho (Braff out)
You're Driving Me Crazy (Braff returns)
NOTE: A recording of these tunes is available but remains unissued.

Manfred Selchow published a photograph from the following performance, showing Ruby with Barney Bigard and Vic Dickenson.[2]

Salute to Duke: Grande Parade du Jazz
July 7, 1979, Jardin des Arénes de Cimiez, Grande Parade du Jazz, Nice, France
Ruby Braff (cnt), Vic Dickenson (tb), Barney Bigard (cl), Jimmy Rowles (p), Slam Stewart (b), Shelly Manne (dm)
Perdido
Mood Indigo
Creole Love Call

Add Illinois Jacquet (ts)
All Too Soon
C Jam Blues

NOTE: A recording of these tunes is available but remains unissued.

Dave Brubeck Group with Ruby Braff: Grande Parade du Jazz[3]
July 9, 1979, Grande Parade du Jazz, Nice, France
Ruby Braff (cnt), Dave Brubeck (p), and others
Unsquare Dance
These Foolish Things

Slam Stewart and Friends: Grande Parade du Jazz
July 11, 1979, 9–10 p.m., Arena Stage, Grande Parade du Jazz, Nice, France
Ruby Braff (cnt), Buck Clayton (tp), Bob Wilber (ss), Peanuts Hucko (cl), Spiegle Wilcox (tb), Ray Bryant (p), Slam Stewart (b), Duffy Jackson (dm)
I Never Knew
I Want to Be Happy

Add Major Holley (b, voc)
Honeysuckle Rose
NOTE: A recording of these tunes is available but remains unissued. This session also includes "What Cha Gonna Do" and "I Got Rhythm" without Braff. Both are bass and vocal duets by Stewart and Holly with piano and drums. In addition a video recording of "I Never Knew" is available.

Ruby Braff: Grande Parade du Jazz
July 13, 1979, Grande Parade du Jazz, Nice, France
Ruby Braff (cnt), Jim Galloway (ss, ts), Jimmy Rowles (p), Slam Stewart (b), Alan Dawson (dm)
Sweet Georgia Brown
I Guess I'll Have to Change My Plans
Thou Swell (Galloway feature)
My Funny Valentine (Rowles feature)
Mean to Me (Braff feature)
Flat Foot Floogie (Stewart feature)
Lover Come Back to Me
NOTE: A recording of these tunes is available but remains unissued.

Ruby Braff with Stan Getz: Grande Parade du Jazz[4]
July 13, 1979, Grande Parade du Jazz, Nice, France
Ruby Braff (cnt), Stan Getz (ts) Lou Levy (p), Chuck Loeb (g), Marc Johnson (b), Victor Lewis (dm)
Willow Weep for Me
There Will Never Be Another You
Ruby Braff does not perform on the following tunes performed by Stan Getz with his group:
Chappaqua
Leaving My Love Behind

There Will Never Be Another You
Pretty City
Empty Shell
O Grande Amor
Infant Eyes
Lester Left Town
Willow Weep for Me
No More
Sea Breeze
Lush Life
NOTE: A recording of the first two tunes is available but remains unissued.

Ruby described this performance in an interview with Steve Voce.[5] He said Getz agreed on a list of tunes to perform but after "Willow Weep for Me" that Stan suddenly announced that they had just received a request and then called something like "Cherokee" at a fast tempo. Ruby did not join in and expressed his displeasure, since there was no time for a request from the audience. On many occasions Ruby praised Stan Getz's artistry; however, he also said he tried to avoid playing with him due to his unpredictable temperament.

But Ruby stated firmly in other discussions that Stan was a genius. Their conversations were limited to "Hello," "Thank you," and "Goodbye." Ruby continued, "We were not buddies, but Stan was wonderful."

From France, Ruby next traveled to England for the Capital Radio Jazz Festival where he was again extensively featured. A copy of the program is available.

Ruby Braff performed at the North Sea Jazz Festival in 1979, but no further information is known. Lacking specific dates for his appearance, I have placed this between his appearances in France and England.

Capital Radio Jazz Festival (Produced by George Wein)
July 17, 1979, Broadcast, Alexandra Palace, North London (Wood Green)
Ruby Braff (cnt), Vic Dickenson (tb), Bud Freeman (ts), Jimmy Rowles (p), Len Skeat (b), Alan Jackson (dm)
The Man I Love (Bud Freeman feature, Ruby out)
Gone with the Wind (Vic Dickenson feature, Ruby out)
You Took Advantage of Me
NOTE: A recording of these tunes is available but remains unissued. Derek Coller noted that the festival's program listed George Duvivier and Duffy Jackson instead of Len Skeat and Alan Jackson.

Capital Radio Jazz Festival[6]
July 19, 1979, Alexandra Palace, North London (Wood Green)
Ruby Braff (cnt), Vic Dickenson (tb), Illinois Jacquet (ts), Jimmy Rowles (p), Slam Stewart (b), Oliver Jackson (dm)
No further information is available.

Capital Radio Jazz Festival[7]
July 20, 1979, Alexandra Palace, North London (Wood Green)
Ruby Braff (cnt), Vic Dickenson (tb), Spiegle Wilcox (tb on 1), George Wein (p), Slam Stewart (b), Alan Dawson (dm)
'Deed I Do
Rose Room
Don't Take Your Love from Me (Wilcox feature)*
I Can't Give You Anything but Love (1)*
Wrap Your Troubles in Dreams
Jeepers Creepers
NOTE: A copy of the ticket for admission is available; Derek Coller noted that program listed Ray Bryant instead of George Wein on piano. A recording of these tunes is available with two exceptions. All remain unissued. "Don't Take Your Love from Me" is not included in the recording available to the author and "I Can't Give You Anything but Love" is incomplete. Both are marked with an asterisk.

Derek Coller noted that Ruby Braff also was scheduled to perform at the Capital Radio Jazz Festival on July 21. The program listed George Wein, Slam Stewart, and Duffy Jackson. Advanced promotion for the festival listed Ruby Braff as a performer on July 22 but not July 21. The listed performances are the only ones available on recordings. No further details are known.

Ruby Braff and Kenny Davern[8]
Possibly July 24, 1979, listed only as "a Sunday in July" from 1979, Liberty State Park, Jersey City, New Jersey
Ruby Braff (cnt), Kenny Davern (cl), Marty Grosz (g), George Duvivier (b), Bobby Rosengarden (dm)
Cottontail
Exactly Like You
Ain't Misbehavin' (MG vocal)
Caravan
NOTE: A recording of these tunes is available but remains unissued.

A photo of Ruby at Tony Bennett's Birthday celebration from the late 1970s exists. Mr. Bennett's birthday is August 13.[9]

Ruby's performances are becoming increasingly limited to jazz festivals and jazz parties. He was a regular participant at Dick Gibson's Labor Day gatherings through 1994.

Gibson Rocky Mountain Jazz Party[10]
September 1–3, 1979, Broadmoor Hotel, Colorado Springs, Colorado
Artists include Ruby Braff, Pee Wee Erwin, Clark Terry, Harry "Sweets" Edison, Red Rodney, Joe Newman, Doc Cheatham, Billy Butterfield (tps), Carl

Fontana, Bill Watrous, Al Grey, Trummy Young, Slide Hampton, Roy Williams, Britt Woodman (tb), Zoot Sims, Flip Phillips, Buddy Tate, Al Cohn, Scott Hamilton, Eddie "Lockjaw" Davis (ts), Budd Johnson (bar, ts), Peanuts Hucko, Buddy DeFranco (cl), Ralph Sutton, Dick Hyman, Roger Kellaway, Teddy Wilson, Ross Tompkins, Jay McShann, Derek Smith (p), Milt Hinton, George Duvivier, Ray Brown, Larry Ridley, Major Holley, Chuck Domanico (b), Cliff Leeman, Gus Johnson, Alan Dawson, Bobby Rosengarden, Jake Hanna, Jackie Williams, Shelly Manne (dm), Chuck Wayne, and John Collins (g)

September 1, 1979, 4:45 p.m., Saturday afternoon
Ruby Braff (cnt), Trummy Young (tb), Kenny Davern (cl), Scott Hamilton (ts, ldr), Ralph Sutton (p), Larry Ridley (b), Jackie Williams (dm)
Lester Leaps In
NOTE: A recording of these tunes is available but remains unissued. Ruby does not perform on other numbers from this set.

September 1, 1979, 11 p.m., Saturday evening
Ruby Braff (cnt, ldr), Roy Williams (tb), Marshall Royal (as), Al Cohn, Zoot Sims (ts), Ross Tompkins (p), John Collins (g), Milt Hinton (b), Cliff Leeman (dm)
Sometimes I'm Happy

Ruby Braff (cnt, ldr), Ross Tompkins (p), John Collins (g), Milt Hinton (b), Cliff Leeman (dm)
Love Walked In
NOTE: A recording of these tunes is available but remains unissued. Ruby does not perform on other numbers from this set.

September 2, 1979, 4:20 p.m., Sunday afternoon
Ruby Braff (cnt, ldr), Britt Woodman (tb), Bob Wilber (as), Al Cohn (ts), Ralph Sutton (p), Chuck Wayne (g), Major Holley (b), Jeff Hamilton (dm)
Jeepers Creepers

Ruby Braff (cnt, ldr), Ralph Sutton (p), Major Holley (b), Jeff Hamilton (dm)
Wrap Your Troubles in Dreams
NOTE: A recording of these tunes is available but remains unissued. Ruby does not perform on other numbers from this set.

September 2, 1979, 1:45 a.m., Sunday evening/Monday morning, September 3
Ruby Braff (cnt, ldr), Britt Woodman, Eddie Bert (tb) Kenny Davern, Bob Wilber (cl, ss), Scott Hamilton (ts), Teddy Wilson (p), Larry Ridley (b) Jeff Hamilton (dm)
Don't Get Around Much Anymore

Ruby Braff (cnt, ldr), Teddy Wilson (p), Chuck Domanico (b) Jeff Hamilton (dm)
This Year's Kisses
NOTE: A recording of these tunes is available but remains unissued. Ruby does not perform on other numbers from this set.

September 3, 7:20 p.m., Monday evening
Ruby Braff (cnt), Doc Cheatham, Pee Wee Erwin (t), Eddie Bert, Roy Williams (tb), Scott Hamilton (ts), Roger Kellaway (p), Major Holley (b), Jeff Hamilton (dm)
The World Is Waiting for the Sunrise

Gus Johnson replaces Jeff Hamilton
You're Driving Me Crazy

Ruby Braff (cnt), Roger Kellaway (p), Major Holley (b), Gus Johnson (dm)
Yesterdays
NOTE: A recording of these tunes is available but remains unissued. Ruby does not perform on other numbers from this set. This set closed the program.

Ruby Braff–*Ruby Plays Bing: Swinging on a Star*[11]
September 18–October 6, 1979, Michael's Pub, 211 East 55th Street, New York
Ruby Braff (cnt), Gene Bertocini (g), John Bunch (p), Michael Moore (b), Mel Lewis (dm)
Too-Ra-Loo-Ra-Loo-Ra
Road to Morocco
Love Thy Neighbor
Woody Allen was featured on Monday nights.

Hanratty's[12]
October 3?–December 18, 1979, 1754 2nd Avenue, New York
Dick Wellstood (p), Ruby Braff occasionally sat in as one of several occasional guests

Dick Wellstood's engagement may have begun earlier in the year; however, *The New Yorker* only began listing it in October. The club had first opened sometime in 1979. After the end of this engagement he returned starting January 2, 1980; however, there are again no details on guest artists listed in *The New Yorker*.[13] Whether Ruby joined him some evenings is unknown. Ruby's next documented appearance at Hanratty's was with Ralph Sutton in January 1983, but there were probably others.

Ruby returned to Texas for the Midland Jazz Classic. Jack Lesberg was the musical director. The following points were mentioned in a review: "To hear Braff in a variety of settings over two days was to be again impressed with the breadth he shares with musicians like Cohn and Sims and, indeed, with most of the players at Midland."[14] Some details of the program are mentioned including several performances with Ruby.

Midland Jazz Classic
Fall 1979, five nights and one afternoon, Midland, Texas—sponsored by Max Christensen and the Midland Jazz Association
Ruby Braff, Pee Wee Erwin (cnt), Joe Wilder (tp), Urbie Green, Al Grey, Bill Watrous (tb), Johnny Mince, Abe Most, Bob Wilber, Al Cohn, Zoot Sims (reeds), Terry Gibbs (vib), Cal Collins (g), Dick Hyman, Dave McKenna, Ralph Sutton (p), Milt Hinton, Jack Lesberg, Michael Moore (b), Jackie Williams, Gus Johnson, Mousey Alexander (dm), Carol Sloane (voc).

Ruby Braff (cnt), Dick Hyman (org)
Chloe

Ruby Braff (cnt), Al Cohn (ts), Terry Gibbs (vib) plus unknown others

Ruby Braff (cnt), Carol Sloane (voc) plus unknown others

Newport All Stars– 5th Anniversary Tribute to Felix Grant[15]
October 15, 1979, Kennedy Center, Washington, D.C.
Ruby Braff (cnt), Vic Dickenson (tb), Illinois Jacquet (ts), George Wein (p), Slam Stewart (b), Panama Francis (dm)
NOTE: Dom Um Romao, Clea Bradford, and Dizzy Gillespie also appeared in this two and one-half hour tribute to the WMAL-AM host on the 25th anniversary of his program.

Charlie Baron produced several recordings on his Chaz Jazz record label that included Ruby Braff, although his major focus was Ralph Sutton with his recordings. The LPs were sold through the mail at the time. The first album featured Ralph and Ruby, launching a partnership that would continue on occasion for over two decades.

Ralph Sutton and Ruby Braff: Duet
October 29, 1979, New York
Ruby Braff (cnt), Ralph Sutton (p)
Get Out and Get Under the Moon
    Chaz Jazz CJ 101, Chiaroscuro CR (D) 211
Think Well of Me
    Chaz Jazz CJ 101, Chiaroscuro CR (D) 211
I'm Gonna Sit Right Down and Write Myself a Letter
    Chaz Jazz CJ 101
Between the Devil and the Deep Blue Sea
    Chaz Jazz CJ 101, Chiaroscuro CR (D) 211

'Tain't Nobody's Business
    Chaz Jazz CJ 101, Chiaroscuro CR (D) 211
'Tain't So, Honey, 'Tain't So
    Chaz Jazz CJ 101, Chiaroscuro CR (D) 211
Royal Garden Blues
    Chaz Jazz CJ 101, Chiaroscuro CR (D) 211
Deep Summer Music
    Chaz Jazz CJ 101, Chaz Jazz 41680, Chiaroscuro CR (D) 211
I Believe in Miracles
    Chaz Jazz CJ 101
Keepin' Out of Mischief Now
    Chaz Jazz CJ 101
Dinah
    Chaz Jazz CJ 101, Chiaroscuro CR (D) 211
Ain't Misbehavin'
    Chaz Jazz CJ 101

NOTE: There are no additional takes or titles available. See next session for additional titles on CR (D) 211. CR (D) 211 is titled *R&R Ruby Braff and Ralph Sutton*. Chaz Jazz 41680 contains issued selections by Ralph Sutton from several different recording sessions.

Ralph Sutton and Ruby Braff: Quartet
October 30, 1979, New York
Ruby Braff (cnt), Ralph Sutton (p), Jack Lesberg (b), Gus Johnson (dm)
Shoe Shine Boy
    Chaz Jazz CJ 102, Chiaroscuro CR (D) 211
What Is There to Say?
    Chaz Jazz CJ 102, Chiaroscuro CR (D) 211
Sweethearts on Parade
    Chaz Jazz CJ 102, Chiaroscuro CR (D) 211
I Ain't Got Nobody
    Chaz Jazz CJ 102, Chiaroscuro CR (D) 211
You Can Depend on Me
    Chaz Jazz CJ 102, Chiaroscuro CR (D) 211
Big Butter and Egg Man
    Chaz Jazz CJ 102, Chiaroscuro CR (D) 211
I Wished on the Moon
    Chaz Jazz CJ 102, Chiaroscuro CR (D) 211
Sunday
    Chaz Jazz CJ 102, Chiaroscuro CR (D) 211
I'm Crazy 'Bout My Baby
    Chaz Jazz CJ 102, Chiaroscuro CR (D) 211
Little Rock Getaway
    Chaz Jazz CJ 102, Chiaroscuro CR (D) 211

I Would Do Anything for You
Chaz Jazz CJ 102, Chiaroscuro CR (D) 211
NOTE: Chiaroscuro CR (D) 211 titled *R&R: Ruby Braff and Ralph Sutton*. Additional titles are included from previous session. "I Ain't Got Nobody" also appears on Chiaroscuro 09145402232 titled *For Dancers Only: A Lindy Hop Compilation.*

While Tony Bennett and Ruby Braff both performed in the next concert, there is no specific information to indicate that they performed together.

We Remember Teddi King: Second Annual Benefit Concert[16]
December 16, 1979, Grand Ballroom, New York Hilton Hotel, New York
Bobby Short, Sylvia Syms, Tony Bennett, Ruby Braff, Marian McPartland, Dardanelle, John Giuffrida, Jimmy Rowles, Jake Hanna, Carol Sloane, George Wein, Richard Sudhalter, Torrie Zito, and the Widespread Depression Orchestra
NOTE: Funds were used to support the SLE Foundation since Teddi King died from lupus. See Figure 16.1 for an advertisement for this concert.

During 1979-80, a television series called *Hart to Hart* starred Robert Wagner. He is a jazz enthusiast and influenced script writers to use the names of several musicians in scripts for the program. Ruby Braff's name is used for a female character in one episode titled "Murder Is Man's Best Friend"; however, Ruby Braff does not appear in either the film or on the soundtrack. The airdate for this episode was January 9, 1980, and a copy of the program has been issued commercially on VHS videotape. At the time of publication, it is also listed for future release on DVD as part of a multiple-disc set containing all episodes aired during the third season; however, these episodes are available for downloading from Amazon.com.

Jazz Artists for Carter–Mondale[17]
Week of January 27, 1980, unknown location, New York

Over 60 musicians participated in a two and one-half hour concert, including Cab Calloway, Teddy Wilson, Ellis Larkins, Ruby Braff, Milt Hinton, Panama Francis, Oliver Jackson, Cecil Payne, Budd Johnson, Jimmy Maxwell, Elvin Jones, Al Grey, Bob Cranshaw, Illinois Jacquet, George Duvivier, Howard McGhee, Charlie Rouse, Sonny Greer, Mel Lewis, Scott Hamilton, Lee Konitz, Sonny Fortune, Billy Mitchell, Eddie Gomez, Major Holley, Roland Hanna, Jo Jones, and Jimmy Owens.

Ruby flew to Stockholm sometime in 1980. The performances are placed here arbitrarily in the absence of more specific information.

Ruby Braff and Bud Freeman in Stockholm
1980, Mosebacke, Stockholm, Sweden

Ruby Braff (cnt), Bud Freeman (ts), Rolf Larsson (p), Arne Wilhelmsson (b), Per Hultén (dm)
The World Is Waiting for the Sunrise

Bud Freeman out
What's New?
You're Driving Me Crazy

Bud Freeman returns
Just You, Just Me

Ruby Braff out
Satin Doll
Tea for Two

Ruby Braff (cnt) returns
Jeepers Creepers
Three Little Words
NOTE: A recording of these tunes is available but remains unissued.

Ruby Braff Interview
1980, Radio Sweden, unknown location, Sweden
NOTE: A recording of this interview is available but remains unissued.

A photograph from the March of Jazz program shows Ruby with Bud Freeman performing on a Swedish ferry boat in 1980, leading to the next entry.[18] A copy of that photo is included in this book's photo section.

Ruby Braff and Bud Freeman in Sweden
1980, performing on a ferry boat in unknown location, Sweden
Further details are unknown.

Hank O'Neal took photos at his Downtown Sound studio on March 13, 1980, in conjunction with his release of the following performances on Chiaroscuro. One shows Ruby posing with his cornet and another shows him standing with Woody Herman. A copy of the latter photo is included in this book's photo section. During an interview by Steve Voce, Ruby claimed that he had arranged this session and worked with Woody to select the titles that were performed.[19] George Avakian played a major role in arranging and supervising the recording.

Ruby Braff and Woody Herman: *It Had to Be Us*
March 12 and 13, 1980, Downtown Sound, New York
Ruby Braff (cnt) Woody Herman (cl, voc), John Bunch (p), Wayne Wright (g), Michael Moore (b), Jake Hanna (dm)

I Can't Believe That You're in Love with Me
Chiaroscuro CR (D) 204
Rose Room (voc)
Chiaroscuro CR (D) 204
Solitude
Chiaroscuro CR (D) 204
I Hadn't Anyone 'Till You (voc)
Chiaroscuro CR (D) 204
As Time Goes By (voc)
Chiaroscuro CR (D) 204
The Sheik of Araby (voc)
Chiaroscuro CR (D) 204
It Had to Be You (voc)
Chiaroscuro CR (D) 204
There Is No Greater Love (voc)
Chiaroscuro CR (D) 204
Wave/Spain (voc)
Chiaroscuro CR (D) 204
I Cried for You (voc)
Chiaroscuro CR (D) 204
'Deed I Do
Chiaroscuro CR (D) 204
The Sheik of Araby #2 (voc)
Chiaroscuro CR (D) 204
Solitude #2
Chiaroscuro CR (D) 204
It Had to Be You #2 (voc)
Chiaroscuro CR (D) 204
George Avakian Jazzspeak
Chiaroscuro CR (D) 204
NOTE: Hank O'Neal often included a track called "Jazzspeak." This included narration pertaining to the background for the session. In this case, the speaker was George Avakian, and Ruby was not present.

The All Stars at the New Jersey Jazz Society Private Jazz Party[20]
March 22, 1980, Downtown Athletic Club, 19 West Street, New York, First Private Jazz Party sponsored by the New Jersey Jazz Society
Ruby Braff (cnt), Vic Dickenson (tb), Sam Margolis (cl, ts), John Bunch (p), Johnny Williams (b), Al Harewood (dm)
Sometimes I'm Happy
Ain't Misbehavin'
When You're Smiling (Margolis feature)
Body and Soul (rhythm)
Love Me or Leave Me
You Made Me Love You (Dickenson feature)

Just You, Just Me (incomplete)
NOTE: A recording of these tunes is available but remains unissued.

Next, Ruby returned to Carnegie Hall as part of a concert called *Mel Tormé and Friends*. Tormé performed with different musicians on March 28 (Gerry Mulligan and the New Concert Band and Carmen McRae) and March 30 (with Woody Herman, Anita O'Day, and Zoot Sims). Tormé sang one or two songs with each guest and performed about half of each concert with his own program. Ruby may have also appeared on March 30; however, I have not found confirmation of that. He did appear on March 29.

Kool Super Nights Jazz Festival: Mel Tormé and Friends[21]
March 29, 1980, 8 p.m., Carnegie Hall, New York (see Figure 16.2)
Mel Tormé, George Shearing Duo, Bill Evans Trio, Teddy Wilson Trio with Ruby Braff and a string ensemble
Avalon (Wilson, Braff, Tormé)

A photograph was published in the *Newport 50th Anniversary Program* from 2004. It shows Ruby with Woody Herman, Buddy Tate, and George Wein but does not specify the date and location. It is likely that it dates from this concert. If so, that adds an additional set, adding those musicians to the above listing.

Kool Super Nights Jazz Festival[22]
March 30, 1980, Carnegie Hall, New York
Mel Tormé, Woody Herman and His Herd, Ruby Braff, and Zoot Sims were featured artists. No further information is available and it is possible that Ruby only appeared the previous night. I list this only because the proximity of the previous recording session may have led to an unplanned appearance.

Toward the end of the next performance, Ruby asked for and received many simultaneous requests from the audience. He good-naturedly replied, "Put 'em all together and you get 'I Cover the Waterfront.'" He promptly began that tune as people laughed.

Classic Jazz Society of Southwestern Ohio: Ruby Braff and Dick Hyman[23]
April 13, 1980, Cuvier Press Club, Cincinnati, Ohio
Ruby Braff (cnt) and Dick Hyman (p, org)
Sunday
Ain't Misbehavin'
It Don't Mean a Thing
You Took Advantage of Me
Just One of Those Things
Tea for Two (organ)
Body and Soul
Bye, Bye Blues

Do You Know What It Means to Miss New Orleans
Muskrat Ramble
What Is There to Say?
I've Got a Feelin' I'm Fallin'
St. Louis Blues
Time on My Hands
Liza (interrupted for tape change)
I'm Gonna Sit Right Down and Write Myself a Letter (organ)
If I Could Be With You (organ)
Persian Rug (organ)
I Cover the Waterfront
Jeepers Creepers
I Want to Be Happy
NOTE: A recording of these tunes is available but remains unissued.

20th Annual Concert of the Duke Ellington Society: *Trumpets No End–An All–Trumpet Tribute to Duke Ellington*[24]
May 18, 1980, 2:30 p.m., New School, 66 West 12th Street, New York
Clark Terry, Art Farmer, Howard McGhee, Buck Clayton (tp), Ruby Braff, Jimmy McPartland (cnt), Marian McPartland or Barry Harris (p), Art Davis (b), Leroy Williams (dm) (Marian McPartland only played on tunes that featured Jimmy McPartland, while Barry Harris played piano at all other times.)
Brown Skin Girl
Daydream
What Am I Here For
Drop Me Off in Harlem
Sultry Serenade

John S. Wilson wrote, "It was Mr. Braff who brought down the house with a set in which the dark, full tones of his low register, his sudden bursts, slides and flutters revealed an unsuspected relationship to Mr. Ellington's Rex Stewart."

Ruby Braff[25]
May 25–31, 1980, Eddie Condon's, 144 West 55th Street, New York
Ruby Braff (cnt), Sam Margolis (ts), Ray Bryant (p), Wayne Wright (g), Jay Leonhardt (b), Mel Lewis (dm)

Ruby again flew to London to appear at Pizza Express for a one- or two-week-long engagement, but not extending to the end of the month because of his next appearance in Los Angeles at the *Playboy Jazz Festival.*

Ruby Braff[26]
June 1980, Pizza Express Dean Street, London
Ruby Braff (cnt), Brian Lemon, Dick Abel (g), Lennie Bush (b), Stan Bourke (dm)

Foolin' Myself
You're My Thrill
Go Fly a Kite
I've Got a Pocket Full of Dreams
Royal Garden Blues

Continuing to later dates adding Scott Hamilton (ts) and Louis Stewart (g)
Yesterdays
Falling in Love with Love
Nancy (With the Laughing Face)
Laura
All the Things You Are
I Want to Be Happy

Ruby may have flown directly to Los Angeles from Pizza Express. There is no trace of any performances between these two engagements. He then returned to New York to appear during the Newport Jazz Festival in a tribute to Fred Astaire at Carnegie Hall.

2nd Annual Playboy Jazz Festival[27] (see Figure 16.3)
June 21–22, 1980, Hollywood Bowl, Los Angeles
Participating musicians included Dizzy Gillespie, Carmen McRae, Chick Corea, Herbie Hancock, Stephane Grappelli, the Brecker Brothers, Toshiko Akiyoshi, Lew Tabackin, Buddy Rich, Benny Goodman, Eddie "Lockjaw" Davis, Illinois Jacquet, Zoot Sims, Richie Cole, Adelaide Hall, Mel Tormé, Bob Crosby, and an all-star swing group with Benny Carter, Teddy Wilson, Shelly Manne, and Ruby Braff. Teddy Wilson led a group including Ruby Braff, Benny Carter, and Shelly Manne.

Interview by Gordon Spencer
June 24, 1980, WBAI Radio, New York
NOTE: A recording of this interview is available but remains unissued.

Newport Jazz Festival: *Puttin' on the Ritz–A Jazz Tribute to Fred Astaire*[28]
June 28, 1980, 8 p.m. and midnight, Carnegie Hall, New York
Ruby Braff (cnt), John Bunch (p), George Duvivier (b), Connie Kay (dm)
My One and Only
I'm Putting All My Eggs in One Basket

Add Clark Terry (tp)
Dancing in the Dark
Some of the other musicians in this concert included Mel Tormé, Rosemary Clooney, Stan Getz, George Shearing, Clark Terry, and Gerry Mulligan.

Ruby Braff at Bechet's[29]
Scheduled to open the club soon after July 1, 1980, but before July 28, Bechet's, 1319 3rd Avenue, New York
A report in *Coda* indicated that the opening was postponed until after October 15 and that Ruby was not rebooked at that time. There may have been other dates that I have not located.

Ruby returned to London and then on to other European venues to appear in festivals produced by George Wein, culminating in other appearances at the Grande Parade du Jazz in Nice where Ruby had become a regular.

Jazz Festival (produced by George Wein)[30]
July 1980, Alexandra Palace, North London (Wood Green)
Ruby Braff (cnt), Benny Carter (as), George Wein (p), Slam Stewart (b), and Duffy Jackson (dm)

Velden Amsee Jazz Festival[31]
George Wein produced the Velden Amsee Jazz Festival in Austria on July 4, 5, and 6 between the performances in Alexandra Palace and the Munich Jazz Festival. He does not mention that Ruby performed there; however, Ruby did not perform at Nice until July 16 and would have been available at this time.

Munich Jazz Festival[32]
George Wein produced the Munich Jazz Festival on July 10, 11, and 12 overlapping the start of the Grande Parade du Jazz in Nice. He does not mention that Ruby performed there; however, Ruby did not perform at Nice until July 16 and would have been available at this time.

Jam Session–Grande Parade Du Jazz[33]
July 16, 1980, Jardins de Cimiez, Dance Stage, Nice, France
Ruby Braff (cnt), Hank Jones (p), Jimmy Raney (el-g), Jack Six (b), Roy Haynes (dm)
You Can Depend on Me

Add Clark Terry (flgh)
Mean to Me
Secret Love (Clark Terry feature)

Omit Braff and Terry
It Could Happen to You (Jimmy Raney feature)
Old Folks (Ruby Braff feature)

Omit Raney
Moose the Mooche (Hank Jones feature)

Add: Terry, Braff, Raney
Take the "A" Train
NOTE: A recording of these tunes is available but remains unissued.

Grande Parade du Jazz: Vanguard Days Revisited: Grande Parade du Jazz[34]
July 18, 1980, Live, Jardin des Arénes de Cimiez, Nice, France
Ruby Braff (cnt), Vic Dickenson (tb), Sir Charles Thompson (p), Jimmy Raney (g), Major Holley (b), Oliver Jackson (dm)
Keepin' Out of Mischief Now
Jeepers Creepers
I Cover the Waterfront
Crazy Rhythm (featuring SCT)
Old Fashioned Love (featuring VD)
Lady Be Good
NOTE: A recording of these tunes is available but remains unissued.

Ruby Braff Sextet: Grande Parade du Jazz
July 18, 1980, Grande Parade du Jazz: Nice, France
Ruby Braff (cnt), Scott Hamilton (ts), Lee Konitz (as), Dave McKenna (p), Slam Stewart (b), Jake Hanna (dm)
Sometimes I'm Happy
Sugar
Sweet and Lovely (Braff and Hamilton out)
Just You, Just Me
Candy (Braff and Konitz out)
NOTE: A recording of these tunes is available but remains unissued.

Ruby Braff Quintet: Grande Parade du Jazz[35]
July 19, 1980, 10 p.m., Grande Parade du Jazz, Nice, France
Ruby Braff (cnt), Vic Dickenson (tb), Dave McKenna (p), Slam Stewart (b), Jake Hanna (dm)

Ruby recalled his next performance on July 21 as a very special evening. When I told him I could provide him with a cassette tape of it (in 2002), he was excited. When I talked with him next, I asked him about the cassette tape I'd mailed to him. He said, "Sometimes when you remember something that is so special you don't want to listen again because you might be disappointed. Well, I decided to listen, and it was just as fine as I remembered." Ruby explored the possibility of releasing the recording, but decided that the sound quality was not up to modern standards. Several photographs are available from that performance, taken by Sir Lawrence Collins. One is a close up of Ruby soloing. The others show Ruby with Hank Jones and Slam Stewart. Two of Sir Lawrence's photos are included in this book's photo section.

Ruby Braff Trio: Grande Parade du Jazz
July 21, 1980, Nice, France
Ruby Braff (cnt), Hank Jones (p), Slam Stewart (b)
Wrap Your Troubles in Dreams
Medley:
 When It's Sleepy Time Down South
 I Want to Be Happy
It's Only a Paper Moon
Medley:
 These Foolish Things
 Chicago
Medley:
 Pennies from Heaven
 Sunday
NOTE: A recording of these tunes is available but remains unissued.

Perhaps it was from this time, either before or after traveling to Nice, that Ruby told me the following story:

> I was talking in a hotel room in Paris one night with Sarah Vaughan and Carman McRae. We were all relaxed and having a good time in Europe, but then one of them started talking about getting some marijuana. Well, I did not object, but in a few minutes they turned to me and offered to pay the cost for me to fly back to New York to make a buy from their source and then return to Paris so that we could enjoy it together. Well, I quickly changed the subject. Sometimes I may have done some crazy things, but this was just not going to be one of them.

As the conversation continued, Ruby talked about problems some musicians have had with alcohol consumption. He made a telling statement: "Tom, how many times in a club have you ever offered to buy a musician a sandwich?"

Carmen McRae Sang with Ruby Braff: Grande Parade du Jazz[36]
July 1980, Grande Parade du Jazz, Nice, France—specific date not known

Concord All Stars: Grande Parade du Jazz[37]
On July 22, 1980, 11 p.m., Dance Stage, Grande Parade du Jazz: Nice, France
Ruby Braff (cnt), Kai Winding, and Vic Dickenson (tb) were guests with the Concord All Stars consisting of Warren Vaché, Jr. (cnt), Scott Hamilton (ts), Dave McKenna (p), Cal Collins (g), John Clayton, Jr. (b), and Jake Hanna (dm).

Ruby Braff Sextet: Grande Parade du Jazz
July 22, 1980, Grande Parade du Jazz: Nice, France (this was the closing day of the festival)
Ruby Braff (cnt), Clark Terry (flgh, voc), Lee Konitz (as), John Lewis (p), Pierre Michelot (b), Alan Dawson (dm)

Lover Come Back to Me
Sweet and Lovely (Konitz with rhythm)
Thou Swell (Braff with rhythm)
Squeeze Me (Terry with rhythm)
Round Midnight (Lewis, Michelot, Dawson)
Perdido
NOTE: A recording of these tunes is available but remains unissued.

There is one report that Ruby appeared with Howard Alden and Frank Tate at Pizza on the Park in July 1980. Howard Alden wrote that he did not begin performing with Ruby until 1984, so this published report likely refers to their appearance ten years later in July 1990. The confusion may result from confusion with Ruby's previously listed appearance in June 1980 at Pizza Express with Brian Lemon, but it was probably a simple typographical error in the article.

Ruby Braff Trio[38] (this entry is unlikely, despite being based based on a published report)
Late July, 1980, Pizza on the Park, London (probably the reported date should have been July 1990 and is listed there, so this engagement cannot be verified)
Ruby Braff (cnt), Howard Alden (g), Frank Tate (b)

Next, Ruby returned to the US, probably from France, since he was again invited to join the musicians at the annual Gibson Jazz Party. I have not traced any performances between these engagements. This is the first time I have documented Ruby playing with Howard Alden; however, it is likely that their paths had already crossed in clubs by this time.

Gibson Jazz Party[39]
August 30 – September 1, 1980, Broadmoor Hotel, Colorado Springs, Colorado
August 30, 4:45, Saturday afternoon
Ruby Braff (cnt, ldr), Vic Dickenson (tb), Buddy Tate (ts), Bob Wilber (cl, ss), Ralph Sutton (p), Howard Roberts (g), George Duvivier (b), Alan Dawson (dm)
Jeepers Creepers
Mean to Me

Out Dickenson, Tate, Wilber
Unknown tune

August 30, 0:35 a.m., Saturday evening/Sunday morning August 31
Ruby Braff (cnt), Bill Watrous (tb, ldr), Peanuts Hucko (cl), Phil Woods (as), Ralph Sutton (p), Michael Moore (b), Grady Tate (dm)
I Want to Be Happy
When You're Smiling

August 31, 4:45 p.m., Sunday afternoon
Ruby Braff (cnt), Bill Watrous (tb, ldr), Budd Johnson (ts, ldr), Scott Hamilton (ts), Dick Hyman (p), Michael Moore (b), Jake Hanna (dm)
Sunday
Them There Eyes

August 31, 11:50 p.m., Sunday evening/Monday morning September 1
Ruby Braff (cnt), Vic Dickenson (tb), Al Cohn (ts), Ross Tompkins (p), Major Holley (b), Jackie Williams (dm)
Rosetta

Add Jack Ackerman (tap dancing)
C Jam Blues

Add Claude Williams (v) and Sandman Sims (tap dancing)
Take the "A" Train

September 1, 6:35 p.m., Monday evening
Ruby Braff (cnt, ldr), Bob Havens (tb, ldr), Peanuts Hucko (cl), Al Cohn, Scott Hamilton (ts), Derek Smith (p), Michael Moore (b), Jake Hanna (d)
Love Me or Leave Me

Ross Tompkins (p) replaces Derek Smith; out Havens, Hucko, Cohn, Hamilton
These Foolish Things (Braff feature)

Ruby Braff (cnt), Bob Havens, George Chisholm (tb), Peanuts Hucko (cl), Al Cohn, Scott Hamilton (ts), Ross Tompkins (p), Michael Moore (b), Jake Hanna (d)
The World Is Waiting for the Sunrise

Ruby Braff[40]
November 25–December 6, 1980, Lyte's, Royal York Hotel, Toronto
Ruby Braff (cnt), Ron Sorley or Carol Britto (p), Danny Mastri (b), Norm Villeneuve (dm)

Likely the pianist changed between reviews by Mark Miller and John Norris. Mark Miller's review was very critical of Sorley and Mastri in this setting. Mark Miller reported the following: "With little support and no challenges from his musicians, the weight of that first set rested solely on Braff's shoulders, and he carried the load with a minimum of fuss. The range of his cornet is remarkable."[41]

Ruby Braff Interview with Ted O'Reilly
December 2, 1980, CJRT-FM, Toronto
NOTE: A recording of this interview is available but remains unissued.

Manassas Jazz Festival[42]
Early December 1980, Manassas, Virginia
Ruby Braff, Earl Hines, Teddy Wilson, Jay McShann, Dick Wellstood, Lionel Hampton, Ralph Sutton, Bud Freeman, Wild Bill Davison, and Sammy Price were announced; however, only Davison actually appeared that year.[43]

Photos taken by Michael Steinman are available from the following performance, showing Ruby with George Duvivier.[44]

Ruby Braff at the International Art of Jazz[45]
December 7, 1980, Ethical Humanist Society, 38 Old Country Road, Garden City, Long Island, New York
Ruby Braff (cnt), Derek Smith (p), George Duvivier (b), Bobby Rosengarden (dm)
Them There Eyes
Tea for Two
You're Sensational
A Day in the Life of a Fool
What Kind of Fool Am I?
This Could Be the Start of Something Big
Come Sunday
They Can't Take That Away from Me
White Christmas
Winter Wonderland
On Green Dolphin Street
Take the "A" Train
NOTE: Recording is held in the Ann Sneed Collection at the Library of Congress. It was not available for auditioning at the time of publication.

Ralph Sutton and the Jazzband
February 1981, Lafayette Club, Minneapolis, Minnesota
Ruby Braff (cnt), George Masso (tb), Kenny Davern (cl), Bud Freeman (ts), Ralph Sutton (p), Milt Hinton (b), Gus Johnson (dm)
Struttin' with Some Barbecue
    Chaz Jazz CJ 113
Keepin' Out of Mischief Now
    Chaz Jazz CJ 113
Ain't Misbehavin'
    Chaz Jazz CJ 113
Muskrat Ramble
    Chaz Jazz CJ 113

The above Chaz Jazz album is taken from a portion of a party organized by Reed MacKenzie. Probably other recordings exist, but they have remained unavailable. A photo from the March of Jazz program dated from the early 1980s may correspond to this party.[46]

Ruby Braff Trio[47]
March 6–7 (7 p.m.) and 8 (3 p.m.), 1981, Struggles, 10 Dempsey Avenue, Edgewater, New Jersey

Ruby was next scheduled to perform at the 10th Boston Globe Jazz Festival; however, Scott Hamilton reported that Ruby suffered his first serious attack of emphysema the night before the festival and did not appear. The organizers arranged for Doc Cheatham to appear in his place. Scott said that he played a set with Zoot Sims and Marian McPartland instead of his scheduled appearance with Ruby.[48]

10th Boston Globe Jazz Festival[49]
March 16, 1981, Berklee Performance Center, Boston
Promotion for the festival lists the following musicians: Ruby Braff, Jimmy McPartland, Marian McPartland, Dick Wellstood, Scott Hamilton, Zoot Sims, Alan Dawson, Vic Dickenson, Al Grey, Bob Wilber, and the Yankee Rhythm Kings. Due to his illness, Ruby was replaced by Doc Cheatham as mentioned.

The promotional flyer for the following concert shows Ruby's first name in large script with the following text: "A diamond in the rough. But oh how his trumpet shines."[50] Ruby had become a regular performer at this series of concerts.

Ruby Braff Sextet: A Heavenly Jazz Concert[51] **(see Figure 16.4)**
March 22, 1981, 5 p.m., The Church of the Heavenly Rest, 90th and 5th Avenue, New York
Ruby Braff (cnt), Teddy Charles (vib), John Bunch (p), John Basile (g), Michael Moore (b), Bobby Rosengarden (dm)
Come Sunday (Bunch and Moore)
Sunday (Braff and Bunch)
Walkin' (Charles, Basile, Moore)
Unnamed selections featured the sextet.

Ruby Braff Trio[52]
June 12–13, 1981, 7 p.m.–3 a.m., Struggles, 10 Dempsey Avenue, Edgewater, New Jersey
Ruby Braff (cnt), John Bunch (p), Michael Moore (b)

Ruby Braff and Friends[53]
June 26–27, 1981, 7 p.m.–3 a.m., Struggles, 10 Dempsey Avenue, Edgewater, New Jersey
Ruby Braff (cnt), John Bunch (p), and Michael Moore (b)

Ruby Braff Trio[54]
July 3–4, 1981, 7 p.m.–3 a.m., Struggles, 10 Dempsey Avenue, Edgewater, New Jersey
Ruby Braff (cnt), John Bunch (p), Jay Leonhardt (b)

Ruby Braff Quintet at the Kool Jazz Festival—Jazzfare II[55]
July 5, 1981, 2–11 p.m. Center for the Arts, State University, Purchase, New York

The day's program features a wide variety of performances, including the following artists, themed sessions, and groups: Joe Albany; a tribute to Eubie Blake with Dick Hyman, Kenny Davern, Bobby Rosengarden, and Milt Hinton; Amherst Saxophone Quartet; Ruby Braff Quintet; John Bunch with Charlie Rouse, Tom Harrell, Bill Pemberton, and Connie Kay; Candido and his V.I.P.'s; Valerie Capers Trio; Junior Cook, and Bill Hardman with Walter Bishop, Jr.; Terry Gibbs and Buddy DeFranco with Ross Tompkins, and George Mraz; Billy Harper Quartet; Louis Hayes; the Julius Hemphill Quartet; Fred Hersch; Robin Kenyatta Quintet; Warne Marsh Quartet; Marian McPartland Piano Jazz with Barbara Carroll and James Williams; Mike Peters' String Fever; Herb Pomeroy Big Band; Gene Taylor; Mal Waldron; Bob Wilber and the Bechet Legacy; "A New Jazz Tap Show" by Jane Goldberg's Changing Times Tap Dance Company; a saxophone workshop with Nick Brignola, Sonny Fortune, and Charlie Rouse; a singers' workshop with Bob Dorough, Stella Marrs, Susannah McCorkle, Marlene VerPlanck, and others. No further details are known. This was the second day of the program.

The next recording documents the final performance of Ruby with Buzzy Drootin. It comes from a party hosted by *Changing Times* magazine. Likely there were other performances not included in the cassette tape that had limited distribution. Following that, he traveled directly to Minnesota to appear at the Emporium of Jazz. No known appearances exist until he next travels to Toronto for a three-week engagement at Bourbon Street, followed by his return to Newport, Rhode Island, after a short interval. After a weeklong engagement in New Jersey at Struggles, he travels with Ralph Sutton for an Australian tour.

Changing Times Summer Jazz Party (see Figure 16.5)
July 8, 1981, Wee Burn Country Club, Darien, Connecticut
Ruby Braff (cnt), Vic Dickenson (tb), Kenny Davern (cl), Al Klink (ts), Ralph Sutton (p), Marty Grosz (g), Jack Lesberg (b), Buzzy Drootin (dm)
When You're Smiling
    private recording from *Changing Times* magazine, Jump JCD 12-29
Mean to Me
    private recording from *Changing Times* magazine

Jeepers Creepers
    private recording from *Changing Times* magazine
Keepin' Out of Mischief Now
    private recording from *Changing Times* magazine
These Foolish Things
    private recording from *Changing Times* magazine
Somebody Stole My Gal
    private recording from *Changing Times* magazine
NOTE: A copy of the complete recording is available. Jump JCD 12-29 is titled *Ruby Braff and His Musical Friends: Recovered Treasures.* See the album notes I wrote for this release in the appendix.

Ruby Braff and Ralph Sutton with the Salty Dogs
July 11–12, 1981, Hall Brothers' Emporium of Jazz, Mendota, Minnesota
Ruby Braff (cnt), Ralph Sutton (p), other musicians added as shown

1st Set, Saturday Night, July 11
'Tain't So, Honey, 'Tain't So
Sugar
Undecided
You Took Advantage of Me

Add Bill Evans (b) and Red Maddock (dm) for the following tune only:
Chinatown, My Chinatown
NOTE: A recording of these tunes is available but remains unissued.

2nd Set, Saturday Night, July 11
Wrap Your Troubles in Dreams
Exactly Like You interpolating Four or Five Times
I've Found a New Baby
Medley:
  Old Folks
  When It's Sleepy Time Down South
You're Driving Me Crazy

Add Bill Evans (b) and Red Maddock (dm) for the following tune only:
Love Me or Leave Me
NOTE: A recording of these tunes is available but remains unissued.

Sunday Afternoon, July 12
Sunday
You've Changed
Louisiana
Medley:
  Please

Pennies from Heaven
Exactly Like You
Save It Pretty Mama
Tea for Two

Add: Bill Evans (b) and Red Maddock (dm) for one title below:
Bugle Call Rag
NOTE: A recording of these tunes is available but remains unissued.

1st Set, Sunday evening, July 12
I Ain't Got Nobody
Don't Blame Me
Jeepers Creepers
Ain't Misbehavin'
As Long As I Live

Add: Bill Evans (b) and Red Maddock (dm) for the following tune only:
I Want to Be Happy
NOTE: A recording of these tunes is available but remains unissued.

2nd Set, Sunday evening, July 12
Confessin'
High Society
Blue Turning Grey Over You
I'm Crazy 'bout My Baby
I Want a Little Girl

Add Charles Devore, Lew Green (cnt), Kim Cusack, Butch Thompson (cl), Tom Bartlett (tb), Bill Evans (b), Red Maddock (dm) for the finale below:
The World Is Waiting for the Sunrise
NOTE: A recording of these tunes is available but remains unissued.

Ruby Braff at Bourbon Street[56]
July 20–August 8, 1981, Bourbon Street, 180 Queen Street West, Toronto
Ruby Braff (cnt), Bernie Senensky (p), Neil Swainson (b), Jerry Fuller (dm)

Ruby Braff Interview with Ted O'Reilly
July 27, 1981, CJRT-FM, Toronto
NOTE: A recording of this interview is available but remains unissued.

Ruby Braff Interview with Phil McKeller
August 4, 1981, CKFM-FM, Toronto
NOTE: A recording of this interview is available but remains unissued.

Newport Jazz Festival[57]
August 22–23, 1981, Newport, Rhode Island
The following artists were included in the 1981 festival: Buddy Rich Orchestra, McCoy Tyner Quintet, Dexter Gordon Quartet with Art Farmer, Mel Lewis Jazz Orchestra with Zoot Sims, Classic Jazz Band (including Dick Hyman, Bob Wilber, Vic Dickenson, Ruby Braff, and Doc Cheatham), Nancy Wilson, Dave Brubeck, Dizzy Gillespie with Milt Jackson, Art Blakey and the Jazz Messengers, Lionel Hampton with All Star Big Band. Partial details of Ruby's appearance follow:

Newport Jazz Festival: Classic Jazz Band with Ruby Braff (guest)
August 22, 1981, (Noon–6:30 concert), Newport Jazz Festival, Newport, Rhode Island
Ruby Braff (cnt), Doc Cheatham (tp), Vic Dickenson (tb), Bob Wilber (ss), Dick Hyman (p), Major Holley (b), Oliver Jackson (dm)

Ruby Braff and Friends[58]
September 18–26, 1981 (7 p.m.–3 a.m.), Struggles, 10 Dempsey Avenue, Edgewater, New Jersey
Ruby Braff (cnt), and unknown other musicians

Ruby Braff and Ralph Sutton were invited to perform in Australia in 1981. Prior to the final concert in Adelaide, they appeared together in at least three other locations, opening in Brisbane, followed by Melbourne but also including a performance for the Perth Jazz Society, perhaps on October 15. This was Ruby's only tour in Australia; however, Ralph Sutton returned several other times.[59]

A copy of Ruby's handwritten letter discussing the trip is available. He wrote the following letter before traveling to London, likely in August 1978, which shows the length of the negotiations:[60]

> Thanks for your letter. When I looked at your address, I found it frightening. The thought of flying that many hours. . . . Well, who knows, maybe there's a way of breaking such a trip up, like stopping here and there and resting. . . . The times I've gone to Japan were distressing enough. That was only 16 hours. Also I rested in Honolulu. . . .
>
> When I play a club in Manhattan I don't work for less than a thousand dollars per week. And I'm home. When I work out of town in my country, I'm paid about 25 hundred a week. When I do individual concerts I've different kinds of money. You see many things determine price. I'm sure you understand.
>
> Now as for your assurance about the quality of the accompanists—Let me quickly point out that your needs and mine are not the same, since you don't play like me. I would like to hear records or something of these people. And don't tell me who liked them. I've heard that before. That's why I usually bring piano players with me.

> Like in England, I usually have Eddie Thompson, because I can depend on him. In the states I have others. This is not to say you don't have pianists that I can play with, I just am no longer accustomed to surprises.

Ruby recalled that he was looking forward to sitting with Ralph on the flight from the US to Australia. He felt that they would have lots to talk about during the long trip. To his great dismay, after boarding the plane, Ralph swallowed a sleeping pill and slept throughout most of the flight, leaving Ruby alone for many hours. For someone who enjoys conversation, that was surely a challenge.

Australian Jazz Expo, National Jazz Festival[61]
October 11, 1981, Cellar Club, Brisbane, Australia
Ruby Braff (cnt), Ralph Sutton (p)
I'm Crazy 'bout My Baby
No further information known

Australian Jazz Expo, National Jazz Festival
October 11, 1981, Cellar Club, Brisbane, Australia
Bob Barnard (cnt), Ralph Sutton (p), Wally Wickham (b), Len Barnard (dm)
Unknown selections without Braff

Australian Jazz Expo, National Jazz Festival
October 11, 1981, Cellar Club, Brisbane, Australia
Ruby Braff (cnt), Chris Taperell (p), Wally Wickham (b), Len Barnard (dm)

A contemporary review in *The Age* reported the following:[62] The real treat was in the cultural exchange which saw Braff and Sutton play with members of the Barnard band."

Ruby Braff and Ralph Sutton[63]
October 12–14, 1981, Beaconsfield Hotel, St. Kilda, Melbourne, Australia
Ruby Braff (cnt), Ralph Sutton (p), John Halliday (dm), Derek Capewell (b)

The other half of the concert featured The Blues Express, led by Peter Gaudion and including Capewell and Halliday. A copy of a photograph of Ruby and Ralph with two members of the audience is available from this engagement.

The following performance was another session that Ruby mentioned to me. He said, "Everyone seems to have a cassette recording of the time that Ralph and I performed in Australia, but the sound is always awful." Fortunately, I was able to contact John Kennedy. He supplied a recording that he made directly from an FM radio rebroadcast of the performance. I shared the recording with Ruby, converting John's CD to a cassette tape for his enjoyment. At last, the sound quality met Ruby's standards. The release on Nif Nuf followed, sharing this wonderful music with the fans of both musicians.

Ralph Sutton and Ruby Braff in Concert[64]
October 16, 1981 Thebarton Town Hall, Adelaide, broadcast by the Australian Broadcasting Corporation, Jim McLeod producer (the final concert on this Australian tour)
Ruby Braff (cnt) and Ralph Sutton (p) duets
I'm Crazy 'bout My Baby (incomplete at start)
Nif Nuf 43/016
Sugar
Nif Nuf 43/016
Honeysuckle Rose
Nif Nuf 43/016
Dinah
Nif Nuf 43/016
It's Wonderful
Nif Nuf 43/016
Royal Garden Blues
Nif Nuf 43/016
Echoes of Spring (RS only)
Nif Nuf 43/016

Add Rob Jeffery (b) and Laurie Kennedy (dm):
You Took Advantage of Me
unissued, recording available
Sweethearts on Parade
unissued, recording available

Omit Jeffery and Kennedy
High Society
unissued, recording available
I Can't Give You Anything but Love
unissued, recording available
Ain't Misbehavin'
Nif Nuf 43/016
I Got Rhythm
Nif Nuf 43/016
What Is There to Say?
Nif Nuf 43/016
Medley (RS only):
Love Lies
Nif Nuf 43/016
Alligator Crawl
Nif Nuf 43/016
Home
Nif Nuf 43/016

Reconstructing the complete concert is a bit problematic. The author has received one cassette tape and two private CDs that contain the music listed above and additional titles. The cassette seems to be from the original FM radio broadcast while the two CDs appear to be from a rebroadcast. Manfred Selchow indicates that the following three titles were also performed at this concert: "Moonglow" (RS only), "Sweet Lorraine," and "Shoe Shine Boy" (incomplete on his recording). These three titles listed by Manfred are neither on the cassette nor the CDs that I have. Two titles on the CDs are duplicated and "What Is There to Say?" is complete on CD2. CD2 is likely the proper sequence from the concert for these two titles; however, it includes two tunes, "Rosetta" and "When You're Smiling" which are not listed among the tunes above. Therefore, both tunes should be added to the listing for this performance along with the three performances mentioned by Manfred.

CD 1 (all titles on this private CD are listed above)
I'm Crazy 'bout My Baby (faded in)
Sugar
Honeysuckle Rose
Dinah
It's Wonderful
Royal Garden Blues
Echoes of Spring (RS only)
I Got Rhythm
What Is There to Say? (fades out)
Royal Garden Blues

Add Rob Jeffery (b) and Laurie Kennedy (dm) for next two titles:
You Took Advantage of Me
Sweethearts on Parade

intermission

Omit Jeffery and Kennedy
High Society
I Can't Give You Anything but Love

CD 2 ("Rosetta" and "When You're Smiling" on this private CD are not included in the initial listing for this performance above)
Ain't Misbehavin'
I Got Rhythm
What Is There to Say?
Medley (Sutton solo):
  Love Lies
  Alligator Crawl

Add Rob Jeffery (b) and Laurie Kennedy (dm) for next three titles:
Rosetta
When You're Smiling (incomplete at start)
Home (encore)

Ruby returned to the United States where he next appeared at Struggles. He did not mention if Ralph took another sleeping pill at the beginning of the long flight home.

Ruby Braff and Friends[65]
October 23–24 and 30–31, 9 p.m., Struggles, 10 Dempsey Avenue, Edgewater, New Jersey

Ruby Braff: *Very Sinatra*
December 12–14, 1981 (LP states December 14–16, 1981), RCA Studio B, New York
Ruby Braff (cnt), Vic Dickenson (tb-1), Sam Margolis (cl-1), Dick Hyman (arranger, p, org), Bucky Pizzarelli (g), Michael Moore (b), Mel Lewis (dm)
Medley:
Street of Dreams
Finesse FW 37988
The Lady Is a Tramp
Finesse FW 37988
This Love of Mine
Finesse FW 37988
I Hear a Rhapsody
Finesse FW 37988
The Second Time Around
Finesse FW 37988
Medley:
New York, New York (1)
Finesse FW 37988
My Kind of Town (Chicago Is) (1)
Finesse FW 37988
Medley:
You're Sensational
Finesse FW 37988
I'll Never Smile Again
Finesse FW 37988
Perfectly Frank
Finesse FW 37988
All the Way
Finesse FW 37988
I'm Getting Sentimental Over You
Finesse FW 37988

Nancy (With the Laughing Face)
Finesse FW 37988
Come Fly with Me (1)
Finesse FW 37988
All titles also on Red Baron JK 53749 (CD) and Red Baron 54739 (cassette) and Finesse JT 53749 (cassette)

The following session delighted Ruby, and the appendix contains extensive information about its background. Joe Bougton asked me to prepare notes for its first release on Jump Records, and that CD included a number of historical recordings that were overdue for release. Dick Hyman also expressed pleasure in knowing that this session would finally be released. This was Ruby's second recording with strings, the first coming 13 months earlier in England. The album notes explain the how Charlie Baron was Ruby's true champion in this project.

Ruby Braff with Strings[66]
December 17, 1981, at RCA Studio B, New York
Ralph Sutton (p), Bucky Pizzarelli (g), Jack Lesberg (b), Mel Lewis (dm) with the Beaux Arts String Quartet: Charles Libove (vln1), Richard Sortomme (vln2), Lamar Alsop (viola), Charles P. McCracken (cello)—arrangements by Dick Hyman, Eastlake Music—session originally recorded for Chaz Jazz
Valse Bleue (Margis)
Jump JCD 12-29
June (Barcarolle) (Tchaikovsky)
Jump JCD 12-29
Ah! So Pure ("Martha") (von Flotow)
Jump JCD 12-29
Waltz No. 9 (Chopin)
Jump JCD 12-29
Stride La Vampa (Verdi)
Jump JCD 12-29
Traumerei (Schumann)
Jump JCD 12-29

Jump JCD 12-29 is titled *Ruby Braff and His Musical Friends: Recovered Treasures.* See the complete album notes I wrote for this release in the appendix for information on the development of this unique recording session. I was honored that Joe Boughton allowed me to be the producer for this release, selecting the tunes, titling the CD, and preparing the text for the back of the jewel case as well as writing the notes.

Ruby Braff Trio[67]
December 31, 1981, Broadway Joe's, 315 West 46th Street, New York
Ruby Braff (cnt), Michael Moore (b), Jimmy Lyon (p)

Lyon was the house pianist and Ruby Braff joined for one night. This led to regular Sunday night engagements

Ruby Braff Trio[68]
January 17, 24, and 31, 1982, Broadway Joe's, 315 West 46th Street, New York
Ruby Braff (cnt), Michael Moore (b), Derek Smith (p)

13th Annual Pee Wee Russell Stomp[69]
February 14, 1982,unknown location in New Jersey

Ruby was honored in his absence by induction into the Jazz Hall of Fame by the New Jersey Jazz Society and the Institute of Jazz Studies.

The following advertisements, handbills, and audio cassette insert depict five of the performances in this chapter:

Figure 16.1: Advertisement
December 9, 1979

Figure 16.2: Advertisement
March 1980

Figure 16.3: Handbill
June 1980

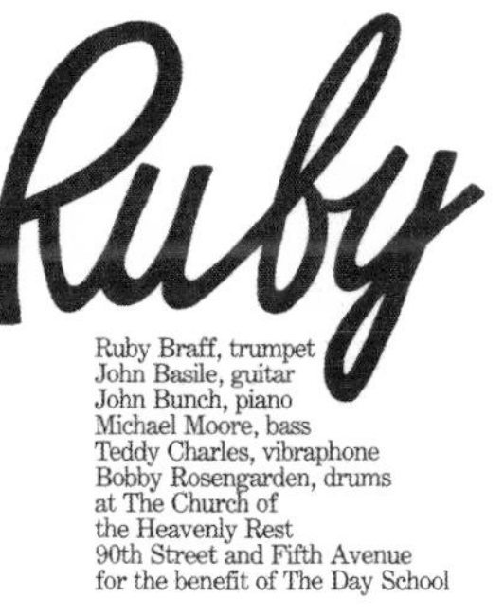

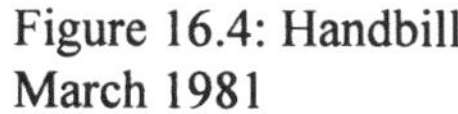
Figure 16.4: Handbill
March 1981

Changing Times Summer Jazz Party
Wee Burn Country Club
Darien, CT
July 8, 1981

1.	When You're Smiling	11:01
2.	Mean To Me	7:56
3.	Jeepers Creepers	7:18
4.	Keeping Out Of Mischief	8:13
5.	These Foolish Things	6:22
6.	Somebody Stole My Gal	8:53
	Total Time	49:53

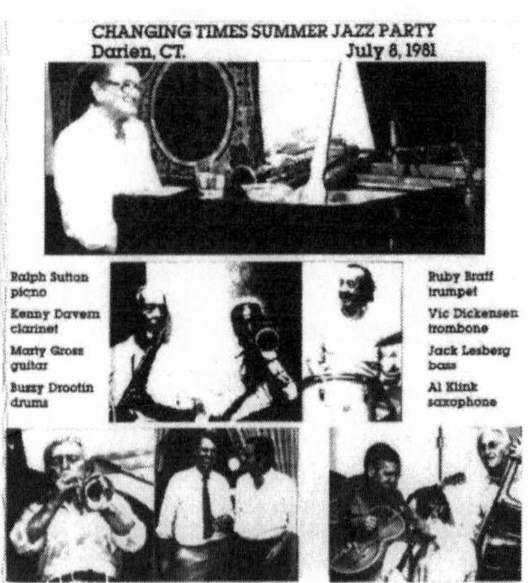

Figure 16.5: Cassette Album Insert from Changing Times Summer Jazz Party, July 8, 1981

Notes

[1] Scott Hamilton quoted in album note for Concord Jazz CJ 274 titled *A First.*

[2] Manfred Selchow, *Ding Ding: A Bio-Discographical Scrapbook on Vic Dickenson* (Germany: Uhle & Kleinmann, 1998), 742.

[3] Information from Michael Frohne.

[4] Personnel and names of additional tunes without Ruby provided by Michael Frohne.

[5] Ruby interviewed by Steve Voce on December 15, 1994.

[6] Information from Derek Coller.

[7] Manfred Selchow, *Ding Ding: A Bio-Discographical Scrapbook on Vic Dickenson* (Germany: Uhle & Kleinmann, 1998), 748.

[8] Edward N. Meyer, *The Life and Music of Kenny Davern: Just Four Bars* (Lanham, MD: Scarecrow Press, 2010), 159. Meyer states that this performance was on a Sunday in July and I have inserted it in an open position in Ruby's documented schedule, following his return from Europe.

[9] Photo, *The March of Jazz Celebrates Ruby Braff's 74th Birthday Party*, Arbors Records, 2001, 25.

[10] Warren W. Vaché, Sr., *Pee Wee Erwin: This Horn for Hire* (Metuchen, NJ: Scarecrow Press, 1987), 370. Details of Ruby's performances supplied by Robert J. Roberts.

[11] *New York Times*, August 26, 1979, and John S. Wilson, *New York Times*, September 20, 1979, September 18, 1979, and September 30, 1979. *The New Yorker*, September 17, 1979, 10, September 24, 1979, 7, October 1, 1979, 6, and October 8, 1979, 8. Al Caiola was listed in *The New Yorker*, whereas Gene Bertocini was listed in other sources.

[12] Edward N. Meyer, *Giant Strides* (Metuchen, NJ: Scarecrow Press, 1999), 137. *The New Yorker* first lists Dick Wellstood's appearances October 8, 1979, 7, and all subsequent issues until December 17, 1979, 8. That issue reports Wellstood's closing date. The listings do not include names of guest artists.

[13] *The New Yorker*, December 31, 1979, 8, January 7, 1980, 8 and subsequent issues.
[14] Doug Ramsey, *Jazz Matters* (Fayetteville, AR: The University of Arkansas Press, 1989), 204.
[15] *Washington Post*, October 16, 1979.
[16] John S. Wilson, *New York Times*, November 15, 1979, and ad in *New York Times*, December 9, 1979.
[17] Associated Press, January 28, 1908.
[18] Photo is reproduced in *The March of Jazz Celebrates Ruby Braff's 74th Birthday Party*, Arbors Records, 2001, 25.
[19] Ruby Braff speaking from his home to Steve Voce, BBC broadcast, Radio Merseyside, December 17, 2000.
[20] Manfred Selchow, *Ding Ding: A Bio-Discographical Scrapbook on Vic Dickenson* (Germany: Uhle & Kleinmann, 1998), 761.
[21] *New York Times*, March 28, 1980, John S. Wilson, *New York Times*, March 28, 1980, and *The New Yorker*, March 24, 1980, 12. A copy of a display advertisement for the concert is available.
[22] William D. Clancy with Audree Coke Kenton, *Woody Herman: Chronicles of the Herds (*New York: Schirmer Books, 1995), 315–316.
[23] John Norris, *Coda Magazine*, June 1980, 38.
[24] Buck Clayton, *Buck Clayton's Jazz World* (New York: Oxford University Press, 1987), 191, John S. Wilson, *New York Times*, May 20, 1980, March 31, 1980, and announcement published on May 16, 1980. *The New Yorker*, May 19, 1980, 10.
[25] *New York Times*, May 25, 1980, *The New Yorker*, May 26, 1980, 7, and June 2, 1980, 10.
[26] Review published in *Jazz Journal International*, June 1980, 21.
[27] Leonard Feather, *Los Angeles Times*, February 7, 1980, and *PR Newswire*, February 7, 1980.
[28] Whitney Balliett, *Night Creature* (New York: Oxford University Press, 1981), 266–267, advertised in *New York Times*, June 15, 1980, John S. Wilson, *New York Times*, June 27, 1980, and June 30, 1980, and *The New Yorker*, June 23, 1980, 9. Ernie Santosuosso, *Boston Globe*, June 30, 1980.
[29] John Norris in *Coda Magazine*, August 1980, 37 and December 1, 1980, 38.
[30] George Wein, *Myself Among Others* (Cambridge, MA: Da Capo Press, 2003), 480–481. Alexandra Palace burned down just prior to the following year's program.
[31] George Wein, *Myself Among Others* (Cambridge, MA: Da Capo Press, 2003), 480–481.
[32] George Wein, *Myself Among Others* (Cambridge, MA: Da Capo Press, 2003), 480–481.
[33] *Hank Jones Discography* and letter from Shin-ichi Iwamoto.
[34] Manfred Selchow, *Ding Ding: A Bio-Discographical Scrapbook on Vic Dickenson* (Germany: Uhle & Kleinmann, 1998), 770. The discography lists "Fascinating Rhythm" in error instead of "Crazy Rhythm."
[35] Manfred Selchow, *Ding Ding: A Bio-Discographical Scrapbook on Vic Dickenson* (Germany: Uhle & Kleinmann, 1998), 771.
[36] *Jazz Journal International*, September 1980, 4, mentioned in review of festival by Sinclair Traill.
[37] Manfred Selchow, *Ding Ding: A Bio-Discographical Scrapbook on Vic Dickenson* (Germany: Uhle & Kleinmann, 1998), 772.

[38] George A. Borgman, "The One and Only Ruby Braff," in *Mississippi Rag*, December 1995, 6.
[39] *Jazz Journal International*, November 1980, 3, mentioned in review by Sinclair Traill. Robert J. Roberts provided details about Ruby's performances at this Gibson party from his notes.
[40] John Norris in *Coda Magazine*, February 1981, 29, and David Lancashire, *Globe and Mail*, November 7, 1980, and Mark Miller, *Globe and Mail*, November 27, 1980.
[41] Mark Miller, *Globe and Mail*, November 27, 1980.
[42] John Norris in *Coda Magazine*, February 1980, 38.
[43] Correspondence with Sonny McGown.
[44] At the time of publication these photos can be seen by scrolling down on the page displayed by visiting http://jazzlives.wordpress.com/tag/george-duvivier/.
[45] Michael Steinman provided initial information. Note that this is listed in *Jersey Jazz* November 1980 with Michael Moore instead of George Duvivier. Moore is also listed in the *New York Times*, December 7, 1980. Titles of tunes provided by Lawrence A. Appelbaum from the Library of Congress.
[46] Photo, *The March of Jazz Celebrates Ruby Braff's 74th Birthday Party*, Arbors Records, 2001, 27.
[47] *New York Times*, March 1, 1981.
[48] Scott Hamilton in personal communication.
[49] Ernie Santosuosso, *Boston Globe*, March 8, 1981.
[50] A copy of the promotional handbill for the concert is available.
[51] Concert handbill and review in the *New York Times*, March 20, 1981, March 26, 1981, *The New Yorker*, March 23 1981, 8, and *New York Magazine*, March 23, 1981, 79.
[52] *New York Times*, June 12, 1981.
[53] *New York Times*, June 21, 1981.
[54] *New York Times*, June 28, 1981.
[55] *New York Times*, June 26, 1981.
[56] Mark Miller, *Globe and Mail*, July 23, 1981, dates of engagement are estimated, allowing for a few days before the cited review and the weekend following the radio interview with Phil McKeller.
[57] George Wein, *Myself Among Others* (Cambridge, MA: Da Capo Press, 2003), 449, *New York Times*, August 16, 1981, and *Boston Globe* August 23, 1981.
[58] *New York Times*, September 13, 1981.
[59] Album notes written by John Trudinger for Nif Nuf 43/016 titled *Ralph Sutton & Ruby Braff in Concert*.
[60] Copy of Ruby's handwritten letter to the organizer.
[61] Information about the Australian Jazz Expo from *The Age*, Tuesday, October 13, 1981, 10, clipping provided by Peter Gaudion.
[62] *The Age*, Tuesday October 13, 1981, 10.
[63] Correspondence with Peter Gaudion, including photos and news clippings. Peter owned the Beaconsfield Hotel, the site for these performances.
[64] John Kennedy and Jim McLeod provided the names of the accompanying musicians. The concert was broadcast on FM radio (ABC).
[65] *New York Times*, October 18 and 25, 1981.
[66] Charles C. Baron; Dick Hyman identified the titles.
[67] *New York Times*, December 31, 1981.
[68] *New York Times*, January 15, 1982, and January 31, 1982.
[69] *Jersey Jazz*, May 1982.

Chapter 17

The Pianists and the Growth of Jazz Parties: February 1982–September 1986

Following his induction to the Jazz Hall of Fame, Ruby flew to London for another appearance at Pizza Express. His appearances in London had become one of his highlights each year.

Ruby Braff[1]
February 1982, Pizza Express, London, England
Ruby Braff (cnt), Brian Lemon (p), Len Skeat (b), Jack Parnell (dm) with Scott Hamilton (ts) as an occasional guest
I Cover the Waterfront
In a Mellotone
Tangerine
Take the "A" Train
Yesterdays
When I Fall in Love

Richard Williams contributed a review to *The Times*:[2]

> The lyric poet of the cornet, Ruby Braff, has been among the most distinguished voices in mainstream jazz since that idiom's renaissance in the middle 1950s. His bejeweled, blue-hour duets with the pianist Ellis Larkins were my first introduction to his work, many years ago, and I remain convinced that his best work is produced in the more intimate settings.
>
> Braff can be found at the Pizza Express throughout this month, performing in a variety of contexts. On Thursday night, for example, accompanied by the Brian Lemon Trio, he was joined by his fellow American Scott Hamilton, the young tenor saxophonist who has earned a large following for his studiously retrospective style.
>
> Firstly it should be said that the quality of the rhythm section was by any yardstick thoroughly outstanding. Lemon's unusually light keyboard touch does not preclude the bluesier emotions and, if one cannot have Larkins, is just

> the thing for Braff; a hushed, responsive beat was maintained by Jack Parnell, the drummer, and Len Skeat, the bassist.
>
> The romantic glow of Braff's playing is often counterpointed by the saltiness of his verbal wit, but on Thursday he was in an expansive mood and at one point invited requests. These elicited an impromptu medley of 'I Cover the Waterfront,' 'In a Mellotone' and 'Tangerine' in which each transition was judged with instinctive wit to create a vehicle of gathering momentum and density.
>
> An interpretation of 'Take the 'A' Train' danced on tiptoe and a lushly mournful 'Yesterdays' found Braff at his best, alternating tricky sotto voce runs with Armstrong-like proclamations. . . .
>
> Braff, of course, dominates everything without seeming to flex the tiniest muscle. He is one of those rare improvisers whose every phrase seems worth preserving.

Ruby resumed his weekend appearances at Broadway Joe's and another of his regular performances in the Heavenly Jazz Concert Series before recording with Dick Hyman for Concord Records.

Ruby Braff Trio[3]
February 28 (Sunday), 1982, Broadway Joe's, 315 West 46th Street, New York
Ruby Braff (cnt), Michael Moore (b), Jimmy Lyon (p)

Ruby Braff Trio[4]
March 7, 14, 21, 28 (Sundays), 1982, Broadway Joe's, 315 West 46th Street, New York
Ruby Braff (cnt), Michael Moore (b), Jimmy Lyon (p)

Ruby Braff Trio[5]
April 4 (Sunday), 1982, Broadway Joe's, 315 West 46th Street, New York
Ruby Braff (cnt), Michael Moore (b), Jimmy Lyon (p)

A photo from the March of Jazz program, taken by Nancy Miller Elliott, shows Ruby rehearsing with Dick Hyman prior to their next performance. A copy is included in this book's photo section.[6]

Heavenly Jazz Concert Series: Ruby Braff and Dick Hyman[7]
April 4, 1982, 5 p.m., Church of the Heavenly Rest, 5th Avenue at 90th Street, New York
Ruby Braff (cnt), Dick Hyman (p, org)
This was the last concert in this season.

Ruby Braff Trio[8]
April 18 (Sunday), 1982, Broadway Joe's, 315 West 46th Street, New York
Ruby Braff (cnt), Michael Moore (b), Jimmy Lyon (p)

Ruby Braff and Dick Hyman: *America, the Beautiful*
April 24, 1982, Keystone Oaks High School, Dormont, Pennsylvania—produced by Ruby Braff, Dick Hyman, and the Pittsburgh Area Theatre Organ Society for the George Wein Collection
Ruby Braff (cnt) Dick Hyman (pipe organ)
When It's Sleepy Time Down South
    Concord Jazz GW 3003, Arbors Records ARCD 19269
When My Sugar Walks Down the Street
    Concord Jazz GW 3003, Arbors Records ARCD 19269
When I Fall in Love
    Concord Jazz GW 3003, Arbors Records ARCD 19269
As Long As I Live
    Concord Jazz GW 3003, Arbors Records ARCD 19269
America the Beautiful
    Concord Jazz GW 3003, Arbors Records ARCD 19269
Louisiana
    Concord Jazz GW 3003, Arbors Records ARCD 19269
High Society
    Concord Jazz GW 3003, Arbors Records ARCD 19269
I'll Be with You in Apple Blossom Time
    Concord Jazz GW 3003, Arbors Records ARCD 19269
I Ain't Got Nobody (Hyman solo)
    Concord Jazz GW 3003, Arbors Records ARCD 19269
This Is All I Ask
    Concord Jazz GW 3003, Arbors Records ARCD 19269
The Yankee Doodle Boy
    Arbors Records ARCD 19269
If Dreams Come True
    Arbors Records ARCD 19269
I'm Confessin'
    Arbors Records ARCD 19269
I've Grown Accustomed to Her Face
    Arbors Records ARCD 19269
Dinah
    Arbors Records ARCD 19269
Medley:
  Don't Get Around Much Anymore
    Arbors Records ARCD 19269
  I Let a Song Go Out of My Heart
    Arbors Records ARCD 19269
Muskrat Ramble
    Arbors Records ARCD 19269
NOTE: All titles released on Concord Jazz GW 3003 also appear on Concord CCD 43003 (CD) titled *A Pipe Organ Recital Plus One* and on Arbors Records ARCD 19269 titled *America, the Beautiful* with additional performances added

as shown. Recorded originally for the Pittsburgh Area Theatre Organ Society, a nonprofit organization dedicated to the preservation of the theater organ. The Concord Jazz CD release is included as one of 30 discs comprising a 30-CD box set titled *30 Concord Jazz Originals: The Rarities*. This set is issued in Korea with catalog number 1796499.

Ruby Braff Trio[9]
April 25 and May 2 (Sundays), 1982, Broadway Joe's, 315 West 46th Street, New York
Ruby Braff (cnt), probably Michael Moore (b), Jimmy Lyon (p)

Teresa Brewer: *Midnight Café / A Few More for the Road*
May 3–4, 1982, New York
Ruby Braff (cnt), Bucky Pizzarelli (g), Slam Stewart (b, voc), Ray Mantilla* (percussion)
Accentuate the Positive
  Doctor Jazz FW 40232
I Dream of You
  Doctor Jazz FW 40232
Come On and Drive Me Crazy
  Doctor Jazz FW 40232
Am I Blue?
  Doctor Jazz FW 40232
My Ship
  Doctor Jazz FW 40232
Flat Foot Floogie
  Doctor Jazz FW 40232
Dream a Little Dream of Me
  Doctor Jazz FW 40232
Life Is Just a Bowl of Cherries
  Doctor Jazz FW 40232
Jeepers Creepers
  Doctor Jazz FW 40232
Hold Me
  Doctor Jazz FW 40232
What Are We Gonna Do?*
  Doctor Jazz FW 40232

Ruby Braff Trio[10]
May 9 (Sunday), 1982, Broadway Joe's, 315 West 46th Street, New York
Ruby Braff (cnt), Michael Moore (b), Derek Smith (p)

Ruby Braff Trio[11]
May 23 (Sunday), 1982, Broadway Joe's, 315 West 46th Street, New York
Ruby Braff (cnt), Michael Moore (b), Derek Smith (p)

Ruby flew to Europe to appear at the Stockholm Jazz Festival. While it is likely he appeared elsewhere, I have not been able to locate any details from this trip.

Ruby Braff at the Stockholm Jazz Festival[12]
July 1982, Stockholm, Sweden
Ruby Braff was included in the list of performers. Others include Maxine Sullivan, Al Cohn, Zoot Sims, Art Blakey, Joe Williams, Flip Phillips, Bud Freeman, and Phil Woods.

Kind words from Warren Vaché[13]:

> Ruby is the best cornet player there is right now. He has an incredible respect for himself, and it shows in his music. He's an entertainer, but he does his entertaining musically, not with funny hats or hokey show-biz bits. The thing that impresses me most about Ruby is his economy. When one note will do, he uses just one note. I tend to get very notey.

Scott Hamilton wrote that George Wein asked Ruby to join a tour that would be billed as the Newport Jazz Festival All Stars and that Ruby and George would be partners, perhaps as a way to deal with past events. Ruby asked for Scott Hamilton to join the tour when Phil Bodner opted out. Other musicians included Ed Hubble, Slam Stewart, and Oliver Jackson. They toured widely across the country, mostly performing at public concerts and subscription series. Scott recalled Laramie, Wyoming, Juneau, Alaska, and Dumas, Texas, and recalled that it probably lasted from October to December of 1982. A UPI story added Elmira, New York to the list of performances.[14] A recording exists for one performance that is perhaps near the beginning of this tour and other performances are confirmed as well.

Newport All Stars
October 9, 1982, McGaw Chapel, The College of Wooster, Wooster, Ohio
Ruby Braff (cnt), Ed Hubble (tb, alto horn), Scott Hamilton (ts), George Wein (p), Slam Stewart (b), Oliver Jackson (dm)
Jubilee
Basin Street Blues
"C" Jam Blues
In a Sentimental Mood
Just You, Just Me (Braff/Wein/Stewart)
Star Dust
Blues (Hamilton)
I'm Gonna Sit Right Down and Write Myself a Letter
Ain't Misbehavin' (Hubble with rhythm)
Flat Foot Floogie (Stewart with rhythm)
I've Got a Feelin' I'm Falling

Medley:
Caravan (Jackson)
Dinah
When a Woman Loves a Man
Nobody Knows You When You're Down and Out (Wein voc with Hubble and rhythm)
Them There Eyes (Braff)
I'm Pulling Though (Braff, Hamilton, Wein)
Lady Be Good (Stewart with rhythm)
The World Is Waiting for the Sunrise (ensemble with Hubble alto horn)
Fine and Mellow
NOTE: A recording of these tunes is available but remains unissued.

Newport All Stars[15]
October 28, Hult Center for the Performing Arts, Eugene, Oregon
No further details are available.

Ambassador Pops: Newport All Stars[16] **(see Figure 17.1)**
November 3, 1982, Ambassador Auditorium, Pasadena, California
Ruby Braff (cnt), Ed Hubble (tb), Scott Hamilton (ts), George Wein (p), Slam Stewart (b), Oliver Jackson (dm)
Phil Bodner (reeds) was advertised but did not perform
In a Sentimental Mood
Star Dust

Leonard Feather reviewed the concert and reported that Ruby was "the savior of the program" and he continued, writing the following in tribute:

> His tone is crystal pure, his taste impeccable, his melodic sense variously evocative of Satchmo and Bobby Hackett. His duet with Wein on 'In a Sentimental Mood' came early in the show, and nothing that followed, not even Hamilton's languorous 'Star Dust,' could top it. . . . But Braff alone made the trip worthwhile. He may well be the last of a vanishing breed.[17]

Newport All Stars[18]
November 5, 1982, El Camino College, Los Angeles
Ruby Braff (cnt), Ed Hubble (tb), Scott Hamilton (ts), George Wein (p), Slam Stewart (b), Oliver Jackson (dm)
Phil Bodner (reeds) was advertised but did not perform.

Newport All Stars[19]
November 6, 1982, Haugh Performing Arts Center, Citrus College, Los Angeles
Ruby Braff (cnt), Ed Hubble (tb), Scott Hamilton (ts), George Wein (p), Slam Stewart (b), Oliver Jackson (dm)
Phil Bodner (reeds) was advertised but did not perform.

Newport All Stars[20]
November 23, 1982, New Hampshire Arts Center in the Palace Theater, 80 Hanover Street, Manchester, New Hampshire
Ruby Braff (cnt), Ed Hubble (tb), Scott Hamilton (ts), Slam Stewart (b) Oliver Jackson(dm)

Ruby Braff Trio[21]
December 31, 1982, Broadway Joe's, 315 West 46th Street, New York
Ruby Braff (cnt), unknown bass, perhaps Michael Moore (b), Jimmy Lyon (p)
Lyon was the house pianist and Ruby Braff joined for one night.

Hanratty's[22]
One night only between January 31 and February 3, 1983, 1754 2nd Avenue, New York
Ralph Sutton (p), Ruby Braff occasionally sat in

Ralph substituted for Dick Wellstood during much of January. Dick returned February 1 but Ralph continued to substitute when he was absent. Dave McKenna joined Ralph on January 29 and 30. Ruby might have appeared on other occasions, but I have been unable to document dates other than earlier appearances with Dick Wellstood in 1979.

Phyllis Condon's 80th Birthday[23]
April 3, 1983, Eddie Condon's Jazz Club on West 54th Street, New York
Balaban & Cats, with guests Ruby Braff, Max Kaminsky, Maxine Sullivan, Buck Clayton, Vic Dickenson, Cliff Leeman, Bob Wilber, and Jimmy McPartland

Teresa Brewer: *American Music Box, Volume 1: The Songs of Irving Berlin*
July 7–8, 1983, New York
Ruby Braff (cnt), Derek Smith (p), Bucky Pizzarelli (g), Martin Taylor (el-g), George Duvivier (b), Grady Tate (dm), substitute Ron Traxler* (dm), Teresa Brewer (voc)
Isn't It a Lovely Day?*
    Doctor Jazz FW 40231
How Deep Is the Ocean?
    Doctor Jazz FW 40231
Blue Skies
    Doctor Jazz FW 40231
All by Myself
    Doctor Jazz FW 40231
Easter Parade
    Doctor Jazz FW 40231

Russian Lullaby*
    Doctor Jazz FW 40231
Always
    Doctor Jazz FW 40231
Say It Isn't So
    Doctor Jazz FW 40231

Buddy Barnes: *Live at Studio B: I've Been to Town*
1983, New York, Teo Macero producer
Buddy Barnes (p and voc), Ruby Braff (cnt), Wayne Wright (g), Jay Leonhardt (b)
I've Been to Town
    Sony EP (VHS video)
Don't Fight It, It's Chemistry
    Sony EP (VHS video)

Add Sylvia Syms (voc)
My Ship
    Sony EP (VHS video)
Pick Yourself Up
    Sony EP (VHS video)
NOTE: Other titles from this video performance do not include Ruby Braff. Buddy Barnes once was Mable Mercer's accompanist.

Ruby Braff and Friends[24]
September 29–October 1, 1983, Struggles, 10 Dempsey Avenue, Edgewater, New Jersey
No further information available

John S. Wilson wrote the following in his review of the next performance[25]:

> Ruby Braff and Dick Hyman are, individually, two of the most distinctive musicians in jazz—Mr. Braff because of a trumpet style that involves dark, somber plunges into the lower register mixed with growls, murmurs and sudden rising shouts, all delivered with closely controlled precision; Mr. Hyman because of the awesome range of musical idioms that he has at his fingertips.
>
> When they come together as a duo, as they did early Friday evening at the New School as part of the *Jazz at Six* series, they combine their personal quirks to create music that is wondrous and delightful.
>
> Starting, as many jazzmen do, with a given theme (their choices ranged from 'I'll Be With You in Apple Blossom Time' to 'America, the Beautiful'), Mr. Braff usually explored bits and pieces of the theme in terms of breathy mutters, soulful moans and precisely organized phrases, while Mr. Hyman supplied a broad background that offered suggestive nuggets to the trumpeter.
>
> Mr. Hyman, in his solo turn, would flow into the theme with deceptive simplicity, using colors to develop ideas that might turn into blues, stride, a

fugue, some Art Tatum runs—all done with calm casualness until Mr. Braff, with renewed energy from his absorption of Mr. Hyman's imaginative goings-on, returned to join in provocative brief exchanges, injecting such broad sounds as a brassy belch or bellow along with his whispered lines.

Their performances were developed with subtle changes of tone and mood. Every phrase seemed a fresh surprise and even when they threw in a hackneyed run it was to produce a surprise. Apparently nothing holds them down to mundane matters because they are always in the process of challenging themselves and their listeners.

Jazz at 6:00 Series: *Fireworks*[26]

November 4, 1983, 6 p.m., New School for Social Research, 66th West 12th, New York

Ruby Braff (cnt), Dick Hyman (p)

The Jazz at Six series and the Heavenly Jazz Concerts were both produced by Paul Weinstein.

Somebody Loves Me
    Inner City IC 1153
I'll Be with You in Apple Blossom Time
    unissued, recording available
Bidin' My Time
    Inner City IC 1153
High Society
    Inner City IC 1153
When My Sugar Walks Down the Street
    unissued, recording available
They Can't Take That Away from Me
    Inner City IC 1153
Lady Be Good
    Inner City IC 1153
Liza (Braff out)
    Inner City IC 1153
Persian Rug
    unissued, recording available
Theme from Swan Lake
    Inner City IC 1153
Sugar
    Inner City IC 1153
America the Beautiful
    unissued, recording available

NOTE: Three tunes from the Inner City LP were also issued on AFRTS basic musical library, P series P-23136 ("Somebody Loves Me," "Lady Be Good," and "Sugar"). All titles from Inner City IC 1153 are also issued on Inner City IC 1153 (CD). A photo from the March of Jazz program about this time is available, dated from the early 1980s.[27]

Colorado Springs Invitational Jazz Party[28]
November 11–13, 1983, Broadmoor Hotel, Colorado Springs, Colorado
Ruby Braff, Billy Butterfield, Bill Allred, Carl Fontana, Kenny Davern, Allan Vaché, Milt Hinton, Colin Gieg, Bert Dahlander, Bobby Rosengarden, and possibly others performed in various combinations at the first Colorado Springs party—further details unknown

Ruby was honored with the mayor of Boston named November 17, 1983, "Ruby Braff Day in Boston." The club in the Hilton Hotel was packed for his performance.

Ruby Braff Day in Boston: Ruby Braff Quartet[29]
November 17, 1983, Satin Doll Room, Back Bay Hilton Hotel, Boston
Ruby Braff (cnt), Gray Sargent (g), Whit Browne (b), Carl Goodwin (dm)
This Could Be the Start of Something Big
Medley:
  Wouldn't It Be Loverly
  I've Grown Accustomed to Her Face
Foolin' Myself
Tea for Two
As Long As I Live
Yesterdays
Lullaby of the Leaves
Topsy

The review published in the *Boston Globe* continues:

> Playing a triumphant return of the native, Ruby Braff came home to a capacity house last night at the Satin Doll Room. Mayor Kevin H. White took appropriate cognizance by proclaiming yesterday "Ruby Braff Day" with a whereas-crammed certificate. A New York resident since his twentieth year, Braff came onstage to an atmosphere of reunion and he reciprocated with a heaping hornful of ideas and waspish whimsy.

Hank O'Neal captured Ruby Braff, John Bunch, Phil Flanigan, and Chris Flory in one of his photographs during the next recording session at Vanguard Studios. A copy is included in this book's photo section. Next, Ruby returned for a week-long engagement Basin Street in Toronto, saving time to record two releases on the Canadian label PediMega and an afternoon live FM radio broadcast from Traders' Lounge. This second PediMega recording was originally only issued on an audio cassette until given broader circulation by John Norris on Sackville.

Next came the first recording that united Ruby with Scott Hamilton and his regular group at the time. They had been jointly touring as members of the Newport All Stars, and their recordings continued later on Concord Records and concluded with Ruby's final recording, released on Arbors Records. The Phontastic release was a wonderful prevue of things yet to come.

Ruby Braff Quintet featuring Scott Hamilton and John Bunch: *Mr. Braff to You*
December 15, 1983, New York
Ruby Braff (cnt), Scott Hamilton (ts), John Bunch (p), Chris Flory (g), Phil Flanigan (b)
China Boy
    Phontastic PHONT7568, PHONTCD 7568 (CD)
Medley (Butterfidia):
  Poor Butterfly
    Phontastic PHONT7568, PHONTCD 7568 (CD)
  Ida, Sweet as Apple Cider
    Phontastic PHONT7568, PHONTCD 7568 (CD)
Goodnight My Love
    Phontastic PHONT7568, PHONTCD 7568 (CD)
Miss Brown to You
    Phontastic PHONT7568, PHONTCD 7568 (CD)
And the Angels Sing
    Phontastic PHONT7568, PHONTCD 7568 (CD)
As Long As I Live
    Phontastic PHONT7568, PHONTCD 7568 (CD)
Emaline
    Phontastic PHONT7568, PHONTCD 7568 (CD)
You Brought a New Kind of Love to Me
    Phontastic PHONT7568, PHONTCD 7568 (CD)

Ruby Braff: *My Funny Valentine*
January 17, 1984, Toronto
Ruby Braff (tp), Gene DiNovi (p)
Medley:
  My Funny Valentine
    PediMega (Can) 2, Marshmallow (J) CEDD 00435, Sackville SK2CD 5005
  My Heart Stood Still
    PediMega (Can) 2, Marshmallow (J) CEDD 00435, Sackville SK2CD 5005
  Be Careful, It's My Heart
    PediMega (Can) 2, Marshmallow (J) CEDD 00435, Sackville SK2CD 5005
Have a Heart
    PediMega (Can) 2, Marshmallow (J) CEDD 00435, Sackville SK2CD 5005
Says My Heart
    PediMega (Can) 2, Marshmallow (J) CEDD 00435, Sackville SK2CD 5005
Nobody's Heart
    PediMega (Can) 2, Marshmallow (J) CEDD 00435, Sackville SK2CD 5005

Break My Heart
PediMega (Can) 2, Marshmallow (J) CEDD 00435, Sackville SK2CD 5005
My Foolish Heart
PediMega (Can) 2, Marshmallow (J) CEDD 00435, Sackville SK2CD 5005
Jazz Classix JC 98023
Sweethearts on Parade
PediMega (Can) 2, Marshmallow (J) CEDD 00435, Sackville SK2CD 5005,
Jazz Classix JC 98023
Blues in My Heart
PediMega (Can) 2, Marshmallow (J) CEDD 00435, Sackville SK2CD 5005
This Heart of Mine
PediMega (Can) 2, Marshmallow (J) CEDD 00435, Sackville SK2CD 5005
Beware My Heart
PediMega (Can) 2, Marshmallow (J) CEDD 00435, Sackville SK2CD 5005
NOTE: The Sackville CD is titled *The Canadian Sessions*. Jazz Classix CD is titled *Ruby Braff Plays Standards and Evergreens.*

Ruby Braff at Bourbon Street[30]
January 16–21, 1984, Bourbon Street, 180 Queen Street West, Toronto
Ruby Braff (cnt and occasional piano), Reg Schwager (g), Steve Wallace (b), Jerry Fuller (dm)
Easy Living

Mark Miller wrote the following:[31]

> Braff's partner on previous visits from New York has been the imperturbable Ed Bickert. Bickert, however, is occupied with Moe Koffman over at George's Spaghetti House this week. Thus, Schwager, Toronto's latest 'coming' guitarist is in the hot seat. Imagine the first time Wayne Gretzky went up against Gordie Howe. It promised to be a little like that.
>
> So what's this? Ruby Braff, at the Bourbon Street piano during Monday's sparsely-attended third set, amiably teaching Schwager some old tunes? 'Do you know. . . ?' he'd ask, rhyming off increasingly obscure titles. 'Oh, you'll like this one,' he'd say, as he laid out the chord sequences, adding the melody, occasionally singing the lyrics, and even doodling out a little improvisation. Schwager, catching on quickly, would play the first solo. Braff accompanied the guitarist for a time and then took up the cornet for a solo of his own. 'Isn't that a nice tune?' he'd ask when the process was complete.... After he thanked the few folks in the house, he made the usual introductions, concluding with a 'Yours Truly, Henry Kissinger.'

Ruby Braff and Jim Galloway
January 21, 1984, afternoon, Trader's Lounge, Toronto, live CKFM Radio broadcast *Toronto Alive* hosted by Jim Galloway
Ruby Braff (cnt), Jim Galloway (ss), Ian Bargh (p), Neil Swainson (b), Jerry Fuller (dm)

Mountain Greenery
Our Love Is Here to Stay
Shine
Laura (Braff out)
Sugar
Liza
All Alone (Galloway out)
No Greater Love
NOTE: A recording of these tunes is available but remains unissued.

Ruby Braff and Gene DiNovi: ***Ruby and Gene Play George and Ira Gershwin***
January 23, 1984, Toronto
Ruby Braff (tp), Gene DiNovi (p, voc-l)
Medley:
  Trumpeter Blow Your Golden Horn (1)
    PediMega FM/C3 (Cassette), Sackville SK2CD 5005
  Do It Again
    PediMega FM/C3 (Cassette), Sackville SK2CD 5005
Medley:
  Love Walked In
    PediMega FM/C3 (Cassette), Sackville SK2CD 5005
  Embraceable You
    PediMega FM/C3 (Cassette), Sackville SK2CD 5005
  The Man I Love
    PediMega FM/C3 (Cassette), Sackville SK2CD 5005
Love is Sweeping the Country
    PediMega FM/C3 (Cassette), Sackville SK2CD 5005
Isn't It a Pity
    PediMega FM/C3 (Cassette), Sackville SK2CD 5005
Of Thee I Sing
    PediMega FM/C3 (Cassette), Sackville SK2CD 5005
For You, for Me, for Evermore
    PediMega FM/C3 (Cassette), Sackville SK2CD 5005
I've Got a Crush on You
    PediMega FM/C3 (Cassette), Sackville SK2CD 5005,
    Jazz Classix JC 98023
Lady Be Good
    PediMega FM/C3 (Cassette), Sackville SK2CD 5005,
    Jazz Classix JC 98023
Maybe
    PediMega FM/C3 (Cassette), Sackville SK2CD 5005,
    Jazz Classix JC 98023
He Loves and She Loves (1)
    PediMega FM/C3 (Cassette), Sackville SK2CD 5005

NOTE: "I've Got a Crush on You" also appears on the album *Cool Jazz for Hot Nights,* Candid Records (UK) 71802 (CD), *Jazz–You Like It*, Emporio (UK) EMPRBX 025 (four-CD set), and *Smooth Jazz for Seductive Nights* on Metro 8458100429. The Sackville CD is titled *The Canadian Sessions*. Jazz Classix CD is titled *Ruby Braff Plays Standards and Evergreens*.

Ruby Braff and Friends[32]
January 27–28, 1984, 9 p.m., Struggles, 10 Dempsey Avenue, Edgewater, New Jersey
Ruby Braff (cnt) and unknown others

Ruby Braff[33]
March 22, 1984, Society for Ethical Culture, 2 West 64th Street, New York
Ruby Braff (cnt), Bucky Pizzarelli (g), John Pizzarelli (g)

Ruby Braff Quintet[34]
March 23–24, 1984, Struggles, 10 Dempsey Avenue, Edgewater, New Jersey

Ruby Braff–Dick Hyman at the New School[35]
April 27, 1984, 6 p.m., New School, 66 West 12th Street, New York
What Is This Thing Called Love?
Blue and Sentimental
Who Cares?
April Showers
When You Wish upon a Star
What a Little Moonlight Can Do
Save It Pretty Mama
Lover Come Back to Me (Hyman)
You Are My Lucky Star
Why Shouldn't I?
If I Love Again
You're Lucky to Me
Come Sunday
Rosalie
When a Woman Loves a Man
High Society
NOTE: A recording of these tunes is available but remains unissued.

Tony Bennett, interviewed by Larry Kart in the *Chicago Tribune*, reported the next special event:[36]

> Ruby is a traditionalist in the sense that he knows the roots and the treasures—Louis Armstrong, Judy Garland, Bix Beiderbecke and all the rest. But then, having learned from them, he takes that knowledge and flies with it in a very modern way. Like all great jazz musicians, Ruby is right in the 'now'—he

moves like nature—and when people get a chance to hear him, they're always moved.

I remember last year, I went to one of those really hardnosed ASCAP (American Society of Composers and Performers) meetings that the Song Writers Hall of Fame puts on. Every big composer was in the audience and a whole bunch of artists performed, but it was more of a social occasion until Ruby came out to back a singer.

He played a few solos and obbligatos, and suddenly it was like everyone was swooning. They didn't know who Ruby was, and then when they heard this magnificent horn, they just went 'Wow!' But that's what Ruby can do to you if he gets a chance.

ASCAP Awards Ceremony
1984, date unknown, probably May 3, Beverly Hills, California

Ruby Braff[37]
May 11–12, 1984, Starlight Roof (Howard Johnson's Motor Lodge), 575 Commonwealth Avenue, Boston
Further details unknown

Scott Hamilton–Ruby Braff Sextet[38]
June 1–2, 1984, 9 p.m., Struggles, 10 Dempsey Avenue, Edgewater, New Jersey

Ruby Braff and Friends[39]
July 13-14, 1984, Struggles, 10 Dempsey Avenue, Edgewater, New Jersey

Vic Dickenson's 78th Birthday Party[40]
August 5, 1984, 4–7 p.m., Eddie Condon's, New York
Ruby Braff attended along with many others including Red Balaban, Johnny Blowers, Joe Bushkin, Buck Clayton, Roy Eldridge, Phil Flanigan, Chris Flory, Marquis Foster, Leonard Gaskin, Keith Ingham, Jane Jarvis, Barbara Lea, Jack Lesberg, Jimmy and Marian McPartland, Joe Muranyi, Rose Murphy, Marty Napoleon, Nancy Nelson, Bucky Pizzarelli, Ed Polcer, Red Richards, Dick Sudhalter, Warren Vaché, Warren Vaché, Jr., Earle Warren, George Wein, and Dick Wellstood.

A published photo of Ruby performing at Vic Dickenson's 78th birthday party exists.[41]

22nd Gibson Jazz Party[42]
September 1–3, 1984, Denver, Colorado
September 1, Saturday afternoon
Ruby Braff (cnt), Scott Hamilton (ts), Barney Kessel (g), Dick Hyman (p), George Duvivier (b), Gus Johnson (dm)
I'm Crazy 'bout My Baby
When I Fall in Love (Braff feature)

The Sheik of Araby
NOTE: A recording of these tunes is available but remains unissued.

September 1, Saturday night
Ruby Braff (cnt), Benny Carter (as), Scott Hamilton (ts), Barney Kessel (g), John Bunch (p), George Duvivier (b), Alan Dawson (dm)
Sunday
Tangerine
Dinah
NOTE: A recording of these tunes is available but remains unissued.

September 2, Sunday afternoon
Ruby Braff (cnt), Buddy Tate, Scott Hamilton (ts), Barney Kessel (g), Dick Hyman (p), Ray Brown (b), Alan Dawson (dm)
Love Me or Leave Me
Yesterdays (Braff feature)
NOTE: A recording of these tunes is available but remains unissued.

September 2, Sunday night
Ruby Braff (cnt), John Bunch (p), George Duvivier (b), Gus Johnson (dm)
Old Folks
Wrap Your Troubles in Dreams
NOTE: A recording of these tunes is available but remains unissued.

September 3, Monday
No details are available for Ruby's final session on Monday.

Ruby Braff and Dick Hyman[43]
September 16, 1984, All Saint's Church, Madison Avenue and 129th Street, New York
NOTE: The program included excerpts from their album, *America the Beautiful.*

New York Jazz Repertory Company: Tribute to Louis Armstrong[44]
September 19, 1984, Spingold Theater, Boston
The program was opened by the Brandeis Jazz Ensemble followed by the New York Jazz Repertory Company including Warren Vaché (cnt), Mel Davis and Doc Cheatham (tp), Kenny Davern (cl), Dick Hyman (p), Panama Francis (dm), and Carrie Smith (voc). Ruby Braff performed with Dick Hyman in the second half of the concert. Tunes performed by Braff and Hyman included the following:
Rockin' Chair
Jeepers Creepers
Sweethearts on Parade
I Can't Give You Anything but Love

Ruby flew to London and then returned to the US to participate in the Floating Jazz Festival on the S/S *Norway*.

Ruby Braff with Jack Parnell Trio[45]
September 22, 1984, Pizza Express, 10 Dean Street, London
Ruby Braff (cnt), Jack Parnell (p), and unknown bass and drums

Ruby Braff and Brian Lemon[46]
September 24, 1984, Pizza on the Park, 11 Knightsbridge, London
Ruby Braff (cnt), Brian Lemon (p)
You're Lucky to Me
Jeepers Creepers
I Got Rhythm
Chicago
I've Grown Accustomed to Her Face

A review by Richard Williams from *The Times* captures the spirit of this evening:[47]

> Ruby Braff is not a singer, but he knows more about songs than most people who make their living that way. At one point, when their conversation abruptly slowed from the chatter of 'Chicago' to the pensive languor of 'I've Grown Accustomed to Her Face,' they even recalled the quality of the classic *Two-Part Inventions in Jazz* recorded by Braff with the pianist Ellis Larkins in 1955: unmistakably invited by his partner's phrasing to double the tempo for the piano solo. Lemon instead stuck to his guns and, profiting from the subtle tension, outlined a chorus which glowed with such rich colors that Braff needed all his artistry to devise an appropriate re-entry. He succeeded, of course, in one of those spellbound moments that define the genius of the art as well as of the artist.

Ruby Braff with Jack Parnell Trio[48]
September 26–29, 1984, Pizza Express, 10 Dean Street, London
Ruby Braff (cnt), Jack Parnell (p), and unknown bass and drums

Floating Jazz Festival[49]
October 20–26 and October 27-November 2, 1984, S/S *Norway*, departing from Miami. There were two cruises, each lasting for one week.

Week 1:

> Woody Herman's big band, Dizzy Gillespie, Al Cohn, Benny Carter, Joe Williams, Jonah Jones and his Quartet, Ruby Braff, Dave McKenna, Bob Haggart, and Hannibal Peterson and His Quintet. Zoot Sims had been scheduled to participate for both weeks; however, his health forced him to cancel the first week. Dizzy Gillespie joined the cruise at St. Thomas.

Week 2:

Mel Tormé, George Shearing, Don Thompson, Clark Terry, Wild Bill Davison, Les Paul, and Doc Cheatham, along with Gillespie, Zoot Sims, Williams, Benny Carter, Ruby Braff, and Dave McKenna

Some information about individual performances can be deduced from photos taken by Hank O'Neal during the cruise. The 1985 Floating Jazz Festival printed program also includes some information about performances during the previous year (1984). Hank O'Neal shared several photographs of Ruby performing with Benny Carter, Scott Hamilton, Bob Haggart, John Bunch, and Bobby Rosengarden. Several other photos showed musicians relaxing outdoors on the deck, including one with Scott Hamilton, Benny Carter, Joe Williams, and Ruby Braff and another showing Hilma Carter, Benny Carter, Shelley Shier, Bobby Rosengarden, Scott Hamilton, and Ruby Braff embarking on a shore excursion. Ruby provided one of Hank's photos for publication in the March of Jazz program.[50] In that personal copy, Ruby used a pen to darken Bob Haggart's white dinner jacket to conform with the tuxedos worn by all the other musicians. Ruby's altered copy of Hank's photo is included in this book's photo section. Ruby simply felt that since all the musicians were asked to wear formal attire, that Haggart should conform to that standard, even long after the fact.

Floating Jazz Festival[51]
October 21, 1984, S/S *Norway*
Ruby Braff (cnt), Benny Carter (as), Scott Hamilton (ts), John Bunch (p), Bob Haggart (b), Bobby Rosengarden (dm)
This sextet performed as a quartet without Carter and Bunch for part of the performance. A few performances were scheduled for the first day of the cruise, but this session opened the main program Sunday night. Hank O'Neal wrote the following:[52]

> Things got into full swing the next day [21st]. Audience reaction had been enthusiastic but not overwhelming the first night. The passengers were used to the ship by Sunday night and everyone was ready to see what the jazz festival was all about. Benny Carter and Ruby Braff were scheduled for the theater, every seat was taken before they began and because it was a formal evening on ship, ninety percent of the audience were in evening dress, as were the musicians. All this made for an elegant atmosphere. At the conclusion of each number there was much shouting which built to a good deal of enthusiasm by the end; a very successful presentation.

Floating Jazz Festival[53]
October 1984, S/S *Norway*
Ruby Braff (cnt), Bucky Pizzarelli (g), Michael Moore (b), Jake Hanna (dm)

Floating Jazz Festival[54]
October, 1984, during second week of the cruise, S/S *Norway*
Ruby Braff (cnt), Benny Carter (ts)

Hank O'Neal wrote the following: "Ruby Braff and Benny Carter [worked] their way through one great melody after another."

Ruby Braff and Dick Hyman at the Floating Jazz Festival[55]
October 1984, S/S *Norway*
Ruby Braff (cnt), Sayyd Abdul Al-Khabyr (cl), Zoot Sims (ts), Michael Moore (b), and others including Scott Hamilton (ts)
NOTE: Sahib Sahib (cl) is listed in the caption to the photo in the March of Jazz program; however, Sayyd Abdul Al-Khabyr is listed in the festival program for that year on clarinet. He is a Canadian musician who recorded with Dizzy Gillespie, Panama Francis, and Mercer Ellington. He also plays flute and tenor saxophone.

Floating Jazz Festival[56]
November 1, 1984, S/S *Norway*
Ruby Braff (cnt), Scott Hamilton (ts), John Bunch (p), Michael Moore (b), Mel Tormé (dm)

Hank O'Neal wrote the following:

> . . . . down in the Saga the farewell jam session was in progress. It led off with a spectacular quartet: Zoot Sims, Bucky, Michael Moore and Jake Hanna. [Zoot] sat all the way through this one on the S/S *Norway* and he was superb. Ruby Braff and Scott Hamilton followed, aided by Mel Tormé, John Bunch, and Michael Moore. Then Wild Bill Davison, the elder statesman on board, wrapped everything up.

The following listing for an appearance at Pizza Express is not confirmed. It is based only on a single caption for a photograph and probably dates from February or March 1982 instead.

Pizza Express, London[57]
Ruby Braff (cnt), Brian Lemon (p), Len Skeat (b), Jack Parnell (dm)

Ruby Braff and Friends[58]
November 9–10, 1984, 9 p.m., Struggles, 10 Dempsey Avenue, Edgewater, New Jersey
Ruby Braff (cnt) and unknown others

Vic Dickenson's Funeral[59]
November 21, 1984, Saint Peter's Lutheran Church, 54th Street and Lexington Avenue, New York
Ruby Braff (cnt), Dick Hyman (org)
When Day Is Done
Memories of You

An article in the *New York Times* that describes Ruby's next engagement at the West End Café, also mentions frequent appearances at Struggles in Edgewater, New Jersey. I have only been able to trace two evenings at Struggles, previously listed on November 9 and 10, so it is likely that Ruby appeared there on other occasions as well. At the West End Café Ruby joined Scott Hamilton's Quintet. They had already recorded for Phontastic a year earlier, on December 15, 1983. The West End Café was located on Broadway at 113th Street, New York, across the street from Columbia University. The details for the overall engagement are shown first, followed by specific information from available recordings that are available for the nights of December 7 and 8.

Scott also reported that this group did play at a private party in New Jersey sometime in 1984. I have not been able to locate further details. Two albums soon followed, on Concord, release in February 1985.

Ruby Braff and Scott Hamilton Quintet[60]
December 4 and 6–8, 1984 West End Café, Broadway at 113th Street, New York–across the street from Columbia University
Ruby Braff (cnt), Scott Hamilton (ts), John Bunch (p), Chris Flory (g), Phil Flanigan (b), Chuck Riggs (dm)

December 7, 1984
Royal Garden Blues
All of Me
Sugar
Chinatown, My Chinatown

New Set:
Them There Eyes
Medley:
  Rockin' Chair
  I Can't Give You Anything but Love
This Is All I Ask (Hamilton featured)
Love Me or Leave Me
Between the Devil and the Deep Blue Sea
NOTE: A recording of these tunes is available but remains unissued.

December 8, 1984
Love Is Just around the Corner

Don't Get Around Much Anymore
The Man I Love
Shine
My Romance (Hamilton featured)
It's Only a Paper Moon
Keepin' Out of Mischief Now
Mean to Me
Lover Come Back to Me
Rockin' Chair
I Love You Porgy (Bunch featured)
Them There Eyes
NOTE: A recording of these tunes is available but remains unissued.

A photo from the March of Jazz program shows Ruby with Scott Hamilton about this time.[61]

Ruby Braff and Dick Hyman[62]
December 16, 1984, West End Café, New York

Scott Hamilton, in personal correspondence, also reported a concert for the Cape Cod Jazz Society about this time with Gray Sargent, Marshall Wood, and Chuck Riggs. He recalls that Benny Waters played the first half of the concert with a Massachusetts band and that toward the end Ruby played the piano behind Gray Sargent. Scott said that it was taped for a public access television station. I have been unable to locate further details.

Scott Hamilton reported that Ruby also substituted for him one night at the West End Café either late in 1984 or early in 1985, prior to the Concord recording session with Scott's band in February when Scott had another engagement with the Newport All Stars. On that night, Scott recalls that there was a live broadcast by WKCR that I have not traced. This leads to the following:

Ruby Braff Substitutes for Scott Hamilton at West End Café
Unknown date late 1984 or early 1985, West End Café, New York (possibly broadcast on WKCR)
Ruby Braff (cnt), John Bunch (p), Chris Flory (g), Phil Flanigan (b), Chuck Riggs (dm)

Ruby Braff and Scott Hamilton: *A First*
February 1985, Penny Lane Studios, New York
Ruby Braff (cnt), Scott Hamilton (ts), John Bunch (p), Chris Flory (g), Phil Flanigan (b), Chuck Riggs (dm)
Romance in the Dark
Concord Jazz CJ 274, CCD 4274 (CD), Snapper Music SMDCD 271, P-23330

When a Woman Loves a Man
    Concord Jazz CJ 274, CCD 4274 (CD)
Rockin' Chair
    Concord Jazz CJ 274, CCD 4274 (CD), P-23330
Dinah
    Concord Jazz CJ 274, CCD 4274 (CD), CCD 4833-2, St. Clair 4515
All My Life
    Concord Jazz CJ 274, CCD 4274 (CD), Snapper Music SMDCD 271
Shine
    Concord Jazz CJ 274, CCD 4274 (CD)
Medley:
  If You Were Mine
    Concord Jazz CJ 274, CCD 4274 (CD), P-23330
  I Wished on the Moon
    Concord Jazz CJ 274, CCD 4274 (CD), P-23330
Bugle Blues
    Concord Jazz CJ 274, CCD 4274 (CD)
When Lights Are Low
    Concord Jazz CJ 296, CCD 4296 (CD), CCD 4833-2

NOTE: St. Clair 4515 is titled *Hoagy Carmichael Songbook,* Concord Jazz CCD4833-2 is titled *Ruby Braff: The Concord Jazz Heritage Series,* and Snapper Music SMDCD271 is titled *I'm Shooting High.* The Snapper release is a reissue of tunes from various Concord Jazz releases. "When Lights Are Low" is also issued on AFRTS Basic Musical Library (16-inch transcription), P series P-23330. Concord included it with the release of tunes from the next session.

Ruby Braff and Scott Hamilton: *A Sailboat in the Moonlight*
February 1985 (one day after the preceding session), Penny Lane Studios, New York
Ruby Braff (cnt), Scott Hamilton (ts), John Bunch (p), Chris Flory (g), Phil Flanigan (b), Chuck Riggs (dm)
A Sailboat in the Moonlight
    Concord Jazz CJ 296, CCD 4296 (CD), CCD 4833-2, CCD 4819-2
Lover Come Back to Me
    Concord Jazz CJ 296, CCD 4296 (CD)
Where Are You?
    Concord Jazz CJ 296, CCD 4296 (CD), Snapper Music SMDCD 271
'Deed I Do
    Concord Jazz CJ 296, CCD 4296 (CD)
Jeepers Creepers
    Concord Jazz CJ 296, CCD 4296 (CD), Snapper Music SMDCD 271
The Milkman's Matinee
    Concord Jazz CJ 296, CCD 4296 (CD)
Sweethearts on Parade
    Concord Jazz CJ 296, CCD 4296 (CD)

NOTE: This album also includes "When Lights Are Low" that was recorded the previous day. Concord Jazz CCD 4833-2 is titled *Ruby Braff: The Concord Jazz Heritage Series* and Snapper Music SMDCD 271 is titled *I'm Shooting High*. The Snapper release is a reissue of tunes from various Concord Jazz releases. Concord CCD 4819-2 is titled *Scott Hamilton: The Concord Jazz Heritage Series*.

Ruby Braff–Dick Hyman Quartet[63]
March 15–16, 1985, 9:30 p.m., 11:00 p.m. and 12:30 am), Struggles, 10 Dempsey Avenue, Edgewater, New Jersey
Details unknown

Nancy Miller Elliott took a photo of Ruby Braff at the Church of the Heavenly Rest. The published caption states that the photo was from 1984, but I have found no record of Ruby performing there in 1984. Thus, I believe it dates from the next performance in 1985.[64] Ruby looks absolutely delighted in the photo. It must have been a very happy occasion for him—and likely for the audience as well.

Another of her photos shows Ruby clowning for her camera from an unknown time and location. His face expresses intense fear.[65] Likely this was taken at about the same time. Of course it is possible that the photos truly date from 1984 during a performance that remains undocumented.

Ruby Braff and Scott Hamilton Quintet: Heavenly Jazz[66]
March 24, 1985, 5 p.m., Church of the Heavenly Rest, 5th Avenue at 90th Street, New York
Ruby Braff (cnt), Scott Hamilton (ts), John Bunch (p), Chris Flory (g), Phil Flanigan (b), Chuck Riggs (dm)
This was the last concert for this season.

Ruby Braff Quintet[67]
March 26–30, 1985, West End Café, 2911 Broadway at 113th Street, New York
Ruby Braff (cnt), Scott Hamilton (ts), John Bunch (p), Phil Flanigan (b), Chris Flory (g), Chuck Riggs (dm)

Ruby Braff Quintet
March 29, 1985, West End Café, 2911 Broadway at 113th Street, New York, WKCR-FM broadcast. Phil Schaap, emcee
Ruby Braff (cnt), John Bunch (p), Phil Flanigan (b), Chris Flory (g), Chuck Riggs (dm)
I Never Knew
Mean to Me
Blue and Sentimental
Rockin' Chair

NOTE: WKCR-FM broadcast a portion of the performance on March 29 and at least a portion of that broadcast is available but remains unissued. Scott Hamilton does not perform on the available tunes.

Ruby next appeared in a concert sponsored by the New Hampshire Library of Traditional Jazz. This library holds the Prescott collection that includes many of the early airchecks from Ruby's performances in Boston listed earlier in this book. Paul Verrette, the producer, must have known that orange was Ruby's favorite color when he designed the program for this appearance.[68] A copy of the program is available—printed on bright orange paper. A recording exists in the library's collection; however, it has not been available to the author so there is no information about the tunes performed.

Ruby Braff with the TJS Quartet: The Traditional Jazz Series
April 15, 1985, Strafford Room, Memorial Union, the University of New Hampshire, Durham, New Hampshire
Ruby Braff (cnt), Jack Bumer (p), Gray Sargent (g), Marshall Wood (b), Chuck Laire (dm)

Rick's Café Americain in Chicago booked Ruby for another repeat performance. A copy of an advertisement is available for this engagement that shows Ruby in a thoughtful pose and also lists the next attraction as Buddy Greco.

Ruby Braff Quintet[69] (see Figure 17.2)
April 29–May 11, 1985, Rick's Café Americain, Chicago
Ruby Braff (cnt), Mike LeDonne (p), Chris Flory (g), Phil Flanigan (b), Chuck Riggs (dm)
My Shining Hour
I've Grown Accustomed to Her Face

Larry Kart reviewed the performance for the *Chicago Tribune*:[70]

> Imagine, for instance, that one could assemble all the key jazz virtues and pack them into one man—beginning with Louis Armstrong's noble virtuosity and adding the wistful grace of Bobby Hackett, the shapeliness of Benny Carter, the romantic passion of Ben Webster and so forth.
>
> If that could be done, the results would sound much like Braff—for he has listened to all the great players and somehow managed to transform their stories into his own personal art.
>
> 'My Shining Hour,' for instance, began with a series of starkly dramatic, Armstrong-like gestures that seemed to make time stand still. Braff suddenly began to make the beat bounce along like a rubber ball—gathering momentum until one wondered how he could keep things under control.
>
> Then, in an instant, it was drama-time again, as Braff indulged in one of his frequent descents into the nethermost regions of the cornet.

> While words can't quite describe the nature of those tones—which not only are cello-like in range but also sound as though they were produced by a bow stroking at strings—their emotional power is obvious. In fact, it was at this point that a very talkative fellow at the bar said, 'Hey, this guy is good,' and proceeded to fall silent for the rest of the evening.
>
> The whole first set was superb, which is what one has come to expect from Braff. But a special spot should be reserved for his version of 'I've Grown Accustomed to Her Face,' which had a muttering, Miltonic eloquence to it—sweepingly complex, multi-noted phrases curved down to form shapes that had a perfectly symmetrical balance.
>
> So to say that Ruby Braff is underrated is to re-state the obvious. He is a master, and if you haven't heard him before, you owe it to yourself to discover him.

Ruby next participated in a fund-raising benefit concert. All proceeds went to Save the Children Africa Relief Fund. Tony Bennett also appeared, but I don't know if they performed together at this concert. A copy of an advertisement for this event is available. Ruby received the fifth billing in the advertisement.

Save the Children: Jazz Stars Come Out for Africa[71] (see Figure 17.3)
May 16, 1985, 7:30, Town Hall, 123 West 43rd Street, New York
Tony Bennett, Gil Evans Orchestra, Hannibal Peterson Quintet, Tommy Flanagan Trio, Ruby Braff with others including Scott Hamilton

Nancy Miller Elliott published an undated photo of Dick Hyman and Ruby Braff, probably from these performances.[72]

Kool Jazz Festival
Ruby Braff and Dick Hyman: A Tribute to Louis Armstrong[73]
June 30, 1985, St. Peter's Church, Lexington Avenue and 54th Street, New York
Nobody Else But You
Beale Street Blues
It's Wonderful
You're a Lucky Guy
I Double Dare You
Blueberry Hill
Save It Pretty Mama

Whitney Balliett reported that this concert consisted of "close to thirty numbers associated with Louis Armstrong." He only named the selections listed above and that this closed "the Manhattan branch of the Festival."[74] John S. Wilson wrote: "The Sanctuary was oversold. Many people had to stand and others could find seats only on steps and in areas where they could not see the performers."[75] Ruby could certainly continue to draw a crowd in New York, although not necessarily one to fill a huge auditorium.

Ruby Braff[76]
July 19–20, 1985, 9 p.m., Struggles, 10 Dempsey Avenue, Edgewater, New Jersey
Further details unknown

Jazz in July: America the Beautiful–Ruby Braff and Friends: *Piano Players and Significant Others: Jazz in July Live at the 92nd Street Y*[77]
July 31, 1985, New York
Ruby Braff (cnt), Dick Hyman (p), Milt Hinton (b), Ron Traxler (dm)
My Shining Hour
 MusicMasters 5042-2-C (CD), Jazz Heritage 512794W (CD)
Yesterdays
 MusicMasters 5042-2-C (CD), Jazz Heritage 512794W (CD)
NOTE: Other unnamed tunes performed at this concert featured Ruby Braff with Dick Hyman playing the organ; however, other performances on this CD do not include Ruby Braff. A copy of a flyer promoting this event is available. The album was also issued on Jazz Heritage 912794F (LP). The publicized billing for the above concert was Ruby Braff, Maxine Sullivan, and Dick Hyman's Perfect Jazz Repertory Quintet (consisting of Dick Hyman, Joe Wilder, Phil Bodner, Milt Hinton, and Ron Traxler). Other tunes mentioned in the review, but not released on the recording, include the following:[78]
 Dooji Wooji
 Carolina Balmoral
 Loch Lomond (Maxine Sullivan)
 O, Take Those Lips Away (Maxine Sullivan)

Edward Meyer stated that this Jazz in July series also included Ruby Braff performing with Dick Wellstood, and probably in other combinations with Joe Wilder, Mike Lipskin, Max Morath, Ralph Sutton, Jay McShann, Carrie Smith, and Bobby Rosengarden; however, the advertisement announcing the various concerts only mentioned Ruby appearing in the listed performances above.[79]

Much later, on July 21, 1987, Dick Wellstood appeared in this continuing series of concerts. Two selections from that date, performed as duets with Dick Hyman, appear on the above CD. Carrie Smith joined them on one tune. These were Dick's final recordings before his untimely death, just three days later on July 24, 1987. But he still performed with Ruby on two documented occasions ahead in 1986, still one year before his passing. Neither of these appearances were listed in Edward Meyer's wonderful book *Giant Strides.*[80]

Allegheny Jazz Society's Conneaut Lake Jazz Festival[81]
August 23–25, 1985, Conneaut Lake, Pennsylvania
The following artists were advertised to appear: Ruby Braff, Billy Butterfield (tp, cnt), Dick Cary (alto horn), Dan Barrett, Bob Havens (tb), Scott Hamilton, Eddie Miller (ts), Dick Hyman, Keith Ingham, Dave McKenna (p), Howard Alden, Marty Grosz (g), Phil Flanigan, Bob Haggart, Michael Moore (b), Nick

Fatool, Jake Hanna, Hal Smith (dm), Maxine Sullivan (voc). But Ruby Braff did not appear at the actual festival.

Ruby performed with Dick Hyman in concerts in September and October before joining the Floating Jazz Festival.

Ruby Braff and Dick Hyman[82]
September 7, 1985, Stony Brook University, Long Island, New York

Ruby Braff and Dick Hyman[83]
October 19, 1985, 8 p.m., State University of New York's Purchase Arts Center, Purchase, New York
NOTE: The date published for the above performance falls in the middle of the upcoming four weeks scheduled for the 1985 Floating Jazz Festival cruises. There would be no direct conflict if Ruby only performed during the final two cruises in the series or if the ship was in port the evening of October19 between cruises. I have not been able to resolve this possible inconsistency.

Hank O'Neal again provided two photographs to supplement the published program for the Ruby's appearances during the Floating Jazz Festival. One photo shows Ruby and Clark Terry clowning with the ship's captain. A second photo shows Ruby at a piano. The program includes a third photo taken the previous year and showing Ruby with Scott Hamilton, John Bunch, Chris Flory, Phil Flanigan, and Chuck Riggs.

Floating Jazz Festival[84]
October 5–November 2, 1985, S/S *Norway*, departing from Miami. There were four cruises, each lasting one week.
Ruby Braff participated in the Floating Jazz Festival on four one-week cruises, beginning October 5 and ending November 2. Other musicians participating all four weeks were Benny Carter, Al Cohn, Scott Hamilton, Clark Terry, Doc Cheatham, George Duvivier, George Masso, Kenny Davern, Svend Asmussen, John Bunch, Cab Calloway, Alan Dawson, Phil Flanigan, Chris Flory, Dizzy Gillespie, Jake Hanna, the Harlem Blues and Jazz Band, Woody Herman, Art Hodes, Major Holley, Dick Hyman, Jack Lesberg, Gerry Mulligan, Flip Phillips, Chuck Riggs, Bobby Rosengarden, Maxine Sullivan, Buddy Tate, Mel Tormé, Joe Williams, Monica Zetterlund, and Eddie Higgins.

The 1985 cruise program stated that Ruby Braff would perform with the following combinations in two of the cruises but his role in the others is unknown:

Floating Jazz Festival[85]
October 20–26 and October 27–November 2, 1985, S/S *Norway*, at unknown times
Ruby Braff (cnt) and Dick Hyman (p and org)

Floating Jazz Festival[86]
October 20–26 and October 27–November 2, 1985, S/S *Norway*, at unknown times
Ruby Braff with Benny Carter, Scott Hamilton, and other musicians

Following the cruise, Ruby and Dick Hyman flew to England for a BBC broadcast and a two-week engagement at Pizza Express. I have not been able to document additional performances in the interval between the broadcast and their opening in London.

Hyman and Braff Inc.: *Euphonic Organization*
November 9, 1985, Broadcast December 13, 1985, Thursford Fairground Museum, Norfolk, England, broadcast on BBC Television, hosted by Russell Davies and directed by Tom Corcoran
Ruby Braff (cnt), Dick Hyman (pipe organ)
When It's Sleepy Time Down South*
Them There Eyes
Louisiana
High Society*
When I Fall in Love
Jitterbug Waltz (Braff out)
Basin Street Blues
America the Beautiful
NOTE: Audio and video recordings of these tunes are available but remain unissued. At the time of publication, the selections marked with an asterisk are available for downloading from YouTube.com.

Ruby Braff and Dick Hyman (they appeared together from November 14–20, 1985)[87]
November 14, 1985, Pizza Express, 10 Dean Street, London
Ruby Braff (cnt), Dick Hyman (p)
As Long As I Live
Somebody Loves Me
Someday You'll Be Sorry
Medley:
  In a Sentimental Mood
  I Got It Bad and That Ain't Good
Medley:
  You're Driving Me Crazy
  The Man That Got Away
High Society
Jitterbug Waltz (Hyman solo)
Medley:
  He Loves and She Loves

The Man I Love
Pennies from Heaven
Old Folks
I Guess I'll Have to Change My Plans
Easy Living
Just You, Just Me
Medley:
Street of Dreams
Can't We Be Friends?
It's Wonderful
I Would Do Anything for You
Rockin' Chair
Liza (Hyman solo)
Medley:
Over the Rainbow
When You Wish upon a Star
If I Only Had a Brain
Dinah (interpolating Honey, Do!)
You're Lucky to Me
Medley:
Memories of You
You Are My Lucky Star
NOTE: A recording of these tunes is available but remains unissued.

Ruby Braff and Dick Hyman [88]
November 15–16, 1985, Pizza Express, 10 Dean Street, London
No further details known

Ruby Braff and Dick Hyman
November 18, 1985, Pizza Express, 10 Dean Street, London
Ruby Braff (cnt), Dick Hyman (p)
I'm Crazy 'bout My Baby
You're a Lucky Guy
High Society
It's Wonderful
Medley:
The Very Thought of You
Tea for Two
Shreveport Stomp (Hyman solo)
Jubilee
Medley:
I Love You, Samantha
You're Sensational
Jeepers Creepers
Thou Swell

Sweet Georgia Brown
Persian Rug
Medley:
  Street of Dreams
  This Is All I Ask
Prelude to a Kiss (Hyman solo)
Swing That Music
Medley:
  The Man That Got Away
  Over the Rainbow
  When You Wish upon a Star
  San Francisco
Big Butter and Egg Man
Medley:
  He Loves and She Loves
  I've Got a Crush on You
  I Got Rhythm
  Bidin' My Time
  But Not for Me
  There's a Boat That's Leavin' Soon for New York
  I Got Plenty of Nothin'
  It Ain't Necessarily So
  Bess, You Is My Woman Now
  I Got Plenty of Nothin'
Medley:
  Someone to Watch Over Me
  Lady Be Good
  Stompin' at the Savoy
NOTE: A recording of these tunes is available but remains unissued.

Ruby Braff and Dick Hyman [89]
November 19, 1985, Pizza Express, 10 Dean Street, London
No further details known

Ruby Braff and Dick Hyman [90]
November 20, 1985, Pizza Express, 10 Dean Street, London
Ruby Braff (cnt), Dick Hyman (p)
Rosetta
Medley:
  On the Alamo
  Indian Summer
  Stompin' at the Savoy
It Had to Be You
Liza
You've Got to Be Modernistic (Hyman solo)

Easy Living
Muskrat Ramble
Medley:
  I Love You, Samantha
  Dream Dancing
Swing That Music
Nice Work If You Can Get It
My Monday Date
Medley:
  Come Sunday
  Swing That Music
Medley:
  In a Sentimental Mood
  Rockin' Chair
  A Pretty Girl Is Like a Melody
Fingerbreaker (Hyman solo)
Emily (Hyman solo)
NOTE: A recording of these tunes is available but remains unissued.

Ruby Braff and Dick Hyman[91]
November 21–23, 1985, Pizza Express, 10 Dean Street, London
Ruby Braff (cnt) with the Jack Parnell Trio
Unknown titles

Upon their return to the US, Ruby and Dick Hyman appeared on a broadcast hosted by John S. Wilson that was subsequently issued by MusicMasters. The program series was titled the *Manhattan Jazz Hour* distributed by American Public Radio.

Ruby Braff and Dick Hyman: *Manhattan Jazz*
December 3, 1985, Manhattan Recording Company, New York
Ruby Braff (cnt), Dick Hyman (p)
Jubilee
    MusicMasters CIJD 60136M
You're Lucky to Me
    MusicMasters CIJD 60136M
Medley:
  The Man I Love
    MusicMasters CIJD 60136M
  How Long Has This Been Going On?
    MusicMasters CIJD 60136M
  He Loves and She Loves
    MusicMasters CIJD 60136M
I'm Crazy 'bout My Baby
    MusicMasters CIJD 60136M

Someday You'll Be Sorry
MusicMasters CIJD 60136M
Don't Worry About Me
MusicMasters CIJD 60136M
Jeepers Creepers
MusicMasters CIJD 60136M
I'm Just Wild About Harry (p solo)
MusicMasters CIJD 60136M
Judy Garland Medley:
The Man That Got Away
MusicMasters CIJD 60136M
If I Only Had a Brain
MusicMasters CIJD 60136M
Over the Rainbow
MusicMasters CIJD 60136M
Blues for John W.
MusicMasters CIJD 60136M
NOTE: All titles on Musical Heritage Society MHS-912122T, Limelight 820 812-2, Jazz Heritage 512794W, and MusicMasters CIJD20136W. "Blues for John W." is named for the broadcast's host, John S. Wilson. There is no available information about other programs in this series.

Ruby Braff and Scott Hamilton[92]
December 26–28, 1985, Regattabar, Charles Hotel, Cambridge, Massachusetts
Ruby Braff (cnt), Scott Hamilton (ts), Gray Sargent (g), Marshall Wood (b), Chuck Riggs (dm)

Ruby Braff and Dick Hyman[93]
January 14, 1986, Wilkes College, Wilkes-Barre, Pennsylvania
Struttin' with Some Barbecue
Squeeze Me
Medley:
Confessin'
Blue Skies
There'll Be Some Changes Made
Sweethearts on Parade
It's Wonderful
Jubilee
Wrap Your Troubles in Dreams (Hyman solo)
If I Could Be with You
Someday You'll Be Sorry
Jeepers Creepers
I Can't Give You Anything but Love
Rockin' Chair
You're a Lucky Guy

Cornet Chop Suey (Hyman solo)
Medley:
  Love Walked In
  The Man I Love
  They Can't Take That Away from Me
St. Louis Blues (incomplete)
NOTE: A recording of these tunes is available but remains unissued.

Ruby Braff and Dick Hyman
January 18, 1986, Struggles, 10 Dempsey Avenue, Edgewater, New Jersey
Ruby Braff (cnt), Dick Hyman (p)
Jubilee
Keepin' Out of Mischief Now
Medley:
  Blue Turning Grey Over You
  How Can You Face Me?
Goose Pimples
Swing That Music
When It's Sleepy Time Down South
Jitterbug Waltz (Hyman solo)
Medley:
  I'm Shooting High
  You're a Lucky Guy
Medley:
  Careless Love
  Old Fashioned Love
Rosetta
Poor Butterfly
Judy Garland Medley:
  The Man That Got Away
  If I Only Had a Brain
  Over the Rainbow
  The Man That Got Away (reprise)
NOTE: A recording of these tunes is available but remains unissued.

Ruby Braff and Friends[94]
March 14–15, 1986, Far and Away, 651 Anderson Avenue, Cliffside Park, New Jersey

Ruby Braff with the Tommy Gallant Trio[95]
Unknown date sometime in the mid–to–late 1980s on a Sunday night, The Pressroom, Portsmouth, New Hampshire
Ruby Braff (cnt), Tommy Gallant (p), Jim Howe (b), Les Harris (dm)

Ruby was a guest in a Sunday night performance with the house trio, led by Tommy Gallant. The engagement was booked by Charlie "The Whale" Lake, who also arranged bookings for the Regattabar in Boston on Friday and Saturday nights. Les Harris wrote that Ruby said he would like to return and enjoyed the performance. No further information is available.

Heavenly Jazz[96]
April 6, 1986, 5 p.m., Church of the Heavenly Rest, 5th Avenue at 90th Street, New York
Ruby Braff (cnt), Scott Hamilton (ts), and other unnamed musicians
This was the final concert in the season.

Jazz at 6: Ruby Braff and Dick Hyman[97]
April 11, 1986, 6 p.m., the New School, 66 West 12th Street, New York
Ruby Braff (cnt), Dick Hyman (p)

Rosemary Clooney[98]
April 29–May 17, 1986 (Tuesdays through Saturdays, with Woody Allen appearing Monday nights, closed Sundays), Michael's Pub, 211 East 55th Street, New York
Ruby Braff (cnt), John Oddo (p), Jay Leonhardt (b) or Michael Moore (b), Joe Cocuzzo (dm)

Since both bass players were mentioned in the review, they likely switched during the engagement.

Condon Reunion[99]
June 10–July 5, 1986, Michael's Pub, New York
Ruby Braff (cnt) and John Bunch (p) performed with other musicians

Ruby was not listed as a participant but could have appeared prior to his departure for Sweden in early July. John Bunch was included in that listing as a guest starting June 24. That is the most likely week for Ruby's appearance, but he could have been present on other occasions. *Newsday* reported that Braff and Bunch appeared with "the Condon gang" in "past months." Thus the reference may apply to these dates during 1986. The club named after Eddie Condon closed the previous year, in 1985, when the site was sold for redevelopment. *The New Yorker* listed several groups of musicians. Starting June 10 were Red Balaban, Ed Polcer, Tom Artin, Kenny Davern, and Maxine Sullivan. June 21 saw other guests, Wild Bill Davison, Art Hodes, Peanuts Hucko, Scott Hamilton, Marty Napoleon, George Masso, and Jack Lesberg, followed by John Bunch, Jane Jarvis, and Joe Muranyi starting June 24. Starting July 1, the group included Kenny Davern, George Kelly, Dick Wellstood, Milt Hinton, and Gus Johnson; however, Ruby would have been on his way to Europe by that time. This series of bookings ended when Anita O'Day and Chris Connor arrived beginning July 5.

Ruby toured Sweden, with performances at the following locations: Mosebacke, Stampen, and Strömsborg (all three in Stockholm), followed by six cities in the south of Sweden. There is a recording from the last performance of the tour in Rackis, Uppsala, July 3. Björn Ågeryd, the drummer on the tour, reported that "Ruby was in a very happy mood all the time and all the boys had a lot of fun."[100]

Ruby Braff and His Swedish Friends
July 3, 1986, Rackis, Uppsala, Sweden
Ruby Braff (cnt), Nils Engström (p), Rolf Berg (g), Pelle Karlsson (b), Björn Ågeryd (dm)
Ain't Misbehavin'
I've Grown Accustomed to Her Face
Tangerine
Medley:
  It's the Talk of the Town
  I Want to Be Happy
I've Got the World on a String
I Can't Give You Anything but Love
Keepin' Out of Mischief Now
Lady Be Good
NOTE: A recording of these tunes is available but remains unissued.

Ruby Braff[101]
August 8–9, 9 p.m., Struggles, 10 Dempsey Avenue, Edgewater, New Jersey

Ruby Braff Quintet[102]
September 5, 1986, Jazzboat, Boston
Ruby Braff (cnt), Scott Hamilton (ts), Gray Sargent (g), Marshall Wood (g), Chuck Riggs (dm)

The 2nd Minneapolis Jazz Party[103]
September 12–14, 1986, Holiday Inn Downtown, Minneapolis, Minnesota
Ruby Braff and other musicians including Dick Hyman, Dick Wellstood, Scott Hamilton, Flip Phillips, Jim Galloway, Milt Hinton, and Carrie Smith among 24 musicians invited to participate
Sponsored by Reed MacKenzie and John Stephens

September 12, 1986, Minneapolis Jazz Party
Ruby Braff (cnt), George Masso (tb), Scott Hamilton (ts), Dick Hyman (p), Jack Lesberg (b), Jake Hanna (dm)
Jeepers Creepers

Ruby Braff (cnt), Carl Fontana (tb), Scott Hamilton (ts), Dick Wellstood (p), Jack Lesberg (b), Gus Johnson (dm)
Royal Garden Blues

Ruby Braff (cnt), George Masso (tb), Scott Hamilton (ts), Bob Wilber (cl), Ralph Sutton (p), Jack Lesberg (b), Jeff Hamilton (dm)
Rosetta
NOTE: A recording of these tunes is available but remains unissued.

September 13, 1986, Minneapolis Jazz Party
Ruby Braff (cnt), Ralph Sutton, Dick Hyman (p), Jack Lesberg (b), Jeff Hamilton (dm)
If Dreams Come True
Sugar
When It's Sleepy Time Down South
Wrap Your Troubles in Dreams

Ruby Braff (cnt), George Masso (tb), Jim Galloway (ss, ts), Dick Wellstood (p), Brian Torf (b), Jeff Hamilton (dm)
Honeysuckle Rose (Galloway ss)
Them There Eyes (Galloway ts)

Ruby Braff (cnt), Flip Phillips (ts), Ralph Sutton (p), Milt Hinton (b), Gus Johnson (dm)
I Can't Give You Anything but Love

Ruby Braff (cnt), George Masso (tb), Scott Hamilton (ts), Bob Wilber (cl), Ralph Sutton (p), Jack Lesberg (b), Jeff Hamilton (dm)
California, Here I Come

Ruby Braff (cnt), Dick Hyman (p), Jack Lesberg (b), Reuben Ristrum (g), Gus Johnson (dm)
Medley:
  Love Walked In
  The Man That Got Away
  Over the Rainbow
  If I Only Had a Brain
  The Man That Got Away (reprise)
Don't Get Around Much Anymore

Ruby Braff does not appear on the next two titles:
Flip Phillips (ts), Ralph Sutton (p), Milt Hinton (b), Gus Johnson (dm)
I Can't Get Started

Kenny Davern (cl), Dick Wellstood (p), Jake Hanna (dm)
Blues My Naughty Sweetie Gave to Me

Ruby Braff (cnt), George Masso (tb), Scott Hamilton (ts), Bob Wilber (cl), Ralph Sutton (p), Jack Lesberg (b), Jeff Hamilton (dm)
Rosetta

Ruby Braff does not appear on the next title:
Kenny Davern (cl), Dick Wellstood (p), Jake Hanna (dm)
Muskrat Ramble
NOTE: A recording of these tunes is available but remains unissued.

September 14, 1986, St. Mark's Episcopal Cathedral, 519 Oak Grove Street, Minneapolis, Minnesota
Ruby Braff (cnt), Dick Hyman (org)
Sunday
Come Sunday
Got a Brand New Suit
Everybody Loves My Baby
He Loves and She Loves
As Long As I Live
When It's Sleepy Time Down South
C Jam Blues
America the Beautiful
NOTE: A recording of these tunes is available but remains unissued.

September 14, 1986, Mendota Days, Mendota, Minnesota
Ruby Braff (cnt), Ralph Sutton (p), unknown (b, dm)
I'm Crazy 'bout My Baby
Keepin' Out of Mischief Now
Way Down Yonder in New Orleans
The above two performances may have taken place during the morning and afternoon of September 14, while the next session was in the evening that day.
NOTE: A recording of these tunes is available but remains unissued.

September 14, 1986 Minneapolis Jazz Party, Holiday Inn Downtown, Minneapolis, Minnesota
Ruby Braff (cnt), George Masso (tb), Scott Hamilton (ts), Kenny Davern (cl), Dick Wellstood (p), Jack Lesberg (b), Jake Hanna (dm)
I Would Do Anything for You

Out Masso, Hamilton, Davern
Blue and Sentimental

Add Masso, Hamilton, Davern
Linger Awhile
NOTE: A recording of these tunes is available but remains unissued.

Ruby did not appear at the first Minneapolis Jazz Party.

This is the last time when there is documentation of Ruby playing with Dick Wellstood. Much later, Ken Gallacher wrote the following:[104]

> CORNETIST Ruby Braff is a walking contradiction, a player of glorious lyricism, and yet, at times, as querulous a person as you could ever meet. His feuds with other musicians are legion and often stem from trivial incidents which Braff somehow transforms into the most lethal of insults against his person. The late pianist Dick Wellstood told me once how George Wein, promoter of the New York Jazz Festival, had called him to offer a prestigious gig at the event as part of a band which had Braff as the nominal leader. Wellstood accepted, only for an embarrassed Wein to call back a few days later to inform him that Braff was refusing to play with him.
>
> Said Wellstood: 'I was puzzled by this. I couldn't honestly think of anything I had done to upset Ruby. I decided I would take the bull by the horns, phone him, and ask what was wrong. He then told me: 'The last time we worked in a group I was taking a solo and when I turned towards the piano you were looking at your watch. I didn't like that.' And that was what it was. He hadn't said anything at the time, and looking back I reckoned I was probably checking to see when the next break was coming. There was no intent to slight but that's how he took it.'

Of course, Dick Wellstood was a very creative artist in his own right, so the lack of future collaborations with Ruby was unfortunate for everyone in the jazz community. Another opportunity was perhaps lost for creating some great musical performances during Dick Wellstood's remaining nine months of life. One of Ruby's principles was "watch me closely at all times" as he signaled changes during the performance. As Ruby saw it, Dick simply broke the rule.

Howard Alden reported that he began performing with Ruby in 1984, "with more frequent gigs from 1986 to 1992, mostly in trio fromat, with Jack Lesberg first, then Frank Tate, starting in 1990."[105] Specific information about those early performances remains to be discovered.

The following advertisements depict three performances in this chapter:

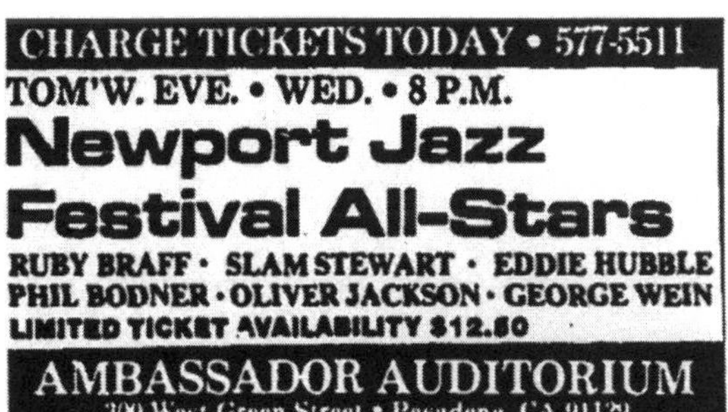

Figure 17.1: Advertisement November 1982

Figure 17.2: Advertisement April 1985

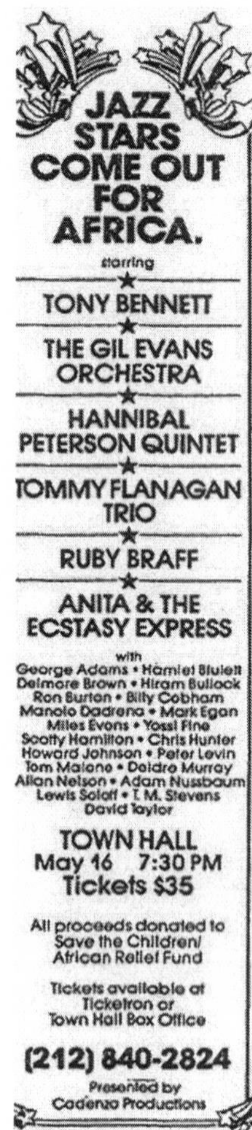

Figure 17.3: Advertisement
May 1985

Notes

[1] Press release containing article by Raymond Horricks and prepared by Loren Schoenberg.
[2] Richard Williams, *The Times*, February 6, 1982, 11.
[3] *New York Magazine*, February 22, 1982, 98.
[4] *New York Times*, March 7, 21, and 28, 1982, and *New York Magazine*, February 15, 1982, 102, March 1, 1982, 105, March 8, 1982, 111, March 15, 1982, 93, March 22, 1992, 90, and March 29, 1982, 119.
[5] *New York Magazine*, April 12, 1982, 98.
[6] A photo from the rehearsal is reproduced in *The March of Jazz Celebrates Ruby Braff's 74th Birthday Party*, Arbors Records, 2001, 25.

[7] Dick Hyman holds a partial recording on a cassette tape. The performance is mentioned in *The New Yorker*, April 5, 1982, 15 and *The New York Times*, April 4, 1982, and *New York Magazine*, April 5, 1982, 109.
[8] *New York Times*, April 4, 1982.
[9] *New York Times*, April 25 and May 2, 1982, and *New York Magazine*, April 19, 1982, 116, and April 26, 1982, 126.
[10] *New York Magazine*, May 3, 1982, 114.
[11] *New York Times*, May 23, 1982.
[12] "20 Years of Jazz! In the World's Most Beautiful Capital," Stockholm, February 14, 2004, http://www.stockholmjazz.com/press_room/?id=2&option=view_entry.
[13] John S. Wilson, *New York Times*, November 19, 1982, quoting Warren Vaché.
[14] United Press International story, September 19, 1982, confirms Scott's recollections.
[15] *Eugene Register-Guard*, October 25, 1982, display ad on 2C.
[16] Advertisement, *Los Angeles Times*, November 2, 1982.
[17] Leonard Feather, *Los Angeles Times*, November 5, 1982.
[18] Advertisement, *Los Angeles Times*, October 24, 1982.
[19] *Los Angeles Times*, October 30, 1982.
[20] Ernie Santosuosso, *Boston Globe*, November 19, 1982.
[21] *New York Times*, December 31, 1982.
[22] *New York Times*, February 4, 1983, and *The New Yorker*, January 31, 1983, 8.
[23] *New York Times*, April 4, 1983.
[24] *New York Times*, September 25, 1983.
[25] John S. Wilson, *New York Times*, November 6, 1983.
[26] Review in *New York Times*, November 6, 1983, *The New Yorker*, October 31, 1983, 8, and November 7, 1983, 8, and *New York Magazine*, November 1983, 126.
[27] Photo, *The March of Jazz Celebrates Ruby Braff's 74th Birthday Party*, Arbors Records, 2001, 26.
[28] Correspondence with Robert Simon.
[29] "Braff, Friends Triumphant," *Boston Globe*, November 18, 1983, and November 11, 1983.
[30] Mark Miller, *Globe and Mail*, January 18, 1984.
[31] Mark Miller, *Globe and Mail*, January 18, 1984.
[32] *New York Times*, January 22, 1984.
[33] *New York Times*, March 22, 1984, and *New York Magazine*, March 26, 1984, 113.
[34] *New York Times*, March 18, 1984.
[35] *The New Yorker*, April 23, 1984, 11, and April 30, 1984, 15.
[36] Tony Bennett quoted in Larry Kart, "Arts," *Chicago Tribune*, April 28, 1985 in article about Ruby Braff.
[37] Ernie Santosuosso, "Weekend: Berman Plans to Sell Sandy's," *Boston Globe*, May 4, 1984.
[38] *New York Times*, May 27, 1984.
[39] *New York Times*, July 8, 1984.
[40] Manfred Selchow, *Ding Ding: A Bio-Discographical Scrapbook on Vic Dickenson* (Germany: Uhle & Kleinmann, 1998), 833.
[41] Manfred Selchow, *Ding Ding: A Bio-Discographical Scrapbook on Vic Dickenson* (Germany: Uhle & Kleinmann, 1998), 833.
[42] Ruby Braff photograph at this party appears in *The Jazz Family Album, Volume 1* (East Stroudsburg, PA: Al Cohn Memorial Jazz Collection, 1992), 26.

[43] *New York Magazine*, September 17, 1984, 170.
[44] Ernie Santosuosso, *Boston Globe*, September 14, 1984 and *The Boston Phoenix*, October 2, 1984, 6–7 Section 3.
[45] *The Times*, September 22, 1984, 19.
[46] *The Times*, September 22, 1984, 19.
[47] Richard Williams, *The Times*, September 26, 1984, 13.
[48] *The Times*, September 22, 1984, 19.
[49] *Boston Globe*, September 9, 1984.
[50] Photo, *The March of Jazz Celebrates Ruby Braff's 74th Birthday Party*, Arbors Records, 2001, 26.
[51] http://www.hankonealphoto.com/fjf_main9.html and http://www.hankonealphoto.com/fjf_main8.html. Also see photo, *The March of Jazz Celebrates Ruby Braff's 74th Birthday Party*, Arbors Records, 2001, 28.
[52] Hank O'Neal, *The Floating Jazz Festival*, 1985, 18.
[53] Photo is reproduced in The *March of Jazz Celebrates Ruby Braff's 74th Birthday Party*, Arbors Records, 2001, 27.
[54] Hank O'Neal, *The Floating Jazz Festival*, 1985, 31.
[55] Dick Hyman and http://www.hankonealphoto.com/fjf_main8.html and http://www.hankonealphoto.com/fjf_main7.html. Also see photo in *The March of Jazz Celebrates Ruby Braff's 74th Birthday Party*, Arbors Records, 2001, 27. PR Newswire release dated March 22, 1985, providing advance publicity for the cruises and reporting the list of musicians who would participate for the entire four weeks—these references, while mentioning 1985, must pertain to 1984 since Zoot Sim's last performance was prior to the sailing date. Accordingly, he was not listed as participating in the 1985 program.
[56] Hank O'Neal, *The Floating Jazz Festival*, 1985, 31.
[57] Photo reproduced in *The March of Jazz Celebrates Ruby Braff's 74th Birthday Party*, Arbors Records, 2001, 27, with caption from 1984 with no month mentioned. This engagement is not yet confirmed from other sources. It may be from February–March 1982 instead.
[58] *New York Times*, November 4, 1984.
[59] Manfred Selchow, *Ding Ding: A Bio-Discographical Scrapbook on Vic Dickenson* (Germany: Uhle & Kleinmann, 1998), 843. "When Day Is Done" is mentioned in album notes by Dick Hyman for *Fireworks* on Inner City and "Memories of You" is mentioned in Dan Morgenstern's *Living with Jazz: A Reader* (Pantheon Books: NY, 2004), 192.
[60] *New York Times*, December 6, 1984, *The New Yorker*, December 3, 1984, 15, and December 10, 8.
[61] Photo, *The March of Jazz Celebrates Ruby Braff's 74th Birthday Party*, Arbors Records, 2001, 27.
[62] Not listed in *The New Yorker* for this date but Dick Hyman has a copy of this recording.
[63] *New York Times*, March 10, 1985.
[64] Suzanne C. Taylor and Kenneth R. Ashworth, Jr., *WKCR Jazz Portraits* (WKCR Books: NY, 1988), unnumbered pages.
[65] Chip Deffaa, *Jazz Veterans* (Fort Bragg, CA: Cypress House, 1996), 199.
[66] *New York Times*, March 22, 1985, March 24, 1985, *The New Yorker*, March 25, 1985, 8, and *New York Magazine*, March 25, 1985, 112.
[67] *The New Yorker*, March 25, 1985, 7, and April 1, 1985, 7.
[68] http://www.izaak.unh.edu/nhltj/pn/pn35.pdf.

[69] *Chicago Tribune*, April 28, 1985, 26 (article reports the engagement will run "for the next two weeks") and Larry Kart, *Chicago Tribune*, April 30, 1985, giving personnel and other details.
[70] Larry Kart, *Chicago Tribune*, April 30, 1985.
[71] Advertisement in *New York Times*, April 28, 1985, and listed May 12, 1985. Also see *The New Yorker*, May 13, 1985, 11, and May 20, 1985, 8.
[72] Chip Deffaa, *Jazz Veterans* (Fort Bragg, CA: Cypress House, 1996), 198.
[73] Dick Hyman has a partial cassette recording, mentioned in *New York Times*, June 21, ,1985, and June 28, 1985. and June 30, 1985. Also see *The New Yorker*, July 1, 1985, 6, and *New York Magazine*, July 1, 1985, 169.
[74] Whitney Balliett, *The New Yorker*, July 22, 1985, 85.
[75] John S. Wilson, *New York Times*, July 5, 1985.
[76] *New York Times*, July 14, 1985.
[77] *New York Times*, July 31, 1985, advertised *New York Times*, May 12, 1985, and July 14, 1985.
[78] *The New Yorker*, July 29, 1985, 6, and August 5, 1985, 6, and *New York Magazine*, August 5, 1985, 81.
[79] Edward N. Meyer, *Giant Strides* (New York: Scarecrow Press, 1999), 170, and *New York Times*, July 14, 1985.
[80] Edward N. Meyer, *Giant Strides* (New York: Scarecrow Press, 1999). The performances from 1986 are not covered in this comprehensive book documenting Wellstood's career.
[81] Advertisement for program in *Jersey Jazz*, July 1985. Joe Boughton indicated that Ruby did not actually appear on the program.
[82] Information from Dick Hyman.
[83] *New York Times*, September 22, 1985.
[84] *Boston Globe*, September 9, 1984, and Hank O'Neal, *Floating Jazz Festival 1985*, 39–62.
[85] Hank O'Neal, *Floating Jazz Cruise 1985*, 50.
[86] Hank O'Neal, *Floating Jazz Cruise 1985*, 41.
[87] *The Times* (London), November 9, 1985.
[88] *The Times*, November 16, 1985.
[89] *The Times*, November 16, 1985.
[90] The final 20 minutes of this evening's performance were not recorded.
[91] *The Times*, November 16, 1985, 19.
[92] *Boston Globe*, December 20, 1985. Nick Puopolo has photos from December 26, 1985.
[93] Information from Dick Hyman.
[94] *New York Times*, March 9, 1986.
[95] Correspondence with Les Harris.
[96] *New York Times*, April 6, 1986, and *The New Yorker*, April 7, 1986, 8.
[97] John S. Wilson, *New York Times*, April 11, 1986, and *The New Yorker*, April 7, 1986, 8.
[98] Paul D. Colford, *Newsday*, May 7, 1986. *The New Yorker* listed the engagement but did not mention Ruby in April 28, 1986, 7, May 5, 1986, 13, May 12, 1986, 5, and May 19, 1986, 8.
[99] *Newsday*, December 23, 1987—further details unknown but probably linked to listings in *The New Yorker*, June 9, 1986, 8, June 16, 1986, 7, June 23, 1986, 5, and June 30, 1986, 6.

[100] Information from Lars Johansson.
[101] *New York Times*, August 3, 1986.
[102] Correspondence with Nick Puopolo. He has photos from September 5, 1986.
[103] John Norris in *Coda Magazine*, December 1986/January 1987, 38.
[104] Ken Gallacher, *The Herald* (England), March 31, 1999.
[105] Personal correspondence with Howard Alden, February 10, 2012.

Chapter 18

The Pianists and the Growth of Jazz Parties: October 1986–August 1988

Following the Minneapolis Jazz Party, Ruby was booked on the Floating Jazz Festivals departing October 11 and 18, 1986. Artists only on the first cruise included Woody Herman, Cab Calloway, and Anita O'Day. Artists only on the second cruise included Dizzy Gillespie, Buddy Rich, and the Milt Jackson Quartet. Appearing both weeks were Joe Williams, and Maxine Sullivan, Al Cohn, Buddy Tate, Flip Phillips, Bob Wilber, Scott Hamilton, Ruby Braff, Harry "Sweets" Edison, Clark Terry, Warren Vaché, George Masso, Tal Farlow, Dick Hyman, Makoto Ozone, Eddie Higgins, Mel Powell, Kenny Davern, Mel Lewis, Jake Hanna, Jack Lesberg, Steve Swallow, Major Holley, Gary Burton, and Svend Asmussen.[1]

Mel Powell: Floating Jazz Festival[2]
October 17, 1986, Saga Theater aboard the S/S *Norway*
Ruby Braff, Warren Vaché (cnt), Bob Wilber, Kenny Davern, Mel Powell (p), Jack Lesberg (b), Mel Lewis (dm), Makoto Ozone (p)
I'll Remember April (interpolating When a Woman Loves a Man) (Powell solo)

Add Bob Wilber and Mel Lewis to accompany Powell
Exactly Like You
Body and Soul
Avalon

Add Jack Lesberg; Wilber out
Too Marvelous for Words
Unknown tune (Makoto Ozone solo)
Honeysuckle Rose (Powell and Ozone duet)
Alone Together (Braff and Powell)
Between the Devil and the Deep Blue Sea (Braff and Powell duet)
Sweet Georgia Brown (full personnel except Wilber)
Scott Hamilton also performed on this cruise and recalled playing with Ruby.[3]

Mel Powell: Floating Jazz Festival[4]
October 19, 1986, Club I aboard the S/S *Norway*
Ruby Braff (cnt), Bob Wilber (cl), Svend Asmussen (v), Mel Powell (p), Howard Alden (g), Phil Flanigan (b), Jake Hanna (dm)
Exactly Like You (featuring Wilber and Hanna)
Body and Soul (featuring Wilber and Hanna)
Avalon (featuring Wilber and Hanna)
Don't Get Around Much Anymore (featuring Asmussen)
What Is This Thing Called Love (featuring Powell and Asmussen)
Limehouse Blues
Lulu's Back in Town

Add Gary Burton (vib)
California, Here I Come (breakdown)
California, Here I Come

Hank O'Neal shared one of his photographs of Ruby Braff and Mel Powel taken on October 23, 1986.

Mel Powell: Floating Jazz Festival[5]
October 23, 1986, Saga Theater aboard the S/S *Norway*
Ruby Braff, (cnt), Dizzy Gillespie (tp), Howard Alden (g), Dick Hyman, Mel Powell (p), Jack Lesberg (b), Buddy Rich (dm)
I'm Crazy 'bout My Baby (Powell and Hyman duet)

Powell, Alden, Lesberg, and Rich
Our Love Is Here to Stay

Add Gillespie
The Lady Is a Tramp

Braff and Powell duet
My Funny Valentine

Add Hyman, Alden, Gillespie, Lesberg, Rich
Liza
Jam Blues (Rich and Gillespie duet)

Hank O'Neal's photographs from the March of Jazz program, taken during this cruise, show both a further session by Ruby Braff with Howard Alden, and Jack Lesberg and Ruby posing with Clark Terry relaxing away from the bandstand.[6] The latter photo is included in this book's photo section.

Zoot Sims Memorial Concert[7]
December 14, 1986, New School, New York
Al Cohn, Gerry Mulligan, Mel Lewis, Lionel Hampton, Scott Hamilton, Jim Hall, Ruby Braff, Tommy Flanagan, and 52 other musicians were scheduled to perform in a four-hour program

Gold Star Sardine Bar[8]
Ruby Braff was reported to appear sometime following January 5, 1987, 666 North Lake Shore Drive, Chicago

Ruby Braff[9]
February 14–15, 1987, 8 p.m. to midnight, Captain Linnell House, 137 Skaket Beach Road, Orleans, Massachusetts
Ruby Braff (cnt), Gray Sargent (g), Marshall Wood (b), Frank Shea (dm)

Ruby Braff and John Bunch[10]
March 30–April 4, 1987, Zinno Restaurant, 126 West 13th Street, New York
Ruby Braff (cnt), John Bunch (p), Michael Moore (b)
Dream Dancing
Rockin' Chair
Liza
Tea for Two

John S Wilson wrote, "Mr. Braff's outgoing personality adds another new dimension to Zinno's musical style. He enjoys himself and shows it with occasional exclamatory shouts or a happy murmuring of lyrics when he is not playing."

Ruby Braff and Friends[11]
May 8-9, 1987, 8 p.m., Struggles, 10 Dempsey Avenue, Edgewater, New Jersey
Ruby Braff (cnt, p), Howard Alden (g), Jack Lesberg (b) with guests: Dan Barrett (tb), Nancy Nelson (voc) as shown
A partial recording is available from this engagement on May 8, 1987:
Final Tunes from Set 1:
Nice Work If You Can Get It
I've Found a New Baby
I'm in the Market for You
Rosetta
Medley:
  Foolin' Myself
  If You Were Mine
My Funny Valentine
Warm Valley (Alden feature)
Jubilee

Set 2:
Shoe Shine Boy
Poor Butterfly

Add Dan Barrett (tb)
Chicago
I Cover the Waterfront
Somebody Loves Me (Braff out)

Add Nancy Nelson (voc)
Stars Fell on Alabama
Keepin' Out of Mischief Now

Nelson out
Jeepers Creepers
Blue and Sentimental (Braff also plays piano)

Set 3 Including Dan Barrett
As Long As I Live
Medley:
  I Can't Give You Anything but Love
  Tea for Two
More Than You Know (Braff out)
High Society
Satin Doll
You're Driving Me Crazy
I'm Pulling Through (Braff plays piano)
What a Little Moonlight Can Do
Give My Regards to Broadway
NOTE: A recording of these tunes is available but remains unissued. Further recordings from the first set likely exist but were not available at time of publication.

Ruby Braff Quintet with Guest Stan Getz[12]
Buddy Rich Memorial Service
May 17, 1987, Saint Peter's Lutheran Church, New York
Ruby Braff (cnt), Stan Getz (ts), others unknown
Blue and Sentimental
Wrap Your Troubles in Dreams

Ruby stated that the above appearance with Stan Getz was the only time other than the Grande Parade du Jazz where they performed together, despite at least two other documented appearances onstage together. He reported that Stan scanned the list of musicians who were slated to perform and requested to play with Ruby.[13]

Ruby Braff and Friends[14]
May 29–30, 1987, Struggles, 10 Dempsey Avenue, Edgewater, New Jersey
No further information available

Loren Schoenberg Big Band, Downtown Uproar: Duke Ellington Society[15]
May 31, 1987, Schimmel Center at Pace University, Spruce Street (between Nassau and Gold Streets), New York
17-piece Loren Schoenberg Big Band featuring Dick Katz (p), Britt Woodman (tb), Barbara Lea (voc), and Ruby Braff (cnt)

The band played reconstructions of Ellington band arrangements. The occasion was the 50th anniversary of the original recording of "Downtown Uproar" recorded by Cootie Williams. Braff, Katz, and Schoenberg (ts) performed in a small group. Arrangements for Barbara Lea's performance were written by Benny Carter.

On his next trip to Europe, throughout July, Ruby performed in the Netherlands, France, and England. He returned to the United States on August 2.

Northsea Jazz Festival[16]
July 10, 1987, Congress Center, The Hague, The Netherlands

Ruby Braff Quintet: Grande Parade du Jazz: Nice Jazz Festival
July 11, 1987, 8–9 p.m., Arena Stage, Nice, France
Ruby Braff (cnt), Mark Shane (p), Howard Alden (g), Jack Lesberg (b), Chuck Riggs (dm)
Shoe Shine Boy
Sugar
Lonely Moments
Miss Brown to You
I'm Pulling Through
Wrap Your Troubles in Dreams
Orange
Sign-off, medium blues
NOTE: A recording of these tunes is available but remains unissued.

Ruby Braff Quintet: Grande Parade du Jazz: Nice Jazz Festival[17]
July 11, 1987, 11–12 p.m., Dance Stage, Nice, France
Ruby Braff (cnt), Mark Shane (p), Howard Alden (g), Jack Lesberg (b), Chuck Riggs (dm)

Ruby Braff and Friends: Grande Parade du Jazz: Nice Jazz Festival[18]
July 12, 1987, 7–9 p.m., Arena Stage, Nice, France
Ruby Braff (cnt), Mark Shane (p), Franz Jackson, Buddy Tate (ts), Howard Alden (g), Jack Lesberg (b), Chuck Riggs (dm)

No recording is known.

Ruby Braff did not appear at Nice on July 13, 1987.[19]

Ruby Braff Quintet: *A Salute to Billie Holiday*—Grande Parade du Jazz: Nice Jazz Festival

July 14, 1987, 7–9 p.m., Arena Stage, Nice, France
Ruby Braff (cnt), Mark Shane (p), Howard Alden (g), Jack Lesberg (b), Chuck Riggs (dm)
Romance in the Dark

Add Scott Hamilton (ts)
Medley:
  If You Were Mine (Ruby out)
  I Wished on the Moon
When a Woman Loves a Man
What a Little Moonlight Can Do

Add Clark Terry (voc)
Them There Eyes (CT voc)

Clark Terry out
Medley:
  Foolin' Myself
  I'm Pulling Through
  The Man I Love

Gerry Wiggins replaces Mark Shane (p)
I've Got a Right to Sing the Blues [incomplete]
NOTE: A recording of these tunes is available but remains unissued.

The Nice program also listed George Wein on piano for at least one tune from this session, but perhaps that is from a portion of the program that was not recorded.

Ruby Braff Quintet plus Scott Hamilton: Grande Parade du Jazz: Nice Jazz Festival

July 15, 1987, 7:30–8:30 p.m., Garden Stage Nice, France
Ruby Braff (cnt), Scott Hamilton (ts), Mark Shane (p), Howard Alden (g), Jack Lesberg (b), Chuck Riggs (dm)
No recording is known.

Ruby Braff Quintet: *A Salute to Louis Armstrong*—Grande Parade du Jazz: Nice Jazz Festival

July 15, 1987, 10–11 p.m., Arena Stage, Nice, France

Ruby Braff (cnt), Mark Shane (p), Howard Alden (g), Jack Lesberg (b), Chuck Riggs (dm)
When It's Sleepy Time Down South

Add Scott Hamilton (ts)
Rockin' Chair
Sweethearts on Parade

Add Doc Cheatham (tp, voc); Scott Hamilton and Ruby Braff out
Sugar (voc DC)
Someday You'll Be Sorry (voc DC)

Add Wild Bill Davison (cnt), Scott Hamilton (ts); Doc Cheatham out
Big Butter and Egg Man
Save It Pretty Mama (voc WBD)

Add Ruby Braff (cnt); Davison out
Medley:
  I Get Ideas
  Blueberry Hill
  Shine

Add Doc Cheatham (tp), Wild Bill Davison (cnt)
When It's Sleepy Time Down South
NOTE: A recording of these tunes is available but remains unissued.

Ruby Braff did not perform on July 16, 1987, at Nice.[20]

Interview with Steve Voce
July 17, 1987, Nice, France
Interview
NOTE: A recording of this interview is available but remains unissued.

Grande Parade du Jazz: Nice Jazz Festival
July 17, 1987, 7–8 p.m., Arena Stage, Nice, France
Ruby Braff (cnt), Scott Hamilton (ts), Mark Shane (p), Howard Alden (g), Jack Lesberg (b), Chuck Riggs (dm)
When You're Smiling
Love Me or Leave Me
Nobody Else But You
Basin Street Blues
You're Driving Me Crazy (incomplete)

Grande Parade du Jazz: Nice Jazz Festival
July 17, 1987, 9–10p.m., Dance Stage, Nice, France

Ruby Braff (cnt), Scott Hamilton (ts), Mark Shane (p), Howard Alden (g), Jack Lesberg (b), Chuck Riggs (dm)
Just You, Just Me
If I Had You

George Wein (p) replaces Mark Shane
I Would Do Anything for You
Sweet Lorraine

Add George Masso (tb)
Take the "A" Train (slightly incomplete)
NOTE: A recording of these tunes is available but remains unissued.

Grande Parade du Jazz: Nice Jazz Festival
July 18, 1987, 6–7 p.m., Arena Stage, Nice, France
Ruby Braff (cnt), Scott Hamilton (ts), Mark Shane (p), Howard Alden (g), Jack Lesberg (b), Chuck Riggs (dm)
Rosetta
The One I Love Belongs to Somebody Else
Don't Get Around Much Anymore
Medley:
  I Cover the Waterfront
  Exactly Like You
  Four or Five Times
You're Lucky to Me
NOTE: A recording of these tunes is available but remains unissued.

Ruby and Scott next travel to London, opening at Pizza Express where they appeared for ten nights. Fortunately their performances were extensively recorded.

Ruby Braff–Scott Hamilton Quintet
July 22, 1987, Pizza Express, London
Ruby Braff (cnt), Scott Hamilton (ts), Harry Smith (p), Len Skeat (b), Jack Parnell (dm)
Just You, Just Me
Wrap Your Troubles in Dreams
I Want a Little Girl
Jeepers Creepers
When a Woman Loves a Man
I've Got the World on a String
Liza
Ain't Misbehavin'
Medley:
  Dancing in the Dark

Love Walked In
Cheek to Cheek
Stars Fell on Alabama
Linger Awhile
Skylark (Ruby out)
Keepin' Out of Mischief Now
Them There Eyes (incomplete)
Medley:
Memories of You
Sweet Lorraine
I Want to Be Happy
Medley:
I've Grown Accustomed to Her Face
Wouldn't It Be Loverly
'Deed I Do
Fine and Mellow
NOTE: A recording of these tunes is available but remains unissued.

Ruby Braff–Scott Hamilton Quintet[21]
July 23, 1987, Pizza Express, London
Ruby Braff (cnt), Scott Hamilton (ts), Brian Lemon (p), Len Skeat (b), Jack Parnell (dm)
Rosetta
Rose Room
Fine and Dandy
I've Got a Feelin' I'm Fallin'
Dream Dancing
Just You, Just Me
Tea for Two
It Never Entered My Mind
All My Life
Someone to Watch Over Me (Ruby out)
All of Me
Blue Lou
They Can't Take That Away from Me
Miss Brown to You
Old Folks
Swing That Music
Closing Blues
NOTE: A recording of these tunes is available but remains unissued.

Ruby Braff–Scott Hamilton Quintet
July 24, 1987, Pizza Express, London
Ruby Braff (cnt), Scott Hamilton (ts), Brian Lemon (p), Len Skeat (b), Jack Parnell (dm)

Jeepers Creepers
When My Dreamboat Comes Home
Basin Street Blues
Thou Swell
All My Life
Muskrat Ramble
Rockin' Chair
Blue and Sentimental
Medley:
  I Wished on the Moon
  This Year's Kisses
Easy Living
St. Louis Blues
Take the "A" Train
Medley:
  What's New?
  Exactly Like You
When a Woman Loves a Man
I Want to Be Happy
Dream Dancing
NOTE: A recording of these tunes is available but remains unissued.

Ruby Braff–Scott Hamilton Quintet[22]
July 25, 1987, Pizza Express, London
Ruby Braff (cnt), Scott Hamilton (ts), Brian Lemon (p), Len Skeat (b), Jack Parnell (dm)
You Can Depend on Me
Medley:
  On the Sunny Side of the Street
  Pennies from Heaven
Blue and Sentimental
Them There Eyes
If You Were Mine (Ruby out)
I Wished on the Moon
Muskrat Ramble
Keepin' Out of Mischief Now
All Alone
Liza
Dream Dancing
Nice Work If You Can Get It
Louisiana
Sweethearts on Parade
Medley:
  He Loves and She Loves
  How Long Has This Been Going On?

The Man I Love (Ruby out)
Medley:
  I've Grown Accustomed to Her Face
  Wouldn't It Be Loverly
NOTE: A recording of these tunes is available but remains unissued.

Ruby Braff–Scott Hamilton Quintet
July 26, 1987, Pizza Express, London
Ruby Braff (cnt), Scott Hamilton (ts), Brian Lemon (p), Len Skeat (b), Jack Parnell (dm)
Someday Sweetheart
Ain't Misbehavin'
The World Is Waiting for the Sunrise
Sunday
Dinah
In a Mellotone
Miss Brown to You
I Can't Get Started
Liza
Love Is Just around the Corner
Medley:
  Skylark
  Take the "A" Train
Yesterdays
Medley:
  This Is All I Ask
  Wouldn't It Be Loverly
NOTE: A recording of these tunes is available but remains unissued.

Ruby Braff–Scott Hamilton Quintet
July 27, 1987, Pizza Express, London
Ruby Braff (cnt), Scott Hamilton (ts), Harry Smith (p), Spike Heatley (b), Jack Parnell (dm)
First Set:
Love Walked In
Mean to Me
When You're Smiling
Medley:
  The Very Thought of You
  Tea for Two
Medium Blues
NOTE: A recording of these tunes is available but remains unissued.

Second Set:
Them There Eyes

You're Driving Me Crazy
What Is There to Say? (Hamilton feature, omit Braff)
The Man I Love
Medley:
  This Is All I Ask
  The Blue Room
NOTE: A recording of these tunes is available but remains unissued.

Third Set:
Medley:
  Don't Get Around Much Anymore
  I Let a Song Go Out of My Heart
Dinah
Honeysuckle Rose
I've Grown Accustomed to Her Face
NOTE: A recording of these tunes is available but remains unissued.

Ruby Braff–Scott Hamilton Quintet
July 28, 1987, Pizza Express, London
Ruby Braff (cnt), Scott Hamilton (ts), Brian Lemon (p), Len Skeat (b), Jack Parnell (dm)
First Set:
Between the Devil and the Deep Blue Sea
Body and Soul
I Want to Be Happy
I Want a Little Girl
Love Me or Leave Me
Sign-off
NOTE: A recording of these tunes is available but remains unissued.

Second Set:
Lester Leaps In
When Your Lover Has Gone
Medley:
  He Loves and She Loves
  How Long Has This Been Going On?
  That Old Feeling
  The Man I Love
Sign-off
NOTE: A recording of these tunes is available but remains unissued.

Third Set:
Nice Work If You Can Get It
Easy Living
Muskrat Ramble

Over the Rainbow
Struttin' with Some Barbecue
Dream Dancing
Sign-off
NOTE: A recording of these tunes is available but remains unissued.

Ruby Braff–Scott Hamilton Quintet
July 29, 1987, Pizza Express, London
Ruby Braff (cnt), Scott Hamilton (ts), Brian Lemon (p), Len Skeat (b), Jack Parnell (dm)
First Set:
I Never Knew
I'm Pulling Through
Jubilee
Body and Soul
Wrap Your Troubles in Dreams
Mean to Me
Sign-off

Second Set:
Avalon
Medley:
  If You Were Mine (Ruby out)
  I Wished on the Moon
  What a Little Moonlight Can Do
Medley:
  Foolin' Myself
  This Year's Kisses
Skylark (Ruby out)
Don't Be That Way
Sign-off

Third Set:
It's Only a Paper Moon
Honeysuckle Rose
I'm Shooting High
You're Sensational
Muskrat Ramble
Wouldn't It Be Loverly
Sign-off
NOTE: A recording of these tunes is available but remains unissued.

Ruby Braff–Scott Hamilton Quintet
July 30, 1987, London

Ruby Braff (cnt), Scott Hamilton (ts), Brian Lemon (p), Len Skeat (b), Jack Parnell (dm)
Crazy Rhythm
Keepin' Out of Mischief Now
All My Life
Dinah
Royal Garden Blues
The Sheik of Araby
You're Lucky to Me
Medley:
  He Loves and She Loves
  How Long Has This Been Going On?
  The Man I Love
I Can't Give You Anything but Love
I Can't Get Started
Undecided
Gone with the Wind
Sophisticated Lady (omit Braff)
Dream Dancing
Medley:
  The Man That Got Away
  Over the Rainbow
  If I Only Had a Brain
I Want to Be Happy
NOTE: A recording of these tunes is available but remains unissued.

Ruby Braff–Scott Hamilton Quintet
July 31, 1987, Pizza Express, London
Ruby Braff (cnt), Scott Hamilton (ts), Brian Lemon (p), Len Skeat (b), Jack Parnell (dm)
First Set:
You Can Depend on Me
Medley:
  Sweet Georgia Brown
  Tea for Two
  Two Sleepy People
Nice Work If You Can Get It
I'm Shooting High
Hey Lawdy Mama

Second Set:
You Took Advantage of Me
High Society
Our Love Is Here to Stay
Medley:

The Man That Got Away
Over the Rainbow
It's Only a Paper Moon

Third Set:
Jubilee
Medley:
Georgia on My Mind
Way Down Yonder in New Orleans
Star Dust (Hamilton feature, Braff out)
Them There Eyes
I've Grown Accustomed to Her Face
NOTE: A recording of these tunes is available but remains unissued.

Ruby Braff–Scott Hamilton Quintet
August 1, 1987, Pizza Express, London
Ruby Braff (cnt), Scott Hamilton (ts), Harry Smith (p), Len Skeat (b), Jack Parnell (dm)
Rosetta
It Had to Be You
Ghost of a Chance
Dinah
Blues
I Want to Be Happy
Embraceable You
I Got Rhythm
Medley:
He Loves and She Loves
How Long Has This Been Going On?
Liza
When You're Smiling
Medley:
Wouldn't It Be Loverly
I've Grown Accustomed to Her Face
Medley:
Poor Butterfly
Tea for Two
Medley:
I'll See You Again
White Christmas
NOTE: A recording of these tunes is available but remains unissued.

Ruby flew back to the United States on August 2 for a ten-night return engagement at Zinno in New York.

Ruby Braff Trio[23]
August 3–15, 1987 (every night except Sunday), Zinno, 126 West 13th Street, New York
Ruby Braff (cnt), John Bunch (p), Michael Moore (b)

Ruby's next recording was released only in Japan and will be unknown to most of his fans. Ruby said that Anli Sugano did not speak English but was very nice to work with during the following session. She sang phonetically.

Anli Sugano: *In Manhattan*
August 26, 27, 28, 1987, New York
Anli Sugano (voc), Ruby Braff (cnt and all arrangements), John Campbell (p), Howard Alden (g), Jack Lesberg (b), Ronnie Zito (dm), Grady Tate (added voc)
Blue Moon
    Philips (J) 28PL-136, 32LD-112 (CD)
Astaire-Rodgers Medley:
  They Can't Take That Away from Me
    Philips (J) 28PL-136, 32LD-112 (CD)
  The Way You Look Tonight
    Philips (J) 28PL-136, 32LD-112 (CD)
  Cheek to Cheek
    Philips (J) 28PL-136, 32LD-112 (CD)
Tea for Two
    Philips (J) 28PL-136, 32LD-112 (CD)
Some Sunny Day
    Philips (J) 28PL-136, 32LD-112 (CD)
Manhattan
    Philips (J) 28PL-136, 32LD-112 (CD)
Sugar (instrumental)
    Philips (J) 28PL-136, 32LD-112 (CD)
Benny Goodman Memories:
  Memories of You
    Philips (J) 28PL-136, 32LD-112 (CD)
  Sometimes I'm Happy
    Philips (J) 28PL-136, 32LD-112 (CD)
  I Cried for You
    Philips (J) 28PL-136, 32LD-112 (CD)
You Go to My Head
    Philips (J) 28PL-136, 32LD-112 (CD)
Orange (instrumental)
    Philips (J) 28PL-136, 32LD-112 (CD)
NOTE: Anli Sugano sings on all titles not indicated as instrumental. Grady Tate sings on "Blue Moon" and "Tea for Two."

WKCR Annual Benefit Concert and Broadcast[24]
August 30, 1987, West End Café, 2911 Broadway, at 114th Street, New York

Jon Pareles wrote the following about the benefit concert:

> Ten groups will perform, led by, among others, David (Fathead) Newman, Percy France, George Kelly and Harold Vick, all saxophonists; Slide Hampton, a trombonist; Ruby Braff, a cornetist; Warren Chiasson, a vibraphonist, and Little Jimmy Scott, an extraordinarily tender and suspenseful singer. The program of swing, be-bop and old-fashioned rhythm and blues—10 hours' worth—will begin Sunday at 2 p.m., and will be broadcast live on WKCR, 89.9 FM; admission, which benefits the station, is $10.

Al White published two photos of Ruby at the 3rd Minneapolis Jazz Party in 1987. The first showed Ruby with Scott Hamilton[25] while another showed Howard Alden, Jack Lesberg, and Ruby playing during one of the sets.[26]

3rd Minneapolis Jazz Party
September 18–20, 1987, Holiday Inn Downtown Minneapolis, Minnesota
Sponsored by Reed MacKenzie and John Stephens. The program began at 8 p.m. Friday and concluded at 11 a.m. on Sunday.

Friday, September 18, 1987
9:25–9:55 p.m.: Ruby Braff (cnt), Scott Hamilton (ts), Phil Bodner (cl), George Masso (tb), Ross Tompkins (p), Howard Alden (g), Jack Lesberg (b), Gus Johnson (dm)
I Never Knew

Hamilton, Bodner, Masso out
These Foolish Things
NOTE: A recording of these tunes is available but remains unissued.

12:00–12:30 a.m.: Ruby Braff (cnt), Kenny Davern (cl), Carl Fontana (tb), Dick Hyman (p), Milt Hinton (b), Howard Alden (g), Butch Miles (dm)
Exactly Like You

Braff and Davern out
Love Walked In

Braff and Davern return
Love Me or Leave Me
NOTE: A recording of these tunes is available but remains unissued.

Saturday, September 19, 1987, 3rd Minneapolis Jazz Party
12:30–12:55 p.m.: Ruby Braff (cnt), Scott Hamilton (ts), George Masso (tb), Jim Galloway (ss, bar sax), Ralph Sutton (p), Howard Alden (g), Jack Lesberg (b), Gus Johnson (dm)
Sugar

Braff, Hamilton, Galloway out
Do Nothin' Till You Hear from Me

Braff, Hamilton, Galloway return
Jeepers Creepers
NOTE: A recording of these tunes is available but remains unissued.

2:30–2:55 p.m.: Ruby Braff (cnt), Flip Phillips (ts), Kenny Davern (cl), George Masso (tb), Dick Hyman (p), Jack Lesberg (b), Howard Alden (g), Gus Johnson (dm)
Crazy He Calls Me (Alden solo)
Rosetta
NOTE: A recording of these tunes is available but remains unissued.

9:30–9:55 p.m.: Ruby Braff (cnt), George Masso (tb), Scott Hamilton (ts), Kenny Davern (cl), Ross Tompkins (p), Howard Alden (g), Jack Lesberg (b). Jake Hanna (dm)
Keepin' Out of Mischief Now*
With Someone New (Hamilton and Alden with rhythm
Dinah
NOTE: Recordings of two of these tunes are available but remain unissued. "Keepin' Out of Mischief Now" is unavailable and is marked with an asterisk.

12:00–12:30 a.m.: Snooky Young (tp), Ruby Braff (cnt), George Masso (tb), Scott Hamilton (ts), Phil Bodner (cl), Ross Tompkins (p), Milt Hinton (b), Jake Hanna (dm)
You Can Depend on Me
On the Sunny Side of the Street (Young and Braff featured)
Lady Be Good
NOTE: A recording of these tunes is available but remains unissued.

Sunday, September 20, 1987, 3rd Minneapolis Jazz Party, Holiday Inn Downtown Minneapolis, Minnesota
9:00–9:25 a.m.: Ruby Braff (cnt), George Masso (tb), Scott Hamilton (ts), Phil Bodner (cl), Ross Tompkins (p), Howard Alden (g), Jack Lesberg (b), Gus Johnson (dm)
You're Driving Me Crazy*
I Can't Give You Anything but Love (Braff feature)
Undecided

NOTE: A recording of these tunes is available but remains unissued; however "You're Driving Me Crazy" is incomplete on the recording available to the author and is marked with an asterisk.

10:30 – 11:00 a.m.: Ruby Braff (cnt), Al Grey (tb), George Masso (tb), Scott Hamilton (ts), Ross Tompkins (p), Howard Alden (g), Jack Lesberg (b), Gus Johnson (dm)
Take the "A" Train (Grey and Masso featured)
When I Fall in Love (Braff and Hamilton featured)
NOTE: A recording of these tunes is available but remains unissued.

Finale: Everybody: Ross Tompkins, Dick Hyman, Ralph Sutton (p), Jack Lesberg (b), Bob Haggart (b), Milt Hinton (b), Gus Johnson, Jake Hanna, Butch Miles (dm), Marshall Royal (as), Snooky Young (tp), Terry Gibbs (vib), Kenny Davern (cl), Irv Williams, Al Grey, George Masso, Carl Fontana (tb), Jim Galloway (ss), Scott Hamilton (ts), Ruby Braff, Warren Vaché (cnt), Flip Phillips (ts), Phil Bodner (cl)
Untitled
Cherry
Sleepy Time Gal (tb feature)
NOTE: A recording of these tunes is available but remains unissued. Irv Williams lived in Minneapolis and was a member of the Fletcher Henderson Orchestra.

Ruby Braff Quintet: Jazz Room Series[27]
November 1, 1987, 4 p.m., Shea Center for the Performing Arts, William Paterson College, Wayne, New Jersey

Ruby Braff Trio[28]
November 9–21, 1987 (except Sundays), Zinno, 126 West 13th Street, New York
Ruby Braff (cnt), Howard Alden (g), Jack Lesberg (b)
God Bless the Child
Jubilee
Smile

The following appearance in the Jazz at 6 series would have been completed before the start of the continuing engagement at Zinno's:

Ruby Braff and Dick Hyman: Jazz at 6[29]
November 13, 1987, 6 p.m., New School, 66 West 12th Street, New York
Ruby Braff (cnt), Dick Hyman (p)
The performance concluded in time for Ruby to reach Zinno for an 8 p.m. set.

Ruby Braff Quartet, Duo and Trio[30]
December 21–24, 26–31, 1987 and January 1–2, 1988, Zinno, 126 West 13th Street, New York
Ruby Braff (cnt), John Bunch (p), Howard Alden (g), Michael Moore (b)

Two reports for an engagement at Zinno listed John Bunch[31] and Howard Alden,[32] but not together. A third article reports that Ruby worked with Michael Moore as a duo.[33] Starting December 28, 1988, John Bunch does not appear with the Trio. On various nights, Ruby performed as part of a duo (Braff–Moore) or a trio (adding either Bunch or Alden to the duo). John Bunch is mentioned only in *Newsday* for the week of December 21–26 (closed December 25). Howard Alden is mentioned during that week and also for January 2 in the *New York Times*, which also reports on the duo. *The New Yorker* lists Howard Alden for the final week. Sundays featured Michael Moore and Gene Bertoncini.

Ruby Braff Trio[34]
February 8–13, 1988, Zinno, 126 West 13th Street, New York
Ruby Braff (cnt), Howard Alden (g), Jack Lesberg (b)

Ruby Braff Trio[35]
February 15–20, 1988, Zinno, 126 West 13th Street, New York
Ruby Braff (cnt), John Bunch (p), Michael Moore (b)

Between his continuing engagements at Zinno, Ruby few to St. Louis to perform in the Mid-America Jazz Festival with Ralph Sutton. Ruby's fans will certainly enjoy watching the video recordings, issued on a DVD by Arbors.

Mid-America Jazz Festival[36]
March 18–20, 1988, Sheraton Hotel, St. Louis, Missouri
Ruby Braff (cnt), Ralph Sutton (p), Milt Hinton (b), Gus Johnson (dm)
First Set (Saturday afternoon, March 19):
Jeepers Creepers
    Arbors Records ARDVD 2 (DVD)
Fine and Dandy
    Arbors Records ARDVD 2 (DVD)
Russian Lullaby
    Arbors Records ARDVD 2 (DVD)
Old Folks
    Arbors Records ARDVD 2 (DVD)
Keepin' Out of Mischief Now
    Arbors Records ARDVD 2 (DVD)

Second Set (Saturday evening, March 19):
The Man I Love
Arbors Records ARDVD 2 (DVD)
Body and Soul
Arbors Records ARDVD 2 (DVD)
Poor Butterfly
Arbors Records ARDVD 2 (DVD)
Rockin' Chair
Arbors Records ARDVD 2 (DVD)

Third Set (Sunday morning, March 20):
Thou Swell
Arbors Records ARDVD 2 (DVD)
All By Myself
Arbors Records ARDVD 2 (DVD)
Sugar
Arbors Records ARDVD 2 (DVD)
Medley:
I Can't Give You Anything but Love
Arbors Records ARDVD 2 (DVD)
Tea for Two
Arbors Records ARDVD 2 (DVD)

Final Set (Sunday afternoon, March 20)
This Is All I Ask
unissued, video available
Sweethearts on Parade
unissued, video available
I'm Crazy 'bout My Baby
unissued, video available
Dinah
unissued, video available

A photo from the March of Jazz program shows Scott Hamilton with Ruby at this festival while another photograph shows Ruby playing with Milt Hinton.[37] Arbors Records ARDVD 2 (DVD) is titled *Ruby and Ralph Remembered.* At the time of publication, all selections from the final set are available on www.YouTube.com.

Ruby Braff Trio[38]
April 18–23, 1988, Zinno, 126 West 13th Street, New York
Ruby Braff (cnt), Howard Alden (g), Jack Lesberg (b)

Ruby Braff Trio[39]
April 25–30, 1988, Zinno, 126 West 13th Street, New York
Ruby Braff (cnt), Howard Alden (g), Michael Moore (b)

Ruby Braff Trio[40]
May 2–7, 1988, Zinno, 126 West 13th Street, New York
Ruby Braff (cnt), Dick Katz (p), Michael Moore (b)

Next, Ruby flew to San Francisco. Mike Lipskin produced several Stride Piano Summit concerts. Ruby was invited to perform in the first one in the series.[41]

Jazz in the City Festival: Stride Piano Summit[42]
June 10, 1988, Davies Symphony Hal in San Francisco
Ruby Braff (cnt), Dick Hyman, Mike Lipskin, Ralph Sutton, Jay McShann (p), Red Callender (b), Eddie Marshall, Sam Shaffer (dm) (Dick Hyman also played the organ on some tunes)

A contemporary review was published in the *San Francisco Chronicle*[43]:

> There were romping two-piano duets—Hyman and Lipskin, McShann and Sutton—that swung on a see-saw of improvised 8- and 16-bar phrases tossed back and forth in the spirit of friendly competition. There were also hot potato numbers, with cornetist Braff, a wiseguy ham who plays like an angel, tossing melodies around the horn to Sutton, Hyman, McShann, Marshall, and Callender. [Braff] carried on like a Catskills comic, pointing to the soloists and cracking jokes while they played, vamping with the crowd and muttering over and over, 'What a racket, what a racket.'

Ruby Braff Trio: *Me Myself and I*
June 1988, Penny Lane Studios, New York
Ruby Braff (cnt) Howard Alden (g) Jack Lesberg (b)
Muskrat Ramble
    Concord Jazz CCD 4381 (CD), CJ 381
Let Me Sing and I'm Happy
    Concord Jazz CCD 4381 (CD), CJ 381
You've Changed
    Concord Jazz CCD 4381 (CD), CJ 381, Snapper Music SMDCD 271
You're a Lucky Guy
    Concord Jazz CCD 4381 (CD), CJ 381, CCD 4833-2
Honey
    Concord Jazz CCD 4381 (CD), CJ 381
No One Else But You
    Concord Jazz CCD 4381 (CD), CJ 381
Me, Myself and I
    Concord Jazz CCD 4381 (CD), CJ 381

When You're Smiling
Concord Jazz CCD 4381 (CD), CJ 381
When I Fall in Love
Concord Jazz CCD 4381 (CD), CJ 381
Swan Lake
Concord Jazz CCD 4381 (CD), CJ 381
That's My Home
Concord Jazz CCD 4381 (CD), CJ 381
Jubilee
Concord Jazz CCD 4381 (CD), CJ 381
Dream Dancing
Concord Jazz CCD 4381 (CD), CJ 381, Snapper Music SMDCD 271
NOTE: Concord Jazz CCD 4833-2 is titled *Ruby Braff: The Concord Jazz Heritage Series* and Snapper Music SMDCD 271 is titled *I'm Shooting High.* The Snapper release is a reissue of tunes from various Concord Jazz releases.

Ruby Braff Trio: *Bravura Eloquence*
June 1988, Penny Lane Studios, New York
Ruby Braff (cnt) Howard Alden (g) Jack Lesberg (b)
Old Man River
Concord Jazz CCD 4423 (CD)
Medley:
Smile
Concord Jazz CCD 4423 (CD)
Who'll Buy My Violets?
Concord Jazz CCD 4423 (CD)
Lonely Moments
Concord Jazz CCD 4423 (CD)
Here's Carl
Concord Jazz CCD 4423 (CD), CCD 4833-2, CCD 4820-2
God Bless the Child
Concord Jazz CCD 4423 (CD)
It's Bad for Me
Concord Jazz CCD 4423 (CD)
I've Grown Accustomed to Her Face
Concord Jazz CCD 4423 (CD), CCD 4833-2
Make Sense
Concord Jazz CCD 4423 (CD)
I'm Shooting High
Concord Jazz CCD 4423 (CD), Snapper Music SMDCD 271
Orange
Concord Jazz CCD 4423 (CD)
Persian Rug
Concord Jazz CCD 4423 (CD)

Travelin' Light
    Concord Jazz CCD 4423 (CD), Snapper Music SMDCD 271
Royal Garden Blues
    Concord Jazz CCD 4423 (CD)
Judy Garland Medley:
  The Man That Got Away
    Concord Jazz CCD 4423 (CD)
  San Francisco
    Concord Jazz CCD 4423 (CD)
  Over the Rainbow
    Concord Jazz CCD 4423 (CD)
  If I Only Had a Brain
    Concord Jazz CCD 4423 (CD)

NOTE: Concord Jazz CCD 4833-2 is titled *Ruby Braff: The Concord Jazz Heritage Series*, CCD 4820-2 is titled *The Sampler: The Concord Jazz Heritage Series*, and Snapper Music SMDCD 271 is titled *I'm Shooting High*. The Snapper release is a reissue of tunes from various Concord Jazz releases.

Ruby returned to Carnegie Hall in a tribute to Louis Armstrong as part of the JVC Jazz Festival. This was a benefit for the Louis Armstrong Project at Queens College. Musicians appearing included Lionel Hampton, Dizzy Gillespie, Wynton Marsalis, Clark Terry, Ruby Braff, Jimmy Owens, Randy Sandke, Jon Faddis, Warren Vaché, Norris Turney, Haywood Henry, Jimmy Heath, Phil Bodner, Kenny Davern, Dan Barrett, George Masso, Jimmy Maxwell, Joe Muranyi, Eddie Bert, Dick Hyman, Milt Hinton, Oliver Jackson, Howard Alden, Carrie Smith, Marty Napoleon, Arvell Shaw, and Eddie Barefield. Phil Schaap also appeared, and Whoopi Goldberg was host. Dick Hyman directed the program and led the New York Jazz Repertory Company in arrangements of Armstrong's classic Hot Five recordings. This was the festival's opening night.

***For the Love of Louis* at the JVC Jazz Festival**[44]
June 24, 1988, 8 p.m., Carnegie Hall, New York

Ruby also appeared at Town Hall on the festival's closing night in a tribute to Billie Holiday. Also appearing on the program were George Wein, Jack Lesberg, Jake Hanna, Mel Lewis, and Haywood Henry. Buck Clayton's Swing Band also performed, including Johnny Letman, Randy Sandke, Warren Vaché, Norris Turney, Chuck Wilson, Joe Temperley, Urbie Green, Dan Barrett, Oliver Jackson, Gerry Wiggins, Eddie Jones, Howard Alden, Doug Lawrence, and Lew Tabackin.

***A Night for Lady Day* at the JVC Jazz Festival**[45]
July 2, 1988, 8 p.m., Town Hall, 123 West 43rd Street, New York
Ruby Braff, Warren Vaché (cnt), Scott Hamilton (ts), Barry Harris, Ellis Larkins (p), Mel Lewis, Jackie Williams (dm), Al Hibbler (voc)

John S. Wilson wrote the following:[46]

> Ruby Braff, the diminutive, garrulous and brilliant trumpeter and cornetist, had waited thirty-four years for his old friend, George Wein, to let him have an evening of his own at the jazz festival that Mr. Wein started in 1954—then the Newport Jazz Festival, now the JVC Jazz Festival. On Saturday evening at Town Hall, he got his wish, and although the program was called *A Night for Lady Day*—that is, Billie Holiday—it was just as much a night for Mr. Braff.
>
> As the producer of the program, Mr. Braff stamped it with his personality and points of view. It reflected his great affection for the music of Billie Holiday, his belief that jazz improvisation is 'adoration of the melody' and his close relationship with the musical children of the swing era who have come to prominence in the last decade.
>
> In Mr. Braff's program there were no singers who tried to sound like Billie Holiday. In fact, there was only one singer, Al Hibbler—who sounded like nobody but Al Hibbler. But Miss Holiday's presence was constantly felt through the evening's songs, every one of which was associated with her.
>
> There were no long solos. At most a soloist got two choruses, and even that was infrequent. More often two soloists shared one chorus. And Mr. Braff twice used quartet formations in a manner that presented closely knit duets and varied challenges.
>
> In one instance, Mr. Braff pitted the drummer Jackie Williams and his own trumpet against the drumming of Mel Lewis and Scott Hamilton's saxophone. In similar fashion, he paired pianist Barry Harris with Warren Vaché on cornet and pianist Ellis Larkins with himself—a quartet that tossed "You've Changed" back and forth to build an increasingly brilliant performance.
>
> Mr. Larkins, who recorded several trumpet and piano duets with Mr. Braff thirty years ago but is rarely heard in New York now, played a fresh, lightly flowing solo on the well-worn 'Lover Man' that was one of the high points of the evening. Another veteran, Buck Clayton, the great trumpeter with Count Basie who is now concentrating on composing and arranging, led a big band in his knowledgeable, craftsmanlike arrangements of Billie Holiday songs.
>
> The band was centered on the young swing-oriented musicians who have given jazz of the pre-bop era a new lease on life—among them Scott Hamilton, Mr. Vaché, Dan Barrett, Randy Sandke, Doug Lawrence, Chuck Wilson, and Howard Alden, along with such relative veterans as Lew Tabackin, Joe Temperley, Urbie Green, Johnny Letman, Jack Lesberg, Oliver Jackson, Gerry Wiggins, Mr. Wein, and the Count Basie bassist of the 1950's, Eddie Jones.
>
> It was a warm, loving, foot-tapping musical event and no one seemed to enjoy it more than Mr. Braff.

Jazz Festival: Ruby Braff and Dick Hyman[47]
July 3, 1988, 6 p.m., Fine Arts Center, Southampton Campus, Long Island University, New York
Ruby Braff (cnt), Dick Hyman (p)

Once again, it time for Ruby to spend July in Europe. This year he again performed in The Netherlands, France and Sweden. This time, his England had to wait.

Northsea Jazz Festival[48]
July 9, 1988, Congrescenter, The Hague, The Netherlands

Ruby was quoted as he spoke with excitement about the Northsea Festival: "Jazz is alive and well everywhere. What is special at this festival is that I've never seen such a variety of music played. I've seen more musicians I know in the past three days than in the past ten years."[49]

Grande Parade du Jazz: Nice Jazz Festival
July 12, 1988, 9–10 p.m., Dance Stage, Nice, France
Ruby Braff, Warren Vaché (cnt), Scott Hamilton (ts), Joe Temperley (bars), Marty Napoleon (p), Howard Alden (g), Jack Lesberg (b), Jake Hanna (dm)
Exactly Like You
I've Got a Right to Sing the Blues
Swing That Music
Medley:
  Fine and Mellow
  St. Louis Blues
NOTE: A recording of these tunes is available but remains unissued.

Grande Parade du Jazz: Nice Jazz Festival
July 14, 1988, 8–9 p.m., Dance Stage, Nice, France
Ruby Braff, Warren Vaché (cnt), Urbie Green (tb), Scott Hamilton (ts), Joe Temperley (bars), Marty Napoleon (p), Howard Alden (g), Jack Lesberg (b), Jake Hanna (dm)
Blue Lou
I Want a Little Girl
Lady Be Good
Ain't Misbehavin'
NOTE: A recording of these tunes is available but remains unissued.

Grande Parade du Jazz: Nice Jazz Festival Tribute to Billie Holiday
July 15, 1988, 9–10 p.m., Garden Stage, Nice, France
Ruby Braff (cnt), Scott Hamilton (ts), Marty Napoleon (p), Howard Alden (g), Jack Lesberg (b), Jake Hanna (dm)
Romance in the Dark
Mean to Me
God Bless the Child
The Man I Love

Add George Wein (p)
Body and Soul
Love Me or Leave Me
Fine and Mellow
NOTE: A recording of these tunes is available but remains unissued.

Grande Parade du Jazz: Nice Jazz Festival
Ruby Braff with Guests
July 15, 1988, 11–12 p.m., Dance Stage, Nice, France
Ruby Braff, Warren Vaché (cnt), Urbie Green (tb), Scott Hamilton (ts), Marty Napoleon (p), Howard Alden (g), Jack Lesberg (b), Jake Hanna (dm)
Jeepers Creepers
Sugar
Sweet Georgia Brown
NOTE: A recording of these tunes is available but remains unissued. The recording of "Jeepers Creepers" is missing the first one and a half choruses.

Grande Parade du Jazz: Nice Jazz Festival
July 17, 1988, 6–7 p.m., Dance Stage, Nice, France
Ruby Braff (cnt), Marty Napoleon (p), Howard Alden (g), Jack Lesberg (b), Jake Hanna (dm)
Yesterdays*
When I Fall in Love

Add: Harry Sweets Edison (tp)
I Never Knew
The Shadow of Your Smile (omit Braff, HE feature)*
Jive at Five
NOTE: A partial recording of this performance is available but remains unissued. Recordings of two tunes have not been available to the author at time of publication and are marked with an asterisk. This performance was rescheduled from 10 p.m. to the actual time listed above.

Grande Parade du Jazz: Nice Jazz Festival
July 17, 1988, 8–9 p.m., Garden Stage, Nice, France
Ruby Braff (cnt), Marty Napoleon (p), Howard Alden (g), Jack Lesberg (b), Jake Hanna (dm)
You're Driving Me Crazy
Medley:
  Sweet Lorraine
  St. Louis Blues
Nobody Else But You (Braff, Alden, Lesberg only)
Dancers in Love (Alden, Lesberg only)
Sunday

Medley:
Foolin' Myself
Lover Come Back to Me
NOTE: A recording of these tunes is available but remains unissued.

Stockholm Jazz Festival[50]
July 1988, Stockholm, Sweden
Ruby Braff was included in the list of performers

Ruby returned to the United States. I have been unable to trace further performances between these documented appearances. Specifically, it appears that Ruby did not appear in London in July 1988 or 1989.

The reviewer of Ruby's next performance at Zinno described him as "a cornetist who makes you lean forward when he descends into the secret chamber that is his lower register and sit up when he rises to a rare high note."

Ruby Braff Trio[51]
August 20–27, 1988, Zinno, 126 West 13th Street, New York
Ruby Braff (cnt), James Chirillo (g), Michael Moore (b)

The reviewer of Ruby's next evening at Zinno noted that Ruby "likes to speak low on his cornet, as if he were transmitting dark, demonic secrets."

Ruby Braff Trio[52]
August 29, 1988–September 3, 1988, Zinno, 126 West 13th Street, New York
Ruby Braff (cnt), John Campbell (p), Michael Moore (b)

Notes

[1] Lawrence Leslie, *Los Angeles Times*, July 27, 1986.
[2] Hank O'Neal for information (digital tape exists in Chiaroscuro's vault).
[3] *Jazz Journal International*, December 1989, 10, interview with Scott Hamilton.
[4] Hank O'Neal for information (digital tape exists in Chiaroscuro vault).
[5] Hank O'Neal for information (digital tape exists in Chiaroscuro vault) and http://www.hankonealphoto.com/fjf_main6.html.
[6] Photo, *The March of Jazz Celebrates Ruby Braff's 74th Birthday Party*, Arbors Records, 2001, 27.
[7] *New York Magazine*, December 8, 1986, 42.
[8] Dave Hoekstra, *Chicago Sun-Times*, December 28, 1986.
[9] Ernie Santosuosso, *Boston Globe*, February 13, 1987.
[10] *New York Times*, April 4, 1987, *The New Yorker*, March 30, 1987, 7, and April 6, 1987, 8, and *New York Magazine*, March 30, 1987, 129, and April 6, 1987, 127.
[11] *New York Times*, May 3, 1987.
[12] Doug Meriwether, *Mister I Am the Band* (North Baltimore, NY: National Drum Association, 1998), 138 (no recording known to exist).

[13] Ruby speaking to Steve Voce in interview on December 15, 1994.
[14] *New York Times*, May 24, 1987.
[15] Jon Pareles, *New York Times*, May 29, 1987, and John S. Wilson, *New York Times*, May 31, 1987, and *New York Magazine*, June 1, 1987, 122.
[16] Listed in ad in *Jazz Journal International* June 24, 1987. The festival ran from July 10–12, but the latter two days Ruby was in Nice, France. Ruby's appearance is mentioned by John Norris in *Coda Magazine*, October/November 1987, 38.
[17] Tony Shoppee provided this time of performance from the festival program. The personnel are presumed to be identical to the 8–9 p.m. performance.
[18] Information from Bob Weir and Tony Shoppee.
[19] Information provided by Tony Shoppee.
[20] Information provided by Tony Shoppee.
[21] The recording of "Just You, Just Me" is missing a few seconds of the performance during a tape change.
[22] Tony Shoppee reported that Ruby had a slight lip injury this night.
[23] *New York Times*, August 2, 1987, *The New Yorker*, August 3, 1987, 6, August 10, 1987, 6, August 17, 1987, 6, and *New York Magazine*, August 3, 1987, 84, August 10, 1987, 87, and August 17, 1987.
[24] Mentioned by Han Schulte and listed by Jon Pareles, *New York Times*, August 28, 1987.
[25] Al White, *Jazz Party* (Little Rock, AR: August House Publishers, 2000), 22.
[26] Al White, *Jazz Party* (Little Rock, AR: August House Publishers, 2000), 23.
[27] *New York Times*, September 20, 1987 and November 1, 1987.
[28] *New York Times*, November 8, 1987, November 12, 1987, and November 15, 1987, *The New Yorker*, November 9, 1987, 13, November 16, 1987, 8, and November 23, 1987, 7, and *New York Magazine*, November 9, 1989, 159.
[29] Dick Hyman and *New York Times*, November 13, 1987, *The New Yorker*, November 9, 1987, 13, and *New York Magazine*, November 16, 1987, 143.
[30] *Newsday*, December 23, 1987, December 27, 1977, *The New Yorker*, December 21, 1978, 13, December 28, 1978, 10, January 4, 1988, 7, *The New York Times*, December 25, 1987, December 27, 1987, and *New York Magazine*, December 19, 1988, 188, and January 4, 1988, 78.
[31] *Newsday*, December 23, 1987.
[32] *New York Times*, December 25, 1987.
[33] *New York Times*, January 1, 1988.
[34] *New York Times*, February 7, 1988, *The New Yorker*, February 8, 1988, 8, February 15, 1988, 8, and *New York Magazine*, February 15, 1988, 112, and February 8, 1988, 127.
[35] *The New Yorker*, February 15, 1988, 8, and February 22, 1988, 8, and *New York Magazine*, February 22, 1988, 100.
[36] Originally taped by Don Wolff.
[37] Photo reproduced in *The March of Jazz Celebrates Ruby Braff's 74th Birthday Party*, Arbors Records, 2001, 28.
[38] *New York Times*, April 17, 1988, April 24, 1988, *The New Yorker*, April 18, 1988, 13, and April 25, 1988, 13, and *New York Magazine*, April 18, 1988, 148, and April 25, 1988, 192.
[39] *The New Yorker*, April 25, 1988, 13, May 2, 1988, 11, *New York Times*, April 24, 1988, and *New York Magazine*, May 2, 1988, 137.

[40] *New York Times*, May 1, 1988, *The New Yorker*, May 9, 1988, 13, and *New York Magazine*, May 9, 1988, 123.
[41] Mike Lipskin in personal conversation.
[42] James D. Shacter, *Loose Shoes: The Story of Ralph Sutton* (Chicago: Jaynar Press, 1994), 284. Also see Herb Caen, *San Francisco Chronicle*, May 25, 1988, June 13, 1988, and *Coda Magazine*, August/September 1988, 26.
[43] *San Francisco Chronicle*, June 13, 1988.
[44] *New York Times*, June 24, 1988.
[45] *New York Times*, June 24, 1988, and *New York Magazine*, June 27, 1988, 197.
[46] John S. Wilson, *New York Times*, July 4, 1988.
[47] Dick Hyman and *New York Times*, July 3, 1988.
[48] Information from Han Schulte.
[49] Galina Vromen (Reuters), *Globe and Mail*, July 11, 1988.
[50] "20 Years of Jazz! In the World's Most Beautiful Capital, Stockholm," February 14, 2004, http://www.stockholmjazz.com/press_room/?id=2&option=view_entry.
[51] *The New Yorker*, August 22, 1988, 7, August 29, 1988, 7, *New York Times*, August 21, 1988, and *New York Magazine*, August 22, 1988, 183 and August 29, 1988, 93.
[52] *The New Yorker*, August 29, 1988, 7, September 5, 1988, 7, *New York Times*, August 28, 1988, and *New York Magazine*, August 29, 1988, 93, and September 5, 1988, 96.

Chapter 19

The Pianists and the Growth of Jazz Parties: September 1988–September 1993

Ruby returned from Europe toward the end of July and had two documented bookings at New York clubs. There may have been other engagements that did not appear in the media. He next returned to Minneapolis for the annual Minneapolis Jazz Party, a festive gathering that reunited Ruby with a number of his musical friends.

4th Minneapolis Jazz Party
Friday, September 16, 1988, Marriott Hotel, City Center, Minneapolis, Minnesota
8:30–8:55 p.m.: Ruby Braff (cnt), Scott Hamilton (ts), Walt Levinsky (cl), Urbie Green (tb), Marty Napoleon (p), Jake Hanna (dm), Howard Alden (g), Jack Lesberg (b)
Rosetta
Ain't Misbehavin'
All of Me
NOTE: A recording of these tunes is available but remains unissued.

10:25 p.m.– 10:55 p.m. : Ruby Braff (cnt), Scott Hamilton (ts), Kenny Davern (cl), George Masso (tb), Ralph Sutton (p), Gus Johnson (dm), Major Holley (b)
You're Driving Me Crazy
I'm Crazy 'bout My Baby (Hamilton, Davern, Masso out)
I Never Knew
NOTE: A recording of these tunes is available but remains unissued.

Saturday, September 17, 1988, Marriott Hotel, City Center, Minneapolis, Minnesota
1:10–1:40 p.m.: Ruby Braff (cnt), Marshall Royal (as), Scott Hamilton (ts), George Masso (tb), Jay McShann (p), Gus Johnson (dm), Howard Alden (g), Jack Lesberg (b)
Wrap Your Troubles in Dreams
I Thought About You

I Cried for You
NOTE: A recording of these tunes is available but remains unissued.

3:30–3:55 p.m.: Ruby Braff (cnt), Kenny Davern (cl), Marshall Royal (as), Christian Plattner (Bar sax), George Masso (tb), Ralph Sutton (p), Gus Johnson (dm), Jack Lesberg (b)
Way Down Yonder in New Orleans
If I Could Be with You
Sugar*
NOTE: Recordings of two of these tunes are available but remain unissued. A recording of "Sugar" was not available at the time of publication and is marked with an asterisk.

9:40–10:15 p.m.: Ruby Braff (cnt), Howard Alden (g), Jack Lesberg (b), Scott Hamilton (ts), Urbie Green (tb), Marty Napoleon (p), Jake Hanna (dm)
Where's Freddie?
Them There Eyes*
NOTE: A recording of these tunes is available but remains unissued. Only a fragment of "Them There Eyes" was available at the time of publication and is marked with an asterisk. Other tunes were probably performed but not recorded.

12:00–12:30 a.m.: Ruby Braff (cnt), Kenny Davern (cl), Christian Plattner (ts), Urbie Green (tb), Dick Hyman (p), Butch Miles (dm), Marty Grosz (g), Milt Hinton (b)
I Would Do Anything for You
Old Man Time (Hinton solo)
Tea for Two
Goodnight Ladies
NOTE: This set closed the Saturday night performances. No recording of these tunes is available at the time of publication.

Sunday, September 18, 1988, Marriott Hotel, City Center, Minneapolis, Minnesota
5:30–6:00 p.m.: Ruby Braff (cnt), Scott Hamilton (ts), Kenny Davern (cl), Urbie Green (tb), Marty Napoleon (p), Jake Hanna (dm), Howard Alden (g), Jack Lesberg (b)
Linger Awhile
Body and Soul (Hamilton feature)
Dinah
NOTE: A recording of these tunes is available but remains unissued. No information is available about performances earlier in the day, either at this location or other sites. It is uncertain if the program began at with this performance.

8:35–9:05 p.m.: Ruby Braff (cnt), Ralph Sutton (p), Kenny Davern (cl), George Masso (tb), Christian Plattner (ts), Jake Hanna (dm), Milt Hinton (b)
Chinatown, My Chinatown
Honeysuckle Rose (Braff, Sutton, Davern feature)
Oh, Baby
NOTE: A recording of these tunes is available but remains unissued.

10:15 p.m. Final–Everyone
Rhythm starts the jam session: Marty Napoleon (p), Gus Johnson (dm), Milt Hinton (b), Howard Alden (g)
Jazz Party Blues
NOTE: A recording of these tunes is available but remains unissued.

Ruby did not appear at the Minneapolis Jazz Party in 1989. Scott Hamilton also recalled a jazz cruise program from about this time in 1988, but may be recalling events in 1984 or 1985 instead, when he participated with both Benny Carter and Ruby Braff; however, I make the following entry just in case other information surfaces in the future.

A Possible Jazz Cruise in 1988[1]
1988, S/S *Norway* (at sea) (one week cruises departing October 20 and 27, 1988)
Ruby Braff (cnt), Benny Carter (as), Scott Hamilton (ts), Bob Haggart (b)
NOTE: This is not listed in the 1988 Floating Jazz Festival Program or the second edition of the Carter discography, so the date must be incorrect. It is based on personal correspondence with Scott Hamilton. Scott may have been referring to Floating Jazz Festivals held in the years 1984–1986, or another cruise altogether, perhaps one he mentioned in an interview in 1989. The following bookings prevent Ruby participating in a cruise in late October or early November 1988.

Dick Hyman and Ruby Braff[2] **(see Figure 19.1)**
October 10, 17, 24, 1988, Fortune Garden Pavilion, 209 East 49th Street, New York
Ruby Braff (cnt), Dick Hyman (p)

At Fortune Garden, Braff and Hyman performed on Mondays while Ralph Sutton soloed for the rest of the week. There is an unresolved conflict in Ruby's performance on October 24, since he was also scheduled to appear at Zinno that day. Perhaps the Fortune Garden Pavilion performance ended earlier.

Ruby Braff Trio[3]
October 24–October 29, 1988, Zinno, 126 West 13th Street, New York
Ruby Braff (cnt), John Campbell (p), Jack Lesberg (b)

Ruby Braff Trio[4]
October 31–November 5, 1988, Zinno, 126 West 13th Street, New York
Ruby Braff (cnt), Gray Sargent (g), Michael Moore (b)

An advertisement for the following performance is available for Monday, November 7.

Ruby Braff and Dick Hyman[5]
November 7, 1988, Fortune Garden Pavilion, New York

Ruby Braff Trio[6]
December 19–24 and 26–31, 1988, Zinno, 126 West 13th Street, New York
Ruby Braff (cnt), Howard Alden (g), Jack Lesberg (b)

John S. Wilson wrote the following: "The cornetist Ruby Braff has found a base in New York during the past couple of years at Zinno, the excellent restaurant on the northern edge of Greenwich Village. He has become a regular there four or five times a year." Dates of some of his appearances at Zinno are reported in this book, but others remain unknown.

Ruby next returned to Europe to perform at the Bern Jazz Festival for the first time.

Newport Jazz Festival All Stars, Featuring Ruby Braff
April 29, 1989, Kursaal, Bern, Switzerland
Ruby Braff (cnt), Howard Alden, Gray Sargent (g), Eddie Jones (b), Oliver Jackson (dm)
Whispering
The Very Thought of You
Ghost of a Chance
You're a Lucky Guy

Add George Wein (p), Scott Hamilton (ts)
I Never Knew (incomplete)

Add Warren Vaché (cnt); Braff, Alden out
Blue and Sentimental
Just a Gigolo (Wein voc, Hamilton out on this number)

Add Norris Turney (as), and Ricky Ford (ts)
I Want to Be Happy
NOTE: A video recording of these tunes is available but remains unissued. Other tunes may have been included in this performance since the concert program also lists Norris Turney playing his clarinet. At the time of publication, all the tunes listed above are available from YouTube.com.

Ruby Braff Trio[7]
June 20, 1989, Mellon Jazz Festival, Academy of Music, Broad and Locust Streets, Philadelphia
Ruby Braff (cnt), Howard Alden (g), Jack Lesberg (b)

Ruby opened the concert and was followed by Nancy Wilson and Joe Williams. In an interview, Ruby is quoted as saying the following:

> I like the word *commercial*. I like money. Is Ella Fitzgerald commercial? Great! Wouldn't any jazz musician like to have a TV program for twenty-three years like Lawrence Welk?

Ruby Braff Interview
June 22, 1989, interview with Ron Della Chiesa, WGBM Radio, Boston
NOTE: A recording of this interview is available but remains unissued. Ruby refers to performing recently at Philadelphia and Pittsburgh with Carnegie Hall "next week" and at Saratoga upcoming with Howard Alden and Jack Lesberg. They also mention the upcoming appearance at the Boston Globe Jazz Festival.

Rosemary Clooney and Ruby Braff at the Boston Globe Jazz Festival[8]
June 23, 1989, Berkeley Performance Center, 136 Massachusetts Avenue, Boston (see Figure 19.2)
Ruby Braff (cnt), Gray Sargent (g), Whit Browne (b), Alan Dawson (dm)
Ruby opened the concert. Rosemary Clooney performed with John Oddo (p), Dave Fink (b), Joe Cocuzzo (dm), with special guests Warren Vaché (cnt) and Ken Peplowski (as, ts, cl). Preconcert publicity reports that Ruby would perform with Fink and Cocuzzo rather than Brown and Dawson.

Ruby had been appearing at the JVC Jazz Festival at Carnegie Hall in a variety of themed concerts for the past several years. This is a testament to both his artistry and ability to attract a loyal audience. This concert presented the music of Gershwin, Porter, Rodgers and Hart, Ellington, and others, performed by Rosemary Clooney, Dave Brubeck Quartet, Phil Woods Quintet, Ruby Braff Trio, Marian McPartland, Urbie Green, Warren Vaché, Jr., Ken Peplowski, Dave Frishberg, and Bobby Short as host. It was a benefit for the Duke Ellington Memorial Fund.

JVC Jazz Festival: *An Evening of Jazz and American Song*[9]
June 27, 1989, 8 p.m., Carnegie Hall, New York
The concert opened with Ruby Braff (cnt), Urbie Green (tb) and Howard Alden (g) performing songs by Irving Berlin.

Ruby also performed at Saratoga as part of the festival. The program included the Ray Charles Show '89, David Sanborn, Wynton Marsalis, Illinois Jacquet

Big Band, Michel Camilo Trio, Yellowjackets, Charles Mingus Super Band, Arthur Blythe Quartet, Tuck and Patti, Ruby Braff Quartet, Kent Jordan, Harper Brothers, Hot Club Quintette, and Jack Wilkins.

Ruby Braff Quartet: Newport Jazz at Saratoga[10]
July 1, 1989, noon to midnight, Saratoga Performing Arts Center, Saratoga Springs, New York
No further information is available about Ruby's performance.

In a letter dated July 2, 1989 to Mel Levine,[11] Ruby says, "I played Saratoga JVC the other day." Ruby's letter includes the following:

> This tragic disease of music is a strange thing. It's very thankless from a monetary point of view. The only reward is in the performer's heart. We play, paint, write, etc., because we have to!!

In this letter, Ruby triple underlined the word *have.* The exclamation points were both his.

Ruby Braff and Dick Hyman: *Music from My Fair Lady*
July 1989, Penny Lane Studios, New York
Ruby Braff (cnt) Dick Hyman (p)
Wouldn't It Be Loverly
    Concord Jazz CCD 4393 (CD), Snapper Music SMDCD 271 (CD)
With a Little Bit of Luck (version 1)
    Concord Jazz CCD 4393 (CD)
With a Little Bit of Luck (version 2)
    Concord Jazz CCD 4393 (CD)
I'm an Ordinary Man
    Concord Jazz CCD 4393 (CD)
The Rain in Spain
    Concord Jazz CCD 4393 (CD)
I Could Have Danced All Night
    Concord Jazz CCD 4393 (CD)
Ascot Gavotte
    Concord Jazz CCD 4393 (CD)
On the Street Where You Live
    Concord Jazz CCD 4393 (CD)
Show Me
    Concord Jazz CCD 4393 (CD)
Get Me to the Church on Time
    Concord Jazz CCD 4393 (CD), Snapper Music SMDCD 271 (CD)
Without You
    Concord Jazz CCD 4393 (CD)

I've Grown Accustomed to Her Face
Concord Jazz CCD 4393 (CD)
NOTE: All titles also on Concord Jazz CJ 393 (LP). The Snapper CD release is a reissue of tunes from various Concord Jazz releases and is titled *I'm Shooting High.*

Newport 1989[12]
Newport All Stars
August 18, 1989, Newport Casino, Newport, Rhode Island—broadcast on Public Television
Ruby Braff (cnt), Urbie Green (tb), Ken Peplowski (ts), George Wein (p, voc), Gray Sargent (g), Eddie Jones (b), Oliver Jackson (dm)
Them There Eyes (Braff and Wein solos featured)
You've Changed (Green feature)*
Nobody Knows You When You're Down and Out (Wein, voc)*
NOTE: "Them There Eyes" was broadcast on Public Television in a program titled *Newport 1989*. The broadcast program also included other artists from this year of the festival. A video VHS tape of performances from Newport 1989, including "Them There Eyes" was distributed by JVC and labeled *not for sale*. Recordings of the other two tunes are not available to the author at the time of publication and they are each marked with an asterisk.

Grande Parade du Jazz: Nice Jazz Festival (probably an error in the published date)[13]
July 1989, Nice, France
A photograph showing Ruby with Vic Dickenson is credited to Nice in 1989; however, there is no indication that Ruby appeared that year. The photo probably dates to their performance together at Nice in 1979. It appears that Ruby did not travel to Europe in 1989 for any engagements.

Jazz Cruise[14]
This is listed here only as a possible, but unlikely, appearance sometime in 1989. There is no further information available beyond Scott Hamilton's mention of a jazz cruise that probably occurred earlier, perhaps during their documented appearances together in 1984 and 1985.

Heavenly Jazz[15]
October 22, 1989, 5 p.m., Church of the Heavenly Rest, 5th Avenue at 90th Street, New York
Ruby Braff (cnt), Dick Hyman (p)
This concert opened the season for this series.

All-Star Tribute to George Wein[16]
November 12, 1989, 5 p.m., St. Peter's Church, Lexington Avenue at 54th Street, New York

Musicians included Lionel Hampton, Howard Alden, Ruby Braff, Jimmy Heath, George Shearing, and others.

Ruby Braff Quartet[17]
December 26–31, 1989, Fortune Garden Pavilion, 209 East 49th Street, New York
Ruby Braff (cnt), Howard Alden (g), and Jack Lesberg (b) and adding Stephen Asch and Richard Wyands (p) on Friday and Saturday December 30 and 31 only

Ruby Braff and Dick Hyman: *Younger than Swingtime: Music from South Pacific*
June 12 and 13, 1990, Penny Lane Studios, New York
Ruby Braff (cnt) Dick Hyman (p)
Bali Ha'i (version #1)
Concord Jazz CCD 4445 (CD)
Some Enchanted Evening
Concord Jazz CCD 4445 (CD)
Cockeyed Optimist
Concord Jazz CCD 4445 (CD)
A Wonderful Guy
Concord Jazz CCD 4445 (CD)
Happy Talk
Concord Jazz CCD 4445 (CD), Snapper Music SMDCD 271 (CD)
Dites-moi
Concord Jazz CCD 4445 (CD)
This Nearly Was Mine
Concord Jazz CCD 4445 (CD), CCD 4833-2
There Is Nothing Like a Dame (solo p)
Concord Jazz CCD 4445 (CD)
Honeybun
Concord Jazz CCD 4445 (CD)
Younger than Springtime
Concord Jazz CCD 4445 (CD), Snapper Music SMDCD 271 (CD)
Bali Ha'i (final version)
Concord Jazz CCD 4445 (CD)
NOTE: Concord Jazz CCD 4833-2 is titled *Ruby Braff: The Concord Jazz Heritage Series*. The Snapper release is a reissue of tunes from various Concord Jazz releases. "Dites-moi" can be translated as "Tell Me."

Piano Spectacular: JVC Jazz Festival[18]
June 23, 1990, noon to 6 p.m., Waterloo Village, Stanhope, New Jersey,
Dick Hyman, Dave McKenna, Derek Smith, Roger Kellaway, Neville Dickie, Jane Jarvis, Barry Harris, Sir Charles Thompson, Bob Haggart, Ed Polcer, Flip Phillips, Ken Peplowski, Bobby Gordon, Ronnie Bedford, George Masso, Jake

Hanna, Howard Alden, Ruby Braff, Jack Lesberg, Randy Sandke, and Kenny Davern

Ken Franckling photographed Ruby at an unknown JVC Jazz Festival event.[19] This photo appears on the webpage that celebrates the 2004 inductees into the New England Jazz Hall of Fame. The text includes references to Ruby's leading a performance that was a tribute to Bobby Hackett held April 9, 2002.

JVC Jazz Festival: ***An Evening of American Song***[20]
June 27, 1990, Town Hall, 123 West 43rd Street, New York
Ruby Braff (cnt), Dick Hyman (p)
Songs from *My Fair Lady* followed by songs by Fats Waller and James P. Johnson, including "Handful of Keys"

Braff and Hyman followed Barbara Lea with Keith Ingham on the first half of the program. Gerry Mulligan concluded the program with his quartet. Braff and Hyman's performance included songs from *My Fair Lady* and compositions by Fats Waller, including "Handful of Keys."

John S. Wilson wrote the following: "Mr. Braff showed his virtuosity by getting through a fast-fingered chorus on cornet before Mr. Hyman gave it his authoritative Waller piano touch."[21]

After the JVC Festival, Ruby traveled to Canada and on to France. He did not perform in Europe in 1989.

Ruby Braff and Dick Hyman: Festival International de Jazz de Montreal[22]
July 7, 1990, Montreal
Ruby Braff (cnt), Dick Hyman (p)
Songs from *My Fair Lady*
Sugar
I Want to Be Happy
I Want a Little Girl

The Alden–Barrett Quintet with Guest Ruby Braff: Grande Parade du Jazz: Nice Jazz Festival:
July 11, 1990, 7:30 p.m., Nice, France
Ruby Braff (cnt), Dan Barrett (tb), Chuck Wilson (as), Howard Alden (g), Frank Tate (b), Jackie Williams (dm)
Big Butter and Egg Man
NOTE: A recording of this tune is available but remains unissued.

The Alden–Barrett Quintet with Guest Ruby Braff: Grande Parade du Jazz: Nice Jazz Festival:
July 12, 1990, 10 p.m., Arena Stage, Nice, France

Dan Barrett (tb), Chuck Wilson (as), Howard Alden (g), Frank Tate (b), Jackie Williams (dm)
Up Jumped You with Love
Chelsea Bridge (Barrett feature)

Ruby Braff (cnt) replaces Barrett, Wilson, and Williams
Blueberry Hill (only about eight bars)
No One Else But You
God Bless the Child

Add Jackie Williams
Miss Brown to You

Chuck Wilson (as) returns
On the Sunny Side of the Street

Dan Barrett (tb) returns
Dinah (incomplete)
Basin Street Blues
NOTE: A recording of these tunes is available but remains unissued. Ruby's few bars of "Blueberry Hill" are blown as a reaction to the overamplified sound carrying over from the adjacent Dance Stage performance by Dave Bartholomew (tp) and his band.

Ruby Braff Quartet: Grande Parade du Jazz: Nice Jazz Festival
July 13, 1990, 8:30 p.m., Garden Stage, Nice, France
Ruby Braff (cnt), Ronnell Bright (p), Eddie Jones (b), Oliver Jackson (dm)
Just You, Just Me
Them There Eyes
Blues in F
Medley:
  I Got It Bad and That Ain't Good
  Take the "A" Train
NOTE: A recording of the first two tunes is available but remains unissued. The following performances were probably not recorded.

Ruby Braff and Clark Terry: Grande Parade du Jazz: Nice Jazz Festival[23]
July 14, 1990, 7:00 p.m., Garden Stage, Nice, France
Ruby Braff (cnt), Clark Terry (tp), Ronnell Bright (p), Steve Novosel (b), Craig McIver (dm)

Following his performances at Nice, Ruby returned to London to resume his July residency at Pizza on the Park. It has been two years since his previously appearances there with Scott Hamilton in 1987.

Ruby Braff Trio[24]
July 1990, Pizza on the Park, Knightsbridge, London
Ruby Braff (cnt), Howard Alden (g), Frank Tate (b)

First Set on Closing Night of the Engagement:
Them There Eyes*
As Long As I Live
In a Sentimental Mood
Ain't Misbehavin'*
Do It Again
Fine and Dandy*
Here's Carl
Closing Theme

Second Set on Closing Night of the Engagement:
Three Little Words
Medley:
  Wouldn't It Be Loverly?
  I've Grown Accustomed to Her Face
Medley:
  Make Believe
  Old Man River
Braff out:
Tears
That Old Feeling
Braff Returns:
Nancy (With the Laughing Face)
'S Wonderful
Medley:
  You're Sensational
  Samantha (Tate feature)
  True Love (Alden feature)
Montage:
  That's My Home
  Sweet Georgia Brown
  Mood Indigo
  Misty
When It's Sleepy Time Down South
Love Me or Leave Me
NOTE: A video recording of these tunes is available but remains unissued. Titles marked with an asterisk are incomplete in that recording. *The Spectator* published a review from an earlier night, mentioning the following tunes played:
Nancy (With the Laughing Face)
Ain't Misbehavin'
Tea for Two

When It's Sleepy Time Down South

Radio Interview
July 1990, London
NOTE: A recording of this interview is available but remains unissued. The interviewer mentions that "tomorrow is the last night" for Ruby's engagement at Pizza on the Park.

I have been unable to discover the dates for Ruby's above engagement at Pizza on the Park; however, they probably began on Saturday, July 15, to capitalize on weekend attendance. If Ruby performed there for two weeks, he would have closed on Saturday, July 29, in time to fly to Los Angeles with Howard Alden for their next appearance at the Hollywood Bowl.

Hollywood Bowl: *Salute to Louis Armstrong*[25]
August 1, 1990, Hollywood Bowl, Los Angeles
Ruby Braff (cnt), Howard Alden (g), Gerry Wiggins (p)
Pennies from Heaven
The program also featured Wynton Marsalis and Doc Cheatham. Emcee was Ossie Davis. Attendance was 15,061.

Newport Jazz Festival: *Salute to Louis Armstrong*[26]
August 17, 1990, Newport Casino, Newport, Rhode Island
Ruby Braff (cnt), Doc Cheatham, Wynton Marsalis, Jon Faddis (tp), Eric Reed (p), Herlin Riley (dm), Reginald Veal (b), Carrie Smith (voc), Ossie Davis hosting—produced by Wynton Marsalis
Struttin' with Some Barbecue (Cheatham and Faddis feature)
Jubilee (featuring all four brass)
Big Butter and Egg Man (Carrie Smith, voc)
Other details unknown

A review in the *Boston Globe* reported the following: "And the version of 'Jubilee,' featuring Cheatham, Marsalis, Faddis, and Ruby Braff, was a joy, full of humor and passion. A tip of the hat to bassist Reginald Veal and drummer Herlin Riley, two of Marsalis' band members. They swung hard all night long."[27]

Ruby was heard performing on the soundtrack of the motion picture *Billy Bathgate.* The film was released in 1991. Ruby does not appear on camera in the film and the film only uses a portion of 'Bye Bye Blackbird.' Ruby is heard playing obligattos behind Rachel York and for the opening portion of his solo. The complete film is available on various commercial releases.[28] The soundtrack CD contains the complete performance of the tune. It is a fine performance that has escaped the attention of Ruby's fans who are generally aware of other collaborations between Dick Hyman and Ruby Braff.

Billy Bathgate
1990, New York, film was released during 1991
Dick Hyman (p, arr), Ruby Braff (cnt), Frank Wess (ts), Howard Alden (g), Jack Lesberg (b), unknown (dm), Rachel York (voc)
Bye Bye Blackbird
    Milan 73138 35611-2 (CD)
NOTE: Ruby does not play on other tunes from the soundtrack.

A photo from the March of Jazz program is attributed to the early 1990s and shows Ruby Braff with George Segal (bjo) performing at the Blue Note in New York to celebrate the rerelease of Segal's album *Touch of Ragtime* by the Imperial Jazz Band; however, Ruby does not appear on that album.[29]

Ruby's comment about the following recording session was simply, "She is a very nice lady."

Teresa Brewer and Friends: Memories of Louis
January 15, 1991, New York
Ruby Braff (cnt), Nicholas Payton, Freddie Hubbard (tps), Clark Terry (flgh), John Hicks (p), Cecil McBee (b), Grady Tate (dm)
I'm Confessin'
    Red Baron AK 48629 (CD)
Ain't Misbehavin'
    Red Baron AK 48629 (CD)
Wrap Your Troubles in Dreams
    Red Baron AK 48629 (CD)
Star Dust
    Red Baron AK 48629 (CD)
NOTE: Other sessions included on this album do not include Ruby Braff. Ruby is only clearly audible on "Wrap Your Troubles in Dreams."

Ruby and Dick Hyman appeared at the Montreal International Jazz Festival, and their performance was broadcast on CBC-FM's program *Jazz Beat* at 8:05 p.m. on a delayed broadcast from a few days earlier

Ruby Braff and Dick Hyman at the Montreal International Jazz Festival
January 26, 1991, Montreal
Ruby Braff (cnt), Dick Hyman (p)
I Want to Be Happy*
Wouldn't It Be Loverly
Dinah
Judy Garland Medley:
  Love Walked In
  Over the Rainbow
  If I Only Had a Brain
  The Man I Love
  Lady Be Good

NOTE: A recording of these tunes is available but remains unissued. The version of "I Want to Be Happy" is incomplete and is marked with an asterisk.

Ruby Braff Trio[30]
February 20–24,1991, Cates, 4200 Wisconsin Avenue, Washington, D.C.
Ruby Braff (cnt), Howard Alden (g), Frank Tate (b)
From the interview, Ruby closed on a Sunday night following what was probably a weeklong engagement.

Ruby Braff Radio Interview with Rob Bamberger
March 2, 1991 (a Saturday night), WAMU Radio, Washington, D.C.
Rob Bamberger interviewed Ruby Braff
NOTE: A recording of this interview is available but remains unissued. Ruby reports an upcoming engagement at the 92nd Street YMCA, so that fixes the date of the interview.

Advertisements exist for the following performance along with a printed program.

Jazz Piano at the Y[31] **(see Figure 19.3)**
March 9, 1991, 8 p.m., 92nd Street YMCA, Kaufmann Concert Hall, New York
Ruby Braff (cnt), Dick Hyman (p)
NOTE: The program consisted of improvisations from *My Fair Lady*, *South Pacific*, and other Broadway musicals.

Jimmy McPartland's Funeral[32]
March 1991 (Following his death March 13), Church of the Heavenly Rest, 5th Avenue and 90th Street, New York
Ruby Braff (cnt), Marian McPartland (p), James Chirillo (g)
Jimmy died on March 13, 1991, and Ruby played at Marian McPartland's request.
These Foolish Things
Other selections are unknown.

A photo from the March of Jazz program is available.[33]

Ruby Braff: *Cornet Chop Suey*
March 27–28, 1991, Penny Lane Studios, New York
Ruby Braff (cnt), Howard Alden (g), Frank Tate (b), Ken Peplowski (cl), Ronnie Zito (dm)
Cornet Chop Suey
    Concord Jazz CCD 4606
Nancy (With the Laughing Face)
    Concord Jazz CCD 4606

Ooh, That Kiss
    Concord Jazz CCD 4606
Do It Again
    Concord Jazz CCD 4606
Love Me or Leave Me
    Concord Jazz CCD 4606, Snapper Music SMDCD 271 (CD)
It's the Same Old South
    Concord Jazz CCD 4606
It Had to Be You
    Concord Jazz CCD 4606
I Must Have That Man
    Concord Jazz CCD 4606
Sweet and Slow
    Concord Jazz CCD 4606
Shoe Shine Boy
    Concord Jazz CCD 4606, CCD 4833-2, Snapper Music SMDCD 271 (CD)
High Society Medley
  You're Sensational
    Concord Jazz CCD 4606
  I Love You, Samantha
    Concord Jazz CCD 4606
  True Love
    Concord Jazz CCD 4606
Lover Come Back to Me
    Concord Jazz CCD 4606

NOTE: Concord Jazz CCD 4833-2 is titled *Ruby Braff: The Concord Jazz Heritage Series*. The Snapper CD release is a reissue of tunes from various Concord Jazz releases and is titled *I'm Shooting High*.

The New Orleans Jazz & Heritage Festival opened April 26. Heavy rain continued from the previous day. Ruby first performed with Doc Cheatham.

Later that day, Ruby performed in a program led by Wynton Marsalis. Two tunes are preserved in video recordings. "Jeepers Creepers" is the only Braff performance included in a television broadcast that was aired on the Arts and Entertainment Network in 1992 as *New Orleans Live!* That program was produced by Chris Blackwell and Liz Heller for Delilah Music Pictures. "Rockin' Chair" is the only Braff performance included on a program issued on a laserdisc titled *New Orleans Live! Jazz* and credited to the same producers in association with Island Visual Arts. It is unknown if Ruby Braff performed any other selections during this concert. Other musicians performing during this concert included Doc Cheatham, Teddy Riley, Greg Stafford, Dr. Michael White, Freddy Lonzo, Nicholas Payton, and Thais Clark. The concert was hosted by Ed Bradley. The program was broadcast in New York on July 21, 1992.

Ruby Braff and Doc Cheatham[34]
April 26, 1991, beginning at 4:26 p.m., New Orleans Jazz & Heritage Festival, Mars, Inc. Jazz Tent, Fairgrounds, New Orleans
Ruby Braff and Doc Cheatham, other musicians unknown

Wynton Marsalis and Friends: *A Tribute to Louis Armstrong*[35]
April 26, 1991, 9:00 p.m., New Orleans Jazz & Heritage Festival, Theater of the Performing Arts, New Orleans
Ruby Braff (cnt), Howard Alden (g), Danny Barker (bjo), Ellis Marsalis (p), Don Vappie (b), Herlin Riley (dm)
Jeepers Creepers
    Unissued, video recording available
Rockin' Chair
    Video Arts (J) Laserdisc VALJ 3344

Ruby Braff: *Ruby Braff and His New England Songhounds, Volume 1*
April 29, 1991, Penny Lane Studios, New York
Ruby Braff (cnt), Scott Hamilton (ts), Howard Alden (g), Dave McKenna (p), Frank Tate (b), Alan Dawson (dm)
I'm Crazy 'Bout My Baby
    Concord Jazz CCD 4478 (CD), Snapper Music SMDCD 271 (CD)
Blue and Sentimental
    Concord Jazz CCD 4478 (CD), CCD 4833-2
This Can't Be Love
    Concord Jazz CCD 4478 (CD)
Thankful
    Concord Jazz CCD 4478 (CD)
Sho-Time
    Concord Jazz CCD 4478 (CD)
My Shining Hour
    Concord Jazz CCD 4478 (CD), Snapper Music SMDCD 271 (CD)
Days of Wine and Roses
    Concord Jazz CCD 4478 (CD), 4791 (CD)
Down in Honky Tonk Town
    Concord Jazz CCD 4478 (CD)
Tell Me More
    Concord Jazz CCD 4478 (CD)
These Foolish Things Remind Me of You
    Concord Jazz CCD 4478 (CD)
More Than You Know
    Concord Jazz CCD 4478 (CD)
Every Time We Say Goodbye
    Concord Jazz CCD 4478 (CD)

NOTE: Concord Jazz 4791 is titled *Swingin' Jazz for Hipsters, Volume 1.* The Snapper CD release is a reissue of tunes from various Concord Jazz releases and is titled *I'm Shooting High.*

Ruby Braff: *Ruby Braff and His New England Songhounds, Volume 2*
April 30, 1991, Penny Lane Studios, New York
Ruby Braff (cnt), Scott Hamilton (ts), Howard Alden (g), Dave McKenna (p), Frank Tate (b), Alan Dawson (dm)
Indian Summer
 Concord Jazz CCD 4504 (CD), P-27478, Snapper Music SMDCD 271 (CD)
Thousand Islands
 Concord Jazz CCD 4504 (CD), P-27478
What's New?
 Concord Jazz CCD 4504 (CD), P-27478
Heartaches
 Concord Jazz CCD 4504 (CD), P-27478
Cabin in the Sky
 Concord Jazz CCD 4504 (CD), P-27478, CCD 4833-2
You're a Sweetheart
 Concord Jazz CCD 4504 (CD), P-27478, Snapper Music SMDCD 271 (CD)
Please
 Concord Jazz CCD 4504 (CD), P-27478
All Alone
 Concord Jazz CCD 4504 (CD), P-27478
Lullaby of Birdland
 Concord Jazz CCD 4504 (CD), P-27478
Nice Work If You Can Get It
 Concord Jazz CCD 4504 (CD), P-27478, 4519 (CD)
As Time Goes By
 Concord Jazz CCD 4504 (CD), P-27478, 4959 (CD)
Keepin' Out of Mischief Now
 Concord Jazz CCD 4504 (CD), P-27478, CCD 4907-2
 Reprise 9 47608-2
NOTE: Concord Jazz 4519 is titled *Gershwin Songbook.* Concord Jazz CCD 4833-2 is titled *Ruby Braff: The Concord Jazz Heritage Series*. Concord Jazz CCD 4907 is titled *Jazz at the 19th Hole.* Concord Jazz CCD 4959 is titled *An Era Remembered from Pearl Harbor to VJ Day.* Reprise 9 47608-2 is titled *Music from the Motion Picture Soundtrack Recording: The Story of Us*. This performance is heard in the movie's soundtrack and included on this CD. The complete motion picture is available on DVD on Universal 20711. The closing credits list Ruby Braff and His New England Songhounds. P-27478 is AFRTS basic musical library, P series. The Snapper CD release is a reissue of tunes from various Concord Jazz releases and is titled *I'm Shooting High.*

It is said that all good things must end, and certainly Ruby's performances were featured with Carl Jefferson's support at Concord Jazz Records. But in life it is not always the case that good fortune calls again, especially when it does so without delay. For in 1993, Ruby found another champion in Mat Domber and Arbors Records.

Ruby moved from New York to Cape Cod in 1991.[36] He reported in a 1994 interview with Steve Voce that he had moved "about four years ago" and that Dave McKenna now lived about a half mile from his home. This was probably prompted by the declining opportunities to perform in Manhattan clubs.

Ruby Braff Tour(with Howard Alden and Frank Tate)[37]
May 4, 1991, The Old Dot, Cambridge, England (with Alden and Tate)
May 5, 1991, Alhambra Studio, Bradford, West Yorkshire, England (details unknown)
May 6, 1991, Grand Hotel, Birmingham, England (details unknown)
May 7, 1991, The Pavilion, Hemel Hempstead, England (20 miles northwest of London), (with Howard Alden (g), Frank Tate (b))

Ruby Braff Trio
May 8, 1991, Bull's Head Pub, Barnes, Southwest London
Ruby Braff (cnt), Howard Alden (g), Frank Tate (b)
Rose Room
Liza
Sugar
When I Fall in Love
You're a Lucky Guy
If I Could Be with You One Hour Tonight
Where's Freddie?
Medley:
  Don't Get Around Much Anymore
  I Got It Bad and That Ain't Good
Do It Again
Medley:
  Body and Soul
  As Long As I Live
Medley:
  Melancholia (Ruby out)
  Dancers in Love (Ruby out)
Keepin' Out of Mischief Now
Medley:
  You're a Sweetheart
  It's Only a Paper Moon

Conversation with his UK fans
NOTE: A recording of these tunes is available but remains unissued. During the conversation Ruby plays a few bars of "'S Wonderful" on piano as he thanks his fans for attending the performance

Ruby Braff Tour[38]
May 9, 1991, Elmwood Hall, Belfast, Northern Ireland
Howard Alden (g) and Frank Tate (b)

Ruby Braff Sextet[39]
May 10, 1991, City Hall, Belfast, Northern Ireland (dance date)
Ruby Braff (cnt), Roy Williams (tb), Bruce Turner (as), Howard Alden (g), Brian Lemon (p), Frank Tate (b), Allan Ganley (dm)
But Not for Me
Dream Dancing
Days of Wine and Roses
Muskrat Ramble (ending first set)
Medley:
  Love Walked In
  My Melancholy Baby
I Found a New Baby
Medley:
  Embraceable You
  Way Down Yonder in New Orleans
A Pretty Girl Is Like a Melody
Rose Room
Medley:
  When It's Sleepy Time Down South
  Too-Ra-Loo-Ra-Loo-Ra
  When Irish Eyes Are Smiling (ending second set)
Rosetta (encore)
NOTE: A recording of these tunes is available but remains unissued.

Roy Williams spoke of this engagement:[40]

> We had a wonderful night in Belfast with a sextet led by Ruby Braff when Ruby announced 'Allan Gainley' on drums! He's since become one of Allan's biggest fans but then he barely knew him. What a night that was! I'll never forget that. We all thought it was going to be a concert, and if I remember we were all wearing evening dress. It turned out to be a dance in the city hall and it had bad echo. But by golly, what a band!

Ruby Braff Trio[41]
May 11, 1991, Royal Marine Hotel, Dun Laoghaire, Co. Dublin, Republic of Ireland
Ruby Braff (cnt), Howard Alden (g), Frank Tate (b)

Ruby Braff Trio[42]
May 12, 1991, All Saints' Church Hall, Woking, Surrey, England (20 miles southwest of London)
Ruby Braff (cnt), Howard Alden (g), and Frank Tate (b)

The 100 Club
May 13, 1991, London
Ruby Braff (cnt), Howard Alden (g), Frank Tate (b)
Where's Freddie?
Sweethearts on Parade (Ruby also plays a few chords on piano)
Do It Again
Dream Dancing

Add Roy Williams, Jim Shepherd (tb), Bruce Turner (as), Brian Lemon (p), Jack Parnell (dm)
Lady Be Good
These Foolish Things

Out Williams, Shepherd, Turner, Lemon, Parnell
The Very Thought of You
Brief Medley of Requests
Isn't It Romantic
Old Man River

Add Roy Williams, Jim Shepherd (tb), Bruce Turner (as), Brian Lemon (p), Jack Parnell (dm)
Big Butter and Egg Man

Out Williams, Shepherd, Turner, Lemon, Parnell
Medley:
  If You Were Mine
  I Wished on the Moon

Add: Roy Williams, Jim Shepherd (tb), Bruce Turner (as), Brian Lemon (p), Jack Parnell (dm)
Closing Medley:
  White Christmas*
  Santa Claus Is Coming to Town*
NOTE: The available recording does not include the closing melody so both tunes are marked with an asterisk. The recording remains unissued.

Ruby Braff Tour (with Howard Alden and Frank Tate)[43]
May 14, 1991, scheduled performance was cancelled, Middlesex Polytechnic, Bounds Green, North London
May 15, 1991, Concorde Club, Eastleigh, Hants (northeast of Southampton), England

Ruby Braff: *Live at University College School / As Time Goes By*
May 16, 1991, University College School, Frognal, Hampstead, North London (Frognal is the name of the street where the school is located)
Ruby Braff (cnt), Howard Alden (g), Frank Tate (b)
Shoe Shine Boy
    CZ 01, Candid CCD 79741 (CD), Jazz Classix JC 98023
Lonely Moments
    CZ 01, Candid CCD 79741 (CD)
This Is All I Ask
    CZ 01, Candid CCD 79741 (CD)
Love Me or Leave Me
    CZ 01, Candid CCD 79741 (CD)
Liza
    CZ 01, Candid CCD 79741 (CD)
As Long As I Live
    CZ 01, Candid CCD 79741 (CD)
I'm Through with Love (Ruby out)
    unissued, recording available
Jeepers Creepers
    CZ 01, Candid CCD 79741 (CD)
My Shining Hour
    CZ 01, Candid CCD 79741 (CD), Jazz Classix JC 98023
Sugar
    CZ 01, Candid CCD 79741 (CD), Jazz Classix JC 98023
As Time Goes By
    CZ 01, Candid CCD 79741 (CD), Jazz Classix JC 98023
Linger Awhile
    CZ 01, Candid CCD 79741 (CD), Jazz Classix JC 98023
Charlie Chaplin Medley:
  Smile
    CZ 01
  La Violettera
    CZ 01
Black Beauty (Ruby out)
    unissued, recording available
Dancers in Love (Ruby out)
    unissued, recording available

Basin Street Blues
CZ 01, Candid CCD 79741 (CD), Jazz Classix JC 98023
High Society Medley:
You're Sensational
CZ 01, Candid CCD 79741 (CD), Jazz Classix JC 98023
I Love You, Samantha
CZ 01, Candid CCD 79741 (CD), Jazz Classix JC 98023
True Love
CZ 01, Candid CCD 79741 (CD), Jazz Classix JC 98023
Medley:
White Christmas
CZ 01
Santa Claus Is Coming to Town
CZ 01
I've Grown Accustomed to Her Face
CZ 01
NOTE: CZ 01 is a cassette tape sold only at Ruby Braff's personal appearances, titled *Live at University College School.* It contains the entire trio performance of that concert. The songs are listed in the order of original performance. Candid CCD 79741 is a reissue of a large portion of that tape, titled *As Time Goes By.* Jazz Classix JC 98023 is a budget CD that also includes several performances from the PediMega LP and cassette. It is titled *Ruby Braff Plays Standards and Evergreens.* "La Violettera" ("Who'll Buy My Violets") is the song from Charlie Chaplin's feature film *City Lights* that played as the tramp bought the blind girl's violets. "This Is All I Ask" also appears on a four-CD anthology titled *Simply Jazz* on Simply 698458240125.

Ruby Braff Trio[44]
May 17, 1991, Stables Theater, Wavendon, England (near Milton Keynes, Buckinghamshire, about 30 miles northwest of London)
Howard Alden (g) and Frank Tate (b)

Bull's Head Pub
May 18, 1991, Barnes, Southwest London
Ruby Braff (cnt), Howard Alden (g), Frank Tate (b)
Lonely Moments
Blue Turning Grey Over You
Whispering
You're a Lucky Guy
Watch What Happens
Once Upon a Time
Dinah
I'll Never Be the Same (Ruby out)*
Keepin' Out of Mischief Now
Wrap Your Troubles in Dreams

Body and Soul
Between the Devil and the Deep Blue Sea
Medley of Requests:
  Tangerine
  Summertime
  Star Dust
  Skylark
  On the Sunny Side of the Street
  Misty
  Tea for Two
God Bless the Child
No Moon at All (Ruby out)*
Medley:
  If You Were Mine
  I Wished on the Moon
Conversation with Fans
NOTE: A recording of these tunes is available but remains unissued. In addition a video recording of "Wrap Your Troubles in Dreams" is also available. Two incomplete recordings during this performance are marked with an asterisk. The final medley may come from another occasion.

Ruby next performed at the JVC Jazz Festival at Town Hall. The program theme for 1991 was a tribute to Doc Cheatham. The program included eight trumpeters including Ruby Braff (cnt), Doc Cheatham, Dizzy Gillespie, Harry "Sweets" Edison, Jon Faddis, Wynton Marsalis, Byron Stripling, and Marcus Belgrave, along with the following musicians: George Wein, Buddy Tate, Al Grey, Britt Woodman, Cyrus Chestnut, Howard Alden, Eddie Jones, Oliver Jackson, Michael Hashim, Joey Cavaseno, Chuck Folds, Bucky Calabrese, Jackie Williams, Arvell Shaw, and Wycliffe Gordon. The evening's host was Phil Schaap.

JVC Jazz Festival: Tribute to Doc Cheatham[45]
June 24, 1991, 8 p.m., Town Hall, 123 West 43d Street, New York
Undecided (Faddis, Stripling, Marsalis, Cavaseno, Hashim, Chestnut, Alden, Jones, Jackson)
West End Blues (Faddis, Stripling)
Yesterdays
St. James Infirmary (Woodman, Grey)
Jumpin' at the Woodside (Tate, Woodman, Gray)
I've Got a Feeling I'm Falling (Cheatham, Folds, Calabrese, Williams)
I Double Dare You (Cheatham, Folds, Calabrese, Williams)
My Buddy (same plus Cavaseno)
The Man I Love (Braff with Alden and Wein)
Tour de Force (Faddis, Striping, Marsalis, Edison, Gillespie, Belgrave)
King Porter Stomp (Marsalis, Gordon, Shaw)

I Can't Get Started (Gillespie, Faddis)
Lover Man (Edison)

Additional tunes were performed by Ruby Braff, who was then joined by all musicians present for the following selections:
Struttin' with Some Barbecue
I Guess I'll Get the Papers and Go Home (Cheatham)

Lenny Solomon stated that he phoned Ruby and they had a very pleasant conversation. Ruby then agreed to join the next recording session. In personal conversations, Ruby told me that Lenny was a nice young kid and he just decided to help him. Given Ruby's insistence on controlling the selection of musicians and tunes, this was quite unusual. But Ruby was also a champion of young musicians who demonstrated commitment to their art. During their time together, Lenny said Ruby referred to the United States being "at war" with Canada. This might refer to Ruby's memory of an immigration incident in July 1978 when he was denied entry to Canada.

Lenny Solomon: *After You've Gone*[46]
June or July, 1991, Toronto
Ruby Braff (cnt), Lenny Solomon (v), Bob Fenton (p), Reg Schwager (g), Shelly Berger (b), Jerry Fuller (dm)
After You've Gone (BF out)
    Bay Cities BCD 2005, Jazz Inspiration Records JID 9316
Georgia on My Mind
    Bay Cities BCD 2005, Jazz Inspiration Records JID 9316
I Found a Million Dollar Baby
    Bay Cities BCD 2005, Jazz Inspiration Records JID 9316
I Found a New Baby
    Bay Cities BCD 2005, Jazz Inspiration Records JID 9316
NOTE: Other performances from this date do not include Ruby Braff.

Ruby returned to England in July or August for a series of performances. I have been unable to trace a date for his engagement with the Concord All Stars, so it is arbitrarily listed first.

Concord All Stars[47]
Summer 1991, Unicorn Hotel, Bristol, England

First Half of Concert:
Scott Hamilton (ts), Dave McKenna (p), Jake Hanna (dm)
But Not for Me
Skylark
Tickle Toe
Chelsea Bridge

Second Half of Concert:
Ruby Braff (cnt), Howard Alden (g), Frank Tate (b)
Ooh, That Kiss
Do It Again
That's My Home

Add Scott Hamilton (ts), Dave McKenna (p), Jake Hanna (dm)
This Can't Be Love
Blue and Sentimental
Just You, Just Me (interpolating Bye, Bye Blackbird)

Concorde Club
August 14, 1991, Eastleigh, Hampshire, England
Scott Hamilton (ts), Dave McKenna (p), Jake Hanna (dm)
A Beautiful Friendship
Medley:
  This Is All I Ask
  Cherokee
Long Ago and Far Away

Same location and date
Ruby Braff (cnt), Howard Alden (g), Frank Tate (b)
It's the Same Old South
I Must Have That Man
This Is All I Ask
Whispering

Ruby Braff (cnt), Scott Hamilton (ts), Dave McKenna (p), Howard Alden (g), Frank Tate (b), Jake Hanna (dm)
Jeepers Creepers
Days of Wine and Roses
Blue and Sentimental
Secret Love (McKenna with rhythm)
Black Beauty (Alden, Tate, Hanna only)
Chelsea Bridge (Hamilton feature, Braff out)
Dream Dancing
Take the "A" Train
NOTE: A recording of these tunes is available but remains unissued.

Ruby Braff Trio with Guests: Brecon Jazz Festival
August 16, 1991, 8 p.m., The Market Hall, Brecon, Wales,
Ruby Braff (cnt), Howard Alden (g), Frank Tate (b)
Just You, Just Me
Yesterdays

Where's Freddie?
When I Fall in Love
You're a Lucky Guy
Old Folks

Add guests Yank Lawson (tp), Scott Hamilton (ts), Dave McKenna (p), Jake Hanna (dm)
Wrap Your Troubles in Dreams
Ain't Misbehavin'
Muskrat Ramble
NOTE: A recording of these tunes is available but remains unissued.

Ruby Braff Trio: *Live at Brecon Jazz 1991*[48]
August 17, 1991, Christ College, Brecon, Wales, United Kingdom, 3:30 p.m.
Ruby Braff (tp), Frank Tate (b), Howard Alden (g)

First Set:
Nobody Else But You*
 unissued, audio and video recordings available
Lonely Moments*
 Storyville SV 6054
You've Changed*
 unissued, audio and video recordings available
Liza*
 Storyville SV 6054
Mean to Me*
 unissued, audio and video recordings available
I've Grown Accustomed to Her Face
 Storyville SV 6054
It's Only a Paper Moon*
 Storyville SV 6054

Second Set:
Nice Work If You Can Get It
 unissued, audio and incomplete video recordings available
When a Woman Loves a Man
 Storyville SV 6054
Orange
 unissued, audio and video recordings available
Miss Brown to You*
 Storyville SV 6054
Charlie Chaplin Medley:
 La Violettera
 unissued, audio and video recordings available

Smile
unissued, audio and video recordings available
Black Beauty (Braff out)
Storyville SV 6054
Judy Garland Medley:
The Man That Got Away
unissued, audio and video recordings available
Over the Rainbow
unissued, audio and video recordings available
If I Only Had a Brain
unissued, audio recording available
Do It Again
Storyville SV 6054
Them There Eyes
Storyville SV 6054
NOTE: Storyville SV 6054 is a videotape in PAL and NTSC formats. Other titles remain unissued. All titles on SV6054 are also issued on Storyville 16054 (DVD). A portion of the program was broadcast on the BBC. The broadcast was similar to the Storyville video recording, except that it did not include the following three selections: "Lonely Moments," "When a Woman Loves a Man" and "Do It Again." At the time of publication, the performances marked with an asterisk are available for viewing from YouTube.com.

Ruby appeared on Marian McPartland's wonderful program *Piano Jazz*. The date is uncertain but probably occurred in fall 1991. There is a spoken reference to the newly released *New England Songhounds, Volume 1* album and Marian remarked that they played together recently at Jimmy McPartland's funeral. The program aired on WGBO New York from 8–9 p.m. on April 23, 1992.[49]

The setting is relaxed, as is typical on this program. Marian interviews Ruby about his early appearances at the Savoy in Boston with Edmond Hall and Vic Dickenson. Ruby commented, "I was always late" and "I substituted for older musicians who had higher paying jobs on some nights." Ruby played piano as well as cornet on the program. With obvious joy, he remarked, "Here I am playing with a professional piano player, and it's the most fun I've ever had." Marian asked a question about Ruby's process of selecting tunes while preparing for recording sessions. Ruby quickly replied, "I'm not interested in a record date. I'm interested in recording a performance." He continued, "I'm a fan of pianists."

Marian McPartland with Her Guest Ruby Braff: *Piano Jazz*[50]
Probably Fall 1991, probably recorded in New York
Ruby Braff (cnt, p) and Marian McPartland (p) except solo piano where noted
Thou Swell
These Foolish Things (Braff, cnt)
This Year's Kisses (Braff, p solo)

This Is All I Ask (Braff, cnt)
Blue and Sentimental (Braff, p duet)
Singing the Blues (McPartland solo)
By Myself (Braff, cnt)
As Time Goes By (Braff, cnt)
Love Is Just around the Corner
NOTE: A recording of these tunes is available but remains unissued.

Los Angeles Jazz Party
November 29, 1991, Friday night, Airport Hilton, Los Angeles
Ruby Braff (cnt), Dave McKenna (p), Howard Alden (g), Milt Hinton (b), Jake Hanna (dm)
I Want to Be Happy (Braff, Alden, Hinton only)
Mean to Me
When I Fall in Love
Alice Blue Gown (Braff out, McKenna feature)
Smile (Braff and Alden only)
Love Walked In
Don't Get Around Much Anymore

Add Dick Hafer (ts)
Nice Work If You Can Get It
Lover Come Back to Me
NOTE: A recording of these tunes is available but remains unissued.

Los Angeles Jazz Party
November 30, 1991, Saturday night, Airport Hilton, Los Angeles
Ruby Braff (cnt), Dave McKenna (p), Howard Alden (g), Milt Hinton (b), Jake Hanna (dm)
Liza (Braff, Alden, Hinton only)
Do It Again (Braff, Alden, Hinton only)
Joshua Fit the Battle of Jericho (Hinton, Hanna only)
Love Me or Leave Me
Medley:
  I've Grown Accustomed to Her Face
  Santa Claus Is Coming to Town
  The Man That Got Away
  If I Only Had a Brain
  I've Grown Accustomed to Her Face

Add Warren Vaché (cnt)
Shoe Shine Boy

Add Kenny Davern (cl)
A Monday Date

NOTE: A recording of these tunes is available but remains unissued.

Los Angeles Jazz Party
December 1, 1991, Sunday morning, final day, Airport Hilton, Los Angeles
Ruby Braff (cnt), Dave McKenna (p), Howard Alden (g), Milt Hinton (b), Jake Hanna (dm)
This Can't Be Love
God Bless the Child
Gone with the Wind
Medley:
  Fine and Dandy
  When You Wish upon a Star
You Go to My Head (Ruby out)
Dream Dancing

Add Dan Barrett (tb)
Dinah
Medley:
  Rockin' Chair
  White Christmas
NOTE: A recording of these tunes is available but remains unissued.

Ruby Braff Quartet[51]
January 7–12, 1992, Eddie Condon's, 117 East 15th Street, New York

Ruby Braff Interview with Ron Della Chiesa
March 12, 1992 (to celebrate Ruby's 65th birthday), WGBH, Boston
NOTE: A recording of this interview is available but remains unissued.

Ron Della Chiesa stated, "Ruby came up from the Cape today just to join our broadcast. Ruby will appear at Chan's this coming Saturday evening in Woonsocket, Rhode Island. He recently moved to the Cape after about thirty years in New York." Ruby injected, "It's just us and the seagulls" and then remarked that the tunes I play "aren't old tunes, but think of them as good literature."

The following performance is the first time I have documented Ruby playing with Jon Wheatley. They would perform together a number of times in the future. After the following engagements in New England, Ruby again headed to England for performances in May and June.

Ruby Braff at Chan's
March 14, 1992, Woonsocket, Rhode Island
Ruby Braff (cnt), Jon Wheatley (g), Alice Ross Groves (p), Marshall Wood (b), Alan Dawson (dm)

Ruby Braff Quintet[52]
May 1992, Yarmouth Inn, Cape Cod, Massachusetts
Ruby Braff (cnt), Bill Davis (p), Fred Fried (g), Rod McCaulley (b), Gary Johnson (dm)

Ruby Braff Tour[53]
May 21, 1992, Ulster Hall, Belfast, Northern Ireland
May 22, 1992, Concorde Club, Eastleigh although listed as Brighton, England

Bull's Head Pub[54]
May 25, 1992, Barnes, Southwest London
Ruby Braff (cnt), Brian Dee (p), Dave Cliff (g), Dave Green (b)
Medley:
  Rose Room
  In a Mellotone
Medley:
  Pennies from Heaven
  Three Little Words
Medley:
  Memories of You
  Ain't Misbehavin'
But Not for Me (omit Braff)
Take the "A" Train
Crazy Rhythm
Embraceable You
'S Wonderful
You've Changed
Medley:
  Ghost of a Chance*
  Exactly Like You*
  Take the "A" Train*
NOTE: A recording of these tunes is available but remains unissued. A trio performance following "You've Changed" was not recorded and these tunes are marked with asterisks. Michael Moore was in the audience for this performance.

Ruby Braff Tour[55]
May 29, 1992 Queen's Hall, Edinburgh, Scotland
Ruby Braff (cnt), Brian Dee (p) possibly with Dave Cliff (g) and Ronnie Rae (b)
Mean to Me
You've Changed
You're Driving Me Crazy
When You Wish upon a Star
Take the "A" Train
The World Is Waiting for the Sunrise
I Want to Be Happy

God Bless the Child
Ain't Misbehavin'
As Long As I Live
NOTE: A recording of these tunes is available but remains unissued.

Ruby Braff Tour[56]
May 31, 1992 Alma Lodge Hotel, Stockport, England

Bull's Head Pub
June 3, 1992, Barnes, Southwest London
Ruby Braff (cnt), Mick Pyne (p), Dave Cliff (g), Michael Moore (b)
There Will Never Be Another You
Medley:
  You're Sensational
  I Love You, Samantha
Jeepers Creepers
Medley:
  I'm Getting Sentimental Over You
  Blue Turning Grey Over You
My Romance
Love Me or Leave Me
Medley:
  Time After Time
  It's the Talk of the Town
  If I Could Be with You One Hour Tonight
  The Very Thought of You
  Tea for Two
  Poor Butterfly
  The Very Thought of You
All the Things You Are (Ruby out)
Medley:
  I Cried for You
  When You Wish upon a Star
NOTE: A recording of these tunes is available but remains unissued.

Ruby Braff Tour[57]
June 5, 1992, Alhambra Studio, Bradford, England
June 6, 1992, Mill at the Pier, Wigan, England

Ruby Braff Quartet
June 7, 1992, Birch Hall Hotel, Oldham, Greater Manchester, England
Ruby Braff (cnt), Mick Pyne (p), Dave Cliff (g), Ronnie Rae (b)
Basin Street Blues
Just You, Just Me
Mean to Me

Dinah
Avalon
Wrap Your Troubles in Dreams
I Cover the Waterfront
You're Lucky to Me
I've Grown Accustomed to Her Face
Keepin' Out of Mischief Now
Dream Dancing
Unknown title (omit RB)*
Sweethearts on Parade*
Indiana*
They Can't Take That Away from Me
All the Things You Are (omit RB)
Medley:
  Memories of You
  The Man I Love
  When You Wish upon a Star (incomplete)

NOTE: A recording of all but three tunes is available but remains unissued. These three tunes are marked with asterisks. The recording of "When You Wish Upon a Star" is incomplete. A videotaped recording of this performance may exist but was not been available to the author at the time of publication.

Ruby Braff Quartet

Ruby Braff (cnt), Mick Pyne (p), Dave Cliff (g), Michael Moore (b)
June 11, 1992, The Garden Room, Burfields Road, Portsmouth, Hampshire, England

Just One of Those Things
Medley:
  I Want a Little Girl
  Dinah
Medley:
  When a Woman Loves a Man
  What Is There to Say?
  'S Wonderful
Poor Butterfly
Rockin' Chair
Between the Devil and the Deep Blue Sea
Medley:
  The Man I Love
  But Not for Me
Medley:
  In a Sentimental Mood
  It Don't Mean a Thing
  I Got It Bad and That Ain't Good

Medley:
  They Can't Take That Away from Me
  Somebody Loves Me
Old Man River
NOTE: A recording of these tunes is available but remains unissued. This recording may have omitted the opening tune(s) in this performance.

Ruby Braff
June 12, 1992, The Stables Theater, Wavendon, Buckinghamshire, England
Ruby Braff (cnt), Jim Shepherd (tb), Dick Morrisey (ts), Brian Lemon (p), Dave Cliff (g), Michael Moore (b), Allan Ganley (dm)

Braff and Moore only
Yesterdays

Braff, Lemon, and Ganley only
The World Is Waiting for the Sunrise

Add Cliff
Keepin' Out of Mischief Now

Add Moore
Old Folks

Add Shepherd and Morrisey
Rosetta
Ain't Misbehavin'
Muskrat Ramble

Omit Shepherd, Morrisey, and Ganley
I Know That You Know
When I Fall in Love

Add Ganley
Thou Swell

Add Shepherd and Morrisey
Jeepers Creepers
I Can't Give You Anything but Love
Take the "A" Train
NOTE: A recording of these tunes is available but remains unissued. This recording may have omitted the opening tune(s) in this performance.

Ruby Braff Tour[58]
June 14, 1992, Football Club, Marlow Bucks, England

Ruby returned to the United States, but I have been unable to locate any engagements until the following appearance in Minneapolis or St. Paul. There are no specific details available for that performance at the time of publication. Then, in January, Ruby used the name *New England Songhounds* from his two Concord recordings for his engagement at the Regettabar. That club would be the site for future engagements as well, in July and also documented in the next chapter.

Ruby Braff[59]
Fall 1992, unknown engagement, Minneapolis or St. Paul, Minnesota
Ruby Braff (cnt), Gray Sargent (g) and perhaps others

Ruby Braff and His New England Songhounds[60]
January 2–3, 1993, Regattabar, Charles Hotel, 1 Bennett Street, Cambridge, Massachusetts
Ruby Braff (cnt), Gray Sargent (g), Marshall Wood (b), Alan Dawson (dm and vibes)
There Will Never Be Another You (Dawson vibes)
Just Friends (Dawson vibes)
Mean to Me (Sargent feature)
It's Only a Paper Moon (Wood feature)
Nobody Else But You
Lonely Moments
Smile
When I Fall in Love

Jazz Society[61]
April 26, 1993, Vero Beach?, Florida
Details unknown

Red Baron Release Party[62]
May 6, 1993, (Thursday), 777 7th Avenue, New York
Ruby Braff (cnt), John Bunch (b), Bucky Pizzarelli (g), John Burr (b), Elise Wood (flute)

Ruby Braff Chamber Quartet[63]
July 30, 1993, Regattabar, Charles Hotel, Cambridge, Massachusetts
Ruby Braff (cnt), Gray Sargent (g), Jon Wheatley (g), Marshall Wood (b)

Teresa Brewer: American Music Box Vol. 2: The Songs of Harry Warren
September 7-8, 1993, New York
Ruby Braff (cnt), John Bunch (p), Bucky Pizzarelli (g), Jay Leonhardt (b), Grady Tate (dm)

Jeepers Creepers
    Red Baron JK 57329
You'll Never Know
    Red Baron JK 57329
I Only Have Eyes for You
    Red Baron JK 57329
Forty Second Street
    Red Baron JK 57329
The More I See You
    Red Baron JK 57329
I'll String Along With You
    Red Baron JK 57329
You're My Everything
    Red Baron JK 57329
September in the Rain
    Red Baron JK 57329
There Will Never Be Another You
    Red Baron JK 57329
Lulu's Back in Town
    Red Baron JK 57329

The following advertisements depict three of the performances in this chapter:

FORTUNE GARDEN
PAVILION Presents...
JAZZ ON 49th ST.
NOW thru SUN. OCT. 30
JAKI BYARD
Coming Tues. Nov. 1 thru Sun. Nov. 6
GEORGE CABLES DUO
w/RAY DRUMMOND
SPECIAL
MONDAY NOV. 7
DICK HYMAN
and RUBY BRAFF
AND FINE CHINESE CUISINE
209 E. 49th
at THIRD AVE.
RES. (212) 753-0101
2 Shows Nightly, 9:30 & 11pm
SUN 7 & 8pm

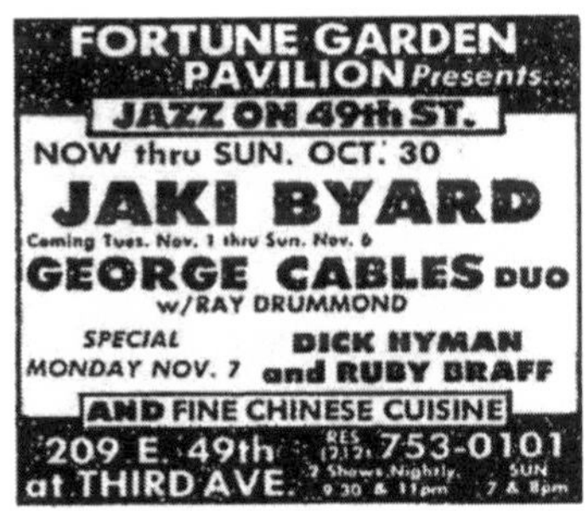

Figure 19.1:
Advertisement
October 1988

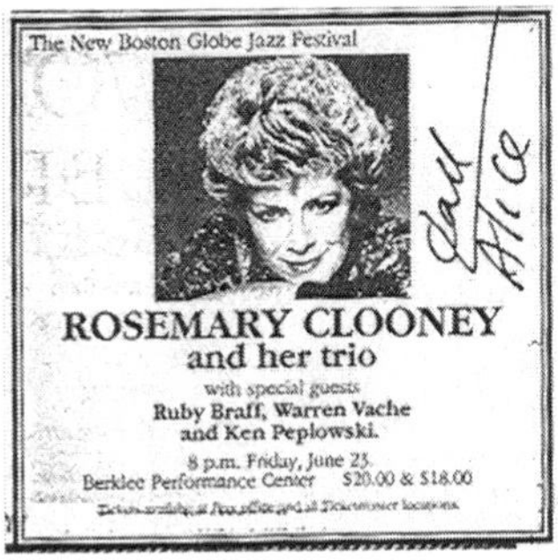

The New Boston Globe Jazz Festival
ROSEMARY CLOONEY
and her trio
with special guests
Ruby Braff, Warren Vache
and Ken Peplowski.
8 p.m. Friday, June 23.
Berklee Performance Center
$20.00 & $18.00

Figure 19.2:
Advertisement
June 1989

Figure 19.3: Advertisement March 1991

Notes

[1] Photo reproduced in *The March of Jazz Celebrates Ruby Braff's 74th Birthday Party*, Arbors Records, 2001, 28—date given only as late 1980s but this photo is from 1984. Scott Hamilton indicates that he and Ruby participated in a jazz cruise in 1988 (see *Jazz Journal International*, December 1989, 10). Other possibilities would be 1984, 1985, 1986, or 1989 (see same *JJI* article). Ruby definitely participated in the Floating Jazz Festivals in 1984–1986. Dates are given in *The St. Petersburg Evening Independent*, September 25, 1984, 1, Section D.

[2] *New York Times*, October 23, 1988, *The New Yorker*, October 10, 1998, 8, October 17, 1988, 8, October 24, 1988, 8, and *New York Magazine*, October 31, 1988, 141.

[3] *New York Magazine*, October 31, 1988, 141, and October 24, 1988, 209.

[4] *New York Times*, October 30, 1988, *The New Yorker*, November 7, 1998, 8, and *New York Magazine*, November 7, 1988.

[5] Advertisement in *New York Times* October 28, 1988, and November 14, 1988, 8, and *New York Times*, November 6, 1989.

[6] *New York Times*, December 18, 1988, December 25, 1988, December 30, 1988, *The New Yorker*, December 19, 1998, 6, December 26, 1998, 11, and January 2, 1989, 7.

[7] PR release, June 20, 1989. Nels Nelson, "Jazz Opens at Academy Joe Williams & Nancy Wilson Vocalize," *Philadelphia Daily News*, June 21, 1981, June 16, 1981, and June 19, 1989.

[8] Fernando Gonzalez, *Boston Globe*, June 15, 1989, and advertisement, *Boston Globe*, June 8, 1989, listed in Calendar, 23.

[9] *New York Times*, June 23, 1989, and a review by John S. Wilson published June 29, 1989, and advertised in *New York Times* May 14, June 3, June 4, June 11, and June 18, 1989.

[10] *New York Times*, June 23, 1989, and advertisement, May 14, 1989.

[11] Mel Levine was one of Ruby's close friends. Mel shared this private correspondence with me.
[12] Fernando Gonzalez, *Boston Globe*, August 19, 1989.
[13] Photograph of Vic Dickenson with Ruby Braff published in *The Jazz Family Album, Volume 5* (East Stroudsburg, PA: Al Cohn Memorial Jazz Collection, 1997), 13.
[14] *Jazz Journal International*, December 1989, 10, in comments from Scott Hamilton.
[15] *New York Times*, October 22, 1989, and *The New Yorker*, October 23, 1989, 31, and *New York Magazine*, October 23, 1989, 202.
[16] *New York Times*, November 12, 1989.
[17] *New York Times*, December 24 and 29, 1989, *The New Yorker*, December 25, 1989, 8.
[18] *New York Times*, June 22, 1990, and *Jazz Journal International*, September 1990, 9, in a report written by Michael Bourne, advertised in *New York Times*, May 6, 1990, and June 17, 1990.
[19] Photo of Ruby Braff at unknown JVC Jazz Festival event by Ken Franckling from http://nejazz.org/2004i.php.
[20] Gary Giddins, *Weather Bird* (New York: Oxford, 2004), 4; date listed in *The New Yorker*, June 22, 1990, June 29, 1990, and July 2, 1990, 13. Advertised in *New York Times* May 20, June 10, 11, 17, 25, and 27, 1990.
[21] John S. Wilson, *New York Times*, June 29, 1990.
[22] Dick Hyman suggests that a full tape recording is probably held in the archives of the Canadian Broadcasting Corporation. Mark Miller, *Globe and Mail*, July 9, 1990.
[23] Source of information Tony Shoppee.
[24] *The Spectator*, August 4, 1990 provided information about the date and three titles performed. Howard Alden supplied further details and a video recording from the date.
[25] Leonard Feather, *Los Angeles Times*, August 3, 1990.
[26] *Los Angeles Times*, May 17, 1990, *Boston Globe*, August 18, 1990.
[27] Fernando Gonzalez, *Boston Globe*, August 18, 1990.
[28] On DVD, Touchstone 27112, and laserdisc, Touchstone Home Video 1337 AS.
[29] Photo, *The March of Jazz Celebrates Ruby Braff's 74th Birthday Party*, Arbors Records, 2001, 28.
[30] Sonny McGown was first to mention this engagement to me. It was also mentioned in a radio interview and in the *Los Angeles Times*, February 19, 1991 (opening later in the week). Dave Robinson provided the dates for the engagement and press release, recalling that he attended Ruby's performance that night with Sonny.
[31] Concert program, *New York Times*, March 3, 1991, advertised in *New York Times*, February 10 and March 3, 1991, and listed in *New York Magazine*, March 11, 1988, 117.
[32] Photo reproduced in *The March of Jazz Celebrates Ruby Braff's 74th Birthday Party*, Arbors Records, 2001, 29. Ruby and Marian mentioned that they played "These Foolish Things" in the *Piano Jazz* broadcast.
[33] Photo, *The March of Jazz Celebrates Ruby Braff's 74th Birthday Party*, Arbors Records, 2001, 29.
[34] Calvin Gilbert, *Baton Rouge Morning Advocate*, April 26, 1991, and *The Incomplete, Year-by-Year, Selectively Quirky, Prime Facts Edition of the History of the New Orleans Jazz & Heritage Festival* (New Orleans: e/Prime Publications, 2005), 191.
[35] Review in *The New Orleans Times-Picayune*, July 19, 1992 and *The Incomplete, Year-by-Year, Selectively Quirky, Prime Facts Edition of the History of the New Orleans Jazz & Heritage Festival* (New Orleans: e/Prime Publications, 2005), 199, and *New York Magazine*, July 20, 1992, 93, for broadcast date.

[36] Ruby Braff interviewed by Steve Voce on October 6, 1994 (*Jazz Panorama*).
[37] "Jazz News," *Jazz Journal International,* May 1991, 4.
[38] "Jazz News," *Jazz Journal International,* May 1991, 4, and confirmed by Ralph O'Callaghan.
[39] "Jazz News," *Jazz Journal International,* May 1991, 4. Likely Dave Bennett recorded additional music from this performance. Ralph O'Callaghan reported that John Barnes also appeared that night.
[40] Steve Voce, "Roy Williams, Acclaimed International Trombonist," *Jazz Journal International*, February 2001, 21.
[41] Tony Shoppee and Alun Morgan provided early information. Details confirming location and musicians supplied by Ralph O'Callaghan, who attended the performance.
[42] "Jazz News," *Jazz Journal International,* May 1991, 4.
[43] "Jazz News," *Jazz Journal International,* May 1991, 4.
[44] "Jazz News," *Jazz Journal International,* May 1991, 4.
[45] Gary Giddins, *Weather Bird* (New York: Oxford, 2004), 25, and a review by Peter Watrous, *New York Times*, June 26, 1991, *Chicago Tribune*, June 26, 1991, advertised *New York Times*, June 12, 16, 19, and 24, 1991.
[46] Lenny Solomon believes that the recording session occurred during either June or July. Only the year has been previously reported in discographies.
[47] *Crescendo & Jazz Music,* volume 28, no 4 (October/November 1991), 4.
[48] BBC aired a shortened version of this program that omits three titles included on the Storyville VHS tape and DVD: "Lonely Moments," "When a Woman Loves a Man," and "Do It Again." Jools Holland was the host for the program and Jonathan Davies from Swansea was the producer. David Griffiths reports that "Do It Again" was included on a broadcast on BBC Cymru in the Welsh language.
[49] *New York Times*, April 23, 1992.
[50] Copy of program provided by Marian McPartland.
[51] *New York Times*, January 5, 1992, *New York Magazine*, January 13, 1992, 94, and January 6, 1992, 89.
[52] George A. Borgman, "The One and Only Ruby Braff," in *Mississippi Rag*, December 1995, 6.
[53] "Jazz News," *Jazz Journal International,* May 1992, 3.
[54] "Jazz News," *Jazz Journal International,* May 1992, 3.
[55] "Jazz News," *Jazz Journal International,* May 1992, 3.
[56] "Jazz News," *Jazz Journal International,* May 1992, 3.
[57] "Jazz News," *Jazz Journal International,* May 1992, 3.
[58] Alun Morgan and Tony Shoppee citing *Jazz Journal International,* May 1992.
[59] Michael Anthony, *Star-Tribune* (Twin Cities Minneapolis–St. Paul), February 19, 1993—he reports that Ruby performed in the Twin Cities "last Fall" with Gray Sargent.
[60] Fernando Gonzalez, *Boston Globe*, January 1, 1993, and January 2, 1993. Also see Daniel Gewertz, *Boston Herald*, January 4, 1993, and personnel from correspondence with Nick Puopolo, who has photos available.
[61] Information from Don Wolff.
[62] Printed invitation (year is estimated by determining the year when March 6 is a Thursday).
[63] Fernando Gonzalez, *Boston Globe*, July 30, 1993.

Chapter 20

Ruby Braff and Mat Domber: Finding Creative Freedom at Arbors Records

The following session is the first new recording by Ruby Braff that was released by Arbors Records. Ruby remarked many times that Mat Domber provided him with unmatched freedom to create unique recordings. This relationship continued for the final decade of Ruby's lifetime. Overall, this was the 30th CD Mat released on his label. Mat came to the recording business from his background as a practicing attorney and he concurrently continued his career managing real estate properties in Florida. A number of jazz musicians and fans recognize Arbors Records as one of the most important small labels in the history of jazz music. In addition, he sponsored and organized a number of live performance events.

Ruby Braff Quartet: ***Live at the Regattabar***
November 22, 1993, Charles Hotel, Cambridge, Massachusetts
Ruby Braff (cnt, p), Gray Sargent (g), Jon Wheatley (g), Marshall Wood (b)
Persian Rug
    Arbors ARCD 19131
It's Wonderful
    Arbors ARCD 19131
Louisiana
    Arbors ARCD 19131
Sweet Sue
    Arbors ARCD 19131
Do It Again
    Arbors ARCD 19131
No One Else But You
    Arbors ARCD 19131
Crazy Rhythm
    Arbors ARCD 19131

Where Are You?
Arbors ARCD 19131
Between the Devil and the Deep Blue Sea
Arbors ARCD 19131
Orange (RB p)
Arbors ARCD 19131
Give My Regards to Broadway
Arbors ARCD 19131

Ruby Braff Interview
November 25, 1993, WGBH, Boston with Ron Della Chiesa
NOTE: A recording of this interview is available but remains unissued.

Ruby Braff & His Buddies / Ruby Braff and His New England Songhounds: ***Controlled Nonchalance at the Regattabar. Volumes 1 and 2***[1]
November 26 and 27, 1993, Regattabar, Charles Hotel, Cambridge, Massachusetts
Ruby Braff (cnt), Scott Hamilton (ts), Dave McKenna (p), Gray Sargent (g), Marshall Wood (b), Chuck Riggs (dm)

November 26, 1993
The Lady Is a Tramp
Arbors ARCD 10134
Blue and Sentimental
Arbors ARCD 10134
It's Only a Paper Moon (McKenna, Sargent feature)
unissued
Ain't Misbehavin'
Arbors ARCD 19311
Them There Eyes
Arbors ARCD 19311
Rosetta
Arbors ARCD 19134, 19192
Sunday
Arbors ARCD 19134
NOTE: A video recording also available for all listed titles except "Rosetta" and "Sunday." The video opens with Ruby playing piano before the performance begins leading into sound check.

November 27, 1993[2]
It's All Right with Me
Arbors ARCD 19311
Mean to Me
Arbors ARCD 10134

Swinging on a Star
Arbors ARCD 19311
If You Were Mine
Arbors ARCD 19311
Familiar waltz (Braff and Hamilton out)
unissued
Struttin' with Some Barbecue
Arbors ARCD 10134
Cocktails for Two (Braff out)
unissued
It Could Happen to You (Sargent and Wood only)
unissued
Winter Wonderland
unissued

Second Set
Jeepers Creepers
unissued
Pennies from Heaven
Arbors ARCD 19311
Ellington Tribute Medley:
In a Sentimental Mood
Arbors ARCD 19311
I Got It Bad and That Ain't Good
Arbors ARCD 19311
These Foolish Things
Arbors ARCD 19311
Take the "A" Train
unissued
What's New? (Braff and McKenna)
Arbors ARCD 19134
I Want to Be Happy
unissued
On the Sunny Side of the Street
Arbors ARCD 19311
Set ends

Love Me or Leave Me
Arbors ARCD 19134
Lester Leaps In
Arbors ARCD 19134
NOTE: "Winter Wonderland" was earmarked for a possible Christmas album. ARCD 19134 is issued as *Volume 1* while ARCD 19311 is issued as *Volume 2*. The second volume was released after Ruby's death. Arbors 19192 is titled *Arbors Records Sampler, Volume 1.* A video recording also available for all

listed titles performed November 27 except, "Love Me or Leave Me" and "Lester Leaps In," including those where no separate audio recording is listed. The tunes are listed in the order of performance in the video.

Regatta Bar[3]
February 1994, Cambridge, Massachusetts
Ruby Braff (cnt), Dave McKenna (p), and possibly others

Mat Domber began a series of jazz parties in 1994. The first event celebrated Bob Haggart's 80th birthday and launched a series that included Ruby Braff in March. Ruby also appeared in 2001 and 2002.

March of Jazz: The All Stars at Bob Haggart's 80th Birthday Party—March 11–13, 1994
March 12, 1994, 10:30–10:55 p.m., St. Petersburg, Florida
Ruby Braff (cnt), Ralph Sutton (p), Howard Alden (g), Jack Lesberg (b), Bobby Rosengarden (dm)
'Tain't So, Honey, 'Tain't So
 unissued, video recording available
Old Folks
 unissued, video recording available
Mean to Me
 unissued, video recording available
Blue, Turning Grey Over You
 unissued, audio recording available
Way Down Yonder in New Orleans
 unissued, audio recording available

March 12, 1994, 11:00–11:25 p.m.
Ruby Braff (cnt), Dick Hyman (p), Bucky Pizzarelli (g), Bob Haggart (b), Jake Hanna (dm)
Love Is Just around the Corner
 unissued, audio recording available
Yesterdays
 Arbors ARCD 19265
I've Grown Accustomed to Her Face
 unissued, audio recording available

Add Dan Barrett (tb), Rick Fay (ts), Kenny Davern, Ken Peplowski (cl)
Muskrat Ramble
 Arbors ARCD 19265
NOTE: ARCD 19265 contains two CDs and also includes performances by other artists from this occasion. It is issued under Bob Haggart's name.

Ruby may not have performed at other times during the 1994 March of Jazz. A photo from the March of Jazz program showing Ruby with Jake Hanna is available.[4]

Ruby was seriously ill, due to emphysema and bronchitis, during April 1994. He was hospitalized at Cape Cod Hospital in critical condition and nearly died. Ruby's recovery from the coma was buoyed by Jack Bradley's decision to supply a number of Louis Armstrong's recordings on tape. Jack played the Decca version of "I Can't Give You Anything but Love," and Ruby regained consciousness, stating that this was not the version he preferred. Jack explained to me that Ruby was referring to the fact that this was not Louis's first recording of the tune.

Regatta Bar[5]
April 17, 1994, Cambridge, Massachusetts (perhaps other nights are included in this engagement)
Ruby Braff (cnt), Jon Wheatley (g), Tad Hitchcock (g), Marshall Wood (b), Jim Gwin (dm), Donna Byrne (voc)

Ruby played from a wheelchair at the Regatta Bar while recovering from his illness.

Next, Ruby was featured in a tribute to Dick Hyman held at Town Hall in New York as part of the JVC Jazz Festival. This had given him some additional time for recovery and Gary Giddins wrote the following about this performance:

> ...before they had finished eight bars of 'Sophisticated Lady' the hall was awash in a roseate glow. Given Braff's idiosyncratic approach to rhythm and melody, it's hard to believe he was often dismissed as a mere traditionalist in the early days. His notes are less played than sculpted, sustained beyond expectation or peremptorily cut off. Every aspect of his pitch is controlled, from attack to decay. The melody notes peal like great bells or small chimes, and his asymmetrical phrasing keeps rhythm in a kind of swinging suspension. He didn't sound like Armstrong on 'My Monday Date' or like Beiderbecke on 'Sunday,' yet he managed to impart both—the power and the reticence. In arousing Hyman's acute antennae, he brought the duets to a state of grace.

While the concert was designed as a tribute to Dick Hyman, it is a certainly true that Ruby was also honored by having been selected to play a significant role in this concert. Ruby had last played with Roger Kellaway and Derek Smith at Waterloo Village in 1990 but obviously he had many occasions to perform with Dick Hyman in their musical partnership.

JVC Jazz Festival: *The Musical Life of Dick Hyman*[6]
June 27, 1994, Town Hall, New York
Ruby Braff (cnt), Dick Hyman (p)
What Is This Thing Called Love (Hyman solo)
Sophisticated Lady

A Monday Date
Sunday
Swan Lake
Liza

Add Howard Alden (g), Bob Haggart (b); Braff out
Idaho
Dardanella
How High the Moon

Ruby Braff (cnt) returns, add Frank Wess (ts)
Just You, Just Me

Dick Hyman (p solo)
Sweet Savannah Sue

Add Roger Kellaway (p)
Chopsticks
In a Mellotone

Add: Derek Smith (p)
Two unnamed standards
Royal Garden Blues

Dick Hyman (p), Frank Wess (ts), Howard Alden (g), Bob Haggart (b)
A Time for Love

Add Ruby Braff (cnt), Derek Smith, Roger Kellaway (p)
Flintstones

Mat and Ruby discussed the earlier recordings Ruby made with Ellis Larkins on Vanguard and Chiaroscuro. Fortunately were able to arrange an encore recording session that spanned four days in New York Studios. Making the most of his trip to New York, Mat recorded Ruby with Dick Hyman the following day on July 2. This is setting a pattern in which Ruby and Mat planned future trips to New York that cluster several days in the recording studio. Following time in the studio, Ruby returned home to Cape Cod for at least one performance I have been able to document.

Jack Bradley's photograph on the covers of the next two CD releases depicted a humorous play on Irving Berlin's last name, showing Ruby and Ellis sitting at a table while they decoded a message received on a shortwave radio.

Ruby Braff and Ellis Larkins: *Calling Berlin, Volume 1*
June 28–July 1, 1994, Clinton Studios, New York
Ruby Braff and Ellis Larkins Duets

Ruby Braff (cnt), Ellis Larkins (p), *add Bucky Pizzarelli (g)
It's a Lovely Day Today*
Arbors ARCD 19139
Blue Skies
Arbors ARCD 19139
Alexander's Ragtime Band
Arbors ARCD 19139
I'm Putting All My Eggs in One Basket
Arbors ARCD 19139
How Deep Is the Ocean?
Arbors ARCD 19139
Soft Lights and Sweet Music
Arbors ARCD 19139
Let's Face the Music and Dance
Arbors ARCD 19139
My Walking Stick
Arbors ARCD 19139
Russian Lullaby*
Arbors ARCD 19139
You're Laughing at Me
Arbors ARCD 19139
This Year's Kisses
Arbors ARCD 19139
Top Hat, White Tie and Tails
Arbors ARCD 19139
They Say It's Wonderful
Arbors ARCD 19139
Steppin' Out with My Baby
Arbors ARCD 19139
Easter Parade
Arbors ARCD 19139

Ruby Braff and Ellis Larkins: *Calling Berlin, Volume 2*
Same dates and personnel
Slumming on Park Avenue
Arbors ARCD 19140
Remember the Night
Arbors ARCD 19140
Change Partners
Arbors ARCD 19140
Cheek to Cheek
Arbors ARCD 19140
What'll I Do?
Arbors ARCD 19140

How About Me?
Arbors ARCD 19140
Isn't It a Lovely Day?
Arbors ARCD 19140
Always
Arbors ARCD 19140
The Song Is Ended
Arbors ARCD 19140
Better Luck Next Time
Arbors ARCD 19140
It Only Happens When I Dance With You
Arbors ARCD 19140
Suppertime
Arbors ARCD 19140
Be Careful, It's My Heart
Arbors ARCD 19140

Ruby and Mat Domber take further advantage of Ruby's time in New York to record another CD, this time featuring Ruby with Dick Hyman.

Ruby Braff and Dick Hyman: *Play Nice Tunes*
July 2, 1994, Clinton Studios, New York
I Want a Little Girl
Arbors ARCD 19141
My Heart Belongs to Daddy
Arbors ARCD 19141
Sweet Savannah Sue
Arbors ARCD 19141
Why Was I Born?
Arbors ARCD 19141
Lotus Blossom
Arbors ARCD 19141
Joseph! Joseph!
Arbors ARCD 19141
Thanks a Million
Arbors ARCD 19141
By Myself
Arbors ARCD 19141
I Must Have That Man
Arbors ARCD 19141
Come Sunday
Arbors ARCD 19141
Save It Pretty Mama
Arbors ARCD 19141

Once Upon a Time
    Arbors ARCD 19141
You're Lucky to Me
    Arbors ARCD 19141
When It's Sleepy Time Down South
    Arbors ARCD 19141

Ruby Braff and Donna Byrne[7]
Mid-July 1994, Christine's, West Dennis, Cape Cod, Massachusetts
Ruby Braff (cnt), Jon Wheatley, Tad Hitchcock (g), Marshall Wood (b), Artie Cabral (dm)
Crazy Rhythm
Love Walked In
Sweet Sue

Add: Donna Byrne (voc)
It's Wonderful
Undecided
When You Wish upon a Star

There is a long gap in Ruby's schedule where I have not located any traces of performances. He enjoyed speaking with Steve Voce in Steve's on-air interviews, perhaps using this as a substitute for his reduced opportunities to perform in clubs. Steve, for his part, enjoyed Ruby's candid responses to questions and his unique sense of humor. Ruby traveled to Denver to perform with Ralph Sutton and then was featured in a surviving benefit concert for needy children carried on a public access television channel.

Ruby Braff Interview with Steve Voce
Broadcast BBC Radio Merseyside
October 6, 1994, Dennis, Massachusetts
NOTE: A recording of this interview is available but remains unissued. In all these interviews, Ruby spoke on the telephone from his home.

Ruby Braff Sextet[8]
October 28–29, 1994, Park Hill Golf Club, Denver, Colorado
Ruby Braff (cnt), Scott Hamilton (ts), Jon Wheatley (g), Ralph Sutton (p), Jack Lesberg (b), Jake Hanna (dm)

This was part of a concert series organized by Ralph and Sunnie Sutton. The series continued for approximately three years, featuring different artists. Further details are unknown.

Ruby Braff Interview with Steve Voce
Broadcast BBC Radio Merseyside

November 10, 1994, Dennis, Massachusetts
NOTE: A recording of this interview is available but remains unissued.

Ruby Braff Interview with Steve Voce
Broadcast BBC Radio Merseyside
December 15, 1994, Dennis, Massachusetts
NOTE: A recording of this interview is available but remains unissued.

The next concert was a benefit for needy children. Ruby Braff had phoned radio host Dick Golden and explained his wish to perform at a benefit concert that would be sensitive to both Jewish and Christian traditions at this time of year. Dick, in turn, contacted Ellen Chahey, then the executive director of the Cape Cod Council of Churches. Ellen later wrote about this concert in *The Barnstable Patriot*[9]:

> We soon made arrangements for a December Sunday afternoon concert at the Federated Church of Hyannis, where I am now one of the pastors. Ruby would play with a who's-who of Cape Cod jazz. . . .
>
> I still remember the moment when we opened the sanctuary doors for the audience. People ran to get the best seats. I looked at the crowd with joy; one of the first, and happiest, people I saw was a man whom I knew had survived Dachau.
>
> True to form, although Ruby's generosity provided a lot of Christmas presents for a lot of children, when I called to thank him for what he had done he chewed me out for not raising enough money. He used language that most people reserve for when they are out of earshot of clergy.
>
> I then, appreciatively, invited him to dinner, along with Dick Golden and Ivy Sinclair, another of the Cape's jazz pillars, and Ruby proved a wonderful guest. He regaled us with stories of Benny Goodman. He loved my stuffed cabbage and my homemade bread and chocolate cake, and warmly praised my husband's choices of recordings for our musical pleasure. He even played our piano.
>
> We wound up scheduling another concert [see it listed in March 1995]. To thank Ruby at his second performance, I gave him a carving of an angel blowing a horn.
>
> 'What the hell is this?' he responded in front of an audience of several hundred at Cape Cod Community College.
>
> I laughed, as did the audience.
>
> 'No, I mean it. What the hell is this?'
>
> Then I told him, and I added what Dick Golden had quipped to me before we'd gone on stage: 'For Ruby, you might as well throw away the angel and just give him the horn.'

Ruby Braff and His All Stars: *Ruby Braff–Plays for Needy Children*, Sponsored by Cape Cod Council of Churches[10]
December 18, 1994 (afternoon), Federated Church of Hyannis, Hyannis, Massachusetts

Ruby Braff (cnt), Dave McKenna (p), Jon Wheatley, Tad Hitchcock (g), Marshall Wood (b), Ron Lundberg (dm), Donna Byrne (voc)
A high school chorus opened the show.
Ruby Braff (cnt), Jon Wheatley, Tad Hitchcock (g), Marshall Wood (b)
Crazy Rhythm
Louisiana
Do It Again

Add Dave McKenna (p)
Quiet Nights of Quiet Stars (Corcovado)
Oh, Little Town of Bethlehem (McKenna solo)

Add Donna Byrne (voc)
Santa Claus Is Coming to Town
The Christmas Waltz
The Best Things in Life Are Free

Ruby Braff (cnt), Jon Wheatley, Tad Hitchcock (g), Marshall Wood (b), Ron Lundberg (dm) open second set
Nobody Else But You
Sweet Sue
When I Fall in Love
Between the Devil and the Deep Blue Sea

Add Dave McKenna (p)
Morning of the Carnival (Manha De Carnival)
Sunset and the Mockingbird (McKenna solo)

Add Donna Byrne (voc)
You'd Be So Nice to Come Home To
I'll Be Home for Christmas (Byrne and McKenna only)
When You Wish upon a Star
America the Beautiful
NOTE: A video recording of the complete program is available but remains unissued.

Joys of Jazz
December 27, 1994, Naples, Florida
Ruby Braff (cnt), Gray Sargent, Jon Wheatley (g), Marshall Wood (b), Chuck Riggs (dm), Donna Byrne (voc)
Crazy Rhythm
Sweet Sue (Wood feature)
I've Grown Accustomed to Her Face

Add Scott Hamilton (ts), Dave McKenna (p)
Struttin' with Some Barbecue (Bossa Nova)

Ruby Braff out
Sunset and the Mockingbird (McKenna solo)
Way Down Yonder in New Orleans (Hamilton feature)

Ruby Braff returns
Limehouse Blues (voc DB)
Wrap Your Troubles in Dreams (voc DB)

Hamilton and McKenna out
Intermission
Liza
Give My Regards to Broadway
Medley:
  Who'll Buy My Violets?
  Smile

Dave McKenna and Scott Hamilton return
Please Don't Talk About Me When I'm Gone
Dinah (McKenna solo)
Dream Dancing (voc DM)
I Have Dreamed (voc DM accompanied by McKenna only)
When You Wish upon a Star (voc DM)
NOTE: A recording of these tunes is available but remains unissued. "Sunset and the Mockingbird" is from Duke Ellington's *The Queen's Suite.*

Joys of Jazz[11]
December 28 or 29, 1994, Sarasota, Florida
Ruby Braff (cnt), Gray Sargent, Jon Wheatley (g), Marshall Wood (b), Chuck Riggs (dm), Donna Byrne (voc)
NOTE: The program was similar to the performance in Naples but no further information is available.

Ruby returned to the Regatta Bar at Harvard Square. Nick Puoplo shared a photograph from January 8, 1995. Ruby then joined Scott Hamilton, John Bunch, Bucky Pizzarelli, and Michel Moore for a jazz cruise on the S/S *Norway* where one performance featured Mel Tormé on drums.

Ruby Braff New England Songhounds[12]
January 6, 7, 8 (the Sunday matinee), 1995 (and perhaps also on the following weekend January 13, 14, 15?), Regattabar, Charles Hotel, Cambridge, Massachusetts

Ruby Braff (cnt), Scott Hamilton (ts), Dave McKenna (p), Gray Sargent (g), Marshall Wood (b), Chuck Riggs (dm), Donna Byrne (voc)
My Funny Valentine
You've Changed
Sunset and the Mockingbird (McKenna feature)
Cherokee (Hamilton feature)

Ruby Braff on S/S *Norway*
January 27, 1995, at sea
Ruby Braff (cnt), Scott Hamilton (ts), John Bunch (p), Bucky Pizzarelli (g), Michael Moore (b), Mel Tormé (dm)
Sultry Serenade (Bunch and rhythm)
Old Folks

Add Scott Hamilton
Just You, Just Me
NOTE: A recording of these tunes is available but remains unissued.

Ruby Braff Interview with Steve Voce
Broadcast BBC Radio Merseyside
February 2, 1995, Dennis, Massachusetts
NOTE: A recording of this interview is available but remains unissued.

Ruby Braff and His All Stars: *Swing into Spring Benefit Concert*[13]
March 1995, Cape Cod Community College, West Barnstable, Massachusetts
Ruby Braff (cnt), Jon Wheatley, Tad Hitchcock (g), Bill Cunliffe (p), Marshall Wood (b), Ron Lundberg (dm)
Special guests: Donna Byrne (voc), Marie Marcus (p), Phil Wilson (tb)
Ain't Misbehavin' (Braff and Marcus)
Other tunes are unknown.

This benefit concert followed Ruby's earlier successful benefit concert December 18, 1994. It was also arranged by Ellen Chahey, then the executive director of the Cape Cod Council of Churches.

There is a published report of Donna Byrne recently touring with the Ruby Braff–Scott Hamilton Sextet. Further information is not available.[14] But they did perform together in Cambridge at the Regettabar in early January 1995 as reported above.

Ruby Braff Interview with Steve Voce
Broadcast BBC Radio Merseyside
April 5, 1995, Dennis, Massachusetts
NOTE: A recording of this interview is available but remains unissued.

Ruby Braff Interview with Steve Voce
Broadcast BBC Radio Merseyside
April 15, 1995, Dennis, Massachusetts
NOTE: A recording of this interview is available but remains unissued.

Ruby Braff Interview with Steve Voce
Broadcast BBC Radio Merseyside
June 8, 1995, Dennis, Massachusetts
NOTE: A recording of this interview is available but remains unissued.

It is fitting that Ruby was able to perform in a concert that paid tribute to Carl Jefferson, who had been such a strong supporter of Ruby during the many years of their association. Ruby was featured on the Concord Jazz label's fifth release.

Ruby indicated that he traveled to California to perform at a concert to honor Carl Jefferson and also to record songs for two albums with Roger Kellaway for Concord Jazz records[15]. Thus, the sessions presently dated September 10–11 should probably be adjacent to the next concert on July 8, either before or after his live performance. If that is true, the date listed in the album *Inside & Out* is probably a date for mixing the tape, not the actual performance. It is unlikely that Ruby would have made a separate flight to California for each booking.

Ruby discussed his frustration that a planned second CD was never released, stating emphatically that the unreleased performances were absolutely the equal of those that have appeared. This is Ruby's last recording for Concord Jazz. I arbitrarily suggest the dates of July 5 and 6 for the following recording session, since it is possible Ruby would have preferred to complete recording prior to his appearance on the next day, a Saturday, at the tribute concert.

Ruby Braff and Roger Kellaway: *Inside & Out*[16]
Perhaps July 5 and 6, 1995 (but listed on CD as September 10–11, 1995), Fantasy Studios, Berkeley, California
Ruby Braff (cnt), Roger Kellaway (p)
Love Walked In
    Concord Jazz CCD 4691
Yesterdays
    Concord Jazz CCD 4691, CCD 4833-2
Memories of You
    Concord Jazz CCD 4691, Snapper Music SMDCD 271 (CD)
I Want to Be Happy
    Concord Jazz CCD 4691, CCD 5219-2
I Got Rhythm
    Concord Jazz CCD 4691, CCD 4833-2, Snapper Music SMDCD 271 (CD)
Always
    Concord Jazz CCD 4691

Between the Devil and the Deep Blue Sea
Concord Jazz CCD 4691
Basin Street Blues
Concord Jazz CCD 4691
Exactly Like You
Concord Jazz CCD 4691
The following titles remain unissued from this session:
The Very Thought of You
Lady Be Good
You've Changed
Looking at You
Old Folks
Orange
If I Love Again
Ghost of a Chance
You Took Advantage of Me
Dinah
Alone Together
NOTE: Concord Jazz CCD 4833-2 is titled *Ruby Braff: The Concord Jazz Heritage Series.* CCD 5219-2 is a 3 CD set titled *Jazz Party Mix* and one of the CDs is sold separately as *Jazz Moods: Cocktail Party* CCD 5218-2. The Snapper CD release is a reissue of tunes from various Concord Jazz releases and is titled *I'm Shooting High.*

Carl Jefferson died in March 1995. The following recording comes from a five-day memorial concert that was held at the Concord Pavilion, a facility he was instrumental in creating 20 years earlier. Musicians waived fees and covered their own travel expenses as a way to show their gratitude to a man who issued over 700 recordings; however, Ruby's travel expenses were likely covered as a result of the adjacent recording session with Roger Kellaway. Without his work with the Concord Jazz label, Ruby's fans would have been denied the opportunity to hear a number of excellent musical performances. Ruby led the session issued as the label's fifth release and he felt that the program was a fitting tribute to this champion of jazz music after owning a successful automotive dealership.

A Tribute to Carl Jefferson[17]
July 8, 1995, Concord Pavilion, Concord, California
Ruby Braff (cnt), Roger Kellaway (p), Michael Moore (b), Frank Capp (dm)
The Very Thought of You
Concord Jazz CCD 7005 (disc 3)
NOTE: Other performances in this four-CD set are by other artists. This was Ruby's only performance at this special tribute concert. This CD is part of a box set titled *Jazz Celebration: A Tribute to Carl Jefferson.*

Ruby Braff Interview with Steve Voce
Broadcast BBC Radio Merseyside
July 27, 1995, Dennis, Massachusetts
NOTE: A recording of this interview is available but remains unissued.

Ruby Braff Quartet[18]
July 1995, Christine's, West Dennis, Massachusetts
Ruby Braff (cnt), Jon Wheatley (g), Marshall Wood (b), Ron Lundberg (dm)

Ruby reported that he was writing arrangements of tunes associated with Louis Armstrong for a 12 piece band. His arrangements were recorded for Arbors Records on April 15 and 16 ahead.

As mentioned, the September dates often reported for Ruby's recording with Roger Kellaway for Concord are probably incorrect. This recording was more likely made when Ruby was in California in July, adjacent to the concert dedicated to Carl Jefferson. Ruby would not have made two separate trips to the West Coast.

Ruby Braff Interview with Steve Voce
Broadcast BBC Radio Merseyside
November 23, 1995, Dennis, Massachusetts
NOTE: A recording of this interview is available but remains unissued.

Jazz Club of Sarasota[19]
December 1995
No recording available

Ruby Braff and His Jazz Celebration of American Song[20]
January 5 and 6, 1996, Regattabar, Charles Hotel, Cambridge, Massachusetts
Ruby Braff (cnt), Urbie Green (tb), Bill Cunliffe (p), Jon Wheatley (g), Marshall Wood (b), Alan Dawson (dm), Donna Byrne (voc)
Couple of Swells (Irving Berlin)

Ruby Braff: You Can Depend on Me
April 7, 1996, Sound on Sound Studios, New York
Ruby Braff (cnt), Bucky Pizzarelli (g), Johnny Varro (p), Bob Haggart (b), Jim Gwin (dm)
You Can Depend on Me
    Arbors ARCD 19165
Little Old Lady
    Arbors ARCD 19165
Big Butter and Egg Man
    Arbors ARCD 19165
Time on My Hands
    Arbors ARCD 19165

The Man I Love
Arbors ARCD 19165
Just You, Just Me
Arbors ARCD 19165
S'posin'
Arbors ARCD 19165
On the Alamo
Arbors ARCD 19165

Ruby Braff: Being with You: Ruby Braff Remembers Louis Armstrong[21]
April 15–16, 1996, Sound on Sound Studios, New York
Ruby Braff (cnt, voc, arr), Jon-Erik Kellso (cnt), Joe Wilder (flgh*), Dan Barrett (tb), Scott Robinson (bar, cl), Jerry Jerome (ts), Bucky Pizzarelli (g), Johnny Varro (p), Bob Haggart (b), Jim Gwin (dm)
I Never Knew (That Roses Grew)
Arbors ARCD 19163
Little One (voc)
Arbors ARCD 19163
Keepin' Out of Mischief Now
Arbors ARCD 19163
If I Could Be with You One Hour Tonight
Arbors ARCD 19163
Hustlin' and Bustlin' for My Baby
Arbors ARCD 19163
When Your Lover Has Gone
Arbors ARCD 19163
Twelfth Street Rag
Arbors ARCD 19163
Royal Garden Blues*
Arbors ARCD 19163
When It's Sleepy Time Down South
Arbors ARCD 19163
Old Folks
unissued
Pennies from Heaven*
Arbors ARCD 19163
St. Louis Blues*
Arbors ARCD 19163
NOTE: According to Mat Domber, "Old Folks" may be issued in the future. Dan Barrett assisted Ruby with the arrangements for this session. Ruby dedicated this album to the memory of his longtime musical friend, Sam Margolis.

Ruby Braff Quintet[22]
April 17–18, 1996, Sound on Sound Studios, New York

Ruby Braff (cnt), Johnny Varro (p), Bucky Pizzarelli (g), Bob Haggart (b), Jim Gwin (dm)
Way Down Yonder in New Orleans
unissued
On the Sunny Side of the Street
unissued
Our Love Is Here to Stay
unissued
What's the Reason? (I'm Not Pleasin' You)
unissued
Sweet Lorraine
unissued
How Can You Face Me?
unissued
Cheek to Cheek
unissued
You Can't Take That Away from Me
unissued
Sweet Georgia Brown
unissued
The Nearness of You
unissued
I'm Getting Sentimental Over You
unissued
It Had to Be You
unissued
There Will Never Be Another You
unissued
Poor Butterfly
unissued
June in January
unissued
NOTE: This session was recorded for Arbors Records for future release. Perhaps one day it will appear.

Ruby Braff Interview with Steve Voce
Broadcast BBC Radio Merseyside
June 27, 1996, Dennis, Massachusetts
NOTE: A recording of this interview is available but remains unissued.

In August, Ruby headed to the UK, first to perform in several sets at the Nairn International Jazz Festival in Scotland and then to return to London and his favorite spot there, the Pizza Express on Dean Street. While there, he also recorded tunes for two CD releases on Zephyr Records.

Nairn International Jazz Festival[23]
August 18, 1996, 8 p.m., Nairn International Jazz Festival, Golf View Hotel, Seabank Road, Nairn, Scotland
Ruby Braff (cnt), Scott Hamilton (ts), and others

The following recording is probably from this occasion, although it was not accurately dated:

Ruby Braff at Nairn Jazz Festival
August 18, 1996, Nairn, Scotland
Ruby Braff (cnt), Scott Hamilton (ts), Bucky Pizzarelli (g), Dave Green (b), Allan Ganley (dm)
Just You, Just Me
Rockin' Chair
Poor Butterfly
Cherokee (Braff out)
Easy Living (Braff and Hamilton out)
Jeepers Creepers
Yesterdays
Medley:
  Sunday
  Take the "A" Train
  Four or Five Times
Indiana
NOTE: A recording of these tunes is available but remains unissued. "Indiana" was played as an encore. In the recording, Ruby said that they would be back to play some more later. The final three performances are part of a subsequent performance. Of course, Nairn would also have become the site of the final performance of his career in August 2002 had his health not forced his withdrawal.

Ruby Braff at Nairn Jazz Festival
probably following the above performance on August 18, 1996, Nairn, Scotland
Ruby Braff (cnt), Scott Hamilton (ts), Bucky Pizzarelli (g), Dave Green (b), Allan Ganley (dm)
Just One of Those Things
Days of Wine and Roses
Skylark (Hamilton feature)
Presumably this performance continues from this point with other selections.
NOTE: A recording of these tunes is available but remains unissued.

Nairn International Jazz Festival[24]
August 18, 1996, lunchtime, Nairn International Jazz Festival, Golf View Hotel, Seabank Road, Nairn, Scotland
Ruby Braff (cnt) and others without Scott Hamilton

Around this time, Ruby Braff also performed at the Soho Jazz Festival; however, I have been unable to locate further details about his appearance.[25]

Ruby Braff at Pizza Express[26]
August–September, 1996, Pizza Express, Dean Street, London—additional details follow through end of September

Ruby Braff with the Brian Lemon Trio at Pizza Express[27]
August 29–31, 1996, Pizza Express, Dean Street, London (opening of engagement)
Ruby Braff (cnt), Brian Lemon (p), Roy Babbington (b), Allan Ganley (dm)

Ruby Braff with the Brian Lemon Trio at Pizza Express[28]
September 4–8, 1996, Pizza Express, Dean Street, London
Ruby Braff (cnt), Brian Lemon (p), Dave Green or Roy Babbington (b), Allan Ganley (dm)
Come Fly with Me
Change Partners

Ruby Braff: *Braff Plays Wimbledon: The First Set and the Second Set*
September 9, 1996, Wimbledon, Southwest London
Ruby Braff (cnt), Warren Vaché (flgh), Roy Williams (tb), Brian Lemon (p), Dave Green (b), Allan Ganley (dm)
Take the "A" Train
    Zephyr ZECD 15
Jive at Five
    Zephyr ZECD 16
I Know That You Know
    Zephyr ZECD 16

September 10, 1996, Wimbledon, Southwest London
Ruby Braff (cnt), Warren Vaché (flgh), Roy Williams (tb), Brian Lemon (p), Howard Alden (g), Dave Green (b), Allan Ganley (dm)
Wouldn't It Be Loverly
    Zephyr ZECD 15, ZECD 10
When I Fall in Love
    Zephyr ZECD 15
I Cried for You
    Zephyr ZECD16

NOTE: ZECD 15 is titled *Braff Plays Wimbledon: The First Set*; ZECD 16 is titled *Braff Plays Wimbledon: The Second Set*; ZECD 10 is titled Zephyr *Swings into 1997* (a sampler containing 12 titles). Howard Alden arrived in the UK on September 10, in time for the second session above.[29]

Ruby Braff Quartet at Pizza Express[30]
September 11–15, 1996, Pizza Express, Dean Street, London
Ruby Braff (cnt), Howard Alden (g), Dave Green (b), Allan Ganley (dm)

Ruby Braff Quartet at Pizza Express
September 12, 1996, Pizza Express, Dean Street, London
Ruby Braff (cnt), Howard Alden (g), Dave Green (b), Allan Ganley (dm)
Here's Carl
You're a Lucky Guy
Memories of You
Mean to Me
Medley:
  A Single Petal of a Rose (Alden solo)
  Dancers in Love (omit Braff)
Lotus Blossom (omit Braff)
Jeepers Creepers (a few bars lost to tape change)
The Very Thought of You
Avalon
No One Else But You
Lonely Moments
Do It Again
There's a Small Hotel
I've Grown Accustomed to Her Face
The Peacocks (omit Braff)
The Song Is You (omit Braff)
Medley:
  It Had to Be You
  Time on My Hands
Jubilee
NOTE: A recording of these tunes is available but remains unissued.

Ruby Braff Quartet at Pizza Express[31]
September 14–15, 1996, Pizza Express, Dean Street, London
Ruby Braff (cnt), Howard Alden (g), Dave Green (b), Allan Ganley (dm) (advertised personnel)

Ruby Braff Quartet at Pizza Express[32]
September 18–21, 1996, Pizza Express, Dean Street, London
Ruby Braff (cnt), Howard Alden (g), Simon Woolf (b), Allan Ganley (dm)
Dave Green (b) was advertised for this session but was replaced by Simon Woolf at least September 18

Ruby Braff Quartet at Pizza Express
September 18, 1996, Pizza Express, Dean Street, London

Ruby Braff (cnt), Howard Alden (g), Simon Woolf (b), Allan Ganley (dm)
Swing That Music
Body and Soul
Fly Me to the Moon
Where or When
Mood Indigo
Avalon
Medley:
  A Single Petal of a Rose (Alden solo)
  Dancers in Love (Braff out)
Lotus Blossom (Braff out)
If Dreams Come True
Here's Carl
Jubilee
Sweet Savannah Sue
Russian Lullaby
You Took Advantage of Me
Rosetta
Do It Again
My Shining Hour (Braff out)
Crazy He Calls Me (Braff out)
Dream Dancing
No One Else But You
NOTE: A recording of these tunes is available but remains unissued.

Ruby Braff Quartet at Pizza Express
September 22, 1996, Pizza Express, Dean Street, London
Ruby Braff (cnt), Howard Alden (g), Dave Green (b), Allan Ganley (dm)
S'posin'
I've Got a Feelin' I'm Fallin'
When You Wish upon a Star
If I Could Be with You
Wabash (omit Braff, Cannonball Adderley composition)
Lotus Blossom (omit Braff)
Louisiana
Between the Devil and the Deep Blue Sea
You're a Lucky Guy
Ooh, That Kiss
Sunday
Foolin' Myself
Russian Lullaby
The Peacocks (omit Braff)
My Shining Hour (omit Braff)
Basin Street Blues
You Can Depend on Me

Body and Soul
NOTE: A recording of these tunes is available but remains unissued. "Basin Street Blues" is missing about 12 seconds on the recording.

Ruby Braff: *Braff Plays Wimbledon: The First Set and the Second Set*
September 23, 1996, Wimbledon, Southwest London
Ruby Braff (cnt), Brian Lemon (p), Allan Ganley (dm)
Someday Sweetheart
    Zephyr ZECD 15
The Very Thought of You
    Zephyr ZECD 15
I've Got a Feelin' I'm Fallin'
    Zephyr ZECD 15
This Is All I Ask
    Zephyr ZECD 15, ZECD 10
It's the Same Old South
    Zephyr ZECD 15
China Boy
    Zephyr ZECD 15
Rockin' Chair
    Zephyr ZECD 16
When a Woman Loves a Man
    Zephyr ZECD 16
Pennies from Heaven
    Zephyr ZECD 16
I'm Pulling Through
    Zephyr ZECD 16
Miss Brown to You
    Zephyr ZECD 16
Save It Pretty Mama
    Zephyr ZECD 16
NOTE: ZECD 15 is titled *Braff Plays Wimbledon: The First Set*; ZECD 16 is titled *Braff Plays Wimbledon: The Second Set*; ZECD 10 is titled Zephyr *Swings into 1997* (a sampler containing 12 titles).

Ruby Braff Quartet at Pizza Express[33]
September 25, 1996, Pizza Express, Dean Street, London

Ruby Braff Quartet at Pizza Express
September 26, 1996, Pizza Express, Dean Street, London
Ruby Braff (cnt), Dave Cliff (g), Simon Woolf (b), Allan Ganley (dm)
Love Me or Leave Me
Lover Come Back to Me
September in the Rain
September Song

I Never Knew
I Got Rhythm
My Funny Valentine
All of Me
Day In, Day Out
Where or When
Medley:
  Take the "A" Train
  Four or Five Times
Cheek to Cheek
NOTE: A recording of these tunes is available but remains unissued.

Ruby Braff Quartet at Pizza Express[34]
September 27, 1996, Pizza Express, Dean Street, London
Ruby Braff (cnt), Brian Lemon (p), Roy Babbington (b), Allan Ganley (dm)

Ruby Braff Quartet at Pizza Express[35]
September 28, 1996, Pizza Express, Dean Street, London
Ruby Braff (cnt), Brian Lemon (p), Roy Babbington (b), Allan Ganley (dm)

Ruby Braff Quartet at Pizza Express
September 29, 1996, Pizza Express, Dean Street, London (closing night)
Ruby Braff (cnt), Brian Lemon (p), Dave Green (b), Allan Ganley (dm)
Fly Me to the Moon
Sunday
The Very Thought of You
Someday Sweetheart
A Beautiful Friendship (omit Braff)*
Between the Devil and the Deep Blue Sea
Medley:
  I've Grown Accustomed to Her Face
  Wouldn't It Be Loverly
I Would Do Anything for You
When It's Sleepy Time Down South
Cheek to Cheek
Medley:
  White Christmas
  Way Down Yonder in New Orleans
Unknown tune (omit Braff)*
Medley:
  Wrap Your Troubles in Dreams (a few bars lost to tape change)
  I Got Rhythm
NOTE: A recording of all but two of these tunes is available but remains unissued. "A Beautiful Friendship" and an unknown tune were not recorded and are marked with asterisks.

This is the closing night for this engagement. Steve Voce reported that Ruby had been ill during this tour and lost over 20 pounds in body weight.[36] John Fordham reviewed the closing performance[37] and referred to a performance at the Soho Jazz Festival that I have been unable to trace:

> Braff is almost the same age Miles Davis would have been. His choice of idiom was unfashionable enough to stunt his career in the fifties, but the following decade saw his exquisite sound and compelling narrative sense more widely recognized. Now jazz-lovers perceive him as a treasure.
>
> Braff's presence in the Soho Jazz Festival has been one of its finest points, and he finished a short run at the Pizza Express on Sunday in the company of a British trio. He likes the middle and lower range and rarely jacks up the volume, preferring a steady, persuasive eloquence that makes constantly creative use of the same phrase-shapes repeated in different registers. At first everyone stepped pretty tentatively around, but when drummer Allan Ganley switched from brushes to sticks on the second tune and Braff threw up his hands in a gesture of mock self-defense, blood came to the cheeks of the music.
>
> Braff's lovely sound, control at whispering volumes and delicately insinuating low notes were all in evidence on the theme statement of 'The Very Thought of You,' and on 'Someday Sweetheart' (a broadly-grinning swinger), pianist Brian Lemon and bassist Dave Green showed why they're so hard to touch in the oblique and intimate arts of small-room, small-band jazz.
>
> Later in the set, Braff began toying with Green's stealthy, padding bass solos by tossing him fragments of 'I Got Rhythm' to chew on, and slowly and patiently turned a rhapsodic slow trumpet rumination into 'Wouldn't It Be Loverly.' Braff guards a neglected area of jazz history with grace and care, and there's almost nobody on the jazz planet who can do it as well.

After Ruby returned home, over seven months passed until he next appeared in a live performance. Quincy is south of Boston. Then another three months passed before he traveled to Chicago to appear in the Chicago Jazz Festival and yet over seven months until his next session in April for Arbors Records in New York. That session is memorable in part for being the first time that Ruby and Kenny Davern recorded together in a studio despite their long association.

Ruby Braff Sextet[38]
May 15, 1997, Raffael's Restaurant, top floor, Solomon Willard Building, State Street, North Quincy, Massachusetts
Ruby Braff (cnt), Dick Johnson (cl, as), Dave McKenna (p), Jon Wheatley (g), Marshall Wood (b), Jim Gwin (dm)

Ruby Braff Interview[39]
June 8, 1997, rebroadcast of a 1983 interview hosted by Loren Schoenberg, WGBO, New York
NOTE: A recording of this interview is available but remains unissued.

Chicago Jazz Festival[40]

August 31, 1997, Vhicago (WBEZ-FM, broadcast on many other jazz stations)
Ruby Braff (cnt), John Bunch (p), Bucky Pizzarelli (g), Michael Moore (b), Jim Gwin (dm)
Blue Skies
Sunday
Medley:
  Chicago
  Fly Me to the Moon
When I Fall in Love
It's Only a Paper Moon
NOTE: A recording of these tunes is available but remains unissued.

While the following session for Arbors Records is the first time that Ruby and Kenny Davern recorded together in a studio, they had performed together regularly since 1960. Three recordings of live performances had already appeared on Chaz Jazz, Changing Times (a cassette recording, partially reissued on Jump Records), and Arbors Records. In Mat Domber's video recording of the following sessions from April 22 and 23, Ruby explained that he asked Kenny to perform only one tune, but that he arrived early and agreed to join the group for several others as shown below. "Romance in the Dark" may appear on a future release with unissued titles from 1996. The next album was named one of six favorites from 1999 by *The New Yorker*.[41] The album that follows was released after Ruby's death. Photos from the March of Jazz from these recording sessions are available.[42]

Ruby Braff: *Born to Play*[43]

April 20-21, 1998, Avatar Studios, New York
Ruby Braff (cnt, voc, arr), Kenny Davern (cl*), Howard Alden, Bucky Pizzarelli, Jon Wheatley (g), Michael Moore and Marshall Wood (b), Jim Gwin (dm)
Avalon*
    Arbors ARCD 19203
The Doodle King*
    Arbors ARCD 19203
Medley:
  Smile
    Arbors ARCD 19203
  La Violettera
    Arbors ARCD 19203
Think
    Arbors ARCD 19203
Jive at Five
    Arbors ARCD 19203

I Want a Little Girl*
    Arbors ARCD 19203
I'm Shooting High
    Arbors ARCD 19203
Born to Lose* (voc)
    Arbors ARCD 19203

Out Kenny Davern
Romance in the Dark
    unissued

Ruby Braff Quintet: *Our Love Is Here to Stay*
April 22, 1998, New York
Ruby Braff (cnt, voc), Chuck Wilson (as), Howard Alden, Jon Wheatley (g), Marshall Wood (b), Jim Gwin (dm)
Linger Awhile
    Arbors ARCD 19426
Gone with the Wind
    unissued, video recording available
All My Life
    Arbors ARCD 19426
Day In, Day Out
    Arbors ARCD 19426
I'm Comin' Virginia
    Arbors ARCD 19426

Ruby Braff Septet: *Our Love Is Here to Stay*
April 23, 1998, New York
Ruby Braff (cnt, voc), Chuck Wilson (as, cl*), Scott Robinson (ts), Howard Alden, Jon Wheatley (g), Marshall Wood (b), Jim Gwin (dm)
I Know That You Know
    Arbors ARCD 19426

Add Jon-Erik Kellso (cnt)
Honeysuckle Rose
    unissued, video recording available
'Deed I Do
    Arbors ARCD 19426
Clear Water
    Arbors ARCD 19426
Medley:
  Our Love Is Here to Stay
    Arbors ARCD 19426
  What Is There to Say?
    Arbors ARCD 19426

Darktown Strutters' Ball*
Arbors ARCD 19426

"Clear Water" is another of Ruby Braff's original compositions. It is a unique melody based on the chords of "Love Me or Leave Me." Before "Clear Water," Ruby performed "Love Me or Leave Me" on the piano and was gradually joined by the other musicians in an informal performance that was captured by Mat Domber's video recording of the session but not captured on the studio recording tapes since the piano was at the rear of the studio and not miked. "Honeysuckle Rose" is a fine performance lasting 16 minutes that might be issued in the future, perhaps accompanied by "Gone with the Wind" or some other unreleased material from Arbor's vault.

I had the distinct honor of being asked to write the album notes for this release and have included them here:

Leading Creative Musical Performances: Ruby Braff in the Studio

Duke Ellington and Louis Armstrong both encouraged people to think of music as "good" or "the other kind." Ellington avoided stylistic labels and even used Billy Strayhorn's words, "Beyond Category," to discourage classification in favor of simply recognizing excellence whenever it occurred. Indeed, you are now listening to good music from a musician who is beyond category. Ruby Braff was an original creative artist. There is no need to argue whether he should be labeled as traditional, mainstream, swing, or modern in his approach. He was all of those and simply used his remarkable skills to create beautiful musical performances. His tone and style are instantly recognizable to anyone who takes the time to listen.

What you have in your hands is an unexpected treat. It presents music recorded on April 22 and 23, 1998, in New York. Ruby's fans will be delighted to have a new studio recording. Because it was not previously documented, they will think of it as a remarkable gift, since Ruby died in 2003. But if this is the first time you have heard Ruby play his cornet, you will be immediately attracted by his creativity and precision. You will enjoy these performances as long as you appreciate good music.

Ruby often told me that he seldom failed to please people who heard him play in clubs and concerts, but he cited a problem when he said that not enough people came in the first place. That may apply to this release as well, but perhaps this will offer an opportunity for Ruby's fans to share this music with a new generation of fans. I certainly hope so, for this is music that everyone can enjoy.

As I mentioned, this recording brings us back to 1998. Mat and Rachel Domber continued to record Ruby regularly, including his final concert performance at Nairn, Scotland (ARCD 19368). Newer projects came along, and these recordings simply remained in their vault. A companion released session, recorded on two previous days, is *Born to Play* (Arbors ARCD 19203). Many of you have already listened to it. That recording featured a somewhat larger group of musicians and was named one of six favorites from 1999 in *The New Yorker*.[44] For that recording, Ruby had prepared a series of arrangements, with the help of Howard Alden on several tunes. But for these final two days in the studio, Ruby wanted a more spontaneous approach. If you listen to both recordings in sequence, you will see that the results are quite different yet equally enjoyable. For this CD, the arrangements were created on the spot. Michael Moore, Bucky Pizzarelli, and Kenny Davern have departed, but Chuck Wilson has been added for both days and Jon-Erik Kellso and Scott Robinson were added for the final day. Before this recording, Ruby had performed with Chuck at the Nice Jazz Festival in 1990. Chuck was then a member of the Howard Alden–Dan Barrett Quartet, but this is the first time they recorded together. Their paths also had crossed in 1988 at the Newport Jazz Festival in New York, although they did not perform together, in a well-received tribute to Billie Holiday. Ruby had recorded with Scott Robinson and Jon-Erik Kellso together once before, on the Arbors release *Being With You* from 1996. Ruby had previously performed on a number of occasions with Howard Alden, Jon Wheatley, Marshall Wood, and Jim Gwin. All appear on some of Ruby's released recordings made for Arbors Records.

Mat Domber captured most of the recording session using his video camera and that gave me a unique opportunity to watch Ruby at work. It is interesting to see that there were several times when the musicians praised Ruby for his creativity during these performances. I find the video fascinating, and it provides an opportunity to examine the way Ruby leads a session and creates the foundation for each tune performed. This music will draw you back to listen more than once. I hope you will enjoy reading about how these performances evolved during the session.

Day One: Avatar Studio, April 22, 1998: Ruby Braff (cnt), Chuck Wilson (as), Howard Alden (g), Jon Wheatley (g), Marshall Wood (b), Jim Gwin (dm)

Mat's video opens while the musicians are gathering. Ruby stood with his back to the control booth while both guitarists were already seated. Jim Gwin took his position opposite Ruby as Marshall Wood arrived. They discussed "Born to Lose," a tune they recorded the previous day. Ruby called it the "suicide tune," describing it as a song that showed no chance of happiness. He joked that he looked out from the 15th floor of his hotel a few times overnight with those lyrics in mind—and loud construction noises in the background. Next, he commented that the studio seemed so empty without the second bass, third guitar, and Kenny Davern. In casual conversation, he praised Don Costa's abilities as an arranger. Soon, he set the tempo for a relaxed rehearsal of "Linger Awhile" as a warm-up for the day. Howard opened. Braff led, followed by Wilson, Alden, Wood, and Wheatley in turn. Then Ruby returned to close. Ruby asked for everyone to move closer to him, changing the microphone setup since yesterday had more musicians and music stands that are no longer needed since there were no written arrangements in today's session. Ruby simply wanted to create a more intimate connection among all the musicians. Nobody used headphones. Everyone was alert and prepared to both lead and support during each performance. Simply put, Ruby was building a team.

Next, Ruby hummed a figure for the performance–something like bo-de-do-de-do-de-do-be–and said that he stole this from Rex Stewart's small group Ellington recording made on November 2, 1940. He remarked, "It was so pretty. We might even end it that way. This was the first record I ever heard of this." Ruby had recorded this tune in 1955 for Vanguard, one of the recordings that catapulted him to fame as a unique jazz artist. The musicians rehearsed twice more. On the first, solos followed an opening ensemble in the following order: Alden, Braff, and Wilson. Ruby stopped the performance and coached the musicians as he outlined the structure he wanted to follow. In the second rehearsal, the opening ensemble led to a different solo order and continues: Alden, Braff leading on the melody with Wilson, then solos from Wheatley, Wilson, Alden, Braff (with a wonderful restatement of Rex Stewart's phrase that leads to a transition with Wilson), then Wood. Braff, and Wilson exchanged ideas, and the ensemble concluded the performance. Ruby remarked, "Yes, something like that." He smiled and provided vocal encouragement throughout. The musicians all moved to the control booth to listen to the playback and return to the studio to discuss the results of the rehearsal.

Now, they became serious and started their work for the day. Take one of "Linger Awhile" began with the ensemble playing Rex Stewart's phrase. Alden stated the melody and soloed, followed by Braff and Wheatley. Ruby stopped the group, saying simply, "Not enough pizzazz." He reworked the head arrangement to include short four-bar exchanges with Wilson and worked out the bridge featuring Braff on top of Wilson. So take two began with an opening ensemble, then Alden for melody and solo, Braff and Wilson for exchanges and joined on the bridge, then Wheatley soloed (with punctuation from Braff), followed by Wilson who started by picking up Braff's figure. Braff started his next solo softly and then interpolated a bit of "Bye Bye Blackbird," then returned to Rex Stewart's figure accompanied by Wilson, next leading to a transition to Wood followed by Braff and Wilson exchanged phrases. Rex Stewart's figure appeared again, leading to exchanges by Braff and Alden and Alden's solo. Next, Braff led the ensemble, and then he asked Gwin to join as they led the ensemble to close. At that, Ruby nodded and said, "That's a good one." So the performance evolved from the earliest rehearsal to a highly interactive performance that is far removed from a simple sequence of solos. This had been accomplished in less than an hour and would not be possible without the great skills of these musicians and their trust in Ruby's musical leadership.

It was now time to relax. During a short break, Ruby walked to a piano in a dark corner of the studio and started to play "All My Life" as a demo. He remarked, "That's a nice tune, isn't it?" The musicians discussed the chords and Ruby continued, "I played it years ago." In fact, he recorded it with Scott Hamilton in 1985. Ruby caught his breath after inhaling some of the medication he used for his emphysema and then outlined the tempo in F. "Let's see what it feels like. One thing we don't need to worry about is keys, because there are so many of them." So, the musicians commenced a rehearsal of the tune. Alden opened, leading to the full ensemble with Braff in the lead. Ruby hummed a descending eighth-note sequence and discussed Bobby Hackett's well-known descending line in "String of Pearls." This framed a transitional unison phrase with Wilson in this performance. Ruby and Chuck rehearsed this phrase, then Ruby outlined a sequence of solos, saying, "And we'll worry about the rest of it as time goes by." Ruby praised Hackett's original line: "You need to really go to college to do that." After a false start and incomplete take, the musicians completed take two of this tune. Alden opened, leading to the ensemble with Braff in the lead using the variation on the Hackett figure supported by Wilson. Wilson soloed; then Braff took the lead with Wilson. Solos continued with Alden and Wilson as Ruby nodded and smiled. Then Braff signaled for Wilson and guitars to stop so that his solo is backed by Wood and Gwin. Next, he signaled for exchanges with Wood and led the ensemble to close. Ruby simply said, "That's fine—don't mess with that one at all. This is not like a rock date where you walk in and ask, 'What's the chord?'"

Next, the musicians focused on "Day In, Day Out." This is Ruby's first recording of this tune. There is a gap in Mat's video recording during an informal run through. Ruby's first vision for the performance included a tempo change that incorporated a Basie-like "Jumpin' at the Woodside" effect. Ruby declared that he set the tempo too fast and joked, "I know, you just want to knock out the trumpet players." The rehearsal continued. Wheatley chorded for the "Jumpin' at the Woodside" effect for the ensemble with Braff in lead for the melody. Then Wilson and Wheatley soloed, and Braff closed using a nice phrase–a very nice performance overall. Ruby said, "Nice tune. Wish I wrote it." One of the other musicians replied, "You almost did." This referred to the creative approach that Ruby had outlined for the performance. With rehearsals done, Ruby called for take one.

The performance began with lots of rhythmic variety. Both guitars opened using a brief samba rhythm that flowed into Braff's lead over ensemble in 4/4 then returned to a samba rhythm. Solos followed by Alden, Wilson, Wheatley, Braff (entering two bars early). Wood accelerated the tempo and led to a transition using the "Woodside" theme as a background as Braff continued his solo, followed by Alden and Wilson. Braff returned to bring the tune to a close with three final notes played by the guitarists, using the effective musical economies associated with Count Basie. Ruby said, "We're making much more of this than is really necessary—just do the tune, swing it, and get out nicely."

This was followed by a short false start. Ruby confirmed that they would retain the opening but not use the "Woodside" motif or the tempo change. The performance now had a simpler structure. It opened with the same rhythmic variety and used both guitars with a short samba opening that transitioned to Braff's lead over ensemble. This was followed by solos from Wheatley and Wilson. Then Ruby soloed with Wood and Gwin, to bring the performance to a close, thus resulting in a much shorter version for this second take of the tune.

What you hear on this CD is a portion of the first recorded take. This begins with Wood setting the accelerated tempo that leads to the "Woodside" theme and it continues as described above. Ruby achieved his goal of "not making too much of this" by simply preserving the most creative part of this performance for you to enjoy.

"I'm Comin' Virginia" came next. It began with an informal run through. Ruby opened with Alden, and the group played a chorus to become familiar with their approach to the tune. Ruby said, "This is nice. I've always wanted to record this one." He did in his Berigan tribute album recorded for RCA in March 1957. Given his many recordings, we should forgive his uncharacteristic memory lapse. In take one, Ruby opened with Alden on the verse, leading to the ensemble entering on the chorus. Solos followed in order: Wilson, Alden, Braff, Wheatley, Wilson, Braff with Alden, Alden, Braff with ensemble to close a beautiful performance. This ended the day's work.

Day Two: Avatar Studio, April 23, 1998: Ruby Braff (cnt), Jon-Erik Kellso (tp), Chuck Wilson (as, cl), Scott Robinson (ts), Howard Alden (g), Jon Wheatley (g), Marshall Wood (b), Jim Gwin (dm)

Ruby sat at piano as the musicians assembled, playing "I Know That You Know" and "Street of Dreams." Scott Robinson joined the group of musicians from the previous day. Ruby mentioned his admiration for Benny Goodman as he played "I Know That You Know." He is very familiar with this tune, having recorded it for Chiaroscuro in 1972 and Zephyr (UK) in 1996. The musicians joined him on the tune for an informal warm-up. Braff led with the melody over the ensemble, followed by Wilson, Robinson, and Wheatley in an incomplete video capture of this performance. Ruby then led a discussion with Wilson and Robinson to establish a harmonized background figure and said, "Just play the chords until we get to that part and then we'll worry about the rest later." Chuck replied, "Slap me if I get too hot." There was lots of laughter and good spirit among the musicians as the second day began.

Two short false starts came next to establish that the saxes harmonize behind Braff's opening. Ruby said to Chuck, "Don't worry. If you worry you'll have grey hair." Take one began with Alden leading into the ensemble with Braff in the lead. Then Wheatley soloed with punctuation by Ruby, Chuck, and Scott. Robinson was next, while Ruby injected a figure in his second chorus and Chuck leaned forward to contribute. Ruby grinned. Wilson soloed, and Ruby smiled at both Scott and Chuck, pleased with what he is hearing. Ruby and Scott added some punctuation to Wilson's solo. Then, Ruby nodded to Howard to take the lead as Chuck's solo approached its end. After Alden's solo, Braff shaped a transition to a series of exchanges in the following order: Wilson, Robinson, Wood, Braff, Wilson, Robinson, Alden, Wood, Wheatley, and Wood. Then, Braff led the ensemble to a close. He used his hand to signal for silence and gave an okay sign with his thumb and finger, adding, "I rather enjoyed that—a good way to start a session." Everyone was smiling.

The musicians entered the playback booth with Kellso now joining them. Ruby expressed his pleasure with the series of exchanges. The musicians discussed whether or not to do another take because Ruby entered slightly early at one point with his support behind Wheatley's solo. Ruby said, "We could do another take because of this one phrase but we don't save things. We just play things. We don't lift things out of bodies like cadavers. We don't graft. The reason we do it over is that we don't like the previous one." The entire group decided to retain this take and continue to the next tune. Ruby was sincere in asking for each musician's opinion on this point.

The CD continues with a performance of "'Deed I Do." Ruby previously recorded this tune with Benny Goodman on the live recordings from Basin Street in 1955, on his own 1955 album for Jazztone, with the Newport All Stars on MPS in 1969, with Woody Herman for Chiaroscuro in 1980, and finally with Scott Hamilton on Concord in 1985. Clearly this is one of his favorites. The group's run through opened with the ensemble with Braff in the lead. Ruby called for take one after saying that he decided to use this tune from a performance the previous night that included Cynthia Sayer performing with several musicians now in the studio. He remarked, "She's a nice person. Okay, kids, let's go." After a false start, the ensemble opened with Braff emerging in the lead on the release with return to the full ensemble. Alden soloed first as Braff, and Kellso added punctuation. Kellso soloed next, followed by Wilson; with Braff, and Kellso again adding punctuation. Wheatley and Robinson followed with Wilson, Braff, and Kellso provided a foundation in the background. Next came exchanges between Braff and Wood as Ruby signaled for the others to stop playing. Then, Gwin entered, joined by the guitars. Ruby interpolated part of the melody from the song "What's the Reason I'm Not Pleasing You," leading to the full ensemble to bring the performance to a close. Ruby said, "All right that's a good one. I like that."

Ruby returned to the piano to explore a mood with the tune, "Love Me or Leave Me." The rhythm spontaneously joined him, followed by Kellso and Wilson. After a while, Ruby left the piano and returned to his position with his back to the control room. He said the following: "That was beautiful. That's the tune and that's the mood we'll play it in. Play behind me just like I played behind you on the piano; then I'll sound good, too. Just keep the mood and let's see what it feels like." They began an informal run through with guitars leading to the ensemble with Ruby in the lead but then stopped. At this point, Ruby surprised them by using the chords from "Love Me or Leave Me" to create an original melody he named "Clear Water." This was performed as a blues, but Ruby instructed, "Don't play the melody anywhere and watch the tempo. Stay downstairs to keep the mood mellow." After three false starts, take one opened with a bass pickup phrase; then guitars and drums entered in sequence, proceeding to the full ensemble with Ruby in the lead to state his original melody. Solos continued in the following order: Robinson, Kellso, Alden, Wilson with ensemble, Robinson with ensemble, Kellso, Wheatley, and Wood. Ruby led the ensemble to close the performance. He then nodded and the others smiled as Ruby said, "Now I need to remember what I played and send it to my publisher."

After a short break for lunch, the musicians resumed their work. Next up was "Our Love Is Here to Stay." Ruby previously recorded this tune with Teddi King for George Wein's Storyville label and later with the Ruby Braff–George Barnes Quartet for Chiaroscuro in 1973. A short run through featured the guitars, then opened to Braff when it stops. Ruby hummed an outline of the opening phrases he wanted to use, saying, "Never go fast or do anything that causes trouble. Stop before there's an accident. I don't care what you do. Just do something beautiful. Then we'll see what happens." He then remarked, speaking to Mat Domber, "What was that tune you were playing at the piano, Matthew? (Mat was noodling on the piano with one finger before the session began playing "The Darktown Strutters' Ball" at a slower than usual tempo.) Remind me of that one later. I've always had to play that one fast in saloons, but what's the hurry here. I like your tempo."

The musicians began take one of "Our Love Is Here to Stay." Braff opened with guitars for four false starts. After the first, Ruby smiled and said, "That chord sounds a little murky." This led to a discussion of the notes for the saxes behind Ruby in the opening, followed by a brief rehearsal as Ruby outlined use of a secondary melody. He asserted, "Don't worry about it. It will work out fine." There was another false start followed by a full take. Braff again opened with guitars and then soloed with rhythm. He interpolated "What Is There to Say?" in his chorus and the others incorporated this in their own playing. Next come Alden, Braff with saxes, Wheatley and Wood. Braff followed and he reverts to the melody line of "Our Love Is Here to Stay" and accelerated the tempo. Alden followed with support from the ensemble. Next, Ruby signaled a series of exchanges in the following order: Robinson, Wilson, Kellso, Robinson, Wilson, Kellso, and Wheatley. Braff entered with rhythm to slow the tempo, ending with "What Is There to Say?" The musicians commented, simply saying, "Nice, Ruby. Really nice juxtaposition." They are all truly working together as a team and their admiration for Ruby's leadership had been consistently evident throughout this session. But now there was only one more tune to perform before the session ended. And it was an unusual choice that appeared to surprise the musicians.

A rehearsal for the opening of "The Darktown Strutters' Ball" began after a short break. The saxes opened with rhythm. Then Ruby entered. Wilson switched to clarinet for a new attempt on the tune for take one. The reeds opened with rhythm; then Braff continued with the ensemble, followed by solos from Kellso and Wilson on clarinet. Ruby grinned while listening to Chuck and he inserted a background figure of "Four or Five Times." Then he followed with the ensemble. Next, Ruby signaled for solos by Alden and Robinson that flowed into exchanges featuring Braff, Robinson, Wilson, Kellso, Ruby with guitars and bass only and finally the full ensemble to close. Watching it unfold on Mat's video recording was a joy for me, as I observed Ruby even slapping his thigh in delight at one point. The rhythm was particularly infectious on this traditional tune. Ruby said, "That was fun. I especially liked the intro. It's as close as we'll get to rock for a while." So, Ruby enjoyed this tune that he had heard Mat play earlier in the day. He had never recorded it before.

It has been over seven years since Ruby passed away. I miss talking with him, but I treasure these recordings as yet another reminder of his artistry. In time, most of us will be forgotten, but Ruby deserves to be remembered through his music for a longer time. My memories of Ruby continue to bring me joy. This recording represents all that Whitney Balliett must have had in mind when he coined the phrase about jazz, the "Sound of Surprise." We delight in receiving this unexpected gift from Ruby, Mat and Rachel Domber, and all the musicians who collaborated in the creation of this wonderful music. Ruby is not able to play for us any longer, but his magnificent music continues to delight many of us and live in our hearts. He was certainly a demanding leader, always direct with his comments, but the results he obtained were often magical. In these performances, combinations of musicians shift from the full ensemble to collections performing as duos, trios, and quartets as Ruby stimulates our interest with his spontaneous instructions to his team. Ruby told me that he would rehearse over 10,000 times a day in his mind, varying tunes, musicians, and combinations to discover ways that he could create unique performances. The results of his dedication are clearly evident here.

In closing, let's recall some words from Louis Armstrong: *"My belief and satisfaction is that as long as a person breathes they still have a chance to exercise the talents they were born with. I speak of something which I know about and have been doing all my life, and that's music. Music has no age. There is no such thing as on your way out. As long as you are doing something that is interesting and good, you're in business as long as you're breathing."* And the music you are hearing on this CD is most certainly good music, performed at the highest level, beyond category.

Finally, I wish to thank Mat and Rachel Domber for giving me the honor of writing these notes. Perhaps some will see this as just another recording by Ruby Braff, but I value each of his recordings as a musical treasure. He brings beauty to the world, and that is a precious contribution to the ongoing history of good music.

Ruby Braff Interview with Steve Voce
Broadcast BBC Radio Merseyside
December 6, 1998, Dennis, Massachusetts
NOTE: A recording of this interview is available but remains unissued.

Ruby Braff Interview with Steve Voce
Broadcast BBC Radio Merseyside
January 3, 1999, Dennis, Massachusetts
NOTE: A recording of this interview is available but remains unissued.

Bob Haggart Memorial Concert
January 24, 1999, Sarasota, Florida
Ruby Braff (cnt), Dick Hyman (p)
The Very Thought of You
    unissued, a video recording is available

Add Panama Francis (dm)
If Dreams Come True
    unissued, a video recording is available
NOTE: A video recording of these tunes is available but remains unissued.

Ruby Braff Interview with Steve Voce
Broadcast BBC Radio Merseyside
March 7, 1999, Dennis, Massachusetts
NOTE: A recording of this interview is available but remains unissued.

A year had passed since Ruby's previous time in the studio. Since he traveled from his home in Cape Cod to New York for recording, he and Mat had determined that an annual multi-day session was an appropriate schedule. This time, three CDs come from the recordings as Ruby planned a different approach for each day.

Ruby Braff and Strings: *In the Wee, Small Hours in London and New York*
March 24, 1999, Clinton Studies, New York
Ruby Braff (cnt), John Bunch (p), Bucky Pizzarelli (g), Michael Moore (b), Kenny Washington (dm) with Robert Chausow, Michael Roth (v), Adria Benjamin (viola), Sarah Hewitt (cello), and arranged and conducted by Tommy Newsom
Love Walked In
    Arbors ARCD 19219

Goodnight My Love
Arbors ARCD 19219
I Married an Angel
Arbors ARCD 19219
Love Thy Neighbor
Arbors ARCD 19219
April in Paris
Arbors ARCD 19219
In the Wee Small Hours of the Morning
Arbors ARCD 19219
I Get Along without You Very Well
Arbors ARCD 19219
My Heart Stood Still
Arbors ARCD 19219
See Pizza session from November 1978 for the rest of the performances included on this CD.

Ruby Braff: *Music for the Still of the Night*
March 25, 1999, Clinton Studios, New York
Ruby Braff (cnt), Howard Alden (g), John Bunch (p), Michael Moore (b), Kenny Washington (dm)
Thinking of You
Arbors ARCD 19221
Can't We Be Friends?
Arbors ARCD 19221
Willow Weep for Me
Arbors ARCD 19221
When It's Sleepy Time Down South
Arbors ARCD 19221
I Wished on the Moon
Arbors ARCD 19221
Linger Awhile
Arbors ARCD 19221
Looking at You
Arbors ARCD 19221
Ghost of a Chance
Arbors ARCD 19221
Fly Me to the Moon
Arbors ARCD 19221
These Foolish Things
Arbors ARCD 19221

Ruby Braff: *The Cape Codfather*
March 26, 1999, Clinton Studios, New York

Ruby Braff (cnt), Kenny Davern (cl), Tommy Newsom (ts), John Bunch (p), Howard Alden (g), Michael Moore (b), Kenny Washington (dm)
My Melancholy Baby
Arbors ARCD 19222
Love Is Just around the Corner
Arbors ARCD 19222
Orange
Arbors ARCD 19222
If Dreams Come True
Arbors ARCD 19222
'Tain't So, Honey, 'Tain't So
Arbors ARCD 19222
As Time Goes By
Arbors ARCD 19222

Ruby immensely enjoyed telling the story behind the design of the cover of his album *The Cape Codfather*. The cover image was produced by combining a new photo of Ruby's head with an existing photo of Marlon Brando's body that was taken from publicity shots surrounding the release of the motion picture *The Godfather*.

Ruby Braff Interview with Christopher Lydon
July 4, 1999, interview on WBUR, Boston, with Chris Lydon on his program *Connections*
NOTE: A recording of this interview is available but remains unissued.

Ruby Braff returned to the United Kingdom where his performances were extensively recorded by Dave Bennett. Dave was gracious in sharing copies with me.

Ruby Braff Quartet: Pizza on the Park
July 26, 1999, Pizza on the Park, London
Ruby Braff (cnt), Paul Sealey (g), Simon Woolf (b), Allan Ganley (dm)
No tape known

Ruby Braff Quartet: Pizza on the Park[45]
July 27, 1999, Pizza on the Park, London
Ruby Braff (cnt), Paul Sealey (g), Simon Woolf (b), Allan Ganley (dm)
Keepin' Out of Mischief Now
Sugar
As Long as I Live
Yesterdays
Just You, Just Me
Jeepers Creepers
There's a Small Hotel

Medley:
  Time on My Hands
  Struttin' with Some Barbecue
Medley:
  The Man I Love
  I've Grown Accustomed to Her Face
NOTE: A video recording of these tunes is available but remains unissued.

Ruby Braff Quartet: Pizza on the Park
July 28, 1999, Pizza on the Park, London
Ruby Braff (cnt), Paul Sealey (g), Simon Woolf (b), Allan Ganley (dm)
Thou Swell
Poor Butterfly
I Want a Little Girl
Don't Get Around Much Anymore
I Never Knew
As Time Goes By
Lover Come Back to Me
I've Got the World on a String
Nice Work If You Can Get It
Blue and Sentimental
Wouldn't It Be Loverly
Liza
NOTE: A recording of these tunes is available but remains unissued.

Ruby Braff Quartet: Pizza on the Park
July 29, 1999, Pizza on the Park, London
Ruby Braff (cnt), Paul Sealey (g), Simon Woolf (b), Allan Ganley (dm)
I Want a Little Girl
As Time Goes By
Lover Come Back to Me
I've Got the World on a String
Nice Work If You Can Get It
Blue and Sentimental
Wouldn't It Be Loverly
Liza
NOTE: A video recording of these tunes is available but remains unissued.

Ruby Braff Quartet: Pizza on the Park
July 30, 1999, Pizza on the Park, London
Ruby Braff (cnt), Paul Sealey (g), Simon Woolf (b), Allan Ganley (dm)
It's Only a Paper Moon
Keepin' Out of Mischief Now
Gone with the Wind
When Your Lover Has Gone

I Want to Be Happy
Don't Get Around Much Anymore
There Will Never Be Another You
You're Driving Me Crazy
Yesterdays*
NOTE: A video recording of these tunes is available but remains unissued. The recording of "Yesterdays" is incomplete and marked with an asterisk.

Ruby Braff Quartet: Pizza on the Park
July 31, 1999, Pizza on the Park, London
Ruby Braff (cnt), Paul Sealey (g), Simon Woolf (b), Allan Ganley (dm)
Ghost of a Chance
Watch What Happens
Dinah
Yesterdays
Take the "A" Train
Lover Come Back to Me
Medley:
  Over the Rainbow
  I've Grown Accustomed to Her Face
Day In, Day Out*
NOTE: A video recording of these tunes is available but remains unissued. The recording of "Day In, Day Out" is incomplete and marked with an asterisk.

Ruby Braff Quartet: Pizza on the Park
August 1, 1999, Pizza on the Park, London (this may actually have been August 2 giving Ruby a day off on August 1 but there is no information to confirm that possibility)
Ruby Braff (cnt), Paul Sealey (g), Simon Woolf (b), Allan Ganley (dm)
Morning of the Carnival
I've Found a New Baby
What Is There to Say?
The Very Thought of You*
Ain't Misbehavin'
NOTE: A video recording of these tunes is available but remains unissued. The recording of "The Very Thought of You" is a fragment and marked with an asterisk.

Ruby Braff Quartet: Pizza on the Park
August 2, 1999, Pizza on the Park, London
Ruby Braff (cnt), Paul Sealey (g), Simon Woolf (b), Allan Ganley (dm)
I've Grown Accustomed to Her Face
Love Me or Leave Me
I've Got a Right to Sing the Blues
Our Love Is Here to Stay (incomplete)

Day In, Day Out*
NOTE: A video recording of these tunes is available but remains unissued. The recording of "Day In, Day Out" is incomplete and marked with an asterisk.

Ruby Braff Quartet: Pizza on the Park[46]
August 3–4, 1999, Pizza on the Park, London
These dates were also listed in *Jazz Journal International.* No further information has been located.

Ruby Braff Quartet: Pizza on the Park
August 5, 1999, Pizza on the Park, London
Ruby Braff (cnt), Paul Sealey (g), Simon Woolf (b), Allan Ganley (dm)
Out of Nowhere
Yesterdays
I Want to Be Happy
Over the Rainbow
Solitude
Someday Sweetheart
'Deed I Do
Pennies from Heaven
Blue Skies*
All of Me
You've Changed
There's a Small Hotel
I Want to Be Happy
You Can Depend on Me
I've Grown Accustomed to Her Face*
NOTE: A video recording of these tunes is available but remains unissued. The recordings of "Blue Skies" and "I've Grown Accustomed to Her Face" are incomplete and marked with asterisks.

Ruby Braff Quartet: Pizza on the Park
August 6, 1999, Pizza on the Park, London
Ruby Braff (cnt), Paul Sealey (g), Simon Woolf (b), Allan Ganley (dm)
Gone with the Wind
When a Woman Loves a Man
Sweet Sue
On the Sunny Side of the Street
Yesterdays
Lady Be Good
Jeepers Creepers
Rockin' Chair
Medley:
  Satin Doll
  Take the "A" Train

NOTE: A video recording of these tunes is available but remains unissued.

Ruby Braff Quartet: Pizza on the Park
August 7, 1999, Pizza on the Park, London
Ruby Braff (cnt), Paul Sealey (g), Simon Woolf (b), Allan Ganley (dm)
Chicago
You've Changed
Sunday
Days of Wine and Roses
Dinah
Gone with the Wind
Mean to Me
I Would Do Anything for You
My Heart Stood Still
You Can Depend on Me
I've Grown Accustomed to Her Face
NOTE: A video recording of these tunes is available but remains unissued.

Jazz Journal International stated that the engagement at Pizza on the Park ran from July 26–August 7, except August 1. If performances occurred August 3 and 4, there are no recordings available. As mentioned, the recording listed above for August 1 is probably from August 2, extending the recordings from that date.

Ruby Braff at Nairn Jazz Festival
August 10, 1999, Highland Conference Center, Nairn, Scotland
Ruby Braff (cnt), John Bunch (p), Frank Tate (b), Louis Stewart (g), Steve Brown (dm)
My Heart Stood Still
Way Down Yonder in New Orleans
Over the Rainbow

Add Joe Temperley (bars)
Jive at Five
It Had to Be You
Between the Devil and the Deep Blue Sea
I Never Knew
I've Grown Accustomed to Her Face
NOTE: A video recording of these tunes is available but remains unissued.

Ruby Braff Interviews
August 10 and 11, 1999, hotel room in Nairn, Scotland
NOTE: A video recording of this interview is available but remains unissued.

Ruby Braff at Nairn Jazz Festival
August 11, 1999, Golf View Hotel, Nairn, Scotland
Ruby Braff (cnt), John Bunch (p), Frank Tate (b), Steve Brown (dm)
Ghost of a Chance
Love Me or Leave Me

Add Joe Temperley (bars)
Blue and Sentimental
It's Only a Paper Moon
When I Fall in Love
Nice Work If You Can Get It
Over the Rainbow
NOTE: A video recording of these tunes is available but remains unissued.

Ruby Braff Interviews
August 13 and 14, 1999, hotel room in Brecon, Wales
NOTE: A video recording of these interviews is available but remains unissued.

Ruby Braff at Brecon
August 13, 1999, Brecon, Wales
Ruby Braff (cnt), Scott Hamilton (ts), John Bunch (p), Dave Green (b), Allan Ganley (dm)
Love Is Just around the Corner*
Between the Devil and the Deep Blue Sea
Who Cares? (Hamilton feature; Ruby out)
I Want to Be Happy
Yesterdays (Braff feature; Hamilton out)
Lover Come Back to Me
Indiana
These Foolish Things
Love Me or Leave Me
My One and Only Love (Bunch feature)
The Man I Love
NOTE: A video recording of these tunes is available but remains unissued. The first tune, "Love Is Just around the Corner" was not recorded and is marked with an asterisk.

Ruby Braff at Brecon[47]
Saturday August 14, 1999, Theatr Brycheiniog, Brecon, Wales
Ruby Braff (cnt), Scott Hamilton (ts), John Bunch (p), Dave Green (b), Allan Ganley (dm)
Just You, Just Me
Mean to Me
Easy Living* (Braff out)
There's a Small Hotel

Lover Come Back to Me*
Someday Sweetheart*
Memories of You* (Hamilton out)
Dinah*
NOTE: A video recording of these tunes is available but remains unissued. The recording of "Day In, Day Out" is incomplete and is marked with an asterisk. The final four tunes marked with asterisks were broadcast on BBC Radio.

Ruby Braff Interview
August 15, 1999, hotel room, Brecon, Wales
NOTE: A video recording of this interview is available but remains unissued.

Ruby returned home following his successful tour and Steve Voce phoned him for an interview on his BBC Radio program.

Ruby Braff Interview with Steve Voce
Broadcast BBC Radio Merseyside
September 12, 1999, Dennis, Massachusetts
NOTE: A recording of this interview is available but remains unissued.

Ruby may have appeared at Ralph and Sunnie Sutton's Denver jazz party, held on Labor Day weekend at the Denver Marriott Hotel. Other musicians in advance publicity included Dick Hyman and Kenny Davern.[48] It is very likely that Ruby did not perform again publically until the next session for Arbors Records in New York. He invited my wife and me to attend the sessions.

Ruby Braff: *Variety Is the Spice of Braff*
July 25–27, 2000, Nola Studios, New York
Ruby Braff (cnt), Skitch Henderson (p), Bucky Pizzarelli (g), John Beal (bowed bass with strings), Frank Tate (b), Sherrie Maricle (dm), and strings: Adria Benjamin (viola), Sarah Hewitt (cello), Robert Chausow (v), Carol Pool (v), Sylvia D'Avenzo (v), Cenovia Cummins (v)
There's a Small Hotel
    Arbors Records ARCD 19194
Happiness Is Just a Thing Called Joe
    Arbors Records ARCD 19194
Moments Like This
    Arbors Records ARCD 19194

Ruby Braff, Randy Reinhart (cnt), Jon-Erik Kellso (pujé), Joe Wilder (tp), George Masso (tb), Kenny Davern (cl), Chuck Wilson (cl, as), Jack Stuckey (as), Tommy Newsom (ts), Scott Robinson (bars), Bill Charlap (p), Bucky Pizzarelli (g), John Beal (b), Sherrie Maricle (dm)
Crazy Rhythm
    Arbors Records ARCD 19194

Liza
Arbors Records ARCD 19194

Ruby Braff (cnt), George Masso (tb), Kenny Davern (cl), Chuck Wilson (cl, as), Jack Stuckey (as), Tommy Newsom (ts), Scott Robinson (bars), Bill Charlap (p), Bucky Pizzarelli (g), John Beal (b), Joe Ascione (dm)
Jumpin' at the Woodside (tk 1)
unissued
Jumpin' at the Woodside (tk 2)
Arbors Records ARCD 19194
I Ain't Got Nobody
Arbors Records ARCD 19194

Out Stuckey and Robinson; add Howard Alden (g)
Somebody Stole My Gal
Arbors Records ARCD 19194

Ruby Braff (cnt), Bill Charlap (p), Bucky Pizzarelli, Howard Alden (g), John Beal (b)
Medley:
It Must Be True
Arbors Records ARCD 19194
Memories of You
Arbors Records ARCD 19194
NOTE: String arrangements by Tommy Newsom, all other arrangements by Ruby Braff. This album was selected as the top jazz CD from 2002 by London's *The Daily Telegraph*, November 23, 2002.

This is the final time that Ruby and Kenny Davern performed together in a recording studio. In some ways, they were both inflexible in their approaches to performance. Both had long since earned the right to select the musicians who accompanied them. They were both acclaimed artists, seen by many as the top performers on their instruments in the world. They both maintained the highest standards for their own performances and required others to make a similar commitment. They both honed their early skills with the support of older, established jazz musicians, probably sharing notes during the earlier days when they lived in the same building in Riverdale. But there were some important differences. While Braff often preferred elements of spontaneity in his performances, Kenny preferred more structure. Ruby was stimulated by the challenges of a wide repertoire, while Kenny (like Louis Armstrong) was more comfortable with familiar tunes. Of course, these are generalizations, and exceptions occurred; however, it is clear that both could be assertive and argumentative if they felt that they were not being sufficiently respected. Perhaps some of the tension between them was due, at least in part, to the fact that each one preferred to be in control of the performance. Sometimes a committed leader, holding a different vision for excellence, can find it hard to conform to another leader's firm and perhaps even unyielding expectations. For more information on Kenny's perspective on their relationship, see Edward Meyer's excellent book *The Life and Music of Kenny Davern: Just Four Bars.*[49] A few words prior to the start of one day of the recording session nearly ended their relationship. Fortunately, they performed together again in Florida in 2001. Both had learned that personal differences could disappear during the joy of creating great music.

A photo from the March of Jazz is available.[50]

Ruby Braff: *I Hear Music*
July 28, 2000, Nola Studios, New York
Ruby Braff (cnt), Tommy Newsom (ts), Bill Charlap (p), Bucky Pizzarelli (g), John Beal (b), Tony DeNicola (dm), Daryl Sherman (voc)
Chicago Medley:
  Chicago
    Arbors Records ARCD 19244
  My Kind of Town (Chicago Is)
    Arbors Records ARCD 19244
We're All Through (voc, DS)
    Arbors Records ARCD 19244
Wouldn't It Be Loverly
    Arbors Records ARCD 19244
Yesterdays
    Arbors Records ARCD 19244
I Hear Music
    Arbors Records ARCD 19244
Baby, Won't You Please Come Home?
    Arbors Records ARCD 19244
I Would Do Anything for You
    Arbors Records ARCD 19244

My wife and I were present as Ruby's guests during the final three days of these recording sessions. We regret that we were unable to attend the following performance at Shanghai Jazz due to other commitments. Ruby wistfully told me, "Tom, it has been over a year since I played in front of real people." He looked forward to this engagement because it was so important to him to connect with an audience. If there is tragedy in Ruby's later years, it is that he did not perform more often and enjoy the support of his many admirers on a more regular basis. He wanted to perform. His fans wanted to hear him perform. But the economics of the current music business stood between them.

During the studio recording sessions, Ruby sat in view of all the musicians, so that they could immediately see his cues. At this point in his life, his lung capacity was greatly reduced due to emphysema. He was in considerable pain due to two cracked vertebrae. He leaned back against a pillow that cushioned the back of the chair. But nobody will hear any signs of these limitations in his playing on the two recordings Arbors released. I feel that these are among the finest recordings in his career.

Prior to the sessions he described his plans to me, saying that he would begin with a large group and gradually reduce the size as the session progressed. *Variety* is an apt title for the first recording. "Jumpin' at the Woodside" was the only performance recorded twice. At one point, Ruby briefly incorporated a few bars of the song "Indiana" in one of his solos—his way of adding his welcoming me when my wife and I entered the control booth. The first take of "Woodside" was deemed too long to fit the CD. Bill Charlap asked if his solo from the first take could be spliced into the second take, but Ruby replied, "We don't do any of that Frankenstein stuff around here."

After completing "I Would Do Anything for You," Ruby entered the control room and told me, "I thought I was going to die" as he referred to his difficulty breathing following his up-tempo performance to end the session. He smiled while recovering his breath, as he listened to the playback. He had invested all his strength and concentration in creating these performances. I personally feel that several of the musicians on this date thought it might be their last opportunity to perform with Ruby in a recording studio, and that this contributed to the spirit surrounding this entire session. Fortunately, Ruby had many more performances ahead of him, and several of these fine musicians were also present at the March of Jazz party in 2001, honoring Ruby on his birthday.

Photos taken by Ruby's friend Al Lipsky exist from this session. One, taken outdoors after the session, shows Ruby relaxed as he rides in a wheelchair to return to his hotel a few doors west of Nola Studio. His smile reflects his pleasure with the quality of the musical performance during the previous four days. A copy of this photo is included in the photo section.

Ruby Braff–Bucky Pizzarelli Quartet[51]
Sunday, July 30, 2000, Shanghai Jazz, 24 Main Street, Route 124, Madison, New Jersey
Ruby Braff (cnt), Ben Aronov (p), Bucky Pizzarelli (g), John Beal (b)
Sometimes I'm Happy
Lover Come Back to Me
Medley:
  When I Fall in Love
  Over the Rainbow
Poor Butterfly
Thou Swell

Second Set:
Wrap Your Troubles in Dreams
Mean to Me
Them There Eyes
Memories of You (incomplete)

NOTE: A video recording of these tunes is available but remains unissued.

A photo from the March of Jazz is available.[52]

The following tunes are mentioned in the following review of Ruby's performance; however, they are not included in the available video recording. Presumably these closed the second set:
I Can't Get Started
On the Sunny Side of the Street
Yesterdays
Just You, Just Me
I've Grown Accustomed to Her Face

George Kanzler described this performance in his online review: [53]

> The cornetist, who has been hobbled by respiratory ailments, was in New York last week, recording what he himself admitted might well be his last sessions. He agreed to further challenge his resources by playing two sets at the Madison club, co-leading a quartet with guitarist Bucky Pizzarelli. . . .
>
> Braff has always gone against the grain as a cornet and trumpet player, eschewing the flamboyance associated with the instrument for intimacy, playing with a soft, burnished tone and favoring whispered low notes over ear-splitting high ones. That preference has become a necessity since he, in the words of one colleague, "is playing on half a lung now."
>
> But through two sets on Sunday night, it was hard to square that 'half a lung' remark with Braff's consistently brilliant, warm, passionate playing. His personal style was marvelously intact, from his lyrical parsing of melodies to his pert, joyously swinging obligatos—casual asides delivered with the brevity and wit of literary aphorisms.
>
> It wasn't just Braff's night either. The quartet was a paradigm of chamber jazz, the co-leaders joined by pianist Ben Aronov and bassist John Beal, with each player given ample solo space, as well as opportunities to match musical wits with Braff. The exchanges were as much epigrammatic dialogue as musical four-bar trades.
>
> The quartet concentrated on American Popular Songbook standards, tunes Braff knows so well he can play hide-and-seek with the melodies, teasing the audience into playing *Name That Tune*. But the cornetist knows them so well his variations have the resonance of equally unforgettable melodies. They are lyrical improvisations of the highest level, as on his interpretations of 'Thou Swell' and 'Yesterdays,' the latter highlighted by a conversational duet between cornet and guitar and a delicate, bowed bass solo.
>
> While Braff usually played the lead chorus, pianist Aronov led off "Poor Butterfly," going right to the lyrical, melancholy heart of that beautiful, too-infrequently heard standard. Aronov also shone on another early standard, "Memories of You," as the quartet pared down, first to cornet and piano, then to a limpid, solo, piano chorus distilling the song's essence.

> If the recordings Braff has been making this past week for Arbors Records are as inspired as his playing at Shanghai Jazz, they should be a capstone of the jazzman's long career.

But, fortunately, this performance in New Jersey was not to be the capstone of Ruby's career. He continued, although it took more and more of his strength during each of the two years that remained in his life. His self-discipline and love of performance took over, and whenever he began playing, he never faltered. Time and again people saw him arrive at various venues during his final tour in 2002 and they worried that his performance would reflect the infirmity visible in his body. In a sense, Ruby delighted in disappointing them because time and again, the sound of his instrument radiated throughout the rooms and auditoriums. The fans were not disappointed. Ruby saw to that. But that is getting ahead of the story.

Ruby Braff Interview with Steve Voce
Broadcast BBC Radio Merseyside
December 17, 2000, Dennis, Massachusetts
NOTE: A recording of this interview is available but remains unissued.

Mat Domber organized a wonderful birthday tribute to Ruby for his annual March of Jazz party. As you will see in the following listing, Ruby was called upon to perform frequently with a wide range of musicians. Everyone who attended enjoyed the entire program. Fortunately recordings survive.

Al Lipsky provided photos from this special occasion. One shows Ruby performing with Jake Hanna and Bucky Pizzarelli. Another shows Ruby with his sister, Susan Atran, and Dan Morgenstern. Still another shows him with his boyhood friend, Nat Hentoff. Other photos capture him in conversation with Jon-Erik Kellso and playing the grand piano as he tests the sound system before performances begin. Copies of both that photo and the one with Nat Hentoff are included in this book's photo section.

The March of Jazz 2001
March 16, 2001, Sheraton Sand Key Resort, Clearwater Beach, Florida
Welcoming Remarks from Ruby
NOTE: An audio recording of Ruby's opening remarks is available but remains unissued.

The March of Jazz 2001
March 16, 2001, Sheraton Sand Key Resort, Clearwater Beach, Florida (since set started after midnight, date is technically March 17)
Ruby Braff (cnt), Joe Wilder (tp), Dan Barrett (tb), Ken Peplowski (cl), Anat Cohen (ts), John Bunch (p), Jon Wheatley (g), Dave Green (b), Allan Ganley (dm)
Sunday

These Foolish Things
Take the "A" Train
On the Sunny Side of the Street
Medley:
  Old Folks
  Rosetta
NOTE: Audio and video recordings of these tunes are available but remain unissued.

The March of Jazz 2001
March 17, 2001, Sheraton Sand Key Resort, Clearwater Beach, Florida
Ruby Braff (cnt), Howard Alden (g), Dick Hyman (p), Phil Flanigan (b), Jack Lesberg (b), Allan Ganley (dm)
Watch What Happens
Wouldn't It Be Loverly
This Year's Kisses
I've Grown Accustomed to Her Face
Rosetta
NOTE: Audio and video recordings of these tunes are available but remain unissued.

The March of Jazz 2001
March 17, 2001, Sheraton Sand Key Resort, Clearwater Beach, Florida
Ruby Braff (cnt), Bill Charlap (p), Jon Wheatley (g), Dave Green (b), Joe Ascione (dm)
Ain't Misbehavin'
Dream Dancing
Just You, Just Me
NOTE: Audio and video recordings of these tunes are available but remain unissued.

The March of Jazz 2001
March 17, 2001, Sheraton Sand Key Resort, Clearwater Beach, Florida (since set started after midnight, technically date is March 18)
Ruby Braff, Jon-Erik Kellso, Bryan Shaw (cnt), Chuck Wilson, Karoline Strassmayer (as), Tommy Newsom (ts), Bill Charlap (p), Joe Cohn (g), Nicki Parrott (b), Joe Ascione (dm)
Lady Be Good
These Foolish Things
Mean to Me
NOTE: Audio and video recordings of these tunes are available but remain unissued.

The March of Jazz 2001
March 18, 2001, Sheraton Sand Key Resort, Clearwater Beach, Florida

Ruby Braff (cnt) Dick Hyman (p), Bill Charlap (p), Jake Hanna (dm)
Looking at You
Yesterdays
Medley:
  Out of Nowhere
  I Cover the Waterfront
Linger Awhile
The World Is Waiting for the Sunrise

Add Bucky Pizzarelli
You're Driving Me Crazy
    Arbors Records ARCD 19260
Between the Devil and the Deep Blue Sea
    Arbors Records ARCD 19260
When I Fall in Love
    Arbors Records ARCD 19260
NOTE: Audio and video recordings of these tunes are available but remain unissued with the exception of the titles released on Arbors Records ARCD 19260 titled *You Brought a New Kind of Love to Me.*

The March of Jazz 2001
March 18, 2001, Sheraton Sand Key Resort, Clearwater Beach, Florida
Ruby Braff (cnt), Ralph Sutton (p)
Tea for Two
    Arbors Records ARDVD 2 (DVD)
Gone with the Wind
    Arbors Records ARDVD 2 (DVD)
Thou Swell
    Arbors Records ARDVD 2 (DVD)

Add: Randy Sandke (tp), Randy Reinhart (cnt), Bryan Shaw (cnt), Jon Wheatley (g), Nicki Parrott (b), Sherrie Maricle (dm)
'Deed I Do
    Arbors Records ARDVD 2 (DVD)
Dinah
    Arbors Records ARDVD 2 (DVD)
NOTE: Arbors Records ARDVD 2 (DVD) is titled *Ruby and Ralph Remembered.*

Treasure Coast Jazz Society
March 20, 2001, Vero Beach (probably), Florida
Ruby Braff (cnt), Tommy Newsom (ts), Kenny Davern (cl), Bill Charlap (p), Frank Tate (b), Joe Ascione (dm)
'Deed I Do
Dinah

Just You, Just Me
'S Wonderful

Second Set:
Three Little Words
Out of Nowhere
Body and Soul (Charlap, solo)
Them There Eyes
Summertime (Davern feature)
I Want to Be Happy
Georgia on My Mind (Newsom feature)
C Jam Blues
I've Grown Accustomed to Her Face
NOTE: Audio and video recordings of these tunes are available but remain unissued.

Ruby flew to Los Angeles for a weeklong appearance with Roger Kellaway at the Jazz Bakery that was professionally recorded at the club. Apart from his performance skills, Kellaway is known by some as the composer of the theme song for the television comedy *All in the Family*, which is named "Remembering You." Ruby had been delighted by their earlier studio sessions for Concord Records.

Ruby Braff and Roger Kellaway
June 26, 2001, The Jazz Bakery, Culver City, Los Angeles
Ruby Braff (cnt), Roger Kellaway (p, voc)
First Set:
I'll Never Be the Same (Kellaway solo)
Love Walked In
Yesterdays
I Want to Be Happy
Mean to Me
Pennies from Heaven
I Got Rhythm
Remembering You (Kellaway solo with vocal)

Second Set:
My One and Only Love (Kellaway solo)
It's a Wonderful World
Sometimes I'm Happy
Memories of You
Between the Devil and the Deep Blue Sea
Lady Be Good
Remembering You (Kellaway solo with vocal)
NOTE: A recording of both sets is available but remains unissued.

Ruby Braff and Roger Kellaway
June 27, 2001, The Jazz Bakery, Los Angeles
Ruby Braff (cnt), Roger Kellaway (p, voc)
First Set:
I Should Care (Kellaway solo)
Struttin' with Some Barbecue
Cherry
Yesterdays
I Got Rhythm
You've Changed
Remembering You (Kellaway solo with vocal)

Second Set:
Here's That Rainy Day (Kellaway solo)
Swinging on a Star
Sugar
Basin Street Blues
Love Walked In
I've Grown Accustomed to Her Face
Give My Regards to Broadway
Remembering You (Kellaway solo with vocal)
NOTE: A recording of both sets is available but remains unissued.

Ruby Braff and Roger Kellaway
June 28, 2001, The Jazz Bakery, Los Angeles
Ruby Braff (cnt), Roger Kellaway (p, voc)
First Set:
How Deep Is the Ocean? (Kellaway solo)
This Can't Be Love
Watch What Happens
Mean to Me
I Never Knew
Liza
Remembering You (Kellaway solo with vocal)

Second Set:
I'll Never Be the Same (Kellaway solo)
I'm Getting Sentimental Over You
Am I Blue?
Gone with the Wind
Fascinating Rhythm
New Orleans
Memories of You
Yesterdays

NOTE: A recording of both sets is available but remains unissued.

Ruby Braff and Roger Kellaway
June 29, 2001, The Jazz Bakery, Los Angeles
Ruby Braff (cnt), Roger Kellaway (p, voc)
First Set:
I'll Never Be the Same (Kellaway solo)
The Man I Love
Where Are You?
How Long Has This Been Going On?
It Don't Mean a Thing
Days of Wine and Roses
Just You, Just Me
Remembering You (Kellaway solo with vocal)

Second Set:
Stella by Starlight (Kellaway solo)
I Want to Be Happy
Willow Weep for Me
Ain't Misbehavin'
In a Sentimental Mood
Tea for Two
I Got Rhythm
NOTE: A recording of both sets is available but remains unissued.

Ruby Braff and Roger Kellaway
June 30, 2001, The Jazz Bakery, Los Angeles
Ruby Braff (cnt), Roger Kellaway (p, voc)
First Set:
New Orleans (Kellaway solo)
Cherry
Where Are You?
Moonlight Becomes You
Watch What Happens
In My Solitude
Strike Up the Band
Remembering You (Kellaway solo with vocal)

Second Set:
Soaring (Kellaway solo)
Struttin' with Some Barbecue
Basin Street Blues
Liza
Confessin'
Always

This Can't Be Love
Remembering You (Kellaway solo with vocal)
NOTE: A recording of both sets is available but remains unissued.

Ruby Braff and Roger Kellaway
July 1, 2001, The Jazz Bakery, Los Angeles
Ruby Braff (cnt), Roger Kellaway (p, voc)
First Set:
I'll Never Be the Same (Kellaway solo)
The Man I Love
Where Are You?
Moonlight Becomes You
Take the "A" Train
In My Solitude
Strike Up the Band
Remembering You (Kellaway solo with vocal)

Second Set:
Days of Wine and Roses (Kellaway solos)
I Never Knew
Basin Street Blues
Liza
Confessin'
Always
This Can't Be Love
Medley:
  Love Walked In
  The Man I Love
Remembering You (Kellaway solo with vocal)
NOTE: A recording of both sets is available but remains unissued.

Original plans called for Bill Charlap to join Ruby's next session in New York on September 12; however, the tragic events on September 11 prevented him from reaching Manhattan until September 13. It is impossible to imagine a more difficult setting for a recording session than New York City at this time. Emergency conditions prevailed, and then the city was in the earliest stages of mourning the loss of so many lives from the destruction of the Twin Towers. The session's opening with "Handful of Keys" was, in many ways, a demonstration of the triumph of Ruby's commitment to artistic performance. Certainly it reflects a spirit of resolve, and it becomes a joyous celebration of life. The vast majority of recordings of Fats Waller's tune have been made by pianists. The most frequent exceptions are recordings by Benny Goodman, mostly, or Jack Teagarden. Ruby performed it only once before, with Dick Hyman at the JVC Jazz Festival. It presents quite a challenge for a cornetist, but

Ruby was determined to use his time in the studio to create a unique performance.

Ruby Braff Quartet: *Watch What Happens*
September 12, 2001, Nola Studios, New York
Ruby Braff (cnt), Dick Hyman (p), Howard Alden (g), Jake Hanna (dm), Daryl Sherman (voc)
Handful of Keys
Arbors Records ARCD 19259
Slumming on Park Avenue
Arbors Records ARCD 19259
Watch What Happens
Arbors Records ARCD 19259
Frankly (aka Perfectly Frank) (vocal, Daryl Sherman)
Arbors Records ARCD 19259
Here's Carl
Arbors Records ARCD 19259
Shadowland (Hyman composition)
Arbors Records ARCD 19259
Over the Rainbow
Arbors Records ARCD 19259
We'll Be Together Again
Arbors Records ARCD 19259
It's All Right with Me
Arbors Records ARCD 19259
The Blue Room
Arbors Records ARCD 19259
What a Little Moonlight Can Do
Arbors Records ARCD 19259

Ruby Braff Trio: *You Brought a New Kind of Love*[54]
September 13, 2001, Nola Studios, New York
Ruby Braff (cnt), Bill Charlap (p), Jake Hanna (dm)
Them There Eyes
Arbors Records ARCD 19260
It's the Same Old South
unissued
Blue and Sentimental
Arbors Records ARCD 19260
Wrap Your Troubles in Dreams
unissued
It's Wonderful
Arbors Records ARCD 19260
You Brought a New Kind of Love to Me
Arbors Records ARCD 19260

An original blues
unissued
Lullaby of the Leaves
Arbors Records ARCD 19260
I Know That You Know
Arbors Records ARCD 19260
The Very Thought of You
unissued
Don't Get Around Much Anymore
unissued

Ruby Braff Performed with Scott Hamilton[55]
September 16, 2001, 5 p.m., Squantum Club, East Providence, Rhode Island
Ruby Braff (cnt), Scott Hamilton (ts), Paul Schmeling (el. p), Whit Browne (b), Jim Gwin (dm)

Scott Hamilton wrote that Ruby was still tired from his recording session. He made several comments to the audience during the performance about the tragic events. Even when we were together for his recordings in 2000, Ruby's chronic emphysema made him acutely conscious of air quality, and this was clearly exacerbated by the tragedy he had seen in Manhattan. He had worried about problems of dust and the possibility that he would not be able to perform. Scott reported that the performance went "quite well" despite Ruby's concerns. To avoid last minute surprises that might be unsettling, Scott had advised Paul Schmeling to let Ruby know in advance that he would need to perform using an electric piano due to the lack of an instrument at the country club that was the location for this performance.

Six months passed without any trace of other performances until the March of Jazz returned in 2002.

March of Jazz 2002
March 15–17, 2002, Sheraton Sand Key Resort, Clearwater Beach, Florida

The March of Jazz 2002
March 15, 2002, Friday opening
Ruby Braff (cnt), George Masso (tb), three bass players, drummer, Dick Hyman conducting
America the Beautiful
NOTE: A video recording of this tune is available but remains unissued.

The March of Jazz 2002
March 15, 2002, Friday, second set, 10:33 p.m.
Ruby Braff (cnt), John Allred (tb), Tommy Newsom (ts), John Bunch (p), Bucky Pizzarelli (g), Frank Tate (b), Jake Hanna (dm)
There Will Never Be Another You

On the Sunny Side of the Street
The Lady Is a Tramp
Sugar
NOTE: A video recording of these tunes is available but remains unissued.

The March of Jazz 2002
March 16, 2002, Saturday, 11:20 p.m.
Ruby Braff (cnt), Dick Hyman (p), Frank Tate (b), Jake Hanna (dm)
Wrap Your Troubles in Dreams
Nancy (With the Laughing Face)
Sunny
Old Folks
Handful of Keys
Gone With the Wind
NOTE: A video recording of these tunes is available but remains unissued.

The March of Jazz 2002
March 17, 2002, Sunday, 4th set, 3:47 p.m.
Ruby Braff (cnt), John Bunch (p), Dave Green (b), Jake Hanna (dm)
Love Me or Leave Me
Time on My Hands
Dream Dancing
The Blue Room
NOTE: A video recording of these tunes is available but remains unissued.

Soon thereafter, Ruby appeared in his hometown, leading a group in a tribute concert to Bobby Hackett. Nick Puopolo supplied a photo of Ruby from that performance. Following the concert, Ruby said that he would like to record with this group in this setting in the future. He enjoyed the gathering, and his comments throughout the concert show that he was very relaxed. This was his final live performance in the USA, although he subsequently entered the recording studios and performed in many locations in England. The concert was a special occasion for all and it was sponsored by the New England Jazz Alliance and organized by Brent Banulis.[56]

Ruby Braff and His Quintet: The New England Jazz Hall of Fame Exhibit and Concert Series: Tribute to Bobby Hackett
April 9, 2002, Tremont Theater, 276 Tremont Street, Boston
Ruby Braff (cnt), Paul Schmeling (p), Jon Wheatley (g), John Repucci (b), Jim Gwin (dm)
Liza
When Your Lover Has Gone
Sugar
When I Fall in Love
There's a Small Hotel

Dream Dancing
I Hear Music
Yesterdays
Memories of You
Dancing on the Ceiling
Gone with the Wind
NOTE: A video recording of these tunes is available but remains unissued.

Brent Banulis wrote a tribute to Ruby that included a description of this concert:

> On April 9, 2002, an ailing Ruby Braff cornet in hand and walking cane by his side delivered one of the most remarkable performances of his sixty-year career when he helped the New England Jazz Alliance pay tribute to NEJA Hall of Fame inductee Bobby Hackett at Boston's Tremont Theater.
>
> Both the audience and the musicians with him on stage went away feeling they had experienced something special, historically as well as musically. In two remarkably spontaneous sets, Braff, sitting upright in a stiffed-back high office chair, set the tone for each of his renditions from the great American songbook with humorous stories and anecdotes pertaining to the songwriters, Louis Armstrong, Bobby Hackett, and other great musicians he had known, and the pretentiousness often found in the music business. Braff truly enjoyed every aspect of the evening and asked NEJA to arrange a return engagement, which he planned to record. Unfortunately for jazz fans everywhere, the 2002 concert proved to be Braff's last public performance in America. Against doctors advice, he did a British tour that summer. He looked as if he couldn't make it from one gig to the next, John Fordham wrote in *The Guardian*. But the moment he lifted his cornet to his lips, all thoughts of frailty and mortality evaporated.
>
> At the Tremont Theater, Braff scolded Gershwin, Porter and Kern. 'They die and they forget about you. I've helped keep their tunes alive, and you'd think they'd thank me once in a while. But they never call me.' Perhaps they have, Ruby.

Notes

[1] Mat Domber provided information about Arbors unissued titles.
[2] Mat Domber provided information about Arbors unissued titles.
[3] Richard P. Carpenter, *Boston Globe,* February 13, 1994. The article refers to a recent performance by Ruby and Dave without any date mentioned.
[4] Photo, *The March of Jazz Celebrates Ruby Braff's 74th Birthday Party*, Arbors Records, 2001, 29.
[5] George A. Borgman, "The One and Only Ruby Braff," in *Mississippi Rag*, December 1995, 8, Larry Ramsdell, *The Patriot Ledger* (Quincy, MA) January 21, 1994, and *Boston Globe*, April 10, 1994.
[6] Gary Giddins, *Weather Bird* (New York: Oxford, 2004), 96; date from *The New Yorker*, June 27 and July 4, 1994 (double issue), 14, Peter Watrous, *New York Times*, June 30,

1994, advertised in *New York Times*, June 5, 1994, and Mary Campbell, Associated Press, June 28, 1994.
[7] George A. Borgman, "The One and Only Ruby Braff," in *Mississippi Rag*, December 1995, 6.
[8] Robert Simon and Norman Provizer, *Rocky Mountain News*, October 20, 1994.
[9]Ellen Chahey, then the executive director of the Cape Cod Council of Churches, described the events, writing about "My Dinner with Ruby Braff" in *The Barnstable Patriot* available at http://www.barnstablepatriot.com/my_dinner_with_ruby_braff_arts_64_11801 .html.
[10] In addition to the above article, Ruby mentioned this performance in an interview with Steve Voce from December 15, 1994. This program was broadcast on C3TV, Cape Cod Community Television. The executive producer was Dick Golden.
[11] Information from Mat Domber.
[12] *Boston Globe*, January 9, 1995, in a review by Bob Blumenthal. Also see Bob Young, *Boston Herald*, January 4, 1995. Donna Byrne was included based on correspondence with Nick Puopolo.
[13] George A. Borgman, "The One and Only Ruby Braff," in *Mississippi Rag*, December 1995, 6. Also see Jack Thomas, *Boston Globe*, April 11, 1995.
[14] *The Providence Journal-Bulletin*, November 10, 1995.
[15] Ruby Braff interviewed by Steve Voce on July 27, 1995.
[16] Unissued titles researched by Nick Phillips, vice president, Concord Records.
[17] Dan Ouellette, *DownBeat*, October 1, 1995.
[18] George A. Borgman, "The One and Only Ruby Braff," in *Mississippi Rag*, December 1995, 7.
[19] Information from Mat Domber.
[20] Bob Young, *Boston Herald*, January 5, 1996, Daniel Gewertz, *Boston Herald*, January 6, 1996.
[21] Mat Domber provided information about Arbors unissued titles.
[22] Information from Mat Domber.
[23] Clive Davis, *The Times*, August 17, 1996.
[24] Clive Davis, *The Times*, August 17, 1996.
[25] John Fordham, *The Guardian*, October 1, 1996.
[26] Steve Voce in *Jazz Journal International*, August 1996, 11, (details not reported in the magazine in any 1996 issue)—"Ruby Braff visits Britain in August to play concerts and a season at the Pizza Express in Dean St., London WI."
[27] Tony Shoppee citing advance publicity. Actual personnel might differ.
[28] Tony Shoppee citing advance publicity. Actual personnel might differ. Clive Davis mentioned two tunes in his brief review and noted that Dave Green played bass, *The Times*, September 7, 1996.
[29] Tony Shoppee in correspondence.
[30] Tony Shoppee reports details. He attended the evening of September 12. Clive Davis, *The Times*, September 14, 1996.
[31] Clive Davis, *The Times*, September 14, 1996.
[32] Tony Shoppee reports details. He attended evenings of September 18 and 22.
[33] Tony Shoppee citing advance publicity. No further information is available.
[34] Tony Shoppee citing advance publicity. Actual personnel might differ.
[35] Tony Shoppee citing advance publicity. Actual personnel might differ.
[36] *Jazz Journal International*, January 1997, 13.

[36] *Jazz Journal International*, January 1997, 13.
[37] John Fordham, *The Guardian*, October 1, 1996.
[38] Jay Miller, *Patriot Ledger* (Quincy, MA) May 8, 1997 and Bob Young, *Boston Herald*, May 9, 1997.
[39] *New York Times*, June 8, 1997.
[40] Correspondence with Manfred Selchow; *Chicago Sun-Times*, August 29, 1997.
[41] "Jazz notes: Six of Our Favorites from 1999," *The New Yorker*, January 10, 2000, 9.
[42] Photos, *The March of Jazz Celebrates Ruby Braff's 74th Birthday Party*, Arbors Records, 2001, 29–30.
[43] Information from Mat Domber.
[44] "Jazz notes: Six of our favorites from 1999," *The New Yorker*, January 10, 2000, 9.
[45] Dave Bennett (second set incorrectly labeled as July 28).
[46] *Jazz Journal International,* July 1999, 2.
[47] Alun Morgan notes that the BBC broadcast was prefaced by a short interview conducted by Alyn Shipton.
[48] *Rocky Mountain News* (Denver), April 23, 1999.
[49] Edward N. Meyer, *The Life and Music of Kenny Davern: Just Four Bars* (Lanham, MD: Scarecrow Press, 2010), 304.
[50] Photos, *The March of Jazz Celebrates Ruby Braff's 74th Birthday Party*, Arbors Records, 2001, 30 and 31.
[51] *The Star-Ledger*, August 1, 2000.
[52] Photo, *The March of Jazz Celebrates Ruby Braff's 74th Birthday Party*, Arbors Records, 2001, 31.
[53] http://www.jazzhouse.org/library/index.php3?read=kanzler2.
[54] Mat Domber provided information about Arbors unissued titles.
[55] *Boston Globe*, September 14, 2001.
[56] Brent Banulis, Nick Puopolo, and the New England Jazz Alliance provided a wonderful setting for Ruby's final concert in the USA. He obviously enjoyed the event and hospitality immensely.

Chapter 21

Reflecting on a Wonderful Career: Ruby's Final Studio Recordings

Anyone seeing Ruby on the street would see someone who appeared very infirm. Anyone seeing him in the studio or on the stage watched him come to life, leading the session, setting the rules, and enjoying the experience. The results reflect an artist at peace with his talent, able to produce music that ranged from intensely rhythmic playing to deep emotional expression. If the words *musical maturity* convey a sense of decline, that would not be an appropriate description for Ruby at this point in his career; however, if those words signal an artist who can effectively draw on the experiences of his entire lifetime, then the description would fit admirably. Ruby did not coast, for he was too committed to his own high standards. But he needed to be efficient, since his strength was limited. His knowledge permitted him to excel, but within his limitations, so that his audiences' appreciation was undiminished. But in contrast to his idol, Louis Armstrong, Ruby never needed to curtail his blowing. Perhaps that is fortunate in another sense, for Louis was the much better vocalist of the two of them.

Ruby's final four days in the recording studio began, fittingly, with a session for Arbors Records. The resulting recording was named one of the best jazz CD releases of 2007 by *The New Yorker.* Al Lipsky provided a photograph of Ruby with Ray, Bucky, and John after the session was completed.

Ruby Braff and the Flying Pizzarellis: *C'est Magnifique!*
June 11, 2002, Nola Studios, New York
Ruby Braff (cnt), Ray Kennedy (p), Bucky Pizzarelli (g), John Pizzarelli (g, voc), Martin Pizzarelli (b), Jim Gwin (dm)—vocal participation by the Oo-La-La Singers: Rachel Domber, Daryl Sherman, Adam and Dan Morgenstern, Al Lipsky, and Gail and Ross Firestone, directed by Scott Robinson
Lulu's Back in Town
  Arbors Records ARCD 19270
(Was I to Blame for) Falling in Love with You
  Arbors Records ARCD 19270

You're a Lucky Guy
    Arbors Records ARCD 19270
When a Woman Loves a Man
    Arbors Records ARCD 19270
C'est Magnifique (Add Oo-La-La Singers)
    Arbors Records ARCD 19270

June 12, 2002, Nola Studios, New York
Same personnel
My Honey's Lovin' Arms
    Arbors Records ARCD 19270
I Didn't Know What Time It Was
    Arbors Records ARCD 19270
They Can't Take That Away from Me
    Arbors Records ARCD 19270
As Time Goes By
    Arbors Records ARCD 19270
Sometimes I'm Happy
    Arbors Records ARCD 19270
Dancing on the Ceiling
    Arbors Records ARCD 19270

Mat Domber invited me to write the notes for the CD release of this Arbors Records session, perhaps because Ruby and Bucky had asked me to write the notes for Ruby's final studio sessions, recorded on the two following days, June 13 and 14 in the same studio and with the same fine musicians. I certainly viewed as an honor to play a small role in both of these final studio recordings. Here is the text I prepared for Mat Domber.

Ruby Braff and the Flying Pizzarellis: *C'est Magnifique!*

It's ultimately all about memories. Ruby Braff wanted to be known for his artistry, not for the personal details of his life. He made that clear to me as we worked to develop a book covering his career. Ruby's gone now. He died on February 9, 2003. While that ended his life, it does not end our celebration of his artistry. This compact disc transports us to two of his final days in the recording studio in June 2002. Not surprisingly, the performances are a delight to hear, despite beginning the final chapter in Ruby's career. These final studio recordings were followed by a successful tour in the United Kingdom. Tony Bennett was one of his fans attending his performances at Pizza on the Park in London, honoring their years of collaboration.

In fact, June 2002 was actually a pretty exciting time in Ruby Braff's life. While his public performances had become infrequent, he had appeared at Mat and Rachel Domber's March of Jazz party in March and was the leader for a "Tribute to Bobby Hackett" sponsored by the New England Jazz Hall of Fame at Boston's Tremont Theater in April. Both audiences were excited to hear him perform. Ruby always told me that he never had a problem pleasing people who attended his performances, only in getting more people to come in the first place. He was looking forward to his extensive UK tour in July and August. So when he entered the Nola recording studio in New York for these sessions, he was excited.

Ruby truly loved his association with Mat and Rachel Domber. He frequently told me that Mat provided him with more creative freedom in the studio than he had ever experienced before. Whenever I mentioned Rachel, Ruby's response almost always began with the sound, "Oooooh. . . ." Then he raved about the cookies and egg salad sandwiches she always provided to help set a relaxed atmosphere in the studio.

On this occasion, Ruby was performing with his longtime collaborators Bucky Pizzarelli and Jim Gwin, but he was also excited to play with the members of the John Pizzarelli Trio for the first time. Ruby had heard them perform on the radio and suggested they record together. Ruby was already convinced of the trio's commitment to producing exciting, creative music, but you can judge for yourself. At last we are able to hear the results.

But these many joys were also accompanied by some deep frustrations. Ruby's health was fragile. His intense lust to create good music overcame his emphysema that should have made playing impossible. His high standards had long limited his opportunities to perform in public, simply because he would not compromise his choice of accompanying musicians and settings. Nor would Ruby ever refrain from explaining to everyone within earshot why certain arrangements were completely unacceptable to him.

Ruby was unwilling to compromise on artistic standards, which is both a reason why he performed less often and why we enjoy his recordings and performances so very much.

But June 2002 was a different story. Ruby was delighted with his plans for this session. Ruby and Bucky first performed together informally at the Upstairs at the Downstairs in New York in 1971 and then at Dick Gibson's jazz party in 1972; however, their first record together was for Sonet Records in 1976. Ruby always enjoyed the rhythmic foundation that Bucky provided. Their paths crossed many times, leading to their final studio collaboration during these days in New York's Nola Studio. This was the seventh time they were teamed on a session for Arbors Records.

Ruby first performed with Jim Gwin in Boston in about 1994. Their first recording together was released on Arbors Records as "You Can Depend on Me." It was recorded at Nola Studio April 7, 1996, and Bucky was also present, along with Bob Haggart and Johnny Varro. That provides similar instrumentation to the present recording, with Ray Kennedy adding his wonderful skills at the piano and Martin Pizzarelli providing a rich foundation with his bass. John Pizzarelli adds a second guitar and his unique vocal talent.

Two guitars—Ruby used that combination to spark some of the finest small group performances in the entire history of jazz music. This album, while departing from the more highly arranged frameworks of the famous Ruby Braff–George Barnes Quartet, sacrifices nothing in quality, while adding lots of spontaneous interplay among the musicians.

Bucky and Jim knew how Ruby ran his recording sessions, seating musicians in a circle and pointing to them when he wanted their musical voice to be heard. But this was a new experience for John, Ray, and Martin who were not accustomed to Ruby's "I point, you play" mode of operations. They quickly understood the need to be ready to take the lead during part of each tune, or to assume specific roles in various combinations in an instant. This inspired a bit of creative tension that added to the vitality of the entire performance. Ruby did not share his thoughts about the tunes to be performed in advance, so everything was spontaneous. In fact, his selection of tunes was special. This CD includes a variety of performances that represent different elements of Ruby's recording career. Three appear in Ruby's recorded repertoire for the first time. One more tune was almost a first for Ruby at the time of this session, while the others have appeared infrequently among Ruby's recordings.

"Dancing on the Ceiling" must have been on Ruby's mind, for he had performed it in his April concert paying tribute to Bobby Hackett. This is a beautiful tune, certainly consistent with Ruby's love for the classic American Songbook; however, this is the first time he recorded it in a studio. "(Was I to Blame for) Falling in Love with You" is almost another first for Ruby. He had recorded it in April 1957 for Columbia Records but that session was never issued and presumed lost by everyone—until Michael Brooks found the tapes in Columbia's vast vault, and Michael Cuscuna included it in a recent boxed set from Mosaic Records. Ruby died before this discovery. He would have loved to hear that original recording, for he spoke fondly of the session. He did record it again in Paris while touring with the Newport All Stars in 1969; however, that record obtained limited European distribution. But that is probably why he decided to share it now. He thought it would be the "first time" for most of us.

Ruby's memory was excellent. He must have been aware that "When a Woman Loves a Man" appeared on his first released recording, in an album by Edmond Hall's All Stars that dates from the Savoy Café in Boston in 1949. But we are not done with history just yet. "Lulu's Back in Town" had appeared on two of Ruby's earlier albums, but one was a 1993 performance that included Bucky Pizzarelli. "You're a Lucky Guy" was a staple in the repertory of the Ruby Braff–George Barnes Quartet. Ruby recorded "I Didn't Know What Time It Was" with Ellis Larkins in a classic performance, but never again until now. Ruby recorded "They Can't Take That Away from Me" with Dick Hyman and

"As Time Goes By" at different times with Scott Hamilton and Woody Herman. But even more important, Ruby also pays tribute to Mat and Rachel Domber, since he released another version of this tune on an earlier Arbors Records release (*The Cape Codfather*). Each of these tunes represents a different time in Ruby's life. It is hard for me to imagine that Ruby was not taking us on a tour of his musical career, celebrating wonderful musical collaborations along the way. Each of these relationships was very important to him.

There are two other songs on this CD that Ruby has never recorded before, "C'est Magnifique" and "My Honey's Lovin' Arms." The former adds the Oo-La-La Singers, an incredibly unusual undertaking in a Braff recording that makes me smile. It forevermore adds voices of some of Ruby's friends and champions to his recorded legacy. Ruby told me once to be careful when I used the word *friends*, for a person was lucky to have only one or two true friends during his entire lifetime. But here, enjoying this recording with Ruby as it was made and now included in Ruby's recorded legacy are Rachel Domber, Daryl Sherman, Adam and Dan Morgenstern, Al Lipsky, and Gail and Ross Firestone, directed by multi-instrumentalist Scott Robinson. Dan has reviewed Ruby's records and performances even longer than I have been a devoted listener. Ruby respected him highly. Ross Firestone is one of Benny Goodman's biographers and has attended some of Ruby's other sessions for Arbors. Al Lipsky is one of Ruby's most devoted friends. I've seen how Ruby has enjoyed listening to Daryl sing, giving her a hug when they meet and again when they part. The chorus was Ruby's idea. Its very informality injects an additional spirit of *joie de vivre* to the session. I missed my chance to join this chorus and to become a footnote in Ruby's discography when I could not attend that day.

That leaves us with "Sometimes I'm Happy." This was a song that Ruby performed frequently in his engagements but recorded only twice before. One of the recordings was only issued in Japan. Maybe that was Ruby's bow to his recollections of past tours throughout the world. Just another memory from a CD filled with many warm associations. I would be surprised if Ruby didn't plan it this way, at least in part.

Each of these selections demonstrates Ruby's commitment to providing variation in the texture of his performances. Musicians are featured in different combinations to create unique coloration, to spark interplay and change both voicings and tempos to keep us listening throughout each tune. So let's look at the *architecture* of Ruby's approach to several of these tunes. This is where his leadership style of "I point, then you play" becomes evident. Ruby's sessions are not just strings of solos, framed by opening and closing choruses.

June 11 marks the first day of recording and "Lulu's Back in Town" is Ruby's choice to begin. This is a familiar tune and a good choice to introduce each musician. Ruby opens the performance. John solos and Ruby returns. Ray continues as members of the John Pizzarelli Trio are introduced to us. Next comes Bucky, and then Martin. Ruby then varies the texture by asking everyone except Martin to cease playing, giving us the rich sound of cornet with a luscious bass accompaniment. Next, in sequence, come John and Ray. Then, Ruby leads the ensemble to a close.

Next comes "(Was I to Blame for) Falling in Love with You." Ruby opens, no surprise there, followed in turn by Ray and John, twice. Then, Ruby caresses the melody over a rich background from the ensemble to close. Bucky and Jim leave no doubt about the rhythmic foundation. No unique combinations this time, but we enjoy everyone's adoration of the melodic heart of this song.

Get ready for a nice surprise. "You're a Lucky Guy" opens with Ruby again in the lead, but the group introduces a strong countermelody of "Perdido." It certainly got my attention. Then Ray, Bucky, Ruby, and John take turns, until Ruby and Jim trade exchanges. Then it's John's turn to trade with Jim, followed by Ruby and Martin. Ruby returns, including the "Perdido" theme to balance this most interesting performance.

Next comes another wonderful ballad, "When a Woman Loves a Man." This time Ruby opens just with Bucky. This flows into the backing of the full group, leading to solos from John, Ray, and Bucky. Ruby closes, including a fine cadenza performed with his patented rapid runs done in the best of taste.

Well, I have already remarked on the unique role of the vocal chorus. Ruby must have been smiling about that unexpected twist. He may also have enjoyed the irony that the chorus was working for him for free. In "C'est Magnifique," Ruby conducts a conversation with the chorus including playful slurs and a legato moment. My mind carries an image of kids enjoying a playground at the first signs of spring. Then, Ray increases the tempo and John leads the group. Ruby reenters, swinging, while maintaining his conversation. Ray increases the rhythmic intensity and builds momentum. Ruby returns with Bucky and John, otherwise unaccompanied, leading in a seamless transition to John's solo with Bucky providing rhythmic counterpoint. Next, Ruby returns to lead the ensemble, until he slows tempo as two guitars provide a supportive foundation for the close. This is a romp throughout that celebrates the joy of this occasion. Treasure it.

June 12, 2002 begins the second day of this session. It opens with a performance of "My Honey's Lovin' Arms." This time, Ruby asks Ray to handle the introduction. That is a sign of respect. Ruby follows in the lead; then come Bucky and Ray. Ruby returns, then passes the baton to John. Martin then collaborates with Jim, with Bucky and Ray providing nice backgrounds. Ruby then enters to trade with Martin. After a brief rhythmic transition, Ruby trades with each member of the group, Bucky, Ray, John, and Jim. Ruby then closes with the final words. Ruby's pointing finger got a workout on this one, but he once again produces constant variety from the interplay of different combinations of these fine musicians.

Ruby leads the opening of "I Didn't Know What Time It Was" with Ray at first then with the full group. Next, comes Ray, then John. Ruby points to Bucky and the two of them continue unaccompanied. John returns; then Ruby caresses this nice melody and brings it to a close.

Next, it is time to enjoy John Pizzarelli's vocal talents. John sings the less celebrated verse of "They Can't Take That Away from Me" with Ray providing support. This is a familiar combination for those who love the music John's trio creates. Ruby then plays a nice solo for the chorus signaling with a trill that John should now sing the familiar part of the lyric. Ruby injects his customary obbligatos over rhythm while John sings. Bucky and Ray take their turns. Then Ruby extends the dynamic range, leading to John's vocal encore, this time augmented by Ruby's powerfully unique punctuation using a series of descending notes. This reminds me of how Vic Dickenson growled with his trombone in a way that Bobby Hackett deeply admired. Bucky, Martin and Jim propel the performance throughout, up to the close with a descending unison line. Listen to Ruby's declaration at the end. "Nice," he exclaims. Don't you agree?

"As Time Goes By" opens with John singing the verse. Ruby seizes the familiar chorus, followed in turn by John and Ray. John returns followed by an interlude filled by Ruby and Ray, unaccompanied. Next, Ruby is joined by everyone. He plays in his most rhapsodic style to close, with Ray's musical voice enriching the foundation until the end. You don't have to remember *Casablanca* to enjoy this performance.

"Sometimes I'm Happy": Seriously, how could you not be happy if you've been listening to these tunes? Ruby opens, trading brief contributions with the group and then assuming the lead. John and Ray follow. Then Ruby returns with both guitars featured, first in a unison figure with John, then with Bucky leading over chorded voicings with John underneath, always supported by Jim's steady foundation. Martin's turn is next, and Ruby closes with the ensemble repeating the earlier unison figure with guitars. It's not just the solos that hold our attention, but the excitement generated by the very structure of this performance.

"In Dancing on the Ceiling," the performance mirrors the title. Ruby opens, followed by John. Then he returns, followed by Bucky and Ray, who lightly dances across his keyboard as he plays. Ruby returns with both guitars and then trades contributions with John and then Bucky. His pointing finger is really busy on this one also, and everyone rises to the challenge. Ruby returns using his strongest voice, supported by everyone, before momentum shifts to Ray. Ruby's close is delicate. Delicious, throughout.

That marks the end of a productive two days in one of New York's finest recording studios. Bryan Shaw, brought from California to Nola Studios for the occasion, captured it all in excellent sound. He was one of Ruby's favorite recording engineers. Whether you choose to listen to this recording intently or play it in the background, you'll find that this disc provides a fine accompaniment to whatever you are doing. You will become enjoined with Ruby's memories as you enjoy the beauty of these performances.

Ruby left us a legacy represented by his uncompromising standards, musical taste, creative imagination, and consummate artistry—nice tunes, beautifully played. He achieved what only some musicians ever accomplish by developing a unique and immediately recognizable style. Whenever we need a reminder of that, we are fortunate to be able to play any of his over 150 released recordings.

These records span a total of 54 years (from 1949 to 2002), a feat almost unmatched in jazz. Louis Armstrong—and Ruby held no musician in higher esteem—recorded over a period of 49 years (from 1923 to 1971), but Ruby would not have wanted to be compared with him on that or any other basis.

While these recordings mark the chronological end of Ruby Braff's remarkable recording career with Arbors Records, they will not be the final recordings that will appear on this label. We are fortunate that Mat Domber still holds unissued recordings—his recorded memories of Ruby—to share with us in the future. I spoke with Larry Ridley who toured with Ruby throughout the US, Europe, and Japan when both belonged to George Wein's Newport Jazz Festival All Stars. Larry said he admired Ruby because "he took no half-steps with his music and had no patience with those who did." Ruby would have liked that. His standards and dedication were legend. After all, he wanted to be remembered for his music, not for his life.

P.S. One more tune was recorded during the second day of this session. It appears on Daryl Sherman's album, *A Hundred Million Miracles* released as Arbors Records ARCD 19279. Check it out if you are either a completist or simply enjoy wonderful music.

Daryl Sherman: *A Hundred Million Miracles*
June 12, 2002, Nola Studios, New York
Daryl Sherman (voc, p), Ruby Braff (cnt), Bucky Pizzarelli (g), Martin Pizzarelli (b), Jim Gwin (dm)
You Are Too Beautiful
    Arbors Records ARCD 19279
NOTE: This recording is released under Daryl Sherman's name. Other selections do not include Ruby Braff.

Ruby's final studio sessions continued for two more days. Al Lipsky provided a photo of Ruby with me and Bucky after the session was completed.

Ruby Braff and the John Pizzarelli Trio with Special Guest Bucky Pizzarelli: *Relaxing at the Penthouse*
June 13, 2002, Nola Studios, New York
Ruby Braff (cnt), Bucky Pizzarelli, John Pizzarelli (g), Martin Pizzarelli (b), Ray Kennedy (p), Jim Gwin (dm)
One O'Clock Jump
    Victoria VC 4348
I Want a Little Girl
    Victoria VC 4348
It's the Same Old South
    Victoria VC 4348

Blue Turning Grey Over You
Victoria VC 4348
Keepin' Out of Mischief Now
Victoria VC 4348
Love Walked In
Victoria VC 4348

June 14, 2002
Same personnel and location
Lady Be Good
Victoria VC 4348
Blue and Sentimental
Victoria VC 4348
Sweet Lorraine (voc John Pizzarelli)
Victoria VC 4348

This is Ruby Braff's final studio recording. It is a spirited, informal session that Ruby's fans should not hesitate to acquire. Bucky Pizzarelli also recorded "One Morning in May" as a solo performance for the producer, Bill Becker, but it is not included in the album. Ruby and Bucky kindly asked me to write the album notes. Ray Kennedy provided a helpful review of my draft. None of us anticipated that Ruby's health would decline following his final UK tour, so the recording shows no evidence of any farewells. This final session resulted from the fact that Mat Domber had only scheduled two previous days for recording and Ruby wanted to record an addition CD. Mat understood Ruby's desire and graciously delayed release of the Arbors CD. The extra recording provided Ruby with additional income prior to his final tour. Al Lipsky took photographs during all four days of the recording sessions. A copy of his photo showing Ruby with Buck Pizzarelli and me on the final day is included in this book's photo section. Here is the text I prepared for Bill Becker for this CD release.

Relaxing at the Penthouse with Ruby Braff and the John Pizzarelli Trio with Special Guest Bucky Pizzarelli

Open your ears and visualize the setting. Ruby Braff sits in the center and faces a semicircle group of musicians. Jim Gwin is to his left behind his drums. Martin Pizzarelli stands next to him with his bass. Bucky and John sit across from Ruby. Ray Kennedy sits to Ruby's right at the piano. Intimacy and direct eye contact are required for playing improvised chamber music at this level. Ruby is clearly the leader. Everyone watches him. Recording begins, and you can hear the results—anytime you wish to do so. The studio was filled with stars, young and old, and they certainly enjoyed performing together.

Now, I am one who views each of Ruby Braff's recordings as a "must buy," so don't look to me for objectivity. Just listen yourself. Ruby strives to make each recording his best. Whenever Ruby Braff has recorded with two guitarists, the results have been special. He loves the melody. He creates drama in his music, calling on each musician at just the right time to create just the right combinations. The energy is electric. But the music resolves the tension. Each musician creates highlights in this collection of performances that you will enjoy hearing time and time again.

When I first met Ruby briefly in the '70s, I told him that he taught me taste in music. Truly, the performances on this CD epitomize great music. But this occasion also reflects several very special qualities.

To begin, Ruby first recorded with Bucky Pizzarelli in 1976, over 25 years ago. They have made 16 recordings together since. This session again demonstrates the magic they create when they play together. Fortunately, this has happened more frequently in studios of late. Each encounter brings special pleasure. This time Bucky also shows his joy to be performing with two of his children. They are quite a family. They have recorded together before, but never with Ruby.

Ruby has encouraged many younger performers over the years. Howard Alden is but one who praises Ruby's support in notes he wrote for one of his own albums. When Ruby began performing professionally in the 1940s, many established jazz stars encouraged him, and he has never forgotten their support. It began with Louis Armstrong. John Hammond became one of his early fans. Here, you can hear Ruby encourage Martin Pizzarelli and Ray Kennedy on "Lady Be Good." Ruby's brief exhortations are infectious. To Martin he said, "Don't quit now," and his words to Ray were an enthusiastic, "Yeah!" When you hear his voice, you will agree that this is high praise, indeed. It comes straight from Ruby's heart. I challenge you to sit still while you listen to this music. Feel Ray's energy as he drives this delightful performance to a close. What a beautiful touch he has. Jim Czak captured Martin's rich bass sound just as I heard him play in the studio, so you share Ruby's pleasure each time you listen to this recording. John, whose recent recordings include performances with both George Shearing and Tony Bennett, beamed with pleasure. After all, this is his trio. John's vocal on "Sweet Lorraine" deserves special notice as well as his contributions throughout the two sessions. Jim Gwin rounds out the sextet. By my count, this is his sixth recording session with Ruby. You certainly can hear why Ruby selected him for this one.

The foundation for this session is provided by the John Pizzarelli Trio. Ruby heard them perform on a tribute to Harry Warren broadcast on National Public Radio. The trio has performed frequently together since January 1993. In addition to releasing nine CDs, they have appeared at the major jazz festivals, in top clubs, and on all the major television news and talk shows. They have also been seen and heard in motion pictures. By any standard, they are stars and are a central force in continuing to remind people throughout the entire world that jazz music is a very special art form and source of wonderful entertainment.

Finally, this recording session returns Ruby to a setting where he plays with two guitars. While he has played with many fine guitarists over the years, his recordings with George Barnes and Wayne Wright (later replaced by Vinnie Corrao) are some of the finest records in the entire history of jazz. Here, "I Want a Little Girl" and especially "Blue Turning Grey Over You" include some marvelous moments of just cornet with guitars. This is improvisation at its best. Ruby plays majestically.

"Lady Be Good" and "One O'Clock Jump" evoke a feeling that would surely have made Count Basie smile, especially when he hears how Ruby injects a few notes from "Hey Lawdy Mama" into his solo on "One O'Clock Jump." You can feel the Count's spirit in the studio. The musicians discussed tunes. Twice someone wrote the chord changes on a sheet of paper. Photocopies were made and quickly distributed. Recording began. First takes were the rule. The music is spontaneous and infectious. The musicians were having fun. Playbacks were relaxed, with Ruby sitting in the center of the control room, listening and smiling and telling stories.

Shortly after this session, Bucky flew to Switzerland and Ruby few to the United Kingdom for a month long tour. The John Pizzarelli Trio resumed its busy schedule of appearances across the country, including the evenings they played at Feinstein's at the Regency during the time this session was recorded. We are truly fortunate that they were able to share the results of these two days of recording with us. I think you will share it with your friends. Do it often. They'll enjoy it with you. You might even develop a habit of buying other recordings by these remarkable artists, for each one brings some special pleasures. This one is a great place to start if you have not yet acquired the habit.

A few notes on the music:

Count Basie recorded all the selections on this CD with the exceptions of "Blue Turning Grey Over You" and "Love Walked In." While his first recorded interpretations typically date from the 1930s and '40s, the Count didn't record "Keepin' Out of Mischief Now" until 1964. "Blue Turning Grey Over You" was recorded by Billie Holiday, Louis Armstrong, and, of course, Fats Waller, so it has developed quite a pedigree over the years even without the Count's endorsement. "Love Walked In" was recorded by Louis Armstrong in 1938, while Ruby first recorded it on a little known record with Larry Adler in 1959.

Ruby recorded "Sweet Lorraine" from the Storyville Club in Boston with Pee Wee Russell in 1952, three years after his earliest released recording from 1949. None of Ruby's recordings since then include that tune, making it one of the rarest in his recorded repertoire. A year later, Ruby accompanied Vic Dickenson in a recording of "Keepin' Out of Mischief Now." That session, made for Vanguard Records, was his first for John Hammond, the legendary producer. Ruby first recorded "One O'Clock Jump," "Blue and Sentimental," and "Lady Be Good" with Benny Goodman in 1955. The first time Ruby and Bucky recorded together was in 1976, and that session also included a performance of "It's the Same Old South." It is nice to reprise that title in 2002, and this is definitely not the "same old" music. While 26 years have passed, the current performance surpasses even the high standards they set back then. Ruby's playing has always been filled with beauty, but there can be no doubt that his mastery has grown throughout the years.

Bucky Pizzarelli's earliest recording that I can trace is with Vaughan Monroe from about 1944. Next came recordings with Joe Mooney and George Barnes, Toots Thielemans, Billy Butterfield, Bobby Donaldson, Rex Stewart, LaVern Baker, Bobby Hackett, Sarah Vaughan, Sir Charles Thompson, Gene Ammons, Etta Jones, Sonny Stitt, Benny Goodman, Lee Wiley, Soprano Summit, Bud Freeman, Zoot Sims, Stephane Grappelli, John Bunch, and Charles Mingus. There are many more sessions, and there is no space to list them all.

John Pizzarelli first recorded with his father in 1980, but in 1983 he hired his father for the date that produced the album "I'm Hip (Please Don't Tell My Father)." The secret is out, and his father now knows. His career has skyrocketed, along with his trio, and releases under his name have appeared regularly since 1985. Martin Pizzarelli first recorded with his brother and father in 1992. Ray Kennedy first recorded with his brother in St. Louis in 1972 when he was only 14 years old. He first recorded with John Pizzarelli in 1994, following two albums with Randy Sandke. In addition to his work with John's trio, he has recorded with Ray Brown and Nat Adderley and appeared with Sonny Stitt, James Moody, and Freddie Hubbard. What an artist he has become. Many place him among the very best jazz pianists performing today. Ray and the Pizzarellis have previously recorded for Victoria Records. Jim Gwin's earliest record dates from Boston in 1988, 14 years and a day before this recording. In addition, he has appeared on three of Ruby's other releases on Arbors Records.

If you follow Marian McPartland's remarkable broadcasts of *Piano Jazz*, you may well know that Ruby, Bucky, John, and Ray have all been featured on her programs. But why read these notes when you have such a treat in store. It's time for you to listen to the music.

Chapter 22

Ruby's Final Tour: Honoring His Audience until the End

Dave Bennett arranged Ruby's final tour, as he had on earlier occasions. It is fitting that Ruby was invited to perform before UK audiences, since many of his fans were able to see him a final time. It is notable that Tony Bennett attended one of the performances in London, and he was again very kind to share them with me. Fortunately, Dave captured recordings of nearly every song performed. Ruby played at a high standard throughout the tour, but was forced to cancel his final festival appearance due to the onset of pneumonia, from which he never recovered. Jon Wheatley accompanied Ruby throughout this tour and has released a few titles on his own CD as shown in the following listings. Hopefully more of this music will be issued in years to come.

Ruby Braff at Pizza on the Park
July 18 and 19, 2002, Pizza on the Park, 11 Knightsbridge, London (two sets nightly)

The announcement said that Ruby Braff would play with a variety of musicians each night of the Pizza on the Park engagement, including Roy Williams (tb), Alan Barnes (cl), John Barnes (as, bs), Brian Lemon (p), Jon Wheatley (g), Dave Green (b).

The full engagement is listed in *Jazz Journal International* and an available handbill, but no details are available for the first two nights above. Details for following evenings follow below.

Ruby Braff at Pizza on the Park
July 20, 2002, Pizza on the Park, 11 Knightsbridge, London
Ruby Braff (cnt), John Barnes (as, bars), Jon Wheatley (g), Dave Green (b), Allan Ganley (dm)
First Set:
Royal Garden Blues
Nice Work If You Can Get It

On the Sunny Side of the Street
Liza
Love Me or Leave Me
Memories of You
Take the "A" Train

Second Set:
Crazy Rhythm
Mean to Me
I Want to Be Happy
It Don't Mean a Thing
I Wished on the Moon
You Can Depend on Me
I've Grown Accustomed to Her Face
NOTE: A recording of these tunes is available but remains unissued.

A review by Jack Massarik described the musicians and his words showed Ruby's commitment to his art.[1] The music they produced was wonderful throughout the entire UK tour, although Ruby's fans were consistently amazed to see the contrast between his limited mobility and his passionate playing:

> He's seventy-five years old and looks every day of it.
>
> An emphysema sufferer, he takes a portable fan onstage to help him breathe. He also plays in a seated position and keeps a wheelchair near the stage to help him up slopes. And for good measure, he now has glaucoma and wears extremely dark glasses.
>
> No, Ruby (short for Reuben) Braff is not a well man, yet his cornet playing and waspish wit seem gutsy enough.
>
> Indeed the irascible Bostonian now jibes at the dead as well as the living. They're all fair game to him, most of his friends having long joined that big jam session in the sky.
>
> 'Richard Rodgers wrote great songs,' he said before playing 'There's a Small Hotel,' 'though I never liked him or his partner, Hammerstein. I was amazed how fast they could work—and how slow they were at paying.'
>
> Flanking him are 'Gangrene' (the rhythm team of drummer Allan Ganley and bassist Dave Green) plus pianist Brian Lemon, an arthritis victim whose hands manage quite delicate solos in a permanently clawed position. There's a grisly fascination about this band. It's like visiting the emergency ward of an old folks' home.
>
> An admirable US guitarist, Jon Wheatley, seems like a sapling beside these gnarled old oaks, but they sound pretty good together. Don't miss Braff. He may be ashen offstage, but when the spotlights come on, so do the smiles, the quips, and the magic. He's still taking a wonderfully elegant solo. Nobody quite knows how.

Ruby Braff at Pizza on the Park
July 21, 2002, Pizza on the Park, 11 Knightsbridge, London

Ruby Braff (cnt), Roy Williams (tb), Jon Wheatley (g), Dave Green (b)
First Set:
Jumpin' at the Woodside
They Can't Take That Away from Me
Ghost of a Chance
Somebody Loves Me
Gone with the Wind
You're My Everything (Braff out)
I've Grown Accustomed to Her Face

Second Set:
Sunday
When Your Lover Has Gone
The Continental (g, b, dm only)
Indian Summer
Medley:
  Memories of You
  Ain't Misbehavin'
Medley:
  Dancing in the Dark
  Pennies from Heaven
I've Grown Accustomed to Her Face
NOTE: A recording of these tunes is available but remains unissued.

During Ruby's UK tours, Dave was always on call to provide support. He related the following example to Steve Voce, who reported it in one of his columns:[2]

> Dave and Anne Bennett settled him in to the hotel they'd booked for him in the city. The Bennetts' phone rang at 5:00 the next morning [July 24] when they were asleep. It was Ruby in a state of rage and agitation. 'You have to get me out of this hotel. It's terrible. The staff are all monsters.' Dave steeled himself. 'OK. Tomorrow I'll fix somewhere for you and then come round and get you.' 'Not tomorrow,' said Ruby. 'Now.' With difficulty, the Bennetts' found a hotel near Slough that would take Ruby in [at this hour]. When they arrived to collect Ruby from the first hotel, they found the staff rattled and white-faced. They never found out what had happened but it must have been one of Ruby's cataclysms. They drove the cornetist out to Slough and settled him in again. All went well the next day but at 3:30 the next morning the Bennetts' phone rang again. The Bennetts' switched on the light and looked at each other in horror. Anne Bennett, who was a teacher, picked it up. It was the headmistress of her school. 'I rang to tell you that the school is on fire and it looks as though it'll be completely destroyed.' 'Oh, thank God,' said Anne with fervor.

Ruby Braff at Pizza on the Park
July 25, 2002, Pizza on the Park, 11 Knightsbridge, London

Ruby Braff (cnt), Roy Williams (tb), Jon Wheatley (g), Dave Green (b), Martin Drew (dm)
The Lady Is a Tramp
Mean to Me
Time on My Hands
Just You, Just Me
This Can't Be Love
I've Grown Accustomed to Her Face

Second Set (only partially recorded):
In a Sentimental Mood
Them There Eyes
Dream Dancing
NOTE: A recording of these tunes is available but remains unissued. "Just You, Just Me" is introduced by Ruby playing "Too-Ra-Loo-Ra-Loo-Ra."

Ruby Braff at Pizza on the Park[3]
July 26, 2002, Pizza on the Park, 11 Knightsbridge, London
Ruby Braff (cnt), Jon Wheatley (g), Dave Green (b), Martin Drew (dm)
First Set:
You'd Be So Nice to Come Home To (Braff out)
Honeysuckle Rose
Skylark
Indiana
Memories of You
Blue, Turning Grey Over You

Second Set:
Limehouse Blues (Braff out)
Come Fly with Me
It Had to Be You
    MACjazz (UK) MAC CD005
Medley
  Chicago
  My Kind of Town (Chicago Is)
Medley:
  Over the Rainbow
    MACjazz (UK) MAC CD005
  The Man That Got Away
    MACjazz (UK) MAC CD005
Ain't Misbehavin'
Yesterdays
    MACjazz (UK) MAC CD005

Take the "A" Train
These Foolish Things
NOTE: A recording of these tunes is available but most remain unissued. MACjazz (UK) MAC CD005 is credited to Jon Wheatley & His Famous Associates and titled *Guitar on the Loose in London.*

Ruby Braff at Pizza on the Park
July 27, 2002, Pizza on the Park, 11 Knightsbridge, London
Ruby Braff (cnt), Roy Williams (tb), John Barnes (bars), Jon Wheatley (g), Dave Green (b), Allan Ganley (dm)
First Set:
The Blue Room (g, b, dm only)
Come Fly with Me
There's a Small Hotel
Gone with the Wind
Just One of Those Things
I've Grown Accustomed to Her Face

Second Set:
Lullaby of Birdland (g, b, dm only)
You Make Me Feel So Young
Skylark
Medley:
  Basin Street Blues
  Nagasaki
Wrap Your Troubles in Dreams
I've Grown Accustomed to Her Face
NOTE: A recording of these tunes is available but remains unissued.

Ruby Braff at Pizza on the Park
July 28, 2002, Pizza on the Park, 11 Knightsbridge, London
Ruby Braff (cnt), Roy Williams (tb), Jon Wheatley (g), Paul Morgan (b), Martin Drew (dm)
First Set:
Sunday
Medley:
  These Foolish Things
  I Want to Be Happy
Keepin' Out of Mischief Now
Lover (g, b, dm only)
Dancing on the Ceiling
I've Grown Accustomed to Her Face

Second Set:
Softly, as in a Morning Sunrise (g, b, dm only)

Come Fly with Me
Sugar
Liza
What's New?
Love Me or Leave Me
As Time Goes By
NOTE: A recording of these tunes is available but remains unissued.

Ruby Braff at the Concorde Club
Wednesday, July 31, 2002, Concorde Club, Eastleigh, Hampshire, England
Ruby Braff (cnt), Roy Williams (tb), John Barnes (bars), Jon Wheatley (g), Kenny Baldock (b), Allan Ganley (dm)
First band set 9–10p.m., second set 10:30–11:30 p.m.
Let's Fall in Love (g, b, dm only)
Avalon
When Your Lover Has Gone
Solitude
Keepin' Out of Mischief Now
I've Grown Accustomed to Her Face

Second Set:
The More I See You (g, b, dm only)
If Dreams Come True
Love Is Just around the Corner
Jeepers Creepers
Isn't It a Pity (tb, g, b, dm only)
Crazy Rhythm
When It's Sleepy Time Down South
NOTE: A recording of these tunes is available but remains unissued.

Ruby Braff at Pizza on the Park
August 1, 2002, Pizza on the Park, 11 Knightsbridge, London
Ruby Braff (cnt), Tony Coe (cl, ts), Jon Wheatley (g), Dave Green (b), Allan Ganley (dm)
First Set:
You Stepped Out of a Dream (as, g, b, dm only)
It's Only a Paper Moon
Out of Nowhere
The Very Thought of You
Watch What Happens
Keepin' Out of Mischief Now

Second Set:
Medley
Exactly Like You
Four or Five Times
Take the "A" Train
As Long As I Live
Autumn Leaves (cl, g, b, dm)
You've Changed
Love Walked In
Cheek to Cheek
When It's Sleepy Time Down South
NOTE: A recording of these tunes is available but remains unissued.

Ruby Braff at Pizza on the Park
August 2, 2002, Pizza on the Park, 11 Knightsbridge, London
Ruby Braff (cnt), Alan Barnes (cl, as), Jon Wheatley (g), Dave Green (b), Allan Ganley (dm)
First Set:
You and the Night and the Music (g, b, dm only)
I Want to Be Happy
Someday Sweetheart
Solitude
Love Me or Leave Me
I've Grown Accustomed to Her Face

Second Set:
A Fine Romance (g, b, dm only)
This Can't Be Love
These Foolish Things
There's a Small Hotel
Nancy (With the Laughing Face) (as, g, b, dm only)
I Wished on the Moon
Dream Dancing
Skylark
I've Grown Accustomed to Her Face
NOTE: A recording of these tunes is available but remains unissued.

Tony Bennett was in the audience for the second set on August 2 to greet Ruby.

Ruby Braff at Pizza on the Park[4]
Pizza on the Park, 11 Knightsbridge, London
August 3, 2002, Pizza on the Park, 11 Knightsbridge, London
Ruby Braff (cnt), Jon Wheatley (g), Dave Green (b), Allan Ganley (dm)
First Set:
What Is This Thing Called Love (g, b, dm only)

The Lady Is a Tramp
What Is There to Say?
You Make Me Feel So Young
Runnin' Wild
Memories of You
Lover Come Back to Me

Second Set:
The Touch of Your Lips (g, b, dm only)
The Very Thought of You
Medley:
  Satin Doll
  Don't Get Around Much Anymore
Nice Work If You Can Get It
If I Could Be with You
This Can't Be Love
Medley:
  When I Fall in Love
  I Want to Be Happy
I've Grown Accustomed to Her Face
NOTE: A recording of these tunes is available but remains unissued.

Ruby Braff at the Woking Jazz Circle
August 4, 2002, Woking Jazz Circle, All Saints Hall, Woodham Lane, Horsell, Woking, Surrey, England
Ruby Braff (cnt), Danny Moss (ts), John Barnes (bars), Jon Wheatley (g), Dave Green (b), Allan Ganley (dm)
First Set:
You and the Night and the Music (g, b, dm only)
Fly Me to the Moon
Ain't Misbehavin'
East of the Sun (Moss feature with g, b, dm only)
You've Changed
Someday Sweetheart
Lover Come Back to Me

Second Set:
Jeepers Creepers
Medley:
  But Not for Me
  Over the Rainbow
  If I Only Had a Brain
My Foolish Heart (Barnes feature with g, b, dm only)
I Would Do Anything for You

NOTE: A recording of these tunes is available but remains unissued.

Ruby's performing career reaches its end with his next appearance. This concludes his tour. But anyone who listens to these recordings will come to understand the contrast between Ruby's lack of ability to walk and his tremendous ability to perform. A photograph of Ruby performing at Nairn Jazz Festival is available.

Ruby Braff at the Nairn Jazz Festival: *Mr. Braff to You*
Wednesday, August 7, 2002 (9:00 p.m.), Nairn Jazz Festival, The Newton Hotel, Nairn, Scotland
Ruby Braff (cnt), Scott Hamilton (ts), Jon Wheatley (g), John Bunch (p), Dave Green (b), Steve Brown (dm)
First Set:
Sometimes I'm Happy
  Arbors Records ARCD 19368
Why Shouldn't I?
  Arbors Records ARCD 19368
Just You, Just Me
  Arbors Records ARCD 19368
I Want a Little Girl
  Arbors Records ARCD 19368
Indiana
  Arbors Records ARCD 19368

Second Set:
Rockin' Chair
  Arbors Records ARCD 19368
Dinah
  Arbors Records ARCD 19368
Yesterdays
  Arbors Records ARCD 19368
The Man I Love
  Arbors Records ARCD 19368
The Man with the Horn (Ruby out)
  Arbors Records ARCD 19368
Honeysuckle Rose (incomplete)
  unissued, recording available
Note: Arbors Records ARCD 19368 is titled *For the Last Time.*

Following this wonderful concert, recorded like the others by Dave Bennett, Ruby determined that he could not complete his tour. In my opinion, when I listened to the recordings, signs of his final pneumonia only were audible in only one earlier performance. Even then, he created wonderful music. Perhaps it is fitting that his final appearance was in front of loyal fans in England, and he returned their passion with a remarkable performance. Fortunately, Arbors Records has released his final performance, with the exception of "Honeysuckle Rose" which was only partially recorded. There may be irony that the final released tune is titled "The Man with the Horn." Ruby certainly was all of that. In retrospect, the musicians paid a most fitting tribute to Ruby and his artistry with that selection. This was the only time in the concert that Ruby did not participate.

Mat Domber has released all available tunes from Ruby's final concert on Arbors Records. I had not seen the artwork for the CDs cover when I prepared the album notes for the CD. Fittingly, Mat used a predominant shade of orange on the cover design, for orange was Ruby's favorite color. Ruby would have smiled at Mat's choice, just as I hope he would be pleased with the design of this book's cover.

Illness kept Ruby from performing at the Brecon Festival for two advertised appearances.

Scott Hamilton shared his thoughts with me about this occasion and his relationship with Ruby Braff:

> Ruby was a mentor, colleague, and close friend from the mid-seventies on. I learned more about what I do from Ruby than anyone else. We met in 1976 when I first came to New York, and worked together many times, most often between 1982 and 1989. I didn't have as many chances to play with Ruby in the last ten years of his life, but we did a gig in Providence right after the World Trade Center disaster and a concert at the Brecon Jazz Festival. Then came the gig in Nairn.
>
> I was hesitant to listen to the tapes at first because I remembered how much trouble Ruby was having on the gig. I had seen him play under a variety of handicaps over the years, but this was the first time I had ever seen him so obviously ill and out of breath. The amazing thing is that none of that comes across on the recording. He sounds very much in control of his instrument and all the tricks he used to stretch the time out just come across as good showmanship. He always knew how to handle a difficult situation (on stage at least).
>
> I am extremely proud of my association with Ruby. I think my best recordings are the ones I made with and as a sideman for him. He knew how to get the very best out of whatever musicians he worked with.
>
> The group on this concert is basically my quartet of the time with Ruby and Jon Wheatley added. It proved a really compatible group—everyone loved Ruby as much as I did and were all pleased to be working with him. Of course, none of us knew it would be his last gig, but the writing was on the wall. Ruby had been fighting emphysema and asthma since 1980 and it was obvious things were getting more serious.
>
> I remember after the gig we all hung out in the hotel bar and Ruby held court. Russell Malone (the guitarist) had come up from Edinburgh to see the concert and we all stayed up for hours—Ruby telling stories had us laughing uncontrollably—just like old times. That was the last time I saw him.

The following is written by Ian King, *Kings Jazz Review* copied from the World Wide Web:[5]

It was 9 p.m. in the Conference Centre of the Newton on Wednesday the 7th of August with over 400 people or folk (not persons) in place for the concert *Mr. Braff to You* when I entered to claim my as usual paid-for seat at the back of the room. The eloquent cornetist who adores playing the melody line had appeared in Nairn in the past, but this year, he would be teaming up with tenor saxophonist Scott Hamilton with backing group, John Bunch (p), Dave Green (bars), and Steve Brown (dm) on stage.

It was sad to see Ruby being wheeled in up to the stage-setting, but well-being, when he slowly with a sparkle in his eye, nestled himself in with pillow as a prop-up to his seating arrangements all set to stomp-in on the opening number this evening.

Up to and until 'I Want a Little Girl' perhaps through apprehensive confidence, and settling-in admiration of this great jazz artist, the first session was lackluster, with only flashes of brilliance of his old-self coming from the Braff cornet.

I heard that it was brandy and not malt which was his fancy at the interval, or was it a read of the *JJI* article of himself presented to him in appreciation that turned him on, whatever, tunes like the Hoagy Carmichael & His Orchestra 'Rockin' Chair' of May 1930 in New York one, showed how Ruby had become his true self, conducting his group in professional style, blowing phrasing qualities, only, that that beautiful Braff cornet tone sound could sound. In being asked by him for a choice of song, someone at the rear of the audience, I shan't say who, but I've known him since before I was born, cried out 'Just Play Nice Tunes—Ruby' perhaps referring to a CD of Mr. Braff with that title, and thereafter, unique to him alone, and always to be remembered, there in front of us for the listening, we heard tunes, played as if they were all coming from heaven.

Ruby Braff was developing a good rapport with his audience, but as he came to announce 'Yesterdays' by US composer of more than a thousand songs, Jerome Kern, whose successful musical in 1927 was *Showboat*, Ruby became infuriated as he mentioned the song of the same title by a famous Pop group, going on to say, that Sir Paul McCartney formerly of that group, the Beatles' effort, coined for a concert this year in the aftermath of the New York twin towers disaster of 11 September last year, that 'a three year old could have written it better.'

Following that outpouring and rage, it was then, that the Ruby Braff rendition of 'Yesterdays' with this group became a masterpiece.

It was on "The Man I Love" that the *Mr. Braff to You* concert ended one half-hour after midnight to a tumultuous applause of appreciation from the crowd.

Finally, I was honored when Mat Domber asked me to write the album notes for the released CDs. That text follows.

Ruby and Scott: *For the Last Time*
Ruby Braff's Historic Final Performance

What a band! This recording brings you Ruby Braff's final performance, a wonderful concert at the Nairn Jazz Festival on August 7, 2002. Except for an incomplete recording of "Honeysuckle Rose," the final number from the second set, you can hear every note and experience the joy of sitting in a front row seat.

Let's be frank. We tend to approach any musician's final recording with some trepidation. Perhaps we even purchase it only because it brings closure an artist's superb career. Well, just set aside any worry you have about the possibility of any sign of diminished talent. This recording lets you hear Ruby performing at the top of his game, joined with wonderful musicians who allow him to reach the heights he always strived to attain. In fact, "Yesterdays" is a masterpiece that can be compared to any performance from any time in his career.

Ruby and Scott had a very special association, from the beginning of Scott's career until this, Ruby's final performance. [Here I inserted the words from Scott Hamilton that I previously cited on page 614. I won't repeat them here.]

Ruby would love those words, for they reflect the way that he touched the lives of musicians as well as his fans. Scott is not the only one of his generation who feels that Ruby was a major influence and career champion.

But we are getting ahead of the story that helps you understand the background for these marvelous performances.

The Setting

My last meeting with Ruby was in New York, at Nola Studios on the occasion of his final studio recording sessions in June 2002. He was excited about his upcoming tour of the United Kingdom, but, because of his continuing health problems with advanced emphysema, he was also apprehensive about the number of performances concentrated in a short interval. But Ruby loved to perform in front of people, and Dave Bennett arranged a schedule that would return Ruby to familiar locations and reconnect him to his loyal UK fans. Dave also arranged Ruby's previous tour of the UK in 1999.

Jon Wheatley recounts how Ruby enjoyed seeing all the musicians who joined him in various performances:

> It was a pleasure to see Ruby reuniting with old friends and collaborators Brian Lemon, Dave Green, Allan Ganley, John Barnes, and Roy Williams, and the

> terrific young drummer, Steve Brown, and then John Bunch and Scott Hamilton in Scotland. He loved these guys. Ruby got into using phrases like "awesome" and "wicked awesome" onstage to show that he wasn't over the hill.
>
> When I hear people say he was always critical, condescending, and rude I sometimes recall a night in Florida when Mat and Rachel Domber, Ruby and I and several others were looking for a spot to relax and have a cocktail after a gig. We went into some decent-looking lounge and had just gotten comfortable when a horrendous one-man band, complete with drum machine and other paraphernalia started performing. Everyone looked at each other anxiously, expecting Ruby to flip out. He just said, 'Oh, it's just some guy making a living. . . no problem' and continued with the conversation. He was a fascinating guy.

I phoned Ruby at his home the night before his departure from the USA. We talked about several things, for Ruby had opinions on nearly any issue you could imagine. When I touched on his tour, he simply said, "I will play as well as I possibly can." From our conversation, it was clear that he had some doubts about his ability to sustain his strength. Then, he changed the subject. Understand that Ruby always strived to make every performance at least as good as the one before. He also treasured every opportunity to perform in front of "real people" as he often said to me. Those occasions were, unfortunately, quite infrequent in the final decade of his life.

The tour was demanding. Beginning July 18, 2002, Ruby performed two sets each night for 12 nights at Pizza on the Park in London and concerts at the Concorde Club and Woking Jazz Circle before this performance at the Nairn Jazz Festival. Dave Bennett, who is also a notable recording engineer, recorded nearly every note of this entire tour. The final concert performance is now in your hands. These recordings are astounding. Jon Wheatley previously issued a few tunes recorded at Pizza on the Park on his own CD, *Guitar on the Loose in London*. The atmosphere during all of Ruby's appearances was festive. He greeted many loyal fans at each performance. He was delighted that Tony Bennett attended one set at Pizza on the Park, renewing their long association that began in 1968.

Ruby loves variety. I was astonished to see that he performed eighty-nine different songs during this tour, even though the stress of nightly performances was taking a toll on his health. A few tunes were repeated two or three times. Only one was featured more often, and that was "I've Grown Accustomed to Her Face." The extent of his repertoire is remarkable and surely shows no sign of any relaxation in his standards and his commitment to delight his audiences. He was aware that many fans would attend more than one performance. Certainly that had been true in the past.

The program on these two discs includes songs that Ruby performed at most one other time during this tour. This alone is remarkable, for after this concert Ruby felt he would be physically unable to perform at his final concert at the Brecon Jazz Festival. Instead, he returned to the USA thinking he could recover. That was not to be, and Ruby entered a hospital and then a convalescent center, where he died on February 9, 2003. It is fitting that his final performances were in front of his appreciative UK fans, for Ruby sadly had come to realize that he would not be able to perform again.

What a Band!

Ruby would not accept engagements when he could not select the other musicians who performed. He refused to tour in the role of a guest artist appearing with local rhythm sections. So, the concert at Nairn featured Ruby with five other musicians he admired. Ruby had previously performed at the Nairn Jazz Festival in 1996 and 1999, so he looked forward to this return engagement. In fact, in 1996 Scott Hamilton and Dave Green accompanied him, while in 1999 he performed with John Bunch and Steve Brown. The 2002 performance was a bit of a reunion for all of them, joined by Jon Wheatley.

Jon, in addition to his musical skills, was Ruby's traveling companion throughout the tour, with him for every flight and hotel booking and playing in every engagement. He told me that being with Ruby was lots of fun. Ruby was an accomplished storyteller and was, after all, a living history of jazz. Due to his long-standing emphysema, Ruby required assistance while traveling and he seldom left his hotel. But Ruby loved to tell stories about his experiences and to discuss current events. Jon first performed with Ruby in 1992, and their first recording together was made for Arbors Records in 1993, a session released as *Live at the Regattabar*. In some of their appearances, Jon was paired with a second guitarist, a format Ruby loved to create. Jon feels that Ruby helped him advance his career. Ruby secured an invitation for Jon to perform at a jazz party in 1994 organized by Ralph and Sunnie Sutton in Denver, thus introducing him to other musicians.

This appearance at the Suttons' party was probably the first time that Jon played with Scott Hamilton. Scott and Ruby produced delightful music. Their performances always reflected the kind of sympathetic engagement that can only be achieved by artists who perform at the very highest level. When one leads, the other provides support, often creating appealing countermelodies that enrich the performance. On several standard tunes, they close with a shift to bop lines that are based on the same chord progressions. You will hear examples of these skills frequently during the Nairn performance.

Scott says that he first performed with Ruby at Condon's and Jimmy Ryan's a few times as a guest artist, starting in 1976. I have traced an early performance to a jazz party in Midland, Texas, in 1977. Scott said that this was his second appearance at a jazz party. This was just at the time that Scott was receiving tremendous acclaim in the US press as a young musician who played saxophone in the tradition of Coleman Hawkins, Ben Webster, and other jazz greats. Of course, this echoed the acclaim for Ruby following his early recordings for Vanguard Records in the '50s. Their paths crossed again at the Kansas City Jazz

Festival in 1979 where they performed together on eight sets in three days. In 1979, both Ruby and Scott toured with the Newport Jazz Festival All Stars led by George Wein and they continued their encounters at the Gibson Jazz Party later that same year. The frequency of their associations increased at festivals and jazz parties in both the US and Europe, but their first recording was not released until 1983 in a session recorded by Hank O'Neal and released in Sweden on the Phontastic label. This recording was also the first to have Ruby Braff, Scott Hamilton, and John Bunch together. The three of them were also joined in two recordings for Concord Jazz in 1985. Ruby and Scott also made two notable recordings for Arbors Records in 1993, drawn from live sets at the Regattabar in Cambridge. There were many other meetings, including the performance at Nairn in 1996. Prior to this final concert, Scott and Ruby last performed together in a club in Rhode Island on September 16, 2001. Following that performance Ruby told me how much he enjoyed playing with Scott, who at that time was considering a possible return to the US from England.

John Bunch and Ruby were also longtime musical friends. John was one of Ruby's favorite pianists. It took considerable skill, patience, and flexibility to arrive at that position. John has a very broad background, including years as musical director and accompanist for Tony Bennett. I believe he first appeared with Ruby at Condon's in New York in 1961. Their first recording together was issued on Sonet and dates from 1978. By then, they had performed again at Condon's, along with the Half Note and various jazz parties. Recordings for Phontastic, Concord (both already mentioned above), Chiaroscuro, Red Baron, and Arbors (three recordings) followed. Shortly before this Nairn concert, they had performed together at the March of Jazz in 2002, organized by Mat and Rachel Domber. In one of those sets, Dave Green accompanied them.

Dave was Ruby's bassist of choice whenever he performed in the UK. His sound on this recording is gorgeous. While their paths may have crossed earlier, I believe their first performance together was at the Bull's Head Pub in 1992 and then with Scott Hamilton at Nairn in 1992. Their first CD is a 1996 release on Zephyr, recorded in the UK on a day that was surrounded by nights performing at Pizza Express in London. Dave, John, Scott, and Ruby performed together for the first time at the Brecon Jazz Festival in 1999 and, without Scott, at the March of Jazz in 2002, a few months before this concert at Nairn.

Ruby praised Steve Brown's talents when they first met at the Nairn Jazz Festival in 1999. John Bunch was the pianist on that occasion. Ruby smiled when he described Steve's musicianship and was taken by the subtlety in his playing. Of all the musicians on this program, Steve is the one with the least experience of playing with Ruby, since Allan Ganley was Ruby's frequent choice when in London; however, Steve subsequently recorded with John Bunch for Arbors Records and Scott Hamilton on Concord and Woodville.

Approaching This Final Concert

Those who listen to Ruby's recordings regularly know how he tries to create unique voicing by combining instruments in different combinations. Here that happens mostly when Ruby and Scott juxtapose their ideas in a fluid manner that never ceases to delight. They are listening to each other in ways that cannot fail to bring smiles to your face each time you listen to these CDs.

If you attended the concert, you might have had some serious concerns when you saw Ruby. He suffered from severe asthma and emphysema since an attack in 1994 that almost ended his life. In his later years he regularly used a wheelchair to conserve energy when he performed. At Nairn you would have seen him wheeled in. He struggled to reach the stage, whereupon he worked to arrange a pillow for support on his chair and properly positioned in a stream of blowing air from a portable fan. He appeared frail. Who would have blamed you if you reduced your expectations? Ruby was aware of growing lung congestion as his tour continued, although he probably had thought that it was due to bronchitis and not pneumonia. His previous performances had consumed much of his energy. He was worried.

Ruby was aware of the audience's startled reaction and he turned it into a joke. He introduced the first tune with a big smile, saying, "Here's another little tune, 'Sometimes I'm Happy.'" The audience laughed in return, perhaps in relief and delight that this frail but legendary performer was showing spunk. They shouted words of encouragement along with warm applause. I am certain that he intended his words to reassure everyone that they would thoroughly enjoy the evening. As the performance began, Dave Bennett observed that Ruby muttered to his horn, "Play ya bastard," willing it to overcome the limitations he was feeling. He had already decided to rise to the occasion, marked by a wonderfully receptive audience and superb musicians onstage.

Yet, Ruby may have made two concessions in this concert program. First, the tunes he selected were ones he had performed many times in his career but at most one other time during this tour. They were familiar to all the musicians in this band. Second, in many of his performances Ruby would often work during each performance to vary the combinations of instruments playing together to vary the musical textures. This concert was more of a jam session, although Ruby and Scott consistently developed rich interplay.

It is useful to draw on Dave Bennett's recollections, as he kindly shared them:

> Being responsible for a tour of Ruby's was never less than a bit traumatic whilst absolutely full of delights, both musical and humorous. His demands, often bizarre, his logic strange but understandable if and when the reasoning became apparent. . . . I collected him, with the help of Jon Wheatley, every night, taking him to the various venues and back. Once onstage with the lighting, sound, and air conditioning adjusted to his satisfaction, he performed as only he could, faultlessly and wonderfully.

By the time of his trip to Scotland his nervousness was apparent, though anyone unaware of the situation would not have sensed it with him appearing to be his usual confrontational self. He was probably for the very first time unsure of his ability to perform. You will hear him comment, "What a great band," a fact beyond dispute and which gave him so much satisfaction. It was the most important thing in life for him to be in such a situation.

For this recording, I used a dummy human head with microphones contained in realistically shaped rubber ears. The idea is to pick up sound in the same way as human hearing. The sound is very lifelike, particularly with listening through earphones. Ruby required a portable fan blowing near him at all times and this can be heard at times during the recording. Unfortunately John's piano is slightly under recorded. Nevertheless, I can enjoy the recording quite comfortably, which makes it doubly important as a document of a great final performance of a truly great jazzman. While waiting for the return flight at the airport, I let Ruby hear some of it on headphones and he was astonished and thrilled by it. How many final performances have been recorded, let alone one as sublime as this?

Anatomy of the Performance

In every selection, these musicians play together, setting rich backgrounds behind each soloist. Ruby injects drama. Scott brings romance. Jon and John use chords and single notes to add depth, while Dave and Steve propel each tune. They all listen while playing, just as you will enjoy listening time and time again.

On "Sometimes I'm Happy," Ruby leads over Scott's harmonies. They reverse roles. Jon's solo brings a rich "Yeah, Jon" from Ruby. Ruby continues, mostly in his lower register, briefly quoting "Do You Want to Know a Secret" as he weaves in allusions to the main melody and extends the tune's harmonics, earning applause. Scott follows with Steve providing wonderful rhythmic punctuations, earning a "Yeah, Scotty" from Ruby. Piano and bass solos follow, with Ruby's "Yeah, Johnny" and "Yeah, Dave" reflecting his delight to be with these artists. Next, Ruby signals exchanges with drums. Ruby starts; then Scott takes his turn as Ruby calls attention to Steve. Ruby leads with Scott's supportive background to close with Ruby's descending cellolike run. What a fine opening.

Next comes "Why Shouldn't I?" Ruby introduces the tune with one of his stories, describing how he originally wanted to play saxophone. He charms the audience. He told stories to provide necessary breaks, so that he could regain his breath. John Bunch must have mentioned this song, and he opens with Ruby exploring the melody before handing the lead to Scott. The lead returns to John who rhapsodizes the melody, followed by Jon and Scott. Then Ruby enters with his delicate runs. He demonstrates convincingly that his strong attack is undiminished. He slows the tempo and closes in tandem with Scott. The audience must be convinced by now that they will enjoy this concert. This is a lovely tune, caressed by each musician.

Ruby asks permission (right!) to play "Just You, Just Me." He chuckles. They begin with Ruby and Scott exchanging the lead as the melody unfolds. Jon takes several fine choruses, while Steve sets a truly infectious rhythm. They earn warm applause. Ruby explores the song's extended harmonics with darting runs and legato effects. Then, Scott enters, swinging and enjoying the strong rhythmic foundation as he builds his solo and briefly quotes "Sometimes I'm Happy" to affirm that this is a joyous musical happening. John comes next, and you can hear Ruby laughing in enjoyment and adding a few handclaps. Dave comes next. You can slightly hear the fan in the background while Ruby and Scott discuss how to close. Ruby and Scott alternate in trading bars with Steve. For his part, Scott briefly quotes phrases from "Let's Fall in Love" and "Honeymoon for Two," the latter picking up from a short musical hint from Ruby. He must be happy. Scott and Ruby then lead to the close by inserting a melodic variation that Coleman Hawkins frequently performed.

Ruby says, "We had a request to do a tune—from me," and he introduces "I Want a Little Girl." John opens and Ruby plays melody in a rhapsodic style. Scott, Jon, and John continue in sequence to extend the melody. Ruby then enters in his lower register and delivers a beautifully constructed solo that contains all his trademarks of trills, runs, slurs, jumps, and delicate shadings. He has always known how to use silence between his notes for dramatic effect. He stretches, and you may hear just momentary weaknesses that do not detract from the emotion he invests in this solo. Scott truly sings with his instrument on this—wonderful. John constructs strings of single notes that evolve into rich chorded patterns, really building his solo and caressing the melody as he finishes. Jon and Dave follow with contributions that explore the textures of this song. Jon consistently provides nice background support for Dave's solos throughout this recording. Then, Ruby returns. He is again rhapsodic as Scott adds his rich harmonies as they close this tune. The applause grows in appreciation of the beauty of this performance.

John opens "Rockin' Chair." Ruby states the melody, over Scott's harmonies. Scott takes over on the release, then returns the lead to Ruby. They are so relaxed and produce such great comfort. Scott solos nicely, followed by Jon. Ruby takes control with precise phrases, whether dancing or sustaining notes as he glides across the melody while in complete control of his instrument. John follows, building then relaxing the intensity, with Jon's nice punctuations throughout. Then Ruby trades with Scott leading to Dave's turn to solo. Finally, Ruby and Scott alternate to close the first CD in this set. Each provides a rich background for the other as we have come to expect.

Ruby opens the second CD with "Dinah." Scott plays a familiar countermelody and Jon is awarded the first solo, with rapidly articulated notes. Ruby enters with swirling notes and rhythmic patterns, including snatches of a melody he knows so very well. He is on top of his game. His playing is even more fluid than the first set. Scott solos next. As he ends, Steve kicks his bass drum three times in approval. Then John extends the momentum. You can hear the relaxed conversation of Ruby and Scott as they plan, but Ruby inserts several verbal exclamations as John builds his solo and ends with a brief quote from "Humoresque." They are talking to each other. Jon solos next. Ruby and Scott build a short transition in unison using a quote from Dizzy Gillespie's "Dizzy Atmosphere." Dave solos, with Jon and Steve propelling the rhythm. Ruby and Scott, using a simple riff, lead exchanges with Steve, who then takes his longest solo. Ruby and Scott quote "Handful of Keys" as they build to the closing. As Ruby says, this tune has "a lot of meat in it."

Now comes a wonderful performance of "Yesterdays." Ruby opens with deep tones accompanied sensitively by Jon. Then Scott enters as they trade melodic lead. At times they both employ cellolike sounds. Ruby then leads into Scott's extended solo before trading with Ruby as they alternate the leading and supporting roles. The playing is very emotional, even mournful at times. Ruby trades with Scott. They tell a story about memories, and I am particularly fond of Ruby's playing during this section just before the middle of this performance. The audience chooses not to interrupt the performance with applause, and I believe that this shows how intently they are following the performance. John comes next choosing beautiful notes that remind us that some memories are whimsical. In a superbly constructed solo, Jon then plays in parallel with the melody but varies his voicing to explore layers in the song. Ruby and Scott enter together with Ruby leading. Then, Ruby slows the tempo for the ending and says to the audience, "The whole thing was like a nice conversation." I certainly agree. This is truly a highlight of the concert. The audience reacts with warm applause. The sound of a cough from someone in the audience brings another joke from Ruby, for he is truly one with the audience now.

Ruby introduces "The Man I Love," displaying his humor with some lines that will be familiar to those who attended his live performances over the years. It is good to have them preserved, for Ruby was a consummate entertainer. The intervals between numbers entertained the audience but also provided a necessary time for him to clear his lungs before beginning the next performance.

"The Man I Love" opens with John's brief introduction. Then, Ruby takes the lead with Scott in support. As has often happened, they smoothly switch roles on the release and then switch back. Jon solos next. Ruby soars on this one with extended runs, laying figures on top of figures with endless variation in his rhythmic pulse. There is absolutely no sign of anything limiting Ruby's imagination on this solo. Scott and then John present swinging solos, and there can be no doubt that these musicians are playing together. This level of collaboration is something that can only be achieved by master musicians. Dave solos next, with Jon's tasty support. Ruby initiates a series of musical exchanges in the following sequence: Ruby then Steve, then Scott, then Steve. This pattern repeats. Ruby and Scott trade lead to the end with each providing a rich foundation for the other. The tune ends with their reference to "Salt Peanuts."

Ruby asks Scott to pick a tune to showcase his talent. Scott selects "The Man with the Horn" as his feature. The beautiful ballad performance also includes an extended solo by Jon, while Ruby gets some needed rest.

The second CD ends with the performance of "Indiana" that actually closed the first set. It is placed at the end of the second CD because the final tune of the second set, "Honeysuckle Rose," was not completely captured in the live recording. Placement here nicely balances the two CDs. John opens and then Ruby takes the lead with Scott underneath. Ruby extends his solo with fluid runs. He darts across octaves with a consistently crisp attack. He hands the lead to Scott as his breath starts to impose limits on his imagination. Next, John and Jon solo in turn. Ruby, playing softly, trades exchanges with Steve and then asks Scott to do the same. Ruby leads this superb band to close with a familiar riff, together with Scott. The warm applause shows how much the audience has appreciated the first set. Ruby says simply, "Thank you so much as we finish our first portion of the set," and introduces the band that has created this wonderful music. If the applause at the end of the concert had been captured, I am certain it would have been even louder.

Several times I encouraged Ruby to record a slow version of "Indiana," the state where I live. Ruby, of course, had his opinion about the possible merits of my suggestion. Of course, he had his way. With this version, he does the Hoosier State proud. Certainly, I will not have a chance to request it any other way again. Every musician in this band is a star.

Conclusion

Ruby wanted to be remembered for his music. Performance was his passion. It is fitting that this final recording proves that he never reduced his standards and always gave his all to pleasing his audiences. If you have not listened to Ruby's recordings in the past, there is no better place to begin than with his many releases on Arbors Records

His last words on the second CD are, "Thank you very much for everything." The band and the audience were perfect. In my opinion, so was Ruby's career. He was dedicated to the creation of beautiful music and, in doing so, he made an indelible mark on the history of jazz. And he loved to perform before people. He said to me, "I don't seem to have any problem making people happy who attend, but sometimes I just wish that there were more of them in the room."

While Ruby cannot read these words, I do think that he became aware of the love, gratitude, and appreciation his fans and other musicians continue to express about his many contributions to the jazz tradition.

Ruby's final two performances were cancelled due to his advancing pneumonia. Tickets had been sold, so fans were disappointed but nothing could be done.

Ruby Braff Quartet with Scott Hamilton (appearance cancelled due to illness)
Friday August 9, 2002, 8:30 p.m., Brecon Jazz Festival, Theatr Brycheiniog, Brecon, Wales
Ruby Braff (cnt), Scott Hamilton (ts), John Bunch (p), Dave Green (b), Steve Brown (dm)

Ruby Braff Trio (appearance cancelled due to illness)
Saturday August 10, 2002, 2 p.m., Brecon Jazz Festival, Theatr Brycheiniog, Brecon, Wales
Ruby Braff (cnt), Jon Wheatley (g), Dave Green (b)

Ruby's Vast Repertoire of Tunes Performed During His Final Tour

Ruby played 89 different songs during his final tour. For Nairn, "Just You, Just Me," "Yesterdays," and "Indiana" had been played one previous time during the tour. The others were only performed at Nairn. The following list shows all the songs Ruby played during his final tour. When songs were repeated, the number of performances is shown. I find this remarkable, but not surprising. Even when ill, Ruby was aware that some people would attend a number of his performances. As I wrote, he loved variety. This presents perhaps a contrast to Louis Armstrong in one other way, for Louis preferred less variety in his repertory, having perfected so many of his solos and routines as the years advanced. Ruby continue to adore the melody and did so with each tune he performed, delighting in the stimulation that variety brought to each set.

1) Ain't Misbehavin' (3)
2) As Long As I Live
3) As Time Goes By
4) Avalon
5) Basin Street Blues
6) Blue, Turning Grey Over You
7) But Not for Me
8) Cheek to Cheek
9) Chicago
10) Come Fly with Me (3)
11) Crazy Rhythm (2)
12) Dancing in the Dark
13) Dancing on the Ceiling
14) Dinah
15) Don't Get Around Much Anymore
16) Dream Dancing (2)
17) Exactly Like You
18) Fly Me to the Moon
19) Four or Five Times
20) Ghost of a Chance
21) Gone with the Wind (2)
22) Honeysuckle Rose (2)
23) I Want a Little Girl
24) I Want to Be Happy (4)
25) I Wished on the Moon (2)
26) I Would Do Anything for You
27) If Dreams Come True

28) If I Could Be with You
29) If I Only Had a Brain
30) In a Sentimental Mood
31) Indian Summer
32) Indiana (2)
33) It Don't Mean a Thing
34) It Had to Be You
35) It's Only a Paper Moon
36) I've Grown Accustomed to Her Face (11)
37) Jeepers Creepers (2)
38) Jumpin' at the Woodside
39) Just One of Those Things
40) Just You, Just Me (2)
41) Keepin' Out of Mischief Now (3)
42) Liza (2)
43) Love Is Just around the Corner
44) Love Me or Leave Me (3)
45) Love Walked In
46) Lover Come Back to Me (2)
47) Mean to Me
48) Memories of You (4)
49) My Kind of Town (Chicago Is)
50) Nagasaki
51) Nice Work If You Can Get It (2)
52) On the Sunny Side of the Street
53) Out of Nowhere
54) Over the Rainbow (2)
55) Pennies from Heaven
56) Rockin' Chair
57) Royal Garden Blues
58) Runnin' Wild
59) Satin Doll
60) Skylark (3)
61) When It's Sleepy Time Down South (2)
62) Solitude (2)
63) Somebody Loves Me
64) Someday Sweetheart (2)
65) Sometimes I'm Happy
66) Sugar
67) Sunday (2)
68) Take the "A" Train (3)
69) The Lady Is a Tramp (2)
70) The Man I Love
71) The Man That Got Away
72) The Very Thought of You (2)
73) Them There Eyes
74) There's a Small Hotel (2)
75) These Foolish Things (3)
76) They Can't Take That Away from Me
77) This Can't Be Love (3)
78) Time on My Hands
79) Watch What Happens
80) What Is There to Say?
81) What's New?
82) When I Fall in Love
83) When Your Lover Has Gone (2)
84) Why Shouldn't I?
85) Wrap Your Troubles in Dreams
86) Yesterdays (2)
87) You Can Depend on Me
88) You Make Me Feel So Young (2)
89) You've Changed (2)

Ruby reached home, strongly believing that he would be able to recover in time. Hank O'Neal sent me an e-mail message to phone Ruby, for one of his associates had just completed a call and reported that Ruby did not sound well. I phoned, but could only leave a message—followed by a few more. Ruby had summoned the paramedics, who took him to a hospital. Following his treatment there, he was transferred to a convalescent center. Soon thereafter, he came to realize that it was very doubtful that he would ever be able to play again. The central purpose of his life had been taken from him due to declining health and damage to his lungs. I was able to speak with him a number of times, with my wife joining in some calls. His medication rendered him incomprehensible on one occasion. We both spoke with him less than a week before his death. When he asked for my wife, I felt that his voice and spirit were stronger than I had heard for weeks. But that was not to be. One of his final callers, and probably his last, was his longtime friend Steve Voce. Steve recounted the call as follows:[6]

> Ruby had told us in the previous October that he would shortly die. At the time I told Dave Bennett that that was nonsense. Dave said, no, that Ruby never said anything unless he meant it. We phoned Ruby for the final time and his nurse gave him the phone at midnight. I spoke to him for a minute or so, but then I broke down, couldn't go on, and handed the phone to my wife, Jenny, of whom he was very fond. She spoke to him for several minutes. He died about four hours later. We must, I think, have been the last of his friends to speak to him.

Ruby had a chance to say something to all of us in his own words, but his music will support our memories for the rest of our lives.

Ruby's passing was widely covered in the media. Apart from jazz publications, long articles appeared in the *New York Times*, *The Wall Street Journal*, and other US newspapers, plus several papers in the UK including *The Times*, *The Guardian*, *The Daily Telegraph*, and *The Independent.* Perhaps not surprisingly, coverage in the UK press was more thoughtful than from newspapers in the US. Regardless, Ruby might have observed that the jazz critics spoke when assured that they would have the final word. Certainly, he would not have liked to read some occasional references to his playing in an old style. His fans, worldwide, cherish their memories of his timeless artistry, which remains fresh and exciting to this day. Together, we can continue to enjoy the body of recorded work he has left us. Most of his fans are not friends, using Ruby's very specific definition, but they are certainly champions of his legacy. Dick Wellstood once wrote the following words that certainly apply to Ruby: "Musicians make music, which critics later label."[7]

Ruby would have been pleased to see an article about John Hammond's "ear for talent" that appeared in the 75th anniversary issue of *DownBeat* magazine. Ruby was mentioned in a short list of Hammond's discoveries, along with (in order of mention) Count Basie, Lester Young, Charlie Christian, Billie Holiday, Ruby Braff, Aretha Franklin, Bob Dylan, Denny Zeitlin, John Handy, George Benson, Bruce Springsteen and Stevie Ray Vaughan.[8]

It is my hope that this book will help keep the memory of Ruby's artistry alive for future generations. For what he accomplished as a musician leaves a mark on the history of jazz:

1. He performed at an incredibility high level for over fifty years and recordings provide the evidence, despite tremendous physical limitations during the final years of his life;

2. With George Barnes, he led one of the finest small groups in the history of jazz;
3. He developed a unique and highly recognizable style, something that only the most notable performers in jazz accomplish;
4. He found a way to survive as a creative artist for his entire adult lifetime without compromising his artistic standards;
5. He was a notable bridge between older and younger artists, learning from some and providing encouragement to others—he was both a student and a teacher of the highest order;
6. He was outspoken in voicing the truth, as he saw it;
7. He was a very honest man; and
8. He was committed to creating beauty in his musical performances.

Ruby, were he alive, would probably want the final word. Perhaps he would choose to remind us of the debt we owe to Louis Armstrong. I'd also like to think that he admired my lack of conformance to the more typical format of a "top 10" list in recounting some of the achievements that define his legacy.

At the time of his final tour in the United Kingdom, he remained the finest cornetist in the world. Years before, Jack Teagarden wrote the following: "If music comes from the heart, it seems to me that there should always be *something* new to say."[9] In an interview in 1958, Pee Wee Russell said, "He'll reach the peak where he can be talked about with Louis, Bix, and Berigan and all those boys. When he gets old and grey, the little giant will be remembered."[10] Ruby never tired of creating beautiful music. He certainly never ran out of things to say. Ruby was a man of high principles, but he will be remembered for his recordings. That is why he took delight in seeing this book develop. He wanted others to enjoy his many recordings and during their lifetimes perhaps even to recall how they enjoyed being present at some of his appearances. Early in our conversations, he stated how he hated it when musicians on the bandstand took time to discuss what to play next, in effect ignoring the audiences that had come to hear them perform. Perhaps this book will help to extend Ruby's conversations with his audience.

Ruby wanted to be known for his artistry, not for the personal details in his life. I have tried to respect his wishes. Readers of this book will certainly agree that he was an amazing artist. That is quite a legacy. He always wanted to honor his fans and audiences.

A copy of the memorial card from his funeral and photograph of his tombstone are available, along with an image of the cover of *Jazz Journal International* that shows him blowing his horn. That is a fitting final image, and one Ruby would like us to remember.

Epilogue

Loren Schoenberg gathered a series of testimonials about Ruby Braff when he was managing Ruby's career. It is useful to capture some of these quotations here:

- **Buddy Rich**: One of my favorite trumpeters, one of the few melodic guys left in the world, as far as I'm concerned.
- **Tony Bennett**: Ruby is my great friend who now holds the reigning position of the best cornet player in the world, in the tradition of Bix Beiderbecke, Louis Armstrong, Bobby Hackett, and now there is only one—Ruby Braff.
- **Cy Coleman**: Musicians like Ruby Braff make writing music a pleasure.
- **Tommy Newsom**: Ruby Braff is one of the unique jazz players of our time, a total individual—he doesn't sound like anyone else and is an extremely melodic and expressive player.
- **Whitney Balliett**: Braff is . . . an extraordinarily precise horn player whose exactness . . . caused Alec Wilder to observe that 'every note he plays is the center of that note.' Braff loves melody and he plays it in a rare and affecting way that lies between embellishment and full-scale improvisation. He does an astonishing thing: he does not, in the manner of many improvisers, impose himself in the tunes he plays; rather he beats them up in such a way that their colors and curves and textures gleam and shine. He points up their treasures, but leaves them intact.
- **John S. Wilson**: Mr. Braff's gently blown open horn conjures up deep singing tones on a ballad.
- **Derek Jewell**: No trumpeter has ever produced a rounder tone at both ends of the scale, and the lazy elegance of the phrasing is quite unlike anything else on the instrument in jazz. The richest gold is his softest playing in the lower register, the sternest test of the lip and control, where much more fashionable players fluff and mumble like men with feet in mud. Braff walks in the sky.
- **Leonard Feather**: Ruby remains today what he has always been, one of the outstanding creative artists on his instrument in the grand tradition of mainstream jazz.

Steve Voce wrote an obituary for Ruby in *The Independent*,[11] part of which follows:

> Braff came in a direct line from Louis Armstrong, Bix Beiderbecke and Bobby Hackett and his playing had all the beauty and eloquence that goes with such a hallmark. His fat sound on the instrument and delicate showers of notes were

> instantly recognizable and he was one of the most melodic improvisers in the history of jazz. Unlike the other three he spawned no imitators, for his sound and the method of creating it were unique and largely uncopyable. Unimpressed by high notes for their own sake, he opened up new depths in the bottom registers of the instrument that others could not reach. . . . and he was one of my best friends. . . . [His] elfin frame was often driven by one of the most surreal senses of humor one could imagine and his spontaneous introductions from the stage invariably had his audiences contorted with helpless laughter. He loved audiences and his happiest moments over the last decade were when he appeared, as he did four or five times a year, on the radio program that I present for BBC local radio in the north.
>
> Here he revealed that he was romantically pursued by the Queen Mother. 'Every time I see her on the television at the races or somewhere she is looking directly into my eyes and I can see that she is singing 'If I Could Be with You One Hour Tonight.'' He mulled over his potential as a member of the royal family. He kept us up to date with the affair over the years, as he did with the frequent occasions when Scotland Yard called him in to advise on how to solve the most impenetrable crimes. Would they ask him to be Chief of Police? He claimed also to have secret underwater rendezvous in their nuclear submarines with another friend, Humphrey Lyttelton, where the two discussed the best actions they should take in directing world affairs.

Mat Domber added his thoughts in tribute, based on a decade long close working relationship:

> The Ruby Braff I knew was a complex individual, at once part angel with a deeply sentimental side who could light the Chanukah candles with me by telephone, and on the other hand, a difficult person whose personality was plagued by a tortured childhood and by the fact that his body was wracked with pain and fears about his emphysema. Through it all, perhaps despite it all, Ruby lived for his music. At the end, after his last performance in Scotland, when he returned to the States suffering from pneumonia, his doctors said he could never play again. For Ruby that was the end. He never again picked up his horn and willed himself to die.
>
> I was fortunate to have worked with and befriended Ruby for almost ten glorious years of music making—many thought some of his most productive work. I think that he enjoyed recording for Arbors Records because, for one of the few times in his career, he had the freedom to select his sidemen and play the music that he felt. Everyone knows about his unique sound and adoration of the melody but for me his playing was the release of emotion and his frustration with life.
>
> Ruby will always remain in my thoughts—a true musical genius—and one who was not only a friend but also a musical mentor.

Ruby had a close relationship with Scott Hamilton, and Scott spoke with Peter Vacher in an interview about Ruby's influence:[12]

> [Ruby] is a musician that's on a level with any of the other trumpet players that are his age, but he chose to do something different. There's been very few people like that. By the time the eighties came around, I was a little bit older and better at what I was doing, so he and I were able really to work together. That's when I felt like I could really keep up with him. I've certainly learned more things from Ruby than anybody, more so than from any of the tenor players I've known. He educated me in a lot of ways.

And of course there could have been more comments included, some of which are already part of this book. It is clear that Ruby's place in the history of American music and, more specifically to jazz artistry, is secure.

One can hope that more recordings will be issued from the stockpiles managed by several record companies:

- Hank O'Neal (Chiaroscuro Records): three recordings remain to be issued, all with extra material: Dick Hyman and Milt Hinton; the first album with George Barnes; duets with Dick Hyman playing organ
- Mat Domber (Arbors Records): several unreleased tunes from various sessions and one complete session
- Concord Jazz Records: one session with Ruby Braff and Roger Kellaway
- Vanguard Records: an unissued session created as a tribute to Johnny Mercer

And, of course there are the myriad live recordings captured over the years, some traced in this book and others yet to surface. Together, these all help to contribute to Ruby's contributions to the history of jazz and such beautiful tunes. He was, indeed, born to play.

Ruby Braff in Memoriam

Born: March 16, 1927
Died: February 9, 2003
First Released Recording; Edmond Hall All Stars, December 1949, Savoy Café, Boston
Final Performance and Recording: Ruby Braff, Nairn Jazz Festival, August 7, 2002
Length of Recording Career: 54 years—a remarkable achievement
Legacy: While Tony Bennett called Ruby the finest cornetist in the world, Ruby would have hastened to add something like this: "Nobody is better than Louis

Armstrong and Bobby Hackett is better than me, if you must keep score." Will Friedwald wrote the following: "Braff sings through his cornet and by any standard is one of the greatest singers of all time." Ruby's obituaries appeared around the world including *The Wall Street Journal* and *The Times* of London. A number of writers labeled him a traditional jazz musician. They were wrong, and those words would have brought a testy response from Ruby. He was a consummate artist who loved to play nice tunes and create beauty for those who listened. He would argue that taste and good music should not be restricted by the word *traditional*. Don't you agree?

Ruby's tombstone gets it right by simply stating "Beloved Musician."

Notes

[1] Jack Massarik, *The Evening Standard*, July 22, 2002.
[2] Steve Voce, *Jazz Journal International*, May 2007.
[3] Steve Voce provided some corrections to the original listing.
[4] Steve Voce provided some corrections to the original listing.
[5] http://dspace.dial.pipex.com/jazzitoria/nairn.htm.
[6] Personal correspondence with Steve Voce.
[7] Dick Wellstood, author of album notes for *Donald Lambert Recorded 1959–1961*, (Storyville Records, 101 8376), unnumbered page 1.
[8] John McDonough, "Benny, Meet *DownBeat. DownBeat*, Benny," *DownBeat* 75th Anniversary Collectors' Edition (July 2009), 47.
[9] Jack Teagarden, foreword to Jay D. Smith and Len Guttridge, *Jack Teagarden: The Story of a Jazz Maverick* (New York: Da Capo, 1987), viii.
[10] Pee Wee Russell quoted in "Louis Armstrong Praises New Ace," *Chicago Defender*, April 19, 1958.
[11] Steve Voce, *The Independent*, February 11, 2003.
[12] Scott Hamilton quoted by Peter Vacher, *Soloists and Sidemen: American Jazz Stories* (London: Northway Publications, 2004), 86–87.

Appendix

Album Notes:

Recovered Treasures

Ruby Braff

and His Musical Friends

Playing Songs Performed by Louis Armstrong and Fats Waller

Featuring Bobby Hackett and Ralph Sutton

Classic Recordings from 1961 and 1981
All Previously Unissued

Ruby Braff:
Recovered Treasures and Musical Friendships

Good things do come to those who wait. This recording offers proof of that oft-used phrase. You will share the pleasure of hearing these previously unissued performances by Ruby Braff, recorded live at Eddie Condon's in New York in 1961 and in a studio and at a jazz party in 1981. All are gems.

In one of our conversations Ruby observed, "When I play a club, I almost never see anyone leave who is disappointed. They like what they hear. They're happy to be there. But the problem is getting more people to come to the club in the first place." That has fueled many discussions about the future of jazz music. But it has also created an opportunity for us to hear some very special performances that, for various reasons, have not previously been released to the public. These recordings have not been discovered by even Ruby's most devoted fans. We'll call them recovered treasures. It is just like having a second chance to enter a club, studio, or party, having missed the original performance. As Ruby suggested, once you begin to listen, you won't be disappointed. The recordings on this CD display the talent of many fine musicians who joined with Ruby on many occasions, leading to very special musical friendships.

Ruby said that he could tell what an audience would like, and generally he created musical performances that were rewarded with great applause and praise from many reviewers. Worldwide. His performances never lacked interest. He talked about how he would prepare for an engagement by rehearsing thousands of tunes each day in his mind, hearing different musicians in a variety of combinations before settling on a program: "What I hate most is when an audience has to look at a group of musicians standing on a stage discussing what to play next." Ruby could enter an established group and change its entire sound by creating new patterns from its instrumental voices.

So Ruby was prepared. He did not disappoint his audiences. He has attracted many loyal fans based on the beauty he created in his recordings and live performances. His repertoire typically included what he called "nice tunes." But Ruby always wanted to reach a wider audience. He described one of his visions in the following way: "I would like to operate a club that would feature many different forms of entertainment, starting with jugglers, then comedians, and ending with musical performances." We never discussed all the acts appearing in between, but it was clear that he enjoyed his memories of the *Ed Sullivan Show*. Ruby did discuss his hopes of making a new recording with strings, citing a goal of collaborating with Robert Farnon. Thus, it is not hard to imagine that Ruby would play with string accompaniment on some occasions. His imaginary club might well have provided this opportunity, perhaps after a demonstration of boxing.

Back to reality. Like many other jazz musicians, Ruby did record with strings—four times. The most recent performance dates from July 2000 in a recording released on Arbors Records titled *Variety Is the Spice of Braff.* The earliest opportunity came in England in November 1978 for the Pizza label. Arrangements on that recording were by Neil Richardson, who Robert Farnon personally recommended to Ruby. Most of the tunes from that recording were reissued by Arbors Records as *In the Wee, Small Hours in London and New York.* That CD also included additional titles recorded with strings arranged by Tommy Newsom, dating from March 1999. But if you have been counting, I've only mentioned three recordings, not four. Before describing the missing session, I would like to tell you a bit more about Ruby.

Ruby probably limited his career by being very selective in his choice of fellow musicians. There are many stories about his demanding standards. He said, "I won't play in a situation where I do not control the selection of musicians and tunes." When I asked Ruby about stories about Benny Goodman's stare—called "The Ray"—Ruby was quick to reply, "Anyone who resented that did not have the faintest idea of what it takes to be a professional musician." The demands he placed on others mirrored the expectations he placed on himself. I spoke with him on the phone the night before he departed for England for his final professional tour. I wished him well. He replied, "I will simply play as well as I possibly can." And he did, at his highest artistic standards.

Ruby's insistence on controlling his musical surroundings got him in trouble in a well-documented encounter with Joe Glaser, Louis Armstrong's manager.

> In 1957, Joe Glaser called Ruby to ask him if he wanted to go to England. Edmond Hall had introduced the two of them at the 1956 Newport Jazz Festival. The call woke Ruby, who later in his life made it known 'no morning calls—I stay up all night and sleep through the morning.' Ruby indicated that he would love to travel with his own octet, but Glaser said Ruby wasn't known enough to support a tour. Glaser was offering a contract to join with Jack Teagarden and Earl Hines, clearly a wonderful opportunity. The conversation quickly became heated and serious insults were exchanged. Ruby suddenly hung up his phone, ending the conversation. Ruby then called back, but ended up exchanging insults again. Nat Hentoff printed Ruby's view of the exchange in *Esquire* magazine, whereupon Joe Glaser phoned and invited Ruby to sign an exclusive representation contract with his booking agency. They met face to face, and Ruby signed. Glaser had a copy of the *Esquire* article on his desk at that moment. Ruby noted it and laughed it off. But Glaser never obtained a booking for Ruby and used his power to reduce Ruby's bookings for the term of the contract. Touring the UK with Teagarden and Hines would have brought Ruby some added visibility, although there is no doubt that Ruby's reputation was still growing in jazz circles.

Ruby and His Musical Friendships: Some Musical Firsts Included on This Recording

I asked Ruby once about his friends. He replied, "Be careful when you use that word, *friends*. A person is fortunate to have one or two of those in an entire lifetime." I did not reach that status in his eyes, but he did introduce me as "his discographer" and we talked regularly. He took considerable pride in the thought that my book would remind people of his recordings after his passing.

But there are some musicians that Ruby clearly regarded as his musical friends and performed with on many occasions. Several are included in the tunes on this CD: Ralph Sutton, Dick Hyman, Dave McKenna, Kenny Davern, Bucky Pizzarelli, Vic Dickenson, Jack Lesberg, Buzzy Drootin, Jake Hanna, and others. With these musicians Ruby never had to worry about them not knowing a tune. They could focus on creating a variety of combinations and textures in their performances. They brought their own ideas but also watched Ruby closely as he worked to create a framework that wove their individual performances into a true collaboration. That combination of richness and variety was a hallmark of Ruby's recorded work. He just called it chamber music. *Bravura Excellence* was one of his aptly titled CDs. These musicians crossed paths many times and in many unique ways. Perhaps you will have interest in learning more about this.

Ruby with Ralph Sutton from 1961 and 1981

Ruby performed periodically at Eddie Condon's club in New York beginning in 1955 when Ralph Sutton was the intermission pianist. But for this CD we advance to a night in January 1961. Ralph was leading a trio for the first three weeks that month, and Ruby was added as a guest artist for the night we hear on this recording. This is the earliest recorded pairing of these two fine musicians, and they joined forces periodically afterwards. Until now, their earliest recorded collaboration appeared on Storyville records from an extended engagement at Sunnie's Rendezvous in 1968. They also performed together at one of the famous Gibson Jazz Parties in 1979 about a month before their first recording for Charlie Baron, in a duet and quartet recording issued on Chaz Jazz (LP) and now mostly available on Chiaroscuro. Their performances together continued, including another Gibson appearance in 1980, a live recording in Minneapolis, and two other wonderful encounters from 1981 that are included in this CD. One of these is a hallmark in Ruby's career, the missing session with strings, but we are still not yet ready to talk about that in detail.

Ruby with Bobby Hackett

Louis Armstrong was Ruby's chief source of inspiration, but Ruby learned his art by playing with many musicians on the radio. Ruby's reputation grew rapidly following release of his recordings for Vanguard Records that were produced by John Hammond beginning in 1954. But before that, Ruby traveled to New York from Boston on weekends. Bobby Hackett often took the same train, boarding at Providence, Rhode Island. Sometimes, Bobby asked Ruby to substitute for him on a date, typically because he had landed a better paying offer somewhere else.

[At this point in the album notes, I included some of Ruby's words that appear at the start of chapter 2 from an interview conducted by Peter Vacher that appeared in *Jazz Journal International*. I won't repeat them here.]

On one occasion I played one of Lee Wiley's rehearsal recordings for Ruby, because it was not completely clear if the accompaniment was by Bobby or Ruby. Ruby listened carefully and then replied with certainty, "That's too good for me. It must be Bobby!" Clearly Ruby regarded Bobby with almost as much respect as he awarded Louis Armstrong. In Ruby's eyes, Louis sat on top of an unreachable pedestal. Ruby said, "I attended the Louis Armstrong University, but there, nobody can ever graduate."

Informal recordings of Ruby with Bobby Hackett are rare, although they performed together on several occasions in the US and in France. They never recorded together, but in 1960 they did advertise that they were accepting students in the New York area. Bobby was booked into Condon's, leading a quartet following Ralph Sutton's departure, starting the final week in January 1961 and closing March 11. This CD includes a performance to treasure from Eddie Condon's club on March 2, 1961, when Ruby was again appearing as a guest artist. In the meantime, Ruby had enjoyed his first club engagement with a new group he fronted with Marshall Brown and was on the threshold of a European tour as a member of George Wein's Newport All Stars. Ruby and Marshall spent a week in Toronto between these two recordings from Condon's. Having Bobby and Ruby together on this recording is certainly a treat, and you will hear the respect that these musicians had for one another. Bobby is plays many roles in this recording, jumping to the fore when leading but showing his incredible talent as an accompanist at other times. This is the only issued recording of these two fine musicians together.

Ruby with Vic Dickenson

Ruby's first major engagement was at the Savoy Café in Boston, with Edmond Hall, Vic Dickenson, Ken Kersey, John Field, and Jimmy Crawford in the late 1940's. That makes Vic one of Ruby's longest standing musical friends. They collaborated many times on record, starting with live sessions in December 1949 from the Savoy Café that were released on Savoy Records, and including the sessions for Vanguard Records from 1953 and 1954 that brought international attention to Ruby's talent. In England, these recordings helped to define the term "mainstream jazz." Ruby liked to tell stories about how he drove Vic Dickenson to the Savoy Café. Vic timed his arrival at the club just in time to reach the bandstand to begin playing with the opening downbeat. Sometimes Ruby drove a car, dropped Vic at the door, but arrived late after taking time to park. But there is no question that Vic Dickenson was one of Ruby's earliest champions. Ruby returned the favors, including Vic in his own session for Vanguard in 1955 and a Bing Crosby tribute album recorded in 1981. Ruby and Dick Hyman performed together at Vic Dickenson's funeral.

Ruby with Kenny Davern

Ruby and Kenny toured the Midwest during part of 1960 and performed together frequently in New York clubs throughout the '70's, including domestic and European appearances with the New York Jazz Repertory Company that included Dick Hyman. They recorded for Chaz Jazz just prior to the *Changing Times* party included in this CD. Their association is also documented by a number of fine recordings that appear on Arbors Records, including a wonderful sessions from 2000 that have been acclaimed by a number of reviewers.

Ruby with Dave McKenna

Ruby and Dave recorded together with Benny Goodman on a session released on MusicMasters. Most of this session remains unreleased, but Ruby described how he encouraged Benny to sing "It's Bad for Me" after the original vocalist had problems with several takes of the tune. They next recorded together in a rare session with Milli Vernon on Storyville, followed by wonderful performances on Ruby's classic Epic Records album *Braff* and a recording on ABC Paramount prior to this date at Condon's. Buzzy Drootin, who also performed on these sessions, is also included in some of the performances on this CD. Ruby and Dave reunited for wonderful recordings on Concord and Arbors Records, and they performed together in various clubs and festivals. Of course, Dave McKenna also recorded with Bobby Hackett and Vic Dickenson. On some occasions when Vic was not present, Bucky Pizzarelli joined them. These musical friendships created treasures in many different combinations.

Ruby with Dick Hyman

Ruby and Dick also recorded together for the first time in a Benny Goodman session for Capitol Records. But their legacy rests with a truly remarkable series of recordings for several labels, Concord Jazz, Atlantic (with the New York Jazz Repertory Company), Columbia, Chiaroscuro, Finesse, Inner City, MusicMasters, Arbors, and a film soundtrack recording for the movie *Billy Bathgate*. They performed in many clubs and festivals, in engagements frequently obtained by Dick Hyman. Dick appears on more of Ruby's recordings than any other musician. That attests to the extent of their musical friendship and Dick Hyman's immense talent, imagination and versatility.

Ruby with Bucky Pizzarelli

Bucky's first recording with Ruby was for Sonet Records in 1976. A few years before, probably in 1971, they performed together in a New York club. The next year they were both invited to one of Dick Gibson's parties. There with other parties and engagements before they joined Vic Dickenson, Dick Hyman, and Mel Lewis on the *Very Sinatra* recording for Finesse. This recording was made just before the very unique strings session recorded for Charlie Baron that is the foundation for this CD release. Bucky and Ruby recorded frequently for Arbors Records and also in Ruby's final studio recordings for Arbors Records and Victoria Records. One of my pleasures in jazz is seeing Bucky perform. His enthusiasm is infectious. His smiles light a room.

Ruby with Jack Lesberg

Ruby and Jack Lesberg toured together as members of the Newport All Stars. Jack was the musical director of some jazz parties where he booked Ruby, Dick Hyman, Dave McKenna, and Ralph Sutton. He appeared on a number of Chaz Jazz and Concord recordings and performs on both the *Changing Times* and strings sessions on this CD. Jack joined Dick Hyman and Ruby on the *Billy Bathgate* soundtrack recording. Fittingly, Jack, along with Dick Hyman and Bucky Pizzarelli and Jake Hanna all appeared at a special jazz party celebrating Ruby Braff's 74th birthday in 2001 organized by Mat and Rachel Domber. Jack set a foundation that made everyone else reach a bit higher.

Ruby with Buzzy Drootin and Jake Hanna

Ruby began performing with Buzzy Drootin in various groups in Boston as early as 1944, and perhaps even earlier. Many of the dates at the Savoy Café and with the Newport All Stars that included Vic Dickenson also had Buzzy on drums. Buzzy was the drummer on many of Ruby's records in the 1950s for Epic, RCA, Columbia, Warner Brothers, and other labels. They were joined by Dave McKenna on several of these albums. Their last performance together that I can trace was the performance for *Changing Times* included in this CD.

Jake Hanna's first engagement with Ruby that I can trace is the performance with Bobby Hackett on this CD. A bit later they performed at the Embers in New York and also in other concert settings. They were together for a time in the Newport All Stars; however, their first studio recording was a wonderful pairing of Woody Herman with Ruby that was issued on Chiaroscuro Records. Jake was Woody's drummer, so he was a natural for that session given his familiarity with Ruby's playing. Jake found himself with Ruby and Jack Lesberg frequently at the Grande Parade du Jazz in Nice as well as other jazz parties where his engaging manner always made him a favorite. Ruby recorded several times with Jake for Arbors Records.

Recovering Some Buried Treasures

Ruby and I were together for several days during his recording sessions in July 2000 for Arbors. Ruby was excited for two reasons when he invited my wife and me to join him in New York. First, he said that we would hear some wonderful music. He planned to begin with a large group of musicians and gradually reduce their numbers as the sessions continued. Second, he said that he was booked to perform at a restaurant in New Jersey, Shanghai Jazz. He said, longingly, "This is the first time I have played in front of real people in over a year."

Well, this CD is not quite what he meant about playing for an audience. Clearly, he is no longer able to play for you in person. But Ruby would like knowing that real people, like all of you, will now have a chance to hear some wonderful creations by many of his musical friends.

Ruby Braff with the Beaux Arts Quartet in 1981

This CD opens with a unique recording of Ruby Braff with strings recorded December 17, 1981, just 13 months after his initial recording with strings in England. It was the very first unissued recording that Ruby mentioned to me as I gathered information during the preparation of a forthcoming book about his career. (Another of his treasured memories was a long lost session for Columbia that has just appeared for the first time on Mosaic Records.) Ruby spoke with tremendous pride about how Charlie Baron had recorded Ruby and some of his best musical friends with the Beaux Arts Quartet. He encouraged me to request a private cassette from Charlie who was kind to send these unique recordings without hesitation. Joe Boughton has now made arrangements to share them with Ruby's fans at last.

At the time Ruby had recorded with Ralph Sutton in various combinations for the Chaz Jazz label. That label's wonderful catalog is being reissued by Hank O'Neal on Chiaroscuro Records. The Chaz Jazz label was created by Charlie Baron, one of Sutton's good friends. Ruby and Ralph had performed together frequently during this period, so it is not surprising that Ruby would approach Charlie to record him with a string quartet and jazz group, including Ralph. They enlisted Dick Hyman, one of the most versatile musicians of all time, to write some special arrangements for the session.

Charlie Baron wrote the following:

> In the early eighties I had Ruby Braff join me at my audio engineer's studio to assist me in editing and balancing the material I was preparing for a forthcoming Chaz Jazz album *The Jazzband* which included Ruby with Ralph Sutton, Gus Johnson, Bud Freeman, Kenny Davern, Milt Hinton, and George Masso. Following our session we repaired to a local West Side gin mill to hoist a few and relax. In the course of our conversation Ruby stated his desire to be featured as a soloist playing with pops orchestras. He believed the range of his style and technique would be compatible with this type of presentation.
>
> At the time André Previn was the director of the Pittsburgh Symphony and somebody told me he was a fan of Ralph Sutton's. A the time I was gainfully employed and making good money in the real world (not the recording business) and was therefore prepared to take an expensive, interesting, but speculative gamble; namely I would back the production of a demo pops package to provide Previn with the long shot odds that he would buy this idea for the Pittsburgh Pops.
>
> I therefore enlisted Dick Hyman to arrange six classic tunes which would be adaptable for a full orchestra presentation. Ruby wanted Mel Lewis and Bucky Pizzarelli to be included with Jack and Ralph in the jazz quartet. We recorded the six pieces at RCA's Studio B with Ralph playing the famous Steinway concert grand that Basie and Peterson used. With Dick conducting,

> the recording went without a hitch in a one-day session. Ruby played extremely well as did the supporting cast.
>
> Hyman and I did the eight-track mix which came out very well. However the bad news is that unfortunately when we were ready to take the pilot to Previn he had left Pittsburgh to conduct the London Symphony, at which point I gave up the venture as a lost cause. I never felt that Chaz Jazz Records was the proper venue to present this material so it has remained in my archives for over twenty years.

Dick Hyman expressed his delight in learning that this session was being released on Jump Records. He was acquainted with the Beaux Arts Trio and had worked in other situations with its director, cellist Charles McCracken. Ruby selected tunes based on his appreciation of their melodies, continuing his fascination with the "nice tunes" he had played throughout his career. All the musicians assembled in the studio for the date. The classical repertoire was a challenge, but Ruby played very well and the arrangements clearly stimulated him.

This is the most distinctive recording of Ruby's career. Without Charlie Baron's sponsorship, we would have never had the opportunity to hear it. It would have remained inside Ruby's head, in some form. But now it has become a very unique part of his recorded legacy.

Ruby Braff at Eddie Condon's Club in 1961

Charlie Baron fortunately made some recordings at Condon's in New York on two nights in early 1961, when Ruby Braff was featured as a guest artist with Ralph Sutton in January and Bobby Hackett in March. These are historic recordings. They include Ruby's first known recording with Ralph and his only released recording with Bobby. These are spirited performances, and the audience is happy. You will need to absorb the sounds of conversation and clinking glasses as part of the ambiance. Think of is as a patina that surrounds these recordings.

Ruby Braff at the *Changing Times* Jazz Party

Changing Times magazine held a series of jazz parties in the early 1980s. In my opinion the most musically successful one featured Ruby Braff with a number of his musical friends. This CD includes one fine performance from that party, which has only circulated privately until this time. Ralph Sutton returns. In fact he is present on every selection on this CD except for Ruby's appearance with Bobby Hackett. Not surprisingly, he provides a firm foundation that anchors this performance. Ruby and Ralph are joined with some of Ruby's long-standing musical friends.

Some Brief Comments about the Performances

This CD contains a unique selection of tunes, uncommon in Ruby's repertory. Nine tunes only appear on this recording: all six titles with the Beaux Arts String Quartet, "You Meet the Nicest People in Your Dreams," "Two Sleepy People," and "Lazy River." In fact the ones with the Beau Arts Quartet are uncommon in the entire history of recorded jazz music. You will quickly see that the selection honors Louis Armstrong and Fats Waller, accompanied by two tunes that Ruby just liked to play. Louis recorded "Save It Pretty Mama," "Lazy River," "Struttin' with Some Barbecue," "Sugar," and "When You're Smiling." Fats recorded "You Meet the Nicest People in Your Dreams," "Two Sleepy People," "I Can't Give You Anything But Love," and "Keepin' Out of Mischief Now." In live performances Ruby enjoyed performing two others: "Lover Come Back to Me" and "Sweet Lorraine" but seldom recorded them. It is fitting that the selections on this CD honor Louis and Fats. Ruby would like that.

You will easily find several favorites on this CD that you will listen to again and again. But here are a few moments that I particularly enjoyed.

In a Studio: Ruby Braff and the Beaux Arts String Quartet, December 17, 1981

Ruby had long enjoyed using the lower reaches of his instrument to produce cellolike tones. This had never been more pronounced than in this performance of Chopin's "Waltz No. 9." The strings provide a lush background to accentuate Ruby's stringlike attack on many of his phrases. Ralph Sutton offers delicious releases from the tension of the more formal passages, sometimes evoking memories of the ragtime feeling of Scott Joplin's approach to music. This is a very unique performance. In contrast, Ralph breaks into a joyous stride solo during Verdi's "Stride La Vampa," balanced by Ruby's staccato notes. "Ah! So Pure" may remind you of a motion picture *Breaking Away,* where it was featured on the soundtrack and linked to the central storyline. This is part of an Indiana theme in this CD that continues with the inclusion of two songs by Hoagy Carmichael.

Club Date: Ralph Sutton Quartet with Ruby Braff, January 1961—Their First Recorded Encounter

Twenty years earlier we are treated to exciting live recordings from Condon's. One of Fats Waller's delightful recordings was "You Meet the Nicest People in Your Dreams." For some reason this song has not been frequently performed since Fats recorded it in 1939. Ruby may have been thinking of a time he played informally with Fats in Boston in the early 1940s. Ralph opens the performance and establishes an infectious rhythm right from the start. If you listen closely you will hear Ruby say "Wow" and soon thereafter announce, "I'll take one." His chorus lifts the performance with a bravura style that evokes the spirit of Louis Armstrong. This leads to exchanges with Ralph that demonstrate the value of their future musical partnership. You'll hear Ruby quote a phrase from Waller's "Handful of Keys" just to establish the allegiance to Fats. Ruby may be the guest here, but he becomes the leader on this number and ends up doing much more than taking one chorus. Listen to his trumpet growls behind Ralph's solo. He is working as a cheerleader to drive the performance, much as Fats did with his vocal inflections on so many of his original recordings. I cannot imagine anyone not enjoying this performance.

Club Date: Bobby Hackett Quintet with Ruby Braff, March 2, 1961—TheirOnly Released Recording Together

Bobby Hackett followed Ralph Sutton into Condon's and Ruby returned as a guest, as he had been doing during the previous half decade. Fortunately this occasion was recorded, for these two artists have never appeared together before on a released recording. Now, if the spirit of Louis Armstrong was present in the preceding session, it is visible in full force in this performance. The session opens with "Struttin' with Some Barbecue." Bobby opens as leader, staying close to the melody, but he offers the first solo to Ruby. He begins with a very soft tone, moves to the rhythmic notes he often used to separate melodic phrases, and leads to Peanuts Hucko's solo. Bobby and Ruby join behind Peanuts to create a nice background and then drop out as Dave McKenna takes charge. The rhythmic intensity increases during Dave's second chorus and Bobby returns in his unique style, followed by Ruby. Rhythm takes over, with Bill Takis soloing. You'll hear Bobby say, "What you say," and Ruby laughs in the background. Ruby returns, then Peanuts, then Bobby as each trades bars in sequence, building the tension over the steady pulse from the rhythm section. Then Ruby takes the lead, with rich background from Bobby and Peanuts, and their voices rise and fall as they complete the performance. Louis would have liked this version of Lil's song.

"Lover Come Back to Me" is a tune Ruby performed in clubs and concerts but seldom recorded. Bobby lets him open, with Dave following. Ruby can be heard as a cheerleader, shouting "Yeah" in the background from time to time. Bobby comes next, with Ruby providing accents in accompaniment. He begins with evenly spaced notes, but moves to more legato-like phrases as he develops his solo. Peanuts comes next, completing the go-around, with both horns providing rhythmic punctuation. Ruby enters in his lower register, then brightens to reach for higher notes, then builds a rhythmic pattern, then closes the performance in his bravura style with a brief quote from "Salt Peanuts."

Jazz Party: Ralph Sutton with Ruby Braff and the All Stars—July 8, 1981

Ralph Sutton returns as part of an all star group with Ruby. This is an extended performance taken from a limited release recording from a jazz party. "When You're Smiling" features many of the musicians that kept mainstream jazz alive. In this performance, Ruby takes the opening solo, with Vic Dickenson making his unique presence felt immediately with his growls. Al Klink follows. Vic comes next, then Kenny Davern with some of his soaring notes. Next comes the rhythm section. Marty gets a chorus, then Jack, before Ralph takes the final solo building nicely as Ruby encourages him with a repeated "Go ahead" and his familiar chuckles along the way. Ruby has the last musical word leading the full ensemble. He'd like it that way.

Ruby would have liked this CD. He was especially proud of the studio session with strings. He always liked performing for people in clubs and at parties. That was his life, and in that part of his life he truly excelled. He left us a legacy of beautiful performances. Yes, good things do come to those who wait.

(Album notes written by Thomas P. Hustad)

Index of Musicians

Index of Song Titles

About the Author

Tom Hustad discovered Ruby Braff's music long before he prepared for his career as a marketing professor and new products management authority. Tom played an instrumental role in the creation of the world's largest association of new product development professionals, the Product Development and Management Association, where he was named the second Crawford Fellow of Innovation. In addition to being the founder and longtime editor of *The Journal of Product Innovation Management*, he is the author of the album notes for the compact discs that contain all the music recorded in Ruby's final four days in a studio and from his final concert performance, issued in three separate releases on Arbors Records and Victoria Records. He wrote notes for another release on Jump Records, which includes unique historical recordings never previously issued. In addition, his notes are included with the most recent Arbors Records CD containing wonderful performances dating from 1998, released for the first time. He has an extensive personal jazz collection and has supplied rare and undocumented recordings to the following CD releases: most of the previously unissued recordings that appeared in *The Complete JATP in the 40s* box set collection on Verve; rare and undocumented recordings that were included in *Bud Freeman 1946* on Jazz Chronological Classics; a previously undocumented Fletcher Henderson alternate take of "Tidal Wave" and dubs of other rare 78s for a box set being developed by Mosaic Records devoted to Coleman Hawkins; and a rare recording of "Time on My Hands" that Don Schlitten added to his CD release of Coleman Hawkins's complete Jazztone recordings, issued as *Jazz Tones* on the Prevue label. Tom was elected as a trustee of the International Association of Jazz Record Collectors and his biography appears in Marquis' *Who's Who in America* and *Who's Who in the World.* He can be found at the Kelley School of Business at Indiana University where his MBA students kindly accepted the jazz music he played before the beginning and following the end of each of his classes. Ruby felt that a marketing professor should be able to broaden the audience for his music. I continue to do my best to honor his wish. To honor Tom's professional work, Nestlé endowed the Nestlé-Hustad Professorship at Indiana University. Tom certainly feels that the creative acts of improvisation in jazz connect with the skills of creating innovative goods and services. His own focus on innovation, while not musical, contributed to his being named a "best bet teacher" by *Business Week* magazine and a past winner of Indiana University's prestigious Eli Lilly Teaching Award.